we got 'em

HISTORY OF
THE SECOND WORLD WAR

BRITISH FOREIGN POLICY IN THE SECOND WORLD WAR

BY

SIR LLEWELLYN WOODWARD

*Fellow of All Souls College
and formerly Professor of Modern History
in the University of Oxford
Professor Emeritus at the Institute for
Advanced Study, Princeton, N.J.*

Volume I

LONDON: 1970
HER MAJESTY'S STATIONERY OFFICE

B.F.P.—A*

First published 1970

© *Crown copyright 1970*

Published by

HER MAJESTY'S STATIONERY OFFICE

To be purchased from
49 High Holborn, London W.C.1
13A Castle Street, Edinburgh EH2 3AR
109 St. Mary Street, Cardiff CF1 1JW
Brazennose Street, Manchester M60 8AS
50 Fairfax Street, Bristol BS1 3DE
258 Broad Street, Birmingham 1
7 Linenhall Street, Belfast BT2 8AY
or through any bookseller

SBN 11 630052 3*

Printed in England for Her Majesty's Stationery Office by McCorquodale & Co., London
H.M. 2946   Dd. 142654   K 32   7/69   McC. 3309

FOREWORD

THIS *History* was written between 1942 and 1950 for official use; a short version of it (with an *Introduction* reprinted in the present volume) was published by H.M. Stationery Office in 1962. When I was invited to write the *History* I asked for and obtained full access to all material in British archives which I might wish to consult and use. In planning and carrying out my work, I was given no brief to defend or attack any person or policy, and in preparing for publication both the shorter version of 1962 and the present long version I have been subject to no censorship.

Most of the material I have used has come from the archives of the Foreign Office, and most of my references are to Foreign Office papers. These papers included, when I was working on them, copies of Cabinet memoranda (many of which, on subjects bearing on foreign policy, had been prepared in the Foreign Office), copies of memoranda and minutes of the Chiefs of Staff Committee, and of minutes exchanged between the Prime Minister and the Foreign Secretary. I consulted in the archives of the Cabinet Office the full records of War Cabinet meetings, Mr. Churchill's correspondence with the American, Russian and other Heads of States, the British records of meetings between these Heads or principal Ministers of States, the record of the proceedings of the European Advisory Commission, the Committee on Armistice and Post-War Reconstruction and other bodies concerned with the preparation of armistice terms, the terms of a post-war settlement and the Charter and organisation of the United Nations. Few memoirs or other personal records were published while I was at work on the *History*, but before I had finished, the first three volumes of Sir Winston Churchill's *The Second World War* were available. I should like to repeat here what I wrote in the preface to the short history about Sir Winston Churchill's book.

'It would be absurd, and graceless, if I did not say how much I have learned from Sir Winston Churchill's own account of his Administration. Sir Winston, on the principle *quia nominor leo*, has rightly allowed himself a personal approach and a freedom of comment from which an official historian is debarred. The six volumes of *The Second World War* cover the main issues of diplomacy— and especially of Anglo-American relations—as well as of battle. A student following only one aspect of war activity through the maze of documents in the archives, finds himself again and again admiring the political insight, fairmindedness, and not least the generosity which Sir Winston Churchill has brought to the story as a whole.'

I had to limit myself in my *History* mainly to British sources and to documents received from Allied or neutral governments. Even if sufficient material from the enemy side had been available, I should not have included it because I was writing not a general diplomatic history of the war, but a history based on the information available at the time to His Majesty's Government and their advisers. Since the short history was merely a summary of the longer work, I made very few additions to it. When I began to prepare this longer history for publication I thought that I ought to use American, German, French and Italian material which was now open to me. I asked myself what would be the best way of incorporating this material in my text. I still wanted to describe British policy as it was formulated and executed in the light of information known at the time, and not to confuse my narrative by introducing 'after-knowledge'. I also could not put more than a part of the new material in the same category as the documents from British archives. The many volumes of memoirs by non-British writers had the usual defects of their kind, and could not be relied upon without confirmation from foreign 'closed' documentary sources. The German documents which had fallen into Allied hands and from which a selection (down to the end of 1941) had been made by British, American and French scholars were of great value. The volumes in the American publication *Foreign Relations of the United States* were even more valuable, but they were only a selection (often of a lavish kind) and obviously did not provide as full a documentation of British or Anglo-American policy as I could get from the whole range of British archives. I decided that the best way of introducing the non-British material was to put it into footnotes. The increase in the number of footnotes—which I had already used to lighten the main narrative—has not made the reading of the text easier, but it does allow anyone who may wish to do so to judge how near to the mark, or how wide of it British Ministers were in guessing enemy plans and intentions or reactions to British policy.

From the beginning of my work I had to choose two ways of treating so large a subject. There is the method of simultaneity; that is to say, a narrative arranged in chronological sequence, in which every chapter covers a limited period of time but carries the whole subject forward from beginning to end of the period. According to this method, each chapter of the book would describe what was happening throughout the world, in every field of policy, during the time covered by the chapter.

There is also the method of analysis. Here again the narrative maintains a chronological sequence, but a single subject is treated over a period of time sufficient to cover a considerable series of changes, and, for purposes of clear analysis, attention is concentrated on one group of events, or developments, as far as possible, without reference to the situation in other fields.

The advantages and disadvantages of either method are obvious. The first method brings out the general flow and interconnexion of things and treats them as they happened; the Foreign Office, for example, had to deal with a dozen major questions at the same time, and the reader is put most nearly in the position of a Foreign Secretary if he also has to keep hold of the threads of a dozen questions simultaneously. On the other hand, from the point of view of a narrative, this simultaneity must be something of a fiction. The historian cannot really follow the flow of events; he must dip into the stream. He can describe only one thing at a time; if he turns continually from one subject to another, he is apt to try to carry too many things forward at once and, to change the metaphor, may easily miss the wood for the trees. So also may the reader. Moreover even the busiest official does not discuss two or three questions at the same time or move from one subject to another without going back in his mind to past analysis. Hence the method of analysis avoids giving the reader an impression of perpetually unfinished business, and allows him to see questions in the perspective in which they were actually treated. At the same time there is in this method a certain danger of over-simplification; questions look neater than they really are; the continuous and kaleidoscopic effects, the confusion and interrelation of affairs tend to be overlooked.

For these reasons I have attempted a compromise. I have taken certain large subjects in order to get a sufficient degree of 'simultaneity'. I have divided these subjects into chapters and sections in order to allow proper treatment of each of the factors into which the main subjects can be analysed. It is open to readers to use the table of contents to assist them, if they so wish, to follow the story more 'laterally' i.e. to see what was happening at a given time in all the major areas of policy, or, conversely, it is possible, by taking each of the larger subjects—for example, relations with Russia—to follow them through from the beginning to the end of the war.

During the composition of the *History* I was helped by a number of people. I wish I could thank each of them individually. It is impossible to name here all the members of the Foreign Office and H.M. Missions abroad who from time to time gave me their personal recollections of the events described in my narrative, but I should like in particular to mention the Rt. Hon. Sir Alexander Cadogan and Lord Strang. My work was much helped by the co-operation of the Librarian and staff of the Foreign Office Library. In the latter part of the work I am most grateful for the watchful assistance of Miss

Anne Orde, M.A., now a member of the History Department of the University of Durham, who had previously shared as Assistant Editor with Mr. Rohan Butler and myself the production of the *Documents on British Foreign Policy 1919–1939*. For the present revision and preparation of the text for publication, I owe a very great debt to Miss Jean Dawson, B.Litt., of the Historical Section of the Cabinet Office, whose good judgment as well as skill and experience in the production of official War Histories have been of the greatest service to me.

I should also add how useful I have found, in correlating diplomacy with military events, the excellent volumes on *Grand Strategy* (History of the Second World War, U.K. Military Series) edited and partially (Volume II and part of Volume III) written by Sir James Butler, which have appeared since 1956, and the volumes by Captain S. W. Roskill, *The War at Sea*. Professor W. N. Medlicott's work on *The Economic Blockade* (History of the Second World War, Civil Series, 2 volumes) has been of similar help in the correlation of diplomacy with economic warfare.

LLEWELLYN WOODWARD

May 1968

NOTE

This History will consist of five volumes. The main contents of volumes II to V will be:

Volume II. Anglo-Russian relations, June 1941 to the end of 1943; Anglo-French relations (Vichy and de Gaulle), 1941 to September 1943; the Far East, 1939–1941; the surrender of Italy; relations with Italy (September 1943 to June 1944).

Volume III. Anglo-Russian relations and Anglo-Polish relations in 1944 and 1945 (to the Potsdam Conference); relations with de Gaulle, Yugoslavia, Greece and Italy (from June 1944).

Volume IV. Relations with Spain, July 1941, to the Potsdam Conference; relations with Portugal, 1939–1945; relations with Turkey and Middle Eastern States, 1942–1945; relations with China, 1941 to the end of the war.

Volume V. British policy regarding (a) a world security organisation, (b) the treatment of Germany; the surrender of Germany; the Potsdam Conference; the surrender of Japan.

CONTENTS

CHAPTER XII. Anglo-American relations from the collapse
of France to the end of 1940: the transfer of American
destroyers to Great Britain and the lease of sites to the
United States in Newfoundland and British Colonial
Territories: Lord Lothian's visit to England in October:
the Prime Minister's letter of December 7 to Mr. Roosevelt:
Mr. Roosevelt's statements of December 17 and 29, 1940.

KEY TO REFERENCES

FOREIGN OFFICE RECORDS

The great majority of the references quoted in this book are to Foreign Office files. These references are always preceded by a letter, indicating the department responsible for the file in question. Thus, A indicates the American department, E the Eastern, N the Northern, etc.

CABINET OFFICE RECORDS

Cabinet	Cabinet Conclusions (pre-war)
CA	Confidential Annex (or Secretary's Standard File) to Cabinet Conclusions
Churchill Papers	Sir Winston Churchill's personal files in the custody of the Cabinet Office.
COS	Chiefs of Staff Committee
DO	Defence Committee (Operations)
Hist(B)	Cabinet Office printed series of Middle East telegrams
PMM	Cabinet Office printed series of Prime Minister's minutes
SWC	Supreme War Council
WM	War Cabinet Conclusions
WP	War Cabinet Papers
WP(G)	War Cabinet Papers, General Series

PRINTED SOURCES

D.G.F.P.	*Documents on German Foreign Policy*
F.R.U.S.	*Foreign Relations of the United States*
Doc. Dipl. Ital.	*Documenti diplomatici italiani*

NOTE

Throughout these volumes, footnotes are indicated in the text by numerals, 1, 2, 3, etc. The marginal notes in brackets, (a), (b), (c), etc., indicate references to sources which are printed at the foot of each page.

INTRODUCTION

THE prime function of the Foreign Office and the British Missions abroad—collectively, in their modern organisation, the Foreign Service—is to advise the Secretary of State for Foreign Affairs and to carry out his instructions on matters affecting the relations between Great Britain and other countries, and to act as a channel of communication and report between the Governments of those countries and that of the United Kingdom. The Foreign Secretary is not a senior official among other officials. As a Minister of the Crown he 'represents in his own person the powers of the Parliamentary majority of the day in the domain of foreign affairs'.[1] Within his Department he carries out his work by methods different in many respects from those of his predecessors even sixty years ago. During the nineteenth century the Department did not lack permanent officials of high ability who exercised a very considerable influence on the determination of policy. The staff in general, however, had little more than routine duties.[2] To-day the permanent officials are a large body of expert advisers, and the arrangement of business ensures the presentation of their advice in a convenient and expeditious form.

It would be a mistake to regard these changes as 'depersonalising' the Secretary of State or putting him, as it were, into committee. The Secretary of State has lost none of his overriding responsibility. He need not and often does not follow the advice of his experts. He has the final word in every decision within the Department as well as the task of convincing his colleagues in the Cabinet, and a majority in Parliament, of the rightness of his policy. He must therefore be a master of the art of choosing priorities, and must trust his advisers to deal with many subjects on lines to which he has given broad approval. He is, incidentally, much handicapped if he is not a rapid reader of papers, but a great deal of his work is done orally, and the record of it may be found only in an outgoing despatch or

---

[1] Lord Strang, *The Foreign Office* (Allen & Unwin, 1955), 152. This book gives an excellent description of the working of the Foreign Office, and of the Foreign Service as a whole.

[2] The staff was small by modern standards. As late as 1914 the Foreign Office employed only 176 people, including doorkeepers, cleaners, etc. The membership of the Diplomatic and Consular Services was just under 450, of whom about a third were 'career' diplomats. In 1953–54 there were over 2,600 members of the Foreign Service above the 'messengerial grades'. Strang, *id.*, 30 and 56–7.

telegram. A historian should thus be on guard against losing sight of the central fact of ministerial responsibility in the mass of departmental material which gathers round almost every question. It is, for example, a good rule to remember that the most lavishly documented subjects are not always the most important, and that the few verbal changes suggested by the Secretary of State in a draft submitted to him may be the most important words in the document.

With this caution one may notice also that the sphere of activities of the Department has widened in the course of time. The services of the experts may be sought outside their own technical field of diplomacy. During the war the Foreign Office and the Missions abroad were used not only to carry out negotiations with Allied and neutral States (neutrality, once a plain term, like black or white, had acquired all manner of subtle shades). They were consulted about the probable political consequences of military action or of moves in what was known as 'economic warfare'. They were also asked to consider and, in some cases, to correct the unforeseen results of decisions taken by other Departments. Thus in the winter of 1939–40 one such decision cut off the import of American apples in order to save dollars, and another decision announced a large-scale purchase of tobacco from south-east Europe. American fruit producers objected to the first of these measures, and American tobacco producers to the second of them. The Department of State in Washington pointed out to the British Ambassador the political importance of the complaints, and the Foreign Office had to measure against the risk of over-spending dollars on 'non-essentials' the risk of alienating important sections of American opinion in the year of a Presidential election. In 1944 Mr. Hull's objection on political grounds to the conclusion of a long-term meat contract between the Ministry of Food and the semi-fascist Argentine Government became a subject of serious controversy involving not only the Foreign Office and the State Department but the Prime Minister, President Roosevelt, and the War Cabinet.

The papers in the Foreign Office archives thus provide a mass of material covering the history of particular questions for a limited time, that is to say, for the period in which such questions were the subject of negotiation between Government and Government, and played a direct and immediate part in the formulation of high policy. In order to give advice or warning, and in order to negotiate at the highest level over matters such as meat or wolfram, the Foreign Office and the Missions abroad had to know the intentions of other Departments. This liaison work was carried out in London partly by interdepartmental committees or by the inclusion of Foreign Office representatives in the departments concerned. Furthermore, although the Foreign Office might act as a clearing house[1] for business of all kinds, and an Ambassador or Minister abroad, in virtue of his opportunities of access, might discuss any question with the Government to which he was accredited, the 'foreign' activities of other Departments during the war were so manifold and of such importance that they created channels of intercourse of their own, not merely for their day-to-day transactions, but for the discussion of large issues of policy. The Ministry of Economic Warfare, with its own political chief of Cabinet (not War Cabinet) rank, its own Intelligence service and Foreign Relations division, was more of an independent kingdom than an outlying satrapy of the Secretary of State for Foreign Affairs. The Ministry corresponded directly (through the Foreign Office) with the diplomatic Missions and sometimes had its own representatives attached to them. Nevertheless the Ambassador himself would take charge of business of high diplomatic importance, and the Ministry always consulted the Foreign Office on the political aspects of trade negotiations.[2]

For a time indeed there was a danger of confusion owing to the number of British Missions—as early as September, 1940, there were nine of them—in the United States reporting directly to Departments other than the Foreign Office. In January, 1941, the activities of these separate bodies (excluding the Ministry of Economic Warfare) were brought under the immediate control, not of the Ambassador, but of a British Supply Council in North America. Mr. Arthur B. Purvis,[3] the Chairman of this Council and, previously, head of the British Purchasing Commission in the United States, was in constant personal contact with Mr. Morgenthau, Jr., United States Secretary of the Treasury. Sir Frederick Phillips, of the British Treasury, came to the United States on two special missions in 1940 to explain and discuss the problems caused by the rapid exhaustion of British purchasing power in gold and dollars. These discussions were the background of the Lend-Lease agreements; four years later Lord Keynes, who undertook five different missions to the United States during the war, went to Washington to put before the United States Treasury the equally difficult problems concerned with the ending of Lend-Lease and the first stages of British economic recovery.

---

[1] There were times when—through the British Missions abroad—the Foreign Office in its capacity as a 'clearing-house' was able to take a rapid initiative in matters normally outside its province. Thus during the German attack on the Low Countries and France in 1940 the Foreign Office began enquiries about the preparation and co-ordination of measures to secure, if possible, the withdrawal from enemy hands of valuable machinery and industrial products.

[2] The actual working of the machinery of blockade (navicerts, etc.) in foreign ports was in the hands of the Consular Service. For a full treatment of these war trade negotiations see W. N. Medlicott, *The Economic Blockade* (History of the Second World War, U.K. Civil Series), 2 vols. (H.M.S.O., 1952 & 1959) (hereinafter referred to as 'Medlicott').

[3] Mr. Purvis, a Scots-Canadian industrialist, was killed in an accident in July, 1941. He has been well described as 'a kind of economic Ambassador'.

Anglo-American economic negotiations—for example, those connected with shipping—were, indeed, never out of range of the Foreign Office.[1] Mr. Morgenthau asked through the British Ambassador in Washington and the United States Ambassador in London for the first of Sir Frederick Phillips's two missions in 1940; early in July, 1940, the Foreign Office transmitted to the State Department a warning of the seriousness of the dollar position, and in October, 1940, the British Ambassador suggested the second series of talks. When, in the summer of 1941, there was a strong current of criticism in the United States that Lend-Lease materials were being used for the benefit of British exports, the American complaints came to the Foreign Office through the British Ambassador, and the undertakings given by the British Government to meet the complaints were transmitted through the same channel. Lord Halifax took part in the critical financial discussions of 1944, just as Lord Lothian had been concerned with those in 1940.

The history of the Anglo-American conversations in 1944 over oil reserves is another example of the practical, if untidy way in which large questions of policy fell partly within and partly outside the sphere of the Foreign Office. On the technical side, the Foreign Office could not do more than 'observe' negotiations about oil reserves. On the political side, they intervened to advise the War Cabinet upon the importance of meeting as fully and as quickly as possible American demands which seemed at first untimely and unreasonable. They had also to put the political aspects of the British case to the State Department. Thus, when in February, 1944, President Roosevelt proposed abruptly that a joint committee of representatives of Cabinet rank should meet in Washington to draw up an oil agreement, Lord Halifax protested to the State Department that the British Government should not be asked to accept a unilateral decision of this kind,[2] and that it was impossible, in view of the nearness of the cross-Channel invasion, to send Cabinet Ministers to Washington.

Early in the summer of 1941 the War Cabinet introduced a new form of devolution by appointing a Minister of State, of Cabinet rank, to act as adviser on political questions to the Commander-in-Chief in the Middle East.[3] The duties of this Resident Minister included the co-ordination of British diplomatic action throughout the area. The

---

[1] There were also Allied Conferences on post-war economic questions, e.g. at Bretton Woods on international financial arrangements and at Hot Springs on food supplies, outside the technical competence of the Foreign Office. Here again, however, much preliminary discussion took place through diplomatic channels, and the Foreign Office was kept informed of the proceedings and consulted about the political aspect of any decisions.

[2] i.e. about the 'level' at which the conversations were to be held.

[3] The term 'Middle East' was used by the military authorities and accepted by the War Cabinet, and therefore by the Foreign Office, to cover an area extending from Malta to the Persian Gulf.

experiment might have led to difficulties. The Minister of State had powers to act on behalf of the War Cabinet in an emergency, but he was without departmental duties, and therefore did not take the place of the Foreign Secretary as the Minister ultimately responsible to Parliament for the formulation and execution of policy in the Middle East. The Minister of State in fact carried out a number of important diplomatic negotiations; thus Mr. O. Lyttelton, Minister of State in Cairo from July, 1941, to May, 1942, negotiated an agreement over the Levant States with General de Gaulle.

The arrangement worked reasonably well in practice.[1] The Minister of State was concerned more with matters requiring administrative co-ordination than with political decisions. He was therefore of service to the Foreign Office and other Departments since he could settle most interdepartmental questions without referring them to London. His advice on political affairs was considered seriously—though it was not always taken—because he was better situated than any of the Heads of Missions to consider questions from the point of view of the Middle East as a whole.[2] The experiment was extended to other areas. A Minister Resident was sent to the Far East, too late, however, to be able to do much before the Japanese conquests. A similar appointment was made for a short time in West Africa. After the North African landings, Mr. H. Macmillan went as Minister Resident to Algiers; his sphere of authority was extended to Italy, and, later, to Greece.

The establishment of a separate and secret organisation dealing with subversion and sabotage and, later, with organised Resistance movements in enemy-occupied countries was necessary in itself, but awkward at times from the point of view of the co-ordination of policy.[3] The Foreign Office had to make representations in the course of 1943 that the action taken, especially in Greece, in support of communist-controlled Resistance groups prejudged and indeed was contrary to the policy accepted by the War Cabinet and likely to have the most serious consequences after the war.

Finally, the highest matters of policy, involving the post-war settlement as well as the immediate conduct of operations, were discussed continuously by direct exchanges or at meetings between

---

[1] There was indeed occasional friction because the Ministers reported directly to the Prime Minister, but their reports generally went through the Foreign Office. They often corresponded directly with the Foreign Secretary, who replied to them as he would reply to Ambassadors. The appointment of Foreign Office advisers to the Ministers did much to avoid confusion.

[2] On the other hand certain Heads of Mission with a long experience of the Middle East, for example, Sir K. Cornwallis at Baghdad, and Sir R. Bullard at Teheran, were, as the Foreign Office realised, better able to judge the repercussions of policy on Moslem opinion.

[3] For a short account of this organisation, known as Special Operations Executive, see J. R. M. Butler, *Grand Strategy*, II (H.M.S.O., 1957), 261, and J. M. A. Gwyer, III, pt. I (H.M.S.O., 1964), 38–48.

the Prime Minister and the President of the United States. Mr. Churchill, with the knowledge of his colleagues in the Cabinet, had begun sending these messages when he was First Lord of the Admiralty. Their purpose had been to give the President information, and throughout the exchanges Mr. Churchill remained the more active of the two correspondents. From May, 1940, he sent over a thousand telegrams to Mr. Roosevelt, and received about eight hundred, most of them in the form of replies.

At least on the British side, however, this correspondence did not lead to any serious confusion of policy. After one or two mild protests from the British Embassy in Washington that the Ambassador, who might himself have to see the President on the questions at issue, should be given full and early knowledge of these special telegrams, Mr. Churchill saw to it that the Foreign Office and the Ambassador were told what he was saying, or at least what he had said. On important matters within his concern the Secretary of State was consulted in advance about the text of the messages.[1] The Foreign Office recognised the value of this personal approach, and there were times when the Prime Minister himself thought it wiser to refuse their suggestions that he should make use of it. Similarly the Prime Minister consulted the Foreign Office and, obviously, the War Cabinet over proposals put to him by the President at their meetings without previous notice.[2] On their side the Secretary of State for Foreign Affairs and his advisers recognised that the Prime Minister was concerned (as indeed they too were concerned) above all else, and, if necessary, at all risks, with the defeat of the enemy. The Foreign Office was often disquieted at the subordination of long-term British political interests to immediate military considerations. A subordination of an equally drastic and dangerous kind took place in economic and financial matters, and had to be accepted as the price of victory.

Thus, in spite of the development of new machinery and of parallel agencies, the Foreign Office and the diplomatic Missions abroad remained the principal instruments for the formulation and execution of policy and the principal channels of communication between Government and Government. From the nature of its work, the first requirements of the Office were that it should be adequately supplied with information, and able to assess this information in depth.[3] An immense mass of material was received, and yet, in spite

---

[1] See also below, pp. xxxix–xli and 334–5.

[2] For an exceptional case (the 'Morgenthau plan') see below, pp. lv–lvi.

[3] The figures of incoming correspondence in 1913 were 68,119, in 1938, 238,879 and in 1944, 402,400. Many of these telegrams or despatches were of a routine character, but the proportion of important material was greater in 1938 than in 1913. A considerable amount of time and money was spent before 1914 in reporting the movements even of minor members of European reigning families.

of it, or perhaps because of it, the level of interpretation was not always sufficiently high. Moreover, owing to the increasing amount of business conducted at a 'Government to Government' level, and to the confusion of world affairs after 1929, the senior members of the service at home and in many posts abroad had been overworked for a long time, and had little opportunity to look outside their day-to-day business. The risk of a superficial approach (though it might not affect the skill and acuteness with which particular questions were handled) was greater because members of the service were transferred at intervals of a few years from country to country or department to department, and not only for the practical reason that otherwise promotion would become a haphazard matter; the foreign service of a country with world-wide interests required that its members should have more than local knowledge and experience.[1] Other defects of the 'machine' might have been corrected earlier; for example, the lack of a special staff or adviser competent to deal with technical economic questions of an international kind. The Foreign Office had thus been at a disadvantage during the years when the problems of German reparation and inter-Allied debts overshadowed the whole field of international relations. Decisions on these questions tended to be left to experts in other departments, or outside them. In such case the political matters on which the Foreign Office could speak with authority might well be given insufficient attention.[2]

In spite of some shortcomings, however, the 'machine' worked well during the war. Mr. Eden, who was Secretary of State from December 23, 1940, to the resignation of Mr. Churchill's adminis-tration in July, 1945, was more of a 'professional' Foreign Secretary than his immediate predecessors in the sense that his parliamentary and ministerial career had centred mainly round the business of the Foreign Office. He had learned much—and discarded not a little—

---

[1] It is often said that British diplomats moved among too narrow social circles in the countries to which they were accredited. There is some truth in this view. It was more true before 1914 than after 1919. It remained true in some countries for reasons outside British control. The Soviet Government isolated the Diplomatic Corps from almost all intercourse with Russians except for the conduct of official business. Even in a parlia-mentary democracy, however, a diplomat has to remember that his first duty is to maintain good relations with the Government rather than to cultivate members of the Opposition. In particular, he must avoid giving cause for suspicion that he is using his position for purposes of political intrigue. During (and before) the war the Germans did themselves more harm than good in this matter, for example, throughout Latin America. M. Maisky allowed himself a freedom of public criticism which would hardly have been tolerated in the case of other Ambassadors, yet one may doubt whether the political value to the Russians of their Mission in Great Britain was really enhanced.

[2] These facts were neither the sole nor the most important reason for the decline in the influence of the Foreign Office in the period immediately before 1939. A historian cannot ignore such a decline, though he would not describe it in terms of an 'eclipse', or regard it as a feature of the actual years of war.

while in office and in opposition to official policy before 1939. One
of his comments on a Foreign Office paper of 1943, 'Let us be most
prudent never to promise in the future what we cannot perform',
sums up the sharpest lesson of these earlier years. He was a realist,
and at the same time inclined by temperament to think in terms of
distant consequences and ultimate considerations. The relations,
personal and political, between Mr. Churchill and Mr. Eden were
exceptionally close. Mr. Eden was thus able to balance, and often to
correct Mr. Churchill's rapid approach and equally rapid conclusions. He was also most fortunate in having Sir Alexander Cadogan
as Permanent Under-Secretary at the Foreign Office. Sir A. Cadogan
had remarkable powers of judgment and lucid expression. His
minutes on paper after paper deal with almost every aspect of foreign
affairs. They stood out at the time, and are likely to stand out in
retrospect, as models of open-mindedness and sound conclusion.
They bear no signs of haste or half-finished reasoning even when the
writer gives a warning that he needs more time for reflection. They
often have a certain irony, never any rancour or prejudice. Only
their modesty is delusive; the reader of these short notes written (they
are very rarely typed) in a firm, quiet hand may not realise at once
how great a mastery they show.

In general the technique of British policy remained—and was
bound to remain—as it had developed over a long period of time.[1]
British diplomatic methods were at once cautious and extremely
flexible, informal and highly professionalised; these habits of caution
and understatement were a part of the tradition of a maritime and
trading community aware of its vulnerability. The wide spread of
British interests throughout the world made it necessary to consider questions of policy from every angle, to show a long patience,
and to accept compromise. Furthermore a cautious policy was
necessary owing to parliamentary control at home and owing to
the ties linking the United Kingdom with the rest of the Commonwealth. The great Dominions—the term was already outmoded as a
description of these independent, sovereign States—made their own
decisions, and their Governments were responsible solely to their
own electorates, but there was still something which could be
called a Commonwealth foreign policy based upon common or
mutual interests as well as upon sentiment and history. The war-
time relations between Great Britain and other members of the
Commonwealth were not merely closer than their respective relations with other Allies; they were different in kind. Ministers of the
Dominions attended meetings of the War Cabinet; Field-Marshal

---

[1] Sir Eyre Crowe's memorandum of 1907 (*British Documents on the Origins of the War,
1898–1914*, III, Appendix A (H.M.S.O., 1927)) remains the best short exposition of
what might be called the 'traditional' British foreign policy.

Smuts was an Elder Statesman of the whole Commonwealth. The initiative in the formulation of policy came largely—though not altogether[1]—from London, since the King's Government in the United Kingdom tended to be more directly informed than the King's Governments overseas. For this very reason the Foreign Office had to take account of the wishes of the Dominions and to ensure that their Prime Ministers were consulted in matters of concern to them.[2]

With the outbreak of war one of the first problems was that of the co-ordination of policy with France. On the face of things this co-ordination should have been easy. British and French Ministers were able to meet within a matter of hours; even in the last confused days of the battle of France two such meetings were held at the shortest notice. In September, 1939, a Supreme War Council came into existence smoothly and without elaborate preparation. In the spring of 1940, Great Britain and France found little difficulty in signing a declaration not to conclude a separate peace. Nevertheless the 'co-ordination of will' between the two Allies was never complete; there was an awkward disagreement on September 2, 1939—the second day of the German attack on Poland—over the time-limit to be laid down in the Anglo-French ultimatum and for most of this same day M. Bonnet was ready, while the British Government refused, to listen to Mussolini's proposal for a conference without any previous withdrawal of the invading German troops.

Until the Germans began their offensive in Norway, Anglo-French differences were less apparent because the military situation did not compel, or rather did not seem to require rapid and unified action. It may well be argued that one of the mistakes of British propaganda in the early part of the war was that it made somewhat futile efforts to discredit Hitler with the German people, but neglected to counter the dangerous German propaganda intended to discredit the British Government and the British war effort in the eyes of the French people. A certain military initiative was open, at least formally, to the Allies, although the French, in particular, did not realise how dangerously limited was their field of choice. There was, however, one limiting factor which each of the two Allied Governments understood. They knew that they could not open a decisive campaign against Germany in 1939 or 1940. In September, 1939, the British Cabinet decided to make plans on the assumption that the war would go on at least for three years. The first year

---

[1] The views of the Canadian Government were of special importance over the whole field of Anglo-American relations.

[2] The Foreign Office also had to consider the views of the Government of India and to defend the interests of the Moslem States in the Middle and Far East with the sovereigns of which Great Britain was in special treaty relationship.

could be only one of preparation. Thus it was possible for the time to evade the question how the war would be won. An evasion of this kind allowed a certain wishful thinking. On the British side one may notice over-confidence in the ultimate efficacy of the blockade as an instrument of victory. On the French side the tendency to evasion took the form of favouring plans which would remove the scene of fighting from the borders of France or redress the balance of numbers to the French advantage. Hence the French proposals for getting the support of the armies of the Balkan States, or for cutting off German oil supplies from Roumania and the U.S.S.R. Hence also the readiness of the French to accept a plan which would deprive Germany of iron ore supplies not only from the port of Narvik but from the northern Swedish ore-fields generally.

These plans came to nothing. Fortunately, as it turned out, British military arguments against becoming involved in war with Russia over Baku, or attempting a diversion at Salonika prevented steps which might have made chances of victory almost impossible. The Scandinavian plans were mishandled, or fumbled, at Cabinet level—both on the political and the military side. On the political side the vacillations and delays were due in part perhaps to a deep and almost subconscious inhibition caused by the hatred of war as such. In any case the British Government hesitated to regard hitherto accepted rules of international law as inapplicable to neutral countries which submitted to illegal pressure from Germany. It was impossible at this stage of the war—before the complete foulness of German behaviour was known—to decide what should be done about the smaller neutrals from whom Germany was extorting by threats or open breach of international law military and economic advantages which the Allies denied to themselves by their scruples. The Allies were fighting for the rule of law and the independence of small States against German aggression; they did not wish to lower their own standards. On grounds of expediency they had also to consider the effect upon neutral opinion generally, and especially upon American opinion, of action against neutral rights. In the last resort indeed the British Government (and the American) failed to see that the enemy would leave them no choice in the matter. If the Germans decided to extend the area of the war, the Allies could not prevent them from so doing.

After the collapse of France the war took a new form for Great Britain. Hitherto the fact that the land war was being fought outside Great Britain created a certain illusion (as in 1914–18) among the British people of a Continental war to which they were lending their assistance. To some extent this illusion—which was not shared in official circles—had an incidental and surprising result. British opinion did not envisage the collapse of France as the defeat of

Great Britain. The escape of the British Expeditionary Force from destruction at Dunkirk was seen, absurdly, but fortunately, almost as a kind of victory—the extrication of a British army from a campaign which was primarily a French affair. Events showed that this reaction, less strange, perhaps, when considered in relation to English history, was neither selfish nor foolishly self-confident. At a time when the world in general took for granted an Allied and not only a French defeat, the value of the 'optical illusion' cannot be over-estimated. It provided the foundation for a new and splendid leadership.

The personal influence of Mr. Churchill was so immense, four-square and noble that it is unnecessary to try to heighten it by disparaging his predecessor. Mr. Chamberlain's words to his colleagues in the Cabinet on September 1 summed up his own personality.[1] His direction of the war and some of his public phrases showed clumsiness and lack of imagination, but in matters of policy and strategy he followed conscientiously the expert advice given to him; his own opinions indeed were shared by most of his advisers. On the other hand Mr. Churchill's judgment throughout the Scandinavian episode was by no means free from fault. Nevertheless in the changed circumstances of the German victory in France and the gravest threat to Great Britain, Mr. Churchill's leadership had about it something absolute and adamantine; something which had not been known in English history since the years 1757–1759. Such power and insight brought a new direction in every branch of the State. This massive driving force manifested itself at once in the attempt to save France, and then to deter the two leading French soldiers as well as a majority of French politicians from the unnecessary immolation of total surrender.

For the Foreign Office these days of military disaster were crowded also with other negotiations; an attempt to discover how far the Soviet Government might change their attitude in view of the dangers which their policy of the previous twelve months had brought upon them; last moment efforts to delay Mussolini's entry into the war; a sudden menace from Japan; acceptance of the attitude of Turkey and of Egypt, and—most significant of all—exchanges with the Government of the United States. Here also the Prime Minister, stronger in temperament and better informed than the Ambassador in Washington about the mood of the British nation, took principal control by means of his direct correspondence with President Roosevelt. The President indeed was more hopeful than his military advisers—including General Marshall—about the survival of Great Britain.

A historian, reading the Foreign Office papers of this time, is struck

---

[1] See below, p. 1, and note 1.

by the way in which, without minimising the extreme gravity of the situation, the negotiations undertaken by the Foreign Office or by the Ambassadors abroad express confidence in ultimate victory.[1] In different circumstances Sir P. Loraine at Rome, Sir H. Knatchbull-Hugessen at Ankara, Sir S. Cripps in Moscow, Sir R. Craigie in Japan, and Sir S. Hoare in Madrid used similar language. From Turkey more could hardly be expected than a friendly neutrality and resistance to German demands. Great Britain asked for a similar resistance from Spain, and could promise in return, with American collaboration, supplies of which the Spanish people were in desperate need and which the Germans were unable to provide. In Japan there was no practical alternative to a stubborn retreat, together with a warning that an attack on Great Britain would mean ultimate disaster to the attacking Power. In the United States the first task was to recreate confidence that Great Britain was a 'good risk', and therefore worth helping. Even after the first mood of alarm had passed, American opinion, in the view of the Prime Minister and the Foreign Office, was too ready to assume that a German invasion would succeed. Against this background, and, incidentally, in the 'pre-election' circumstances of American politics, the Foreign Office also had to try to secure American diplomatic support in restraining Japan and in influencing Marshal Pétain's Government against further surrender to German demands, especially with regard to the French fleet.

The question of the French fleet was of the highest importance to British survival, just as the question of the British fleet loomed large in American calculations about their own chance of defeating Axis attack. The British Government had not anticipated the terms which the Germans laid down about the fleet in the armistice with France. These terms (like those providing for an 'unoccupied' area in France) were adroitly devised in order to allow the French Government the illusion that they could 'contract out' of the war, while escaping the consequences of military defeat, and, incidentally, keeping their promise to Great Britain not to allow their fleet to fall into German hands.[2]

This clever German move succeeded only too well. In fact the Germans could put inescapable pressure on the French, and the

---

[1] The calmness of tone and manner of the Foreign Office papers in the weeks of extreme danger is almost ironical. Indeed the only external evidence of crisis is a certain confusion in the filing system when, as a result of instructions (not in themselves unnecessary) for the practice of greater economy in the use of paper, the Registry gave up its excellent but lavish system of including only a few papers under a single jacket. The results of this change of method soon became so chaotic that Sir A. Cadogan ordered a reversion—with due care for economy—to the previous practice.

[2] The Germans did not intend to limit themselves ultimately to the terms of the armistice. They contravened these terms at once in the illegal charges levied as part of the cost of their army of occupation.

British Government could not avoid—without enormous risk—taking action to prevent as many warships as possible from reaching French metropolitan ports. One of the results of British preventive action was the tragic engagement at Oran. This event intensified French anger with Great Britain, and the more so because the French Government put out an untrue version of the facts. It is, however, doubtful whether, if the engagement at Oran had been avoided, the policy of Marshal Pétain's Government towards Great Britain would have been any less hostile.[1] Darlan's anglophobia was increased by the French losses at Oran, but Laval was not an admiral, and his policy of Franco-German collaboration was not based on sentiment—least of all, a sentiment of blind revenge. In 1940 Laval, Darlan, and Marshal Pétain himself believed that Germany would certainly win the war. For some time after their own surrender Marshal Pétain and his Government expected a British defeat almost at once. They remained convinced throughout 1941 of the unlikelihood of a British victory, and would not have refused the price of any real German concessions merely in order to prolong British resistance. They even regarded the prolongation of this resistance as dangerous to France, and as a threat to the stability of Europe.[2] Marshal Pétain's confused and half-hearted efforts by secret negotiation to arrange a kind of *modus vivendi* with the British were mainly an attempt, once again, to 'contract out' of the blockade and to establish with Great Britain the same relations of quasi-neutrality which he hoped to secure from the Germans. At best they could be regarded as a reinsurance when the British defeat was surprisingly delayed, and the French Ministers began to be afraid that Great Britain and Germany might come to terms at French expense; in other words, that the British Government would treat France as Marshal Pétain's Government had been willing to treat Great Britain.[3]

One fact of this time is indeed often overlooked. The situation throughout German-occupied Europe in the latter half of 1940 and the first half of 1941 would have been more serious for Great Britain—

---

[1] Marshal Pétain's Government had already shown, among other military measures favourable to Germany, by a breach of the French promise to ensure that German air pilots captured in France should be transferred to custody in Great Britain, that they would do nothing to prevent the strengthening of the German forces of invasion.

[2] M. Paul Baudouin's diary (*Neuf mois au Gouvernement* (Paris, 1948), 309) contains a revealing comment on a speech by Mr. Churchill on August 20, 1940. Mr. Churchill had spoken of fighting a long war until victory. M. Baudouin broadcast: 'Les années défilent sous ses yeux comme un programme de destructions: 1940 . . 1941 . . 1942. S'il devait en être ainsi, si la guerre devait continuer ses ravages sur l'Europe et sur le monde pendant tant de mois, c'est la misère qui triompherait. Aucun homme d'Etat soucieux de ses devoirs envers son peuple . . . ne peut, même en esprit, adhérer à ce fatalisme de destruction.'

[3] The German attack on Russia made no difference to the attitude of the French Government. They expected a Russian defeat. In any case, a German defeat at the hands of the Russians would have been, from Marshal Pétain's point of view, a disaster for France, since it would certainly have resulted in the collapse of the conservative Vichy régime.

and the task of the Foreign Office more difficult—if the Germans had behaved in accordance with the illusions of the Vichy Government, that is to say, if they had acted in a manner likely to reconcile the conquered nations to a Europe organised and dominated by the German Reich. Great Britain might have been isolated in neutral—including American—opinion as an intransigent and selfish Power fighting only for her own imperial interests. Even the German explanation of their attack on Russia might have carried some conviction.

The Germans put out propaganda in and after the autumn of 1940 about a New Order which they intended to establish in Europe —a united Europe under German hegemony with immense economic advantages to all concerned. This propaganda never made much headway. It trailed a great deal of doctrinaire talk about *Lebensraum* and *Grossraum* and other favourite terms of the Nazi theorists. Hitler himself was not much interested in it; conquest and the stark employment of power—the everlasting tramp of heavy-booted police and soldiers—were more satisfying to him than the conciliation of conquered peoples. The Germans were not even on good terms with their Italian allies; they distrusted and despised them, and, in return, the Italians (including Mussolini) quickly realised that their place in the New Europe was not likely to be much better than that of the French.

In any case the Germans soon dropped the pretence of a New Order. The organisation of such an order depended on victory, and from the early winter of 1941–2, the complete victory—which had receded unexpectedly in the autumn of 1940—looked more distant. The planning of a New Order had to give way to the immediate requirements of war. The treatment of the occupied countries became more severe. The Germans began to meet sabotage and organised underground resistance. Their response was savage and brutal, and, in a last analysis, ineffective. The 'New Order' took the political form of mass executions of hostages, the imposition of torture, and, economically, the exploitation of subject labour on a vast scale. Meanwhile the answer to the Germans had been made, at the suggestion of the United States, in the Atlantic Charter, and to this affirmation of human rights the Germans could make no effective reply.[1]

---

[1] It is an interesting example of the difference between British and American ways of thinking that the Foreign Office had proposed a broadcast by Mr. Keynes explaining that Great Britain had more to offer Europe in the form of an order based on sterling, and linked with the free nations of the Commonwealth, than Germany could offer in a new order based on the mark and the subordination of the rest of Europe to German economic domination. Some of Mr. Keynes's economic arguments were used by Mr. Eden in a speech of May 29, 1941; the main broadcast was never delivered because the President—while not disagreeing with the British view—wanted a statement in broad terms of human rights. Sir R. F. Harrod, *Life of J. M. Keynes* (Macmillan, 1951), 503–4 and 509–10.

The Prime Minister has written that, on hearing of the Japanese attack on Pearl Harbour, his first thought was that Great Britain could not now lose the war.[1] This was the view of most Englishmen, and especially of those in a position to measure the dangers through which the country had passed since the spring of 1940. Hitherto all that could be done since the collapse of France had been to gain time, win tactical successes, and wait for a great strategical opening, after Hitler had made some large and irretrievable mistake. It was not unreasonable to hope that such a man would make such a mistake, though, when Hitler actually made it in his attack on Russia, the fact was realised more quickly in the Foreign Office than by military opinion. Most—not all—military experts in Great Britain thought that the Russian armies would be defeated within a few months.[2] The German position would then be much stronger, and an Allied victory would require even greater sacrifice in the face of a long war. On the other hand the British Government wisely acted on the assumption that Russian resistance would be prolonged. Within a few hours of the German attack the Prime Minister promised the fullest assistance which Great Britain could provide, although every item supplied could be spared only at a risk to the rapid equipment of the British Forces.[3]

The entry of the United States into the war was—as seen from Great Britain—a more certain guarantee of victory because at this very time Hitler had failed to break Russian resistance, and was unlikely to do so—if at all—until Germany had suffered more and heavier losses, and the western Powers had gained invaluable time. The Prime Minister, however, had always thought that the United States would be compelled in American interests to enter the war as a full belligerent. In the event American entry was delayed much longer than Mr. Churchill had at one time expected, and the delay was partly the result of the successful defence of Great Britain. Nevertheless throughout the months of extreme crisis, even as a myth, the idea that American belligerency might be close at hand was of service in the formulation of policy and the fight for survival.

Mr. Churchill has also written—and the two statements are not inconsistent—that he found the strain of war greater during the period of defeat in 1942 than in 1940 and 1941.[4] The length of time for which this strain had already been endured was no doubt one

---

[1] The Prime Minister's words are more positive: 'So we had won after all.' Winston S. Churchill, *The Second World War*, III (Cassell, 1950), 539. (These volumes are referred to hereinafter as 'Churchill'.)

[2] See below, p. 620.

[3] The President seems to have decided independently to help the Russians if they were attacked, but the effect on American opinion of the Prime Minister's prompt action is a fact to which the Russians at least have never given sufficient weight.

[4] This was also the view of the Foreign Office.

reason why it seemed heavier. There was also a sense of disappointment and humiliation over the losses of 1942. Above all the Prime Minister's responsibilities were extended in and after 1942 to cover a new situation. Once again—and to their good fortune—Great Britain and the Dominions were fighting with powerful Allies, but the alliance brought with it, as always, serious problems of unity among its members. The Prime Minister had the heavy burden of persuading the Americans to give up an impracticable strategic plan, and to accept something more within the compass of Allied resources in 1942. He had to argue—with the prestige of resistance in 1940 receding into the background and without the prestige of victory—against proposals put forward by the President and his most trusted military adviser, General Marshall, and obviously supported by Stalin.

The discussions on high strategy have been fully described elsewhere, and in any case were mainly outside the sphere of the Foreign Office. So also were the arrangements made for the establishment of a Combined Chiefs of Staff Committee at Washington upon which the British Chiefs of Staff would have permanent representation. There was no counterpart, and, for obvious reasons, there could hardly be a counterpart in the political sphere to this close and continuous military collaboration, or to the Combined Boards dealing with production and the allocation of resources. The British Embassy in Washington and the United States Embassy in London already provided machinery for political consultation.

These existing channels of communication, however, were different in kind from those provided by the Combined Chiefs of Staff. The business of the Foreign Office and of the Department of State extended from the particular and temporary ends of military collaboration into wider questions of permanent national interest. The function of the British diplomatic Mission in Washington was not to work out with the Department of State a 'combined' policy, but to transmit and explain the views of the British Government, and, through the Foreign Office, to inform the British Government of American views. There was a common political purpose—the defeat of the enemy in war—but 'victory' was by no means a simple term; it had one meaning for the United States, another for Great Britain, and—disastrously, as it turned out—a third meaning for Russia. To some extent, indeed, the close and friendly Anglo-American collaboration over immediate tasks—the 'combination' in military plans, and in the production and supply of things necessary for the defeat of the enemy—was delusive because it tended to conceal the differences in political interests and outlook. When, in the last stages of the war, the immediate purposes of 'combination' were coming to fulfilment, their temporary nature was shown with disconcerting suddenness, for example, by the abrupt termination of Lend-Lease.

Nonetheless the existence of a very close liaison on the military side without any corresponding political instrument—a committee working, day to day, as the Combined Chiefs of Staff worked, on an agenda—was bound to have important consequences and the more so because the business at the meetings between the Prime Minister and the President was primarily military. The Chiefs of Staff therefore attended with a team of assistants; the Foreign Office and the State Department were not always represented by their political heads, and sometimes only by relatively subordinate officials. The Prime Minister was more guarded, but the President was apt to take decisions carrying with them important political implications without consulting his expert advisers. Political questions could not in fact be separated from military decisions. Even during the informal and non-binding staff conversations held at Washington in the early part of 1941 the American representatives were warned by their own authorities that 'it is to be expected that proposals of the British representatives will have been drawn up with chief regard for the support of the British Commonwealth. Never absent from British minds are their post-war interests, commercial and military. We should likewise safeguard our own eventual interests.'[1]

It is thus unlikely that the British Embassy in Washington could have done more to clear away prejudices and misunderstandings in the minds of the President and his advisers over the motives of British policy. In any case the Prime Minister was to a large extent his own interpreter. His personal messages to Mr. Roosevelt were of the greatest political service, especially during the year and a half between the collapse of France and the entry of the United States into the war. On the political side, however, there was a certain danger that the President would take the Prime Minister's arguments and predilections as formal statements of British policy, and also that he might feel afraid of being over-persuaded to support proposals which American public opinion would regard as more in British than American interest.

As the war went on, and the development of American power increased, Mr. Roosevelt showed some restiveness, even perhaps a little jealousy at the Prime Minister's initiative.[2] Mr. Winant, in a conversation with Mr. Law[3] on August 23, 1943, also made the comment that the machinery of the Department of State was much

---

[1] M. Matloff and E. M. Snell, *Strategic Planning for Coalition Warfare* (Department of the Army, Washington, D.C., 1953), 29–30.

[2] Mr. Stettinius, in May, 1944, spoke plainly on this matter.

[3] Mr. R. Law, M.P.

complicated by the direct line of communication between the Prime
Minister and the President. He suggested that the complication was
less in London because the Prime Minister and the Foreign Secretary
were always in the closest consultation, whereas in Washington there
were no daily talks between the President and the Secretary of State.
If they 'saw each other once a month, their relations could be considered very close'.[1] The situation, as far as British observers knew,
had not changed a year later. Mr. Stettinius, shortly after his appointment to the Secretaryship of State in December, 1944, told Admiral
Leahy that, with the President's approval, he was appointing Mr.
C. E. Bohlen to act as a special liaison officer between the White
House and the State Department. Admiral Leahy thought the plan
'an excellent idea', and described it as an effort by Mr. Stettinius
'to get in closer contact with the President who had been handling
much foreign affairs business without consulting the Department of
State'.[2] The United States Chiefs of Staff were themselves often
unaware of what the President and the Prime Minister were discussing. General Deane, who was United States Secretary of the
Combined Chiefs of Staff until 1943, has written that he had a very
close working arrangement with his British colleague whereby he
obtained 'much information from British sources concerning the
subjects of communications between President Roosevelt and Prime
Minister Churchill. For some reason our President often kept our
Chiefs of Staff in the dark on these matters until the die was cast,
and, at times, the advance information that I could obtain was
invaluable.'[3] Since the British Embassy in Washington communi-

---

[1] From other American sources this statement would appear to have been an exaggeration, but 'once a week' might not have been wide of the mark. Mr. Winant, in this
conversation, showed that he did not feel that he was himself receiving the full confidence
of the President. (It is worth remembering that during the first World War Mr. Page,
United States Ambassador in London, suffered—though for different reasons—from a
similar lack of confidence on the part of Mr. Wilson.) From the British point of view, the
President's liking for 'one-man Missions' did not provide an adequate substitute for a
continuous and fully informed political liaison on what might be called the 'highest
official levels'. Mr. Hopkins, in particular, was generally of great service in smoothing
over differences of opinion and in interpreting British views to the President as well as
American views to the Prime Minister. Mr. Hopkins's position, however, as a friend and
personal adviser to the President, and his bad health—he was always in danger of physical
collapse—made his intervention somewhat haphazard and uncertain. Moreover his own
relationship with the President was less close after his long illness in the first half of 1944.

[2] W. D. Leahy, *I Was There* (Gollancz, 1950), 281. Admiral Leahy, while Ambassador
at Vichy, had written frequently to the President (at the latter's request), and also to Mr.
Welles. He does not seem to have corresponded personally with Mr. Hull or with anyone
else in the State Department, *id.*, pp. 14–15. See also *Foreign Relations of the United States*
(hereafter referred to as *F.R.U.S.*), 1944, I, 811 and 833.

[3] J. R. Deane, *The Strange Alliance* (New York, 1947), 9. General Deane's first intimation that he was being sent to the Moscow Conference of 1943 as Mr. Hull's military
adviser reached him from a telegram (sent by the Prime Minister in Washington) which
was shown to him by his British colleague. For the lengths to which Mr. Roosevelt went
in withholding information from Mr. Hull, see Leahy, *op cit.*, 173. The Foreign Office
was aware of the differences between British and American procedures, and also of
personal differences within Mr. Roosevelt's administration. These matters, however, were
not of British concern, and the Foreign Office, obviously, had to accept them.

cated normally with the State Department, Mr. Churchill's direct access to the President had advantages in bringing before him arguments which might otherwise not have reached him. Nevertheless one result seems to have been that the Secretary of State and his officials—as well as the American Chiefs of Staff—tended to take a kind of defensive attitude towards the Prime Minister, and not less so because they knew his masterful powers of persuasion. Admiral Leahy's comment on Mr. Hopkins is typical of a general American feeling: 'Nobody could fool him [Mr. Hopkins], not even Churchill.'[1]

The fear of being over-persuaded to support British interests may be seen in the American attitude at the three meetings of heads of Governments—Teheran, Yalta, and Potsdam. At Teheran, where their views on strategic policy had brought the Americans closer to the Russians than to the British on the main issues under discussion, the records give the impression that the President and his military advisers came away with a curiously favourable view of Stalin.[2] At and after Yalta the American suspicions of British policy were even more serious. The President seemed to find in British doubts about Russian policy little more than an outmoded anxiety over the balance of power and to regard the more cautious British attitude towards the demands of Italian politicians, and the action taken by the British forces in Greece as due in no small part to Mr. Churchill's predilection for constitutional monarchy. Mr. Roosevelt believed that, if handled tactfully, and brought within the legal arrangements of the proposed World Security Organisation, the Russians would be no danger to European stability. Hence on almost every point in the discussions at the Conference where the Prime Minister and Mr. Eden were prepared to resist Russian claims or to insist upon con-

---

[1] Leahy, *op. cit.*, 138. This defensive feeling came out in the American view that the British had a better 'military-political organisation', and were more clear-headed in working out a national policy. At the time of Mr. Eden's visit to Washington in March, 1943, Admiral Leahy wrote: 'Eden, like other British political officials (*sic*) of high position that I came to know, seemed to have a better understanding of the general policy of his country than was the case with many of our own leaders. Anthony Eden knew what Britain wanted. There were times when I felt that if I could find anybody except Roosevelt who knew what America wanted, it would be an astonishing discovery.' Leahy, *op. cit.*, 156. See also Gordon A. Harrison, *The European Theatre of Operations, Cross-Channel Attack* (Department of the Army, Washington, D.C., 1951), 3–6 for an interesting summary of the difference between British and American procedures.

[2] Admiral Leahy gives an account of the first view of Stalin taken by the Americans. After the opening session of the Conference Admiral Leahy wrote: 'The talk among ourselves . . . was about Stalin. Most of us, before we met him, thought he was a bandit leader who had pushed himself up to the top of his government. That impression was wrong. We knew . . . that we were dealing with a highly intelligent man who spoke well, and was determined to get what he wanted for Russia.' Leahy, *op. cit.*, 205. General Deane also noticed that the Americans were 'all considerably and favourably impressed' by Stalin, 'probably because he advocated the American point of view in our differences with the British. Regardless of this, one could not help but recognise qualities of greatness in the man.' Deane, *op. cit.*, 43. It is also, perhaps, significant that General Deane noted that Mr. Churchill's oratory lost effect when it was turned into Russian by an interpreter. *id. ib.*, 42.

cession for concession the President gave only half-hearted support or took the Russian side. Mr. Churchill was left alone to argue in favour of allowing the French a place in the Allied Control Commission for Germany, though the President said that the United States army of occupation would be removed after two years, and French support of Great Britain was thus obviously necessary to maintain the balance of military power in Europe against the Russians.[1] The President was much more willing than the Prime Minister to commit himself to Russian proposals for the dismemberment of Germany, and was readier to accept the extreme Russian demands for reparation. Even on the Polish question, when the President had a domestic political interest in getting a settlement satisfactory to the five or six millions of people of Polish descent in the United States, the Prime Minister was firmer in attempting to secure a Polish Government of real independence. Towards the end of the Conference the President embarrassed the British Ministers by insisting on closing the proceedings, not in order to return quickly to the United States, but in order to see King Ibn Saud, King Farouk of Egypt, and the Emperor of Ethiopia on his way home.

On March 13, after his return to the United States, Mr. Stettinius—according to Mr. Forrestal[2]—described the Yalta meeting as most successful, especially as regards Russo-American relations. There was 'every evidence of the Russian desire to co-operate along all lines with the United States'. Three days later—again according to Mr. Forrestal's notes[3]—the President 'indicated' to his Cabinet 'considerable difficulty with British relations. In a semi-jocular manner of speaking, he stated that the British were perfectly willing for the United States to have a war with Russia at any time, and that, in his opinion, to follow the British program would be to proceed toward that end.'

Such was one of the misunderstandings which had arisen in the course of settling the affairs of the Grand Alliance by the method of personal discussion between the three Heads of Governments. It is impossible to say whether, if President Roosevelt had lived longer, there would have been any change, at the highest level, in this American distrust of British aims or in the belief that the Russians

---

[1] Mr. Roosevelt himself seems belatedly to have realised this fact. At a later stage in the conference he withdrew his opposition to inviting the French to join the Control Commission, and also qualified, somewhat vaguely, his statement about a two-year limit of occupation by saying that, if a World Organisation were established on satisfactory lines, the American public might be more willing to take a full share in the organisation of peace through the world.

[2] *The Forrestal Diaries*, ed. W. Millis and E. S. Duffield (Cassell, 1952), 53.

[3] *Id.*, 36–7. Mr. Forrestal was not present at the Cabinet meeting. The note recorded in the *Diaries* was taken by Mr. Hensel, Assistant Secretary of the Navy.

were more amenable to American than to British influence, and that the first care of the United States should be, in President Truman's phrase, to avoid 'ganging up' with Great Britain in an anti-Russian policy.

In the latter part of May, 1945, Mr. Truman and most of his advisers still regarded British policy as an obstacle to satisfactory Russo-American relations.[1] On May 23 the President sent Mr. Hopkins on a visit to Moscow in order to learn more about the Russian attitude. The primary reason for taking this step was the deadlock over the Polish question, but Mr. Hopkins himself told Mr. Forrestal on May 20—before leaving for Moscow—that he was 'sceptical about Churchill, at least in the particular of Anglo-American-Russian relationship', and that he thought it of vital importance that 'the United States should not be manoeuvred into a position where Great Britain had us lined up with them as a *bloc* against Russia to implement England's European policy'. Mr. Truman, at the same time, sent Mr. Joseph E. Davies on a special mission to London. Mr. Davies, a former American Ambassador to Russia and a leading supporter of Russo-American collaboration, was not very successful. He brought with him a proposal, which the Prime Minister was certain to reject, that before the proposed tripartite meeting of Heads of Government, the President should see Stalin alone. The Prime Minister tried to explain to Mr. Davies that the differences between Great Britain and Russia were over matters of principle for which the Western Powers had been fighting the war, and that the United States Government was not just dealing with two 'foreign Powers of which it might be said that both were equally at fault', but Mr. Davies thought Mr. Churchill 'basically more concerned over preserving England's position in Europe than in preserving peace'.[2]

Thus when Mr. Truman reached the tripartite Conference, after refusing to visit Great Britain on his way to Berlin, he continued to see himself as a mediator, from outside the troubled countries of Europe, between the British and the Russians over 'special interests' which were of little direct concern to the United States. After his first meeting with Stalin, Mr. Truman seemed to think that he and Stalin could come to a satisfactory agreement. In his own account of the Potsdam Conference he implies that this settlement would have been made between the United States and Russia, with Great Britain on the side-lines. He did not underrate the difficulties and realised that he would be faced as chairman with many problems arising out

---

[1] In spite of warning messages about Russian policy received from Mr. Harriman, United States Ambassador in Moscow. Mr. Truman has written in his *Memoirs*, I (Hodder & Stoughton. 1955), 164, that at the end of April, 1945, he was trying to persuade Churchill to forget power politics.

[2] Leahy, *op. cit.*, 380. Admiral Leahy also thought that Mr. Churchill wanted to keep the American army in Europe because he saw in its presence 'a hope of sustaining Britain's vanishing position in Europe'.

of the conflict of interests. He knew that Stalin and Churchill[1] would have special interests that might clash. He was clearly impressed by Stalin's direct manner and speech, and felt hopeful that an agreement could be reached satisfactory to the world and the Western Powers.[2]

The Prime Minister also carried on a correspondence with Stalin during the period after the German attack on Russia.[3] This correspondence was different in character from the exchanges with Mr. Roosevelt. For one thing, there was no personal meeting between the two men until the Prime Minister's visit to Moscow in August, 1942. This visit, at a time of great difficulty and disappointment, was, on balance, a success: it may indeed be described as one of the most outstanding achievements of Mr. Churchill during the war. There was also very little common ground with the Russians, and on the Russian side, no store of goodwill. The Russians, while accepting all the help which Great Britain and the United States could provide—and indeed making impossible demands—had not responded with much eagerness to the Prime Minister's offer of loyal collaboration. From their own rigid standpoint they had no reason to do so. They were fighting solely because the Germans had attacked them. Before this attack they had been willing to assist Hitler. They had no interest in the idealist motives which were as genuine a part of the British will to victory as the motive of self-preservation. They were perhaps more hostile to western capitalist democracy than to national socialism. Their main wish—after the desire to expel a savage and brutal invader—was that the Western Powers, fascist and anti-fascist, should be not less exhausted than the Soviet Union after the war. M. Maisky told a foreign diplomat in London in December, 1940, that he added up British and German losses not in two columns, but in a single column. The confusion, not the recovery, of the West seemed the safest guarantee of Soviet security. If the military effort of repelling an invasion should inflict upon Great Britain immense losses in manpower and resources, so much the better, in the long run, for the Soviet Government.

There was thus an element of irony in the Russian appeals for a 'second front'. The Russians were in fact bearing the weight of the

---

[1] The order of mention is of some interest.

[2] Truman *Memoirs*, 267, 275. Later Mr. Truman wrote less hopefully that the personal meeting with Stalin and the Russians was significant for him because it enabled him to see what we and the west had to face in the future. *Id., ib.,* 342.

[3] The Prime Minister sent a personal message, before the German attack, conveying to Stalin information received by the British Government that this attack was likely to take place. For an earlier letter, see below, pp. 466–7.

German attack on land. They had fallen into the danger which, at some humiliation, they had tried to avoid. They were now asking from their Allies sacrifices which they had never themselves intended to make. When their demands for a second front were not and could not be met, the Russians began to taunt their Allies, particularly Great Britain, with cowardice and even to hint at treachery. Mr. Churchill's difficulty in persuading the Russians that an invasion resulting only in defeat could be of no help to them was not lessened by the continued American misjudgment of the extent of the preparations necessary for success and the time which these preparations would take.

Stalin's protests against the postponement of the invasion were most strident after the Anglo-American discussions in Washington in May, 1943, when the project of a cross-Channel expedition in the early autumn of that year faded out, and the main operation was fixed for the spring of 1944. It is impossible—without greater knowledge of what the Russians really thought—to say whether Stalin's charges of bad faith at this time were or were not genuinely made, that is to say, whether he believed, in spite of the guarded statements always made by the Prime Minister, that he had been given an assurance of a second front in France in 1943, and that the military situation in June, 1943, was more and not less favourable to the opening of this front than had been expected when the assurance was given. Sir A. Clark Kerr pointed out that, as seen from Moscow, there was a certain weakness in the Allied case. This weakness lay 'not in our inability to open this second front, but in our having led [Stalin] to believe that we were going to' open it.

The Prime Minister now told Sir A. Clark Kerr that he assumed the 'Churchill-Stalin correspondence' to have come to an end. Stalin himself, however, may have seen that he had gone too far in provoking his Allies—whose assistance he still needed—or he may have been impressed by the results of their Mediterranean strategy, and have realised that, in view of his own successes, he could more easily afford to wait until the spring of 1944 for a large-scale operation in the west. Anyhow, the 'Churchill-Stalin' correspondence was resumed, though, as earlier, the Russian response had none of the cordiality of Mr. Churchill's approach.[1]

In his correspondence with Mr. Roosevelt the Prime Minister, while consulting and informing the Secretary of State, was inclined to set out his own views and ideas. The correspondence with Stalin was much more of an exposition of British policy, almost in the form

---

[1] The Russian distrust was lasting. M. Mikolajczyk, in a memorandum recounting a party given by Stalin to the Polish Ministers at the Potsdam Conference on July 27, 1945, noted that Stalin said to him, *à propos* of the change of government in Great Britain, 'Churchill did not trust us, and, in consequence, we did not fully trust him'. *F.R.U.S., Potsdam Conference*, II, 1531.

of diplomatic notes addressed to the head of the Russian State. The
British Government had found that unless they could reach Stalin
directly through the Prime Minister, they could not be sure that
their requests and explanations ever got to him at all. Even so,
Stalin's answers at times gave the impression that they were written
by another and more unfriendly hand. The Russians made very few
concessions to British requests, and hardly any of them were secured
without this direct intervention. The official contacts between the
British Embassy in Moscow and the Soviet leaders were infrequent,
stiff, and formal. M. Maisky and his successor M. Gusev saw far
more of the British Ministers and high officials in the Foreign Office,
but there is little evidence that the reports of their representatives
in London carried much weight with the Soviet Government.

Mr. Eden, as well as the Foreign Office, inclined to regard Stalin,
at all events before 1944, as more reasonable than M. Molotov, and
even as 'comparatively co-operative'.[1] There is no doubt about the
genuineness on the British side of the wish for co-operation. The War
Cabinet and the Foreign Office were generally agreed—and for the
most obvious reasons — that the future peace and prosperity of
Europe, the prevention of future German aggression, and the larger
plans for the organisation of world security, required the maintenance of good Anglo-Soviet relations on the lines of the treaty of
1942, and that every possible effort (which meant, in practice, every
possible concession) should be made to convince the Soviet Government of the sincerity of the British desire for collaboration. In view
of the Russian attitude the Foreign Office could not be sure that
the Russians really wanted collaboration—which would imply concessions on their side—but the British were prepared to act on the
view that nothing would be lost and a great deal might be gained
by assuming Russian sincerity.

In some respects the Foreign Office held longer than the Prime
Minister to this assumption. They were readier to acquiesce in the
Russian control of the states of south-east Europe — excluding
Greece—partly because it was physically impossible for Great Britain
to prevent this control, and therefore imprudent for her to become
engaged in an attempt to do so. The Foreign Office were also more
conscious than the Prime Minister of the dismal history of representative institutions and the treatment of minorities in these States,
and less inclined to think that notwithstanding the poverty and

---

[1] The Prime Minister reported optimistically to the War Cabinet after the Yalta
Conference about the prospects of post-war collaboration with Russia; his optimism, however, was not unqualified, and rested, as before, largely on the belief (which was shared by
other members of the British Delegation) that Stalin himself showed more personal good
will than his colleagues. The Prime Minister warned the War Cabinet that there might
be a change if for any reason Stalin were no longer in control of Russian policy. Mr.
Churchill had specially in mind that Stalin had kept to his undertaking to regard Greece
as within the British sphere of influence.

confusion of Europe matters would be much better after the defeat of Germany if only the Russians did not interfere. Moreover, as Sir A. Clark Kerr—a very shrewd observer—pointed out from Moscow as late as March, 1945, however 'disappointing and even disturbing' the attitude of the Soviet Government might be, they did not seem to have given up all idea of collaborating with the Western Powers after the war. Their policy of establishing Soviet influence in the Balkans was one of limited objectives which did not endanger British interests. They would not give way as far as these limited objectives were concerned; on the other hand they wanted British support against a possible revival of German aggression.

In the autumn of 1944, with the assurance of Allied victory, the question of Russian post-war co-operation had become more urgent and more ominous. There was clear evidence that the Russians intended to keep under their political and military control the satellite states into whose territories they were advancing. Their treatment of Poland raised even more serious issues with the western Powers, and especially with Great Britain whose immediate reason for entering the war had been the defence of Polish independence. Mr. Churchill, while doing what he could for the Poles in argument with Stalin, thought that the Polish Government in exile had been unwise in refusing to accept, explicitly and without delay, the heavy Russian demands on the pre-1939 Polish eastern frontier, but the Russians were now (as the Poles had always feared) going beyond territorial claims and aiming at the establishment of a Russian-controlled communist régime on 'police-state' lines in the country. They set up a puppet committee of Polish communists, and as they advanced westwards across Poland 'recognised' this committee as the sole legal authority and provisional Polish government. They had given no help to the desperate Warsaw insurrection of August 1 –October 3, 1944,—though they were at least partly responsible for its outbreak—and put obstacles in the way of the slight assistance which the western Powers were able to provide. Mr. Churchill disapproved of the puppet committee, but his own and Mr. Roosevelt's willingness to accept within a short time Stalin's version of the character and outbreak of the Warsaw insurrection showed the Russians how little attention they need pay to Anglo-American protests. At the Yalta Conference Great Britain, in particular, insisted upon a broadening of the basis of the Russian-sponsored Polish Provisional Government to include more representative Poles; the formula adopted for the purpose was, however, not wholly without ambiguity and the Russians showed immediately after the Conference that they did not intend to give the Poles genuinely free institutions. In Mr. Churchill's words, the Russians, having deprived the Poles of their frontiers, were now trying to take away their freedom.

The fact that he was in close touch with two other Heads of Governments in the Grand Alliance who had centralised in themselves the power of decision almost inevitably brought the Prime Minister to treat the whole field of foreign affairs as within his immediate province, although the circumstances—the emergence of liberated States—were at last allowing the Foreign Office to resume its ordinary place in the conduct of policy. Mr. Churchill was still concentrating on the decisions to be taken in the military field where his grasp of detail was unrivalled. He was less concerned as yet with the manifold and remoter—one might almost say quieter—calculations upon which long-range foreign policy must be based. Moreover he was not easily open to persuasion. His closest personal friends were men of forceful character, but without his unmatched political insight. He was, as ever, most careful of his constitutional position and of constitutional practice. No man since Mr. Gladstone has dominated Parliament so magnificently. There was perhaps some danger in this remarkable control, even though Mr. Churchill, again like Mr. Gladstone, was most sensitive to the rights and opinions of the House of Commons. It would, however, be wrong to say that the Prime Minister disregarded expert advice from the Foreign Office or that he encroached upon its functions; nevertheless a good deal of the time and energy of the Foreign Secretary—and, still more, of the Permanent Under-Secretary[1] and the staff of the Office—was taken up in efforts to persuade him that not all his proposals were suited to British interests, or adequate to meet the many important factors in a situation.

The differences of outlook and emphasis between the Prime Minister and the Foreign Office were concerned occasionally with the actions of individuals—the most important case of this kind was the prolonged refusal of Mr. Churchill to agree to a change of British representation in the Levant States when the Foreign Office regarded such a change as essential to the establishment of good relations with the Free French. In a larger issue—the transfer of British support from General Mihailovic to Marshal Tito—there is perhaps room for

---

[1] The fact—in itself salutary—that Mr. Churchill and Mr. Eden left London whenever possible for week-ends at their respective country houses did not lessen the labour of the Permanent Under-Secretary whose chances of rest were too often broken by telephone calls giving the 'sudden thoughts' of one or both of these Ministers. The Foreign Office staff also found some cause of strain in the Prime Minister's urgent demands for drafts of important telegrams. Thus one of the most hard-pressed senior members of the staff commented in April, 1944: 'We are nearly always working [on the question of joint Anglo-American action with regard to Spanish exports of wolfram to Germany] with a margin of minutes. For example, the reply to the last message to the President had to be drafted between 11.15 a.m. and midday today when the Prime Minister left for Chequers. Similarly a brief drawn up by the Cabinet was finished only five minutes before the Cabinet meeting.'

doubt. It may well be that, owing to the deep-rooted bitterness of internal political disputes in Yugoslavia, especially between Serbs and Croats, and the general dislike of the pre-1941 régime, the British Government could not have adopted at any time a policy which would have avoided the alternatives either of civil war or of the totalitarian—or at least dictatorial—rule of one party in the country after the invaders had been turned out. It is also possible to hold, as the Foreign Office was inclined to think, that, on balance, neither General Mihailovic nor Marshal Tito was of very great military value to the Allies since each—while wanting the defeat of Germany and Italy—was concerned at least as much with internal political feuds, and preoccupied with securing a dominant position in the control of Yugoslavia after the war.

At all events the papers in the Foreign Office archives suggest that the Prime Minister may have listened too readily to the opinions of a few advisers of whose opportunities for obtaining full evidence the Foreign Office was less sure. Resistance in Yugoslavia was a military matter, and the decision about the military advantages or disadvantages to be gained from the support of Marshal Tito rested primarily upon the recommendations of the military authorities, but Marshal Tito's advocates with the Prime Minister seemed to the Foreign Office inclined to disregard the extenuating circumstances in the case of General Mihailovic's failure to act against the enemy, and the political risks of supporting a communist dictatorship any-where in south-east Europe. These matters were not easy to judge.[1] After an interview with Marshal Tito the Prime Minister somewhat changed his own view. He wrote to Mr. Eden about the responsibility which would rest on Great Britain if Marshal Tito, having secured control of Yugoslavia, used the arms which he had obtained from British sources to suppress his non-communist opponents. Mr. Eden's answer was that the Foreign Office was well aware of the danger, and that not they, but the Prime Minister himself, had 'pushed' Marshal Tito.[2]

In his attitude towards General de Gaulle the Prime Minister seemed at times to the Foreign Office to show less than his usual generosity, and also to come near to risking British long-term interests

---

[1] It has been pointed out that the terms 'resistance' and 'collaboration' acquired a moral significance during the second World War which they had not possessed in the first war. One reason was the existence of a 'collaborationist' government in France, and that of Quisling in Norway, for which there was no parallel in the first war. The change was also due to the nature of 'total war', the illegal demands made by the Axis Powers upon the countries in their occupation, the savagely oppressive character of this occupation, and the widespread organisation of underground activities.

[2] It is typical of the Prime Minister's quick and masterful judgment that in another case of disagreement with the Foreign Office—the question of the regency of Archbishop Damaskinos in Greece at the end of 1944—he changed his mind at once after a personal meeting with the Archbishop in Athens. The Prime Minister took this journey to Athens—in mid-winter—though he was overwhelmed with business at the time owing to the German counter-offensive in the Ardennes.

in order to meet a certain prejudice on the part of President Roosevelt. Before 1943 Mr. Churchill had become impatient with General de Gaulle, though he never ceased to respect him. General de Gaulle was responsible for this exasperation. He spoke, wrote, and acted too often with a disregard for political and military realities—British and French—and with an abruptness of manner which could not be excused by the fact that he was causing offence not to the weak but to the strong. General de Gaulle had not even the justification that within the narrow field open to him he was doing his utmost for the Allied cause. He was not always a good judge of men, and not able to prevent intrigue within his own Movement. For very different —and prouder—reasons he was as obstinate as Marshal Pétain in refusing to face the humiliating but inevitable consequences of French surrender. Marshal Pétain assumed that, having accepted the armistice, France would be left free to work out her own regeneration through suffering. General de Gaulle assumed that, having rejected the armistice, the Free French could maintain the honour and integrity of France by a complete separation from the Vichy defeatists. Marshal Pétain ignored the facts that the Germans could not leave France alone, and had no interest in the moral regeneration of Frenchmen. General de Gaulle, in expecting the Allies to subordinate all other considerations to the maintenance of French honour in his Movement, forgot at times that, however lofty his claims, he could not undo the facts of surrender, and that the recovery of France would be achieved not by French but by British and American arms.

The Prime Minister had shown a noble sympathy with France in the great distress of 1940. He has also described General de Gaulle in discerning terms.[1] During the war he was for a long time very tolerant of the General's obstinacy and his exaggeration, or so it seemed, of the immediate requirements of French sovereignty, but he came understandably, though without full cause, to distrust and suspect his political aims, and was not very willing to use his personal influence with Mr. Roosevelt to try to change the latter's attitude towards the Free French. On the other hand, the President, and, for a long time, Mr. Hull refused to see the Vichy politicians and collaborationists among the *haute bourgeoisie* for what they were. The United States Government were not well informed about French opinion generally by Admiral Leahy during his time as Ambassador at Vichy, and the President paid too much attention to the Admiral's reports. Nonetheless there is something remarkable in the American insensitiveness to the fineness of General de Gaulle's conception of his Movement and to the shame which the Vichy Government had brought upon France.

---

[1] Churchill, IV, 611.

The American failure to realise the point of honour—the honour of France which General de Gaulle claimed to have in his keeping—had its worst consequences in the clumsy deal made with Admiral Darlan at the time of the North African invasion. Here again it was argued, though the point can be disputed on military grounds, that the recognition of Darlan's 'legitimate' authority saved many British and American lives at a most critical moment in the campaign. The damning fact, however, as General de Gaulle and British opinion saw it, was that the American military chiefs and their political advisers did not seem to realise that they were surrendering on a matter of principle, and that the surrender would look like a betrayal of the cause for which the European Allies were fighting.[1]

The Prime Minister, in view of his wish to avoid, whenever possible, differences with the President, and owing to his own experience of General de Gaulle's intransigence, inclined to underrate the effect of the Darlan episode upon the General's behaviour, if indeed this behaviour was more ungracious after than it was before the end of 1942. The documents show that the Foreign Office had more sympathy with General de Gaulle in spite of his relentless suspicions of British policy. The Foreign Office realised more quickly the change which had come over the Gaullist Movement after the Free French began to make closer contact with the Resistance groups in France. The political situation was now more favourable to the transformation of the Free French National Committee, under General de Gaulle's leadership, from a dissident group into something like a genuine Provisional Government. With the German move into the occupied zone, the Vichy Government lost even the shadow of independence; Marshal Pétain's programme of 'regeneration' was already discredited. De Gaulle had been right, and Pétain wrong in their respective forecasts. Neither the Allies nor the majority of Frenchmen wanted a communist government in France after the war. General Giraud, whom the Americans had expected to take a lead in North Africa, was a failure and totally unsuited either for military or political command. There was thus no alternative to General de Gaulle if he secured the support of the Resistance Movement.

One of the sharper differences between the Prime Minister and Mr. Eden arose out of the recognition of this change, and of the subsequent claim of the French Committee that before the cross-Channel invasion the Allies should negotiate with them an agreement which would recognise their control of civil affairs in liberated France. The Foreign Office, and, for that matter, General Eisenhower, as

---

[1] A Foreign Office memorandum sent to Lord Halifax in Washington summed up the matter in these words: 'We are fighting for international decency, and Darlan is the antithesis of this.'

Commander-in-Chief of the cross-Channel expedition, regarded the early conclusion of such an agreement as necessary for military as well as political reasons. The State Department, including at long last Mr. Hull, came round to this view early in 1944, but the President remained unwilling to face the facts, and, for some considerable time, the Prime Minister refused to assert firmly the British point of view and to reject the President's instruction to General Eisenhower to deal with any authority in France (other than Vichy) whom he might think fit to employ. Mr. Duff Cooper— to the Prime Minister's annoyance—described the President's action as a deliberate insult to the French Committee. Mr. Eden was finally able to persuade the Prime Minister to approve of a compromise which saved the situation with the French and enabled the President to climb down without loss of prestige.[1]

It is important, however, to remember that, apart from the immediate strain of the pre-invasion period (the documents show the deep anxiety of the Prime Minister during this time), the Foreign Office was more free than the Prime Minister to put long-range considerations affecting the post-war situation in Europe before matters of immediate military relevance. The Prime Minister—and not the Foreign Office—had been carrying the burden of persuading the President and the American Chiefs of Staff to accept military proposals which on the British side seemed essential to the success of the expedition. Mr. Churchill knew that these arguments between Allies would not end with the liberation of France; he was unwilling to expend his capital of goodwill with the President on issues which he did not consider of the first importance. The Foreign Office, on the other hand, as soon as they were released from conducting what might be called the diplomacy of survival, reasoned and planned by habit in terms of the long-range political interests of Great Britain.

This difference of outlook is clear in another field of action, or at all events discussion. In 1943, and through most of 1944, the Prime Minister was unwilling and indeed unable to give much thought to the post-war settlement of Europe and problems of the international organisation of security. His general opinion was that these problems could not be decided in any detail until after the Allied victory had been assured. He was therefore willing to consider them only to the extent to which pressure from the United States and, to a lesser degree, the Dominions and the smaller European Allies compelled

---

[1] The Prime Minister did not expect the Allies to hold at first more than a small area of French territory. For this reason he considered that the question of civil administration could be settled after the Allies had landed in France. During the final stages of this controversy General de Gaulle himself behaved with a lack of tact and an odd misunderstanding of the strength of his own position.

him to do so. He held strong but vague opinions about the conditions to be imposed upon Germany, and equally strong views about the need for European unity. He was also determined not to surrender any part of the British Empire to an international trusteeship; one of his reasons for not wanting to oppose President Roosevelt on matters which he (the Prime Minister) regarded as secondary was that he expected to have to resist American proposals hostile to the recovery of British territory.

The Foreign Office developed, in a somewhat haphazard way, efficient machinery in 1943 and 1944 for considering the question of a post-war security organisation to take the place of the League of Nations. Their proposals were ably worked out with a view to avoiding the faults of procedure which had contributed so much to the weakness and collapse of the League. The major premise in all these plans was that it was desirable to accept, in the more optimistic formula that peace was indivisible, the grim conclusion that wars could no longer be localised. In any case it was clear that the United States would not come into an organisation unless it were world-wide.

The Prime Minister accepted this major premise. He was more concerned, however, in practice, with re-establishing the importance of Europe in the balance of world power, and, at the same time, maintaining the closest Anglo-American co-operation. He was much attracted by pre-war proposals for the establishment of a United States of Europe, and believed that only through such means, including the federation of the smaller States, would Great Britain and Western Europe generally be able to deal on equal terms with the immense 'continental' resources of the U.S.S.R. and the United States.[1] His plan therefore was to set up a World Council based on subordinate Councils of Europe, the Americas, and the Pacific. He described the arrangement as a kind of 'three-legged stool', and, in order to secure the essential co-operation of the United States in European affairs, suggested American membership of the Council of Europe.

The Prime Minister broadcast his ideas in March, 1943, and argued in favour of them during his visit to Washington in May. The President was at first attracted by the plan, but from the point of view of American public opinion there was an important difference between the participation of the United States in a World Security Organisation, and membership of a European Council involving direct and continuous interference in European affairs.[2]

---

[1] The Prime Minister was influenced by Count Coudenhove-Kalergi's ideas on pan-European union.

[2] Mr. Hull, whose main purpose, as far as concerned post-war organisation, was to secure the removal of trade barriers, was afraid that a large and powerful European organisation might develop an economic policy for Europe which would be damaging to American trade interests.

The Foreign Office on the other hand thought that these proposals for Europe were not in British interests; they would cause great suspicion in the U.S.S.R., and would lead, sooner or later, to a renewed German domination of the Continental States outside Russia. This difference of view involved a good deal of argument of which the Prime Minister was somewhat impatient. He was willing to leave the question of a World Organisation to discussions at an official level—which committed none of the governments concerned—and to await a meeting with President Roosevelt and Stalin at an easier time before taking any binding decisions.

For similar reasons Mr. Churchill was disinclined in 1943 and 1944 to give much consideration to the plans put forward for the future of Germany. At the Casablanca meeting early in 1943 he had acquiesced in the statement by the President that the Allies would demand the unconditional surrender of Germany. It is now known— though Mr. Churchill does not appear to have known it at the time—that this statement was not an *impromptu* move by the President, and that he had been considering it before he left Washington. The Prime Minister consulted the War Cabinet by telegram about the expediency of such a demand, and suggested that it might be applied to Germany and Japan, but not to Italy. Mr. Attlee replied on behalf of the War Cabinet in favour both of the use of the term and the extension of it to include Italy.

It has been argued that, whatever the advantages of this formula in leaving the Allies free to decide upon the conditions to be applied to the Germans after their surrender, the early announcement of the demand was a tactical mistake and that it left the Allies no room for manoeuvre and the peoples of the enemy countries no motive for getting rid of their governments. In fact the Italians did get rid of their fascist government when they realised that the invasion of the mainland of Italy was certain, and, although unconditional surrender was enforced on them, they knew that, by 'working their passage' on the Allied side, they would obtain—considering their heavy responsibilities—not overharsh terms. The satellite States also surrendered on terms which were not in practice unconditional, though, except in the case of Finland, the terms of surrender were much less significant than the military circumstances which allowed a Russian occupation and control. In Japan there was no chance of a successful movement for the overthrow of the government, and when at last the unexpected and terrible weapon of the atomic bomb brought a rapid Japanese surrender, the Allies agreed not to require the deposition of the Emperor.[1]

---

[1] It is possible that, if a more explicit statement had been made at the Potsdam Conference about the maintenance of the dynasty, the Japanese might have surrendered before the dropping of the atom bombs. See Volume V, Chapter LXIX.

In Germany the failure of the military *coup* against Hitler in July, 1944, was not connected with the demand for unconditional surrender. A second *coup* was unlikely at least until Nazi control had been broken by military defeat. The Nazi leaders knew that they could expect no mercy for themselves—they deserved none—and no future for their régime. In the final stages of the war the overwhelming sentiment of the Germans was not so much anxiety about the consequences of unconditional surrender to the Western Allies as fear—amounting to panic—of the revenge which the Russians would take on German territory for the crimes committed by the Germans themselves in Russia.

Thus nothing in the course of events suggests that the Nazi control of Germany lasted longer owing to the Allied demand for unconditional surrender. The Prime Minister indeed in 1943 and 1944 regarded this demand as likely to be less alarming to the Germans than the publication of the actual terms already under discussion on the Allied side. Finally the demand for unconditional surrender was also a consequence of the endless German harping on the treaty of Versailles. The Allies did not intend to repeat the error of 1918 when they had accepted a German surrender on unnecessarily vague political terms to which the Germans subsequently gave their own interpretation.

In view of his care not to commit himself to any particular statement about the terms to be imposed on Germany after surrender, it is surprising that the Prime Minister should have given even a tentative approval to a drastic American proposal not only that Germany should be dismembered politically but that she should be transformed into a country 'primarily agricultural and pastoral in its character'. This proposal was made to the President shortly before the Quebec Conference of 1944 by Mr. Morgenthau. The plan provided that all the industrial equipment of the Ruhr not already destroyed during the war should be dismantled or removed. The mines would be completely wrecked, and the whole region 'so weakened and controlled' that it could not 'in the foreseeable future' again become industrialised.

President Roosevelt and the Prime Minister gave a general assent on September 15, 1944, to this plan for the 'pastoralisation' of Germany. During the discussion Mr. Churchill was mainly concerned with the future of Lend-Lease after the defeat of Germany, and the grave economic situation in which Great Britain would certainly be placed after the war. Mr. Morgenthau's proposal was put to him as part of a general arrangement which would allow

British economic recovery. Mr. Eden, who was not present when the President and the Prime Minister discussed the plan,[1] pointed out to Mr. Churchill the calamitous effects which the proposal would have not only in Germany but in the rest of Europe. Mr. Hull and Mr. Stimson were equally critical on the American side. There was no likelihood that the Allies would accept the plan; the tentative endorsement of it by the Prime Minister and the President would have mattered little if the main facts had not appeared almost at once in the American press. Although the leakage gave Nazi propaganda an opportunity to warn the German people what could happen to them after unconditional surrender, it was already clear that the Nazi leaders intended to fight to the last, and that until the final hours of defeat no group—military or civil—in Germany would be able to overthrow them. The Morgenthau plan thus had no effect in prolonging German resistance.[2]

After the practical repudiation of the Morgenthau plan the President gave instructions that for the time all detailed planning in the Department of State on the future of Germany should cease. The Prime Minister did not lay down any such rule for the Foreign Office, but, in effect, until the Allies had decided at least in the most general terms what they intended to do the Foreign Office could not go beyond the preparation of memoranda. They assumed that there would be a peace conference at which post-war questions hitherto held in suspense would be discussed. The Foreign Office also agreed with the Prime Minister on the expediency of postponing, as far as possible, all disputable matters, and especially territorial claims, until this discussion had taken place. Any other policy might have meant either a serious crisis with the Soviet Government (involving— as a consequence which the Allies could not exclude—the possibility of a separate peace between the U.S.S.R. and Germany) or a surrender to all the Russian demands.

On the other hand the weak point in the policy of delay, as the Prime Minister came increasingly to realise, was that, combined with the American failure to understand the significance of the question of a post-war European balance of power, it allowed the Russians to obtain practical possession or control of such large areas in Europe that no decisions other than those desired by the Soviet Government were likely to be taken when a Peace Conference met. In the circumstances, however, the dangers of a large-scale *fait*

---

[1] The Prime Minister was influenced by Lord Cherwell's support of the plan. The Foreign Office was sharply critical of Lord Cherwell's activities in connection with it.

[2] The President—with the American elections close at hand—could not risk any charge that he was treating Germany too leniently. He did not repudiate the Morgenthau plan, but said in a speech of October 21, 1944, that the Allies were not planning to enslave the German people.

accompli had to be accepted, though they might perhaps have been lessened in the critical three months before the Potsdam Conference if the Americans had approved of Mr. Churchill's proposals for standing on the farthest lines of military advance. As things were, the main hope was that the Russians themselves would continue to see advantages in co-operation and in common membership of a World Security Organisation directed primarily against a recurrence of German and Japanese aggression. The Allies also continued to reckon on their bargaining power, especially in the form of economic aid and the allocation of German reparation in kind from the industrial zone in the west, which they could use in discussions with the Soviet Government.

The Foreign Office, while regarding the Prime Minister's far-reaching schemes for the integration of Europe as impracticable, had been concerned since the end of 1942 with the provision of machinery for the immediate purpose of meeting the confusion—and the risks of chaos and anarchy—certain to occur at the end of the war. In order to secure a common policy, and, in particular, to prevent unilateral action by the Russians, the Foreign Office had put forward at the beginning of 1943 a proposal for a United Nations Commission for Europe. At the Moscow Conference in 1943 Mr. Eden took the lead in bringing these practical questions to an issue, and suggested the establishment of a European Advisory Commission.

The Foreign Office appointed one of their ablest officials—Sir William Strang—to represent Great Britain on this Commission. The primary business of the Commission was to draw up the detailed terms of surrender to be imposed upon Germany, and to settle the arrangements for the Allied occupation and control of the country (and, where relevant, Austria). The Commission carried out this work, and attempted, less successfully, to deal with armistice terms imposed on the satellite States. The Commission was not asked to consider the general post-war problems of Germany or of the rest of Europe, but throughout 1944 it might have been able to do something to clear and define Allied policy, and indeed to carry out its more limited tasks less slowly if the Soviet Government had been less obstructive and the United States Government had given more positive backing. Mr. Winant, who represented the United States on the Commission, nearly always supported Sir William Strang; the President rarely allowed him to take the initiative in making proposals.

The Prime Minister, although he could spare little of his time for matters not directly concerned with defeating the enemy, had set up a Cabinet Committee in August, 1943, for the consideration of armistice and immediate post-war problems.[1] The committee, under the chairmanship of Mr. Attlee, Deputy Prime Minister, did much useful work in calling for memoranda and in co-ordinating the activities of a number of departmental committees engaged in studying particular aspects of the post-war situation. It provided instructions for the British representative on the European Advisory Commission. It was also of considerable negative value in giving an opportunity for some of its own members to bring forward proposals about Germany which did not stand up to close analysis. Even so, the most decisive document submitted to the War Cabinet on the treatment of Germany was a memorandum from the Treasury. In this memorandum, which was drawn up after the Yalta Conference, the Chancellor of the Exchequer, Sir John Anderson, pointed out the incompatibility between the proposals put forward for reparation and those for the dismemberment of Germany, and the danger that, if the Russians had their way, much of the burden of German reparation would in fact fall upon the British people.

The history of war-time diplomacy ends with the Potsdam Conference, and the surrender of Japan. The Allies had won the war, but were in disagreement about the purposes to which they would put their victory. The Russians had maintained their hold on the satellite states, and after having arrested a number of non-communist Polish politicians with whom they were nominally in negotiation, finally agreed to the admission of a few non-communists to their Provisional Polish Government. They were also pledged to allow free elections in Poland, but there was little likelihood that they would fulfil this pledge or that the non-communist Ministers would have any influence on policy, Mr. Churchill had wanted the Allied armies to stand on the lines they had occupied, and not to withdraw to their allocated zones of occupation before obtaining a genuine fulfilment of the Yalta obligations, but Mr. Truman still hoped for a tripartite agreement and suspected British motives in opposing the Russians. In anticipating what he had described to President Truman as a 'show-down' at the tripartite Conference, Mr. Churchill had contemplated a good deal of plain speaking, and also a final bargain, at which, after much manoeuvring, the British and Americans would exact concession for concession to the full extent of their power. The bargaining took place, as Mr. Churchill had expected, but the critical point was not reached until after he and Mr. Eden had left Potsdam. The final compromise was proposed

---

[1] This committee, which continued the work of an *ad hoc* committee dealing with the immediate terms of surrender for Italy, was given wider terms of reference in April, 1944, and was known from that date as the Armistice and Post-War Committee.

by Mr. Byrnes. Mr. Attlee and Mr. Bevin accepted it, though with misgivings, especially in regard to Poland.[1] Mr. Churchill—writing some eight years later[2]—has said that he would never have conceded the western Neisse frontier to Poland, and that, if necessary, he would have had a 'public break' over the matter.[3] It is most probable that, if he had remained at the Conference, he would have tried to get more from Russia in return for the very large concessions made to her. How far would he have succeeded? He had been unable to persuade the Americans to accept his view of the need to meet at once the grave threat from the U.S.S.R. to the future of Europe and the peace of the world. British views now counted for less than at any time in American decisions. Anglo-American relations expressed in terms of power had changed to the disadvantage of Great Britain. In spite of her victories and her armies, which were beginning to melt away, Great Britain was, temporarily at least, near to the end of her resources and dependent economically upon American help to tide over the period of recovery.[4]

The President and his advisers were conscious of the world predominance of the United States and of their ability—and perhaps their duty—to take decisions for themselves; they were also dangerously sure that they knew what was best for Great Britain and Europe. At all events they took their decisions, and with a certain impatience that, whatever they did for Europeans, must be done once for all, and must not commit them to perpetual interference in the domestic affairs of a Continent which, for historical reasons, they distrusted.

The difficulty of speculating on what might have happened at the Potsdam Conference if Mr. Churchill had been returned to office is increased by the need to ask another question. What would have happened at Potsdam if the Japanese surrender had taken place three weeks earlier? In such case the Russians would have lost a great deal of their bargaining power since their aid would no longer have been needed in the war against Japan, and the Americans would have had less reason to avoid committing themselves further

---

[1] Mr. Bevin made a strong—and shrewd—attempt to do what he could to safeguard the freedom of elections in Poland.

[2] Churchill, VI, 581–2.

[3] Technically, Mr. Byrnes's proposal did not make this concession, since the final delineation of the frontier was left to the Peace Conference. In fact the concession was made by allowing the Polish claim to extend their administration to the western Neisse.

[4] A paper submitted to the War Cabinet on August 14, 1945—the day before the Japanese surrender, and three days before Mr. Truman gave instructions that Lend-Lease should end in a fortnight—stated that, without substantial new aid from the United States, Great Britain would be 'virtually bankrupt, and the economic basis for the hopes of the public non-existent'. Sir W. K. Hancock and M. M. Gowing, *British War Economy* (H.M.S.O., 1952) (History of the Second World War, United Kingdom Civil Series), 546–9.

to action in Europe on behalf of their own principles and of the kind of settlement which they regarded as likely to ensure peace. The news of the successful explosion of an atomic bomb in the New Mexican desert was reported to the Prime Minister at Potsdam on July 17, the opening day of the Conference. The President and the Prime Minister discussed together the most tactful way of letting Stalin know something which they had previously concealed from him. Mr. Truman told Stalin the news in the presence of Mr. Churchill. Mr. Churchill does not think that Stalin realised the significance of this new weapon. The weapon changed the balance of military power, at least for a time, overwhelmingly in favour of the western Allies. If Hitler had developed the atomic bomb, the Allies would have lost the war. If the Russians had possessed it, they would probably have made it their final political argument. It is outside the task of a historian of British diplomacy during the war to consider whether use might have been made at the Potsdam Conference, or after, of this *ultima ratio* of the western democracies in warning the Soviet Government that the western Powers could compel them to fulfil the agreements made at Yalta, and that the Russian *glacis* of puppet States had lost much of its military value. A warning of such gravity, with such a sanction attached to it, would have been out of keeping with all the habits and hopes of the western democracies, and the implementation of any threat—when the Allies had added to their store of the weapons—would hardly have been practicable politically in view of the attitude of public opinion in the United States and Great Britain. As for the moral implications of a threat of ultimate force, the historian can give no answer. He would be prudent to limit himself to one of the very few generalisations which apply inevitably, and, as it may seem, blindly to the fate of all nations at all times: "Ὀψὲ θεῶν ἀλέουσι μύλοι, ἀλέουσι δὲ λεπτά.[1]

---

[1] The mills of the gods grind late, but they grind small.

CHAPTER I

The alignment of forces: September—December 1939

(i)

The Anglo-French notes of September 1 to Germany: the Italian proposal for a conference: Anglo-French differences of view with regard to a time-limit to an ultimatum: the British and French notes of September 3, 1939.

THE British Government, with the support of the British people, and of the Governments and peoples of the Dominions, declared war against Germany on September 3, 1939. They did not make this declaration lightly; nevertheless they could not avoid it. Although the actual note of warning of September 1 which preceded by a day and a half the declaration of war came from the Allied side, the responsibility of deciding between peace and war lay with Hitler. In this respect there was a difference, real as well as formal, between the situation immediately before the outbreak of war in 1939 and the situation in 1914. Until the German violation of Belgian neutrality on August 3, 1914, the British Government retained at least formal freedom of decision, and, in fact, neither the Cabinet nor the country at large was unanimously agreed that in the circumstances as then known Great Britain was morally committed to go to war in support of France and Russia. There were no such doubts about the British obligation in September 1939. When the Cabinet met shortly before noon on September 1, after hearing the news of the German attack on Poland, the Prime Minister used the words 'our consciences are clear, and there should be no possible doubt where our duty lies'.[1]

The position was also different from that of the previous year. In the long-drawn crisis over the Sudetenland, the British Government had to decide whether they would allow Hitler to enforce demands which they thought unreasonable and dangerous in substance and outrageous and threatening in the manner in which they were presented. It is possible to hold different views about the morality, or the expediency, of the British decision to accept the terms of the Munich settlement which was a virtual surrender to the German demands, but the British Government had not stated in plain terms

---

[1] Mr. Chamberlain had begun by saying that the event against which we had fought so long and so earnestly had come upon us. One might notice a personal significance in the Prime Minister's employment of the term 'fought' to describe an effort not to win a war but to avert it.

that an attempt by Hitler to enforce such demands would inevitably mean war with Great Britain. With their guarantee to Poland in March, 1939, the British decision had been taken and made public. Great Britain (and France) had engaged themselves to defend Polish independence against German attack. They would honour their engagement. Thenceforward the decision between peace and war rested with Hitler. If he attacked Poland, he would be at war with the Western Powers.

The task of British diplomacy, therefore, in the critical weeks and hours before September 1 was to try to restrain Hitler from bringing upon the world the fearful calamity of war. There was no question of giving way if Hitler chose war.

The invasion of Poland began in the early hours of September 1. Great Britain did not declare war on Germany until September 3.[1] During these two days, or rather, during the first twenty-four hours after the opening of the German attack, there seemed to the Foreign Office a very faint chance that, on realising that the two Western Powers intended to fulfil their guarantee to Poland and to declare war on Germany, Hitler might agree to a resumption of negotiations on terms which the British, French and Polish Governments could accept.[2] After twenty-four hours this faint chance of a peaceful settlement disappeared. It was clear that Hitler would not break off his attack on Poland; the formal declaration of war therefore followed, though it was delayed owing to the insistence of the French Government.

(a)   The Cabinet met just before noon on September 1; until this hour Ministers were engaged in the executive work necessary for putting war measures into effect. At their meeting the Cabinet discussed the terms of a communication to be made to the German Government. They agreed that the communication should be sent as soon as we had concerted action with the French. They considered whether the communication should include a time-limit for a reply but decided that this question also should be settled with the French. The Prime Minister thought that the Germans might attack our merchant shipping and ships of war as soon as they had received the communication.

---

[1] For a documentary record of the negotiations between September 1 and the British declaration of war, see *Documents on British Foreign Policy, 1919–1939*, Series III, VII, ch. VII (H.M.S.O., 1954).

[2] Hitler and Ribbentrop appear to have thought that the announcement of their agreement with Russia would deter Great Britain and France from going to war. The Italian Ambassador in Berlin reported to Ciano that the news on August 25 of the signature of the British alliance with Poland was a 'fulmine in ciel serena' (*Documenti diplomatici italiani*, 9th Ser., I, No. 21). Hitler's short postponement of the attack on Poland while he made an 'offer' to the British Government was a final attempt to get Anglo-French agreement to a settlement on his own terms. He had no intention of calling off the attack if the offer was rejected.

(a) C13238/15/18; Cabinet (39) 47.

The Cabinet considered 5 p.m. as the best time for the communication; they finally authorised the Prime Minister and Lord Halifax to take such action as they thought fit after consulting the French Government. They also arranged for the Dominions to be informed at once of their action.

Sir N. Henderson was therefore instructed at 4.45 p.m. that he (a) would receive the text of a communication which he and the French Ambassador were to deliver at once to the German Government. He was told to ask for an immediate answer. In reply to any questions, he could say that the communication was 'in the nature of a warning', and was 'not to be considered as an ultimatum'. For his own information, he was also told that, if the German reply were unsatisfactory, the next stage would be either an ultimatum with a time limit or a declaration of war.

The communication (which was telegraphed to Sir N. Henderson at 5.45 p.m.) stated that 'by their action' in attacking Poland, the German Government had 'created conditions (viz., an aggressive act of force against Poland, threatening the independence of Poland) which call for the implementation by the Governments of the United Kingdom and France of the undertaking to Poland to come to her assistance'. Then followed the warning: 'Unless the German Government are prepared to give His Majesty's Government satisfactory assurances that the German Government have suspended all aggressive action against Poland and are prepared promptly to withdraw their forces from Polish territory, His Majesty's Government in the United Kingdom will without hesitation fulfil their obligation to Poland'.

The 'warning' was drawn up as a joint Anglo-French communication. M. Bonnet, whom M. Corbin, the French Ambassador in London, had consulted by telephone, agreed to the terms and instructed M. Coulondre, French Ambassador at Berlin, to join Sir N. Henderson in presenting an identical communication. The Ambassadors asked to be received together, but Ribbentrop refused (b) their request. The British communication was therefore presented at 9.30 p.m.: M. Coulondre followed at 10 p.m. Sir N. Henderson asked for an immediate answer. Ribbentrop said he would submit the communication to Hitler; he also claimed that the Poles had invaded German territory on August 31.

Meanwhile it had been necessary to say something more to Mussolini about a proposal which he had made on the previous day for a conference. This proposal was that, if the British and French Governments would agree to the return of Danzig to the Reich, Mussolini would ask Hitler to accept a conference (to be called for (c) September 5) 'for the revision of the clauses of the treaty of Versailles

---

(a) C12609/15/18. (b) C12713/15/18. (c) C13099, 12529/15/18.

which were the cause of the present great troubles in the life of Europe'. Lord Halifax had replied to Ciano by telephone—apparently about 7 p.m.—on August 31 that he had discussed Mussolini's proposal with the Prime Minister, and that the Prime Minister felt it impossible to ask the Poles to give up Danzig in advance of negotiation. Lord Halifax said that 'it was Hitler's methods, in part, that made it impossible to recommend such a course. The Danzig question must be negotiated as part of a general discussion.' The Polish Government had agreed to a discussion of this kind; there was no reason why the German Government should not give the Polish Ambassador their proposals 'if indeed they had any.' Before telephoning this verbal answer, the Prime Minister and Lord Halifax had asked the French Ambassador to call at No. 10 Downing Street. M. Corbin knew nothing of the Italian proposal, but, on telephoning to Paris, found that M. Bonnet had heard from Rome of the Italian suggestion and had spoken by telephone about it to M. Coulondre. M. Coulondre did not believe that the matter was of such urgency as the Italians had suggested. M. Bonnet wanted to consult M. Daladier, who might wish to know the views of his colleagues. Thus the French reply might therefore be delayed for several hours. The Prime Minister told M. Corbin that 'his first reaction was that it was impossible to agree to a conference under the threat of mobilised armies', and that 'a preliminary condition in any case would have to be a measure of demobilisation'.

(a)   M. Daladier had sent a message to the Prime Minister about 3.30 p.m. that he would rather resign than accept this 'invitation to a
(b) second Munich'. On the evening of August 31, however, M. Bonnet told Sir E. Phipps, British Ambassador at Paris, that the French Government after the session of the Council of Ministers felt that they would not decline 'off-hand' the Italian proposal. They would therefore send for the approval of His Majesty's Government a draft of their reply in which they would probably accept the proposal for a conference, on the conditions that Poland should take part in it and that it should have a wider agenda. They did not favour a demand for demobilisation. At 9 p.m. M. Bonnet telephoned to M. Corbin that the French would accept the proposal, if the direct German-Polish negotiations failed, on the two conditions stated to Sir E. Phipps. Later M. Corbin told M. Bonnet that an answer—in addition to the message telephoned to Ciano—would be sent by His Majesty's Government on the morning of September 1.
(c)   On the morning of September 1, Sir P. Loraine, British Ambassador in Rome, was instructed to say to Ciano that, in view of Hitler's attack on Poland, it seemed impossible to go further with Mussolini's proposal. Ciano answered that he would ask Mussolini

---

(a) C12544/15/18.   (b) C12556/15/18.   (c) C12637, 12636/15/18.

whether in the changed circumstances he could telephone the proposal to Hitler. Ciano appeared to think that the French Government were more favourable than the British Government to the plan.

There was, in fact, a divergence (for which, in the view of the Foreign Office, M. Bonnet was responsible) between the respective attitudes of the two Governments. The French Government had decided on September 1 to send the reply on which the Council of Ministers had previously agreed. The reply was telephoned to M. (a) François-Poncet, French Ambassador at Rome, at 11.45 a.m.; it made no reference to the German attack on Poland. At 3.40 p.m. M. Bonnet telephoned to M. Corbin that—on information from Rome—the Italian Government still thought it possible, if they had the consent of the British and French Governments, to revive their proposal of the previous day. They had asked whether the French Government had the approval of the Polish Government for the plan. M. Bonnet—without consulting the British Government—made enquiries about the Polish attitude; M. Beck's reply was that, since Poland was at war as the result of unprovoked aggression, the need was not for a conference, but for common action by the Allies against this aggression.

The Polish reply did not reach M. Bonnet until the afternoon of September 2. Meanwhile, as far as the British Government were concerned, the matter had ended with their instructions to Sir P. Loraine. The French Government, however, issued a communiqué during the night of September 1–2 through the Havas agency that they had given a 'positive' reply to the 'Italian initiative'.

The Germans did not reply to the warning note of September 1. The British Government therefore had to concert with the French the ultimatum which was the inevitable consequence of the German refusal to suspend hostilities and to withdraw their troops from Poland. Here there were divergencies of view about a time-table. Sir E. Phipps telephoned at 9.35 a.m. on September 2 that the French Parliament was meeting in the afternoon and that the proceedings (b) might take longer than had been expected. Sir E. Phipps said that there was no doubt about the final result of the deliberations, but that an attempt to curtail the discussion in Parliament would be resented by public opinion and would not be in the true interests of Great Britain or France or Poland. Furthermore every hour which allowed French mobilisation to continue unhindered was precious. An answer was sent at 11.55 a.m. to Sir E. Phipps:

'For your own information: the delays in Paris and the attitude of the French Government are causing some misgiving here. Shall be grateful for anything you can do to infuse courage and determination

---

(a) C12855/15/18. (b) C12710/90/17.

into M. Bonnet. If the French Government are disposed to delay by reports of disaffection and indecision in Germany, please inform them that in our view that situation can only be turned to account by firm and immediate action on our part. That alone might yet save the day.'

(a) Sir E. Phipps replied at 12.45 p.m. that the French Government agreed with the statement—telephoned by M. Corbin to M. Bonnet—which the British Government proposed to make to Parliament in the afternoon of September 2. At 1.30 p.m. Sir E. Phipps telephoned French agreement that in the afternoon of September 2, after the meeting of the French Chamber, the British and French Ambassadors should present identical notes to the German Government. They strongly urged a time-limit of forty-eight hours before the expiry of the ultimatum to be contained in the notes. The French General Staff wished for this period of forty-eight hours in order to allow time for the evacuation of large towns and for general mobilisation. Sir E. Phipps did not think that there were any other reasons for the suggestion of so long a time-limit.

Lord Halifax had already told M. Corbin that he thought the German delay in answering the Anglo-French warning might be due to a desire to gain time for an advance into Polish territory after which Hitler would make a new offer of negotiation. Lord Halifax said that the British Government would insist on the withdrawal of troops from Polish territory before any negotiations could take place.

(b) A quarter of an hour before the time (2.45 p.m.) at which the British statement was to be made in Parliament, Ciano telephoned that the Italian Government had informed the German Government that they still thought it possible to call a conference if the Germans would accept it. Sir P. Loraine then took Ciano's place at the telephone. He said that the Italian Ambassador in Berlin had told Ribbentrop—for information, and not as a proposal—that Mussolini believed that, if Hitler would suspend hostilities and agree to a conference, Great Britain and France would accept the plan, and would obtain Polish agreement to it. The Ambassador had now reported that Hitler would not refuse to consider the plan if the British and French notes were not to be regarded as an ultimatum. The Ambassador had seen Sir N. Henderson who had authorised him to say that the British note did not have the character of an ultimatum. Ribbentrop wanted Sir N. Henderson's statement to be confirmed. He asked also whether Germany would have time to consider Mussolini's proposal, for example, up to noon on September 3. Ciano had put these points to M. Bonnet who had agreed to each of them (i.e. M. Bonnet had not

---

(a) C12862, 12783, 12791, 12782, 12939/15/18. (b) C13150, 12879/15/18.

stipulated for the withdrawal of the German armies).[1] Lord Halifax replied to Sir P. Loraine that he felt sure that the British Government would insist on the withdrawal of German troops from Polish territory. Ciano said that he did not think it possible to obtain this withdrawal.

The statement in the House of Commons was now postponed in order to allow time for discussions with the French over Ciano's proposal. Lord Halifax telephoned about 4 p.m. to M. Bonnet. M. (a) Bonnet thought that Hitler would not accept the withdrawal of German troops, and that the essential point was that Poland should be represented at a conference. On this condition his view was that a conference might be considered. We ought to do everything possible to convince public opinion that we had tried our utmost to avoid war. M. Bonnet then asked whether the British Government would agree that our eventual ultimatum should contain a time-limit of forty-eight hours.

The Cabinet met again at 4.15 p.m. The Prime Minister thought (b) that we should insist upon the withdrawal of German troops as a preliminary condition of a conference, and that, since Hitler was not likely to accept the condition, it would be undesirable to give the Germans beyond midnight on September 2–3 to consider their reply. The Cabinet agreed with the Prime Minister. Sir A. Cadogan therefore telephoned these conclusions to M. Bonnet at 5 p.m. M. Bonnet (c) said that the French Government had given a favourable reply on August 31 to Mussolini's proposal for a conference. Since then the Germans had invaded Poland. The French Government were about to consider ('va délibérer') whether the retirement of the German troops should be a necessary condition to their acceptance of the proposal for a conference.

M. Bonnet argued very strongly that an ultimatum should have a forty-eight hours time-limit. Sir A. Cadogan said that the British Government intended to fulfil their obligations to Poland if Hitler had not replied by midnight on September 2–3. M. Bonnet said that, if the British Government insisted on this time, they would incur a grave responsibility, since French evacuation[2] would not be completed for another two days. The French Cabinet would reach their decision about a time-limit by 9 p.m. Sir A Cadogan asked whether

---

[1] In the version of this conversation reported by the French Ambassador in Rome, M. Bonnet said that his answer about the time-limit was subject to the approval of M. Daladier. Ciano told Hitler on October 1, 1939, that Bonnet had informed Rome at 2 a.m. (apparently on September 2) through the Italian Ambassador in Paris that he believed France could agree to the Italian proposal 'if the German troops were withdrawn at least symbolically, by the withdrawal of a "single flag or gun" '. (*Documents on German Foreign Policy, 1918–1945*, Series D, VIII, No. 176. (H.M.S.O.) These documents are referred to henceforward as *D.G.F.P.*) For the Italian proposals, see *D.G.F.P.*, VII, Nos. 535, 539, 541, 554, and 568.

[2] i.e. the evacuation of women and children from the cities.

(a) C13081/15/18. (b) C13239/15/18; Cabinet (39) 48. (c) C13452/15/18.

9 p.m. was the earliest hour at which the British Government could be told of the decision. M. Bonnet then said 'perhaps 8 p.m.'.

(a)   At 6 p.m. Lord Halifax telephoned to Sir E. Phipps that the line taken by the French Government was 'very embarrassing'. We did not know whether they would agree that the withdrawal of German troops was an 'essential preliminary condition of a conference'. We also did not know what time-limit they would require. Sir E. Phipps was asked to see M. Daladier, and to try to persuade him that the ultimatum should expire at midnight on September 2–3.

Shortly after 6.30 p.m. Lord Halifax again telephoned to Ciano.
(b) He put the condition about the withdrawal of the German troops, and added that Danzig must also revert to the *status quo* of two days earlier. Ciano said that Hitler could not accept the condition about the withdrawal of troops. At 9 p.m. M. Bonnet told Ciano that the French would also insist on this condition. Later in the evening Ciano told
(c) Sir P. Loraine and M. François-Poncet that, in view of the conditions attached by Great Britain and France to acceptance of his proposal, Mussolini had decided not to take any further steps in the matter. Sir P. Loraine reported that, according to M. François-Poncet, Ciano thought the French Government more willing than the British Government to accept the proposal. The Foreign Office comment was that the impression was correct at least as far as M. Bonnet was concerned.

There remained, therefore, only the question of the time-limit. The Prime Minister made a statement in the House of Commons at 7.44 p.m. He reported Mussolini's proposal, the conditions which we had laid down for acceptance, and the fact that we were still in communication with the French about a time-limit.

The statement was badly received, and the delay in fixing a time-limit was largely misinterpreted as a sign of weakness and hesitation about the fulfilment of the guarantee to Poland. The Prime Minister and Lord Halifax therefore met at once to consider the situation. The
(d) Foreign Office had also heard at 8 p.m. from Sir H. Kennard, British Ambassador at Warsaw, that he and the French Ambassador had been told by M. Beck that the Polish armies were suffering from German superiority in the air. M. Beck hoped that we should soon enter the war and find it possible to draw off a considerable proportion of the German aircraft from the Polish front.

At 9.50 p.m. the Prime Minister telephoned to M. Daladier that it
(e) would be impossible to obtain agreement in Parliament for a time-limit of forty-eight hours from mid-day on September 3. The Prime Minister proposed as a compromise that we should announce that our

---

(a) C13084/15/18. (b) C12876/15/18. (c) C12806/15/18. (d) C12808/15/18.
(e) C13088/15/18.

Ambassadors had been instructed to present an ultimatum at 8 a.m. on September 3 with a time-limit of four hours. M. Daladier said that the French Government had told Ciano that they could not accept a conference unless the Germans evacuated Polish territory. Ciano said that there was still some hope of an agreement on the German side if the Anglo-French ultimatum were delayed until mid-day on September 3. The French Cabinet had endorsed this view. M. Daladier thought it better to fix a time-limit of some hours after mid-day on September 3 in order to delay air attacks on the French armies.

At 10.30 p.m. Lord Halifax spoke to M. Bonnet. He said that it was (a) necessary to make some announcement during the evening, and to state a definite hour at which our ultimatum would expire. Our proposal was to deliver at 8 a.m. on September 3 an ultimatum expiring at noon. If the French Government could not accept this time-table, we suggested separate British action on the understanding that the French would follow within twenty-four hours. M. Bonnet 'gravely deplored' our proposal, and asked whether we could not wait until mid-day on September 3. Lord Halifax said that 8 a.m. was the latest time we could accept. M. Bonnet therefore agreed that we should act at 8 a.m. and the French at mid-day.

The Cabinet met at 11.30 p.m. The Prime Minister explained what had happened. He also said that the Chiefs of Staff thought that (b) we should give the Germans too much notice if we announced at midnight that Sir N. Henderson would be presenting a note to Ribbentrop at 8 a.m. The Chiefs of Staff suggested 2 a.m. on September 3 for the presentation of the ultimatum, and 6 a.m. for the hour of expiry. On the other hand a long interval between our own and the French action would have a bad political effect. After some discussion the Cabinet agreed that Sir N. Henderson should present the note at 9 a.m., and that the ultimatum contained in the note should expire at 11 a.m.

Sir N. Henderson had previously been warned to be ready at any (c) time to present a note to Ribbentrop. He was instructed at 5 a.m. to deliver the note at 9 a.m. and also informed that the French note would not be delivered until noon, and that it might contain a time-limit of six to nine hours.

The French Government did not settle their time-limit until (d) September 3. At 8.45 a.m. on September 3 Sir E. Phipps reported a statement by M. Bonnet that the time-limit would be 5 a.m. on September 4. At 12.14 p.m. Sir E. Phipps sent a further message that the French Government had decided upon 5 p.m. on September 3 in order that there might be as little divergence as possible between the action of the two Governments.

(a) C13089/15/18. (b) C13240/15/18; Cabinet (39) 49. (c) C12811/15/18. (d) C12805, 12820/15/18.

(a)   Sir N. Henderson carried out his instructions at 9 a.m. He found it difficult to make contact with Ribbentrop. Finally, he was told that Dr. Schmidt, the official interpreter at the Ministry, had authorisation to accept on Ribbentrop's behalf any communication which Sir N. Henderson might make. At 11 a.m.—the hour at which the ultimatum expired—Ribbentrop asked Sir N. Henderson to call on him. Ribbentrop then presented him with a long memorandum which attempted, in general terms, to justify the German attack on Poland.

(ii)

The Russian invasion of Poland: the collapse of Polish resistance: Hitler's peace offer of October 6, 1939.

The Germans who had chosen war in 1939 had the initiative in waging it. Except at sea the two western Allies had little freedom of military choice. The terrible consequences of this loss of initiative were not realised at once. Apart from a small-scale French advance into the outpost region of the Siegfried Line followed by a withdrawal in mid-October under German pressure, the Allies gave no help to the Poles. The British Government had never expected, after the Russo-German agreement, to save Polish independence at the beginning of the war; they could hope only to restore it after they had defeated Germany. They had indeed exaggerated the possible duration of Polish resistance (on September 4 the War Cabinet thought that this resistance might last for three or four months) but it is fair also to remember that they did not themselves expect to escape from the ordeal of battle. They had anticipated heavy air attacks on the ill-defended centres of population in Great Britain, followed probably by an assault in force on the western front.

In fact, within a week of their invasion of Poland the Germans occupied the industrial areas of Silesia, and were approaching Warsaw. On September 17 the Russians invaded eastern Poland. Henceforward the Poles could make only a heroic last stand against a circle of enemies. On October 5 Polish organised resistance was at an end.

(b)   The Russians alleged in justification of their own aggression that events had shown the 'internal bankruptcy of the Polish State'; the Polish Government, together with the Polish State, had 'disintegrated'. On this hypothesis the agreements between Poland and the

---

(a) C12817, 12941/15/18. (b) C13953/13953/18.

U.S.S.R. no longer operated; Polish territory had become 'a suitable field for all manner of hazards and surprises which might constitute a threat to the U.S.S.R.'.

The first warning of Russian intentions came with a report from Sir W. Seeds, British Ambassador at Moscow, on September 9, of a (a) partial mobilisation of the Russian Army on their western front. A week later the Soviet Government concluded an armistice with Japan to end the fighting on the Manchukuo border. In any case, the Allies could have no clear idea of Russian plans or of the extent to which Russo-German collaboration might develop. In particular they had no knowledge of a secret additional protocol to the Soviet-German non-aggression pact of August 23 which had envisaged a new partition of Poland with the rivers Narew, Vistula and San as the approximate boundaries between the Soviet and German spheres. Clause 2 of this secret protocol stated that 'the question whether the interests of both parties make desirable the maintenance of an independent Polish State, and how such a State could be bounded, can only be definitely determined in the course of further political developments. The two parties will resolve this question by means of a friendly agreement.'[1] The Russians themselves seem to have been surprised at the determination of the Allies. On September 2 M. Molotov appeared to think that Great Britain and France would (b) accept Italian mediation and that, in any case, they would not go to war. Two days earlier, in a speech to the Supreme Council of the U.S.S.R., M. Molotov had said that, in the event of war, the U.S.S.R. would observe strict neutrality. At this stage the Foreign Office inclined to the view that, at all events for some time, the U.S.S.R. would remain in isolation, but that they might be willing to sell war material to Poland or to allow the transit of British material through Russian territory. Sir W. Seeds had been asked to make indirect soundings in the matter. He had found that there (c) was little chance of getting Soviet consent to either suggestion.

The British Government now had to consider whether they should regard this Russian attack on Poland as a *casus belli*. According to the terms of a secret protocol attached to the Anglo-Polish treaty of alliance the British guarantee of assistance to Poland applied only in the case of aggression by Germany. The British Government were free to decide whether they would or would not declare war on the U.S.S.R. The determining factor (as Lord Halifax told Count Raczynski, Polish Ambassador in London) in their decision had to be whether a declaration of war would or would not help towards the defeat of Germany.

---

[1] *D.G.F.P.*, VII, No. 229.

(a) N4282/4030/38. (b) C12902/15/18. (c) C13315, 13319/110/55.

There could be no doubt at this time about the answer to the question. War with the U.S.S.R. would not save Poland and might make the situation of the Polish people even more terrible. The defeat of Germany would be rendered more difficult by forcing the U.S.S.R. into close alliance with Germany (and thus greatly weakening the effects of the Allied blockade), and by the diversion of Anglo-French forces to meet Russian attacks in the Near or Middle East. In these circumstances even a note of protest to the Soviet Government was useless. The French Government asked for an explanation of the Soviet action, but received no reply. The British Government limited themselves to the issue of an official statement (September 19). The statement ran as follows:

'The British Government have considered the situation created by the attack upon Poland ordered by the Soviet Government. This attack made upon our ally . . . cannot be justified by the arguments put forward by the Soviet Government. The full implication of these events is not yet apparent, but His Majesty's Government take the opportunity of stating that nothing has occurred which can make any difference to the determination of His Majesty's Government, with the full support of the country, to fulfil their obligations to Poland, and to prosecute the war with all energy until their objects have been achieved.'

These words were carefully chosen; they made it clear that the British Government had no intention of accepting the Russo-German partition of Poland, and that they would not listen to peace overtures at Polish expense. The need for plain language was shown by the treaty which Ribbentrop concluded with the Russians at Moscow on September 28. The treaty established friendly relations between Germany and the U.S.S.R. on the basis of common interest in protecting their territorial gains against third parties. The Soviet Government promised to give Germany economic support and to consult with her regarding measures to be taken if Great Britain and France refused to bring the war to an end.

This reference to consultation in the event of a prolonged war might mean that the U.S.S.R. intended to join Germany. On the other hand it might be no more than a verbal support to Hitler's attempt to get peace on German terms. The most likely hypothesis was still that the Soviet Government did not intend to go to war but were acting on the policy of securing everything they wanted while Great Britain and France were unable to check them. On the day of the signature of the new Russo-German treaty, the Soviet Government concluded a pact with Estonia for the lease to the U.S.S.R. of naval bases on the islands of Ösel and Dagö and at Baltic Port.

On October 5 a similar pact with Latvia secured to the U.S.S.R. the right to establish naval bases at Libau and Windau and to build aerodromes on Latvian territory. Five days later Lithuania gave permission for the maintenance of Russian land and air forces at agreed points on Lithuanian territory.[1]

Meanwhile on October 6 Hitler had made the offer of negotiations foreshadowed in the Russo-German treaty. He put this offer in a speech to the Reichstag which, as usual, showed his failure to measure the depth of feeling which had brought the British people to accept war with Germany for the second time in twenty-five years. Hitler's argument was that Great Britain and France had gone to war to save Poland. They had not saved Poland. Hence they had no reason to continue fighting. There was some evidence that Hitler and his entourage really believed that the British Government would listen to a dishonourable proposal of this kind.[2] The War Cabinet never even considered the possibility of accepting such an offer; in any case they regarded all Hitler's offers and promises as worthless. The (a) only question was whether to make a reply. They decided to reply in order to reaffirm their position and to establish the fact that responsibility for the fearful slaughter now to be expected in the west would rest with Germany. The Prime Minister therefore spoke in these terms on October 12. He was careful to avoid language which might give the impression of assenting, even tentatively, to the idea of negotiation. He safeguarded himself by saying that it was no part of British policy to exclude from her rightful place in Europe a Germany which would live in amity and confidence with other nations; he also stated plainly that we would not surrender to wrong-doing or agree to an uneasy truce interrupted by further threats. After this statement neither the Germans nor the Russians could go on believing that Great Britain would acquiesce in the destruction of Poland or agree to peace on German terms. Hitler's delusions reappeared after the collapse of France, but from October 1939 to June 1940 he made no more 'peace-feelers'.[3]

---

[1] On October 7, 1939, Ribbentrop instructed the German Ministers in Estonia, Latvia and Finland that these countries and Lithuania fell within the Russian sphere of interest 'for the eventuality of a territorial and political reorganisation in these areas'. *D.G.F.P.*, Series D, VIII, No. 213.

[2] On the other hand Hitler told Ciano on October 2 that he did not expect his forth-coming speech to 'make a deep impression on the enemy'. He was delivering the speech 'only in order to place the enemy in the wrong'. *D.G.F.P.*, *id.*, No. 224.

[3] See Volume II, Chapter XXV, for other and later German suggestions for a 'compromise peace'.

(a) WM(39)40, C15985/13005/18; WM(39)42, C16215/13005/18; WM(39)43, C16325/13005/18; WM(39)44, C16457/13005/18; WM(39)45, C16489/13005/18.

(iii)

Unsuccessful attempts to open staff conversations with Belgium, September–
December 1939: the 'alarm' of November 8–11, 1939.

After the rejection of Hitler's peace offer, the general impression
in Great Britain was that the Germans might use their initiative by
attacking at once in the west.[1] There was every likelihood that this
attack would come through Belgium. The main fortified system of the
Maginot Line did not extend to the north-west beyond Longuyon.
The Franco-Belgian frontier, although not without protection, was
much more open to attack and the Germans, who in 1914 had
violated Belgian neutrality, would not hesitate to do so again. Hence
on the British side the most important diplomatic action directly
concerned with military strategy was an attempt to persuade the
Belgian King and Government to consent to staff conversations on
the question of meeting a German attack. Great Britain and France
had reaffirmed in April 1937 their guarantee to Belgium, although
Belgium herself was released from any obligation to France. It was
assumed, however, in 1939 that the Belgians would resist invasion
and call upon the Allies to fulfil their guarantee. The Allies would
then wish to send troops into the country, but the line which the
troops would try to hold could not be improvised. In any case the
British and French air forces would have to attack the German
invaders. If they did not know the Belgian plans of defence they
could not avoid the risk of bombing Belgian troops and civilian
refugees on the roads. The question thus affected the Allied forces
as a whole; the British Government were directly concerned, since
the British Expeditionary Force would be on the left flank of the
Allied armies, and a German occupation of Belgium would bring a
renewal of the dangerous position in the war of 1914–18 when
Zeebrugge and the Bruges Canal were used as submarine bases.

The Foreign Office was well aware of the Belgian attitude.
Attempts to open staff conversations in February and May 1939 had
failed. Although the Chief of the Belgian General Staff and the
Minister of Defence had been favourable to them, the King, the
Court, and the majority of the Belgian Cabinet had taken the
opposite view. They thought that the Germans would hear of the
conversations and treat them as a breach of Belgian neutrality.[2]
Early in September 1939 the War Cabinet considered the advisa-

---

[1] On October 9, 1939, Hitler gave orders for the preparation of an attack on the
northern wing of the Western Front through Belgium, Holland and Luxembourg. The
attack was to be carried out as soon as possible. *D.G.F.P.*, *ib.*, 248–50.

[2] The Belgian Government announced on June 23, 1939, that they intended to pursue a
policy of independence and saw no justification for modifying such a policy, and that there
was no question of establishing contacts with foreign General Staffs.

bility of sending a special emissary to Belgium and also of asking (a)
His Majesty The King to write a personal letter to King Leopold. On
the advice of the Foreign Office this plan was given up and the
subject was raised, without success, through ordinary diplomatic
channels. Lord Halifax spoke to the Belgian Ambassador in London
on September 23 and, three days later, to M. van Zeeland.[1] (b)
M. van Zeeland answered that, in order to secure Belgian unity in the
event of an invasion, the Government must be able to say that the
attack was entirely unprovoked. M. van Zeeland, however, suggested
that contacts between the Belgian and British staffs might be made
through a civilian intermediary in each country.

Meanwhile, Sir R. Clive, British Ambassador at Brussels, had been
instructed to repeat the arguments as strongly as possible to the
Belgian Government. He left an *aide-mémoire* with M. Spaak, the
Belgian Foreign Minister, on September 20; M. Spaak repeated the
argument that the Germans would learn of the conversations through
their espionage system in Belgium and might decide to forestall what
they would assume to be a plan for an Allied attack through Belgium.
On September 29 M. Spaak gave Sir R. Clive an official reply to his
aide-mémoire. The reply stated that the Belgian Government did not (c)
expect the Germans to attack through Belgium, and that staff conversations were unnecessary because the Belgians themselves had decided
upon all the measures of defence required against invasion, and were
putting these measures into effect. Therefore the guarantor Powers, if
called upon, could send their forces into Belgium without risk of
surprise attack by land. M. Spaak, in conversation with Sir R. Clive,
added that the Belgian and Dutch Military Attachés in Berlin had
been told on September 28 that Germany intended to respect the
neutrality of their respective countries, but feared an Allied attack
through them. Hence the Belgian Government thought that there
were greater risks in holding staff conversations than in waiting upon
events.

The Belgian attitude on this question of staff conversations did not
change during October. The King of the Belgians even complained to
the British Government, and personally in a letter to His Majesty The (d)
King, that we were inviting the Belgian Government to act dis-
honourably in going 'behind the back of the Germans, who had
equally guaranteed Belgian neutrality', and in holding staff conversations with us.

---

[1] M. van Zeeland, a well-known economist and business man, had been Belgian Prime
Minister from March 1935 to November 1937. Although he did not at this time hold an
official position, he acted as an informal adviser on economic matters to the Belgian
Government.

(a) WM(39)16, 19, 20; C14088, 14089, 14101, 14295, 14343, 14467, 14468, 14605,
14686, 14839/209/4. (b) WM(39)29; C15153, 15260/209/4. (c) C15265, 15279,
15525/209/4. (d) C16212, 17657/209/4.

Early in November, however, there was a new development. On
(a) November 7 M. Spaak told Sir R. Clive that a German attack on
Belgium and the Netherlands seemed imminent. The Germans had
been massing troops on the Belgian frontier for some days, and had
made reconnaissance flights over the country. The Dutch were even
more disturbed, and, at the invitation of the Queen of the Netherlands, King Leopold and M. Spaak had gone to The Hague on the
previous day. Here they had agreed to send a joint offer of mediation
to the three belligerent Powers.[1]

M. Spaak said that this offer was an attempt to gain time and to
hold back a German attack in the belief that the Germans might
hesitate to attack the two countries which had offered their good
offices for mediation. He hoped that, if the British Government
found it impossible to accept the proposal, they would not give a hasty
refusal. Sir R. Clive suggested that, if matters were so serious, it was
surely desirable for the British and Belgian military authorities to
meet.

(b)   On the following evening Sir R. Clive again saw M. Spaak. M.
Spaak was still anxious about the situation. Sir R. Clive asked what
the Belgian Government would do if the Dutch alone were attacked.
M. Spaak asked what the Allies would do. Were they prepared to
send a sufficient force to defend the Netherlands? Sir R. Clive said
that we could not do so without the consent of Belgium. Would the
Belgian Government agree to the passage of Allied troops across
Belgian territory?

M. Spaak thought the Belgian Government would agree; Sir R.
Clive then suggested that he should ask the British Government to put
the question officially. M. Spaak hesitated, but made no objection.
Sir R. Clive again asked why the Belgians had not made a move
during the day to establish military contacts with the Allies. M. Spaak
said that he hoped contact would very shortly be established in Paris,
but that 'there was still opposition from a certain quarter'. At 12.30
a.m. on November 10 the Foreign Office instructed Sir R. Clive to
speak again to M. Spaak on the question of concerting plans with the
Belgian military authorities in order that the Allies might be able to
give effective support to Belgian and Dutch resistance.

(c)   Sir R. Clive carried out his instructions at once. M. Spaak said
that he was personally in favour of immediate contacts, but that the
opposition came from the military side. The Belgian Military
Attaché in Paris, however, had been instructed to see General Gamelin, and the attitude of the Belgian military authorities would depend
on the question whether the British and French forces could come

---

[1] See Volume II, Chapter XXV. The Germans had in fact just begun troop movements for an offensive to be opened on November 12, but had postponed the date.

(a) C17984/12907/18. (b) C18035/12907/18. (c) C18199/209/4.

immediately and in sufficient force to the assistance of Belgium. On the morning of November 11 M. Spaak sent an official note to Sir R. (a) Clive to the effect that the Belgian Commander-in-Chief would receive with the greatest interest any information which the British Military Attaché could give about the extent of Allied support in the event of an appeal from the Belgian Government. Colonel Blake, the Military Attaché, therefore arranged to see the Belgian Chief of Staff. Before this interview took place, Colonel Blake was asked to go (b) to General van Overstraeten, the King's personal military adviser. General van Overstraeten said that he—not the Chief of Staff—had received authority from the King as Commander-in-Chief to discuss the position. The general gave very little information about Belgian military plans, but repeated the question about the amount of help which the Allies could send and, in particular, what support we could provide for the defence of the Albert Canal zone.

Colonel Blake saw General van Overstraeten again on November 12. He asked that the French should be brought into the discussion. (c) The general thought that the best plan would be for Colonel Blake to talk to him, and for the Belgian Military Attaché to deal with General Gamelin. He promised to speak to King Leopold about tripartite military conversations, but doubted whether the King would accept them.

Although the War Cabinet regarded this plan as unsatisfactory, they were willing to give way to the King's wishes about procedure, on the understanding that our own military authorities would keep in close touch with the French, since we did not know what answer General Gamelin had given to the Belgian question. In fact the Belgian Military Attaché limited himself in his interviews with General Gamelin to this question about the extent of Allied assistance, and refused to discuss the related question of concerting military action.

In any case, the Belgians drew back when the German attack did not take place, and the German Government issued a communiqué that they would respect Belgian and Dutch neutrality as long as the two countries showed that they were capable of maintaining their neutral attitude. The War Cabinet thought it desirable that Admiral Sir R. Keyes, who was a personal friend of the Belgian royal family, should go to see the King in order to explain the position, and to try to make him realise why we regarded it as important that Belgium should consider a German attack on the Netherlands as a *casus belli*. M. Spaak changed his ground a little when Sir R. Clive raised this (d) latter point with him again on November 14. He said that the Belgian Government could not take an absolute decision in the matter

---

(a) C18251, 18258/209/4. (b) C18263, 18291/209/4. (c) C18277/209/4.
(d) C18530/18243/18.

until they knew what the Dutch would do. M. Spaak thought that the Germans had phrased their communiqué in a way which left an excuse for aggression and that the danger of attack remained even though, owing to the weather conditions and the time of year, military operations on a large scale were daily becoming more difficult.

(a)   King Leopold told Sir R. Keyes that he held the view that the Belgians would regard an attack on the Netherlands as a *casus belli*, but that the Belgian Government had not yet come to a decision. The King said that the decision could not be taken before the Germans attacked, and therefore could not be announced in advance. He believed that the Germans had intended to attack the Netherlands and, probably, Belgium, on November 11, and that they had refrained from doing so only when their air reconnaissance had shown the great strength of the Albert Canal position and of the French concentrations on the left flank of the Allied line. The King seemed fairly confident that the Germans would not attack before the spring of 1940. Sir R. Keyes told the King that the British military authorities attached great importance to the preparation of a strong defensive line between Wavre and Namur,[1] The King promised that the existing defences should be strengthened as soon as possible; he also wanted the liaison between Colonel Blake and General van Overstraeten to continue. He did not wish the French Military Attaché to be brought into these talks in Brussels, though he agreed to further discussions in Paris between the Belgian Military Attaché and General Gamelin, and a British representative.

At the same time the King still hoped that he might go on with his attempts to bring about an acceptable peace. He realised that the British and French rejection of the Belgian and Dutch proposals for mediation was absolute, and that Hitler was unlikely to make an offer acceptable to the Allies. Nevertheless he thought that the opening of negotiations would be in the interests of the Allies and of Belgium, and might induce Hitler to wait before committing himself to an intensified 'Blitzkrieg'.

The result of these inconclusive discussions was unsatisfactory. The Belgians apparently learned from the French that the Allies, if they received an invitation in time, would come to their support on the Antwerp–Namur line;[2] they wanted, if possible, support on the line of the Albert Canal (from Antwerp to the Meuse north of Liège) and although the King had given Sir R. Keyes to understand that he would certainly approve of resistance to a German attack on Belgium,

---

[1] This was the area to which the B.E.F. might advance if it came to the assistance of the Belgians.

[2] This 'line' extended south of Antwerp along the river Dyle through Louvain to Wavre, and thence to Namur; from Namur it followed the Meuse to Givet on the French frontier.

(a) C18644, 18597/:8243/18.

he would not pledge himself to action in the event of an attack on the Netherlands, and clearly hoped that somehow or other the war might end in a compromise peace which the Allies would accept. With this idea in mind, the King was unwilling to go very far in detailed military conversations.

General Gamelin's plan (which was approved by General Ironside) for an advance to the Antwerp–Namur line in the event of a German attack on Belgium was definitely accepted at a meeting of the Supreme War Council on November 17 in London. The British Government had suggested this meeting because they wanted to be clear about the military action to be taken,[1] and also because differences of opinion had arisen between the British and French experts on the use to be made of the British long-range bombers. At the meeting Mr. Chamberlain explained the extreme gravity—for Great Britain and France—of a German occupation of Belgium, and put forward the proposal that, as soon as the German attack began, British long-range bombers should attempt to destroy the railways and industrial establishments of the Ruhr. He thought that the effect of this bombing would be an outcry from the German people for the evacuation of Belgium or at least for the return of reinforcements for the defence of Germany. Mr. Chamberlain realised the risks of German retaliation once we began to attack objectives containing large civilian populations; he therefore would not put the plan into effect unless it were absolutely necessary.

M. Daladier was unwilling to accept this proposal, since in his view it would not succeed in destroying the Ruhr industries or in saving Belgium; on the other hand the Germans, with their greatly superior air strength, could do much more harm to British and French industry. M. Daladier, however, entirely agreed about the importance of preventing the Germans from occupying a substantial part of Belgium; he thought that at least the Allies should hold the Antwerp–Namur line, and that they had every chance of holding it. Mr. Chamberlain said that he must again emphasise the importance, from the British point of view, of keeping the Germans out of Belgium, but that he was satisfied with M. Daladier's statement that every effort would be made to hold the Antwerp–Namur line. The Supreme War Council therefore formally adopted a resolution that, in view of the importance of keeping the Germans as far east as possible, the Allies (a) would do all that they could to defend the Antwerp–Namur line in the event of a German invasion of Belgium. Here the matter remained until the next 'alarm', in January 1940.

---

[1] I have not dealt here with the Anglo-French military discussions or with the views of the British Chiefs of Staff before this date on the question whether military action should consist in holding the line of the Scheldt or the more advanced Antwerp–Namur line. See *Grand Strategy*, III, ch. VIII, and L. F. Ellis, *The War in France and Flanders, 1939–40* (H.M.S.O., 1954), chs. II and III.

(a) C375/9/17 (1940).

(iv)

British policy towards Italy, September-December 1939.

The prolonged attempt to improve the defensive position in the west had failed because the Belgians knew the Germans to be stronger in numbers and material than the Allies. As long as the Germans held this superiority they could terrorise their smaller neighbours. Although these neighbours could not trust German assurances, they hoped that, if they took care not to provoke Hitler, they might even yet evade calamity. They played for time in the hope that the war might come to an end, or at all events that the Allies might become so strong that the Germans would be forced to the defensive, and that the small nations could then 'creep out into the sun again'.

Against this state of mind the Allies could do little or nothing. On the other hand they had at least the advantage that in the case of Belgium they were dealing with a friendly State. Whatever the hesitations of the Belgian King and Cabinet, there was no reason to suppose that they were considering the possibility of joining the enemy. In the case of Japan and Italy, it was necessary to take this possibility into account. During the first few months of the war the danger of Japanese intervention did not appear to be great. The Russo-German agreement had shocked Japanese opinion: Japan was occupied in China and even the Japanese military extremists, although reckless in the largest decisions, moved cautiously, and step by step, in their actual tactics.[1] In the case of Italy the danger also did not seem immediate. There was no doubt about Mussolini's personal inclinations, or that, at this stage in his career, his judgment was distorted by vindictiveness against Great Britain as the country which had tried to enforce sanctions against Italy. Furthermore, an Allied victory would endanger Mussolini's own position and that of the Fascist régime, whereas a victory for the Axis Powers would be a proof of his good judgment in making an alliance with Germany and would also secure him some at least of his demands at the expense of Great Britain and France.

On the other hand, Mussolini had not encouraged Hitler to go to war in September 1939, and had made it clear that, at all events for the time, he did not feel obliged to fight at the side of his ally. Although this 'stepping down' was described in high-sounding terms, the facts were obvious. The Italian people had no wish for war, but this consideration did not matter much to Mussolini, since he knew that they would obey his orders, and that without political revolution —for which there were no leaders—they could not do otherwise.

---

[1] See Volume II, Chapter XXII for British policy towards Japan in the first year of the war.

Mussolini's main reasons for hesitation were that Italy was not ready for war either from an economic or from a military point of view, and could not get help from the Germans at sea or reckon on sufficient supplies from Germany by land to withstand an Allied blockade. Above all, Mussolini could not be sure that Germany would win the war. It is probable that at any time between the outbreak of war and the German successes in Norway, he would have preferred a negotiated peace without military victory for either side.[1] As the price of using his influence to secure such a peace, he might hope to obtain concessions from Great Britain and France. Italy would thus strengthen her position and in the uneasy balance which would follow a compromise peace Italian bargaining power would be an important factor, while Germany would continue to exist as a barrier against Communism.

At all events, the British Government had reason to expect that Mussolini would remain 'malevolently neutral', or non-belligerent, unless the Allies took some action directly contrary to Italian interests or unless the Germans appeared to be winning the war easily and quickly. Italian bargaining power was a 'wasting asset'; Mussolini could not wait too long, but in the first few months of the war there were no obvious signs of a rapid victory for either side. German military inaction after the defeat of Poland surprised Italian opinion and even suggested doubts whether after all the Allies were going to lose the war. The much boasted German air force did little. At sea the Allies had held their own against submarine attacks and countered the new danger of the magnetic mine within a few weeks. The victory of the British 8-inch and 6-inch gun cruisers against the 11-inch guns of the pocket-battleship *Admiral Graf Spee* on December 13, 1939, was a warning to the Italians of the risks of an engagement with the British Navy.

There were arguments in favour of compelling Mussolini to choose at once between open war or full collaboration with the Allies. A 'knock-out' blow against one of the Axis Powers would certainly affect the morale of the other and would immensely strengthen the position of the Allies in south-eastern Europe. Furthermore, unless Mussolini were compelled to submit to the full exercise of the Allied rights of belligerency at sea, the blockade of Germany would remain

---

[1] The Italian Ambassador in Berlin told the German Foreign Office on September 15, 1939, that Mussolini still hoped that 'a really magnanimous' peace offer might have chances of success with the Western Powers. The Ambassador did not go into details, but said that the proposals must not 'bear the character of far-reaching intentions of conquest' (*D.G.F.P.*, VIII, No. 73). The Ambassador continued to make these suggestions. On his third attempt Weizsäcker noted that Mussolini had made similar suggestions to the German Military Attaché in Rome (*D.G.F.P.*, *id.*, No. 127). From the other side Lord Halifax gave Ciano a hint for Mussolini and himself on November 25 that, if they saw any opportunity for Anglo-Italian co-operation to the mutual advantage of both countries he (Lord Halifax) and Mr. Chamberlain would give it full sympathy (*Doc. Dipl. Ital.*, 9th Series, II, No. 338). For the changes in Mussolini's attitude, see below, pp. 147–54.

imperfect, and the Italians would be enabled to increase their own reserves of essential commodities.

Once more, however, the resources of the Allies on land and in the air were not sufficient to allow them to take the initiative. The Allies were still too weak in relation to Germany to permit any large-scale diversion from the main objective of building up an overwhelming concentration in the west. Hence the wiser policy was to accept the Italian attitude and, while trying to minimise its disadvantages from the point of view of the blockade, to avoid action which would force Mussolini to make his choice. The War Cabinet therefore decided at (a) an early stage to say nothing on the political issue, but to offer discussions on questions of trade.[1] The acceptance of this offer seemed to justify a policy of silence on the larger issue in spite of Italian military concentrations in Libya. Ciano told Sir P. Loraine on November 13, that the 'present purpose' of the Italian Government was to 'carry on the life of the country' on a basis of 'non-belligerency'. If a change in policy were made—in other words, if Mussolini were intending to enter the war on the German side—Ciano would tell Sir P. Loraine in time to allow an 'exchange of views'. This promise might be no more than a form of reinsurance for the Italians, and the 'exchange of views' might well turn out to be merely an attempt at blackmail, but there was as yet no change in the Italian policy of 'non-belligerency'.

(v)

Anglo-French policy with regard to the Balkans, September–December 1939: the Anglo-Franco-Turkish Treaty of October 19: the question of a Balkan bloc.

The loss of initiative which compelled the Allies to deal cautiously with Mussolini also affected their policy in south-eastern Europe. Here there was a certain divergence of view between the British and French Governments. This divergence was due ultimately to the anxiety of the French to draw the main centre of warfare away from the western front and also to secure the help of the armies of the Balkan States as a means of redressing the numerical balance of forces in favour of the Allies. As long, however, as the Germans did not attack in south-east Europe, the two Governments were agreed that their interests would best be served by the creation of a Balkan *bloc*

---

[1] The economic negotiations with Italy before the Italian entry into the war are described in Medlicott, I, ch. VIII. I have therefore dealt with them only as far as is necessary to explain Anglo-Italian political negotiations.

(a) WM(39)5, R7177/1/22.

resolved to defend itself against German attack. They were agreed also that any encouragement given to the formation of such a *bloc* must not be such as to supply Italy with a reason or even a pretext for abandoning her neutrality. The difference between British and French policy lay in their respective estimates of what could be done to encourage the Balkan States within the limits of Allied resources and without giving provocation to Italy. The question was touched upon at the first meeting of the Supreme War Council at Abbeville (a) on September 12, and discussed more fully at a second meeting of the Council held at Hove on September 22. M. Daladier then explained his view that the Allies ought to have a force either at Salonika or at Istanbul to meet a German advance towards the Mediterranean or the Straits. Such a force would 'act as a cement' for the Balkan States who might otherwise give way to German demands or fail to unite against a German attack.

Mr. Chamberlain pointed out that the Allies could do nothing to prevent a German advance through Yugoslavia; that the maintenance of a force at Salonika or Istanbul would put a very heavy strain upon Allied shipping and naval escorts; that Salonika was not a good base or starting point for offensive operations, and that in any case the use of either place must depend upon the attitude of Italy and Turkey. Furthermore it was impossible to combine the plan of a neutral Balkan *bloc* with the presence of Allied forces in one of the Balkan States. No decision was therefore taken other than to 'explore' the position through diplomatic channels at Rome and Ankara. Even on this point there was not complete agreement, since the British Government were inclined to question the association of General Weygand[1] with the approach to be made by the French Ambassador at Ankara.

Apart from the limited help which the Allies could provide, there were other obstacles in the way of the formation of a Balkan *bloc*. All the States of south-eastern Europe were afraid of Germany and, like Belgium, were concerned primarily with avoiding anything likely to provoke a German attack. Roumania was equally nervous of Russia, and Yugoslavia and Greece were nervous of Italy. Furthermore, Hungary and Bulgaria had territorial claims against their neighbours and might think it worth while to join or even to initiate an attack against them. Roumania and Greece had British guarantees, and Turkey might be expected to assist in the defence of Roumania against an attack likely to be a prelude to a German advance against the Straits. Great Britain and France had treaties of mutual assistance

---

[1] General Weygand was at this time in command of the French forces in the Levant.
(a) C373, 374/9/17 (1940).

with Turkey, but the difficulties in the final stage of negotiating these treaties justified the caution of the Foreign Office in refusing to be led into wishful thinking about the possibilities of co-operation in south-eastern Europe.

At the outbreak of the war Great Britain and Turkey were on the point of concluding a Treaty of Mutual Assistance. The history of the negotiations showed on the Turkish side a break with the policy of association with Germany and a return to the older tradition of friendship with Great Britain. The decision to make this change had been taken before the death of Atatürk in November 1938. President Ismet Inönü, Atatürk's successor, had brought new men into his Government, but otherwise—with differences of temperament—had continued the main lines of his predecessor's policy. Turkey, however, would probably not have entered into a new commitment in foreign affairs if Italy had not invaded Albania. Mussolini's speeches in favour of an Italian occupation of Anatolia had not been forgotten, and the Italian occupation of the Dodecanese was a threat as well as a source of discontent to Turkey. The seizure of Albania was even more serious, since it affected the *status quo* in the Balkans. Hence the Turkish Government were willing to join Great Britain in a declaration that the two countries would conclude a long-term agreement, and that meanwhile 'in the event of an act of aggression leading to war in the Mediterranean area, they would be prepared to co-operate effectively and to lend each other all aid and assistance in their power'. The two Governments also recognised that it was necessary 'to ensure the establishment of security in the Balkans'; they were 'consulting together with the object of achieving this purpose as speedily as possible'.

This declaration was made on May 12, 1939. The French Government agreed with it, and would have shared in it, but difficulties had arisen between France and Turkey over the cession to Turkey of Hatay (the Sanjak of Alexandretta) in Syria. On June 23, after the cession had been arranged, a Franco-Turkish declaration was announced in terms similar to that between Great Britain and Turkey.

The British Government had suggested that the procedure following the declaration should be (i) an 'interim understanding', (ii) a meeting of experts to discuss the practical execution of an agreement, (iii) the final negotiation of the agreement. They found it better to dispense with an interim understanding and, as the discussions between experts were already taking place, to deal with the terms of the final agreement. One reason why these negotiations were so much prolonged was that Turkey needed economic assistance on a large scale. Germany took nearly half of Turkish exports. She was acquiring them on terms disadvantageous to Turkey, but the

Turks could not break away from these terms unless they found other customers. Their most important export was tobacco—one-third of which went to Germany; the trouble in this case was that, after Turkey joined Germany in the First World War, and Great Britain had to rely largely on American tobacco, the taste of British smokers changed. It was therefore much less easy to dispose of the Turkish tobacco crop in Great Britain, and a new change in taste would now mean heavy and permanent loss to American tobacco growers, and therefore difficulties with the United States. Furthermore, by joining Great Britain and France and thereby incurring military obligations, Turkey would have to rearm on a scale beyond her own resources. Since Turkish military needs could not be met entirely by Great Britain and France, and Germany would no longer be a main source of supply, the Turkish Government wanted to be able to use armaments credits for purchases in the United States, Belgium and Sweden.

At the outbreak of war the political and military terms of the Anglo-Franco-Turkish Treaty were largely agreed, but the financial and economic terms were still unsettled. The Turkish Government maintained their original demands for loans and war material, and for markets in which to dispose of the commodities they could no longer sell to Germany. They asked for a gold loan of £15 million and for the inclusion in the treaty of a 'suspense clause' providing that Turkey should not be obliged to go to war under the treaty until she had been adequately supplied with war material. The Foreign Office considered the terms very high, but not too high a price to be paid for the political and military advantages of the treaty. Hence the terms were accepted by the British and French Governments and a tripartite treaty was initialled on September 28.

According to the treaty (i) Great Britain and France promised help to Turkey in the event of 'an act of aggression' against her by a European Power; (ii) Great Britain and France on the one part, and Turkey on the other part promised mutual assistance in the event of 'an act of aggression by a European Power leading to war in the Mediterranean area' involving the signatories; (iii) Turkey promised to aid Great Britain and France in the fulfilment of their guarantees to Greece and Roumania; (iv) if Great Britain and France were at war with a European Power in consequence of an aggression by that Power to which provisions (ii) and (iii) did not apply, the signatories would consult together, and Turkey would observe at least a benevolent neutrality toward Great Britain and France. A protocol was added that the obligations undertaken by Turkey were not to have the effect of compelling her to go to war with the U.S.S.R.[1]

---

[1] Protocol 2: 'The obligations undertaken by Turkey in virtue of the above-mentioned Treaty cannot compel that country to take action having as its effect, or involving as its consequence, entry into armed conflict with the Soviet Union.'

It had been intended to keep this protocol secret, but the fact of its existence was made public by the Turkish Government.

The treaty was accompanied by a military convention defining certain military measures to be taken if a *casus foederis* should arise, and by a financial agreement in which the British and French Governments promised Turkey £25 million[1] credit for the purchase of war material in the United Kingdom and France, a gold loan of £15 million,[2] and a loan of £2 million from His Majesty's Government and the equivalent in francs of £1½ million from the French Government for liquidating frozen Anglo-Turkish and Franco-Turkish balances. A Turkish mission would come to London immediately to draw up a programme of war material to be purchased under the £25 million credit. Particular regard was to be given to the needs of Turkey for the defence of her Thracian frontier. Until war material for this purpose had been delivered a 'suspense' condition would apply to the treaty.

The treaty was not signed until three weeks after it had been initialled. The delay was due to another disturbing factor in the Balkan situation. At the end of September the Soviet Government had (a) invited M. Saracoglu, the Turkish Foreign Minister, to Moscow in order to discuss 'matters of common interest', including a Russo-Turkish pact. On October 1 M. Saracoglu had an interview with Stalin and Molotov. The Russians then went through the text of the Anglo-Franco-Turkish treaty clause by clause. Molotov raised a number of objections, but Stalin waved them aside, and made only two demands. He wanted the Turkish undertaking to support Great Britain and France in the execution of their guarantees to Roumania narrowed down to provide only for consultation. He also asked that the protocol exempting Turkey from taking part in war against the Soviet Union should be widened to secure the suspension of the treaty as a whole if the Soviet Union were engaged in war with Great Britain and France.

The Foreign Office considered that if we insisted upon the maintenance of the treaty in the terms in which it had been initialled, we should be putting too great a strain on Russo-Turkish, and, to some extent, on Anglo-Turkish relations. On balance it seemed best to accept the Soviet demands on condition that the Turkish Government allowed us to see the text of their own agreement with the U.S.S.R. and that this agreement did not preclude Turkey from coming into the war on the Allied side.

---

[1] The French Government agreed to provide £9 million of this sum. The total included £10 million already granted by the British Government and 460 million francs already granted by the French Government.

[2] The French Government agreed to provide £4 million of this sum.

(a) WM(39)36, R8444/661/67; WM(39)38, R8522/661/67; WM(39)39, R8523/661/67; WM(39)42, R8677/661/67; WM(39)43, R8678/661/67; WM(39)49, R8947/661/67; WM(39)50, R8986/661/67; WM(39)51, R9079/661/67.

The War Cabinet and, after some hesitation, the French Government accepted this plan. It was not put into effect because the negotiations between Russia and Turkey broke down on two points raised by Stalin and then withdrawn. M. Molotov had raised them again, but had agreed, subject to Stalin's consent, to withdraw them. Stalin had then in turn become unwilling to drop them and finally the Turkish Government had refused to accept them. The two points were that the Russo-Turkish pact should include a 'suspense' clause on the lines of the Anglo-Franco-Turkish treaty exempting the Soviet Union from taking part in a war against Germany, and that Turkey, under Article 21 of the Montreux Convention,[1] should deny passage through the Straits to warships and transports other than those of Black Sea Powers. According to this article, Turkey had the right, if she were a belligerent, to allow or refuse passage to warships.

After the breakdown of the negotiations with Russia, the Turkish Government were willing to sign the Anglo-Franco-Turkish treaty. The treaty was signed on October 19 in the form in which it had been initialled. The conclusion of the treaty and the loyalty of the Turkish Government were matters of satisfaction, but it seemed unlikely that Stalin would have given up the Russo-Turkish pact if he had not made some arrangement with Germany for joint Russo-German action in the Balkans. Hence it was even more desirable, and at the same time more difficult, to secure a Balkan *bloc*.

The French Government continued to put forward plans for Allied action in the Balkans. At the third meeting of the Supreme War Council on November 17 M. Daladier had suggested that the Allies should consider the possibility of a German attack in south-eastern Europe. He did not regard a Salonika front as possible, but thought that we might lay down munition dumps in Turkey, or Thrace, or prepare air, naval, or even land bases in these areas, or in Syria or Palestine. Mr. Chamberlain pointed out that, if Turkey remained neutral, we could not establish the dumps or prepare bases on Turkish territory, and that in any case we were short of material, and could put it to better use on the western front. The Supreme War Council did not discuss the matter further, and resolved only that

---

[1] The Montreux Convention, signed on July 20, 1936, brought to an end the international control of the Straits established under the Treaty of Lausanne in 1923. By it all the Black Sea Powers obtained substantial privileges over other nations in respect of the passage of warships, but the effective control of the Straits passed into the hands of Turkey. Under Article 19 of the Convention, belligerent warships, in a war during which Turkey remained neutral, might pass through the Straits only to fulfil obligations under the League Covenant, or to help States to whose assistance Turkey was herself bound by treaties concluded within the framework of the Covenant. Article 20 empowered Turkey, if herself at war, to control the passage of all warships at her discretion. Under Article 21 Turkey might exercise this control if she considered herself in imminent danger of war. A protocol permitted Turkey to refortify the demilitarised zone of the Straits. Italy, alone of the signatories to the Treaty of Lausanne, was not a party of the Convention, which was to remain in force for twenty years subject to revision at five-year intervals.

the Allied military authorities should study what could be done to
meet a German offensive in south-east Europe.

The British military authorities, however, remained nervous of
General Weygand's activities, and on November 30 the War Cabinet
(a) agreed to ask the French Government to ensure that there was no
departure from the agreed Anglo-French policy with regard to the
Balkans. Before the fourth meeting of the Supreme War Council in
(b) Paris on December 19 the War Cabinet therefore examined the
whole matter once again in the light of a full review by the Chiefs of
Staff of policy in the Middle East. It was thus possible to consider
Balkan policy in a larger setting.

In this larger setting the Chiefs of Staff suggested that the strategic
importance of Singapore was greater than that of the Mediterranean,
and that Turkey and Iraq were of greater interest to us than the
Balkan countries. Without Italian neutrality we could give little help
to Turkey or Greece. Germany had sufficient resources to allow her
to embark upon a Balkan offensive. She could do so quickly since, in
the despatch of troops, 'the train always beats the ship'. Turkey alone
could offer serious resistance to German aggression but the Turkish
military authorities appeared to underestimate the danger of German
attacks on her communications. In Greece we could probably not
hold Salonika, but we might defend a line from Euboea to Corinth.
We could do nothing directly to help Hungary, Yugoslavia or
Roumania.

(c)   The Prime Minister therefore went to the fourth meeting of the
Supreme War Council with the support of the War Cabinet for the
policy previously laid down, that is to say a policy which would avoid
provocation to Italy or any action likely to extend the war to the
Balkans. Mr Chamberlain found M. Daladier anxious to make
preparations for helping the Balkan countries if they should wish to
resist aggression. Preparation would take the form of joint diplomatic
action in Turkey, Roumania, Greece and Yugoslavia; material help
to these countries; a study of the forms in which assistance could be
given to them, and an effort to persuade them to unite in order to
resist attack. Mr. Chamberlain tried to bring more precision into the
discussion. He asked whether M. Daladier wanted to encourage
Yugoslavia to resist German attack or whether he proposed that we
should promise the Yugoslavs an Allied force. He pointed out that
each of the countries concerned was differently situated and unlikely
to agree to enter a *bloc* merely on the strength of mutual support.
Would Yugoslavia agree to join the *bloc* when she could get nothing
more than certain war supplies from Great Britain and France?
M. Daladier referred to the ninety divisions which could be put into

the field by the Balkan countries, but Mr. Chamberlain pointed out that the military value of these divisions was unequal, and that there seemed little prospect of the emergence of a united Balkan force which could, for example, defend Yugoslavia. Before an undertaking was given to the Balkan countries it was necessary to ensure at least the benevolent neutrality of Italy. Otherwise we might find it impossible to fulfil promises which we had made. If, however, we put a direct question to Italy, the answer would be that the Italian attitude largely depended upon the intentions of the Allies in the Balkans.

Mr. Chamberlain therefore wanted to approach the Italian Government with a statement of Allied intentions. M. Daladier, on the other hand, thought it better to begin preparations and to watch the Italian reaction to them. Finally it was agreed that Sir P. Loraine should make an informal approach to Ciano and that, until this approach had been made, no new staff conversations should (a) be opened with the Balkan States, but the French General Staff might continue normal conversations already in progress with Yugoslavia and Roumania. Diplomatic action in the Balkan States for the formation of a Balkan *bloc* would best be carried out through Turkey, and the first step would be to secure Turkish co-operation in the matter.

Thus the more cautious British policy was maintained. The Foreign Office, however, were doubtful about an informal approach (b) to Italy. Italian policy had remained as Ciano had described it, but, if Mussolini still hesitated to take the risk of war, he was as closely bound as ever to Germany, and was continuing to protest against British contraband control. He was likely to pass on to the Germans every hint given to him about the Allied plans, and also to prevent the Allies from putting their plans into effect. In any case at this time the War Cabinet were considering the possibility of an expedition to Scandinavia. Since we would not send expeditions both to Scandinavia and to the Balkans, the best policy seemed to be to say nothing to Italy.

There was less need for Sir P. Loraine to make an approach since on December 24 M. François-Poncet, French Ambassador at Rome, (c) took the chance of discussing the Balkan situation informally with Ciano. Ciano said that he did not expect a Russo-German invasion of Roumania in the near future. Germany had given Italy some assurances on the subject, and the U.S.S.R. was occupied in Finland. Ciano agreed upon the desirability of a Balkan *bloc*. Italy could not disinterest herself in the Balkans, and would intervene if the Russians invaded Bessarabia. On the other hand, the question of co-operation with the Allies was very 'delicate'.

(a) R11805/2613/67. (b) R11838/2613/67. (c) R12073, 12131/2613/67.

(a)   In view of this conversation, Sir P. Loraine did not raise the matter with Ciano until December 29. He then mentioned M. François-Poncet's talk because he had been given a hint from the Italian Ministry of Foreign Affairs that the Allies were suspected of 'preparing something' in the Balkans, and that the Italian Government would rather hear of any move from Great Britain than from

(b)   France. On January 9, 1940, Ciano told Sir P. Loraine that Mussolini was not yet prepared to discuss the Balkan question. He added '. . . but little by little', and left the sentence unfinished.

Sir P. Loraine's opinion was that Mussolini's unwillingness to enter into discussions was due to a wish to keep his freedom of manoeuvre. He did not want a Russian or Russo-German move against Hungary or Roumania, but he could neither give up the chance of German support against Russia nor act alone and against German wishes. He was still bound, for personal and political reasons, to the German side, that is to say, he wanted a German and not an Allied victory, though a negotiated peace with the balance tipped on the German side would have been the best solution. He would therefore continue as long as possible without committing himself. Sir P. Loraine considered that Ciano, Balbo and Grandi would try to persuade Mussolini to go further towards a *rapprochement* with the Allies, but that they would remain loyal to him whatever he might decide.

The Foreign Office agreed that there was no reason to change their estimate of Italian policy. They were not disposed to alter their

(c)   view as the result of a curious hint, in private conversation, from Signor Bastianini, the Italian Ambassador in London, that Great Britain might take the place of Germany in the Anti-Comintern pact, and thus create a new London-Paris-Rome Axis which would also be joined by Spain. The Foreign Office considered the suggestion entirely impracticable. It would mean signing pacts with General Franco and Japan as well as with Italy. We should be aligning ourselves with Japan against China and would lose American support. Hence the only reply given to Signor Bastianini was that we were 'interested' in the suggestion; and the purpose of this non-committal answer was, if possible, to get some further disclosure of Italian intentions. Here the matter ended.

(a) R67/5/67 (1940). (b) R512/5/67. (c) R464, 1103/60/22.

CHAPTER II

The Russo-Finnish war and the question of an Allied expedition to Scandinavia

(i)

Introduction.

THE fact that in December 1939 the British Government were considering an expedition to Scandinavia illustrates the unexpected course of events during the first three months of the war and also the efforts made by the Allies to find some way of gaining the initiative. From the French point of view a diversion in Scandinavia, like the proposed action in the Balkans, had the advantage of attacking the Germans in an area far distant from France. For the British a Scandinavian expedition offered a chance of using the greater mobility given to them by sea-power as a means of wasting the enemy's resources and cutting off his supplies. Although historical analogies are dangerous, it is possible to notice that the whole Scandinavian project suffered from many of the defects which had led to disaster in the case of British overseas expeditions in the early stages of previous wars. The plan was considered in relation to conditions which very quickly changed. It took too little account of enemy counter-moves. It was neither pushed rapidly to execution nor abandoned when the actual opportunity had passed. From first to last it remained an affair of improvisation. There was insufficient study behind it, and a lack of conviction in the preparations made to carry it out.[1]

The occasion, or rather opportunity, out of which this Scandinavian project arose was, broadly speaking, the Russian attack on Finland and the strong Finnish resistance in the early stages of the campaign. The Finns could not hold out indefinitely without Allied help. It was unlikely that, in spite of their sympathies with the Finnish cause, the Allies would have felt justified in diverting any of their resources to Finland, and in risking war with Russia, if there had not been a further consideration of great importance. The Allies could reach the main area of operations in Finland only by passing through Norway into northern Sweden. Across this route

---

[1] The lack of adequate 'security' precautions about the plans also had unfortunate results. French officials in Stockholm seem to have talked openly in the third week of February about plans to occupy Narvik. See also below, p. 96, note 1.

lay the iron ore-fields of Kiruna and Gällivare. These fields were one of the main sources of German supply. The ore was taken by rail either to the Norwegian port of Narvik or to the Swedish port of Lulea (and other smaller ports) in the Gulf of Bothnia. Narvik was ice-free; Lulea was closed during the winter months. An Allied expedition, therefore, which landed at Narvik, and followed the railway to the Gulf of Bothnia would, literally, take the ore-fields in its stride and thus deprive the Germans of a commodity essential to their war production.[1] Before the Russian attack on Finland there had been some consideration of the possibility of stopping supplies from Narvik by means of a minefield, but a proposal to land troops in Norway and transport them into Sweden was never considered; Norway and Sweden would have refused to allow a breach of their neutrality which would certainly have involved them in war with Germany. Hence no thought had been given to the requirements of such an expedition or to the possible counter-moves by Germany. After the Russian invasion of Finland, the circumstances changed. The League of Nations had authorised its members to give assistance to the Finns; hence there would be no legal violation of Norwegian or Swedish neutrality if Allied forces crossed Scandinavian territory into Finland.

The Scandinavian States might themselves be more ready to allow the passage of assistance to the Finns, since they were alarmed at the prospect of a Russian advance beyond Finland, and thus might welcome Allied help either in support of the Finns or in the defence of northern Norway and Sweden after a Finnish collapse. There was reason to think that the plan might not mean war with the U.S.S.R. elsewhere than in Finland. The Allied assistance might take the form of 'volunteers' on the lines of German and Italian help to Spain. In any case the apparent weakness of the Russian war machine as well as the unexpected hesitation (as it seemed) of the Germans to risk an attack in the west led the Allies at least for a time to look with less anxiety at the possibility of fighting the U.S.S.R. as well as Germany. Such, in outline, was the origin of the Scandinavian project. In order to understand the details it is necessary to go back to the relations between Great Britain and the U.S.S.R. at the beginning of the war, and the effect of Russian policy on these relations.

---

[1] According to British estimates Germany imported 22 million tons of iron ore in 1938. $9\frac{1}{2}$ million tons came from sources which the Allies were able to cut off; 9 million tons came from Sweden. If the supply from Narvik were stopped, the loss would be between $2\frac{1}{2}$ and $3\frac{1}{2}$ million tons. A report compiled for Admiral Raeder early in 1940 estimated an approximate loss of this magnitude, but, though it would obviously be a serious matter, Admiral Raeder did not regard it as catastrophic for German industry.

(ii)

Anglo-Russian relations from the outbreak of war to the Russian invasion of Finland.

The statement made by the British Government on September 19 at the time of the Russian attack on Poland had reaffirmed the intention of Great Britain to fulfil her obligations to Poland, and had rejected the pretexts by which the Russians tried to justify their aggression. On the other hand the statement did not threaten the Soviet Government or even preclude the possibility of improving Anglo-Soviet relations.

There were economic as well as political and military reasons why the British Government were anxious to avoid a breach with Russia. The Soviet Government had already taken a strong and unfriendly attitude towards the British measures for the enforcement of the blockade against Germany. They seemed to be considering a denunciation of their trade agreement[1] with Great Britain and forbidding the (a) export of timber to British ports. This latter action would have been very serious from the British point of view owing to the need of large imports of Russian timber. The Russians were already holding up cargoes of timber on the plea that we were refusing to allow the export of machinery and machine tools ordered by the Soviet Government. As a way out of this difficulty, the British Government proposed to the Soviet Government an *ad hoc* agreement under (b) which the timber would be shipped in return for the release of the machinery and raw materials (including rubber) required by the Russians.[2] After some delay in negotiation, the Soviet Government accepted this proposal.

The willingness of the Soviet Government to discuss an *ad hoc* agreement showed that at all events they were not intending to use the immediate commercial dispute as a pretext for war. It was however possible that their need of machinery and raw materials made it expedient for them to postpone a break for which they could find an excuse at any time. Hence on September 23 Lord Halifax (c) put to M. Maisky, Soviet Ambassador in London, certain questions including a definite enquiry whether the Soviet Government would be ready to discuss a general war trade agreement. M. Maisky replied (d)

---

[1] This agreement, which had been concluded in July, 1936, provided for the placing of orders by the Soviet Government in Great Britain to the value of £10,000,000 under guarantees given through the Export Credits Guarantee Department. The position at this time was that goods to the value of £7,600,000 had already been shipped to Russia, and that the Soviet Government's obligations under the agreement, including interest, were more than £9,000,000.

[2] The British Government would not release tools for the machine tool industry.

(a) N4281/96/38; N4286, 4287, 4351, 4390/4030/38. (b) N4494, 4510/92/38; N4535, 4939, 5169/92/38; WM(39)19, 32, 43. (c) N4736/1459/38. (d) N4803/1459/38.

four days later that the Soviet Government would enter into such discussions if His Majesty's Government really desired them. The genuineness of this offer seemed doubtful in view of the second visit of Ribbentrop to Moscow, the conclusion of a new Russo-German treaty, and the Russian propaganda that the Allies alone were responsible for continuing a war which they were fighting for 'imperialist' reasons. In fact 'imperialist reasons' seemed to be determining Russian policy, since the Soviet Government were quickly extending their military control over the Baltic States. The British Government had held out in the negotiations of the previous summer with the Soviet Government against an infringement of the independence of the Baltic States, and had no liking for the Russian 'indirect aggression', but they could do nothing to prevent it. Moreover, from the point of view of the Allied prosecution of the war against Germany, a Russian advance in the Baltic would have no adverse consequences and might indeed have some indirect military advantage if, as was likely, it caused dissension between Germany and the U.S.S.R.

The Russian plans, however, also included demands on Finland. The Soviet Government informed the Finnish Minister in Moscow on (a) October 5 that 'owing to changes brought about by the war', they wished to discuss with Finland 'certain political questions'. They asked that a Finnish representative should be sent to Moscow as soon as possible. The Finnish Government sent M. Paasikivi, Finnish Minister at Stockholm; they let His Majesty's Government know that they would refuse to make an arrangement on the lines of the Russo-Estonian pact. The Finns were taking military precautions which did not amount to mobilisation. The Finnish delegation went back to Helsinki on the night of October 14–15. They told Sir W. (b) Seeds that some of the Russian demands were unacceptable; they did not say what the demands were.

These rapid moves and the uncertainty with regard to Russian intentions raised in more urgent form for the British Government the problem of restoring some kind of political contact with the Soviet Government. The only way of regaining contact appeared to be through trade negotiations, but there was an obvious risk that an approach in this direction might meet with open rebuff. M. Maisky, (c) however, took the initiative in the matter by hinting at the possibility of developing trade relations on the lines of the 'barter' arrangement (d) for timber and rubber. On October 16 Lord Halifax explained to M. Maisky that the principal difficulty on the British side was the risk that anything sent to Russia might be passed on to the Germans. M. Maisky recognised this difficulty and said that, if the Soviet

(a) N5025, 5190, 5260/991/38.   (b) N5278, 5388/991/38.   (c) N5296, 5426/92/38.
(d) N5342/92/38; N5343/1459/38.

Government made a trade agreement, they would do so in 'their own interest'. He also argued that Russian policy in the Baltic was defensive. To the question why such defensive policy was necessary M. Maisky answered that 'it was an uncertain world, and no friendship was secure in these days'.

Lord Halifax reported M. Maisky's views to the Cabinet on (a) October 20 and 21. On October 24 the Cabinet agreed that, unless a speech which Ribbentrop was making at Danzig showed that the U.S.S.R. was committed to far-reaching economic concessions to Germany, Lord Halifax should say to M. Maisky that His Majesty's Government had a plan for the improvement of Anglo-Russian relations, but that this plan could be put into effect only if political conditions allowed. The Soviet Government would thus understand that the negotiations would lapse if they attacked Finland. M. Maisky would then be told, in guarded terms, that His Majesty's Government would be willing to send a trade delegation to Moscow.

Lord Halifax saw M. Maisky on October 25.[1] He said that his (b) own interest, as Secretary of State for Foreign Affairs, in the trade proposals was primarily political. He was concerned, 'if possible, to effect some improvement' in Anglo-Russian relations, or at least to prevent them from getting worse. M. Maisky told Mr. Stanley, President of the Board of Trade, that he would have to refer the question to Moscow. The crisis in the Russo-Finnish negotiations, however, put an end to the plan. The Finnish delegation went again to Moscow on October 21 and five days later brought back new (c) proposals to Helsinki. They returned to Moscow for a third visit on October 31. On this day M. Molotov gave a review of Russian foreign policy to the Supreme Council of the U.S.S.R. He said that Finland had refused a mutual assistance pact with the U.S.S.R. The Soviet Government had also asked, not for the Aaland Islands, but for an extension of the Russian frontier in the Leningrad area, in exchange for a part of Russian Karelia, and a lease of certain islands, with the right to establish naval bases in the northern part of Finland. Finland was willing to grant only a part of these requirements. The Soviet Government had modified their proposals, but if the Finns continued to reject them, they would do harm to the cause of peace and to themselves.

The Russo-Finnish dispute was not the only obstacle to the attempt

---

[1] It is of some interest that, at this time, M. Maisky, whose words always reflected the policy (as far as he knew it) or the propaganda of the Soviet Government, explained to Signor Bastianini, the newly arrived Italian Ambassador in London, the reasons why he thought that Germany could not defeat Great Britain. (*Doc.Dipl.Ital.*, 9th Ser., I, No. 878).

(a) N5517, 5609/92/38; WM(39)54, 55; WP(G)(39)50. (b) N5634, 5678/92/38. (c) N5518, 5617, 5635, 5841, 5896/991/38.

of His Majesty's Government to improve Anglo-Russian relations.
(a) On the night of October 25–26 Sir W. Seeds was given a note of protest, signed by M. Molotov, against the British contraband list and the method of examining neutral shipping. The Soviet Government claimed that the inclusion of 'fundamental articles of popular consumption' as contraband was contrary to international law. In fact no Russian ship had been brought to a port of examination and the question whether this exemption should continue was under discussion in the War Cabinet. It was difficult either to leave Russian ships alone without raising demands for similar treatment from other neutral states or to be specially lenient to Russian cargoes without allowing Germany to use the Soviet Government as a channel for the evasion of Allied contraband control. Since Russian seaborne trade was not great and was actually diminishing, the War Cabinet were able to delay a decision until November 22. It was then agreed
(b) to accept the views of the Foreign Office and the Ministry of Economic Warfare and to instruct the contraband authorities to avoid, as far as possible, action likely to lead to serious disputes with the Soviet Government.

This decision was taken after considering the strategical situation which would arise in the possible event of a Russian attack on Finland. The British Government were already committed to a declaration that they would regard a German attack on Norway as
(c) equivalent to an attack on Great Britain. The declaration, to which the Norwegian Government had made no reply, was made on September 16 after consultation with the Chiefs of Staff Committee. The purpose of the declaration had been to secure Norwegian co-operation in blockade measures. The Chiefs of Staff thought that Germany might reply to an attempt to stop the transport of Swedish ore from Narvik (a) by a seaborne expedition; (b) by sporadic attacks against Norwegian ports and ships; (c) by air attack; (d) by the seizure of Stavanger aerodrome or the establishment elsewhere of air or submarine bases. We could not give direct protection against air attack but it appeared that 'all other forms of possible German action against Norway [fell] into the category of operations which it would be in our own interest to combat, and which we could undertake with a reasonable chance of success'.

Early in October the Cabinet asked the Chiefs of Staff Committee for a general appreciation of the possible consequence of Russian participation in the war on the side of Germany, and also for special consideration of the position which would result from a Russian

---

(a) N5637, 5638, 5853/5637/38; N5609/92/38. (b) N6584/5637/38; WM(39)91.
(c) N4218/64/63.

move in the Balkans either alone or in concert with Germany. The Committee decided to add an estimate of the damage which the Russians might do to Allied interests while remaining nominally neutral. The Committtee were told by the Foreign Office that they could make three political assumptions: Japan would do nothing to help Germany and the U.S.S.R., but would try to get as many concessions as possible from the Allies; Italy would dislike a Russo-German combination but might join it if it appeared to be the winning side; Turkey would be unlikely to go to war with the U.S.S.R.

The Chiefs of Staff reported on October 9 that the 'abiding aim' (a) of the Soviet Government was world revolution, and that this aim would be served by the exhaustion of Germany and of the British Empire. The Russians would probably limit themselves to a benevolent neutrality towards Germany which would leave them free to extend their control to all the Baltic States, and to lock up Allied forces in the Middle East. On the other hand Russo-German economic co-operation, and possible Russian assistance to German submarines—such as the use of Murmansk—would weaken the effects of our blockade. The Cabinet was not wholly satisfied with (b) this report since it did not seem to take enough account of political factors, notably the possibility of Russo-German dissensions, which might operate in our favour. The Chiefs of Staff were therefore asked to prepare another report in collaboration with the Foreign Office and the Dominions Office.

For this second report the Foreign Office drew up a note (October 19) on the actual state of Russo-German relations. The evidence was scanty and conflicting. There was no doubt, for example, that the Soviet Government had acted in close collaboration with Germany to remove any risk to either Power from the provisional Anglo-Franco-Turkish agreement. A number of German experts had gone to Russia to assist in the reorganisation of heavy industries. The Russian press was becoming increasingly abusive of the Allies. On the other hand, in spite of their talk of economic solidarity with the Germans, the Russians were still ready to supply Great Britain with timber and other materials. They had not broken off contact with Turkey. Their expansion in the Baltic was a strategic threat to Germany, and there was no support for rumours of a Russo-German agreement for the partition of Scandinavia. Obviously the Soviet Government did not want a strong and victorious Germany; they probably wished to hold the balance in order to be able to 'bolshevise' an exhausted Europe, but Stalin's personal motives were obscure. In a final analysis, it could be said that, although the U.S.S.R. had helped Germany, Russian policy might

---

(a) WP(39)74.   (b) C16324/15/18, WM(39)43.

be given an interpretation 'very unfavourable to German interests in the long run'.

(a)　　Before the Chiefs of Staff Committee had finished their report they were also asked to consider the question of a declaration of war upon the U.S.S.R. in the event of Soviet aggression against Finland

(b)　or other Scandinavian countries. They concluded their report on October 31. They regarded a Russian attack on Finland and the Scandinavian states as unlikely, especially in winter. An attack on Finland involved no military threat to the Allies. In any case we could give no direct help to the Finns. If a Russian attack on Finland were followed by the invasion of Sweden and the occupation of the Swedish ore-fields or even of the port of Narvik, there would be no material change in the military situation between the Allies and Germany, but we could not be sure that Narvik would be the limit of the Russian advance. The Germans were unlikely to agree to the complete domination of Scandinavia by the U.S.S.R., and might invade the Scandinavian countries from the south if Russia invaded them from the north. Although these moves would be dangerous to us, a decision upon war against the U.S.S.R. would have to take account of wider issues. We should have to meet increased submarine activity, and Russo-German economic collaboration would lessen the effects of the Allied blockade. Russian intervention might block the way for the Germans in south-east Europe, but it would protect their flank and rear; the west would then be 'more than ever' the decisive front. In Iran, Iraq and Afghanistan we should be faced, on our existing resources, with an insoluble problem even if Italy remained neutral. In the Far East, although there was no danger of a German-Japanese alliance, the lapse of Russian interest in China would give greater freedom to Japan. Hence the Committee thought that we could not assume additional burdens and that from a military point of view we should avoid war with the U.S.S.R. The situation would be different if the United States entered the war.

(c)　　On November 1 the War Cabinet discussed the report and agreed with its recommendation. As late as November 1 the view of the War Cabinet was that we ought not to encourage the Finns to oppose any reasonable demands from the U.S.S.R., but that we could not press them to give way on matters which they thought vital to their national independence. The Foreign Office were less inclined to think that an increase of Russian strength in the Baltic would be indirectly to our advantage, but there was general agreement that our policy towards the U.S.S.R. should be as forthcoming as possible. The course of events in Finland during the next month therefore must be considered against this background.

(a) N5594/991/38, WM(39)57.　(b) N5908/991/38, WP(39)107.　(c) WM(39)67.

(iii)

The outbreak of the Russo-Finnish war, November 30: the Finnish appeal to the League of Nations, December 2–14, 1939.

The Finnish delegation left Moscow for the last time on November 13. A week earlier the Comintern had issued a manifesto alleging that the ruling circles in Great Britain and France were fighting to preserve their 'slave empires', and the ruling circles in Germany to redistribute the wealth of these Empires in German interests. The Italian bourgeoisie was waiting to seize part of the spoil from the loser, and the American bourgeoisie wanted to prolong the war for the sake of profits from the sale of arms. The working class ought to unite against the 'imperialist bourgeoisie' and against the Social Democratic leaders without whose 'treacherous help' the war could not have been started. The 'peace policy' of the U.S.S.R., and especially the pact with Germany, had localised the war, and had thus encouraged the workers of all nations.

The counterpart to this picture was given by Marshal Voroshilov's warning on November 7 that the U.S.S.R. was surrounded by capitalist countries and must be ready for any emergency. Finally, the stage was set for aggression against Finland by press attacks upon the Finns, their British and American supporters (including President Roosevelt), and the 'Scandinavian lackeys of British and American capital'.

The Russian demands were now confirmed from the Finnish side (a) as the cession of territory along the Karelian isthmus, and an agreement for the demilitarisation of the frontier on either side; cession of the Finnish part of the Kola peninsula; cession of islands in the Gulf of Finland; the grant of a naval base at the outlet of the gulf. The first demand meant the surrender of carefully prepared and very valuable defence works. The second demand offered no serious difficulty. The Finnish Government were prepared to give up Petsamo. They were also willing to offer dockyard facilities at Åbo and to cede certain islands in order to meet the third and fourth demands. They refused to cede Hangö.

As the danger of a Russian attack increased it became clear that neither Sweden—in spite of early manifestations of sympathy—nor Norway would go to war on behalf of Finland, although they regarded the Russian demands as a threat to Finnish security. The Finns themselves did not expect a Russian attack in the winter. On November 26 however, the Soviet Government alleged that Finnish (b) artillery on the Karelian isthmus had fired on Russian troops and demanded the withdrawal of Finnish forces to a line twelve or

---

(a) N5910, 6285, 6007, 6010, 6537/991/38. (b) N6623, 6665, 6671, 6687, 6689/991/38.

fifteen miles behind the frontier. The Finnish Government claimed that the firing came from the Russian side, but stated their willingness to discuss a mutual withdrawal of troops and to submit the question of the Karelian frontier to a neutral mediator or to a conciliation commission. Nevertheless on November 28 the Soviet Government denounced the Russo-Finnish non-aggression treaty of 1932, and, on

(a) November 29, broke off diplomatic relations with Finland. On the following day Russian troops and aircraft attacked Finland.

Before this attack took place the British Government had contin-
(b) ued, in spite of Soviet press attacks, to do everything possible to remove Russian suspicions, but they had received no answer to their suggestion for the holding of trade talks. They still wanted a trade agreement, and, for this reason, Lord Halifax decided to invite M. Maisky to the Foreign Office for a general discussion. This discussion took place on November 27. M. Maisky gave Lord Halifax the official defence of the Russian policy towards Finland. Lord Halifax said that he would not comment on the merits of the rival (Russian and Finnish) contentions, but that if the dispute developed into war, it would be very difficult for His Majesty's Government to improve Anglo-Russian relations by means of a trade agreement. Lord Halifax denied that we had influenced the Finnish decisions and pointed out that suspicion of Soviet intentions was not surprising in view of the Soviet action in Poland and in the Baltic States. After raising the question of the arrest by the Russians of Polish trade union leaders, Lord Halifax spoke about the attitude of the Russian press and wireless towards Great Britain. M. Maisky answered that this attitude only reflected the general feeling in the U.S.S.R. that British diplomacy was working against Russian interests in every part of the world. Lord Halifax said that this charge was untrue. We had been 'shocked', as most of the world had been, at the Soviet Government's proceedings in Poland, but 'in spite of all that had happened since the signature of the German-Soviet pact', His Majesty's Government had tried to work for better relations. We had made proposals for a trade agreement, but no response had come from the Soviet side. 'If anyone had a right to complain that Anglo-Soviet relations were not what they might be, it was His Majesty's Government, and not the Soviet Government.'

The Russian attack on Finland destroyed the chance of an immediate improvement in Anglo-Russian relations. British public opinion was overwhelmingly on the Finnish side. Moreover it was impossible to avoid a formal condemnation of the Soviet Government, since on December 2 the Finnish Government appealed to the League

(a) N6733, 6745/991/38.   (b) N6602/92/38; WM(39)91; N6717/991/38.

of Nations. On the previous day the Russians had set up a so-called (a)
'Finnish People's Government' under a certain Kuusinen, a Finnish
Communist and former secretary of the Comintern. The Finns based
their appeal against Russian aggression upon Articles 11 and 15 of
the Covenant. In answer to the appeal the Secretary-General of the
League announced that he was summoning a meeting of the Council
on December 9 and of the Assembly on December 11. M. Molotov
replied on December 4 that the U.S.S.R. was neither at war with
Finland nor threatening her. The Soviet Government had made a
pact with the 'Finnish People's Government' which had asked for
military assistance to liquidate the danger created by the former
Finnish Government. Hence the Soviet Government would not take
part in the proceedings of the Council.

The British and French Governments accepted the invitation to
the meetings although they could not hope for any effective help to (b)
Finland from the League. The Foreign Office thought that the appeal
would merely advertise 'the failure, at the moment, of the ideas of (c)
consultation and co-operation in the face of a number of gangster
Great Powers. Each meeting of this kind brings the League into
greater disrepute, and will make it harder to set up anything in its
place after war.'

The Scandinavian Governments, after meeting to decide upon (d)
common action, agreed to work for a resolution registering the fact
of Russian aggression, asking the Soviet Government to withdraw
their troops, and suggesting direct negotiations between the U.S.S.R.
and Finland. It was, however, clear that other States would urge the
expulsion of the U.S.S.R. from the League. Uruguay and Argentina
stated that, unless the U.S.S.R. were expelled, they would leave the
League. Most of the Central and South American States would
follow their example. On the other hand the Scandinavian and
Balkan States did not want to antagonise the Soviet Government and
were opposed to the mention of sanctions or expulsion.

For practical reasons, therefore, the Foreign Office hoped that
there might be general agreement to authorise every country to give
what help it could to Finland, but that there would be no proposals
to impose sanctions or to expel the U.S.S.R. Sanctions would be
ineffective, and their imposition would only discredit the League.
Expulsion, as matters stood, would be slightly ridiculous; nevertheless, if it were proposed, the British representatives would vote for it.
The War Cabinet accepted this view.

On December 11 the Assembly of the League appointed a (e)
committee to consider the Finnish appeal. The committee invited
the Soviet Government to accept negotiations under the mediation

---

(a) N6865, 6886, 7284/991/38. (b) N7035/991/38, WM(39)103. (c) N7200/991/38.
(d) N7126, 7127, 7128, 7196, 7111/991/38. (e) N420/1/56 (1940).

of the League, but M. Molotov repeated his previous reply. On December 13 the Assembly referred to their committee a proposal by the delegate of Argentina for the expulsion of the U.S.S.R. The committee drew up a resolution for the Assembly urging every member of the League to give all possible help to Finland; stating that the U.S.S.R. had by its own action 'placed itself outside the Covenant' and asking the Council to pronounce on the consequences of this situation.

The Assembly accepted the resolution and the Council met on December 14 to consider it. The Council associated itself with the condemnation of the U.S.S.R. by the Assembly and found that by its act the U.S.S.R. had placed itself outside the League and was therefore no longer a member. Mr. R. A. Butler supported the resolution on behalf of the United Kingdom. He did not refer directly to the question of expulsion, but promised that His Majesty's Government would give to Finland the greatest assistance in their power.

The British Government had begun to send material help to the Finns before the meeting of the League. The Finnish Government had asked for the removal of administrative delays holding up the
(a) shipment of goods already ordered in Great Britain. The Foreign Office had approached the departments concerned in the last week of October. On the outbreak of war with the U.S.S.R. the Finnish Government again asked for a quicker clearance of supplies ordered from overseas and held up by the contraband control. They also wished to obtain certain essential commodities from Sweden—their nearest source of supply—and asked the British Government to allow the import into Sweden of an equivalent amount of the commodities in question. This request was also accepted.

The Finnish forces were in particular need of aircraft. From December 4 the Finnish Government made a series of appeals for immediate reinforcements, especially in fighters. In spite of the difficulty of meeting these appeals at a time when it was impossible to supply aircraft to Turkey, the British Government authorised the despatch of a number of fighters and bombers, together with large quantities of other war material.

(iv)

The question of German supplies of iron ore from Sweden (September 19–December 18, 1939).

Meanwhile the War Cabinet had been considering the general implications of the Russo-Finnish war. From statements by M. Prytz,

---

(a) N5631, 6967, 7034, 7081, 7228, 7319, 7356/194/56; N7054/991/38; WM(39)103, 104, 111.

Swedish Minister in London, it seemed clear as early as December 5 that Sweden was unlikely to go to war on behalf of Finland. Norwegian participation was equally improbable. The Russian move against Finland might be the prelude to schemes of expansion in south-eastern Europe or in Asia. Unless these schemes were put into effect, there was no reason for the Allies to change the policy of avoiding war with Russia. Thus at first the War Cabinet did not discuss the possible strategic connexion between the control of the Swedish ore-fields and intervention on behalf of the Finns against Russia. Since they were, however, considering means of stopping the Narvik traffic to Germany, and also the means of sending help to Finland, the larger project of cutting off the whole of the German ore supplies from Sweden was bound to suggest itself.

The first proposal for direct action to stop the traffic from Narvik had come from Mr. Churchill as First Lord of the Admiralty. On (a) September 19 Mr. Churchill told the War Cabinet that, if we could not prevent the passage of ore ships to Germany by putting pressure upon the Norwegian Government, we might lay mines in Norwegian waters. Mr Churchill said that this action had been taken in the war of 1914–18 (after the United States had become a belligerent) in order to drive ships outside the territorial limit.[1]

Neither Mr. Churchill nor the War Cabinet appear to have discussed (b) the subject again at all fully until the middle of November. The matter was not given detailed consideration partly because the shipments from Narvik to Germany temporarily ceased, and mainly because we were negotiating an arrangement with Norway for the chartering of merchant ships and with Sweden for a trade agreement. If the negotiations with Sweden had been as successful as we had hoped, most of the ore supplies to Germany would have been cut off.[2] The Foreign Office had asked the Admiralty on September 28 whether ships bound for Germany could not be intercepted at two points where they left territorial waters. The Admiralty was uncertain at this time whether the passage from Narvik to German ports necessarily involved an exit from territorial waters at any point where interruption was feasible.[3] On November 19 (c) Mr. Churchill submitted to the War Cabinet a note in favour of

---

[1] The Norwegian Government had agreed to this minelaying at the end of September (d) 1918, but had stipulated that they themselves would lay the mines and had also emphasised that they were doing so exclusively in Norwegian interests, and that their action did not imply a recognition of the right of the belligerent countries to request such action.

[2] For an account of these negotiations, and of their bearing on the iron ore question, see Medlicott, op. cit., I, Ch. IV.

[3] On January 5, 1940, the First Sea Lord told the War Cabinet that there was no (e) point in this passage at which it was necessary to leave territorial waters.

(a) N4607/490/42, WM(39)20.   (b) WP(39)143, N6741/64/63.   (c) N6726/64/63, WP(39)126.   (d) N6726/64/63, WP(39)126.   (e) N258/19/63 (1940), WM(40)4.

setting up the 'Northern barrage'—a minefield extending from the Orkneys to the Scandinavian coast which had formed part of the blockade against Germany in 1914–18. About six months of preparatory work would be necessary before the minelaying operations could begin. Hence there was no need as yet to raise with the Norwegian Government the question of completing the barrage by a

(a) minefield in Norwegian territorial waters. On November 29, however, Mr. Churchill made a suggestion to Lord Halifax that mines might be laid at once at a point in these waters in order to prevent the passage of ore ships from Narvik after the freezing of the Gulf of Bothnia.

(b)   The War Cabinet agreed on November 30 to authorise preparations for the 'Northern barrage'. Mr. Churchill again raised the question of mining Norwegian territorial waters. Lord Halifax pointed out the difficulties in the proposal. The Norwegian Government would certainly refuse their permission, and the Germans would retaliate. The War Cabinet therefore asked the Chiefs of Staff to report on the military factors involved in stopping the traffic either by means of a naval force at the Vest Fjord (at the head of which lay Narvik) or by mining territorial waters. The Ministry of Economic Warfare was asked to consider the economic aspects of the proposal.

The Chiefs of Staff did not submit a report until December 20.

(c) Meanwhile Mr. Churchill had brought forward for consideration a third method of dealing with the ore traffic to Germany. Two British and one Greek ship had been torpedoed in Norwegian waters. We could therefore claim a similar latitude of attack on German shipping. The Admiralty proposed to send destroyers to arrest in Norwegian waters ships with cargoes of ore for Germany. They wanted to act at once since the Norwegian Government were said to have plans for convoying ships in their territorial waters.

(d) Mr. Churchill suggested later to Lord Halifax that, in view of the risk of a clash between our patrols and the Norwegian escorting vessels, it would be better to revert to the minelaying plan. The Foreign Office doubted the expediency as well as the legality of this latter plan. We could not describe a minefield as a measure to prevent the operations of German submarines in Norwegian territorial waters, and we might become involved in a serious incident if the Norwegians began minesweeping and we tried to stop them. In any case the minefield would be laid only at one point, where continuous watch would be difficult; if we employed patrols, German ships would not be safe anywhere. We could advise the Norwegians privately not to start a convoy system. On December 16

(a) N6741/64/63.   (b) N6818, 6819/64/63; WM(39)99.   (c) N7523/64/63, WM(39)116. (d) N7522/64/63.

Lord Halifax asked the War Cabinet to postpone a decision until (a
the Chiefs of Staff had completed their report.

Even at this date the War Cabinet do not appear to have discussed the possibility of action by land forces to cut the German ore
supplies at their Swedish source. On December 11, however,
Mr. Churchill had raised the general question of the strategic (b)
results of an extension of the war by a Russian attack upon Norway
and Sweden. The War Cabinet asked the Foreign Office to draw up
a memorandum on the political aspects of the question, i.e. developments which might follow the Russian invasion of Finland and a
possible extension of the war to Scandinavia.

The evidence upon which the Foreign Office had to base their
estimate was uncertain and, in some respects, conflicting. The (c)
Russian attack on Finland seemed to have taken the Germans by
surprise; the German leaders were divided in their views about it.
They had tried, and failed, to use the Russian move as an opportunity
for blackmailing the Scandinavian countries into economic subservience to Germany. There was now a desire at least in some
quarters—Göring, for example—to help the Finns.

The Swedish attitude was more clearly defined. Sir E. Monson,
British Minister at Stockholm, was told on December 12 that the (d)
Swedish Foreign Office hoped that His Majesty's Government would
remain 'at peace' with the U.S.S.R., since a declaration of war
would force Germany to support Russia and bring Sweden into the
field of operations. The Swedish view was that the Allies could not
help Sweden. A British expeditionary force was out of the question
and Germany was 'much nearer'.

The Foreign Office memorandum was circulated to the War
Cabinet on December 15. The main conclusions were as follows:
Norway would resist an attack upon herself, but unless she were
definitely threatened, would do little to help Finland. Sweden would
do everything possible short of war. The Soviet Government would
probably ignore Swedish assistance to Finland as long as they
continued to believe that they could quickly overcome Finnish
resistance. They were likely to find their operations unexpectedly
difficult. They might then put the blame on Sweden and demand
complete Swedish neutrality. Public opinion in Sweden might not
allow the Swedish Government to give way, and Sweden might
become involved in war with the U.S.S.R. The Swedish and
Norwegian Governments expected the U.S.S.R., after defeating
Finland, to demand some control of Narvik and of the railway from
Narvik to the Baltic. Germany would probably not intervene unless

---

(a) N7567/64/63, WM(39)117. (b) N7320/5542/63, WM(39)111. (c) N7615/5542/63,
WP(39)164. (d) N7422/991/38.

the Russians made unacceptable demands on Sweden. If such demands were made and resisted by Sweden, the Germans would probably ask Sweden to allow herself to be 'protected' by German bases on her territory. The Swedes were unlikely to agree and might ask for help. Germany would thus try to prevent Russia from making demands on Sweden, but Russia was bound to make them if she wanted to take Narvik, since she could reach it only through Swedish territory. Russia already had Murmansk, and was therefore less interested in the Norwegian ports north of Narvik. Thus, even after a Finnish collapse, the general situation was unlikely to change. Allied assistance to Norway or Sweden would raise very serious military problems; this fact was an additional reason why we should try to maintain Finnish resistance.

(a)   The War Cabinet considered this memorandum on December 18. They also had before them a memorandum of December 16 from Mr. Churchill in favour of stopping the ore traffic to Germany both from Narvik and from the ports in the Gulf of Bothnia.[1] Mr. Churchill thought that, with our command of the sea, we need not fear German retaliation and that we could meet a German invasion of Scandinavia. At all events we could take and hold islands or suitable points on the Norwegian coast and thus make absolute our northern blockade of Germany. Mr. Churchill proposed that the question should be reviewed by the military experts.

The War Cabinet now asked the Chiefs of Staff to make a general report on the practicability of Allied action in Scandinavia.

(b) Meanwhile the French Government had also raised with the Foreign Office, in addition to the provision of help to Finland, the possibility of concerted diplomatic action in Stockholm and Oslo. The French Government were afraid of a Russo-German move whereby Germany would secure the Swedish ore-fields and Russia the nickel mines of Finland. Hence they wished to encourage Norway and Sweden to assist Finland and to plan resistance to any further Russian advance.

(v)

The fourth meeting of the Supreme War Council, December 19: French views on the prospects of occupying the Swedish ore-fields and proposals for an approach to the Scandinavian Governments: acceptance of the French proposals by the War Cabinet on December 22, 1939.

In their review of the possible consequences of the Russo-Finnish

---

[1] Mr. Churchill's proposal was that a minefield could be laid by submarines in the Gulf of Bothnia.
(a) N7615/5542/63, WM(39)118; N7567/64/63, WP(39)162. (b) N7521, 7568/991/38.

war upon the Allied war against Germany, the War Cabinet had reached the point of discussing the question of an extension of the war to Scandinavia, but they still had in mind primarily the use of sea-power to cut the Narvik supply route to Germany. The French Government had also been considering these matters, and had come to a more definite conclusion with regard to the problem of the ore-fields. They stated their views to the British representatives—Mr. Chamberlain, Lord Halifax and Admiral Chatfield, Minister for the Co-ordination of Defence[1]—at the fourth meeting of the Supreme War Council in Paris on December 19. This meeting was called especially to discuss the Scandinavian problem. It was held at a time when the Russians had met with very sharp reverses. The Russian plan of campaign had been to make five separate attacks on Finland. The main attack across the Karelian Isthmus was held up in front of the fortified Mannerheim Line. A second attack north of Lake Ladoga was also held up. A third attack, in the centre of Finland, was no more successful. The fourth attack, from the Russian frontier west of Kandalaksha on the head of the White Sea, had had some success, and a fifth, in the far north, had established a Russian force in the Petsamo area. The Allies, therefore, could reckon on the pro-longation of Finnish resistance, though it was clear that, after the winter, the Russians would overwhelm Finland unless the Finns had help from Great Britain and France.

At a meeting of the Council the British representatives suggested a joint Anglo-French examination of the question of strengthening (a) Scandinavian resistance in view of the possibility that Russia might try to stop the passage of supplies to Finland across Sweden and that Germany might intervene to safeguard her own access to the Swedish ore supplies.

M. Daladier not only agreed with this suggestion, but put forward a proposal which went beyond anything hitherto considered by the British Government. He explained that the French Government had been informed of a report by Herr Thyssen, a well-known German industrialist, to Hitler and Göring that German ore supplies were far short of requirements and that the war would be won by the country which secured control of the Swedish ores. This report appears to have been written before the war. M. Daladier stated that Herr Thyssen, who had taken refuge in Switzerland on the outbreak of war, had been promised full restitution of his property and position if he would destroy all copies of the report, since the German leaders regarded it as so very damaging. It would appear—though the evidence is uncertain—that the Allied Ministers did not submit the report to a very critical examination, and that they did not realise

---

[1] The French representatives were M. Daladier, General Gamelin and Admiral Darlan.
(a) N7842/5542/63; C941/9/17 (1940).

that Herr Thyssen was not regarded in Germany as an authority of great weight on technical subjects. On the other hand the conclusions in the report agreed generally with those held at this time by Allied experts. M. Daladier was not going beyond the British view when he described the question of the ore-fields as being of paramount importance. If Germany seized them, she might be able to prolong the war by one or even two years. M. Daladier had therefore prepared draft instructions for the French representatives in Norway and Sweden. A diplomatic *démarche* to these Powers would probably lead to demands for material help. After reading the French draft the Prime Minister said that he would have to consult his colleagues about it, since the adoption of the French proposals would involve a considerable change in the attitude hitherto adopted by His Majesty's Government with regard to war against the U.S.S.R. It was decided that the instructions would be examined by His Majesty's Government through normal diplomatic channels.

(a)   The French draft reached the Foreign Office on December 20. The draft stated that the British and French Governments were studying the means of giving the greatest possible help to Finland and that they hoped for Swedish and Norwegian collaboration. The Swedish and Norwegian Governments could not be indifferent to the fate of Finland, and probably wished, in their own interests, to examine the menace which would be caused by a Finnish defeat. Since the attitude of the Allies would be an important factor in a study of the situation, the British and French Governments considered it desirable to state that they regarded the preservation of the independence and integrity of Norway and Sweden as an important element in European security and that they were ready to consider what help they could provide against any possible consequences of Swedish or Norwegian assistance to Finland.

The Foreign Office view of this draft was that it invited Norway and Sweden to go to war with the U.S.S.R. and pledged Allied support to them. This policy might save Finland and enable us to intervene in Scandinavia in more favourable conditions than if we intervened to save Norway and Sweden after a Finnish collapse. It would also solve the ore problem by allowing us to establish ourselves at Narvik and Lulea. On the other hand acceptance of the French plan would mean abandoning the policy recommended by the Chiefs of Staff that we should avoid war with the U.S.S.R. There were indications that this development—war with Russia—was just what the Germans wanted.

The Foreign Office also drew up a memorandum in answer to

Mr. Churchill's paper of December 16. The Foreign Office agreed (a)
with Mr. Churchill's view that we could not fight the war on the
basis of allowing Germany to break all the rules of international law
while we kept them; that there was a difference between violations
of law such as the torpedoing of merchant ships without warning and
the infringement, without danger to life, of national rights in territorial waters. If our action were not inhumane, we could now
consider a policy with regard to the Narvik ore traffic according to
the balance of advantage to ourselves. On the other hand the
advantages did not seem to be considerable. We could cut off a
million tons of German supplies over a period of four months, but
this loss would be made good from the Baltic ports, and unless we
could deprive Germany of her Baltic supplies, the plan was not worth
while. If, however, we decided to intercept the Narvik traffic, the
method of patrols would be better than that of minelaying.

The figures on which the Foreign Office based their opinion were
taken from a report of December 18 by the Ministry of Economic (b)
Warfare. This report suggested that, if the Narvik supplies were cut
off at once, and if Lulea—the most important of the Baltic ports—
became ice-bound at the usual time, German steel production would
be seriously curtailed in the spring of 1940. If the Baltic traffic was
also cut, German industry might well be brought to a standstill and
in any case the cutting off of the ore supplies would have 'a profound
effect upon the duration of the war'.[1]

The report of the Chiefs of Staff Committee on December 20 dealt (c)
with the two questions put to them by the War Cabinet. On the first
question (the military factors involved in stopping the ore traffic) the
Committee thought that the best method would be the use of a naval
force in the Vest Fjord, but that this force might have to meet
Norwegian resistance. We should therefore find it easier to intercept
the traffic further south, but the Germans would then have more
chance of evading our patrols, and could attack the patrol ships by
sea or air. The Chiefs of Staff pointed out, however, that 'generally
speaking' the Admiralty favoured the laying of minefields in Norwegian territorial waters rather than the use of patrols, since the
former method involved less risk of 'armed clashes' with the Norwegians. We could not stop the traffic by sabotage against the main
generating station serving the mines and the railway because the
installations were connected by a grid with other power stations. If
we destroyed the railway, we should be depriving ourselves of supplies
from Narvik.

---

[1] The Foreign Office pointed out that during the four winter months when Lulea was
closed large quantities of ore were shipped from the more southerly Baltic ports. If the
Narvik shipments were cut off, the amount shipped from these Baltic ports would be
increased.

(a) N7696/64/63, WP(39)168.   (b) N7567/64/63, WP(G)(39)162.   (c) N7653/64/63,
WP(39)169.

On the question of Allied action in Scandinavia the Committee pointed out that the Germans might insist that Norway should assert her rights as a neutral. The Norwegian Government would then have to resist us or tell Germany that they could not protect their neutrality or they would have to come into the war on one side or the other. The Germans would also put pressure on Sweden to develop the ports and railways on the Baltic side of the ore-fields. Norway and Sweden might then turn to Germany because they feared Russian encroachment and because we could promise only naval help.

Our only counter-measure against Russian action at Narvik or in the ore-fields would be to reach these areas before the Russians. The Germans might then invade southern Norway or southern Sweden by air. They could establish aerodromes and naval bases at Oslo, Christiansand, Stavanger, and Haugesund, and increase their air and naval activity against our ships. The Committee also repeated their previous views about possible Russian action in non-European areas.

The War Cabinet discussed these various memoranda on December 22. At Mr. Churchill's request the Prime Minister gave the War Cabinet a summary of Herr Thyssen's views that victory in the war would go to the side which obtained control of the Swedish iron ore. Mr. Churchill then said that if we could deprive Germany of these supplies we had a great chance of shortening the war and possibly saving very heavy casualties on the western front. He suggested that, as a first step, we should urge Sweden and Norway to give all possible help to Finland and that we should offer them a guarantee that we would go to their assistance if as a result of their help to Finland, or later on, Russia or Germany should invade them. We should also tell the Norwegian Government of the action which we proposed to take to stop the Narvik traffic. Our best method of stopping this traffic would be by patrols. We should also make plans for cutting off all German supplies from Sweden. Germany would probably try to coerce Sweden by threats, and then by bombing, and, finally, by landing a force at Lulea to seize the ore-fields. We should have to meet such an attempt, but there was no reason why we should not be able to send and maintain the necessary military and naval forces; in many ways there would be advantages in conducting operations in Scandinavia, where we could use our sea-power, rather than on the western front. Mr. Churchill did not think that if we sent an expedition to Scandinavia we should necessarily be involved in war with the U.S.S.R. In general Mr. Churchill considered that we should at once take the first step of intercepting the Narvik supplies, although we could not know precisely what our next step would be. The Germans might reply by seizing Stavanger and thus increasing the range of their aircraft and bringing Scapa Flow within closer range,

(a) N7862/64/63. WM(39)122.1, C.A.

but this would not be more decisive than the threat of air attack to which London was already exposed. The Chief of the Imperial General Staff also pointed out that the Germans were inexperienced in combined operations, and that an invasion of southern Scandinavia would be a very large commitment for them.

Lord Halifax took a different view from Mr. Churchill. He thought that stoppage of the Narvik supplies was in itself of little importance, and should be considered in relation to the larger question of cutting off the Baltic supplies. Lord Halifax said that, if we were to adopt Mr. Churchill's proposals for preventing Germany from seizing the ore-fields, we should have to land a force at Narvik, and send it by the railway to the ore-fields. We could hardly make this landing without Norwegian consent. Lord Halifax doubted whether Norway or Sweden would want to receive a guarantee from us against Germany; hence we should take care not to prejudice our larger plan by immediate action at Narvik. Lord Halifax proposed that we should give all the assistance in our power to Finland, and that we should approach Norway and Sweden on the lines suggested by the French, but that, until we saw the results of our approach, we should not take action at Narvik.

The Prime Minister said that the question of the ore supplies was of the highest importance; he was much impressed by Herr Thyssen's memorandum, and considered that we might have a chance of striking a decisive blow against Germany. He too doubted whether Sweden would accept an Anglo-French guarantee against Germany, since it might very quickly involve her in war. We must, however, get Sweden into the war on our side if we were to cut off the ore supplies, since we could not otherwise send our expeditionary force. How could we bring Sweden into the war? In considering this question we should have to calculate very carefully the effects of action against the Narvik traffic. Mr. Chamberlain agreed with Lord Halifax that we ought to avoid hasty action against the Narvik traffic until we knew the Swedish and Norwegian reactions to a guarantee on the lines proposed by the French and that we should also hint that we intended to take drastic action to cut off ore supplies to Germany.

The discussions in the War Cabinet ranged somewhat loosely round the two questions whether immediate action against the Narvik traffic was desirable, and what form we should give to our approach to Norway and Sweden. Finally the War Cabinet decided to send the communications proposed by the French to the Scandinavian Governments and also to tell these Governments that we intended to take measures to stop the supply of iron ore from Sweden to Germany. Lord Halifax was asked to settle the method of making these communications, i.e. through His Majesty's Ministers at Oslo and Stockholm, or through a special emissary or personally to the

Norwegian and Swedish Ministers in London. Meanwhile no action would be taken to interfere with the Narvik traffic.

The War Cabinet also asked the Chiefs of Staff to give further consideration to all the military implications of an attempt to stop the export of Swedish ore to Germany, and to the character and extent of the assistance which Great Britain might give to Finland or to Sweden and Norway as a protection against possible consequences of assistance given by them to Finland.

CHAPTER III

The development of Allied policy with regard to Scandinavia: hesitations and delays

(i)

The response of the Scandinavian Governments to the Allied offer of assistance.

IT will be seen that the decisions of December 22 did not commit the War Cabinet either to the 'larger' plan of assistance to Finland on a scale and by methods which would ensure an Allied occupation of the ore-fields, or to the 'smaller' plan of interfering with the Narvik traffic. The War Cabinet had indeed decided, at least by implication, to cut off the Narvik supplies, but here also they had resolved not to act without previous notice to the Scandinavian Governments. The diplomatic *démarche*, as originally proposed by the French Government, was, in form, nothing more than an offer of assistance, on certain conditions, to Norway and Sweden.

Nonetheless from this time the two plans became entangled, and the execution of the smaller plan was hampered and delayed by considerations affecting the larger project. The plan to cut off the Narvik supplies might or might not have been, on balance, a wise move for the Allies: at all events it was an exercise of sea-power, limited in scope, and in itself requiring no great diversion of forces. It did not directly concern Sweden, or require the active co-operation of Norway. On the other hand the Norwegians could not prevent the British navy from carrying it out. On the Allied side, the plan could be abandoned if political or military reasons made its abandonment desirable. Although they could not forecast German counter-measures, the Allies did not expect a German invasion of Norway merely as a means of restoring free communication with Narvik.

The larger plan was a far more difficult undertaking from which it would be impossible to withdraw without an admission of major defeat. The fate of Poland might have been a warning to the British Government of the risk of undertaking political commitments involving promises of military aid without first calculating very carefully how far these promises could be fulfilled. The *démarche* to the Scandinavian Governments was not an actual commitment, yet it implied a promise to consider military aid, and indeed, especially on the French side, the reason for the approach was to secure the consent of Norway and Sweden to measures which would certainly involve those countries in war.

It is thus curious that the Allies did not take into account the effect of the fate of Poland upon the Swedes and Norwegians. The attitude of the Belgian King and Government had shown that the small nations would try to keep out of the war as long as possible and that they were afraid even of precautionary measures in their own defence, since they regarded the risk of provoking a German attack as much more immediate and serious than the risk of leaving themselves unprepared later on to meet such an attack. The Allies could have brought large-scale assistance to Belgium within a few hours: they could not possibly reach Scandinavia as quickly or in such force. Furthermore in the winter of 1939–40 a German march through Belgium appeared much more likely than a German attack on Norway and Sweden if these two Powers behaved discreetly towards Hitler. Hence it was most improbable that the Allied *démarche* would meet with anything more than an emphatic and anxious refusal. In retrospect one may feel surprise that the Allies thought it worth while even to make their approach, and that the British Government should have postponed the execution of the Narvik operation in the hope of persuading the Scandinavian States to accept the larger plan.

The War Cabinet had left the Foreign Office to settle the best means of making the communication to the Scandinavian Govern-
(a) ments. The Foreign Office instructed the British Ambassador in Paris[1] in the evening of December 22 to tell the French Government that they accepted the French proposal and that they also intended to give the Scandinavian Governments an 'oral hint' that the Allies regarded the iron ore question as vital to the 'prosecution and shortening of the war'. The French Government agreed at once to
(b) this suggestion of an 'oral hint', but the evidence at least from Sweden did not suggest that the hint would be well taken or the offer of assistance well received. Sir E. Monson, British Minister in Stock-
(c) holm, reported that the Swedish Government continued to be very nervous about the possible consequences to themselves of any help which they might send to Finland. They asked for less publicity about the assistance given by the British Government to the Finns. M. Boheman, Secretary-General at the Swedish Foreign Office, told a member of the staff of the British Legation that more definite action by Sweden in support of Finland would be 'suicide' and that Sweden did not want Allied assurances 'at this stage'. The King of Sweden, in
(d) conversation with Sir E. Monson, thought that in due course Russia would attack Sweden and that the Swedes were not strong enough to resist. The King 'spoke wistfully of the possibility of peace with Germany' and suggested that a conference might be proposed. In

---

[1] Sir R. H. Campbell had succeeded Sir E. Phipps as Ambassador in Paris on November 1.

(a) N7747/5542/63.   (b) N7788/5542/63.   (c) N7554/194/56;   N7814/5145/42.
(d) N7786/1818/42; N220/124/42(1940).

such event Sweden might get help against Russia. The King agreed that Hitler was not to be trusted, but said that Göring was very different. He did not agree with Sir E. Monson's suggestion that, if the Russian danger ceased to exist, Germany would remain a menace to Europe. Sir E Monson concluded that when the King spoke of 'getting help', he meant help from Germany.

In view of this information the Foreign Office decided that it would be better not to say anything to the Scandinavian Govern- (a) ments about our intention to stop the ore traffic. The main pre-occupation of the Swedish Government was not to do anything which might have the effect of involving them in a war from which they still hoped to escape. Our 'hint' might therefore cause a violent and hostile reaction and might prejudice the success of our diplomatic approach on behalf of the Finns. Therefore until we knew from the Chiefs of Staff whether the project of a military expedition was feasible, we had better not arouse Swedish and Norwegian suspicions.

The Chiefs of Staff Committee also reported against telling the Scandinavian Governments that we intended to stop the ore traffic to (b) Germany. Owing to the unexpected resistance of the Finns, the danger of a Russian invasion of Scandinavia had temporarily receded. The Swedes thus had no immediate reason to fear that the Russian drive would reach the ore-fields. Hence they would be less favourable to our advances for co-operation, and we should have less reason for sending a force to northern Sweden. If we now told them of our intention to stop the ore traffic, we might turn them again towards Germany and the Germans might get news of our plans.

The War Cabinet discussed the matter again on December 27. It then appeared that there had been some misunderstanding about the (c) action agreed on December 22. The Prime Minister said that he had not envisaged anything more than an offer of assistance and, at the same time, an oral statement that, in view of the action of Germany in sinking our own and neutral ships in Norwegian territorial waters, we proposed to enter these waters in order to stop all traffic to Germany. The statement to Sweden would be made out of courtesy since the ore would have left Sweden before we interfered with it. Lord Halifax and the Foreign Office had regarded the oral com-munication as a warning that we intended to take measures generally against the ore supplies to Germany. The Chiefs of Staff held similar views and had assumed that our communication would be made at a time when Sweden was seriously threatened by Russia, and likely to agree to the landing of Allied troops in order to occupy the mines.

This difference of interpretation shows the lack of clarity with which the whole Scandinavian project was handled, but it had little

---

(a) N7788/5542/63.   (b) N7928/64/63, WP(39)175.   (c) N7869/64/63, WM(39)123.1, C.A.

effect on the immediate decision. Lord Halifax thought that even if we limited the oral communication to the Narvik traffic, we might prejudice our chances of getting Sweden into the war against Germany. Mr. Churchill, on the other hand, expected the Germans to invade southern Scandinavia as soon as we interfered with the Narvik traffic; we should then have full justification for the 'larger' plan of occupying the ore-fields. The War Cabinet, after some discussion, decided that the communication about an offer of assistance should be made at once, and that, unless the question were raised by the Norwegian and Swedish Ministers, the oral communication should be delayed until the following week and should take the form of a proposal to stop coastwise traffic as a counter-measure to German violation of Norwegian territorial waters. We should make preparations to follow up this oral communication, but should not actually decide about it until we knew the Scandinavian reactions to our communication.

(a) Lord Halifax made the communication about an offer of assistance to the Norwegian and Swedish Ministers in London in the afternoon of December 27. The communication was in the form of an *aide-mémoire* in the following terms:—

'His Majesty's Government and the French Government, having regard to the resolutions voted by the Assembly and Council of the League of Nations regarding the assistance to be afforded to Finland against the attack made upon her by the Soviet Union, are for their part disposed to afford unofficially to Finland, for the defence of her national independence, all the indirect assistance in their power.

The details of this assistance, which will in the normal way take the form of the despatch of technical missions and the supply of material on credit or otherwise, are at present under examination. In any case, however, it will be put into effect with all possible speed; and the two Governments, in informing the Norwegian[1] Government of their action, trust that they will find them similarly disposed to help Finland and ready to afford all necessary facilities for help from other sources.

His Majesty's Government and the French Government are indeed convinced that the fate of Finland could in no circumstances be a matter of indifference to the Norwegian Government, in view of the threat to the whole of Northern Scandinavia which the subjugation of Finland would involve; and they have no doubt that the Swedish and Norwegian Governments, while reserving to themselves the right to take, when necessary, such measures as their own interests demand, will be prepared to examine immediately, in a spirit of mutual solidarity, the situation prejudicial to the Scandinavian community which has already arisen. In this examination the attitude of His

---

[1] Or, here and below, 'the Swedish Government'.

(a) N7866, 7867/5542/63.

Majesty's Government and the French Government will, of course, be an important consideration; and they accordingly desire to assure the Swedish and Norwegian Governments that the preservation of the integrity and independence of Sweden and Norway, no less than that of Finland's independence, constitutes in their view an important element in European security. They are therefore prepared to consider in what circumstances and in what form an assurance could in practice be given to Sweden and Norway of Franco-British help against the possible consequences to those countries of giving such direct or indirect assistance as they might afford to Finland.'

On receiving the *aide-mémoire* M. Prytz, the Swedish Minister, repeated to Lord Halifax that the Swedish Government were doing everything possible for Finland short of going to war. They were now less nervous about German intervention but still afraid that their help to Finland might involve them in the war between Germany and the Allies.

The Swedish Government replied to the Anglo-French offer of assistance on January 4. They stated that the maintenance of their (a) neutrality would best further Finnish as well as common European interests. If Allied assistance were given to Finland in such a way that Sweden was associated in common action against the U.S.S.R., the latter Power and Germany might take counter-measures which would not merely involve Sweden but lead also to the collapse of Finnish resistance. M. Prytz, in delivering the reply, said that the Swedish Government were disquieted about suggestions in France that more help should be given 'officially' to the Finns. Lord Halifax said to M. Prytz that the Swedish reply had not made any very explicit reference to the Allied offer. M. Prytz answered that neither Germany nor Russia had put direct pressure on Sweden and that it seemed too early to discuss an eventuality that had not yet arisen.

M. Prytz also said that some Swedish papers were suggesting that 'the Allies thought it would be an advantage to them to create a new Scandinavian front'.[1] Towards the end of the conversation Lord Halifax told M. Prytz that he was glad to hear that the Swedish Government were doing their best to slow up deliveries of ore to Germany. M. Prytz asked whether there was not a point where ships from Narvik to German ports had to leave territorial waters. Lord Halifax said that His Majesty's Government were examining the question and that, if and when a decision were reached, he would ask M. Prytz 'to discuss the matter further'.

---

[1] Sir C. Dormer, British Minister at Oslo, had reported on January 2 that the 'German-inspired press' was asserting that the Western Powers were trying to extend the war (b) against Germany into Scandinavia, and were using the desire to help Finland as a means of bringing Norway and Sweden into the war. They could then cut off German ore supplies and establish submarine bases on the Norwegian coast. Germany, however, would not be caught unprepared.

(a) N240/2/63. (b) N214/211/30.

(a)   The Norwegian reply was not received until January 15. M. Colban, Norwegian Minister in London, then left an *aide-mémoire* to the effect that, in accordance with the Hague Convention of 1907, the Norwegian Government would not object to the transit of material across Norwegian territory to Finland or to the passage of technicians in a private capacity. They asked for the avoidance of publicity in order to prevent 'the possible misconception that Norway was participating in military action against the U.S.S.R.'. They were grateful for the Anglo-French assurance with regard to 'the preservation of the integrity and independence of Norway', but did not at present wish to have this assurance 'more precisely defined'.

(ii)

Further discussion of the Narvik plan in the War Cabinet: views of the Chiefs of Staff: communications to the Norwegian and Swedish Governments on the stoppage of the Narvik traffic (December 29, 1939–January 6, 1940).

The War Cabinet had decided that their oral communication about the Narvik traffic should follow the offer of assistance to the Scandinavian Governments. Nonetheless they debated the whole question again, and once more their discussions give an impression of hesitancy and lack of direction. The initiative and driving force in proposing to take action against the Narvik traffic had come from Mr. Churchill. If Mr. Churchill had been Prime Minister, he would have been in a position at least to secure immediate execution of the plan once he had persuaded his colleagues to accept it. Mr. Churchill was not Prime Minister. He could persuade his colleagues, but he could not give to their collective decisions his own intensity of purpose and sense of urgency. If his colleagues (and, in particular, Mr. Chamberlain) had been weaker men, Mr Churchill might have dominated the War Cabinet and given to the Chiefs of Staff the leadership which was needed throughout these months. It is one of the misfortunes of the early conduct of the war that Mr. Churchill's influence was strong enough to deflect the course of policy, but not sufficiently strong to control it. In other words British policy at this stage might have been more fortunate if Mr. Chamberlain had given either more or less weight to Mr. Churchill's advice.

On the Narvik question this advice was sharp and clear-cut. Mr. Churchill wanted immediate action. He hoped that this action would provoke a German counter-move against Scandinavia. He was prepared to go ahead with a northern expedition even against

_____
(a) N617/2/63.

Scandinavian opposition. He wrote to the Prime Minister on
December 29 suggesting a timetable. He proposed that the diplo- (a)
matic communication about an offer of help should be made at
once (it had, in fact, been made on December 27) and should be
followed on January 1 by a notification to the Norwegian Government (and, for reasons of courtesy, to the Swedish Government) of
our intention to retaliate for German sinkings in Norwegian territorial waters. On January 2 we should send flotillas into these waters
to arrest German ships, and on January 3 at the latest we should
begin our measures against the Baltic port of Oxelösund. Meanwhile
we should study the report of the Chiefs of Staff on the larger
project, and await German reactions to our measures. Thus the
interruption of the Narvik traffic, so far from hindering the larger
plan, would be the best means of setting in train German reactions
which would guide our future decisions. The Prime Minister,
however, considered that the matter was less urgent and that it
would be better to wait until the War Cabinet had discussed the
reports from the Chiefs of Staff on the larger operation.

The War Cabinet considered these reports on January 2. The
Chiefs of Staff recommended the larger plan if its success were (b)
decisive for the issue of the war. If the plan were adopted,
Scandinavia would become for a time the main centre of operations.
It would therefore be more difficult for us to fulfil our obligations
to Turkey if Germany invaded the Balkans. It might also mean war
with Russia. In this event we should find it hard to provide the
necessary air reinforcements for India. Time was the crucial factor.
Germany might decide upon 'desperate measures' to defeat us before
she herself went down in defeat owing to the loss of her ore supplies.
The question was whether the loss of the Swedish ore supplies would
bring about a German collapse quickly enough for us. The operations
that we should have to undertake in southern Sweden would not be
desirable from a military point of view but they were the price of
Swedish co-operation. Since Swedish and Norwegian co-operation
was essential, the Committee did not recommend the minor operation, i.e. the stoppage of the Narvik traffic, if we intended to
undertake the larger plan. Action against the Narvik traffic might
antagonise Norway, and possibly Sweden, and give the Germans a
pretext for demands on either or both of these countries. The
Germans might require Norway, under threat of air bombardment
or invasion, to give them bases from which to operate against Great
Britain. Norway would then ask us for help. We should have to say
that we could do nothing effective until March. Norway and Sweden
might then accept the German demands in the hope that at least
they would be protected from Russia. The War Cabinet were also

---

(a) N75/19/63. (b) WM(40)1.1, C.A.; N95/19/63; WP(39)179, 180.

told that, in the view of the Ministry of Economic Warfare, Germany could probably hold out for a year after the stoppage of ore supplies, and for a longer time if she were not undertaking serious military operations.

The discussion in the War Cabinet dealt with the likelihood of German retaliation to our interference with the Narvik traffic. The Germans might invade southern Norway and thereby greatly compromise our naval control and the security of any bases we might establish at Trondhjem. Moreover, a German invasion of Norway might bring Sweden over to the German side. Mr. Churchill considered that we could then seize the Swedish ore-fields, whatever the attitude of Norway and Sweden, but the military view was that an expedition to Scandinavia against the wishes of the inhabitants would be 'a very hazardous affair'. Mr. Churchill wanted immediate action against the Narvik traffic, and suggested that the Chiefs of Staff should reconsider the possible effect on us of a German occupation of bases in southern Norway and also say what could be done to mitigate or prevent these disadvantages on the assumption that we acted at once against the Narvik traffic.

The War Cabinet agreed to this suggestion. The discussion was then adjourned until the following day. At this second discussion the
(a) Prime Minister concluded, from the views expressed by the Chiefs of Staff, that if the German occupation did not get beyond Christiansand and Oslo, the military consequences would be less unfavourable. The Germans would not have the use of aerodromes or submarine bases on the west coast. It was pointed out that in summer aircraft from Christiansand and Oslo could threaten our shipping. The War Cabinet then considered whether the Germans might seize the southern Norwegian ports in any case (i.e. irrespective of Allied action against the Narvik traffic), since we could not prevent them from doing so. The C.I.G.S. said that the Germans might well have a project for the invasion of Norway later in the year but for the time the weather would make such an operation very difficult.

The general view of the War Cabinet was that Germany did not wish the war to spread to Scandinavia. Lord Halifax did not regard the possibility of a German seizure of bases in southern Norway as a vital factor. The main consideration was the effect of the stoppage of the Narvik traffic upon our chances of carrying out the major project. Although action against this traffic would attract German attention to the whole question of Swedish ore, the Germans would not improve their position by going to war with Sweden or by occupying bases in southern Norway. Mr. Churchill now thought that the Germans would not invade southern Norway in retaliation for our stoppage of the Narvik traffic, though he would be glad if

(a) WM(40)2.1, C.A.

they did so. An invasion of Norway would not be in their interests, since it would involve them in a serious commitment, and, if they tried to secure the control of the Swedish ore by conquest, they would ruin their chances of getting much of it in 1940. Meanwhile the loss of the Narvik ore would embarrass them until the ice melted, and we should be able to take further action.

The Prime Minister concluded from the report of the Chiefs of Staff that we should be able to forestall Germany in the occupation of the western ports of Norway, and that, in such an event, the results of action at Narvik would not be to our serious disadvantage. He also agreed with Mr. Churchill that it was in German interest to keep the war out of Scandinavia. Therefore he did not regard a German invasion of southern Norway as likely, especially in the winter. He thought that we should tell the Norwegians what we proposed to do, and await their reply before we came to a final decision. If we decided to stop the Narvik traffic, we should get ready the forces wanted for the occupation of Bergen and Stavanger. The War Cabinet finally agreed to this plan, with the addition of Trondhjem to the two Norwegian ports which it might be necessary to occupy.

On January 3 the Foreign Office gave the French Ambassador the text of the proposed communication to the Norwegian Government. Two days later the Ambassador said that the French Government (a) agreed in principle with the communication; they thought it better to represent our action not as a reprisal, but as something which 'necessarily resulted from German acts of piracy in neutral territorial waters'. The War Cabinet accepted this change of wording and on (b) January 6 Lord Halifax gave the communication, in the form of an *aide-mémoire*, to the Norwegian Minister. The *aide-mémoire* began by (c) stating that His Majesty's Government viewed 'with grave concern the recent action of German naval forces, which have, on more than one occasion, indulged in flagrant violation of Norwegian territorial waters'. Then followed details of the torpedoing—without warning—of two British and one Greek ship in those waters. The *aide-mémoire* continued:

'By these hostile acts German naval forces have made Norwegian waters a theatre of war and have in practice deprived them of their neutral character. His Majesty's Government accordingly find themselves obliged to take account of the situation thus created and to extend the scope of their naval operations into waters which have thus become a theatre of operations for the enemy's naval forces. His Majesty's Government are therefore taking appropriate dispositions to prevent the use of Norwegian territorial waters by German ships and trade. To achieve this purpose it would be necessary for His Majesty's naval forces at times to enter and operate

(a) N262/2/63.   (b) WM(40)5.5, C.A., N315/7/63.   (c) N301/2/63.

in these waters. His Majesty's Government have been naturally reluctant to take this action; but they see no other means of dealing with the situation created by the operation of the enemy's naval forces, in disregard of the recognised rules of maritime warfare, to which they have referred.'

(a) On the same day Lord Halifax gave the Swedish Minister an *aide-mémoire* in identical terms, but with the addition of the words: 'His Majesty's Government feel it incumbent on them, as a matter of courtesy, to communicate the foregoing to the Swedish Government, seeing that considerable quantities of goods of Swedish origin are shipped to Germany from Norwegian ports.'

(b) The reaction of the Scandinavian Governments to the *aide-mémoire* was unexpectedly strong. M. Colban impressed Lord Halifax by the seriousness with which he received the communication. His first argument was that British aircraft had violated Norwegian territory; neither the Norwegian Government nor His Majesty's Government—nor even the Germans—had regarded this violation as having turned Norway into a 'theatre of war'. Lord Halifax pointed out the difference between an accidental crossing of the territorial limit and the deliberate acts of piracy of which the Germans had been guilty. We did not wish to see the disappearance of Norwegian neutrality, but we could not allow the Germans to benefit by rules of neutrality which they themselves disregarded. His Majesty's Government did not doubt the will of Norway to defend her neutrality; the question was one not of will but of capacity, 'and the facts of geography . . . made it almost impossible to believe that the neutrality of the waters along the whole Norwegian coast could be adequately protected against a Power determined to violate it'.

M. Colban then said that His Majesty's Government had allowed three weeks to pass since the last of the three cases cited in the *aide-mémoire;* could they not wait a little longer in order to see what the Norwegian Government could do to ensure respect for their neutrality? Lord Halifax answered that the *aide-mémoire* referred to these three cases since they were well authenticated, but that we held that these cases were possible owing to the general use of Norwegian waters by German submarines. We realised the difficulties of Norway, yet our own position should be considered. 'Could we, fighting for our lives, be expected to overlook the determination of the enemy to stick at nothing to destroy us, regardless of the rights of neutrals, and allow him to benefit by our respect for those rights, regardless of his conduct?'

M. Colban admitted that German ruthlessness was a fact to be taken into account; this fact did not prove that Norwegian waters

(a) N322/2/63. (b) N301/2/63.

were a theatre of war. If British ships now entered Norwegian waters to search and divert ships, the Germans would not remain passive, and the result would be the end of Norwegian neutrality. Lord Halifax said that he did not see why our action should bring Norway into the war. He assumed that the Norwegian Government were protesting to the German Government against the violation of Norwegian waters by German submarines. Although they would probably feel it necessary to protest to His Majesty's Government, they would not thereby be brought into the war.

Lord Halifax explained to M. Prytz the reasons for the British (a) decision and asked him what he thought of M. Colban's view that this decision might involve Norway in the war, and what would be the probable effect of this action upon Sweden. M. Prytz's first reaction gave no indication of the strength of feeling shown later in the official Swedish reply. He said that, speaking unofficially, he had expected such a step to be taken by the British Government and had so informed his Government as soon as he had heard of the sinkings in Norwegian territorial waters. He did not think that there would be much reaction in Sweden. The Germans might try to protect their commerce and risk a naval engagement in Norwegian waters, but only a German invasion of Norway need compromise Norwegian neutrality. The test of our action in Swedish and Norwegian opinion would be whether our object was solely to defend ourselves against German illegalities and to tighten the blockade of Germany but not to bring Scandinavia into the war. Lord Halifax replied that 'our intentions were to protect ourselves and to harm Germany, but not to bring the Scandinavian countries into the war against their will'.

Two days later M. Colban brought Lord Halifax a letter in which he had embodied the views of the Norwegian Government. He also (b) presented a letter from the King of Norway to His Majesty the King.[1] M. Colban's letter contested the facts about the sinking of two of the three ships and stated that, even if these facts were fully established, the implication would not be that the Germans had made the coast of Norway a theatre of war and deprived it of its neutral character. The Norwegian Government did not consider that infractions of their neutrality by one belligerent authorised another belligerent to violate it. They also could not believe that Great Britain would 'drive a small neutral country into a war, as would be the result if the action mentioned in [the] *aide-mémoire* were taken'.

M. Prytz also gave Lord Halifax on January 8 a memorandum from the Swedish Government. The latter appealed to His Majesty's (c) Government not to adopt the proposed measures, since they would 'lead to unpredictable consequences not only with regard to the

---

[1] This letter repeated the arguments set out by M. Colban.

(a) N322/7/63. (b) N330/7/63. (c) N331/7/63.

maintenance of Swedish trade relations with Great Britain but also to the position of the Scandinavian States in their policy of neutrality. Taking into account the military and political situation in Northern Europe as well as the concern for Finland in her struggle with the Soviet Union, manifested in British quarters, it would seem to the Swedish Government as though it were not in the British interest to create such a situation.'

M. Prytz also said that he had been instructed to state that if, nevertheless, His Majesty's Government carried out their proposed action, the Swedish Government hoped that they would do so with as little publicity as possible and, above all, without previous public announcement. Lord Halifax pointed out that it was difficult to avoid publicity in such actions and that in any case the Norwegian Government would hardly accept the Swedish view. M. Prytz suggested that we might seize a few ships and, in reply to Norwegian protests, promise to take no further action if the Germans would agree not to use Norwegian waters. Lord Halifax said that no value could be given to German assurances. M. Prytz asked whether we would wait to see whether the assurances were kept. Lord Halifax repeated that the 'fundamental question' was 'whether the Germans could be allowed to "get away" with illegal and inhumane acts, while the Allies watched impotently a great volume of German trade proceeding through the waters where these acts had been committed'.

On the day before this interview M. Boheman had told Mr.
(a) Montagu-Pollock[1] that, in his view, the consequences of the proposed British action would probably be a German occupation of Denmark and, possibly, the end of the independent existence of all the Scandinavian States. M. Boheman then commented: 'I should have thought that the British Government had the fate of a sufficient number of smaller States on their consciences as it is'.[2] M. Boheman considered that it would be better for us 'to slip in and sink ships on the quiet' rather than to claim that we were justified in so doing. Other suggestions from the Swedish side were that shipments from
(b) Narvik might be forbidden to all belligerents or that the British authorities should buy off the pilots working in the dangerous channel in territorial waters south of Narvik.

---

[1] Sir E. Monson left Stockholm at the end of December 1939. He was succeeded as Minister by Mr. V. Mallet. Mr. Mallet arrived in Stockholm on January 16, 1940. During the interval Mr. Montagu-Pollock was Chargé d'Affaires.

[2] As a result of information from Swedish sources the Foreign Office were not inclined to treat M. Boheman's outburst very seriously.

(a) N295/19/63. (b) N367/19/63.

(iii)

Decision to postpone action against the Narvik traffic, January 12: further representations to the Scandinavian Governments: British aid to Finland and the transit of volunteers.

On January 9 the War Cabinet considered the question of opera- (a) tions against the Narvik traffic in the light of the communications from the Scandinavian Governments. Lord Halifax explained that hitherto we had not thought that the Germans were planning an invasion of Scandinavia. There was now evidence that they might be doing so. If they did take this action, it would be the best thing from our point of view, since we should avoid incurring the odium of being the first to take drastic steps in Scandinavia, and we should avoid also the risk of losing Norwegian goodwill.[1] The Foreign Office view was that, if we intended to carry out our larger plan against the ore-fields, we ought to avoid creating a feeling of bitterness in Scandinavia. We should certainly create this feeling if, as a result of our action against the Narvik traffic, Norway and Sweden became involved in war with Germany.

The War Cabinet agreed with this view, and adjourned their discussion until the following day. Meanwhile on January 9 a meeting was held at the Foreign Office with members of the Ministry of (b) Economic Warfare to discuss the advantages and disadvantages of the proposed action in Norwegian territorial waters. The general conclusion reached at this meeting was that action against the Narvik traffic was worth while in itself since it would deprive Germany of considerable supplies of ore. It also allowed the possibility of carrying out the larger scheme if the Germans reacted by attacks on Scandinavia (as the Swedish and Norwegian Governments professed to fear). If the Germans did not react in this way, the Scandinavian Governments would lose some of their fears of Germany.

It was also suggested that before we began operations in Norwegian territorial waters we might put to Norway and Sweden themselves alternative suggestions. The Norwegian Government might be asked to prohibit all exports of ore from Norway, or prevent Norwegian pilots from embarking on German ships. The Swedish Government also might be asked at least to guarantee that shipments of ore from the Baltic ports did not make up for the German loss of supplies from Narvik.

In the adjourned discussion at the War Cabinet on January 10 Lord Halifax recommended that we should try these alternatives. (c)

---

[1] It should be noted that the Foreign Office at this time accepted the military view that Germany would not act against Norway without also invading Sweden, and that an invasion of Sweden was not in the German interest.

(a) WM(40)7.8, C.A.; N368/19/63. (b) N560/7/63. (c) WM(40)8.1, C.A.; N450/19/63.

Mr. Churchill thought that the Scandinavian Governments would not accept them, and that we should be wasting more time. We had already been discussing the question for six weeks. We ought to take naval action at once and await the results. It was very questionable whether our action would bring about a German invasion of southern Norway and, in any case, such an invasion would be to our general advantage. We should not allow neutrals to tie our hands while we were fighting to defend their liberty. We ought also to tell the Swedish Government that we were determined not to allow the Germans to get ore from the north Swedish ore-fields. The stoppage of these supplies would shorten the war and save an enormous number of casualties on the western front. We had the necessary force and could promise support to Sweden in the event of a German attack. It was just possible that if we showed our determination in this way, Sweden might agree to cut off supplies to Germany by destroying the ore-fields. We might wait for the visit of M. Wallenberg,[1] and hear what he had to suggest, but very little was likely to come of his visit and we ought then to put into effect our naval measures against the Narvik traffic.

The War Cabinet decided to postpone a decision until after M. Wallenberg's visit. Meanwhile they asked for the advice of the Chiefs of Staff about the preparations necessary for sending a force (i) to the ore-fields, (ii) to southern Sweden. M. Wallenberg saw
(a) Lord Halifax and Mr. Cross, Minister of Economic Warfare, on January 11. Lord Halifax explained that His Majesty's Government could not allow the Germans the benefit of breaking the rules of war while the Allies kept them. They had therefore told the Swedish Government of their intention of stopping German trade in Norwegian territorial waters. They had been surprised at the Swedish attitude towards their statement of intention and wanted an explanation.

M. Wallenberg said that the Swedish Government were afraid that the Germans, who already had plans for the invasion of Scandinavia, might regard British action in Norwegian territorial waters as a first step in an Allied plan to establish themselves in Scandinavia. If Germany attacked Sweden, Sweden could not help Finland, and there would be no chance of maintaining Finnish resistance to Russia. Lord Halifax asked M. Wallenberg whether he could suggest any way of cutting off German ore supplies except by action in Norwegian territorial waters. M. Wallenberg had nothing to suggest. Lord Halifax pointed out that the Swedish Government appeared to

---

[1] M. Marcus Wallenberg, a Swedish banker, had been a member of the Swedish delegation to London for the negotiation of an Anglo-Swedish war trade agreement. He returned to London to discuss the situation created by the British statement about the proposed action against the Narvik traffic.

(a) N706/19/63.

assume that the Allies were following two incompatible aims. They wanted to do as much damage as possible to Germany; they wanted also to strengthen Finland and Sweden against Russia. The Swedish Government thought that the pursuit of one of these policies would risk the failure of the other. His Majesty's Government, however, had made an offer of help to Sweden if she were involved in war with Germany as the result of help to Finland. If, from the Swedish point of view, the defeat of Germany was as desirable as that of Russia, would it not be wise for the Swedish Government to consider the British offer? Germany might well think in the spring, irrespective of anything the Allies might do at Narvik, that she ought to make sure of her ore supplies. With this possibility it might be worth while for Sweden to contemplate taking help from the Allies or at least to discuss with them what might be done.

M. Wallenberg did not dispute this reasoning, but said that many Swedes would argue that the immediate necessity was to keep Germany quiet. He agreed that the Germans would hesitate before invading Sweden, yet they could do so, especially if their armies were not occupied elsewhere. What help would the Allies be able to give? Lord Halifax thought that by the spring the Allies could give a great deal of help, but that it was essential to concert plans at once. M. Wallenberg discussed the question again at the Foreign Office on January 11, 12 and 15, without suggesting a satisfactory alternative method of stopping the ore traffic. He was given a further explanation of the British attitude. We were becoming impatient of the constant appeals to us to refrain from injuring the Germans because the Germans might injure some third party. It was for the Swedish Government, if they felt so strongly on the matter, to suggest some means of achieving part at least of the objectives at which we were aiming without involving them in the risks which they feared.

The War Cabinet discussed on January 11 the effect upon our own industries of the prohibition of the export of ore from Narvik to all (a) belligerents. It was agreed that, although there would be a temporary dislocation in certain branches of the steel industry, the effect would not be lasting. Mr. Churchill again wanted action at once, and expected nothing more than protests against it. Next day the dis- (b) cussion was continued. Lord Halifax said that his conversation with M. Wallenberg had led him to decide against the Narvik plan owing to its probable effects upon Swedish opinion, and upon the power of Sweden to help Finland. There was also 'an apparent possibility'— Lord Halifax would not use a stronger term—that we might be able to open negotiations with Sweden and bring her to our side.

(a) WM(40)9.5, C.A.; N506/19/63. (b) WM(40)10.1, C.A.; N553/19/63.

The War Cabinet was also informed that the Chiefs of Staff inclined to the view that the Narvik plan would prejudice the larger project for which the active co-operation of Norway and Sweden was essential. The Germans might also retaliate by sabotage against the Narvik-Gällivare railway, which could not be guarded at all points.[1] Without the use of the railway we could not send a force to the ore-fields. Furthermore action in Sweden might develop into a very large commitment and would divert forces from the decisive western front. On the other hand a diversion in Scandinavia would be strategically sound and would probably rule out the possibility of large-scale offensives elsewhere by the Russians or Germans.

Mr. Churchill said once again that the Narvik plan had been talked about for six weeks. He did not think that Sweden would ever willingly allow us to go through with the larger plan. It was not right that we should bear the whole burden of fighting the Germans on behalf of the small neutrals, while they did nothing to help us. Ever since the beginning of the war we had allowed Germany to keep the initiative. If we opened a new theatre of operations in Scandinavia, we had a good chance of forcing Germany into situations which she had not foreseen and of seizing the initiative for ourselves.

The Prime Minister thought that, if we carried out the Narvik plan, Germany might retaliate, not by the invasion of Sweden, but by an offer to 'protect' Sweden against Great Britain as well as against Russia. The Swedes might say that our action had forced them to accept the German offer. We should then have lost all chance of carrying out the larger project. In any case we could not take action at once on the Narvik plan since the Dominions wished to be able to express their views about the probable effect upon neutral opinion. The Prime Minister suggested that we should send a Minister to Sweden[2] to open conversations with the Swedish Government which might well lead to active Swedish co-operation.

Mr. Churchill thought that if we sent a mission to Sweden before taking naval action we should merely be advertising our interest in the German ore traffic and encouraging the Swedes to continue their protests. Mr. Churchill accepted the general view of the War Cabinet not to put the Narvik plan into effect at once, or without carrying the Dominions with us. He said that hitherto we had thought time on our side. He was not sure that time would continue to be on our side. He asked whether it was certain that, after six months of war, we should have improved our air position with regard to Germany. The central position of Germany allowed her to deliver thrusts in several directions. Mr. Churchill thought that we might well have a much

---

[1] The railway ran through mountainous country.
[2] The Prime Minister suggested that Sir S. Hoare should be sent.

graver situation ahead of us, and that we ought to redouble our efforts to guard against it.

In taking the decision to postpone action against the Narvik traffic, since they might thereby be risking the success of the larger plan, the War Cabinet agreed that they would not inform the Scandinavian Governments. They also asked Lord Halifax and Sir S. Hoare for a report on the suggestion of a mission to Sweden and the Chiefs of Staff for their views on the possibility of capturing the ore-fields against Swedish and Norwegian opposition.[1] This question of a mission was discussed again on January 17. (a) Mr. Churchill thought that if the mission were sent, we ought to tell the Scandinavian Governments that, if the Allies were beaten, Germany and Russia would be able to divide the world between them. Were they (Norway and Sweden) willing to assist in bringing about this situation? They were in fact contributing to it, and were sending hundreds of thousands of British and French soldiers to their death. We ought to tell the Scandinavian Governments that we could not tolerate for an indefinite period their supplying Germany with the means of continuing the war. We might also point out that Finland was being destroyed before their eyes, and that sooner or later the Scandinavian countries were almost certain to become involved in the war.

The Prime Minister said that he could not agree to a proposal (which Mr. Churchill seemed to have in mind) to seize the ore-fields against Norwegian and Swedish opposition. His reasons were that the Chiefs of Staff were opposed to such an operation, and that the effect upon opinion in the Dominions and in the United States would be very bad. He also thought that there were small prospects of attaining our object—the possession of the ore-fields—by the dispatch of a mission. Lord Halifax suggested that, as a first step, he might explain our case firmly to the Swedish and Norwegian Ministers in London.

The War Cabinet agreed with this view. Lord Halifax therefore saw M. Prytz and M. Colban at the Foreign Office on January 18. (b) Lord Halifax summed up the case for the proposed action at Narvik and said that, if the Norwegian Government objected to it, we had the strongest grounds for asking them to do something to remedy the situation. M. Colban admitted that the real question for Norway was not one of law, but of the extent to which Norway could be expected to compromise the neutral position upon which alone she

---

[1] It is not clear why this report was asked for, since the Chiefs of Staff had already given their view that they regarded Swedish and Norwegian co-operation as essential. Lord Halifax's opinion was that, whatever the military arguments might be, he could not contemplate war with Norway to capture Narvik. It will be seen that on January 17 the Prime Minister repeated the previous statement of the views of the Chiefs of Staff.

(a) WM(40)16.9, C.A.; N740/19/63.   (b) N790/7/63.

relied to avoid becoming involved in the war. Lord Halifax agreed
that the matter was not one of law. We had indeed a right to demand
that the Germans should not be permitted to break all the rules
and commit acts of inhumanity everywhere on the high seas while
we were expected to refrain even from the smallest technical violation
of international law. We also had a right to expect that the Norwegian
Government, knowing that a German victory would mean the end
of Norwegian independence, would take action in their own vital
interests to deal with the ore traffic.

Lord Halifax repeated the same arguments to M. Prytz. He
(a) referred specially to undertakings given by Sweden at the time of the
signature of the Anglo-Swedish War Trade Agreement, to limit and,
as far as possible, reduce the export of ore to Germany from Sweden.
He said that the Swedish Government always met our requests with
arguments about the danger from Germany or the danger to Finland.
We had offered help in protecting Sweden from the first of the
dangers. The Swedish Government had not accepted our offer and
were now even showing signs[1] of going back on their undertaking to
allow passage of volunteers from Great Britain to Finland, 'apparently
from fear of those very reactions from Germany, the consequences of
which they had been unwilling to discuss with us. . . . It was time
that the neutral Governments applied their minds to considering the
best means of helping rather than hindering a cause which they
could not wish to see defeated.'

Lord Halifax then suggested that in the spring Hitler might find
it desirable to secure German ore supplies by offering 'protection' to
Sweden. M. Prytz said that Sweden would refuse such an offer. Lord
Halifax replied that the Swedes would then have to turn for help to
the Allies. The Allies would help them—they must do so for their
own sakes—but they could not help effectively without previous
discussions with the Swedish Government. These discussions could
be secret; they must be held 'if we were not to be taken by surprise by
the development of a situation which could hardly remain static'.[2]

The discussions in the War Cabinet and the conversations with the
Scandinavian Ministers took place against the background of the
Finnish war. Although there were unconfirmed reports of German
mediation in mid-January, the general impression of the British

---

[1] See below, pp. 71–2.

[2] As an example of the nervousness of the Swedish Government at this time, it may be
mentioned that M. Prytz called Lord Halifax's attention to an article in *Le Nord* of
November 1939, saying that the supply of scrap iron was more important to Germany than
(b) that of iron ore. The writer of the article later admitted to Swedish friends that he had
written it at the request of the Swedish Foreign Minister in order to divert Allied interest
from the ore traffic.

(a) N789/7/63. (b) N1666/7/63.

Government during this period was that Finnish resistance could be continued at least during the winter months, and, in view of the lateness of the northern spring, until April or May. Nevertheless the question of assistance to Finland was urgent, and the British Government did their best not only to provide material aid from their own resources,[1] but also to encourage and facilitate help from other sources, including the United States and Italy as well as the Scandinavian states.

The possibility of some kind of assistance from Italy arose out of a question from Ciano reported by Sir P. Loraine on January 14. Ciano had asked whether the Finns were in need of men. Sir P. (a) Loraine thought that he was considering the possibility of sending airmen with experience of the Spanish war. Sir P. Loraine was instructed on January 16 to tell Ciano that the Finns urgently needed men and that we were hoping to facilitate the recruiting of volunteers in Great Britain, provided that they could be given passage in small groups across Norway and Sweden. The Finnish Government were also advised to ask whether Italy would release any aeroplanes. Sir P. Loraine was told to support any request in this matter from the Finnish Minister at Rome. He was informed by the Finnish (b) Minister on January 24 that the Italian Government was ready to release aircraft from stocks but that the process of release was rather slow and the prices rather high. Lord Lothian was instructed on (c) January 17 to ask President Roosevelt whether the United States Government could let the Finns have any fighters on order for the U.S. army. Although Mr. Cordell Hull promised to make enquiries, no decision had been reached at the end of January.

On January 12 the War Cabinet decided to inform the Swedish and Norwegian Governments that unofficial recruiting for volunteers was being authorised in Great Britain and that His Majesty's (d) Government assumed that these volunteers would be given passage across Scandinavian territory. The Scandinavian Governments were, however, nervous about the reactions of Russia and Germany towards volunteers from Sweden and Norway. In the latter country the volunteer movement was not of much political significance. In Sweden the numbers were large, but not as great as had been expected. Even so the Soviet Government sent notes to Sweden and Norway protesting against the recruitment of volunteers in these (e) countries and the despatch and transit of war material. The answers of the Scandinavian Governments were not very vigorous. In the

---

[1] Up to January 31, in spite of our own urgent needs, we had released in all 116 aeroplanes for Finnish use. Only 20 of these aircraft had reached Finland at the end of January.
(a) N548/9/56. (b) N995/9/56. (c) N586, 779, 1335/9/56. (d) WM(40)10; N543, 537/9/56. (e) N483, 532, 764, 862/9/56.

Swedish reply (published on January 15) it was stated that the Soviet Government appeared to be exaggerating the number of the volunteers; that the Swedish authorities were not assisting the movement, and that officers and men in Swedish service were not taking part in it.

The Norwegian Government replied at first to the British Govern-
(a) ment that they would allow the passage of volunteers travelling singly or in small numbers and as civilians. On January 15, however, Sir C. Dormer was told that this answer was not final and that the Norwegian Government must consult Sweden. On the Swedish side,
(b) Mr. Mallet was informed that the request was 'rather embarrassing'. The passage of large numbers of volunteers would cause difficulties with Germany and Russia, while small numbers would be of no use to the Finns. Hence the Swedish Government were unlikely to give a favourable answer.

The Foreign Office were most dissatisfied with this reply. The Swedish Government had asked us not to get them into difficulties about Narvik on the ground that they might be 'embarrassed' in their efforts to help Finland. They were now pleading that our own help to Finland would embarrass them. Finally the Swedish Government agreed, on January 23, to allow the passage of several hundred British volunteers if they came in small groups and wearing civilian clothes and if they were not members of the Allied armed forces. A reply was received on January 25 from the Norwegian Government that they also would allow the passage of 'technicians and persons in a similar position' travelling to Finland, including volunteers, if they could produce Finnish and Swedish visas and were travelling as individuals or in small groups.[1]

(iv)

Allied decision to prepare an expedition to assist Finland and to seize the ore-fields: fifth meeting of the Supreme War Council, February 5, 1940.

The War Cabinet again discussed the Scandinavian question on
(c) January 19. They had before them the answers of the Chiefs of Staff to their questions about the size of the force necessary for operations in Scandinavia on the assumption of Norwegian and Swedish co-operation, and about the practicability of seizing the ore-fields against Scandinavian opposition. The Chiefs of Staff thought that, ultimately, two divisions might be required for the force to be landed at Narvik; five battalions would be needed in southern Norway and at least two

---

[1] The British Government did not expect the number of volunteers to exceed 1,000.

(a) N547, 656/9/56.   (b) N657, 985, 1048, 1071/9/56.   (c) WM(40)18.10, C.A., N835/19/63; WP(40)23, N837/19/63.

divisions in southern Sweden. The total air support would be 3 fighter, 2 bomber, and 2 army co-operation squadrons, together with 4 heavy bomber squadrons operating from home bases. The forces would require a very large amount of shipping and there were great difficulties in making plans without holding staff talks with Sweden.

The Chiefs of Staff did not think that an attempt to seize the ore-fields should be made against Scandinavian opposition. A landing at Narvik would be possible, though difficult; it might also be possible to break through Swedish and Norwegian opposition on the route to Gällivare, but the operation could not be carried out in time to forestall the Germans in the ore-fields during the coming spring.

The Foreign Office at this time pointed out the need for 'disentangling' the various Scandinavian projects. The need was greater because the French had suggested yet another plan or, rather, had given their support to a plan proposed to them by the Finns. On January 5 the French Ambassador had asked whether the British (a) Government would reconsider their decision not to allow Polish ships serving with the Royal Navy and based on British ports to take action against the U.S.S.R. in the Arctic. The Foreign Office pointed out the reasons against revising the decision, but on January 18 the French Ambassador brought another memorandum from his Government in (b) favour of a 'more active and effective policy' in Scandinavia. The memorandum referred to the possibility that action at Narvik might lead ultimately to the control of the ore-fields. Delay in taking this action after the Norwegian Government had been told of our decision would only do us harm. Similarly we were losing the chance of helping the Finns by means of Polish action in the Arctic. Finnish resistance could not last indefinitely against increasing Russian pressure. The defeat of Finland would have very serious consequences for the Allies because they had publicly assured Finland of their support, and because they would be unable to prevent Germany and Russia from controlling the whole of the Scandinavian peninsula and thereby securing supplies for continuing the war almost indefi-nitely. Thus the French Government wished to tell His Majesty's Government most urgently and seriously that they regarded Scandin-avia as of 'capital importance' to the final issue of the war, and that the Allied Governments would be 'under a heavy responsibility' if they missed the opportunities offered to them.

Lord Halifax explained to the Ambassador that we agreed about the importance of developments in Scandinavia but that, in view of the unexpectedly violent protests from Norway and Sweden, there was a danger that our proposed action against the Narvik traffic

---

(a) N264/9/56. (b) N792, 1008/7/63.

might have a serious effect upon neutral opinion, especially in the United States. A false step over the Narvik plan might also prejudice the larger project—for which we needed Swedish co-operation—of stopping the Baltic ore supplies to Germany.

(a) The Ambassador also suggested a meeting of the Supreme War Council to discuss the Scandinavian question. The War Cabinet accepted this suggestion and asked the Chiefs of Staff to work out in greater detail the plans necessary for the Scandinavian operations. They thought that the French might not realise that operations in Scandinavia on a large scale in May would involve considerable diversion of our war effort from France.

(b) Meanwhile the Foreign Office received more information at least upon the Norwegian attitude. M. Colban left an *aide-mémoire* on January 19 repeating the previous statement about the lack of evidence that the Germans had torpedoed ships in Norwegian territorial waters. The Norwegian Government maintained that they had now taken adequate measures to protect their neutrality. They also appealed again to the British respect for international law, and for the rights of small states. The *aide-mémoire* concluded with the words: 'The circumstance that Great Britain is fighting for its life cannot give it a right to jeopardise the existence of Norway.'

(c) On the same day M. Koht, Norwegian Foreign Minister, spoke very strongly in the Storting about the right of Norway to expect that all belligerent Powers would refrain from violating her neutrality. The official version of M. Koht's speech communicated to the diplomatic missions in Oslo contained the words: 'When a ship is blown up and the crew are killed, we have no proof left of who is responsible, and we cannot address our complaints to any one Government; we can only blame the war itself.' The Foreign Office instructed Sir C. Dormer on January 24 to point out the bad impression made in Great Britain by this speech and to say that 'if the Norwegian Government's conception of neutrality is that both belligerents earn equal blame for action known to be taken by one of them, the other will have less inducement to respect Norwegian interests'.

(d) The Swedish Government also showed no disposition to run risks in the cause of Finland. M. Wallenberg told Lord Halifax on January 23 that the Swedish Government would feel doubtful about the suggestion for staff talks. They would be afraid of publicity, and would be uncertain whether we could in fact give them much help.

(e) The Swedish Foreign Minister said to Mr. Mallet on January 23 that he was a little surprised and anxious at the attention which the British press was paying to Scandinavia. The Swedish press was

---

(a) WM(40)18.10, C.A., N835/19/63.   (b) N1027/7/63.   (c) N825, 1813/7/63.
(d) N984/19/63. (e) N1070/9/56.

commenting adversely on Mr. Churchill's broadcast of January 20.[1] M. Günther thought that Germany was less dependent upon iron ore than was believed in Great Britain. On January 26, when Mr. Mallet (a) was presenting his credentials, the King of Sweden repeated the official Swedish view. He hoped that, as soon as the weather allowed, the Allies would land volunteers at Petsamo and make this port a base for the infiltration of men and materials. Sweden could not go to war openly in support of Finland; such a course would be too dangerous with Germany waiting to pounce upon her. The King hoped that we should not take our proposed action against the Narvik traffic since it would lead to immediate German reprisals against Sweden. He was most anxious to find some way of ending the war before it led to general ruin.

The Foreign Office view at this time was that, if the Finns held out through the winter, the Germans would intervene in the spring (b) because they would want to have forces available to prevent the ore-fields from falling into Russian hands, and—even more urgently— to prevent the Allies from sending an expeditionary force to save Finland. German intervention to end the Russo-Finnish war would probably take the form of a demand to Finland, under threat of force, to accept German mediation. As a first step, the Germans might try to get a 'Munich' settlement which would allow a Finnish state to exist until Germany and Russia decided upon the ultimate fate of the country. It was clearly in Allied interests to prevent German mediation. We could do so only by encouraging the Finns to appeal to us before committing themselves to peace discussions with Russia or with any third party, but a Finnish appeal would be useless if we were not ready to make an immediate and substantial offer of military help, and to implement this offer, if necessary, by means of Swedish and Norwegian co-operation or at all events connivance.

Furthermore, we had to recognise the connexion between assistance to Finland and the control of the ore-fields. In each case interference in Scandinavia would be to our advantage. We could not, however, get control of the ore-fields without at least the tacit acquiescence of the Norwegian and Swedish Governments. It was in our interest to receive an invitation from the Scandinavian Governments which would allow us to occupy northern Sweden.

---

[1] In this broadcast Mr. Churchill mentioned the German attacks on neutral shipping and threats to the independence of neutral states. He said that the neutrals 'bowed humbly and in fear to German threats of violence, comforting themselves with the thought that Britain and France would win'. He asked what would happen if the neutrals 'were . . . to do their duty according to the Covenant and stand together with the British and French Empires against aggression and wrong?'

(a) N1826/124/42. (b) N2306/1/56.

Owing to their fears of Germany, Norway and Sweden were unlikely to give this invitation. One reason for their fear of Germany was that the Scandinavian Governments doubted whether our help could reach them in time. It was therefore essential for us to remove this impression; the best way to remove it would be to prepare a force which, to the knowledge of the Scandinavian Governments, would be ready to go to their aid.

(a)   On January 29 the War Cabinet considered the enlarged version of the report of the Chiefs of Staff on the detailed preparations for an expeditionary force to Scandinavia. In its new form, and under the title 'Intervention in Scandinavia', the report dealt with the despatch of a force to Narvik for the occupation of the ore-fields, and of another force to co-operate in the defence of southern Sweden, and of smaller bodies of troops for the occupation of Trondhjem, Bergen and Stavanger.[1] The requirements would be up to 40 escort destroyers, an Anglo-French force of 100,000 (5 divisions and 2 brigades), 3 fighter squadrons, 1 army co-operation squadron and 1 flight, 2 bomber squadrons, and 4 heavy bomber squadrons (the latter to be based in Great Britain). It would be necessary to establish bases at Trondhjem and Namsos before sending a force into Sweden and also to occupy Bergen and to destroy the aerodrome at Stavanger.[2] In order to reach the Baltic port of Lulea before the breaking of the ice at the end of April, the expedition would have to reach Narvik by March 20; the Swedes would require our aid at the same time in southern Sweden.

The Chiefs of Staff were now in favour of the operation since it would give us our 'first and best chance of wresting the initiative from the Germans and of shortening the war'. On the other hand the risks and difficulties were considerable. We could not act without Norwegian and Swedish co-operation. Owing to their own lack of protection against German air attack, neither the Norwegians nor the Swedes would give their consent unless we could promise substantial help to meet this attack. We could not give much direct help but we might promise indirect help; we might, for example, declare that, if Germany bombed Scandinavian cities as she had bombed Polish cities, we should retaliate on Germany. This move on our part might lead to unrestricted air warfare. It was also possible that, if Finland collapsed, Sweden might appeal to us for protection against a Russian invasion and as an alternative to

---

[1] The report did not discuss the question of an advance into Finland. A separate report by the Chiefs of Staff on aid to Finland dealt almost entirely with the French project of an expedition to Petsamo.

[2] It was suggested that after the destruction of the aerodrome, we should withdraw from Stavanger.

(a) WM(40)29, N1207/2/63; WP(40)35.

accepting German 'protection'. We ought to be able to act at once in defence of the ore-fields against Russia and Germany.

The War Cabinet took notice of this report on January 29 but deferred further consideration of it in view of discussions about to take place with the French military authorities. These discussions were necessary because the French had brought forward proposals for (a) a landing at Petsamo which would mean war with Russia. The Chiefs of Staff did not regard the French plans as practicable and thought that a meeting with General Gamelin should be held before the session of the Supreme War Council. They therefore asked the Foreign Office to prepare for them an estimate of the probable political repercussions in other countries of help to Finland, or, although the words were not used, war with Russia.

The Foreign Office view[1] was that, if Norway and Sweden agreed (b) to the Allied use of their territory, they would be ready to risk the danger of German retaliation. Their fear of such retaliation had been their reason for not inviting Allied co-operation in the defence of Finland. If Norway and Sweden did not agree in advance, and if, nevertheless, we occupied a Norwegian fjord as a base for refuelling ships at Petsamo, Norway might acquiesce, after protest, on the ground that we were using territorial waters, not for operations against Germany, but to help the Finns in accordance with the League resolution to which Norway was a party. On the other hand, Norway would be likely to oppose a landing at Narvik and Sweden an advance across Swedish territory to Finland. A landing at Narvik would undoubtedly lead to a German attack on Sweden and Norway. German intervention would be less likely if we occupied a fjord near Petsamo as a naval base, but the Germans would probably wait only until the Gulf of Bothnia was open. They would then send an expedition to Lulea in order to seize the ore-fields and to hold the Swedish-Finnish frontier.

The repercussions on other countries were likely to be as follows:

(1) Turkey was anxious that her relations with the Allies should not damage her relations with Russia: in any case Turkey could not be expected to follow the Allies into war with Russia unless she were attacked by Russia.

(2) The Iranian and Afghan Governments were afraid of Russia, though public opinion in each country was anti-Russian. The Russians might occupy northern Iran.

(3) Public opinion in Italy would be favourable, but the Italian

---

[1] The estimate was asked for at very short notice. Some sections of the Foreign Office memorandum were modified in a second draft. The summary given above is based on the second draft. In its amended form the memorandum was dated February 3.

(a) N994/2/63, MR(J)(40)15; N1193/9/56; N1103/2/63; WM(40)26, N1206/9/56.
(b) N1638/9/56.

Government would probably dislike war between the Allies and Russia, since Italy could not join the Russian side and would therefore lose her main bargaining power with the Allies.

(4) Hungary and Roumania would also favour the Allied move, unless Roumania had reason to fear an immediate Russo-German attack.

(5) Opinion in the United States and in Latin America would be favourable.

(6) In the Far East the Japanese would welcome war between the Allies and Russia, but might show even less regard for Allied interests in China. China might be unable to get help from Russia and might ask us for more assistance. We should have to try to provide it even at the cost of increased Japanese hostility.

(a)   The Foreign Office added a note on the effect upon Russo-German relations of war between the Allies and Russia. The Germans would welcome such an event in the hope that it would lead to a closer Russo-German alliance with Germany as the main partner. On the other hand there was little chance that the Allies could secure Russian friendship except at a price which they would be unwilling to pay.

(b)   The military discussions in Paris showed a certain vagueness in General Gamelin's plans. Although he proposed to send three to four divisions of volunteers into Finland, he had no clear idea where these volunteers would be found or how he could get them across Sweden if the Scandinavian States objected. The French also seemed to make light of the consequences of war with Russia and indeed even to welcome the prospect since it would give the Allies an opportunity to bomb Baku and thus make it impossible for Russia to spare oil for Germany. General Gamelin did not give much consideration to the difficulties which Russia might cause in India. He was also less certain that the Germans would attack on the western front in the spring, and felt that there was much to be said for ending the stalemate on land by opening up new fields of operations.

(c)   On February 2 the War Cabinet considered the reports of the Chiefs of Staff and the result of the discussions in Paris. They did not accept the French plan for an expedition to Petsamo, since it seemed likely to involve us in war with Russia without enabling us to give decisive help to Sweden or to secure control of the ore-fields. On the other hand, they agreed in the main with the report of the Chiefs of Staff. They considered that it was of the utmost importance to save Finland and that this could be done only by sending trained men to Finland through Norway and Sweden. We should have to send units

(a) N1360/40/38. (b) N1350, 1351/9/56. (c) WM(40)31.1, C.A., N1636/2/63.

of our own armed forces as 'volunteers' on the analogy of the Italians in Spain. This measure would give us the most likely opportunity of securing the ore-fields; we could carry it out only with the co-oper-ation of Norway and Sweden. We ought therefore to make it clear both to the Finns and to Norway and Sweden that the prospects of help depended upon such co-operation. We should not mention the ore-fields to Norway and Sweden, but should make it clear that, if these countries were attacked by Germany, we could help them with substantial forces.

The British Ministers[1] explained these decisions to the Supreme (a) War Council in Paris on February 5. The Prime Minister said that we agreed upon the importance of saving Finland. A Finnish collapse would mean a loss of morale, especially in the Dominions and in the United States, and would be regarded throughout the world as an Allied defeat. Our primary purpose, however, was the defeat of Germany. We wanted therefore to combine help to the Finns with the stoppage of iron ore supplies to the Germans. An expedition to Petsamo would almost certainly mean war with Russia; it would be technically difficult and would not result in the occupation of the ore-fields.

The Prime Minister then outlined the possibilities of an expedition to Narvik. This expedition would require Scandinavian consent and must be undertaken, if this consent were to be secured, ostensibly to help the Finns. The force must be substantial, and must consist of regular divisions, although they would go as 'volunteers'. Russia therefore need not declare war against the Allies unless she wished to do so.

The German reaction would be one of 'consternation'. They might occupy points in southern Norway. The Allies would have to guard their lines of communication from Narvik and leave a force near the ore deposits. The Germans would find it hard to turn out this force. We should, however, have to tell Sweden that we were prepared to defend Swedish territory against German attack. Hence we should have ready for instant action a force to defend the line of the lakes in southern Sweden.

The Prime Minister then asked how we should get Scandinavian consent to this plan. He considered that our approach should be through the Finnish question. We should point out the effect upon Norway and Sweden of a Finnish collapse which might be followed by a Russian or German attack upon Scandinavia. We should explain that the Allies wished to help Finland, and could do so only through Norwegian and Swedish territory. Hence their demand for

---

[1] The Prime Minister, Lord Halifax, Mr. Churchill, Mr. Stanley and Sir Kingsley Wood. They were accompanied by naval, military and air chiefs.

(a) C3999/89/18, S.W.C.(40)1.

right of passage. The Finns would be told of this demand, and would make their own appeal to the Scandinavian Powers not to oppose the only action which could save Finland. The Prime Minister doubted whether Norway and Sweden could resist these appeals. Public opinion in the two countries was ahead of their Governments and the Allies could meet the argument of danger from Germany by offering help against a German attack. The two Scandinavian Governments might hesitate through fear of German air attacks on their southern cities. They might stipulate that such attacks should be followed by immediate reprisals against Germany. If Sweden and Norway became embroiled with Germany, the Allies would gain by the diversion of German forces and by the stoppage of supplies vital to the Germans. There was also likely to be 'a much enhanced degree of support for the Allied cause throughout the world'.

M. Daladier agreed with the proposals, but asked what the Allies would do if either or both of the Scandinavian countries refused right of passage to the expedition. The Prime Minister said that this risk had to be taken; Norway, for example, could destroy the Narvik railway (which had already been mined), and Sweden could take equally decisive action to block the plan. The Prime Minister thought actual refusal unlikely, although the two countries might make public protests. M. Daladier said that, in the event of refusal, he would ask the Supreme War Council to reconsider the possibility of an expedition to Petsamo.

Thus the British plan was accepted, and preparations for its execution were agreed upon. The third week of March was taken as the latest date for the arrival of the force in Norway. As soon as the military preparations were complete, diplomatic action would begin on the lines proposed by the Prime Minister.

CHAPTER IV

The collapse of Finland: French insistence upon action in Scandinavia: sixth meeting of the Supreme War Council, March 28, 1940, and the decision to lay mines in Norwegian territorial waters

(i)

Further consideration of the proposed Scandinavian expedition: the Altmark *incident: declaration by the King of Sweden (February 19): refusal of the Swedish Government to allow passage to an Allied expedition to Finland: further postponement of action in Norwegian territorial waters, February 10–29, 1940.*

THE Allies had now spent over two months in deliberating over their policy. They had decided at last upon the 'larger plan' which, in one form or another, would involve them in heavy military commitments. Their communications to the Scandinavian Governments had lost them the advantages of surprise. The Scandinavian press was commenting on their plans and public opinion in Norway and Sweden was becoming alarmed at the prospect of war. The Finnish position was more dangerous; the Russians had brought up stronger forces and on February 2 had reopened their offensive against the Mannerheim line; the Finns, for all their courage and determination, could not hold out alone against the attack and the Allies could not reach them soon enough or in sufficient force to turn the situation. The Germans might attack on the western front within two months; indeed, if the Allies were right in their view of the paramount importance of the ore-fields and of the embarrassment which an Anglo-French expedition to northern Sweden would cause to German war industry, they could expect an attempt to force the issue in the west as soon as the weather allowed a grand offensive.

In any case the Allies had hardly begun to take stock of their own resources for a campaign in the snows of Scandinavia. Even if they had possessed sufficient forces for specialised action of this kind, they had collected neither the men nor the equipment; further delay would thus have been necessary in the most favourable political circumstances. The political circumstances, however, were obviously unfavourable. It is difficult to understand why the War

Cabinet should have expected that the Scandinavian states would suddenly change their policy and risk the displeasure of Germany and Russia when the military prospects for the Finns were much less favourable than in mid-December.

This optimism on the Allied side is the more remarkable because, three days before the meeting of the Supreme War Council on

(a) February 5, there was more evidence that Norway at least would persist in avoiding any breach of neutrality. M. Colban had brought to the Foreign Office a note from the Norwegian Government reaffirming their duty to abide by the legal rules of neutrality. They had declared Norwegian neutrality because it was 'the unanimous will of the Norwegian people that Norway be kept out of the war'. The question of preventing iron ore from reaching Germany affected Sweden as well as Norway; the Norwegian Government had no suggestions to make in the matter but would examine any proposals compatible with their neutrality.

(b) On February 10 M. Prytz, on his return from a visit to Stockholm, said that the Swedes were equally resolved to maintain their neutrality. They did not feel responsible for the conditions which had led to the war in Europe. They could not intervene openly on the side of Finland against Russia because their intervention would bring Germany into the Russo-Finnish war. Germany could reach Sweden more quickly than the Allies; in any case, the Swedish Government could not take action which would make Sweden a theatre of war. They were also unable to discuss with the Allies the possibility of military assistance in a situation arising out of aid given by the Scandinavian countries to Finland. 'Negotiations regarding military assistance from one of the belligerents in the present great war could hardly be regarded as compatible' with neutrality. M. Prytz admitted that Swedish policy might not seem to the Allies 'very heroic, nor perhaps wholly in accordance with purely Allied interests'.

M. Prytz left with the Foreign Office an *aide-mémoire* elaborating his arguments. These arguments had already been put on February 7

(c) to Mr. Mallet by the Swedish Foreign Minister. M. Günther thought that Great Britain or France could not help Sweden in the event of a sudden German attack. The Germans would obtain immediate and complete domination in the air and could destroy every city in Sweden. It would take the Allies five months to bring 100,000 men into Sweden;[1] before this time the country would have been overrun by the Germans.

(d) Mr. Mallet had telegraphed to the Foreign Office on February 8 his general view of the position. He thought that Sweden was more

---

[1] i.e. on the assumption that Norwegian ports would be available.

(a) N1353/7/63. (b) N1718/19/63. (c) N1651/9/56. (d) N1697/9/56.

afraid of Russia than of Germany, and would do almost anything to make herself safe from Russian attack. The first step to safety would therefore be a settlement of the Russo-Finnish war, possibly with Sweden as mediator and Germany putting pressure on Russia to offer reasonable terms. A Finnish collapse would not involve Sweden in war, if the Russians did not advance beyond Finland. The Swedes would argue that the fate of Finland was another instance of the inability of the Allies to help the smaller Powers. They might then be tempted to give way to German demands. The only way in which we might be able to persuade them to stand up to Germany was by showing that we really could send them assistance, and the best evidence of our ability to do this would be the provision of help to the Finns. Neither Sweden nor Norway would allow the passage of a force from Narvik, but they might permit the 'filtering' of several thousand volunteers in small numbers. Mr. Mallet therefore advised this policy if we were sure that the maintenance of Swedish neutrality was not more to our interest, and that in committing ourselves to a serious military effort in Sweden we were not taking too great risks.

Meanwhile the Foreign Office was beginning to doubt whether the Finns could hold out until the spring. Mr. Noel-Baker, M.P., and Sir W. Citrine[1], who had visited Finland, brought back (a) encouraging reports early in February, but M. Gripenberg pressed very strongly on February 10 for increased Allied help, and said that, although as yet the military position was 'pretty good', Field-Marshal Mannerheim could not 'speak with certainty about the future'.

Lord Halifax told the War Cabinet on February 12 that he was (b) afraid that Norway and Sweden would refuse passage to our expedition in the spring, and that we might find ourselves in March still unable to help Finland. He thought that we ought to send larger numbers of 'official volunteers', and that we could persuade the Scandinavian Governments to let them go through into Finland. It was pointed out that in the spring the Finns would need 30–40,000 men and that we could not send this number of volunteers. In any case only volunteers used to skis were of any use, and of these we had under 400. Mr. Churchill thought it worth while to send fairly small bodies through as soon as possible, since from a strategic point of view the important thing was 'to get our foot into the doorway into Scandinavia'.

On February 16 the War Cabinet discussed the proposed (c) Scandinavian expedition at length. They considered the military time-table, and the arguments for and against an early diplomatic

---

[1] At this time General Secretary of the T.U.C.

(a) N1714, 1705, 2148/9/56. (b) WM(40)39.6, C.A., N1753/9/56. (c) WM(40)43.1, C.A., N2149/2/63.

approach to Norway and Sweden. In view of the close inter-relation between the political and military factors in the time-table, they asked for a joint report on the question of the time-factor from the
(a) Chiefs of Staff and the Foreign Office. This report was submitted on February 18. On the military side it suggested that the expedition should sail between March 15 and March 29. On the political side the report pointed out that we needed Finnish agreement to our intervention with regular troops. We might not get this agreement because the Finns might think our proposed assistance not enough to counterbalance the risk of war with Germany. If we did not get it, we should have to reconsider our whole plan. On the assumption that the Finns agreed to appeal to us, and, simultaneously, to Norway and Sweden, the appeal should be timed to allow about a week for getting the consent of the Scandinavian Governments to our passage, but we should have our forces ready, as soon as the Finnish appeal was received, to forestall the Germans at Stavanger, Bergen and Trondhjem. It would be inadvisable to send a brusque ultimatum to Norway or Sweden, since we could not enforce our demands. Even passive non-cooperation or a failure to supply electric power or the removal of rolling stock from the railways could prevent the movement of our forces inland.

(b) The War Cabinet considered this report on February 18. In answer to a question about the possible scale of German air attacks upon Trondhjem, it was explained that, in the view of the Chiefs of Staff, the risks were considerable, but were worth taking if we could secure the ore-fields. Mr. Churchill thought that, if the Germans forestalled us by occupying aerodromes in Norway and southern Sweden, a German violation of Scandinavian territory would be on balance to our advantage, since it would give us full justification for entering Sweden to secure the ore-fields. Mr. Churchill agreed about the risks of German air attack in southern Sweden but thought that this risk was much less serious—even if we had not Scandinavian co-operation—on the lines of communication from Narvik to Gällivare. In the course of the discussion doubts were raised about the practicability of the expedition to southern Sweden and about the extent to which the troops forming the expedition would have been adequately trained. It was also pointed out that the Swedish General Staff, realising the great difficulties in the way of our operations, might doubt whether we could make good our offer of help.

The general attitude of the Scandinavian Governments was illustrated at this time by the correspondence arising out of the

---

(a) WP(40)59, N2271/9/56.   (b) WM(40)45.1, C.A., N2085/2/63.

rescue of British prisoners of war from the German ship *Altmark*. This auxiliary naval vessel of about 18,000 tons had served as a supply ship to the *Admiral Graf Spee* and had taken on board about 300 British seamen from merchant ships sunk by the *Graf Spee*. After the destruction of the latter ship, the *Altmark* attempted to reach Germany with the prisoners, but H.M.S. *Cossack* intercepted her in Norwegian waters. The captain of H.M.S. *Cossack*, according to instructions from the Admiralty, proposed that the *Altmark* should go to Bergen under a joint Anglo-Norwegian guard in order that the circumstances of her passage through Norwegian waters might be investigated. On February 16, after further proposals which did not get a satisfactory answer, a party from H.M.S. *Cossack* boarded the *Altmark*, and took off the prisoners.

The Norwegian Government protested against this action. His (a) Majesty's Government replied that they were justified in ordering the commander of H.M.S. *Cossack* to secure the release of the prisoners because the Norwegian Government had failed to compel the *Altmark* to observe the conditions under which the warships of belligerent Powers could enter and pass through neutral waters. The Norwegian Government refused to admit failure on their part and suggested on February 24 that the difference of opinion between the two Governments should be submitted to arbitration. His Majesty's Government would not agree to this proposal, but recorded their 'regret that they should have had no option but to adopt a course, which, although in their opinion fully justified by the circumstances, admittedly involved taking action in Norwegian territorial waters'.

The reports received by the Foreign Office from Stockholm during the second half of February showed that the Swedish Government were as determined as ever not to be drawn into the war through their own or Allied intervention in Finland. M. Wallenberg told Mr. Mallet on February 14 that the Swedes were not in the least con- (b) vinced that the Allies could help them if the Germans invaded or bombed Sweden. Sweden would merely become a shambles like Poland. Two days later Mr. Mallet reported an interview with M. Boheman. M. Boheman referred to rumours that the French (c) intended to send troops to Finland. He considered that if this plan were carried out, it would lead at once to German intervention, but that the Swedish and Norwegian Governments would refuse passage to troops from Narvik.

Mr. Mallet thought the Swedish Government were now much alarmed at the possibility of a Finnish collapse and were trying belatedly to prevent it. Their policy was (i) to avoid open war with

---

(a) W2906, 3369, 3389/2854/49.   (b) N1943/9/56.   (c) N2069/9/56.

Russia; (ii) to concentrate on a more rapid supply of Swedish volunteers and material; and (iii) to put every obstacle in the way of open intervention by the Allies, but to encourage them to supply the Finns with aircraft and war material.

Any hopes of a change in Swedish policy were checked by a declaration issued by the King of Sweden on February 19, after a

(a) press statement that Sweden had refused a Finnish request for military aid. The King regarded it as his 'imperative duty to make the utmost endeavour' to keep Sweden out of the war between the Great Powers. He had warned the Finnish Government 'from the very first' not to count on Swedish military intervention. If Sweden were to intervene in Finland, she might become involved in war with Russia and also in the war between the Great Powers. In such case she would probably not be able to continue to send volunteers or material to Finland.

(b) Mr. Mallet thought that this declaration did not rule out the possibility of passing Allied volunteers in large numbers through Sweden, but that, if we wanted Swedish consent to direct intervention, we should have to convince the Swedes that we could protect them against a combined Russo-German attack. As yet they were 'a very long way' from accepting our assurances. They also suspected our motives in trying to persuade them. The best way of getting their confidence was to go on supporting Finland by every means which the Scandinavian Governments would allow. Unless we could be sure of saving Finland, it would be unwise to do more than the Swedes themselves in providing help. At worst our failure would leave us in the same position as Sweden. Direct intervention on a large scale, involving the violation of Scandinavian neutrality, could be justified only by success. Otherwise we should lose all sympathy in Sweden and throw the Swedes into the arms of Germany.[1]

The misuse of Norwegian territorial waters by the German commander of the *Altmark* raised once again the question of Allied

(c) action against the Narvik traffic. M. Corbin told Lord Halifax on February 20 that, in the opinion of the French Government, the *Altmark* case gave the Allies a chance of refusing to recognise the inviolability of Norwegian waters. Two days later M. Corbin left

(d) at the Foreign Office a memorandum from the French Government suggesting that the Allies should declare their intention of protecting the neutrality of these waters since the Norwegians were unable to do so. The Norwegian Government would probably refuse

(e)   [1] Sir C. Dormer agreed with these views.

(a) N2120, 2381, 2383/9/56.   (b) N2229/2/63.   (c) N2185/7/63.   (d) N2266/2/63, WP(40)65. (e) N2536/9/56.

to admit the claim. We could then occupy the Norwegian ports and thereby show that we were in a position to help Sweden.

The Foreign Office doubted whether such action was advisable as long as there was the slightest chance of getting the Scandinavian Governments to agree to the passage of our troops through Narvik to Finland. The War Cabinet was also uncertain. On February 21 they (a) agreed to the drafting of a communication to the Norwegian Government pointing out that we had done everything possible to refrain from the violation of Norwegian territorial waters, but that their continued violation and abuse by Germany had brought about a situation which we could not accept. It was suggested that the statement should end in such a way as to leave it open to us to take action within a few days.

The War Cabinet considered this draft on February 23. They had (b) before them also a telegram from Lord Lothian. Lord Lothian thought that, although our explanation of the *Altmark* incident had been well received in the United States, further action, such as the laying of a minefield, in Norwegian territorial waters might meet with a less good reception and strengthen the growing sentiment for American neutral rights against high-handed British interference. The War Cabinet agreed to postpone a decision until early in the following week.

The delay in deciding about the Narvik plan did not in fact make any difference to the fate of the larger project. The increasing weight of the Russian attack on Finland and, with it, the increasing fears of the Swedish Government over the prospect of action which might involve them in war destroyed the remaining chances of getting Scandinavian consent to an expedition across Norwegian or Swedish territory.

Mr. Mallet[1] was told once again by M. Günther on February 23 (c) that Sweden could not send official help to Finland on a scale sufficient to save the Finns, and that, if she allowed the passage of Allied troops, she would become involved in war with Germany for which she was totally unprepared. Mr. Mallet and Mr. Macmillan thought that Sweden hoped for a 'Finnish Munich' which would give time for the Scandinavian States and the Allies to build up their strength against further German aggression. On February 26 (d) Mr. Mallet and Mr. Macmillan saw the Swedish Prime Minister. M. Hansson's attitude seemed to them 'rather defeatist'. He would

---

[1] Mr. Mallet was accompanied on these visits to M. Günther and M. Hansson, the Swedish Prime Minister, by Mr. H. Macmillan, M.P. Mr. Macmillan was returning from Finland.

(a) WM(40)48, N2267/7/63. (b) WM(40)50, N2319/7/63, WP(40)61, N2273, 2283/7/63. (c) N2331, 2514/9/56. (d) N2430/9/56.

not commit himself to the extent to which volunteers would be allowed passage through Sweden, although he did not object to the passage of small groups.

Meanwhile there were already signs of the end of Finnish powers of
(a) resistance. M. Maisky had told the Foreign Office on February 22 the terms on which Russia would be willing to make peace. These terms included the surrender of Sortavala, Viborg and the whole of the Karelian isthmus and the western half of the Ribachi peninsula, and a lease of Hangö. M. Maisky suggested that the British Government might communicate these terms to the Finns. He also spoke generally on the Russo-German trade agreement which had been signed on February 11.[1] He said that this agreement was limited to economic questions and that the Soviet Government did not intend to make a military alliance with Germany or to give up their neutrality unless they were attacked, or to invade Scandinavia.

The British Government refused officially to communicate the Russian terms to the Finns. The Foreign Office instructed Mr. Vereker,[2] British Minister at Helsinki, to mention M. Maisky's
(b) *démarche*, but to state the terms only if the Finnish Government asked for them, and then to give them only for information. The question did not arise because the Finnish President had already heard the terms from a Swedish source. Mr. Vereker explained to the Finnish Government on February 25 the Allied proposal for an appeal from Finland. The Finnish Ministers asked what would be the strength of the Allied contingents and when they would arrive. Mr. Vereker said that they would arrive in mid-April, and that they would be about 20,000 strong and well armed.[3]

M. Tanner went to Stockholm on the night of February 25 in order to enquire about the Swedish attitude to the proposed appeal.
(c) He came back on February 28 with the reply that the neutrality of the Swedish Government did not allow the passage of Allied troops through Sweden; permission would be given only to small groups of
(d) unarmed volunteers. Meanwhile the Finnish President had told Mr. Vereker that the Finns had to choose between accepting the Russian terms or making an appeal on the lines proposed to them by the Allies. It seemed clear, from M. Tanner's visit to Sweden, that they would not make an appeal unless they were sure of Scandinavian

---

[1] See below, p. 108.

[2] Mr. Vereker had succeeded Mr. Snow in this post. He arrived at Helsinki on February 24.

[3] The Foreign Office thought that Mr. Vereker's statement to the Finnish Prime Minister was somewhat misleading. They telegraphed to him on February 27 that the proposal was that the Allied contingents should concentrate in Finland between the middle and end of April, and that they would amount to between 12,000 and 13,000 well-armed men supported by considerable forces in Sweden.

(a) N2252, 2329/1/56.   (b) N2333/9/56; N2329/1/56.   (c) N2565, 2535, 2601/9/56. (d) N2424/1/56.

consent to the passage of Allied troops, but that they were sure that this passage would be refused.

The situation with which the Allies were now faced would in any case have been dangerous; it was much more disastrous owing to their own hesitancy and miscalculations. If from the start they had made it clear that, for geographical reasons alone, they could do nothing to save Finland, the collapse of Finnish resistance would have been a less serious blow to Allied prestige, and a less terrifying example to other European neutrals who were more favourably placed for receiving British and French help. There would also have been more likelihood of a rift between Germany and Russia.

As matters had turned out, the Allies had talked of their intention to save Finland, and had done little or nothing. They had shown their interest in the Swedish ore-fields, and were now unable to reach them. They had announced their intention of stopping the Narvik traffic, and the Narvik traffic was continuing without interference. Even at this stage, a more resolute leadership might have grasped the facts of the situation, withdrawn at once from the larger project, and taken immediate action against the Narvik traffic if it were clear that interference with this traffic would have a really serious effect upon German war industry.

It may be said that the position of the British Government was (a) more difficult because the French, for internal political reasons, were particularly concerned with the repercussions on French opinion of an Allied failure to save Finland. The French Government thus took the lead in trying to counter the effects of the Swedish refusal to allow passage to an Allied expedition. They instructed the French Minister at Helsinki to point out to the Finnish Government that if the Finnish appeal were to depend upon the previous consent of Norway and Sweden to the passage of Allied troops, the plan might break down. Norway and Sweden were known to fear the consequences to themselves of Allied intervention, and to hope that Finland would accept the Russian terms. Therefore they would try to prevent a Finnish appeal. On the other hand, if Finland were to make the appeal and to leave the Allies to discuss ways and means with the other Governments concerned, the responsibility for refusing the appeal and for the ruin of Finland would rest entirely upon Norway and Sweden. It would be difficult for these countries to accept public responsibility for opposing the immediate Allied help upon which the safety of Finland depended.

M. Corbin asked the Foreign Office on February 28 whether Mr. Vereker could support the French Minister. Instructions were

---

(a) N2537, 2497/9/56.

sent to Mr. Vereker accordingly, but with little hope that the Swedish Government could be moved to change their policy. The Foreign Office indeed were considering what should be done in the event of (a) a Scandinavian refusal. They were concerned primarily with the political rather than with the strategic aspect of the matter. They accepted the view of the Chiefs of Staff that we could certainly defend Norway, if not Sweden, against German retaliation. They realised the strength of the French arguments that a Finnish collapse would have serious political consequences for the Allies; one of the consequences, if we did nothing to prevent this collapse, would be a severe strain on Anglo-French relations. A suggestion was made in the Foreign Office—though not put forward to the War Cabinet— that we should send volunteers, unarmed and in civilian clothes, to Stavanger, Bergen, Trondhjem and Narvik. The Norwegian Government would be informed on the day before the arrival of the convoys in which the volunteers would sail. If the Norwegians fired on them or otherwise opposed their landing, we could say that they had prevented us from going to the help of the Finns and we could use the incident as an excuse for doing as we wished in Norwegian territorial waters, If, as appeared more likely, the volunteers were allowed to land, we could act as the Italians had done in Spain. On the whole, however, the view of the Foreign Office was that we should wait to see whether the Finns made an appeal. If the Finns made this appeal, and if we felt sure of carrying American and Italian opinion with us, we might then put our plan into effect by determined action which would enable the Scandinavian states to say that they could not stop us. If, on the other hand, it seemed clear that American and Italian opinion would not approve our action, and if we were not sure of success in the face of Scandinavian non-co-operation, we should be unable to carry out our plan, although we could clear ourselves morally of responsibility for the Finnish collapse.

(b)   On February 29 the War Cabinet again discussed the proposal for action in Norwegian territorial waters. After taking into account the views of the High Commissioners and Commonwealth Prime Ministers and of the Parliamentary opposition at home, they decided once again upon postponement. Their reasons were (i) the risk of prejudicing even the small chance that Norway and Sweden would grant the Allies passage through their territories, (ii) the likelihood that American reactions would be unfavourable, (iii) the loss of our own iron ore supplies from Narvik through German retaliation on Norway. The Prime Minister thought that nothing very formidable was to be feared from this retaliation, but that Norway

---

(a) N2813, 2595/9/56. (b) WM(40)55, N2607/7/63.

might cut off our supplies, and refuse to sign the impending War Trade Agreement or to allow us the use of Norwegian tankers.

Mr. Churchill was in favour of action. Our northern policy was petering out. The period of quiescence would not necessarily be prolonged by a decision not to lay mines in territorial waters; meanwhile it was dangerous to give the Germans an opportunity quietly to prepare and perfect their plans for large-scale operations.[1]

(ii)

Final refusal of the Scandinavian Governments to allow passage to an Allied expedition to Finland: the end of Finnish resistance (March 1–13, 1940).

During the period between March 1 and the Finnish acceptance of the Russian terms on the night of March 12–13 the Allies failed to persuade the Finns to make an appeal for help or the Scandinavian Governments to change their policy of refusing passage.

At the end of February the Allies had no certain information whether the Finns were intending to appeal to them. On the evening of February 28 the Finnish Minister in Paris thanked M. Daladier, (a) on behalf of the Finnish Prime Minister, for the Allied offer of help, and hoped that it could be accepted. At the same time the French Minister at Helsinki reported an interview with M. Tanner in which the latter had said that the Finns had no alternative to negotiations with Russia because they could look for very little Allied help. M. Daladier wanted to take the message of thanks as sufficient to allow us to begin diplomatic action in Scandinavia and thus to avoid responsibility in the event of a Finnish surrender.

The War Cabinet were unwilling to act on M. Daladier's view (b) without further enquiry. Mr. Vereker was instructed on the evening of February 29 to ask whether the Finnish Prime Minister's message (c) was intended to be the appeal for which we were asking, and whether the Finnish Government had appealed, or were about to appeal to the Scandinavian Governments to allow the Allies the right of passage. On this evening Mr. Mallet telegraphed from Sweden that (d) the majority of Swedes accepted the policy of the Government and were prepared to face criticism 'for much the same reasons as His Majesty's Government after Munich'. It would therefore be unwise to count upon an explosion of public feeling strong enough to force the hands of the Government. The Government could excuse their

---

[1] In view of the decision to postpone action, the proposed statement (see above, p. 87) was not communicated to the Scandinavian Governments.

(a) 2567/9/56.   (b) WM(40)55.6, C.A.   (c) N2647/9/65.   (d) N2602/9/56.

abandonment of the Finns by saying that the interests of the Allies in Finland were not purely altruistic.

(a) The Finnish Minister in London went to see Lord Halifax in the morning of March 1. He said that the military situation was very difficult, and that, in view of the Swedish refusal, there was little chance of getting Allied help. In any case, the Allied forces would not arrive in time, and appeared to be limited to 12,000 men. Hence the Finns had to consider whether they would open discussions with Russia.

(b) The War Cabinet met later in the morning. They agreed to tell the Scandinavian Governments that we were prepared to send forces to help Finland and to support Norway and Sweden if their attitude should lead to German aggression against them. After this meeting

(c) Lord Halifax again saw the Finnish Minister. M. Gripenberg now said that, according to messages from Helsinki, the military situation was such that the Finns had to decide within twenty-four hours whether they would discuss terms with Russia. The Finnish decision depended upon the prospects of immediate and extensive help from Great Britain. M. Gripenberg had been instructed to ask whether the Allies could send 100 bombers and their crews at once and 50,000 men to reach Finland in March, with reinforcements later, whether this force could fight anywhere in Finland, whether the British Government thought that they could persuade Norway and Sweden to allow passage to the Allied forces, and whether the refusal of passage would change Allied policy.

Lord Halifax pointed out that, owing to conditions of disembarkation and transport, it would be impossible to send 50,000 men to Finland in March. He could not say whether we should refuse the Finnish appeal if Norway and Sweden were unwilling to allow us passage. A certain measure of co-operation on their part was necessary—for example, on the railways.

(d) The War Cabinet met again on the evening of March 1 and discussed M. Gripenberg's questions. They also heard at this meeting that M. Daladier had told the Finnish Minister that the French

(e) Government would agree to all the Finnish requests and were prepared to override the objections of Norway and Sweden; that the French troops were ready and were awaiting British transports, and that he (M. Daladier) was considering whether he could spare more bombers and was urging the British Government to hasten the despatch of their forces.

The War Cabinet thought the French answers most disquieting. Their promises seemed to be bluff and to have been made in the knowledge that they could blame us for the failure to redeem them.

<hr/>

(a) N2623/9/56. (b) WM(40)56.1,C.A. (c) N2648, 2645, 2639/9/56. (d) WM(40)57, C.A. (e) N2655/9/56.

We could neither spare the bombers nor transport 50,000 men to Finland in March. If Allied troops operated in the south of Finland, they could be cut off by the Germans in the Gulf of Bothnia after the melting of the ice. We should therefore need more than 20,000 men to hold our line of communications. It was therefore impossible to meet the Finnish requests.

After discussing the matter at length the War Cabinet decided to explain to the Finnish Government that the limiting factor in our offer was the transport facilities in Scandinavia; that the despatch of Allied forces would mean that the British Empire and France were wholeheartedly behind the Finns and would do everything in their power to support them; and that we had approached Norway and Sweden. It was thought that a message in these terms would be more encouraging than a detailed reply to the Finnish requests, since such a reply would be a refusal. The message was sent to Mr. Vereker (a) during the night of March 1–2. At the same time the Foreign Office instructed Mr. Mallet and Sir C. Dormer to approach the Scandin- (b) avian Governments with a statement of our intention to ask for passage and an offer of assistance if this grant involved them in war with Germany.

The replies of the Scandinavian Governments were known during the night of March 2–3. M. Koht would not commit himself. He said (c) that he must consult the Swedish Government, and also that the consent of the Storting was necessary for the passage of foreign troops across Norwegian territory. It was, however, clear that this answer was really a refusal. The refusal was given officially to Sir C. Dormer on March 4. The grounds were that a grant of passage would be (d) incompatible with Norwegian neutrality and would involve Norway in war with Germany and Russia.

M. Günther's answer to Mr. Mallet was that the Swedish Govern- (e) ment would not agree to the passage of troops, but that he must consult the Swedish Cabinet and the King of Sweden before giving a considered answer. M. Günther was sure that the Allies could not send adequate help. He also implied 'very politely' that we were more interested in using Scandinavia as a battleground for 'our war' with Germany than in saving Finland. Mr. Mallet replied that 'our war' was of vital interest to Sweden. M. Günther's answer was that he did not think it in Swedish interests that the Germans should be utterly defeated, since the result would be a Communist Germany too weak to act as a counterpoise in Eastern Europe to a strong Russia. The danger to Sweden from Russia would then be worse than the danger from Germany in the event of a German victory.

(a) N2648/9/56. (b) N2435/9/56. (c) N2654/9/56. (d) N2725, 2812/9/56. (e) N2666, 2872, 2810/9/56.

M. Günther said that he had been 'considering the hope' of an early peace settlement which would save Finnish independence, although the Finns would have to give up Hangö and probably Viborg. Mr. Mallet said that these terms would mean ruin for Finland. M. Günther considered this to be better than allowing the Allies to turn the whole of Scandinavia into a battlefield. In the
(a) afternoon of March 3 Mr. Mallet was asked to call on M. Boheman. M. Boheman then stated, orally and officially, that the Swedish Government would neither allow the passage of Allied troops through Swedish territory nor hold staff talks.

Mr. Vereker had carried out on March 2 the instructions sent to
(b) him to support the French Minister in representations to the Finnish Government not to make their appeal dependent upon previous Scandinavian consent to right of passage. He thought that the Finnish Government might agree, but that they were uncertain whether to throw in their lot with the Allies. On the night of
(c) March 3–4 he reported the Finnish reply to the answer which he had been instructed to give to their questions. The Finnish Ministers again asked for 100 bombers at once. Mr. Vereker suspected that they were trying to gain time in relation to their negotiations with Russia and also to learn the Scandinavian reactions to our proposals.
(d) The War Cabinet agreed on March 4 that they could not decide to send more bombers to Finland unless they knew whether the Finnish Government intended to make an appeal. They also agreed that, in the event of an appeal, Norway and Sweden should be asked what they would do if we sent an expedition in spite of their refusal to grant us passage, and what they proposed to do themselves in response to the Finnish appeal.
M. Daladier still wanted to tell the Scandinavian Governments
(e) that we intended to carry out our plans whatever their attitude might be. The French views were set out in notes which M. Corbin brought to the Foreign Office on March 4 and 5. M. Daladier also spoke very strongly to Sir. R. Campbell. He thought that too much attention should not be paid to military objections. 'War involved risks' and, if we let Finland go today, the turn of Roumania would come tomorrow, and, probably after Roumania, Turkey. The psychological effect upon the neutrals of the Finnish collapse would be disastrous. Italy would be likely to turn to Germany; the U.S.S.R. would be free to develop military and economic collaboration with Germany and to take joint action with her in the Balkans. The Allies would lose the chance of cutting off German ore supplies from

---

(a) N2667, 2811/9/56. (b) N2651, 2652/9/56. (c) N2690/9/56. (d) WM(40)59.6, C.A.
(e) N2728, 2754, 2815/9/56.

Sweden or oil supplies from the Caucasus. The French did not regard the Scandinavian answers as refusals. The Scandinavian Governments were too afraid of Germany to consent openly, but they appeared ready to tolerate our passage if their responsibility were not publicly involved.

The Foreign Office were less hopeful about the question of passage. Sir R. Campbell was instructed on March 6 to tell M. Daladier that we agreed upon another approach to Norway and Sweden if the Finns appealed to us, but we could not act in the event even of passive resistance to our passage, since we depended upon the use of the Scandinavian railways. It was true that we should lose prestige if Finland collapsed owing to lack of help from us; the loss of prestige would be greater if we landed in Scandinavia and were unable to advance.

The Foreign Office also considered that, unless we could give an (a) answer to the Finnish demand for more bombers—this demand was repeated on March 6—we should not go on arguing with the Finns about an appeal. In any case, since we had no hope of obtaining Scandinavian consent to our passage, was it in our interest to get a Finnish appeal?

The War Cabinet again postponed a decision about the bombers. (b) Mr. Vereker continued to think that the Finns would not appeal. On the morning of March 7 Mr. Vereker reported that the Finnish (c) Government had received from Russia proposals for peace. The discussion of the terms would take a long time: the Finnish Government therefore wanted to know whether they could postpone until March 12 their decision about an appeal. They also asked again for 100 bombers.

The War Cabinet met on March 7 before the receipt of this report, (d) but Lord Halifax had already heard the facts from M. Corbin[1]. The (e) War Cabinet now decided in favour of sending up to 50 bombers, and of asking the Finns for an answer about the appeal within a specified time. The Chiefs of Staff Committee also met on March 7 to consider the question of assistance. They summed up their views in a report (f) which the War Cabinet discussed on March 8. The report stated that our original plan was to cut off German supplies of ore. For this purpose we were prepared to risk war with Russia and to weaken our forces on the western front. The arrangements for carrying out the plan were complete, but we needed an appeal from Finland and the co-operation of Norway and Sweden. We could now send 50 bombers to Finland as a bargain in exchange for an appeal or merely to keep up Finnish resistance. From a military

---

[1] The information had reached the French Government through the French Minister at Helsinki.

(a) N2895, 2830, 2753/9/56.   (b) WM(40)61.5, C.A.   (c) N2830, 2847/9/56.
(d) WM(40)62.7, C.A.   (e) N2893/9/56.   (f) N2891/9/56, WP(40)86.

point of view every effort should be made to go ahead with the Scandinavian expedition, since it would give us a chance—which might not recur—of seizing the initiative from Germany and depriving her of important raw materials. If we could be sure that we should be able to send our expedition across Scandinavia, the despatch of the bombers would be worth while, but, apart from the chance of getting our expedition to Gällivare, the maintenance of Finnish resistance offered only the military advantage that Russian resources would not be available to Germany. If, however, we were not established in Scandinavia and Finland,[1] the Germans could stop the Finnish war at any time after the Gulf of Bothnia had become ice-free. Hence the Chiefs of Staff did not favour sending bombers merely to keep up Finnish resistance.

The Finnish Minister in London brought a message to the Foreign
(a) Office in the afternoon of March 7 that the Finnish Government expected to hear the Russian terms within a few days. They did not suppose that these terms would be acceptable, but they must postpone their appeal until March 12. Meanwhile they hoped that
(b) the Allies would continue their preparations. The War Cabinet, after reviewing the situation again on March 8, agreed to tell the Finnish Government that they must decide upon an appeal before March 12, that, if they made an appeal, we would send 50 bombers,[2] that Scandinavian opposition or even failure to co-operate with us might prevent us from sending the expeditionary force which we had prepared, but that we would put all possible pressure on the Scandinavian Governments to secure their co-operation. A message
(c) to this effect was sent to Mr. Vereker on the evening of March 8. On this same evening the Foreign Office heard that a Finnish delegation had started for Moscow in order to discuss peace terms. Mr. Vereker was therefore told to ensure that the message sent to him reached Field-Marshal Mannerheim and the Finnish delegation in Moscow as well as the Finnish Government.

No further news of importance was received on March 9. On
(d) March 10 M. Gripenberg gave to the Prime Minister and Lord Halifax a message from the Finnish Government suggesting a public

---

[1] There was at this time no change in the Swedish and Norwegian attitude. Mr. Mallet reported, however, that details of his representations—including proposals for staff talks and for securing the Norwegian ports—were publicly known. The Belgian Minister knew
(e) the plans very accurately and had probably heard of them from M. Boheman. A leading newspaper editor had told a member of the British Legation staff that we proposed to land troops at Trondhjem and Stavanger on March 11, and the Swedish press, under official inspiration, was pointing out that the Allies had an interest in the prolongation of the Finnish war irrespective of the interests of Finland or Sweden.

[2] Mr. Vereker was told that eight could be sent on the fourth day after the decision to send them, and the remainder within the following ten days. In order to avoid delay arrangements for despatching the aircraft were put in hand at once, so that the first eight could have been despatched on the first suitable day after March 11.

(a) N2976/9/56. (b) WM(40)63.4, C.A. (c) N2994, 2936/9/56. (d) N3047/9/56.
(e) N2832, 2962/9/56.

announcement of the Allied decision to make the fullest response to an appeal for help from Finland. The Finnish Government thought that this announcement would strengthen them in their negotiations with the Russians and would also hearten their army. M. Gripenberg once again asked whether a few bombers could be flown to Finland immediately.

In the afternoon of March 10 the Foreign Office heard from Mr. Vereker of the delivery of the message sent to him on the evening (a) of March 8. M. Tanner had told him and the French Minister that the Finnish delegation had met the Russians on March 8. The Russian terms were 'far-reaching and oppressive', but did not involve Russian interference in the foreign policy or internal affairs of Finland. M. Tanner said that the Finnish Government would certainly come to a decision by March 12 about an appeal. Meanwhile he hoped that the Allies would continue their military preparations. 'There was no armistice, and the Finnish army was full of fight and not yet defeated.'

The French Government were most anxious that we should send (b) some bombers at once, and that, if we received an appeal from Finland, our expedition should start even though Norway and Sweden had refused us passage. M. Corbin repeated to the Foreign Office on March 11 the French view that the British answers had been unnecessarily discouraging to the Finns. He was told, in reply, that we thought it unfair to hold out false hopes to the Finns and that the French seemed to have made promises—even to the extent of a force of 200,000 men—which they could not fulfil. M. Corbin said that, if nothing were done to save Finland, M. Daladier would be compelled to resign.

The time for discussion was now running short both for the Finns and the Allies. On March 11 the War Cabinet agreed that they (c) would make known their decision to respond to a Finnish appeal,[1] and that they would send eight bombers at once and continue preparations for sending 42 others. They also considered the question of sending our expedition in spite of the refusal of right of passage. The Prime Minister thought that we ought not to abandon the expedition merely because we had received this diplomatic refusal. The War Cabinet asked the Chiefs of Staff to report on the desirability of landing at Trondhjem, Bergen and Stavanger as well as at Narvik.

---

[1] The announcement took the form of an answer to a parliamentary question on March 11. The Prime Minister stated that His Majesty's Government and the French Government had informed the Finnish Government that, in response to an appeal from them for further aid, they were prepared to proceed immediately and jointly to the help of Finland, using all available resources at their disposal.

(a) N3022/1/56. (b) N3045, 3131/9/56. (c) WM(40)65.6, C.A.

(a)   Meanwhile on March 10 Sir C. Dormer and Mr. Mallet had been asked what, in their opinion, the Scandinavian States would do if we continued our plan, i.e. would they try to obstruct our entry into a Norwegian port, or would they oppose our landing? Or would they try to make railway transport unusable, and would such steps be effective? Or again, would Scandinavian public opinion be strong enough to prevent the Governments from resisting us?

(b)   Sir C. Dormer replied on the night of March 11–12 that he did not expect serious obstruction or resistance, but that the railway line (from Narvik) could easily be wrecked by sabotage.[1] Mr. Mallet thought that the Swedes would not resist us by force, but that they were likely to make railway transit very difficult. If the Russo-Finnish peace negotiations failed, the action of the Swedish Government would depend upon the opinion of the Swedish people whether the Finns were right in refusing the Russian terms. The Swedish Government might defend themselves by quoting the British, and more particularly, the French press as evidence that the Allies were not in earnest about Finland and cared only about bringing Scandinavia into the war against Germany owing to the iron ore position. If, however, the Swedish public strongly approved of a Finnish decision to go on fighting, the Government might think it safe to send 2–3 divisions into Finland and ask the Allies to remain in the background in order to send help, if necessary, through Petsamo. M. Boheman had told Mr. Mallet on March 11 that the Swedes had been warned in Berlin that, if they allowed passage to any Allied formations, they would at once get a declaration of war from Germany. In spite of anti-Russian feeling, most Swedes approved of the policy of neutrality towards Germany. Hence the Government could not agree to, or facilitate, our passage. Moreover, the Swedish army was 'alarmingly unprepared' for war.

Before these answers had been received in London, Mr. Vereker
(c)   telegraphed (March 11) a message from the Finnish Government asking the Allies to make another appeal to the Scandinavian Governments to allow passage to an expedition to Finland. Sir C. Dormer and Mr. Mallet were instructed to put this request immediately.[2] Sir C. Dormer was unable to see M. Koht, but left

---

[1] Mr. Mallet reported on March 12 that a War Office transportation expert who had visited Stockholm gave the impression that he foresaw difficulties in maintaining a force in
(d)   Finland. The line in the Lulea-Boden 'bottleneck' was heavily overloaded, and resolute enemy air action could reduce traffic 'to a mere trickle'. All the railways from Norway to Sweden could be sabotaged.

[2] After these instructions had been sent, M. Corbin told the Foreign Office that the French Government were unwilling to agree to the appeal because they thought it a
(e)   Finnish manoeuvre intended to provide arguments for the party in favour of surrender. The War Cabinet decided on March 12 to cancel the instructions, but Sir C. Dormer and Mr. Mallet had already acted on them.

(a) N3025/9/56.   (b) N3106, 3118/9/56.   (c) N3053, 3058/9/56.   (d) N3107/9/56.
(e) WM(40)66.2, C.A.

a note with the Secretary-General of the Norwegian Foreign Office. (a)
Mr. Mallet saw M. Günther, and found him bewildered at the
appeal because he thought that the Russo-Finnish negotiations were
on the point of succeeding. He had told the Finnish Government
'ten times' that Sweden would not allow passage to the Allies. He
thought that the Finnish Government had made the appeal merely
to save their faces with their own people. Mr. Vereker's reports
on March 11, however, were that, according to the General Staff, (b)
the Russian terms were unacceptable, and would probably be
rejected on March 12. The Finnish Government would probably
then make their appeal.

On March 12 the War Cabinet decided that a landing should be (c)
made at first only at Narvik and that we should not attempt to land
at Trondhjem until we knew the result of the operations at Narvik.
The forces for Stavanger and Bergen should be held in readiness but
not actually sent. Mr. Vereker was told at 12.30 p.m. to hint con-
fidentially to the Finnish Government that, even if the Scandinavian
refusals were maintained, we should not abandon our plans for giving
rapid effect to a Finnish appeal for the despatch of troops.

On the night of March 12–13 Mr. Vereker telegraphed that the (d)
Finnish Government had not yet decided whether to make their
appeal. Mr. Vereker had asked for a decision by midnight. He
thought, however, that the Finns were sure that, even if immediate
passage were granted by Norway and Sweden, the Allies could not
arrive in time to save the south of Finland.

The Finnish Government could indeed have no hope that Allied
assistance would reach them in time; Field-Marshal Mannerheim,
who had directed their defence with great courage and skill, advised
them to accept the Russian terms. On the morning of March 13 Mr. (e)
Vereker was told that armistice terms had been signed on the
previous night and would come into force at 11 a.m. M. Tanner
apologised to Mr. Vereker and the French Minister for the trouble
caused to the Allies in the preparation of an expeditionary force. He
said that unfortunately the Finns could make no use of our offer of
help. Their army was exhausted and short of officers, and would have
been compelled within a fortnight to withdraw and to leave Helsinki
open to the Russians. The Finns could not have held out for 4–5
weeks while Allied help was arriving. In any case, the attitude of
Norway and Sweden would have prevented the passage of Allied
troops.

(a) N3122, 3097/9/56. (b) N3054, 3066/9/56. (c) WM(40)66.2, C.A. (d) N3119/9/56.
(e) N3156, 3195/1/56.

(iii)

French proposals for action in Scandinavia and in the Caucasus: consideration of the general position, March 27, 1940.

(a)   From the point of view of the Allies, one of the most serious results of the collapse of Finland was the depressing effect upon French morale. The Foreign Office fully realised this fact; they had received warning from French sources that the failure to seize the initiative would mean a strengthening of the movement in favour of a compromise peace. The French attitude might seem unreasonable, but French public opinion had been more uneasy than opinion in Great Britain over the inaction of the first six months of war. We had been creating and equipping an army; the French had a large army in the field, but had no results to show except continuing economic dislocation.

The Foreign Office also understood the tendency of the French Government to suggest operations in areas away from the western front. They now expected the French to press for a change in our Balkan policy. It was, however, impossible to take the initiative in the present state of Allied resources; action against the Gällivare orefields would be more likely to drive Norway and Sweden to the

(b) German side. Sir R. Campbell was therefore instructed on March 14 to tell the French Government that we should now disperse the force collected for the Scandinavian expedition.

The French Government, however, were not prepared to give up the plan. On March 15 M. Corbin brought a note to the Foreign

(c) Office suggesting that we should carry out the proposed minelaying in Norwegian territorial waters, and take advantage of the probable German reaction to put into effect our larger project of obtaining control of the ore-fields. The Foreign Office did not support the French proposal. It seemed useless to offer help to the Scandinavian states in the event of further Russian aggression. Norway and Sweden were too much afraid of Germany to accept our help. We could, however, make these countries realise that in certain circumstances they might find themselves in direct conflict with Great Britain or France. We should say that we should consider as an unfriendly act any political agreement which the Scandinavian states might make with Germany and we should tell them that a Russian attempt to obtain an Atlantic port or an increase in the supply of iron ore to

---

(a) N3064/9/56; N3616/2/63, C4408/9/17.   (b) WM(40)66.4, C.A., N3259/9/56.
(c) N3333/2/63.

Germany and a decrease in the supply to us would be against our vital interests.

The War Cabinet considered the French note on March 19. They (a) agreed that the French proposals were impracticable, but thought that we might send notes to the Scandinavian Governments on the lines suggested by the Foreign Office. They considered the possibility of action elsewhere. Lord Halifax referred to the project of bombing the Caucasian oilfields,[1] and thus cutting off German oil supplies from Russia, and preventing any further Russian offensive action. It was, however, uncertain whether we could carry out a plan of this kind successfully without committing ourselves to an expedition to the Black Sea and Baku. Similarly we could do nothing in the Balkans until we and the Turks were more prepared. The most promising line of attack was therefore the plan for dropping mines into German inland waterways.[2]

In view of the political situation in France—where a change of administration was likely—the War Cabinet decided not to send a written answer to the French Government, but to tell M. Corbin orally that we were opposed to action in Norwegian territorial waters, and that we suggested a meeting of the Supreme War Council to consider the general situation. This meeting was delayed owing to the resignation of M. Daladier's Government on March 20. On March 21 M. Reynaud formed a new administration in which he took the Ministry of Foreign Affairs and M. Daladier was Minister of War and Defence.[3]

On the night of March 25–6 M. Reynaud sent to the British Embassy in Paris a memorandum, signed by himself, on the future (b)

---

[1] See below, pp. 104, 108, 111–13.

[2] This plan (suggested by Mr. Churchill) was to float mines into the Rhine from the French bank, and also drop them from the air into the Rhine and other rivers. For reasons of secrecy the plan was described as the 'Royal Marine Operation'. The plan had already been mentioned to the French Government; they had not approved of it since they thought that it would lead to retaliation against French factories. It is doubtful whether the plan, although it was an ingenious reply to the German attacks on British seaborne traffic, could ever have caused more than minor interference with the German transport system. The fact that it came to considerable prominence in Allied discussions was due mainly to Mr. Churchill's desire (in contrast with the passivity of his colleagues) to do something, even if it were only of a harassing kind, which would give the impression of an Allied initiative. The reluctance of the French Ministers to accept even a small measure which might provoke retaliation, while at the same time they were ready to risk war with the U.S.S.R., again illustrates their deep anxiety to keep the fighting away from the borders of France. German bombing of French factories might have done much damage, but the drain upon French resources would have been far greater if the French had added Russia to their enemies. Moreover, the behaviour of the Germans at sea had shown that, if they considered it worth while to begin the bombing of war factories, they would do so without waiting for an excuse.

[3] For Sir R. Campbell's views on the political situation in France at this time, see below, Chapter VII, section (iii).

(a) WM(40)72, C4256/5/18. (b) C4615/1101/17. WP(40)109.

conduct of the war. M. Reynaud repeated the considerations already put forward with regard to the Finnish collapse, and proposed once again immediate action in Norwegian territorial waters, with the probable consequence of German retaliation which would give the allies an opportunity to take control of the ore-fields. M. Reynaud also suggested that we might cut off Russian oil supplies to Germany by bombing the Caucasian oil centres and thereby paralysing the economy of the U.S.S.R. before Germany had time to mobilise it to her advantage. Since action against the oil centres could not be undertaken at once, M. Reynaud proposed the immediate despatch of Allied submarines to the Black Sea.

(a)   On March 27 the War Cabinet met to consider the policy which the British representatives should recommend to the Supreme War Council. They had before them memoranda from the Foreign Office on the questions of Scandinavia and of south-east Europe. They also had M. Reynaud's memorandum, but there had not been time for detailed consideration of it by the Foreign Office or the Chiefs of Staff.

(b)   The first of the two Foreign Office memoranda contained a draft reply to the French note of March 15. It pointed out that, although we agreed with the French desire for vigorous action to re-assert Allied authority after the 'grave check' resulting from the Russo-Finnish treaty, the proposed action in Norwegian territorial waters would be justified only if the results were commensurate with the criticism which we should receive from neutrals, and especially from the United States, and with the effects of German counter-action. It was doubtful whether German violations of Norwegian territorial waters were sufficiently numerous, recent, and well-authenticated to justify retaliation on our part. Furthermore, our action would have only a limited effect since Lulea would soon be open to traffic. On the other hand, we considered that the time had come for a change in the policy of the Allies towards Norway and Sweden. Hitherto this policy had assumed Norway and Sweden to be free agents, ready to exercise a benevolent neutrality towards the Allies. We had now seen their subservience to Germany, and would therefore be compelled to take special precautions for the defence of our vital interests and requirements. The memorandum then continued with a draft note of warning[1] to be communicated to the Norwegian and Swedish Governments, and suggested that meanwhile we should not announce the dispersal of the expeditionary force intended for Finland; we should thus give the impression that the force was being kept to

---

[1] The terms of this draft were almost identical with the text adopted at the meeting of the Supreme War Council on March 28. See below, pp. 111–12.

(a) WM(40)76, N3688/2/63. (b) WP(40)107, N3617/2/63.

enable us to protect our interests in Scandinavia at a moment's notice. Vigorous action against neutrals would be ineffective unless we also took direct action against Germany. Hence we proposed to ask the French to give further consideration to the British plan for dropping mines in German inland waterways.

The memorandum on south-east Europe pointed out that the (a) attempts to secure a neutral *bloc* in the Balkans had not been altogether unsuccessful. Hungary and Bulgaria had not joined Germany, and were not convinced of a German victory. They were, however, equally uncertain of an Allied victory, and the Russian successes in Finland would increase their doubts. We should therefore find it hard in the next few months to maintain the ground we had gained if we did not win any military successes, and our prestige would fall in the event of a reverse such as a German invasion of the Netherlands.

The main objective of the Balkan countries was to keep out of the war and to maintain their independence. No other considerations were of comparable importance to them; only Hungary and Bulgaria wanted to gain territory. Hence, unless our military actions in the Balkans were effective and decisive, we should merely lose the sympathy of the Balkan states, since we should be bringing on them a German occupation. In any case our action must depend, as hitherto, on securing the benevolent neutrality of Italy, the active support of Turkey, and at least the consent of Greece. Italy appeared to be less inclined to remain neutral. We could not expect Turkey to fight unless vital Turkish interests were in danger. Greece needed arms and Greek policy would probably be determined by the chances of an early victory. It was thus not to our interest to initiate action until we could intervene in strength.

On the enemy side the Germans, apart from their interest in keeping Russia out of the Straits, were concerned with south-east Europe mainly from the point of view of supplies, and especially of oil. They could put pressure on Roumania, with Russian collusion, and also through Bulgaria; hence, probably, the rumours of a guarantee of the Balkan states by Russia, Germany and Italy. Such a guarantee would provide a basis for Italo-Russian collaboration and might be accepted by the Balkan states. Their acceptance would be very dangerous for us, since it would be not merely a diplomatic defeat but would go far to nullify our blockade. It was difficult to see how we could secure the rejection of an offer of this kind by the Balkan states. Our main hopes were in the increase of our own strength, and in bringing Turkey into close relations with the Balkan states, so that she could form a rallying-point between these States and the Allies.

(a) WP(40)110, R3856/5/67.

(a)   In the discussion of this memorandum Lord Halifax thought it important for our prestige that we should 'show the flag'. He suggested that it might be desirable for him to pay a visit to Turkey. The War Cabinet agreed with this proposal, and considered that Lord Halifax might possibly extend his visit to the Balkan countries and also to Rome. Meanwhile our attitude to the French proposals about the Black Sea and the Caucasus would be to ask how the proposals could be carried out and to say that we would be willing to prepare plans but could not commit ourselves to them.

The War Cabinet did not discuss further these French proposals
(b) for action against Russian oil supplies. A memorandum on the general aspects of the question had been prepared by a member of the Foreign Office staff. The view taken in the draft was that, on balance, the advantages of bombing the Caucasian oilfields appeared to out-weigh the disadvantages if we could be sure that the operation would have a decisive effect on the Soviet economy and thus avert the danger of an increase in Russian oil supplies to Germany.

This draft was shown to the Prime Minister (with a note that it was not a 'final conclusion') but was not circulated to the War Cabinet because Lord Halifax considered that it was too optimistic in its view of the decisive results which would follow from the operation and that it also overrated the arguments in favour of taking action against the U.S.S.R. Lord Halifax thought that more information was needed before even a tentative decision could be reached in the matter. He also wished to avoid any action which would antagonise Turkey, and considered that the Turkish Government would not join in or give facilities for an attack on Baku. Sir H. Knatchbull-
(c) Hugessen was asked on March 25 for an estimate of the probable Turkish reaction to an attack on Baku if it were not made from
(d) Turkish territory. He replied on March 27 that in his opinion the Turkish Government would not join in or give facilities for such an attack, but that they would probably be willing to allow and even to participate in an attack when Turkey was more prepared for war.

The British Ministers thus went to the meeting of the Supreme War Council with a less optimistic view than their French colleagues about the possibility of taking the initiative in any new field of attack against Germany. Although they realised the possibility of closer Russo-German co-operation, with serious consequences, in particular, upon the effectiveness of the Allied blockade, they were much more doubtful than the French about the advisability of an offensive measure which would bring Russia into the war on the German side. On the other hand, they viewed the general situation of the Allies

---

(a) WM(40)76, R3942/5/67.   (b) N3698/40/38.   (c) N3588/40/38.   (d) N3619/40/38.

with less disquiet than the French. Their 'overall view' was summed up in a memorandum drawn up by the Chiefs of Staff and submitted to the War Cabinet on March 27. This memorandum began (a) by pointing out that, in the event of a war against Germany and Italy, we had known that we should have to remain on the defensive, except at sea and in the economic sphere, while we were building up our resources. This phase would be a long one, but we had felt that time was on our side. The War Cabinet had decided at the outbreak of war that our programme should be based on the assumption that the war might last for three years.

The Germans had not yet launched a major land or air offensive and had given us a valuable and unexpected breathing space in which to make good some of our many deficiencies. We were, however, still far short of our essential requirements, even for defence, and we could assume that the Germans were also taking advantage of the period of military inactivity and that, if this period continued, they might be able to exploit Russian resources. Except in the invasion of Poland, the direction of the war by the German High Command had not been impressive and had not shown a determination to force a quick decision. The German attacks at sea and in the air appeared to aim at cheap and spectacular successes. They had thrown away the surprise value of the magnetic mine by using it prematurely on a very small scale. Their failure to attack our destroyers on their return from the *Altmark* affair suggested a lack of co-ordination and a weakness in countering a surprise situation. Hence we might secure far-reaching results by enterprises on our part which would mystify the Germans, play on their nerves, and prevent them from organising at leisure.

At sea we had the measure of the submarine campaign, and need not expect that, even with an increase in the number of submarines, our communications would be in serious danger. Similarly we were getting the better of the German minelaying. An intensified air attack on our shipping in home waters, and possibly our ports, was a very grave danger, and might force us to divert shipping to our western harbours.

On the other side of the balance our blockade was already aggravating German economic difficulties, but we had not a satisfactory control of Italian imports or exports. We had no control of trade across the Black Sea and in the Far East could only detain a few ships bound for Vladivostok. There was a possibility that in 1941 German exploitation of Russian resources, especially of oil, might largely nullify our blockade. The Chiefs of Staff stated that they were examining this question; they considered that in any case Allied diplomacy should aim at dissolving the Russo-German coalition and at creating a situation in Turkey which would enable us, if necessary,

(a) WP(40)111, R4666/5/67.

to go to war effectively with Russia. The Chiefs of Staff did not suggest how either of these diplomatic aims could be realised.

The memorandum then considered the air position, and pointed out that we should be unwise to take the initiative in undertaking an air offensive on a large scale. Our air forces overseas were also not strong enough to allow us to carry out operations on a serious scale.

Similarly we could not open an offensive on the western front in 1940, though, taking into account the French frontier fortifications, the Allied forces now in the field ought to be capable of stopping a German offensive against France. Elsewhere the Germans would have sufficient forces for a two-front war, although it was doubtful whether their railway system in its present condition would allow the transfer of large forces from the west to the south-east of Europe. The Chiefs of Staff then called attention again to the importance of Turkey, especially in view of the difficulty of attacking at the source Russian oil supplies unless we had Turkish collaboration.

The Chiefs of Staff considered, as before, that the entry of Italy into the war would be a serious embarrassment to us. The Italian army was worth little, but Italian action at sea and in the air might compel us temporarily to withdraw naval units from the North Sea and to use the Cape route for our merchant shipping.

In conclusion the Chiefs of Staff gave a warning that time was on our side only if we took the greatest advantage of it to build up our resources. In view of the close Russo-German collaboration we ought to pass to the offensive as soon after 1940 as possible. Meanwhile we should resist pressure to undertake operations which would use up our resources without bringing decisive success.

(iv)

Anglo-Russian relations during the Finnish war: Sir S. Cripps's visit to Moscow: Russian proposals for trade talks, March 27: sixth meeting of the Supreme War Council, March 28, and acceptance by the War Cabinet of proposals for action against the Narvik traffic involving, in the event of German action, the occupation of certain Norwegian ports, March 29–April 2, 1940.

Although the draft reply to the French memorandum did not refer to the French proposals of March 25 for operations against Russian oilfields in the Caucasus, the War Cabinet had in fact been considering the general question of Anglo-Russian relations. Throughout the Finnish war these relations were near to breaking point. Sir W.

Seeds left Moscow on leave at the end of 1939 and did not go back. His Majesty's Government were represented by a chargé d'affaires until the appointment of Sir S. Cripps as Ambassador in June 1940. M. Maisky remained in London, but after Lord Halifax's conversation with him on November 27, and until the third week of February 1940, there appear to have been only two important exchanges of a general political kind between British and Russian official representatives.

The first of these interviews took place on December 31, 1939, when Sir W. Seeds paid a farewell call on M. Molotov. Sir W. Seeds (a) said that, after the breakdown of the Anglo-Soviet negotiations, he had been prepared for strict neutrality on the part of the U.S.S.R., but that he had been 'distressed by the ever-increasing attacks in the press and speeches in spite of attempts made by His Majesty's Government to show good-will'. He asked whether M. Molotov could give him a message to Lord Halifax which might relieve the tension. M. Molotov, 'after claiming that the Soviet Union was the greater sufferer by a hostile press and speeches . . . could only say that his Government bore no enmity to Great Britain, but was convinced by our acts all over the world that His Majesty's Government was unfriendly to Russia'. M. Molotov complained that Great Britain had encouraged Finnish hostility and was supplying Finland with munitions. Sir W. Seeds pointed out that Russia was supplying Germany; M. Molotov answered that Russian supplies to Germany were 'only in pursuance of a commercial agreement'. He refused to accept Sir W. Seed's statement that the initiative in excluding Russia from the League was not Anglo-French, and that we had tried to meet Russian wishes in our treaty with Turkey.

The second conversation took place on January 30 between (b) Mr. R. A. Butler and M. Maisky. After complaining about the detention of a Russian ship in Far Eastern waters,[1] M. Maisky talked generally about Anglo-Soviet relations. Mr. Butler said that the Finnish war, following the Russo-German agreement, was bound to put a strain on these relations. M. Maisky spoke of the importance of isolating 'sources of difference'. At the beginning of the Spanish Civil War he had agreed with Mr. Eden 'to put the war into a compartment by itself, but otherwise to try to maintain the necessary contacts between Great Britain and the Soviet Union'. He hoped

---

[1] This ship, S.S. *Selenga*, carrying a cargo of wolfram, was stopped off Formosa by a British warship on January 13, 1940. M. Maisky said that the cargo was for the use of the Soviet Government. On December 10 the Soviet Government had protested against the British decision to seize German exports carried in neutral ships and to compel vessels with cargoes from ports or states to which Germany had access to go to British or French ports for examination.

(a) N40/40/38. (b) N1390/30/38.

that we might treat the Finnish war in the same way. 'We might object to what the Soviet Government were doing in Finland and might even help the Finns; but we must not be too spectacular, and on the rest of the front both sides must try to maintain their diplomatic relations.' There was 'nothing sentimental in the German-Soviet *rapprochement*'. The Soviet Government intended to keep their hands free and to pursue only Soviet interests. Mr. Butler asked whether recent messages from the Soviet Government supported this view. M. Maisky reported that the Soviet Government would be actuated entirely by their own interests, adding that we lived in a period of change, that anything might happen, and that in the jungle the strangest of animals got together if they felt their joint interests made this advisable.

On February 11 the Soviet Government signed an economic agreement with Germany. This agreement provided for the exchange of Russian raw materials for German industrial products. An article

(a) of February 13 in *Pravda* stated that, even in its first year of operation, the agreement would allow a turn-over between Germany and the U.S.S.R. greater than at any time since 1914, and that it was intended still further to increase the volume of goods exchanged between the two countries.

In view of this agreement, and of the fact that the U.S.S.R. was now free from the commitments of the Finnish war, the War Cabinet were bound to consider whether we should gain or lose by action which would cut off Russian oil supplies to Germany and at the same time involve the Allies in war with the U.S.S.R. As a first step towards answering this question, the War Cabinet had already received on March 8 from the Chiefs of Staff a report on the military implications of war with Russia in 1940, with particular reference to the defeat of Germany which was the primary aim of the Allies. In the early stages of the preparation of this report the Chiefs of Staff consulted the Foreign Office on the political side, but stated that the Foreign Office might not agree with their conclusions. These

(b) conclusions were that, even with a considerable amount of German help in reorganising their transport system, the Russians were unlikely to be able to increase their supplies to Germany in 1940. We could bomb the Caucasian oilfields, and thus ultimately bring about a Russian economic and military collapse which would deprive Germany of all supplies from the U.S.S.R., but we could not take any action against the U.S.S.R. which would bring about an early German defeat. Meanwhile our military strength in 1940 might not be sufficient to deal with Germany alone. We had also to consider Italy and could not provide without risk forces adequate to meet Russian threats in the Middle East until late in 1940.

(a) N2004/360/38.   (b) WP(40)91, N3313/40/38.

The Foreign Office view was that the Russians would do nothing to involve themselves in war with the Allies, since they did not want to facilitate or hasten the victory of either side. The War Cabinet (a) agreed with this view on March 12 in their discussion of the report from the Chiefs of Staff. They considered that it was not to our interest to declare war on Russia, but that the risk of a declaration of war on us by Russia need not deter us from action which might be to our advantage elsewhere. Since this risk in the near future was not great, we need not send bombers to the Middle East in preparation for operations there against Russian objectives.

Before this meeting of the War Cabinet suggestions of a possible change in Russian policy reached the Foreign Office through Sir S. Cripps. Sir S. Cripps, while on a tour in the Far East, had seen the Soviet Ambassador at Chungking and had come to the con- (b) clusion that the Russians wanted a *rapprochement* with Great Britain. He offered to fly to Moscow to see M. Molotov. The offer was accepted and Sir S. Cripps arrived in Moscow on February 15. He saw M. Molotov on the following day. M. Molotov produced the usual arguments in defence of Russian aggression against Finland and of the Russo-German agreements, but said that the Soviet Government were ready to make a trade or political agreement with Great Britain, if Great Britain would act in a friendly way to Russia.

The Foreign Office thought Sir S. Cripps too hopeful about the possibility of an agreement. The first official approach therefore came from M. Maisky after the Finnish war. The approach was in two stages. M. Maisky began on March 18 by protesting against the (c) detention of the *Selenga* and of another Russian ship, the *Mayakovsky*, with a cargo of copper and molybdenum. This ship had also been detained because the British authorities believed that the cargo was bound for Germany via Siberia. M. Maisky offered to give a formal assurance that it was intended solely for Russian use. He then discussed Anglo-Soviet relations in general and once more described Russian policy as one of independence.

On March 27 M. Maisky told Lord Halifax that the Soviet Government would be prepared to enter into a trade agreement if (d) His Majesty's Government would settle certain problems which had arisen in the conduct of Anglo-Russian trade. He could give no details about these problems except that they included the question of the two detained ships. Lord Halifax pointed out that Anglo-Russian trade relations were complicated by the very close economic relations between the U.S.S.R. and Germany. The Soviet Govern-

---

(a) WM(40)66, N3208/40/38.   (b) N2779, 2780, 2781/40/38.   (c) N3485/40/38.
(d) N3706/5/38.

ment appeared deliberately to be working against the attempts of
the Allies to cut off German trade. M. Maisky thought that the
Soviet Government would be willing to meet the requirement that
goods sent to Russia by the Allies were for Russian use only. He
again said that Russian policy was independent and that there was
no foundation for the talk of a Russo-German military alliance.

The Foreign Office did not expect much to come from M. Maisky's
suggestion. Russian policy clearly aimed at prolonging the war
between the Allies and Germany to the advantage of the U.S.S.R.
On the other hand, it might be to our advantage to increase our
trade with Russia and to secure an agreement rationing the import
of valuable materials into Russia and restricting the deliveries of oil
to Germany. The War Cabinet accepted this view and authorised
(a) the Foreign Office to explore possibilities of an agreement.

(b)   The sixth meeting of the Supreme War Council was held in
London on March 28.[1] The Prime Minister opened the meeting
with a general survey of the position after the Finnish collapse. He
thought that we should consider actions which could injure Germany
and impress the neutrals and also maintain the courage and determination of our own people. These actions should, if possible, 'be in the
nature of surprises'. He suggested that we should begin at once with
the 'Royal Marine Operation'. This operation would confuse the
Germans and put a great strain on their railways. The German
retaliation would be directed against Great Britain rather than
against France.

We could not now occupy the Gällivare ore-fields as an incidental
consequence of sending an expedition to Finland, but we might tell
the Scandinavian Governments that we reserved our right to take
such measures as we thought necessary to prevent Germany from
obtaining advantages from Sweden and Norway. In other words, we
should be warning them in general terms that we intended to stop
the ore traffic to Germany. It would be a fairly simple operation
at any time to block Norwegian waters at certain points with mines
and seize German ships which would be driven out into the open sea.
This action would not affect traffic from Lulea, but the possibility
of interfering with this traffic was under consideration.

German oil supplies came from Roumania, Galicia and Baku.
Roumania could not fight Germany. Turkey was not sufficiently
armed, and we ought not to act in the Balkans without consulting
her or before she was ready. His Majesty's Government proposed

---

[1] For other decisions of the Supreme War Council at this meeting, see p. 140.

(a) WM(40)77, N3738/40/38. (b) C5988/9/17.

a study of the possibilities of an attack on Baku, and an attempt to get Turkish support for Roumania.

Finally the Prime Minister said that we should be unwise to think that we could win the war by short cuts. Our main weapon must be the blockade; we must be patient because the effects of this weapon were slow. On the other hand, a 'patched-up' peace would be the worst conclusion of the war.

M. Reynaud agreed that the war must be fought to the end. He agreed also that the Finnish collapse had had a bad effect on morale. The French had to face German propaganda that Germany had no quarrel with France; that the war had arisen out of a British 'blank cheque' to the Poles, and that France had been dragged into it, and could not carry it to a finish. The German plan seemed to count upon the discouragement of six million Frenchmen under arms and the emergence of a government which would make a 'compromise peace' at the expense of Great Britain.

The French were also asking how we could win the war. The German army was growing more quickly than the Allied armies; it would be a very long time indeed before we should have manpower enough for operations in the west. In these circumstances it was impossible to maintain a belief in the power of our blockade unless we compelled Germany to draw on her stocks of oil and raw materials. We must therefore do something 'new'. The French Conseil de Guerre had opposed the 'Royal Marine Operation' because it would bring reprisals upon France; they might agree to it if the French proposals were also accepted.

M. Reynaud accepted the plan for a minefield in Norwegian territorial waters and wanted it to be put into effect immediately and to be followed by action against the Baltic traffic. He then discussed the question of oil. He thought that it might be possible to destroy the whole Baku oil region. He wanted a rapid decision and suggested that we should send the necessary bombs to Syria at once. He also wished to tighten the blockade by establishing a system of quotas for neutrals who were accumulating stocks.

The Prime Minister had already agreed to a 'study' of the position; he refused to commit himself to an attack on Baku. He asked whether it was in our interest that the war should spread to Russia and that Russia and Germany should be brought closer together. He pointed out the possibilities of Russian action, especially in operations which did not involve fighting against the armies of a first-class Power, and also the existence of signs that Russia wanted to improve her relations with the Allies.

M. Reynaud said that he understood British objections to war with Russia. He agreed that the operation against Baku ought not to be undertaken unless it were decisive. He believed that an attack on the oil supplies would disorganise Russian agricultural economy and might even help in bringing Russia to the side of the Allies.

The Prime Minister then mentioned M. Maisky's approach on the question of a trade agreement. He asked whether we might propose to the Soviet Government the restriction of supplies of oil and other commodities on the basis of rationing. M. Reynaud thought it impossible to trust the Soviet Government. They would merely spin out the negotiations and might even be trying to gain time in which to complete their defences in the Caucasus. The Prime Minister then suggested that we also might spin out the negotiations until the Allies had decided upon their policy with regard to the Caucasus. M. Reynaud agreed with this view.

The Council finally agreed—subject to the approval of the French Conseil de Guerre—that the notes to the Scandinavian Governments should be sent on April 1 or 2; that the 'Royal Marine Operation' should begin on April 4; and that a minefield should be laid in Norwegian waters on April 5.

(a) On March 29 the War Cabinet accepted the decisions of the Supreme War Council. They also considered the possibility— though they did not think it likely in view of the lateness of the season[1]—that the Germans would reply to the Allied action in Norwegian territorial waters by an invasion of Norway with a view to establishing sea and air bases. If the Germans retaliated in such a way we should be able to land troops in Norway with the consent of the Norwegian Government.

(b) The War Cabinet approved on April 1 a plan of operations put forward by the Chiefs of Staff in the event of this opportunity—as it then seemed—being open to us. The plan envisaged the occupation of Narvik and an advance on the railway to the Swedish frontier, and, as a defensive measure to forestall the Germans, a raid to prepare the aerodrome at Stavanger for demolition, and the occupation of Bergen and Trondhjem. The Chiefs of Staff were not sure whether we should be able to reach Stavanger in time. They had little doubt that we could reach Bergen and Trondhjem before the Germans; they did not even consider the possibility of a German attempt to get to Narvik. They recommended—and the War Cabinet agreed—that no landings should be attempted against serious Norwegian opposition.

Preparations for these landings were made at once. One British brigade of three battalions and a French force, with one light anti-

---

[1] i.e. the blocking of the Narvik traffic would not have serious economic effects since all the Swedish Baltic ports would soon become available.

(a) WM(40)77.2, C.A.   (b) WM(40)78, WP(40)115.

aircraft battery, were regarded as sufficient for Narvik. Five British battalions were assigned for the southern occupation. No artillery was considered necessary; there was no mention of air support. The expedition to Stavanger would be ready to start on April 5; the other forces would sail as soon as possible after April 5.

Note to Section (iv). Abandonment of the 'study' of the proposal to attack the Caucasian oilfields.

Within a very short time after the meeting of the Supreme War Council the German successes in Norway, and their consequences, ruled out of practical consideration the project for an attack on the Caucasian oilfields. The study suggested by the Supreme War Council therefore seems to have 'faded out' after April 10. The project was also discussed in general terms at a meeting of His Majesty's Representatives in Turkey, Hungary, the Balkan States and Italy at the Foreign Office on April 8 and 11. The view taken by all present at the meeting was that, unless intensive warfare developed, Germany had oil supplies for several months; that Turkey would object to the project, and that public opinion in Great Britain would regard as unjustifiable an act of aggression against the U.S.S.R.; that, in view of our policy of building up our reserves until we could take the initiative with success, it would be better (again on the assumption that intensive warfare had not meanwhile begun) to drop the project for the time and to reconsider it in the autumn when the German oil position would be more critical and both the Allies and Turkey would be stronger.

M. Reynaud raised the question at the eighth meeting of the Supreme War Council on April 22, but there was obviously no possibility of putting the plan into effect, even if the British Government had been more favourable to it.

(v)

Reports of German concentrations against Scandinavia: the Allied notes of April 5 to Norway and Sweden: the German invasion of Norway.

In the last few days before the German attack on Norway and Denmark the Allies again hesitated before putting their plans into effect. The delay came from the French side, but neither the British nor the French authorities took sufficient notice of the reports of German preparations for a *coup* against Scandinavia. These reports were, of course, not received for the first time; they came now in a more definite form, and it is strange that the Allies did not pay more attention to them in view of the fact that there had been so much public talk about their own plans.[1] On March 26

(a) Mr. Mallet had transmitted a report from Swedish naval sources that the Germans appeared to be concentrating aircraft and shipping for an operation which might be aimed at the seizure of Norwegian aerodromes and ports. The pretext would be that the disclosure of Allied plans for the occupation of Norwegian territory had compelled Germany to act not merely for her own sake but in the interest of the Scandinavian States. Mr. Mallet thought that these preparations might have been intended as a counterstroke to our expedition to Sweden or that they might foreshadow a new German initiative.

(b) Two days later Mr. Mallet wrote that he could not confirm the
(c) reports. On March 29 the Norwegian Chief of Naval Staff admitted that he had heard these rumours; they did not disturb him because he believed that the Germans had made their preparations in connexion with the proposed Allied help to Finland.

(d)   On April 2 Mr. Mallet reported information which had reached the Swedish Ministry of Foreign Affairs from Berlin that for more than a week there had been a concentration of about 200,000 tons of shipping, with troops on board, at Stettin and Swinemünde. The Swedish Minister in Berlin had been instructed to ask the German Government their intentions with regard to this concentration. Baron von Weizsäcker said that the Swedish Government underestimated the danger from the Allies in northern Sweden; he refused on military grounds to discuss the concentration of troops. The Swedish Foreign Office did not think that the Germans would use

---

[1] Admiral Raeder proposed to Hitler on October 10, 1939, a German occupation of submarine bases on the Norwegian coast. Hitler did not accept the proposal because it would have led certainly to British naval attacks on the Narvik traffic and probably to attacks elsewhere on the long Norwegian coast. Raeder suggested the plan again in December. He now had support from Rosenberg, who was a friend of Vidkun Quisling. Quisling, a former Norwegian Minister of War, was leader of a small and unimportant Norwegian fascist party. The Germans never had much confidence in Quisling's promises of a revolutionary movement in Norway favourable to their intervention, but his assertions that the British were planning intervention seem to have impressed Hitler. At all events Hitler appears to have accepted the idea of getting into Norway primarily in order to forestall a British invasion of the country. The final German decision to carry out their plan was not taken until February 20, 1940, after the *Altmark* incident (see above, p. 85); the order to complete the preparations was given on March 1. The Germans had intended to begin the invasion on March 20, but, owing to the severe winter, were prevented by ice in the Baltic and the Great Belt. In any case, after the end of the Russo-Finnish war the Germans believed that for the time there was no immediate danger of a British landing in Norway; on the other hand the Germans could no longer use the danger to justify an invasion by their own forces. Towards the end of March, however, they began to fear British action against German shipping in neutral waters leading, under some new pretext, to a landing in Norway. Sooner or later, therefore, Germany would have to occupy the Norwegian coast. On Admiral Raeder's advice Hitler decided to act at once. The date fixed for the opening of the German attack (which would include the invasion of Denmark) was April 9. The first German movements at sea began on April 3. Hitler did not settle on the actual date—April 9—until April 2. The Allies had received a number of reports about German plans, but so many rumours of German action were current that it was difficult to place confidence in any of them.

(a) N3602, 3603/2/63.   (b) N3695/2/63.   (c) N3772/2/63.   (d) N3816, 3941/2/63.

this force for a landing in Norway, Sweden or Denmark, if the Allies merely stopped the passage of German ore supplies through Norwegian territorial waters.

Meanwhile there was delay on the Allied side in putting into effect the Scandinavian plans as accepted at the meeting of the Supreme War Council because the French Government refused to agree to the 'Royal Marine Operation'. The opposition came mainly from M. Daladier. He maintained his view in spite of a personal message from the Prime Minister that this minelaying in German waterways (a) was an essential part of the combined operations, and that it would deflect American opinion from criticism of the action in Norwegian territorial waters. After further discussion His Majesty's Government agreed on April 5 to postpone the 'Royal Marine Operation' and to (b) send the notes to the Scandinavian Governments at once. The mine-laying in Norwegian waters would begin at dawn on April 8.

The notes began by stating that events had shown that the German Government did not allow Sweden and Norway 'that liberty of (c) action in foreign affairs to which they were entitled'; the Scandin-avian Governments therefore were not, 'in present circumstances, entirely free agents'. The Allies would not accept a situation in which Germany could draw from Sweden supplies essential to the pre-servation of the war. The time had come to notify the Scandinavians 'frankly of certain vital interests and requirements which the Allied Governments intend to assert and defend by whatever measures they may think necessary'. The Allies could not acquiesce in (i) a further Russian or German attack on Finland, or, if such an attack were to take place, a refusal by the Swedish or Norwegian Government to facilitate Allied help to Finland or an attempt to prevent such help; (ii) an 'exclusive political agreement' with Germany, or a Scandin-avian alliance providing for the acceptance of German help; (iii) a Russian attempt to obtain from Norway a footing on the Atlantic seaboard; (iv) a Norwegian refusal to provide reasonable commercial and shipping facilities.

'Further, the Allies, seeing that they are waging war for aims which are as much in the interests of the smaller States as in their own, cannot allow the course of the war to be influenced against them by advantages derived by Germany from Sweden or from Norway. They therefore give notice that they reserve the right to take such measures as they may think necessary to hinder or prevent Germany from obtaining in these countries resources or facilities which, for the purpose of the war, would be to her advantage or to the disadvantage of the Allies.'

The British and French Ministers at Stockholm and Oslo delivered these notes at 7 p.m. on April 5. At the same time copies were given

---

(a) C4983, 5026/5/18. (b) WM(40)80.5, C.A. (c) N3986, 3987/2/63.

to the Swedish and Norwegian Ministers in London. Sir C. Dormer
(a) reported that M. Koht protested against the tone and wording of the
(b) note. Mr. Mallet telegraphed that M. Günther's first remark was:
'This brings our countries very close to war'. M. Günther then asked
where, how, and when the Allies would exercise their 'right' to stop
the export of Swedish ore. M. Günther said that he 'would never
have expected to receive such a note from two Governments which
he had always regarded as Sweden's friends'.

(c)   During the night of April 5–6 Mr. Howard-Smith, British
Minister at Copenhagen, telegraphed that, according to information
from a 'well-placed' neutral source, Hitler had ordered on the
previous night a division in ten ships to move unostentatiously at
night in order to land at Narvik. Jutland would be occupied on the
same day, but Sweden would be left alone. Mr. Howard-Smith said
that the Danes were nervous at the presence of warships and
transports at Baltic ports, but that they did not appear to feel any
real anxiety.[1]

On April 6 Lord Halifax told the War Cabinet of the Swedish
(d) reception of the note. M. Günther wanted to publish it. The War
Cabinet agreed that the best course would be to persuade the
Swedish Government not to do so at the moment. As soon as we had
laid our minefields the Germans would be likely to ask the Norwegian
Government whether we had given notice of our intention. This
enquiry would probably lead to publication, but it would then be
clear that for the time we were doing no more than lay a minefield
in Norwegian territorial waters.

Mr. Mallet was instructed in the evening of April 6 to tell
M. Günther that our note was not a preliminary to action against
Sweden. We did not intend to land forces in Scandinavia unless the
Germans compelled us to do so by taking hostile action against
Norwegian or Swedish territory. Mr. Mallet reported on April 7
(e) that this explanation had reassured M. Günther. He admitted that
he had judged the note too hastily, and agreed not to publish it.

On April 8 the Admiralty gave notice of the laying of a minefield
in Norwegian territorial waters. The minefield was laid at the entrance
to the Vest Fjord between 4.30 a.m. and 5.0 a.m. on April 8 by four
destroyers. On the previous evening British air reconnaissance had
located an enemy naval force moving northward across the Skag-
gerak toward the Naze. In spite of the report received from
Copenhagen it seemed unlikely that this force was making for

---

[1] Copies of this telegram were sent, according to usual custom, by the Foreign Office to
the War Cabinet Office and to the Service Departments. The report was not believed
since it seemed most unlikely that the Germans would attempt to reach a point as far north
as Narvik.

(a) N3909/1804/59.   (b) N3978/2/63.   (c) N3990, 4002/2/63.   (d) WM(40)83,
N4097/2/63. (e) N4047/2/63.

Narvik, but naval counter-measures were taken to meet it. On the morning of April 8 further information showed that the Germans were in fact aiming at Narvik. The Admiralty therefore expected a naval engagement 'on terms not unfavourable for us'. It was thought that Hitler might have ordered the capture of Narvik as a measure preparatory to the occupation of Lulea after the ice had melted, but there was as yet no realisation on the British side of the extent and completeness of the German plans. In any case the British counter-measures were hampered by storms and bad visibility, and the Germans were able to carry out their landings on the west coast of Norway without much interference.

During the morning of April 9 the whole German plan was revealed; German transports under naval escort had landed troops at Oslo, Christiansand, Stavanger, Bergen, Trondhjem and Narvik, and a German army had invaded Denmark. The Allies had lost the initiative in Scandinavia.

CHAPTER V

The Allied defeat in Norway and its political consequences

(i)

The German invasion of Norway and Denmark: Allied plans to expel the Germans: seventh, eighth and ninth meetings of the Supreme War Council, April 9, 22–3 and 27; withdrawal of the Allies from Norway, (April 9—June 8, 1940).[1]

(a)   THE first news from Sir C. Dormer of the German invasion of Norway reached the Foreign Office in a telephone message at 3.25 a.m. on April 9. The Resident Clerk transmitted the message at once to the War Cabinet Office and to the Duty Officers at the Admiralty, War Office and Air Ministry. Sir C. Dormer's message was to the effect that M. Koht had told him that four large German warships were coming up Oslo Fjord.[2] The Norwegian defences had fired on the ships and might succeed in resisting them. Five ships were also approaching Bergen, and at least one was approaching Stavanger. M. Koht added 'so we are now at war'. Sir C. Dormer asked whether the Norwegian Government intended to remain at Oslo. M. Koht answered 'Yes', and said that he thought the defences 'strong enough'.

(b)   The War Cabinet met at 8.30 a.m. and again at noon on April 9. At this stage they took an optimistic view of the situation. Lord Halifax thought that our chances of reaching Gällivare were now better than at any time. Mr. Churchill held the same view. He pointed out that we could not have prevented the German landings unless we had instituted large and continuous naval patrols off the Norwegian coast, but that we could liquidate the landings in a week or so. The War Cabinet also considered the position with regard to Denmark, where the Government had capitulated to the German invaders. It was decided to occupy the Faroe Islands in order to forestall a German occupation, and to inform the Icelandic Government that we would be prepared to assist them in maintaining their

---

[1] Since this chapter is not a military history of operations in Norway, I have excluded most of the telegrams in which Sir C. Dormer transmitted military information.

[2] The position in Narvik was still uncertain. Before the second meeting of the War Cabinet a small German force was known to have landed there.

(a) N4068/1110/30.   (b) WM(40)85 and 86.

independence, but that for this purpose we should need facilities in Iceland.[1]

At 12.55 p.m. Sir C. Dormer was instructed to assure the Nor- (a) wegian Government that, in view of the German invasion of their country, His Majesty's Government had decided to extend their full aid to Norway and would fight the war in full association with her. His Majesty's Government were taking immediate steps to deal with the German occupation of Bergen and Trondhjem, since they considered this action to be the most useful immediate help which they could give to Norwegian resistance. They hoped that they could count on the active co-operation of the Norwegian Government and people.

In the afternoon of April 9 Sir C. Dormer reported the fall of Oslo (b) and the removal of the Norwegian Government to Hamar, 15 km. from Oslo. He also transmitted a message from the Norwegian Government urging the need for strong and quick assistance before the Germans had established themselves in Norway. Meanwhile the Foreign Office had informed the French Embassy of the military and diplomatic steps which were being taken and the Ambassador had brought a message from M. Reynaud suggesting a meeting of the (c) Supreme War Council at once.

This meeting was held in London during the afternoon. M. (d) Reynaud explained that he had asked for the meeting in order to examine the measures to be taken as a result of the German attack on Norway.[2] He thought that the Allies should not lose sight of their 'essential aim' of cutting off German ore supplies and that we should act promptly to avoid a collapse of the neutrals, e.g. in the Balkans. The French Conseil de Guerre had decided in principle in favour of moving forward into Belgium if we could secure the co-operation of the Belgian army. If the British Government agreed with this plan, the French would accept the 'Royal Marine Operation'. The Prime Minister agreed that a communication should be made to the Belgian Government.[3]

After discussing the military situation, the Council agreed upon a reply to the Norwegian appeal for help, and considered the dis-

---

[1] On May 6 the War Cabinet decided to land a small force in the Reykjavik area of Iceland in order to forestall a possible German invasion. The landing took place on May 10. His Majesty's Government explained to the Icelandic Government that our action was necessary to prevent Iceland from becoming a battleground, since, if the Germans arrived first we should have to turn them out, whereas they could not send an expedition to turn us out. His Majesty's Government also gave full assurances with regard to the independent status of Iceland after the war.

[2] The Supreme War Council took the view that the Germans would have carried out their intention of occupying Norway even if the Allies had not laid their minefield, but that they (the Germans) would have found a pretext more difficult.

[3] See below, section (iii) of this chapter.

(a) N4119/1110/30. (b) N4100, 4101/1110/30. (c) N4092/2/63. (d) C5513/9/17; SWC (40)3.

tribution of forces for a counterstroke in Norway as soon as the
necessary information had been received. The first objective would
be the recapture of the ports but the forces for this purpose would not
leave until the naval position had been cleared up.[1] The Council
recognised the particular importance of Narvik with a view to subsequent action to deprive Germany of access to the Swedish orefields.

(a)   Meanwhile Mr. Mallet had been instructed at 12.40 p.m. to ask
the Swedish Government what they proposed to do about the German
invasion of Norway. Mr. Mallet was not in Stockholm but Mr.

(b) Montagu-Pollock and the French Minister had already seen M.
Günther. M. Günther said that the Germans had assured the

(c) Swedish Government that they would not interfere with Sweden.
Later, after a meeting of the Foreign Affairs Committee and a secret
session of the Riksdag, M. Günther told Mr. Mallet that Sweden did
not intend to enter the war on behalf of Norway. Norway had no
army and was already practically in German hands. Sweden would
maintain a 'watchful neutrality' and would fight only if attacked. M.
Günther did not trust the German assurances and admitted that
Sweden might be at war within a week. He welcomed Allied help to
Norway and thought that we should not have much difficulty in
recapturing the ports.

(d)   On the morning of April 10 the French Minister at Stockholm
gave M. Günther a note promising help in the event of a German
invasion. M. Günther asked Mr. Mallet whether he had been
instructed to deliver a similar note. Mr. Mallet said that he had no
instructions, but that he could associate himself with the French
Minister's assurances. The Foreign Office instructed him on April 11
to confirm this statement. On the night of April 10–11 the French
Government informed Sir R. Campbell that they had decided to
send a mission to Sweden in order to encourage the Swedish Govern-

(e) ment to remain firm in their attitude to Germany.
Sir R. Campbell had told the French Government that this
mission should include British representatives. M. Coulondre and
General Mittelhauser, the French representatives, came to London
on the morning of April 11 for a discussion on policy. M. Coulondre
proposed to tell the Swedes that in the event of a German attack the
Allies could promise assistance within a definite period. The Prime
Minister thought that it would be a dangerous mistake to underrate
the strength of the position which the Germans had already built
up in Norway. If they had not done so, they could soon reinforce
Stavanger, Bergen and Trondhjem, and we could not easily dis-

---

[1] I have not dealt with the technical matters involved in these discussions, e.g. whether
the Admiralty were rightly informed about the German naval strength at Bergen and
Trondhjem, and whether a naval attack on these places on April 10 might have succeeded.
(a) N4119/1130/30.   (b) N4112/124/42.   (c) N4135/1130/30.   (d) N4195/4179/42.
(e) N4306/4179/42.

lodge them. At any moment we might have a great offensive in the west. We therefore ought not to disperse our forces. If we urged Sweden to declare war on the assumption that the Allies would come to her aid, we might be committed to operations on a considerable scale. The French had said that they could not provide air assistance; Great Britain could do so only by weakening forces needed for the west. If we told the Swedes that we would retaliate for air attacks on Sweden by bombing Germany, we should raise the whole question of 'total war'. Hitherto the Allies had agreed that it was not in their interest to start 'total war'. Hence we should advise the Swedes to maintain their neutrality unless the Germans tried to reach the ore-fields. In the latter event we should give all possible assistance to Sweden.

M. Coulondre agreed with this view. The War Cabinet took a similar line. Mr. Mallet was therefore instructed on the night of April 11–12 that the Mission should not try to persuade the Swedes (a) into a policy of provoking Germany to action, but should say that, if at any time the Swedish Government decided to go to war with Germany, they could count on Allied assistance. The Allies could not yet reach Sweden through the southern ports of Norway, but an entry would shortly be affected by whatever ports might be found suitable as a result of a reconnaissance now being made. Thereafter we intended to open other ports.

The Anglo-French Mission arrived in Stockholm on April 12.[1] Meanwhile Mr. Mallet had transmitted a telegram from Sir C. (b) Dormer reporting that he had joined the King of Norway and the Norwegian Government (which had left Hamar) at Nybergsund, near the Swedish frontier. The Norwegian authorities, who had appeared earlier to be vacillating, were now showing more deter- (c) mination and wished to establish themselves at Trondhjem as soon as the Germans had been expelled, but they could not cope with the invaders if British support were confined to naval operations. Sir C. Dormer urged the extreme importance of the recapture of Trondhjem.

The Foreign Office also considered Trondhjem rather than (d) Narvik to be the key to the situation. As long as the Germans held Trondhjem, our possession of an isolated base at Narvik would not enable us to establish contact with the Norwegian Government, while communications with Sweden could be more conveniently secured from Trondhjem than through the long and precarious route from Narvik. Opinion in Italy and among the neutrals of south-

---

[1] The British representatives on the mission were Admiral Sir Edward Evans, Major-General Lewin, and Wing-Commander Thornton, Air Attaché in Stockholm.
(a) N4242/4179/42. (b) N4281/1130/30. (c) N4178/1130/30. (d) N4299, 4352/4125/30.

eastern Europe would regard the occupation of Narvik and the Faroes merely as a sign of our inability to deal with the main problem of turning the Germans out of Norway. Unless we succeeded in retaking Trondhjem it was doubtful whether Norwegian resistance could continue for long, and still more doubtful whether Sweden would resist German demands.

(a)   These views were put to the War Cabinet on April 12. Lord Halifax pointed out that the operations at Narvik, although militarily sound, would have much less political effect than an attempt to clear the Germans out of southern Norway. The Admiralty view, however, was that a landing at Trondhjem without adequate preparation might lead to a severe repulse, while we could be reasonably sure of success at Narvik and would clearly show thereby that we should be able ultimately to re-occupy all the ports. The War Cabinet agreed that, for the time, the main effort should be made against Narvik.

(b)   Later on April 12 Mr. Mallet telegraphed that the members of the Allied Mission to Sweden agreed with Sir C. Dormer's view that the recapture of Trondhjem was more important than that of Narvik. They thought that it was necessary above all to stiffen Norwegian resistance. The collapse of Norway would shake the morale of Sweden; in any case, the Swedes were expecting German demands for the use of their railways, and might not resist these demands if we had not opened a way to help them through Trondhjem. The (c) first interview between M. Coulondre, Head of the Allied Mission, and M. Günther, on April 12, confirmed this view.

The War Cabinet considered the position again on the morning of (d) April 13. The Prime Minister drew attention to the views of the Allied Mission and Lord Halifax said that, from a political point of view, early action must be taken against Trondhjem, while it seemed that, if necessary, operations at Narvik could wait. Mr. Churchill thought that we should first make sure of Narvik. He also explained that plans were being made for landings in the Trondhjem area. The War Cabinet therefore decided to tell the Swedish and Norwegian Governments that we intended to take both Narvik and Trondhjem. We recognised the supreme importance of Trondhjem, but we wanted to secure Narvik as a base for our naval operations. In order to reassure the Swedish Government, Mr. Mallet could add that our Narvik force would not cross into Swedish territory against the wishes of the Swedes.

(e)   The Foreign Office thought that the French were insisting too much upon the expedition to Narvik and upon the possibility of (f) reaching the ore-fields. In the afternoon of April 13 Sir R. Campbell

---

(a) WM(40)90.3, C.A.   (b) N4289/1130/30;   N4317/4125/30.   (c) N4316/4179/42.
(d) WM(40)91.3, C.A.   (e) N4259/1130/30.   (f) N4325/4125/30.

telegraphed that the Conseil de Guerre now considered the re-capture of Trondhjem to be more urgent than that of Narvik. The Norwegian Commander-in-Chief continued on April 13, 14 and 15 to (a) point out the urgency of recovering Trondhjem. On the night of April 14–15 Mr. Mallet was told that operations to this end were 'now starting'. These operations were, however, delayed owing to another change of plan. On April 13 a British naval force completed the destruction of the German flotilla at Narvik.[1] Mr. Churchill told the War Cabinet on the following day that the 'altered situation' at (b) Narvik gave more hope of operations in the Trondhjem area; the naval staff had now suggested a landing at Trondhjem itself. Mr. Churchill thought at this time that the risks were not 'unjustifiable', particularly if, as seemed possible, the railway to Trondhjem was still in Norwegian hands.

On the morning of April 15 Mr. Churchill was less optimistic. He (c) explained that we could not reckon on recapturing Narvik without resistance. The War Cabinet then discussed plans for the recapture of Trondhjem. Lord Halifax again spoke of the political importance of establishing ourselves in the Trondhjem area, but the War Cabinet accepted the military argument in favour of postponement. In the afternoon of April 15 Lord Halifax met the members of the (d) Allied Mission on their return from Sweden. M. Coulondre explained that the German attack had taken the Norwegian Government by surprise; that resistance was feeble and fragmentary and without co-ordination. There were, however, signs that the Government was regaining a little confidence. For this reason the recovery of Trondhjem was of the greatest importance.

On April 17 the War Cabinet again discussed the military position. (e) Mr. Churchill outlined plans for a direct attack on Trondhjem, with diversions already proposed to the north and south, and gave April 22 as the provisional date for the attack. On April 18 the War Cabinet (f) was informed that the attack could not take place before April 24 and (g) on April 19 the date was postponed until April 25. On April 20 (h) Mr. Churchill told the War Cabinet that the Chiefs of Staff had recommended the abandonment of the plan of a direct landing at Trondhjem in favour of an enveloping movement from the north and south[2]. This operation would take about a month.

---

[1] An action on April 10 had already sunk two destroyers, six merchantmen and an ammunition ship.

[2] This decision was taken in the afternoon of April 19. Mr. Churchill had then obtained the consent of the Prime Minister. Landings of troops had already been made on April 17–18 at Namsos and Aandalsnes. On April 21 Mr. Churchill told the War Cabinet that, (j) owing to air attack, the position at Namsos was less favourable. A day later Mr. Churchill (k) said that the situation there was most difficult but not desperate.

(a) N4326, 4330, 4339, 4402/4125/30.   (b) WM(40)92.5, C.A.   (c) WM(40)93.4, C.A. (d) N4576/4125/30.   (e) WM(40)95.3, C.A.   (f) WM(40)96.3, C.A.   (g) WM(40)97.3, C.A.   (h) WM(40)98.3, C.A.   (j) WM(40)99.4, C.A.   (k) WM(40)100.3, C.A.

(a)   The change of plan increased the disquiet of the Foreign Office at the inability of the naval and military authorities to act more quickly against Trondhjem. The technical aspects of the matter were outside the sphere of the Foreign Office, but it appeared doubtful whether the chances of success would be greater after the Germans had been free for a month to bring in reinforcements. Moreover within a month the Germans might have invaded the Low Countries and our failure to get a decision in Norway might bring Mussolini into the war.

(b)   A meeting of the Supreme War Council was held in Paris on April 22 and 23. M. Reynaud had asked for this meeting in a personal letter of April 18 to the Prime Minister. In his letter M. Reynaud suggested that the German plan was to 'conquer' the ore deposits. In order to defeat this attempt the Allies should first recapture Trondhjem as the easiest port of access to Sweden. Since we must be able, with the Scandinavian forces, to oppose the Germans in equal strength, the French would agree that British forces in France might be withdrawn for a northern expeditionary force. The Foreign Office did not accept M. Reynaud's reasoning. The Germans were unlikely to have planned to reach the ore-fields through Norway when, in a month's time, the Gulf of Bothnia would be open. The French view seemed to be affected too much by the question of the ore-fields and by a desire to keep active military operations away from the western front. The Foreign Office were in full agreement about the recapture of Trondhjem and the re-establishment of the Norwegian Government in northern and central Norway, but considered a considerable advance southwards too dangerous owing to difficulties of supply over the Norwegian railways.

(c)   At the Supreme War Council M. Reynaud repeated his opinion that the Allies should concentrate upon Norway.[1] He said that the French could spare forces for the operations and that our object should be to cut off the ore supplies or destroy the electrical installations necessary for working the mines. We could help Sweden to protect herself and, perhaps, with Swedish assistance, we should try to expel the Germans from the whole of Scandinavia. Meanwhile, the capture of Trondhjem was urgent. If we did not act decisively within two or three weeks, the Germans would be too firmly established for us to turn them out of Scandinavia.

The Prime Minister agreed that the key to the position of Germany was the security of her oil and iron ore supplies; oil was

---

[1] The Council made a general survey of Allied policy. See below, sections (iii) and (iv) of this chapter.

(a) N5004/1130/30. (b) W4916/31/49. (c) C6205/9/17.

perhaps more vital than iron ore. Our main objective in Scandinavia was the ore mines, but the operations had become in some measure a test of Allied strength; a withdrawal would have a bad psychological effect. We had decided at first to make our main effort at Narvik. We had then seen that the recapture of Trondhjem was necessary to preserve Norwegian and Swedish morale and to keep the Germans from the control of central Norway. We had planned landings at Namsos, Aandalsnes and Molde in combination with a direct attack on Trondhjem from the sea. We had given up the direct attack in favour of a pincer movement from north and south, but heavy air attacks at Namsos, where we had no anti-aircraft protection, had upset this movement. Although we had destroyed all the German warships at Narvik, the Germans were strongly fortified in the place, and we could not yet attack them. We should need specially trained troops for an advance from Narvik through the snow to the Swedish frontier. The Gulf of Bothnia would not be ice-free for a month, but the Germans might not wait before giving an ultimatum to Sweden. We might therefore have only a fortnight in which to advance from Narvik, and we should have to arrive on the Swedish frontier in great strength as soon as possible if, in the event of a German invasion of Sweden, we were to reach the mines before the Germans and destroy the means of producing the iron. The Prime Minister pointed out that the Germans could reinforce their troops by sea and air more quickly than the Allies.

The Council agreed to aim at the capture of Trondhjem and Narvik and at the rapid concentration of a force on the Swedish frontier. They also 'took note' of the practical limitations set by the inadequate landing facilities.

The military position in central Norway continued to get worse and, in spite of the resolutions of the Supreme War Council, the British military authorities had to consider the possibility of evacuation. On April 26 the Prime Minister told the War Cabinet the military view of the situation. If we took Trondhjem, we should (a) have to provide 50 heavy and 80 light anti-aircraft guns for the defence of the place as a base; even so we should find it difficult to use the port against air attack on a heavy scale. We should need most of our Home Fleet to maintain our force, and we should be exposing the fleet to risks which we ought not to take in view of the chances that Italy might come into the war against us. We could not deal with Italy and at the same time maintain forces at Trondhjem and Narvik. On the other hand, without Trondhjem we could do little in central Norway.

(a) WM(40)104.3, C.A.

The conclusion therefore was that we should be prepared to evacuate our forces at Namsos and Aandalsnes. This withdrawal would be a serious blow to our prestige but we could mitigate its effects if we could show that we had landed in central Norway only in order to gain time for the capture of Narvik. Meanwhile the operations at Narvik depended to some extent on the thaw. Finally, the Prime Minister said that the C.I.G.S. was going to France to explain the situation to General Gamelin.

(a) The French Conseil de Guerre were strongly opposed to withdrawal. They sent General Gamelin to London in the evening of April 26 to put the French view to His Majesty's Government. After discussions in London it was decided to hold another meeting of the

(b) Supreme War Council in the afternoon of April 27. At this meeting the Prime Minister said that at their previous discussions on April 22-3 he had thought the setback at Namsos only temporary and the position south of Trondhjem satisfactory, but matters had become worse almost at once owing to the unexpected rate of the German advance and the weight of their air attacks. It was now clear that in face of this type of attack operations feasible in the last war could not be carried out. Unless we had an aerodrome we could not provide fighter support or land heavy material. We could not therefore take Trondhjem, and sooner or later we should have to withdraw from southern Norway. The position at Narvik was better, although we might not be able to reach Gällivare. The Germans were now more able to attack Sweden and might induce the Swedes to keep us out of the ore-fields, but we must try to reach them. The psychological effect upon the neutrals of a failure in southern Norway would be bad. We had a report[1] that Italy would enter the war on May 1-2 and attack Malta and Gibraltar, possibly with Spanish collaboration. We were not strong enough at sea or in the air to fight at the same time in central Scandinavia and in the Mediterranean. The entry of Italy would therefore compel us to leave central Scandinavia. The Council had not considered the question of an Italian attack on the Allies; they had discussed only the reply which we might make to Italian aggression against Dalmatia or Corfu. We ought not to limit ourselves to the consideration of one aspect of the war. If we left central Scandinavia, we must divert our attack elsewhere, possibly to the very heart of Germany. We might attack, among other objectives, stocks and sources of supply in Germany and navigation on the Rhine.

After discussion the Council agreed (i) to give up the attack on Trondhjem; (ii) to delay the evacuation of Aandalsnes as long as possible; (iii) to ask the Allied staffs to consider the question of a

---

[1] See below, p. 151.
    (a) WM(40)105 and 105.2, C.A.   (b) C6476/9/17.

gradual northward withdrawal of the Namsos force; (iv) to try to take Narvik and to concentrate a force on the Swedish frontier, and (v) to consider asking the Swedish Government—if the Germans invaded Sweden—to destroy the mines or to allow the Allies to do so on promise of compensation for the losses thereby caused.[1]

The proposal to evacuate central Norway caused great anxiety in the Foreign Office in view of the political consequences likely to (a) follow such an acknowledgment of defeat. The information from His Majesty's Missions in neutral countries confirmed these fears, but the military situation made it necessary to leave central Norway even sooner than had been anticipated at the meeting of the Supreme War Council. On April 28 the Prime Minister told the War Cabinet that (b) the military authorities, with the assent of General Gamelin, had decided on the previous evening to evacuate Namsos and Aandalsnes at once. M. Reynaud protested to Sir R. Campbell against this (c) decision. He thought that the entry of Italy into the war, and possibly the whole issue of the war, might depend on success or failure in Norway. Sir R. Campbell was instructed in the afternoon of April 29 to tell M. Reynaud that we could not maintain our troops without air or artillery support south of Trondhjem against the German forces advancing from Oslo, but that we hoped to withdraw slowly northwards from Namsos in accordance with the decision taken at the Supreme War Council. This latter plan could not be carried out owing to lack of petrol and the badness of the roads. The Namsos force was therefore withdrawn on the night of May 2–3; the Aandalsnes force had been taken off on the previous night.

The withdrawal was bound to have a most depressing and indeed bitter effect upon the Norwegians. Lord Halifax explained the military position to M. Colban on the evening of April 29. Sir C. Dormer telegraphed on the same evening that M. Koht considered (d) that, if we abandoned the area south of Trondhjem, the Norwegian Government might have to give up fighting. On the night of (e) April 29–30 General Paget explained the plans for evacuation to the Norwegian Commander-in-Chief. The Commander-in-Chief said that he would advise his Government to continue the war if there were further hope of Allied intervention in Norway in the near future. Otherwise he would advise surrender. The War Office replied at once that the Allies were resolved to continue their support and to go on with the war in northern Norway. Lord Halifax spoke in the same sense to M. Colban.

---

[1] The Council also discussed the position with regard to Italy and the Balkans.

(a) N5034/227/42; N5129/40/38. (b) WM(40)106.10, C.A. (c) N5172/1130/30.
(d) N5277, 5231/1130/30. (e) WM(40)108.3, C.A.

M. Mallet's reports from Stockholm on May 3 showed the effect upon Scandinavian opinion of the abandonment of operations against Trondhjem. M. Hambro, President of the Norwegian Parliament, (a) told him that the Norwegian Government had gone secretly to Tromso; he asked whether there was any truth in the rumour that we were advising them to come to terms with Germany. Later in the evening of May 3 Mr. Mallet reported that M. Hambro had held a meeting of members of the Norwegian Parliament, including four members of the Foreign Affairs Committee. They had decided to telegraph to the Norwegian Government in favour of continuing resistance on the understanding that the Allies did not intend to abandon Narvik and northern Norway. Mr. Mallet asked whether he could give M. Hambro an assurance to this effect. On May 4 (b) the War Cabinet instructed the Foreign Office to give this assurance. The Foreign Office therefore told Mr. Mallet to say that the rumour that His Majesty's Government had advised the Norwegians to (c) surrender was a 'malicious falsehood'. Mr. Mallet replied on May 6 that M. Hambro welcomed our assurance but doubted whether we could hold Narvik after we had recaptured it. On May 6 Lord (d) Halifax told M. Koht, who had flown to London, that our aim in capturing Narvik was 'to establish ourselves as firmly as we might on territory in northern Norway in order to be free to develop the situation as circumstances might permit'.[1]

After their withdrawal from central Norway the Allies were thus committed to the capture of Narvik and to the maintenance of their hold on northern Norway.[2] The growing seriousness of the French

---

[1] Mr. Mallet also reported some Swedish criticisms of the Allied withdrawal. He was instructed on May 6 that, if he wished to add anything to his own answers to these criti- (e) cisms, he could say that we knew very well the reasons for Swedish policy since the outbreak of war. This policy had not enabled Sweden to avoid grave danger to herself and did not place her in a position to criticise us. We had done our best to help in conditions which Sweden had not made easier. On May 7 Mr. Mallet telegraphed a confirmation by the Swedish Ministry of Foreign Affairs of a German report that the King of Sweden had (f) exchanged letters with Hitler in the latter half of April. In these letters the King emphasised the intention of Sweden to maintain her neutrality and Hitler promised to respect this neutrality. According to a statement by General Bodenschatz which was reported to the Foreign Office, the King had told Hitler that Sweden would resist a British advance into the country.

[2] The withdrawal from central Norway was announced by Mr. Chamberlain in the House of Commons on May 2 (Parl. Deb. 5th ser. H. of C., vol. 360, cols. 906–13). A debate on the failure of the attempt to expel the Germans took place on May 7 and 8. The Government was strongly criticised and in the division on a general motion their majority fell to 81; 33 Conservatives voted against them, and some 60 abstained. On May 9 Mr. Chamberlain decided to form a National Coalition Government, or to resign if he failed to get sufficient support for his own leadership of such a Government. On the morning of May 10, after failing to get Labour support, Mr. Chamberlain decided to resign. Later in the day Mr. Churchill formed a coalition administration.

(a) N5393/1130/30; N5395/4125/30.   (b) WM(40)112, N5504/1130/30.   (c) N5395/4125/30.   (d) N5483/1110/30.   (e) N5394/1130/30.   (f) N5503/227/42.

position made it impossible for Great Britain to fulfil this undertaking. On May 9—the day before the opening of the German offensive in the west—the Foreign Office received a note from the French (a) Government on the decisive importance of the operations at Narvik for Allied prestige, especially in Italy and in the Balkans, and on the desirability of covering Narvik by an occupation of the coast between Mosjoen and Bodö. M. Corbin said to Lord Halifax that the French Government were afraid that we might be thinking of abandoning Narvik. Lord Halifax answered that we had no such intention.

In effect the War Cabinet had decided, on the advice of the Chiefs of Staff, that it would be possible to hold Narvik, even against heavy air attack. They were also considering the possibility of making the ore-fields unusable by air attack from Narvik if Sweden gave way to German demands for the transit of reinforcements through Swedish territory. Mr. Mallet was asked on May 13 whether we should strengthen Swedish opposition to these demands if we warned (b) the Swedish Government that acceptance of them would free us from our undertaking to respect Swedish neutrality. Mr. Mallet (c) thought it unnecessary to give this warning since the Swedish Government were refusing German requests for the passage of munitions to Narvik and had told the Germans that an attempt on the ore-fields would be met by immediate and complete sabotage.

Before the evacuation of Narvik became necessary, Mr. Mallet reported a proposal, which was said to come from M. Mowinckel,[1] a former Norwegian Prime Minister, for the neutralisation of (d) northern Norway. According to this plan, all foreign troops were to be withdrawn from northern Norway to a line roughly south of Mosjoen, and the Germans would leave Norway free to the north of this line. Narvik would be occupied by the Norwegians, or, temporarily, by Sweden; the port would be open, but no ore would be shipped.

Mr. Mallet first heard of this plan on May 14 from Norwegian sources, and, later, from M. Günther. He told M. Günther that the British Government would refuse to consider the plan and that the mere suggestion of it would make them suspect Swedish collusion with Germany. The Foreign Office realised the strong objections to the proposal but thought that there was something to be said for it. If we recaptured Narvik, the maintenance of a force there would be a considerable effort, especially at the cost of aircraft and anti-aircraft defences needed in Great Britain and France. The plan would allow the Norwegian Government to remain in Norway, though not as an ally; the question of Allied prestige mattered less

---

[1] The plan may have been suggested to M. Mowinckel from Swedish sources, or it may have occurred to more than one person.

(a) N5549/1130/30.   (b) N5559/1130/30.   (c) N5596/227/42.   (d) N5606/1130/30.

in view of the German successes on the western front. A Swedish occupation of Narvik would, however, be essential since if Germany forced Sweden into the war we should then be able to use Narvik and the railway to the ore-fields.

On May 19, however, the Prime Minister[1] wrote to Lord Halifax that the proposal would be 'most detrimental to us. The main (a) remaining value of our forces in Norway is to entice and retain largely superior German forces in that area away from the main decision. Norway is paying a good dividend now and must be held down to the job.'

On the instruction of the War Cabinet the Norwegian and Swedish (b) Governments were informed that the British Government would not consider the plan. We were determined to take Narvik and to (c) establish a cover behind which the Norwegian Government could function in safety. If we accepted the plan we should be surrendering to the Germans advantages which they were unable to win by force of arms. In any case, we could not trust the Germans to keep their part of the bargain.

On May 21 Sir C. Dormer and Mr. Mallet were told to avoid further discussion of the plan, since it might after all be of use if, for military reasons, we found it necessary to withdraw from Narvik. On (d) May 23 the Chiefs of Staff proposed to the War Cabinet a withdrawal from Norway after the capture of Narvik. Lord Halifax suggested that in these circumstances we might ask the Norwegian and Swedish Governments about the practicability of the 'Mowinckel plan', but the War Cabinet considered that, in view of the need for keeping our intentions secret and of the unlikelihood that the Germans would accept the plan, no further soundings should be made.

The capture of Narvik on May 28 to some extent simplified the problem of withdrawal. At all events we should leave after a victory, and it would be clear that events in France and not our own failure to obtain a hold in northern Norway had determined our policy. We could also consider the 'Mowinckel plan' more easily since we were in possession of the most important area with which the proposal was concerned. At the same time the increasing completeness of their victory in France made it less likely that the Germans would accept the proposal.

(e) On May 30 the War Cabinet agreed to withdrawal from Narvik. They did not then discuss the 'Mowinckel plan', but M. Prytz spoke (f) about it to Mr. Collier in the Foreign Office on May 30 and to Lord Halifax on the following day. Lord Halifax asked M. Prytz

---

[1] Mr. Churchill.

(a) N5636/54/30.   (b) WM(40)129.   (c) N5636/54/30.   (d) WM (40)135.9,   C.A.
(e) WM(40)148.9, C.A.   (f) N5644/1130/30.

whether there was reason to suppose that the Germans would keep their word. M. Prytz thought that a Swedish occupation of Narvik would be a good guarantee. The Soviet Government also might support the plan because they wanted both to keep the Germans away from Lulea and the British away from a base on the Atlantic coast of Norway.

Lord Halifax gave an account of this conversation to the War (a) Cabinet on May 31. He suggested that the plan would enable us to get out of Norway without discredit. Northern Norway would remain free for the King and his Government. We should keep access to Sweden and prevent the Germans from coming too far north for our security. The War Cabinet agreed to continue with the plans for evacuation and to advise the Norwegian Government to enter into discussions with the Germans over the neutralisation proposals at once, i.e. before the Germans heard of our intention to withdraw. The Norwegian Government approached the Swedish Government (b) and the latter agreed on June 4 to make enquiries at Berlin. On the evening of June 4 Mr. Mallet telegraphed that the German Government did not intend to reply to the enquiries since they had heard that the Allies were withdrawing from Narvik.

After this failure, the King of Norway and the Crown Prince decided to stay in Norway. The King thought that ultimately the Allies would win the war but that, after the Allies had withdrawn and the Norwegians had no ammunition, Norway must give up fighting and negotiate with the Germans. Later on June 5, however, the King and Crown Prince agreed, under strong British pressure, to come to England. They left Norway on June 7.[1]

(ii)

The Allies and Belgium: the alarm of January 13–14 and the offer of guarantees to the King of the Belgians (January–March, 1940).

The German attack on Norway and Denmark had a paralysing effect upon the attitude of the smaller European neutral countries, and especially upon the Belgians and the Dutch who were all too likely to be the next victims of German aggression. The Germans had no political grievances against Belgium or the Netherlands, but they had now shown—though, indeed, there need have been no

---

[1] The British withdrawal from Narvik was completed on June 8.

(a) WM(40)150, C.A. (b) N5606, 5730, 5745/1130/30; N5738/5443/30; N5852/1130/30.

previous doubts about the matter—that, if it suited their military plans, they would break their engagements to respect the neutrality of their neighbours. The methods which the Germans had used in their invasion of Norway also suggested that an attack would be made without warning, and that it would be carried out by the new 'fifth column' methods of infiltration by civilians, and the employment of traitors—'quislings'—within the country concerned as well as by direct military assault.

In these circumstances the Belgian and Dutch Governments might have been expected to turn at once to the Allies, and to be more ready at least to co-ordinate plans for resistance while there was time. Such considerations applied especially to Belgium, where the chances of Allied help were greatest. Owing, however, to the vacillations of King Leopold and the defeatism of some of his advisers, it is doubtful whether the Belgian Government would have decided upon a resolute and logical policy even if the Allies had been able to turn the Germans out of Norway. Fear of German ruthlessness outweighed all considerations of logic. The Belgian King and Government still clung to the hope that they could escape the fearful choice between surrender and war. As the chances of escape narrowed, the moral and emotional burden of decision increased; so also did the temptation to postpone almost from day to day action which might be interpreted, or misinterpreted, as unneutral, and draw the Germans into immediate retaliation.

There are responsibilities which cannot be evaded; moreover the Belgian King and Government might have reckoned that if, as in 1914, the Germans had laid their plans for the invasion of Belgium, they would be deterred only by military reasons from carrying them out—in other words, they would give up the invasion of Belgium only if it seemed likely to fail. On the other hand, if the German plans did not involve an invasion of Belgium—or the Netherlands— these plans would not be changed by any defensive measures which the Belgians or Dutch might take in conjunction with the Allies. Thus the policy of avoiding all possible provocation of Germany was pointless since the Germans would neither trouble to look for an excuse for an attack nor make such an attack merely because the Belgians increased their precautionary measures.

A detailed attribution of responsibility on the Belgian side is not a matter for an English historian. It is fair, in any case, to remember that when they were faced at last with the choice which they had risked so much to avoid, the Belgians, like the Dutch, decided to fight for their liberties, and that they took this decision after the Allies had failed to save Norway, and after German air-power had appeared to justify the propagandist claims made for it as an invincible and decisive instrument of war.

The refusal of the Belgian King and his advisers to face facts, and their fear of bringing upon themselves and their country the choice which, in the end, was forced upon them, had continued after the 'scare' of November 1939, when the British and French Governments had failed to persuade King Leopold to agree to a declaration that Belgium would enter the war if the Germans invaded the Netherlands.[1]

During December 1939, the Belgian authorities discouraged even normal contacts between their General Staff and the British and French Military Attachés. At the beginning of January 1940, the French Government heard through Count Ciano that the Germans (a) were 'about to launch a grand-scale offensive'. This report did not seem very probable. The Foreign Office agreed with the French view that it was more likely to be a prelude to a new peace move, but on January 6 the Netherlands Government announced that rumours in the 'foreign press' were raising doubts about the resolution of the Dutch to resist attack; the Netherlands Government therefore reaffirmed that the integrity of their country was not a matter for negotiation. An attack on the Netherlands would 'meet with the most obstinate armed resistance'.

On January 8 Lord Halifax told the Belgian Ambassador that, in the opinion of His Majesty's Government, the Belgian Government (b) would do well to state that, if the Dutch were attacked, Belgium would support them. A few days later the question of a German attack on the Low Countries became a matter of urgent consideration. On January 10 a German aeroplane made a forced landing[2] at Mechelen-sur-Meuse. After the landing two officers in the aeroplane tried to burn some papers which they were carrying. A Belgian officer seized the papers and found that they contained plans for an offensive from the North Sea to the Moselle, and for the occupation of the Netherlands and an air attack on Great Britain.

The Belgian Government took no immediate steps after the discovery of these papers. On the morning of January 13, however, the Belgian Foreign Minister, through his Chef de Cabinet, let His (c) Majesty's Government know his alarm at the accumulation of evidence suggesting a German attack on Belgium and the Netherlands on January 15, or at the latest, early in February. At midnight on January 13-14 M. Spaak asked Sir L. Oliphant[3] to come to (d)

---

[1] See Chapter I, Section (iii).

[2] The Belgian Government did not think that the landing was 'staged'. The Germans had, in fact, fixed January 17 as the date for the opening of the offensive which had been postponed in November.

[3] Sir L. Oliphant succeeded Sir R. Clive as Ambassador at Brussels on December 1, 1939.

(a) C169/89/18.   (b) C434/31/18.   (c) C677/677/18.   (d) C678/677/18.

see him. He said that he wanted to inform His Majesty's Government that the Belgian Government had grave reason to expect a German attack next morning; if such an attack took place, Belgium would look to Great Britain and France for help.

At midday on January 14 Sir L. Oliphant was instructed to tell the Belgian Government that we should fulfil our obligations to Belgium, and that it was necessary to hold staff conversations at once. Mean-
(a) while the King of the Belgians had asked Sir R. Keyes to come to Belgium. Sir R. Keyes arrived on January 13 and, after seeing King Leopold, went to British General Headquarters in France. Here at
(b) 2 a.m. on January 14 he telephoned to Mr. Churchill a message from the King asking whether His Majesty's Government would agree, if Belgium were involved in the war, (i) not to open peace negotiations without Belgian participation, (ii) to give guarantees for the complete restoration of the territorial and political status of Belgium and the Belgian colonies, (iii) to promise help in the economic and financial restoration of Belgium. On these terms Sir R. Keyes thought that the King could persuade his Ministers to invite the Anglo-French armies into Belgium 'at once'. The Prime Minister, however, whom Mr. Churchill consulted, felt that the time was not one for giving guarantees other than those of a military alliance and that the most useful step would be to begin staff conversations. Sir R. Keyes was therefore instructed to give the King a message in this sense.

The War Cabinet met on the morning of January 14.[1] They decided to ask M. Daladier's views on the King's three conditions, and to find out from the British and French military authorities how soon a move into Belgium could take place after an invitation had been received; they also gave instructions that Sir R. Keyes should tell the King that his questions were under consideration, but could not be answered at once. Unfortunately the War Cabinet failed to notice an ambiguity in Sir R. Keyes's message. Sir R. Keyes had received this message from King Leopold at a time when the King and his Ministers thought that Belgium might be invaded within a few hours. It seemed therefore, from the message, and from M. Spaak's statement to Sir L. Oliphant, that the King had in mind an immediate entry of Allied troops into Belgium. The War Cabinet did not consider the possibility of a different interpretation. The term 'at once' might mean 'as soon as the Germans attacked'; in other words, if there were no German attack, there would be no invitation. The attack which the Belgians had expected had not taken place. The War Office had already doubted the authenticity of the main evidence upon which the expectation of attack had been based, and the

---

[1] The Prime Minister was not present, but agreed by telephone to the decisions.
(a) WM(40)11.5, C.A., C871/31/18. (b) WM(40)12.1, C.A., C872/31/18.

French had reported that there were no enemy movements of a kind (a) likely to be the prelude to an attack. Hence, whatever the King had meant by the words 'at once', when he thought a German attack imminent, he might again draw back as soon as the alarm had subsided.

The King, in fact, did withdraw his invitation, or at all events did not proceed with it when the emergency had passed. The Allies, on the other hand, acted for a short time on the assumption that the invitation held good if they accepted the three conditions. The War Cabinet met again in the afternoon of January 14. The Prime (b) Minister reported that the French agreed to give the assurances required by the King:[1] they also thought that it would be a great military advantage to move into Belgium, but that the move must be made as soon as the invitation had been received. Although the War Cabinet still accepted the literal interpretation of the King's 'at once', they began to doubt whether the invitation would be maintained now that there seemed to be no immediate risk of a German attack. Nevertheless they decided to tell the King that the Allied Governments were ready to accept an invitation for the entry of Allied troops into Belgium, that the required guarantees went further than anything we had promised to France, but that we would give them, subject to our ability to carry them out at the end of the war, and that the value of the invitation would be seriously discounted if it were not given at once.

Late in the evening of January 14 Sir L. Oliphant telegraphed that (c) he had carried out the instructions sent to him at midday and that M. Spaak thanked His Majesty's Government for their promise of support but said that he would have to refer the question of staff talks to his Prime Minister. He also said that he had received reports of the postponement of the German attack. Meanwhile, the French Government were under the impression that, since the Allies had accepted the King's conditions, they would receive the invitation 'at once'. General Gamelin had therefore ordered French troops to the Belgian frontier where they were in an exposed position (in very cold weather) and vulnerable to air attack. Hence on the morning of January 15 M. Daladier told the Belgian Ambassador that the (d) troops must either move into Belgium or return to their previous positions. The Belgian Government sent an oral answer that they could not give an invitation for a move into Belgium. General Gamelin therefore withdrew the French forces on the night of January 15–16.

The confusion did not end here. The British Government had no answer to their message to King Leopold until the evening of January (e)

---

[1] King Leopold had not informed the French Government or General Gamelin of his conversation with Sir R. Keyes.

(a) C689/677/18. (b) WM(40)13.1, C.A.; C873, 895/31/18. (c) C696/31/18. (d) C774, 775, 869, 1050, 1051, 1207/31/18. (e) C893/31/18.

15. Sir L. Oliphant then telephoned a report from Sir R. Keyes. The King said that he had not asked for the guarantees through official channels and on behalf of the Belgian Government. He could not accept the provision that the guarantees would be given only if the Belgian Government agreed to the immediate occupation by the Allies of strategic points in Belgium. This demand would have a very bad effect upon the Belgian Government since it would mean that Belgium must again become the battlefield of Europe. The King said that his Government would not enter the war as long as there was a hope of averting it from Belgium. Any other course would be unfair to the Belgian people.

The War Cabinet considered this report on January 16. They also
(a) had a message from Sir L. Oliphant that M. Spaak had asked him to call at 10.30 a.m. on January 15, but had twice postponed the interview. Sir L. Oliphant had heard later that an answer to the request for staff talks would have been a refusal. The King held the view that sufficient preparations had been made for co-operation; all the necessary information was ready in envelopes to be handed to the service attachés without delay in the event of a German attack. The King explained that he could not compel his Government to agree to staff talks, but that he would do his utmost to attain the same end
(b) without talks. The War Cabinet considered the King's reply to be deplorable, but that the occasion should be used to secure close co-operation, even if we could not get staff conversations. Sir R. Keyes was therefore instructed to insist that the information in the envelopes should be given to the service attachés at once.[1]

(c)   [1] These instructions crossed a telegram from Sir L. Oliphant that, although M. Spaak had refused staff conversations, he had promised to answer questions put by British and French Military Attachés. The King's words about preparations already made for co-operation evidently referred primarily to military information supplied through General van Overstraeten in answer to questionnaires given to him and to other information obtained by the French military authorities.

(d)   In September 1941 the Belgian Government informed His Majesty's Government that in March 1940, General Delvoye, Belgian Military Attaché in Paris, had been instructed to see General Gamelin in order to recapitulate the information already supplied to him and, after reviewing the results obtained by previous contacts, to ensure that there were no lacunae and no misunderstandings. General Delvoye asked General Gamelin whether, on the hypothesis of a German attack, and in accordance with the dispositions envisaged, French and British forces would advance beyond the Antwerp–Namur line. General Gamelin's answer showed that he was entirely clear on the situation and that there were no ambiguities. The Belgian Government therefore maintained that the plan of operations carried out by the Belgians on May 10, was in full conformity with General Gamelin's statement.

(e)   The Belgian Government made a further statement to His Majesty's Government on February 9, 1942, that these conversations took place between General Delvoye and General Gamelin during the period from the end of February to the end of March. In view of General Gamelin's request for an invitation as soon as possible after a German attack had begun, the Belgian authorities had taken steps to ensure that the invitation could be transmitted by several other ways if the Germans had destroyed ordinary telephone communications.

(a) C783/292/4.   (b) WM(40)15.7, C.A.   (c) C870/292/4.   (d) C10460/10460/4 (1941). (e) C1585/460/4 (1942).

The confusion over the King's invitation and demand for guaran- (a)
tees was not cleared up until Sir R. Keyes explained to Lord Halifax
on February 21–2[1] that the phrase in his message that the King might
be able to persuade his Ministers to invite Allied troops into Belgium
'at once' represented his (Sir R. Keyes's) own opinion and not a
statement by the King to this effect.

After this explanation the Foreign Office considered that Sir L.
Oliphant should tell King Leopold of the misunderstanding and
should offer him a revised statement of the proposed guarantees. He
could repeat that the effectiveness of Allied help depended upon the
promptness with which it was requested and the extent to which
military arrangements between Belgium and the Allies had been
co-ordinated. A communication on these lines might reassure the
King and promote the exchange of military information. It might
also lessen the risk of a Belgian surrender to German demands and
thus increase the chances that Belgium might call on us for help
before a German invasion or even in the case of a German attack on
the Netherlands. The final text of the guarantees was in these terms: (b)

'(1) We are ready to accept an invitation to British troops to enter
Belgium, and we understand that the French attitude is the same.
(2) We are asked to give guarantees to Belgium which go further
than anything we have promised to France, and which we might not
be in a position to carry out at the end of the war. Subject to the
above, we are ready to promise as follows if such an invitation were
given:

(i) If Belgium thereupon becomes involved with the Allies in
hostilities with Germany, neither of us will open peace
negotiations without the participation of the other.
(ii) We will do our utmost to maintain the political and territorial
integrity of Belgium and her colonies.
(iii) If, after the war, Belgium is in need of economic and financial
assistance, we will include her in any assistance we may be
able, in conjunction with our Allies, to render in these respects.

The King will realise that the value of an invitation will be seriously
discounted, from the point of view of Belgium as well as of ourselves,
unless the invitation is given in sufficient time to enable the British
and French troops to secure all the strategic advantages of position
before any German attack begins.'

Sir L. Oliphant made this communication to the King on March (c)
22. The King was unwilling to give an immediate answer, but said
that he would consider the question. No answer was, in fact, given.

---

[1] This delay in giving an explanation was due partly to the fact that Sir R. Keyes had
written an account of his interview with King Leopold in a letter to Mr. Churchill, and
that he had intended this letter to be shown to the Prime Minister and to Lord Halifax.

(a) C1421, 2044/31/18; C1871, 1932, 2520, 2879, 3243, 3404, 4013/292/4. (b) WP(40)
98, C4180/292/4; WM(40)72, C4257/31/18. (c) C4725/31/18.

(iii)

*Possible action in the event of a German invasion of the Netherlands:
sixth and seventh meetings of the Supreme War Council, March 28 and
April 9: Allied decision to ask the Belgian Government for an immediate
invitation into Belgium: refusal of the Belgian Government to give this
invitation: eighth meeting of the Supreme War Council, April 22–3, 1940:
consideration of Allied policy.*

Although the Belgian fears of invasion in mid-January were not
borne out by events, and although reports[1] of a German offensive
in February seemed no more than a part of the German 'war of
nerves', there remained the possibility of an attack on the western
front in March. Military information showed that the Germans had
massed on the Dutch and Belgian frontiers troops enough for an
offensive. There was no information suggesting an attack on the
Maginot line; the most probable areas for an offensive were the
Dutch, Belgian and Luxembourg frontiers, and little additional
preparation would have been necessary there for launching a full-
scale attack.

In the middle of March—and while the War Cabinet were
deciding upon a revised offer of guarantees to the King of the
Belgians—there were signs that the Belgian Government was again
(a) becoming nervous. M. Spaak said to Sir L. Oliphant on March 16
that the difficulty of getting help to Finland across neutral territory
had caused him to ask what would be the attitude of Great Britain
and France if Germany attacked the Netherlands but did not
attack Belgium, while Belgium wished to go to the assistance of the
Dutch? Would the Allies then send troops across Belgium?

Sir L. Oliphant answered that he must refer the question to the
(b) Foreign Office. Lord Halifax raised the matter at the War Cabinet
on March 18. On March 19 the War Cabinet authorised the Foreign
(c) Office to reply that His Majesty's Government could not answer
M. Spaak's questions fully until they had consulted the French
Government. They could say at once that, if the Belgians went to the
assistance of the Dutch in the event of a German attack on the
Netherlands, the Allies would come immediately to the help of
Belgium, and that if, contrary to our expectation, the Belgians did
not assist the Dutch, His Majesty's Government, in response to a
Dutch appeal, might send air forces across Belgium and troops into

---

[1] An investigation of the sources of reports of a forthcoming large-scale air offensive
against Great Britain pointed to an attempt by the Germans to spread these reports from
neutral capitals in the second week of February.

(a) C4020/31/18.   (b) WM(40)71.6, C.A., C4185/31/18;   WM(40)72, C4257/31/18.
(c) C4020/31/18.

Belgian territory both to help the Dutch and to protect themselves. In either case Allied action would depend upon Dutch military dispositions of which the Allies had no knowledge. The Belgian Government should therefore advise the Dutch to give us the necessary information. At the same time the Foreign Office let M. Daladier know of M. Spaak's questions and of the provisional answers to them.

Sir L. Oliphant gave the answers to M. Spaak on the evening of (a) March 20. M. Spaak was willing to consider an approach to the Netherlands Government, but said that they were 'very taciturn'. He 'bridled considerably' at the suggestion that in the event of a German invasion of the Netherlands the Allies might assume a right of passage across Belgium.

The War Cabinet reconsidered the question on March 21. It was (b) pointed out that we had told the Belgians that the effectiveness of our aid would depend upon the promptness with which an invitation was given to us. This statement might imply that without an invitation we should not enter Belgium, but we had also said that we might do so in the event of a German invasion of the Netherlands even if the Belgians did not give active help to the Dutch. It would therefore be logical for us to enter Belgium without an invitation if the Germans invaded the country. Lord Halifax said that the Foreign Office had always taken this view and that our message to the King of the Belgians had been worded in such a way that it did not imply that we should necessarily wait for an invitation. The War Cabinet considered that we should make sure by enquiry that the French Government agreed with our view of the matter, since General Gamelin, who would be responsible for giving orders to advance into Belgium, would be acting under French instructions.[1]

There was some delay in getting the French views owing to the resignation of the French Government on March 20. On March 23 (c) M. Reynaud told Sir R. Campbell that he agreed with the provisional answer given to M. Spaak, but that he must consult his colleagues. Three days later Sir R. Campbell reported M. Reynaud's acceptance of the British view. M. Reynaud thought that, if the Low (d) Countries, owing to German intimidation, did not defend their neutrality with full force, they ceased to be neutral because their 'passivity' was of assistance to the enemy. General Gamelin, however, considered that from a military point of view it would be useless to enter Belgium, if the Dutch were attacked, without an

---

[1] The question was also raised whether we should have a right to enter Dutch or Belgian territory if the Dutch or Belgian Governments accepted German demands which threatened their neutrality. The Foreign Office view was that, if the Dutch agreed to a gross breach of their neutrality, we should be legally justified in entering their territory to attack German bases established in it, but that, without a Dutch appeal for help, we should have no legal justification for entering Belgian territory in order to reach the Netherlands.

(a)C4319/31/18. (b)WM(40)74, C4389/31/18. (c)C4393, 4390/31/18. (d)C4560/31/18.

invitation.[1] The Allied forces would have to cross 100 miles of Belgian territory to help the Dutch. They would have to construct defence positions. Without a Belgian invitation these operations would take place in potentially hostile country, with the Belgian fortresses on our flank, and would lose us time so that we could do no more than occupy the line of the Scheldt, and therefore be of no assistance to the Dutch.

(a)   The War Cabinet agreed on March 27 that the matter should be raised at the forthcoming meeting of the Supreme War Council. They also authorised Sir N. Bland, British Minister to the Netherlands, to discuss officially with the Netherlands Government the question of Allied assistance.[2] Sir N. Bland was given the official

(b) answer on March 30. The Netherlands Government considered that they must maintain their traditional policy of independence and that, for this reason, they could not engage themselves with Belgium. Sir N. Bland pointed out that it was possible to hold preliminary talks without making engagements, but the Netherlands Foreign Minister, M. van Kleffens, said that His Majesty's Government must already know what help the Dutch would need.

(c)   The Supreme War Council met on March 28. In the course of their discussion of future policy in the offensive conduct of the war they considered the action which they would take in the event of a German attack on Belgium or the Netherlands. Their resolutions summed up the situation before the German invasion of Scandinavia: (i) If Germany invaded Belgium, the Allies would enter the country without waiting for a formal invitation. They would not make their intention known in advance to the Belgian Government, since they wished to avoid the impression that it was a matter of indifference whether they did or did not receive a formal invitation. (ii) If Germany invaded the Netherlands, and the Belgians went to the help of the Dutch, the Allies would support Belgium at once. (iii) If the Belgians did not go to the help of the Dutch, the Allies would regard themselves as entitled to enter Belgium for the purpose of assisting the Dutch, but would reserve their liberty of action on the course to be adopted. (iv) The grant of naval or air bases to Germany by the Dutch would be an unneutral act entitling the Allies to take such counter-action as they might think necessary in the circumstances. (v) The contingencies in (iii) and (iv) were to be the subject of study by the British and French staffs: the question of a move through Belgium to the Netherlands was thus, in fact, left

---

[1] Lord Gort agreed with General Gamelin's view.

[2] Sir N. Bland had found the attitude of the Dutch Government in unofficial conversations more favourable than he had expected in view of previous statements that they would not ask for Allied help 'until the last possible moment'.

(a) WM(40)76; C4639, 4342, 4020/31/18.   (b) C4624, 4726/31/18.   (c) C5988/9/17.

in suspense, and no communication was made to the Belgian Government. On April 5, however, the Foreign Office sent to the War Cabinet Office the draft of a communication which they proposed to make to M. Spaak. The draft stated that, if Germany invaded the Netherlands and Belgium went to her assistance, the Allies would (a) support Belgium immediately with all their forces; the Allies were unwilling to believe that Belgium would not go to the help of the Dutch in the event of a German attack on the Netherlands, but if this should be the case the Allies reserved full liberty of action, whether for the purpose of helping the Dutch or of safeguarding their own security and vital interests.

The Foreign Office considered that this form of words avoided any apparent contradiction about the question of receiving an invitation before entering Belgium, and that Sir L. Oliphant should be instructed to say—if M. Spaak raised the matter again—that he had nothing to add to the text. On April 9 General Ismay agreed to the text on behalf of the Chiefs of Staff.

On the morning of the German invasion of Norway and Denmark, the French Conseil de Guerre decided in favour of an immediate (b) move into Belgium if the co-operation of the Belgian Government were assured. M. Reynaud asked the French military, naval and air commanders whether they approved of this move in spite of Allied air inferiority. Their approval was based on the view that the addition of 18–20 Belgian divisions to the Allied forces would practically cancel out German military superiority in numbers on the western front.

At the seventh meeting of the Supreme War Council[1] on April 9 (c) M. Reynaud proposed an immediate Anglo-French communication to the Belgian Government asking for an invitation into Belgium. He said that the entry of Allied troops would shorten the line of defence and protect the vulnerable industrial regions of northern France. M. Daladier also added that, according to French reports, a German offensive on the western front was about to open and might settle the problem of getting an invitation from the Belgian Government. The Prime Minister asked what the Allies should do in the event of the refusal of an invitation. M. Reynaud thought that our action must depend on the attitude of the Belgian Army. The army might be willing to co-operate even if the Government refused to invite us into Belgium. Without the collaboration of the army, Allied inferiority on land and in the air, and perhaps also in munitions, would make action impossible.

---

[1] For the meeting of the Supreme War Council, see also section (i) of this chapter.
(a) C5077/9/17; C5228/31/18. (b) C5226/31/18. (c) C5513/9/17.

The Council decided to act upon the French suggestion. At
(a) 9.30 p.m. Mr. Aveling, Chargé d'Affaires while Sir L. Oliphant was
on leave in England, was instructed, in concert with the French
Ambassador, to point out to M. Spaak that German aggression
against neutral States was spreading and the threat to Belgium
imminent. The efficacy of Allied help depended very largely upon
the ability of the Allies to move forward in good time to take up a
suitable line. The Allied Governments thought it indispensable to the
security of Belgium that they should receive an invitation at once for
their troops to enter the country. The Belgian Government would
realise their grave responsibility if, owing to their hesitation, they
did not get the assistance now offered to them in conditions necessary
to make it effective.

Mr. Aveling saw M. Spaak at 1 a.m. on April 10. M. Spaak said
(b) that an invitation to the Allies would bring a German invasion in
which one half of Belgium would be overrun, since the Allied forces
would presumably occupy the Antwerp–Namur line. The Belgian
General Staff did not think an attack imminent. From a political
point of view acceptance of the Allied proposal would 'place Belgium
in a lamentable moral situation'. It was impossible to reconcile an
invitation to the Allies with the Belgian engagements to which the
United Kingdom and France had given formal recognition on
April 24, 1937.[1] In answer to questions from Mr. Aveling, M. Spaak
said that the Belgian Government might be more ready to consider
the proposal if they could be assured of an Allied advance to the
more easterly line of the Albert canal (from Antwerp to the Meuse),
and that the Belgian Government would call in the Allies if they
were sure that an invasion was about to take place.

The Foreign Office enquired whether M. Spaak had spoken in a
similar way to M. Bargeton, the French Ambassador, whom he had
seen immediately before his conversation with Mr. Aveling. They
found that M. Spaak had not done so, possibly because M. Bargeton
had not put the questions to him. Sir R. Campbell was therefore
asked on the night of April 10–11 to enquire from M. Reynaud
whether the French would agree to occupy the Albert canal line.
(c) M. Reynaud sent an officer at once to General Gamelin's headquarters and reported an hour later that the French could promise
to do everything in their power to give satisfaction to the Belgian
desideratum. M. Reynaud said that he must also consult M. Daladier.
(d) In the evening of April 11 Sir R. Campbell reported M. Daladier's
agreement.

The Belgian Government, however, issued communiqués to the
press on April 10 and 11 announcing their intention to adhere to a

---

[1] See above, Chapter I, section (iii).

(a) C5252/31/18. (b) C5291/31/18. (c) C5300/31/18. (d) C5377/31/18.

policy of strict neutrality. M. Spaak told Mr. Aveling during the (a) afternoon of April 11 that the Belgian Cabinet had endorsed his provisional answer unanimously and almost without discussion. A new situation would arise if Belgium could be assured of really effective Allied help on the Albert canal line but M. Spaak could not commit his Government to a question which was at present 'hypothetical'. He repeated that there seemed to be no immediate danger of a German attack.

Mr. Aveling, on the instructions of the War Cabinet, told M. Spaak (b) in the afternoon of April 12 of the French assurances. M. Spaak said that they did not tally with the French Ambassador's statement to him.[1] On the following day the Belgian Ambassador in London came to the Foreign Office to say that during the previous forty-eight hours, while there had been no sign of a reinforcement of the Germans, Allied troops had been moved up close to the Belgian frontier and that no information of the reason for this move had been given. The Belgian Government wished to be assured that the Allies would not enter Belgium without an invitation. The Ambassador also mentioned comments in Belgium about the reinforcement of the British armies in France.

A written reply was sent from the Foreign Office to the Ambassador on April 14 ignoring the Belgian demand for an assurance but saying that Allied troop movements were not intended as a means of pressure upon Belgium. The Ambassador, however, asked again for a definite answer to his question. Later on April 14 Lord Halifax repeated the assurance already given viz. (i) that in the event of a German attack on Belgium we should instantly come to the help of the Belgian Government (who had already said they would ask for help); and (ii) that in the event of a German attack on the Netherlands, we should immediately give help to Belgium if the Belgians went to the help of the Dutch. Lord Halifax pointed out to the Ambassador that the Belgians ought to want us to have as large a force as possible in France. He also said that we could not answer questions about action on our part which would depend upon the attitude of the Belgians themselves unless we knew what their attitude would be. For example, what would Belgium do if Germany attacked the Netherlands without invading Belgium? Or again, the Dutch might allow the Germans to establish themselves in the Netherlands as they had occupied Denmark. Would the Belgian Government expect the Allies to do nothing, even though the German action might affect the whole issue of the war?

---

[1] The difference appears to have been one of emphasis. Mr. Aveling seems to have emphasised the French promise to try to reach the Albert canal line; the French Ambassador, on the other hand, while also saying that the French would try to reach the line, emphasised that they could give no undertaking to do so.

(a) C5417/31/18. (b) WM(40)89; C5508, 5291, 5478, 5482, 5490, 5522/31/18.

The Foreign Office, at the Ambassador's request, summarised these points in a note for the Belgian Government. Two days later
(a) Sir L. Oliphant sent a report, from a reliable source, that King Leopold and his advisers had decided not to go to the assistance of the Dutch in the event of a German attack on the Netherlands. M. Spaak had also said in the Senate that Belgian policy was one of absolute neutrality and that the Belgian Government would accept no proposal leading to an abandonment of this course.

The Foreign Office had thought it desirable, even before M. Spaak's conversation of April 12 with Mr. Aveling, to tell the Belgian Government definitely that, if Belgium did not go to the help of the Dutch,
(b) the Allies would nevertheless enter Belgium, not only to assist the Dutch but to safeguard their own security as well as that of Belgium. On April 12, after receiving the Belgian reply of that day, they had instructed Sir R. Campbell to propose to the French Government that they should make a joint communication to the Belgians. This communication would begin in the terms of the Foreign Office draft already approved by the Chiefs of Staff,[1] but would also state definitely that, even if the Belgians did not go to the help of the Dutch, the Allies would feel obliged to enter Belgium for the purpose of going to the assistance of the Dutch, and also of safeguarding the security and vital interests of Belgium and of the Allies themselves. The French Government had replied on April 13 that they still thought it inadvisable to make this statement, since the Belgians would continue to refuse to commit themselves, and another rebuff would make our action later even more difficult. On hearing Sir L. Oliphant's report, however, it seemed to the Foreign Office necessary to leave no doubt about our intentions.

The War Cabinet considered the question on April 18. In view of
(c) the great danger to us if the Germans established themselves in the Netherlands, they regarded it as essential that we should enter Belgium if the Germans attacked the Dutch. They were somewhat concerned that the French seemed doubtful about going in if the Belgians remained neutral. They were also sure that if we went in, the Germans would attack Belgium. They decided first to confirm French agreement, since it appeared uncertain whether M. Reynaud really intended a move into Belgium as soon as the Germans invaded the Netherlands. The second step would be to ask the Belgians to tell us what they would do. If the Belgians assumed that, by concessions to Germany, they could avoid being drawn into the war, we should put an end to their complacency by pointing out that, if the Netherlands were invaded, Belgium would certainly be involved.

---

[1] See above, p. 141.

(a) C5719/31/18.   (b) C5362, 5492, 5504, 5511, 5512/31/18.   (c) WM(40)96, C5984/31/18.

Sir R. Campbell was therefore instructed on the night of April (a)
18–19 that His Majesty's Government wanted a clear statement from
the French Government on three points: (i) If Germany invaded the
Netherlands, and not Belgium, was it agreed that the Allies should
enter Belgium at once? (ii) If the Dutch ceded bases to Germany, was
it agreed that the Allies should enter Belgium at once? The Supreme
War Council had decided that in this latter case, the Allies should reserve freedom of judgment. His Majesty's Government now considered
that no difference should be made between cases (i) and (ii). (iii) Was
it agreed that General Staff talks about air action should apply to all
circumstances in which the Allies might enter Belgium?[1] Sir R.
Campbell was told that there was a danger that Germany might
acquire by intimidation or invasion most valuable bases in the
Netherlands for an attack upon Great Britain. The Belgians might
accept German assurances and the Germans might then consolidate
their position in the Netherlands. For this reason it seemed 'very
desirable to disillusion the Belgian Government by showing them
that we shall feel bound to make a move which will certainly expose
them to German invasion'. Hence we were asking the French to
reconsider their decision not to reopen the question with the Belgian
Government.

The French Government gave an affirmative answer on April 19 to (b)
the questions put to them. They still thought, however, that it would
be better not to make a statement of our intentions to the Belgian
Government. If the Germans heard of such a statement they might
compel the Belgians to say that they would oppose any violation of
their neutrality. The Allies might therefore find themselves hindered
at the moment of action by Belgian opposition.[2] For the time, His
Majesty's Government accepted the French view.

The possibility of a German attack on the Netherlands was discussed at a meeting of the Supreme War Council on April 22–3. The (c)
British view at this time was that such an attack—as a prelude to a
full-scale air offensive against Great Britain and British shipping—
was likely to be the next German move. M. Reynaud repeated the
French argument against letting the Belgian Government know our
intentions. If we made a statement to them, they might refuse to

---

[1] On April 12 His Majesty's Government had asked whether M. Reynaud agreed that, (d)
in the event of a German attack on Belgium or the Netherlands, air attacks should be made
on military objectives in Germany, and the 'Royal Marine Operation' should be carried
out. On April 13 the French Government accepted these proposals subject to agreement
between the General Staffs upon the nature and military importance of the objectives and
to an understanding that the Allies had no interest in initiating action which might affect
the civilian population. Owing to the French hesitation, Mr. Chamberlain raised the question of air action at the Supreme War Council on April 23.

[2] The British view was that an Allied statement, if known to the Germans, might deter
them from action.

(a) C5724/31/18.   (b) C5850, 5851, 5852, 5867, 5889, 5890/31/18.   (c) C6205/9/17.
(d) C5362, 5491/31/18; C5493/5/18.

admit us into Belgium or make our entry conditional upon a request from the Dutch for help. The Dutch might not ask for help, while the Allies needed the twenty divisions of the Belgian army.

The Prime Minister said that we had accepted the French decision not to make a statement, but that we wanted to be clear whether they proposed an Allied occupation of the Antwerp–Namur line if the Netherlands were invaded. M. Daladier said that if the Belgians did not go to the assistance of the Dutch, the Germans might reach the mouth of the Scheldt before the Allies had taken up position: the Belgian defences would then be outflanked. If the Belgians agreed upon our entry, we should be assured of the co-operation of their twenty divisions and could move rapidly to the Antwerp–Namur line. Without this co-operation it would be difficult to do so.[1]

The Prime Minister pointed out that the question of the Netherlands was more important to Great Britain than to France, and that we should have to take air action to hamper a Dutch occupation. M. Reynaud wanted consultation with the French high command before we attacked objectives in German territory. Our attacks might bring retaliation on French aeroplane factories. American equipment was being installed in these factories. If it was destroyed, replacement would take a long time; the transfer of the factories to safer regions would not be completed for several months. M. Reynaud agreed that German marshalling yards might be attacked.

The Prime Minister explained that we did not propose indiscriminate bombing of German factories, but that we wanted to attack certain vital objectives in Germany while conditions for attack were still favourable; for example, a lightning blow against the nine oil refineries in the Ruhr might upset the internal economy as well as the military effort of Germany. M. Reynaud agreed that attack on these refineries might be carried out without previous Anglo-French consultation if the Germans attacked the Netherlands or Belgium. The Council also resolved (i) that, if the Germans attacked the Netherlands, the Allies would enter Belgium at once without further consultation between themselves and irrespective of the Belgian attitude; the extent of their advance, however, would depend on this attitude; (ii) that the Belgian Government was not to be approached in advance with a request to agree to the entry of the Allies in the event of an attack on the Netherlands, but that a joint Anglo-French note should be prepared for delivery at the time of the Allied entry.

Thus after months of negotiation the relations between Belgium and the Allies were still not satisfactory, and the Belgian King and Government, in the hope of avoiding attack, had lost the most favourable chances of protecting themselves even on the Antwerp–

---

[1] i.e. it might not be possible to establish a line beyond the Scheldt.

Namur line. In these circumstances the Germans made their 'lightning' move into the Low Countries, and the French and British armies came out to meet them with consequences far more disastrous to the Allied cause than defeat in Norway.

(iv)

The Allies and Italy: Mussolini's increasing hostility: breakdown of Anglo-Italian trade negotiations: Anglo-French discussions on the question of an Italian attack on Yugoslavia.

The German successes in Scandinavia excited Mussolini as much as they depressed the King of the Belgians. Mussolini had begun earlier to emphasise more strongly the malevolent element in his neutrality, or 'non-belligerency'.[1] He showed the change in his attitude towards trade negotiations with Great Britain. Early in January Sir W. Greene, Master of the Rolls, went to Italy in order to discuss Anglo- (a) Italian commercial relations. The main points of negotiations were the stoppage of seaborne exports of German coal to Italy, the War Trade Agreement with Italy, the purchase from Italy of war material, and the chartering of Italian shipping. On his return Sir W. Greene (b) gave his opinion that there was little chance of success in the negotiations unless we spent up to £5 million in buying Italian fruit and vegetables.[2] In spite of the objections to this purchase, Sir W. Greene thought that we should have to agree to it. The War Cabinet accepted the proposal as part of a general agreement.

At the beginning of February it appeared fairly certain that this agreement would be made. On February 2 Mussolini had made no objection to a contract with the Caproni firm for the supply of training aircraft to Great Britain. Six days later, evidently under German pressure, Mussolini changed his mind, and refused to allow the contract to be signed. Sir P. Loraine telegraphed on February 8 that, according to Ciano, Mussolini was not prepared to consider (c)

---

[1] For the shifts in Mussolini's attitude, see *The Ciano Diaries* (English transl., Heinemann, 1947), and *D.G.F.P.*, VIII, *passim*. On January 31, 1940, Mussolini wrote a letter to Hitler criticising German policy.

[2] The Italians insisted on this purchase since they would otherwise have no market for the produce hitherto exchanged for German coal. (I have not dealt in detail with these trade negotiations, since they fall within the scope of other war histories.) The decision to stop German exports of coal followed the general action taken after November 27, 1939. against German exports in retaliation for the German violation of international law at sea. The decision had not been enforced against coal exports to Italy in view of the negotiations with the Italian Government over a war trade agreement.

(a) R301, 1200/48/22. (b) WM(40)26; R1"80⁵ 1390/48/22. (c) R1882, 18883, 2040. 2075, 2076, 2134, 2135/48/22.

these sales for another six months. He did not wish either to expose himself to 'misunderstanding' with the Germans or to denude Italy of modern armaments. Ciano assumed that Mussolini's decision would mean the stoppage of coal exports to Italy. Sir P. Loraine answered that this would be so, and that it was not certain that Great Britain would be willing to reopen discussions in six months' time. Sir P. Loraine thought that the Italian decision might be reconsidered in view of the economic difficulties in which Italy would be placed, but on February 13 Ciano repeated that Mussolini felt that, in view of Italo-German relations, he could not 'honourably' sell armaments to Great Britain. On February 19 the War Cabinet
(a) decided to stop German seaborne coal exports to Italy on March 1. At Sir P. Loraine's suggestion, British coal exports would be con-
(b) tinued for a month and would then cease because the Italians would be unable to pay for them.

The British decision brought a strong protest from Italy that the embargo on coal imports and British contraband measures in
(c) general would 'disturb the economic and political relations between Great Britain and Italy as set up by the agreements of April 16, 1938'.[1] The Foreign Office were uncertain whether Mussolini's change of mind was due to German pressure or whether it was an attempt to bluff over the coal question, or, again, whether Mussolini thought that the Germans were about to launch an offensive and that, in the event of a large German success, he could bring Italy into the war more easily if he had worked up a feeling of grievance against Great Britain. On the other hand Mussolini might be doing no more than showing his 'nuisance value' or even giving way to a fit of bad temper. In any case there could be no question of calling off the embargo on German coal. At the same time there appeared to be a misunderstanding over the actual date of the stoppage of the German coal exports. Thirteen coal ships which would have sailed before March 1 from Dutch ports with coal already paid for were held up because bad weather had delayed loading operations. These ships were intercepted and taken to British ports. The Foreign Office suggested that the ships might be released on the understanding that the Italians
(d) promised not to buy any more German seaborne coal. The War Cabinet agreed that this compromise should be offered to Italy. Mussolini accepted the arrangement on March 9. His acceptance was more significant because Ribbentrop was known to be coming to Rome, and Ciano did not hide his wish to get the matter settled before Ribbentrop's arrival.

On March 18 Hitler and Mussolini met at the Brenner Pass.

[1] See Command papers 5726 and 5793.
(a) WM(40)46, R2423/48/22. (b) WM(40)47, R2424/48/22; R2313, 2314/76/22. (c) R2815, 2959/51/22; R2814/76/22. (d) WM(40)61, R2991/76/22; WM(40)62, R3070/76/22; WM(40)63, R3085/76/22; WM(40)65, R3261/57/22.

Hitler told Mussolini of his intention to finish the war quickly by a rapid defeat of Great Britain and France. Mussolini said that Italy would enter the war soon, not to help Germany (since she did not need help) but because Italian honour required intervention.[1] Ciano assured Sir P. Loraine after this meeting that Italian policy had not changed. There would be no 'surprises' or *coups de théâtre*. (a) For the time Ciano's assurances were borne out by the facts, and, at all events before the German successes in their attack on Norway, there was nothing to show that Mussolini had come to a decision to bring Italy into the war.

In the first days of the German attack on Norway the evidence of Mussolini's intentions still seemed conflicting. On April 12 the Italian Ambassador in London was sure that Italy would not take any (b) 'final decision' in the immediate future, but reports from other sources suggested that Mussolini had been much impressed by the brilliance of Hitler's plans and had promised at the Brenner meeting to come in on the German side. There were rumours of discussions between Mussolini and other highly placed fascists on the expediency of Italian participation in the war.

The Foreign Office considered at this time that Italy was unlikely (c) to attack the Allies directly or, indirectly, by an attack on Corfu which would bring the Allied guarantee to Greece into operation. It was less certain that the Italians would not attack the Dalmatian coast. If such an attack took place, the Allies would not be in a position to intervene; all they could do would be to reserve their liberty of action. The French Government, who were also afraid that Italy would attack Yugoslavia, thought that the Allies should find out what Yugoslavia would do in the event of an attack, and what would be the attitude of Turkey, Greece and Roumania. They suggested on April 16 that these four States should be told that the individual (d) safety of each of them was bound up with that of the Balkan States as a whole. Allied assistance would depend upon the resources available as a result of the co-operation of the four States.

The Foreign Office did not regard the French proposals as practicable. The attitude of the four Balkan States would depend on Allied action and, if we tried to force them to commit themselves in advance, they would merely suspect us of wanting to get them involved in the war. We could not therefore merely wait to see what action the four States took among themselves. The War Cabinet agreed with this

---

[1] *Documenti diplomatici italiani*, 9th Ser., III, No. 524. According to the German record of the meeting Mussolini told Hitler, somewhat naively, that he would 'lose no time' after the Allies had been so shaken by the German attack that it 'only needed a second blow to bring them to their knees'. (*D.G.F.P.*, Series D, IX, p.15). In a memorandum of March 31 to the King of Italy, Mussolini described Italian entry into the war as inevitable.

(a) R3563/57/22. (b) R4882/60/22. (c) R4698/58/22; R4748/1961/7. (d) R4826/58/22.

(a) view. They suggested on April 18 that the French and British staffs should consider whether we should be well advised to go to war with Italy in the event of Italian aggression against Yugoslavia, i.e. were the military disadvantages of war with Italy less than the political disadvantages of allowing Yugoslavia to be overrun? If the answer were in favour of supporting Yugoslavia, we should find out whether we could count on Turkish help, and, if this were the case, we should inform the Yugoslav Government that, if they resisted attack, they would have British, French and Turkish support. The French Government agreed with this proposal as a first step.

(b)   At the meeting of the Supreme War Council on April 22–3 the French Government again raised the question of an expedition to Salonika. Mr. Chamberlain pointed out that the Greek Government might be unwilling to allow an Allied landing at Salonika if the Italian attack were directed against Yugoslavia and not against Greece. It was agreed that the Allied Governments should ask whether the Greeks would accept an Allied force at Salonika, and that the British and French staffs should consider the practical considerations (with special reference to shipping) involved in the despatch of such a force.

   Mr. Chamberlain told the French representatives at the Supreme War Council that His Majesty's Government did not consider it desirable to go to war with Italy in the event of an Italian attack on

(c) Yugoslavia. Before the next meeting of the Council on April 27 the British Chiefs of Staff had recommended that no approach should be made to the Greek Government about a possible landing at Salonika until the military aspects of the question had been examined by the Allies. The experience of air attack in Scandinavia showed that we could not establish or maintain a force at Salonika if we were at war with Italy. On the other hand a direct air attack on factories in north-west Italy might be the best way of 'knocking out' Italy at once. For this attack it would be necessary to use French aerodromes close to the Italian frontier.

   The War Cabinet decided on April 27 to put these views to the

(d) Supreme War Council which was meeting later in the day. There Mr. Chamberlain explained that he was not asking for an immediate decision, but that, if the Allies did no more than protest against an Italian attack on Yugoslavia, they would lose all influence in the Balkans, and, if they declared war on Italy, they ought not merely to impose severe economic pressure, since this would give Mussolini the chance of uniting the Italian people by telling them that they were being starved again by sanctions.

   The French representatives agreed to postpone the approach to

---

(a)WM(40)96, R4985/58/22. (b)R5004/58/22. (c)WM(40)105, R5464/5/67. (d)C6476/9/17.

Greece and to consider the question of an air attack on Italian industry in north-west Italy, but they made it clear that the French Air Ministry would oppose the latter plan until they had been able to remove to safer areas the machine tools received from the United States.

Meanwhile, although for a time the news from Italy had appeared more reassuring,[1] there were reports on April 26 that Mussolini had (a) persuaded the Fascist Grand Council to approve the entry of Italy into the war on May 1–2 and the opening of hostilities by attacks on Malta and Gibraltar. In view of these reports the War Cabinet (b) decided upon measures for the diversion of merchant shipping from the Mediterranean. After the meeting of the Supreme War Council they considered once more what should be done in the event of an Italian attack limited to Yugoslavia. The Foreign Office view was (c) that in the latter case we should declare war at once. On April 30 the War Cabinet thought that the balance of military advantage lay (d) in delivering a heavy blow immediately but that we could not do so unless the French agreed to our proposals for air attack. Otherwise we should be unable to give direct help to Yugoslavia and thereby to encourage the other Balkan States. The Germans would get control in Italy and we should have to meet German aircraft and submarines in the Mediterranean. The War Cabinet felt unable to come to a decision until they had more recent information about the military action which we could take against Italy, and until we knew more about the attitude of Turkey. The Turkish Government had replied (e) to a question whether they thought a declaration of war against Italy would be advisable. Their reply was, broadly speaking, that (f) they wanted to know more about the effect of an Italian entry into the war on the general chances of an Allied victory over Germany. The War Cabinet decided to agree to open staff talks with Turkey on this basis.

At the time of their concession to Italy on the coal ships detained after March 1, the War Cabinet had decided that in dealing with economic and contraband questions they would continue to be 'as friendly and helpful as possible' short of giving the impression that they would 'make any further concessions without some substantial *quid pro quo*'. Hence discussions went on about possible purchases in

---

[1] Mussolini was reported, from a French source, to have said: 'The Germans are trying to drag me into the war by the hair: luckily I am bald'.

(a) R5425/58/22.　(b) WM(40)105, R5465/5413/67.　(c) WP(40)141, R5581/58/22. (d) WM(40)108, R5630/58/22.　(e) R4826/58/22.　(f) R5297/58/22.

Italy, and in the third week of March, Mr. Playfair, of His Majesty's Treasury, went to Rome in order to resume conversations about a Clearing Agreement. Sir P. Loraine suggested that Mr. Rodd[1] should go back to Italy at the beginning of April. Mr. Rodd did not leave at (a) this time because on April 4 the War Cabinet authorised a general examination of Anglo-Italian economic relations, with special reference to contraband control.

(b)   The committee appointed to make this examination reported later in the month. In a review of the political situation they pointed out that Italy had been 'gradually modifying' her attitude of 'non-belligerency' in a sense favourable to Germany. Italian newspapers and broadcasts had taken on a decidedly anti-Allied tone, and were generally supporting the German aggression in Norway and Denmark. This change of tone might be intended merely to increase Italian 'nuisance value' and to counteract the swing of public opinion away from Germany. At all events the decision about peace or war remained with Mussolini. The King of Italy, Ciano, and most of Mussolini's advisers were against war; this could be said also of Catholic opinion and of public opinion as a whole, particularly in the industrial north. Mussolini could rely on the young men who formed the majority of the Fascist party and upon the rural population whose interests he had been careful to foster. On balance therefore it was unsafe to assume that he could not carry the nation with him into war on the German side. The question of reopening trade negotiations therefore had to be considered against this background of increasing menace.

On the Allied side economic relations with Italy were unsatisfactory. Control of contraband was becoming more and more ineffective. There was increasing evidence of leakage of imports into Germany and of German exports passing through Italy. Italy's own imports, especially oil, had improved considerably her war potential. Our treatment of Italian ships and cargoes had exposed us to neutral criticism that we showed favour to countries of which we were afraid; unless we tightened our control as regards Italy, we had no moral ground for tightening it elsewhere. Any further development of contraband traffic through Italy might have serious strategic consequences. We had therefore to choose between another attempt to reach an agreement with Italy and the enforcement of our control on a scale not less effective than that employed with regard to minor neutral Powers.

A decision between these alternatives would depend largely upon an estimate of their ultimate effect upon keeping Italy out of the

---

[1] Mr. Rodd had been in charge of negotiations in Italy on behalf of the Ministry of Economic Warfare.
(a) WM(40)81. (b) WP(G)(40)109, R5017/60/22.

war, i.e. should we try for an agreement in order to make it more difficult for Mussolini to get Italian support for a war policy or should we tighten up our controls in order to increase our economic pressure on Germany and to prevent Italian war potential from reaching a point at which Italy could safely consider entering the war? Each policy involved risks. The first alternative would not ensure that Italy stayed out of the war but would make an early entry less likely. On the other hand it would strengthen Italy and weaken our blockade against Germany. The second alternative would risk an 'early explosion' on the part of Mussolini, but would weaken Italy and make our blockade of Germany more effective. The committee recommended the first alternative for the immediate future.

On April 24 the War Cabinet accepted this view as the best (a) practical way of dealing with a situation for which there were no legal or political precedents. International law assumed only 'enemies' or 'neutrals': there were no provisions for meeting the case of 'pre-belligerency'. The War Cabinet decided to move cautiously and not to allow Italy to increase her war potential. We would also try to make a good bargain and would not let the Italians get the impression that we were offering concessions out of weakness. Lord Halifax therefore gave the Italian Ambassador an *aide-mémoire* (b) on April 26 summarising the British attitude and suggesting that Mr. Rodd should shortly go back to Rome.

Italy did not enter the war on May 1, but it was impossible to tell which—if any—of the conflicting rumours about Mussolini's intentions was correct. The general view of the Foreign Office on May 1 was that Mussolini's policy had three objectives. He was trying by (c) bluff and intimidation to induce us to make more concessions to Italy over contraband control and to approach him with offers to discuss Italian 'claims'; he was collaborating with Hitler to distract our attention and attract our forces to the Mediterranean and away from the North Sea; he was preparing the unwilling Italian nation to come into the war. Our own policy towards Italy was also threefold. We were trying to propitiate Mussolini by offering another trade agreement and by reducing our contraband control to a formality; we were taking precautionary measures such as the diversion of shipping and the proposed despatch of two battleships to the eastern Mediterranean; we were also trying to bring personal pressure to bear on Mussolini.[1]

---

[1] Lord Lothian reported that on April 29 President Roosevelt had sent a message to (d) Mussolini stating his 'considered opinion' that, if Italy entered the war, the war would spread until it included both North and South America, and that, in the end, Germany could not win. See *F.R.U.S.*, 1940, II, 691–2.

(a) WM(40)102, R5314/48/22. (b) R5429/48/22. (c) R5920/60/22. (d) R5547/58/22.

It was unlikely that Mussolini would go to war over contraband control. If it were essential for military reasons to avoid war with Italy, we might have to try to buy her off by satisfying some of her 'claims'. Meanwhile we should pay no attention to them. Our policy for the time should be to offer Mussolini a trade agreement, but otherwise to maintain both our contraband control and our precautionary measures.

In the few days preceding the German western offensive there were more rumours of a conflicting kind about Italian intentions. (a) On May 8 Sir P. Loraine, who had been home on leave prolonged by illness, had a long conversation with Ciano. Sir P. Loraine said that during the last month the possibility of an Anglo-Italian war had reappeared. Ciano's answer was that Mussolini stood by his pact with Germany and would fulfil all his obligations to Germany, that he had taken complete and sole control of Italian policy and would come to his decision 'at his own time and in his own way'. For the moment Italian policy was unchanged. Ciano could not say how long it would remain unchanged—'perhaps two months, perhaps four, perhaps six, maybe even two years'. Neither Ciano nor Mussolini thought that the 'real war' had yet begun. Ciano hinted that Mussolini's attitude would depend on what happened when the 'real war' began. Meanwhile Mussolini would discuss trade matters, but would 'reject and resent anything that looked like an attempt to bribe him away from his obligations to Germany'.

(a) R5933, 5925/58/22.

CHAPTER VI

Anglo-American relations to the beginning of the German offensive in the West

(i)

The first three months of war: the evolution of American opinion: amendments to the Neutrality Act: the Panama declaration.[1]

AT the outbreak of war the British Government knew that the great majority of Americans sympathised with the Allied cause and desired the defeat of Hitler. On the other hand this sympathy was based primarily on American ideas of right and justice, not on a calculation of American interests. Indeed, one of the problems of the Foreign Office in dealing with Anglo-American relations in the first stages of the war was that public opinion in the United States did not realise the extent to which American strategic and economic interests were bound up with an Allied victory.

To British observers it seemed obvious enough that in the event of an Allied defeat there would be no limit to the possibilities of expansion by the Axis Powers. The smaller European countries would fall directly under German or Italian domination. Two of these smaller countries, Belgium and the Netherlands, had colonies of great strategic and economic importance. These colonies, together with those of Great Britain and France, would be at the disposal of Germany and Italy. No help could be expected from Russia; if the Russians had made an agreement with Hitler when they could have had British and French support in resisting him, they were unlikely to dare to oppose him after he was master of the rest of Europe. Any concessions offered to Japan, in order to obtain freedom of action for the United States armed forces in the Atlantic area, would be bought at great ultimate risk to American security in the Pacific; the Japanese might indeed refuse American offers, and seize the occasion to fight their own war in conjunction with the Axis Powers.

Egypt, Iraq, Iran, and all Arabia would also become subservient to the victors, and the United States would no longer be assured of

---

[1] In dealing with the large subject of Anglo-American relations, I have excluded, as far as possible, here and in later chapters, the history of economic and financial relations, since these subjects are treated in other War Histories. I have therefore referred to them only to the extent necessary to explain the background of Anglo-American political relations.

supplies of rubber, tin, copper and other raw materials or of access to the oil resources of the Middle East or the Dutch East Indies. Furthermore, German influence would be strong in South America, where the Germans could offer markets on a barter basis which would give them great economic control, and where also they would have considerable means of extorting political concessions by threats or even, in some cases, by direct attack.

The danger to American ideas and institutions would thus be very great. There were no limits to Hitler's ambition. The possession of vastly increased resources would only strengthen his dreams of world mastery. He would know that criticism of National Socialism and its methods was most vocal in the United States. Since Hitler was likely to impose by force some kind of totalitarian régime upon Great Britain and France, the countries of North America would alone remain free to continue their criticism and to threaten the permanence of German hegemony. It was therefore certain that at the least Hitler would do all he could to interfere with American freedom of action and to undermine the structure of free government in the United States.

President Roosevelt and the Administration might be aware of these considerations; American opinion in general, while detesting the internal and external policy of the dictators, was still unwilling to face the possibility that the United States might be drawn into the European war in order to defend American interests, since in the last resort these interests could not be defended adequately by others. There was a widespread belief—fostered by German propaganda ever since the treaty of Versailles—that American participation in the first World War had been unnecessary and that Great Britain and France had misused a victory won with American help. To most Americans the risk of being involved in war a second time by mistakes in their own policy appeared more real and more serious than the risks which the United States would run in the event of an Allied defeat. Few people, indeed, outside a small circle of business men and technicians impressed by the German Air Force, envisaged such a defeat, at all events on the scale of the French collapse in May and June 1940. It was assumed that at the worst the United States would have a long time for preparation and that even if the Allies failed to destroy the Nazi régime or to stop German aggression in Europe, there was no immediate danger that the whole of the eastern Atlantic seaboard would fall under German control.

The extent to which President Roosevelt and his Administration, or certain members of it, had taken account before 1940 of the consequences of an Allied defeat is still a matter upon which historians may disagree. It is, however, certainly true that the President, who knew well enough how ill-prepared America was for war, had tried to focus public attention upon the menacing situation in Europe. Even so, the centre of discussion was not whether the United States should interfere either to prevent war or to secure an Allied victory if war came. In the summer of 1939 the President and the Administration attempted—unsuccessfully—to persuade Congress at least to remove some of the disadvantages which the American effort to 'legislate themselves out of war' would place upon the Allies.

The debates during the first half of the year 1939 over the amendment of the Neutrality Act of 1937 showed the strength of 'isolationist' views. The Act of 1937 represented the extreme point reached by 'isolationism'. The principal provisions of the Act were that, on the outbreak of a war, the President was bound to issue a declaration naming the belligerents. Thereafter the supply of arms, ammunition and the implements of war to the parties named in the declaration was illegal. The President also had power to declare that certain other materials could be supplied to belligerents only on the 'cash and carry' principle;[1] in other words, these materials could be carried solely in non-American ships and after all American interest in the title to them had been transferred.

The President and Administration made it clear that they wanted the amendment of the Act, and, in particular, the repeal of the embargo on the export of war material. A large body of opinion shared this view, on the ground that the embargo would prejudice the democratic States—since Great Britain and France, through their sea-power, could alone benefit by the freedom to import such material, and in any case could prevent it by their blockade from reaching their enemies. In view of the European situation, it was desirable to remove this handicap upon the democratic Powers as soon as possible. On the other hand a considerable isolationist element in Congress, and especially in the Senate, argued that the removal of the embargo might allow the President to lead the country into war. There were also domestic political reasons of a party kind for opposing a proposal which the President was known to support.

In the belief that the growing tension in Europe would convince Congress of the expediency of getting rid of the embargo, the Administration waited for a time before beginning their campaign. They were, however, unable to persuade the Senate. On July 11, 1939, the Senate Committee on Foreign Relations decided by 12 votes to 11 to defer until the next session of Congress proposals for the amendment of the Act. After a meeting on July 18 with the majority and minority leaders in the Senate, Mr. Roosevelt decided that it was useless to attempt any action.

---

[1] This last provision expired on May 1, 1939.

On the outbreak of war Mr. Roosevelt issued the prescribed proclamations and called a special session of Congress for September 21. In his opening message to Congress Mr. Roosevelt made it clear that he wanted as soon as possible the repeal of the embargo and other amendments to the neutrality legislation. Senator Pittman introduced into the Senate proposals to this effect on October 2. The bill passed the Senate on October 27, and was approved, after a much shorter debate, on November 2 by the House of Representatives. The new Act repealed the embargo on the export of arms, reimposed the 'cash and carry' principle and made it applicable to all materials, but exempted certain 'safe' belligerent areas from the operation of this clause. The President was given power to define 'combat areas' into which American ships and citizens might not enter. The Act continued the prohibition of loans to belligerent Governments, the collection of funds in the United States for such Governments except for relief purposes, and the use of American ports as supply bases by belligerents.

The counterpart to the view that America could keep out of the war was the belief that the war could be kept out of America. To this end an attempt was made soon after the outbreak of war to establish a 'security zone' within which the peace of the western hemisphere would be undisturbed. The President had considered a plan of this kind before the outbreak of war, and had indeed consulted the British Government about it at the beginning of July, 1939. He had proposed American air and naval patrols over the Western Atlantic in order to deny these waters to the operations of belligerents. In order to enable the patrols to be carried out he had asked for the use of bases at Trinidad, Santa Lucia, Bermuda and Halifax, and at Fernando Noronha in Brazilian territory.[1]

The British and Canadian Governments had agreed to provide the required facilities, though they made certain reservations with regard to their own belligerent rights in the area to be patrolled. Mr. Roosevelt obviously had more than one reason for his proposal, but he made it clear in conversation with the British Ambassador that he regarded it as in the interest of Great Britain, especially in the matter of obtaining information about the presence and location of German submarines in the patrolled area.

The question of a security zone was raised on a pan-American basis in the first month of the war, when the Governments of the United States, Argentine, Brazil, Chile, Colombia, Cuba, Mexico, Peru (and subsequently Panama) joined in inviting the twelve other American Republics to hold a meeting of their Ministers of Foreign Affairs. The invitations were accepted and the Conference opened at Panama on September 23.

---

[1] See below, p. 340.

The Conference at once resolved itself into three sub-committees to discuss neutrality, the protection of the peace of the Western Hemisphere, and economic co-operation. The United States Government were represented on each of the three sub-committees. The proceedings were secret; the German Minister to the Central American Republics asked to be allowed to attend as an observer but was refused. The local press, however, published (in English) daily accounts of the resolutions brought forward to the sub-committees. The most important resolutions were those put forward by the United States and Cuba for the establishment of a 'maritime security zone' and by Argentina, Chile and Uruguay for the exemption of foodstuffs and other materials from lists of contraband.

On October 2 the Conference in plenary session adopted five resolutions: (1) the Declaration of Panama defining the maritime security zone, (2) a general declaration of neutrality and (3) a resolution co-ordinating regulations for the maintenance of neutrality, (4) and (5) resolutions on contraband and on the 'humanisation of war'. The third resolution was of local concern in the countries affected; the fifth was an appeal to the belligerents and the fourth mainly a statement of view. The general declaration of neutrality called for the respect of the Republics as neutrals and specified certain forms of neutrality, acknowledged by the American States, including the right of purchase of belligerent merchant ships if effected in American waters and without intention of reversion to the original flag.

The Declaration of Panama laid down that the interests of neutrals should prevail over those of belligerents; 'the character of the present conflagration . . . would not justify any interruption whatever of inter-American communications'. As a measure of 'continental self-protection', the American Republics had the 'inherent right' to keep all belligerent activities away from their waters[1] and at a considerable distance from the shores of America. The area covered by this security zone would extend to a distance of 300 miles from the eastern and western coasts of the American Continent. The American Governments agreed 'to endeavour to secure' from the belligerents the observance of the provisions of the Declaration and to permit 'individual or collective patrols' within their respective waters.

The idea of a 'safety zone' did not carry much conviction either in the United States or in Latin America. Mr. Cordell Hull told Lord Lothian on October 6 that in his view there were great practical difficulties in the way of making a pan-American patrol effective. Mr. Hull said that the main interest of the United States had been to create a patrol which would give the American Governments inform-

---

[1] Other than the territorial waters of Canada and of the colonies and possessions of European States.

ation about what was going on in the Atlantic. If the proposal to belligerents were rejected or if acts of war took place within the safety zone, the American Governments would confer together. Mr. Hull did not object to Lord Lothian's statement of the British view that, unless the patrol were effective, we should retain the full right of pursuit of enemy vessels within the zone. The British Government therefore accepted the plan as a whole, and indeed welcomed the possibility that they might thereby obtain information privately as a result of the United States patrols.

One of the problems which confronted the British Government especially in the early stages of the war was that of explaining their policy to the American public. There was no difficulty at the highest levels; Mr. Churchill's personal correspondence with President Roosevelt[1] (which became of the greatest importance later on) was already of service in supplementing the information supplied through diplomatic channels. At the beginning of the war Lord Lothian had (a) pointed out the danger of attempting to influence American opinion by direct propaganda or criticism. The Foreign Office realised the danger and warned the French Government on the matter, though the warning was at this time unnecessary since the French Government was equally aware of the facts. There was indeed an opposite danger that in a country of vivid publicity methods the Allied case might be given insufficient attention if it were set out in the colourless form of information bulletins. In any case it was of the greatest importance to watch American opinion, if only to be able to form some idea of the possible reaction of the United States to important Allied decisions of policy. Owing to the delicate balance between the Executive and the Legislative in the American constitution, public opinion had a direct and immediate effect upon the action of the Administration to a degree unknown in Great Britain. Hence the Administration would not go any appreciable distance beyond the limits approved by public opinion in helping the Allies; it would also refuse to acquiesce for long in Allied action which might be legitimate in itself but caused public outcry in the United States.

Lord Lothian sent home frequent analyses of the general direction and movement of public opinion. Until mid-December there was little broad change in the position; American opinion continued to show sympathy with the Allies and, at the same time, a determination to keep out of the war. In mid-December, while there was still no general change, Lord Lothian observed two contradictory (b) currents of 'minority' opinion. One view was that the Allies were losing the war. They had won no 'victories' on land, and at sea the German magnetic mine was a serious threat to them. The other view

---

[1] See below, p. 334, note 1.

(a) A7053, 8614, 8946/7052/45. (b) A9115/7052/45.

was that Hitler had lost the war to Russia, if not to the Allies, in making an agreement with the Soviet Government, and that the United States could safely go back to a policy of isolation since the European war did not threaten American security. This return of a sense of safety brought a certain resentment at the Allied treatment of American trade, and even a suspicion that the blockade was being manipulated in British interests against the trade of the United States. The ordinary business man was irritated by delays in the examination of ships, the interruption of cable and telephone services, the 'navi-cert' system, the embargo on exports to Germany and the restriction of British purchases of staple agricultural commodities in the United States.

The Russian attack on Finland had also affected American views on the war between the Allies and Germany. Some 'big business' interests even thought that the Allies should come to terms with Germany and combine with her against the U.S.S.R. For this reason Lord Lothian recommended that British Ministers should continue to make speeches explaining why we were fighting and why we refused to make peace with Nazi Germany. He also urged that we should do everything possible to minimise our interference with American shipping and communications.

(ii)

American protests against the British exercise of belligerent rights: Lord Lothian's despatch of February 1, 1940.

During the third week of January, 1940, the mood of annoyance over the dislocation of American trade and economy by the war, and particularly by the British interpretation and exercise of belligerent rights at sea, affected the State Department and brought a short but somewhat sharp reminder that the United States expected more consideration from Great Britain. *The New York Times* of January 21 contained a statement that 'a feeling of intense irritation with Britain, (a) which, it is feared, is spreading in the United States . . . has developed in official quarters here over the adamant British attitude towards joint problems'. The statement then referred to British stiffness in dealing with United States mails, to restrictions upon American imports into Great Britain, and to delays in the examination of ships. An *aide-mémoire* of January 19 from the State Department to the British Embassy set out the same grievances, and was published (b) on January 23 before the Embassy could reply.

(a) W1203/8/49. (b) W1113, 1299, 2431/8/49.

(a) Lord Lothian telegraphed that the State Department appeared to have prompted the comments in the press. He did not think that there was need for serious alarm. The State Department had to show that they were protecting American rights and wished also to warn us that we were inclined to rely too much upon the known sympathies of the United States for the Allied cause and to pay more attention to protests from neutrals, e.g. Italy, possessing a greater nuisance value. In fact the press agitation met with little public response, and soon died down.[1]

(b) On January 22 Mr. Cordell Hull asked Lord Lothian to see him. He spoke of the various causes of friction and mentioned disputes about the censorship of mails; the diversion of American ships into the combatant zone; delays and discrimination in the examination of ships at Gibraltar; the navicert system, and the restrictions upon the purchase of agricultural commodities, especially tobacco. Lord Lothian pointed out that, owing to the limitations imposed by American legislation, His Majesty's Government must restrict the use of their dollar resources and avoid buying in the United States foodstuffs and raw materials which they could buy elsewhere. Turkey was also 'a vital bastion in the Allied system of defence' and His Majesty's Government had been compelled to make her a large loan and to buy tobacco from her. Lord Lothian was also able to show that there was little, if any, justification for the view that American ships were less well treated than Italian ships.

Lord Lothian's comment on this interview was that by improving our arrangements we should try to meet American complaints about the use of belligerent rights at sea and that we should reassure the State Department of our agreement with their view that the maintenance of multinational trade was necessary as the basis of post-war recovery. Lord Lothian suggested that we should give President Roosevelt a full statement of the future course of British policy in the matter of American purchases. We should explain that we knew that this policy must affect the economy of the United States and that we wanted American advice about it.

(c) In a letter to Lord Halifax on January 27, 1940, Lord Lothian summed up the change which these discussions marked in Anglo-American relations. Hitherto sentiment in the Administration and in the United States generally had been dominated by a desire to escape the risk of war at almost any price. This phase was disappearing. There was no longer a fear that—except in the event of the defeat of Great Britain at sea—America would be 'dragged into' the European war. The policy of the Administration towards us had

---

[1] For the views of the Ministry of Economic Warfare about the whole incident, see Medlicott, *op. cit.*, I, 350 *et seq.*

(a) W1203/8/49. (b) W1298/8/49. (c) A1164/434/45.

not altered in the sense that there would be insistence on American rights to the point of crippling our war effort. It was felt, however, that we had been needlessly inconsiderate of American interests and that we were trading too much upon American goodwill.

Lord Lothian thought we should have to do more to prove to the United States that action taken by us which affected American interests was really necessary for winning the war. We could not merely impose restrictions and expect American acquiescence. Our position was in some respects more difficult than in the war of 1914 because the Neutrality Act had eliminated 'counter-friction' with the Germans.

On January 30 Lord Lothian had a long discussion with Mr. Hull (a) about the subjects of detailed complaints. On the general question of restriction of purchase Mr. Hull agreed that a statement was desirable; he hoped, in view of American opinion, that it would soon be made. He understood the British difficulties, but pointed out the importance in Congress of the agricultural interests which were seriously affected by the restriction.

On February 1 Lord Lothian sent a despatch to the Foreign Office (b) covering a wider range of subjects. He began by repeating the phases through which American opinion had passed.[1] He then mentioned four factors making for further change:

(i) There was a belief that the war would be greatly intensified in the early spring. One view was that the Germans would make a tremendous assault by sea and air on the British navy and merchant shipping and on British ports. There might or might not be simultaneous attacks upon France and the Low Countries: the main objective would be to secure the surrender to Germany of the British navy and British bases as the quickest way to world empire. Another view was that the German High Command had already decided that they could not compel Great Britain to surrender and that their objective must be to show also that Great Britain could not bring about the defeat of Germany by blockade, partly because Germany was able to get enough supplies from Russia and the Balkans, partly because the Germans could force upon Great Britain such an expensive defence organisation for the protection of her imports that Germany would stand the strain longer than the British. These considerations had caused an undertone of alarm which had been intensified by Admiral Stark's statement to a Congressional Committee that in preparing its defence programme the United States had to take into account the possibility of a British defeat at sea.

---

[1] This restatement did not wholly agree with his previous analyses, but the inconsistencies were not relevant to his main conclusions.

(a) W1780/8/49. (b) A1190/131/45.

(ii) The Russian attack on Finland (as Lord Lothian had previously reported) had deeply stirred American opinion and had cleared away all that was left of the argument that the war was only between British and German imperialism. Nevertheless, the strengthening of the view that the war was a struggle of the free peoples against totalitarianism had not made any difference to American determination to keep out of it.

(iii) On the recent 'flare-up' over interference with American trade Lord Lothian repeated the views which he had written to Lord Halifax.

(iv) Americans had come to realise that the United States now had to take the lead in the Far East and that, if they pressed Japan to the point of retaliation, such retaliation would be directed, not against themselves but against the British, French and Dutch; the United States would then have to choose between coming to the assistance of the latter Powers or acquiescing in Japanese expansion in the Southern Pacific.

Lord Lothian discussed the probable future of American policy and the conditions in which the United States might find it necessary, in spite of the intense wish to remain neutral, to enter the war. He repeated his warning against attempting propaganda. Americans wanted information; they insisted on being left alone to make up their own minds. They would be glad to see an early end of the war, but only a small minority thought peace desirable at any price. American opinion would require the restoration of independence to Poland and Czechoslovakia, and real guarantees against a renewal of Nazi aggression. Practically no one expected Hitler to concede these terms and the President's gestures in the matter were mainly to placate pacifist opinion.

(iii)

Mr. Sumner Welles's visit to Europe, February–March, 1940: Lord Lothian's despatch of April 29, 1940.

As far as the State Department was concerned, the wave of irritation over British high-handedness soon spent its force; in March the British and French Governments sent a joint mission to Washington to discuss the machinery of the blockade as it affected American interests. The mission, under the leadership of Mr. Ashton-Gwatkin of the Foreign Office and Professor Charles Rist, stayed for seven weeks, and secured general agreement on most points in dispute. Meanwhile, however, a new question had caused a good deal

of anxiety on the British side. On February 1 President Roosevelt told (a)
Lord Lothian that, according to information from Germany, and
particularly from people who had seen Göring, the Germans felt that
they must go on fighting to save their country from partition. An
offensive, directed especially against Great Britain, was in preparation. This offensive, and the retaliatory action which it would
bring, would make peace more difficult. In order to satisfy himself
that everything possible had been done to end the war, Mr. Roosevelt
had decided to send Mr. Sumner Welles[1] to Europe. Mr. Welles
would leave the United States on February 17, and would visit
Rome, Paris, Berlin and London. He would make no proposals, but
merely report to the President. Mr. Roosevelt wanted the Prime
Minister to know of his plan before he announced it officially. He
added that informal diplomatic conversations between neutrals were
under discussion. These conversations were not concerned with
terms for ending the war; they were intended as a means of learning
the views of the neutrals about the principles of a final peace
settlement.

Lord Lothian said that such discussions were to the good if they
did not end in proposals for 'whittling away' the Allied blockade.
Mr. Roosevelt explained that his ideas of peace were practically the
same as those of His Majesty's Government: a restoration of freedom
to the Czechs and Poles; guarantees against the renewal of aggression
and the establishment of the 'four freedoms'.[2] Mr. Roosevelt was not
hopeful of results, but, if Germany proved an obstacle to peace, he
could issue a statement to this effect on Mr. Welles's return.

The Prime Minister sent a reply to Mr. Roosevelt on February 4
that His Majesty's Government had received information from
Germany similar to that obtained by the President. In fact, no
Allied statesman had suggested a partitioning of Germany. The
suggestion of a great offensive was part of the German 'war of nerves'
against the neutrals who might fear that they would become involved
in the war. In this way Germany hoped to mobilise world opinion
against the Allies. The main difficulty, however, lay in the question
of guarantees. A demand for the removal of the Nazi Government
might encourage the Germans to overthrow the régime; it was more
likely, owing to Hitler's propaganda, to unite them in a common fear
of Great Britain and the United States. Our plan hitherto had been
to state conditions which 'considerable elements' in Germany would
not reject, but which Hitler could not accept. The Prime Minister

---

[1] Mr. Welles was Under-Secretary of State.

[2] Freedom from fear: freedom of religion: freedom of information (press and public
meetings): freedom from want. President Roosevelt had laid down these conditions of a
settlement in an address to Congress on January 3, 1940.

(a) C1839/285/18.

hoped that Mr. Welles would also see representatives of the Polish Government. He suggested that, in view of the strong feeling about Russian aggression in Finland, Mr. Roosevelt might wish to 'extend Mr. Sumner Welles's enquiry in that direction'. Finally, the Prime Minister said that Mr. Welles's mission would cause a sensation; that it was likely to embarrass the democracies and to be of advantage to German propaganda.

At the same time the Foreign Office sent special instructions to Lord Lothian. These instructions mentioned the reports received by the British Government from German sources, including the entourage of Göring (whose 'moderation' was now completely suspect), suggesting that an irresistible offensive was being planned, but would be called off if peace talks were started. Other information[1] through German intermediaries and neutral sources hinted that, if the Allies were not aiming at the dismemberment of Germany, the German army would overthrow or modify the present régime and bring into power a government with whom the Allies could negotiate. These stories seemed part of the German 'war of nerves'. Hitler was using the wishes of the neutrals for an early peace, even if this peace were inconclusive and precarious. The neutrals would hope to escape present loss and danger. Italy might think that an inconclusive peace would give her chances of 'profitable manoeuvre'; other neutrals hoped that peace would bring a crusade against bolshevism. Hitler would try to secure a peace which would leave the German armed forces intact, and establish him in a position from which he could renew the war at will before the Allies were again ready. We had thus been expecting a peace move from the Italian Government or the Pope or from the President but we had not anticipated anything so spectacular as a public mission fully advertised in advance. We were afraid that President Roosevelt was doing just what Hitler wanted him to do, and that he might have been influenced by Americans of 'dubious' political views or connexions.

Lord Lothian gave Mr. Roosevelt the Prime Minister's message on February 6. Mr. Roosevelt was in general agreement with the British view. He would not use the word 'peace' in any published instructions to Mr. Welles. He would consult the Polish Government but thought that the inclusion of Finland and the U.S.S.R. would make Mr. Welles's field of enquiry too wide. Mr. Welles would make it clear to the German Government that an attack on the Allies which showed prospects of success would bring the United States near to intervention.

(a)

---

[1] See Volume II, Chapter XXV.

(a) C1987, 3072/285/18.

On February 7 the Prime Minister sent another message to the President. He explained that the Allies intended to try to bring help to Finland through Scandinavia, and said that we were afraid that Mr. Welles's mission might affect the attitude of Norway and Sweden towards our demand for passage. Mr. Roosevelt told Lord Lothian on February 8 that his proposal would avoid the dangers (a) which we feared. He would make it clear that Mr. Welles was not going on a 'peace mission', and that the United States would have nothing to do with a precarious and inconclusive peace.

Mr. Welles's mission was announced on February 9. He left New York in an Italian liner and arrived in Rome on February 25 with Mr. Myron Taylor, whom the President was sending on a special mission to the Pope. Mr. Welles saw Ciano and Mussolini, and then (b) left for Berlin. Here he had an hour's conversation with Ribbentrop on March 1.[1] After seeing Hitler on March 3 he went to Paris via Lausanne. He was received by the President of the Republic, and visited MM. Daladier, Reynaud, Blum, Chautemps and Bonnet. He also saw General Sikorski and M. Zaleski. He reached London on March 10. He was received by His Majesty the King, and had conversations with members of the Government and of the Opposition. He went back to Rome through Paris, and, after an audience with the Pope and another visit to Mussolini, sailed for the United States from Italy on March 20.[2]

Before Mr. Welles's arrival in London the United States Military Attaché asked whether he might be given, for Mr. Welles's infor- (c) mation, a statement of the composition of the British forces and an outline of their proposed expansion. The War Cabinet decided that they could not supply general information of this kind, though they (d) were willing to answer questions on detailed points. Mr. Kennedy, the American Ambassador, in discussing the arrangements for Mr. Welles's visit, said to Lord Halifax that Mr. Welles was coming in order to put the President in a position to know whether there was any possibility of a settlement. Lord Halifax pointed out that Mr. Kennedy must himself know that Great Britain would not accept

---

[1] On February 29 Hitler ordered great reserve in dealing with Mr. Welles; 'concrete' questions such as the future of Poland should be avoided, and there should be no discussion of Austria or the German Protectorate of Bohemia and Moravia. Hitler suggested that Mr. Welles should be left to do most of the talking, but according to the German records of the meetings between Mr. Welles and Hitler and between Mr. Welles and Ribbentrop (who spoke in German for more than two hours without interruption except for the translation of his discourse by the interpreter) the Germans took up most of the time with their usual exposition of Nazi aims. After the meeting with Ribbentrop Mr. Welles told Weizsäcker that, if the German Government really believed that its objective could be realised only by a military victory, his (Welles's) visit to Europe was pointless (*D.G.F.P.*, VIII, No. 642, and *F.R.U.S.*, 1940, I, 42).

[2] Mr. Welles's report of his interviews is printed, with omissions, in *F.R.U.S.*, 1940, I, 21–117.

(a) C2124/285/18.   (b) C3117/82/18.   (c) C3538/89/18.   (d) WM(40)58; C3346, 2465/17; C3349/89/18.

a 'patched-up' peace. Mr. Kennedy asked whether it might be possible to get 'mechanical guarantees' which would deprive the German nation of the power of doing again what they had done. Lord Halifax answered that he was not clear about the meaning of 'mechanical guarantees'. Our own test was that, after the war, the German Government must not be able to tell the German people that 'they had on the whole done pretty well out of it'.

(a) On March 9 the Foreign Office received an account of Mr. Welles's conversations in Paris. Mr. Welles seemed to be surprised at the determination of the Allies. The French Ministers thought that he had been impressed too easily by Mussolini's arguments,[1] and that our own insistence upon our difficulties and upon the need for American help had inclined opinion in the United States to believe that we had to choose between a 'compromise' peace and social and economic ruin. While in Paris Mr. Welles had given M. Reynaud the text of a memorandum on the essentials of the economic policy of the United States. This memorandum argued in favour of a restoration of the conditions of multilateral trade. Mr. Welles had asked whether the French Government approved of it and would agree to its publication. The French Government had agreed, but in order to make it plain that the Allies were not fighting only for economic purposes, they had added that the principles of economic freedom were 'part of those for which the Allies were fighting'.

(b) In his first conversation with Lord Halifax on March 11, Mr. Welles said that Mussolini wanted to keep out of the war, but felt that it would be difficult for him to do so; therefore he wished to end the war. Mr. Welles asked what, in Lord Halifax's opinion, would be the Italian demands at a peace conference. He also mentioned, incidentally, Gibraltar, but Lord Halifax said that we could not consider a suggestion that we should surrender Gibraltar to Spain or accept an international arrangement with regard to it. Lord Halifax said that we could not trust the Nazi régime or make peace on terms which would allow Germany to continue the policy which had caused the war.

Mr. Welles asked what material guarantees would give general confidence. He suggested, as an example, disarmament by means of the destruction of offensive weapons on a qualitative basis, the restriction of national air forces, and the creation of an international police force. The United States would be ready to share in the work

---

[1] The Polish Government also thought that Mr. Welles had been unduly impressed by (c) Mussolini.

(a) C3654, 3688, 4011/89/18. (b) C3814/89/18. (c) C3750, 3998/89/18.

of international inspection during the process of disarmament. Mr. Welles agreed that the restoration of Poland was a necessary condition of peace. He thought 'Bohemia'[1] a more difficult question. He also quoted a German view that the Allies wanted the dismemberment of Germany. Lord Halifax said that this was not the case.

During a later conversation (at which Mr. Kennedy was present) with the Prime Minister and Lord Halifax on March 11 Mr. Welles (a) gave more details of a possible mode of ending the war. The Germans should withdraw their troops from Poland and Bohemia within an area to be agreed. There should be a rapid and progressive disarmament of the belligerents by means of the destruction of weapons and of the factories where they were produced. An international air force would also be created. During this interim period the armies would remain mobilised and the blockade would continue. A plan of economic reconstruction would be linked with the measures of disarmament. Mr. Welles thought that the Germans, when they saw their troops leaving Bohemia and Poland, would realise that force did not pay, that the destruction of weapons, together with the collaboration of the United States, would give a physical guarantee against the resumption of a policy of aggression, and that the 'economic carrot' would attract the Germans.

The Prime Minister said very strongly that we could not trust Hitler; that even with a considerable measure of disarmament Germany could overrun a weak country like Roumania, and that nothing would restore confidence—the essential condition of disarmament—as much as a change of government in Germany.

Mr. Welles and Mr. Kennedy had another conversation with the Prime Minister and Lord Halifax on March 13. The Prime Minister (b) again said that disarmament of itself would not produce confidence and was possible only after confidence had been restored. The first practical requisite of confidence was that Great Britain and France should be strong enough to make it 'clearly not worth while' for the Germans to resume a policy of aggression. Disarmament must therefore begin with Germany. The Germans might ask about their own security in relation to Great Britain and France, and might not be satisfied by a direct Anglo-French undertaking not to attack them. We might give a formal undertaking to the United States not to attack Germany, but the terms would have to be defined with care in order to leave us free to carry out obligations of assistance to a third party which might be the victim of German aggression.

We could not, however, deal with the existing German régime. Mr. Welles asked whether this refusal would still hold if satisfactory

---

[1] The Foreign Office called attention to Mr. Welles's use of this term.

(a) C3815/89/18. (b) C3999/89/18.

arrangements could be made in other respects. The Prime Minister said that, in his view, it would be impossible to deal with the régime; in any case we could not be satisfied with a settlement which did not show clearly that Hitler's policy had been a failure. Lord Halifax added that we should require restoration and reparation for Poland and Bohemia and Moravia and freedom of decision for Austria, an Anglo-French superiority in strength relative to Germany, and a real restoration of liberty to the German people. They must be freed from the Gestapo and the whole system of persecution, and must be able to recover knowledge of the outside world. 'If these several conditions were realised, Hitler's policy would be so clearly reversed that we should not be justified in refusing discussion.' The Prime Minister said that he would not differ from Lord Halifax's view, but that such a transformation would be 'in the nature of a miracle'. Mr. Welles thought that there was a '1 in 10,000' chance of peace on this basis: Mussolini had regarded a settlement of this kind as 'not impossible'.

Lord Halifax said that we should also want evidence of a German desire to resume co-operation not only in the economic field (as Mr. Welles had suggested) but also in the political field through the League or some new instrument of international order. Mr. Welles said that he had been told in authoritative quarters of a similar desire in Berlin. He thought that in the economic field the Germans had in mind some kind of preferential position in the countries adjoining Germany. The Prime Minister said that before the war he had thought there would be no real difficulty in making an arrangement between Germany and her neighbours which might in some degree be held comparable with that between Great Britain and parts of the British Empire. All these preferential arrangements seemed to Mr. Welles undesirable, but it was difficult to resist them in one area if they prevailed in another.

(a) The Foreign Office summed up the impressions left by Mr. Welles's conversations in a telegram to Lord Lothian on March 27. Mr. Welles seemed to have been affected to some extent by Mussolini[1] and to have been impressed in Berlin with the pretended invincibility of Germany. Mr. Kennedy had also spoken to him a good deal of the chances of general ruin if the war continued. It seemed likely that Mr. Welles would suggest to the President that he should outline peace terms which would not require the elimination of Hitler's régime but would give security to the Allies. Mr. Welles thought that even without an American guarantee disarmament could precede security,

---

[1] According to Ciano (*Diary*, March 16, 1940) Mr. Welles gave the impression in Rome that Great Britain and France were less uncompromising than their press and the speeches of their political leaders suggested, and that, if they had guarantees of security, they would give in, and accept the *fait accompli* [of the war].

(a) C4564/89/18.

and that the United States would share merely in the supervision of disarmament and in economic reconstruction.

There was an unexpected sequel to the Prime Minister's suggestion that German demands for security might be met by a pledge given by (a) Great Britain to the United States. On April 3 Mr. Roosevelt, in the presence of Mr. Hull and Mr. Welles, told Lord Lothian that he wanted to discuss the Prime Minister's proposal. Mr. Welles had been impressed in Germany by the general belief that the Allies wanted to break up the Reich. Mr. Roosevelt also agreed about the importance of trying to convince the Germans that the Allies had no such intention. Mr. Welles held that an assurance of this kind was required from the point of view of 'powerful elements in Germany' as well as of the German people as a whole. Hence Mr. Roosevelt was much attracted by the Prime Minister's suggestion for a dramatic declaration on the subject. He thought that, for reasons which included 'political considerations in the United States', the Prime Minister should make his proposed declaration in a letter to all Heads of neutral States, and that the French Prime Minister should make a similar declaration. The Prime Minister might say that 'without entering into the question of possible peace terms, the object of the Allies was to create a system which (a) gave security for national unity to all nations large and small, including Germany, (b) would remove by suitable measures of disarmament once and for all the terror which reigned in men's hearts everywhere that men in the future would have to live underground and that their children would have no prospect of a free and happy life, (c) would secure to all nations equality of access to raw materials and markets so that none could be starved into dependence. The Allied objective, in fact, was security in the widest sense for all nations.' Mr. Roosevelt thought that the declaration might also refer to the abolition of offensive weapons as a method of disarmament, the possibility of an international police force, the necessity of a lasting peace, and the right of all nations to free information about what was going on in the world.

Lord Lothian pointed out the difficulty of drafting a declaration of this kind which would not give the impression that it was a proposal for peace. Mr. Roosevelt agreed that it would be necessary to explain that the declaration was concerned not with the conditions of peace but with the aims of the Allies.

The Foreign Office considered that Mr. Roosevelt had misunderstood the Prime Minister's proposal. This proposal had nothing to do with German fears of dismemberment; it was brought forward with a view to the post-war security of Germany on the assumption that

(a) C5073/89/18.

the Germans must disarm before the Allies. We had already made public statements on the general lines of Mr. Roosevelt's suggested statement of war-aims. The difficulty about an undertaking to all the neutrals was that some of them might refuse to act as 'stake-holders'. It would then be less easy for the United States to accept the proposal. Even if all or most of the neutrals accepted, the conception of 'collective security' had fallen into such disrepute that a general guarantee would be less effective than a direct and solid guarantee from the United States. Furthermore, the position of 'stake-holder' must involve the United States in taking some action or using some 'suasion' if Great Britain broke, or appeared to be breaking, her guarantee.

For obvious reasons the Foreign Office did not wish to give Mr. Roosevelt the rebuff of a plain refusal. The German invasion of Scandinavia changed the situation, and made it unlikely that the President would want to maintain his suggestion. The Foreign Office therefore instructed Lord Lothian on April 20 to say that in the altered circumstances Mr. Roosevelt would probably regard a declaration as inopportune. Another German act of aggression had taken place, and further attacks upon neutrals were very likely. Hence a statement primarily intended to reassure the German people would be open to misconstruction. The 'further attacks' took place within a short time, and Mr. Roosevelt did not continue with his proposal.

(a) On April 29 Lord Lothian wrote[1] that the general appreciation which he had sent on February 1 still held good. 'The United States is 95 per cent anti-Hitler, is 95 per cent determined to keep out of the war if it can, and will only enter the war when its own vital interests are challenged, though those vital interests include its ideals.' The invasion of Norway and Denmark, however, had profoundly affected American opinion. This opinion still regarded the European war as the concern of Great Britain and France; there was no greater readiness to intervene in it, but events had revived the old feeling that sooner or later America would be 'dragged into the war'. On the other hand, 'the hysteria about keeping out becomes more intense as the precipice seems to be nearer'.

Lord Lothian thought that, if the United States became involved in the war, the entry would be by different methods from those of the first World War. There would be no crusading demonstrations but a firm defence of American interests—possibly without a declaration of war. For example, the United States would at once attack German

---

[1] This despatch was received on May 10.

(a) A3202/131/45.

forces attempting to occupy Greenland or the Dutch West Indies. Or again, if necessary, the United States would certainly make loans or provide credits or even gifts to the Allies, especially if this could be done without direct participation in the war; a move of this kind, however, would not be made until we had sold our gold, our investments and other saleable overseas assets.

An Italian success in an attack on Gibraltar would greatly affect American opinion, since it was now understood that American security in the Atlantic depended upon the predominance of the British fleet and that the possession of Gibraltar by one of the totalitarian states would be a threat to the Monroe doctrine. If Great Britain and France could not hold the Atlantic, the United States would have to decide between running grave risks there or bringing back part of their fleet from the Pacific and thereby abandoning China, the Dutch East Indies and the Philippines to the Japanese.

Meanwhile, for the time, public discussion was being stifled by the presidential election, and no public man in the country dared to call the attention of the public to the facts. It was therefore unlikely that, although American interests required an Allied victory, the United States would take far-sighted defensive action. Italian entry into the war would much increase the chances that the United States would be compelled to fight, and to do so under more formidable conditions, yet the American people could not be persuaded that the best way of keeping out of war would be to tell Mussolini that if he entered the war the United States would at once help the Allies to blockade Italy.

Lord Lothian summed up his views as follows:

'The United States is still dominated by fear of involvement and incapable of positive action. On the other hand the war is steadily drifting nearer to them and they know it. They are not pacifists; on the contrary, they are highly belligerent by temperament. The point at which they will be driven to say, as we did after Prague, "Thus far and no further" depends mainly on the dictators and the events they precipitate. The President would like to take action vigorously on the lines of his own principle "Everything short of war". This is also true of Mr. Hull. All the other candidates,[1] and especially the Republicans, none of whom are familiar with international affairs, are paralysed by fear of being charged with a desire to get the United States into war. That does not mean that if they were elected they would not deal with the situation in a practical and realist manner.'

---

[1] i.e. for the elections of 1940.

CHAPTER VII

The first month of the German offensive in the West

(i)

Summary of the German offensive in the west from May 10 to June 4, 1940.[1]

DURING the three weeks before the opening of the German western offensive the Foreign Office received reports from a number of sources about German intentions. Reports of a coming offensive had been current for months past and were indeed part of the German methods of propaganda. The more recent information, however, pointed with increasing definiteness to a large-scale attack in the west, and suggested also that Italy and Spain

---

[1] Both France and Great Britain were on May 10 in the process of changing governments. Mr. Chamberlain decided on the morning of May 10 to resign, and later in the day Mr. Churchill formed a coalition administration (see p. 128, note 2). Mr. Churchill at once introduced an important change in the organisation of the higher direction of the war. Mr. Chamberlain had appointed a Military Co-ordination Committee at Ministerial level in October 1939, to serve as a link between the small War Cabinet (set up at the beginning of the war) and the Chiefs of Staff sub-Committee which had previously reported to the Committee of Imperial Defence. (This body more or less went into suspense on the outbreak of war.) In fact the new 'link' did not relieve the War Cabinet of consideration of much unnecessary detail, but added to the delay in taking decisions because matters now had to be discussed in three committees. In any case, for some unexplained reason, the Military Co-ordination Committee did not include a representative of the Foreign Office. At the beginning of April 1940, Mr. Churchill was appointed Chairman of the Military Co-ordination Committee. The appointment of the (civilian) head of one of the Service departments to be in charge of a committee which had to advise the War Cabinet on the general conduct of the war was unlikely to work satisfactorily and within a week the Prime Minister was taking the chair at the meetings of the Committee. Furthermore, the Chiefs of Staff Committee did not even secure co-ordination between the Services. During the Norwegian campaign the Naval and Military Chiefs of Staff appointed their respective commanders without mutual consultation, gave them separate directives, and went on issuing separate orders to them. At the end of April—when the disastrous results of this confusion were all too clear—Mr. Chamberlain laid down that Mr. Churchill should take the chair as his deputy at meetings of the Co-ordination Committee and also give guidance and direction to the Chiefs of Staff Committee. This plan, which was no more satisfactory than its predecessor, faded out with the change of government.

Mr. Churchill took the new title of Minister of Defence as well as that of Prime Minister. He maintained a small War Cabinet (reduced at first from nine to five members—including the Prime Minister himself—but later enlarged again to eight). He replaced the Co-ordination Committee by a Defence Committee under his own chairmanship. The Committee, which included (after a short time) the Foreign Secretary, worked in two sections dealing respectively with operations and supply. The Chiefs of Staff and the three Service Ministers attended the meetings dealing with operations. The Chiefs of Staff Committee had under it joint Planning and joint Intelligence sub-committees; the chairman of the latter was a member of the Foreign Office. (See *Grand Strategy*, II, 180–1.)

might come into the war on the German side.[1] In the first week of May there were indications of an offensive within a few days. On May 7 Sir N. Bland transmitted a Dutch report—confirmed from (a) elsewhere—that, if flying conditions were good, a German attack on the Netherlands, Belgium and the western front would begin on the following day. During the night of May 7–8 Sir N. Bland telegraphed that there was no unusual activity on the German side of the Dutch frontier. The Dutch General Staff did not believe the report of an offensive on May 8 but had stopped military leave. Sir N. Bland repeated his telegrams to Sir R. Campbell and Sir L. Oliphant, who informed the French and Belgian Governments of the report. M. Reynaud said that on the French front there were no indications 'such as would normally precede an attack against the Maginot Line'. M. Spaak gave the information that, according to the Belgian (b) Ambassador in Berlin, the Germans were drafting a note for presentation to the Belgian and Netherlands Governments.

On the evening of May 8 Sir N. Bland reported that the Secretary- (c) General of the Netherlands Foreign Office had no 'startling' news. On the other hand the Secretary-General was inclined to believe that the reports of an imminent invasion were not just part of the German 'war of nerves'. Later in the night of May 8–9 Sir L. Oliphant telegraphed that M. Spaak's Chef de Cabinet thought the situation a (d) little easier, at least for the moment. The only new development of a 'disagreeable' kind was a tank concentration in the Saar area. During the night of May 8–9 the Foreign Office heard that an (e) ultimatum, of which the terms and time of expiry were unknown, had been delivered in the afternoon to the Netherlands Government. The Foreign Office believed the report to be a garbled version of the more probable story of the preparation of a note for presentation to the Belgians and the Dutch. Sir N. Bland was asked to make enquiries; he telegraphed on the morning of May 9 that the (f) Secretary-General had described the report as 'sheer fantasy'. On the other hand the Secretary-General thought that the war had reached a turning-point and that something was bound to happen soon and in the west rather than in the Balkans.

About mid-day on May 9 Sir L. Oliphant telegraphed that, (g) according to M. Spaak's Chef de Cabinet, the situation appeared to be easier. At 2.40 a.m. on May 10, however, Sir L. Oliphant reported (h)

---

[1] One report, from a reliable source, described a conversation in which General Bodenschatz had said that Hitler still regretted that he was fighting England. The source considered that the Germans hoped that England might see that the war 'did not pay' and, after bombardment of the British ports, might agree to terms which would secure the (j) Nazi régime and at least part of the German gains.

(a) C6596/31/18.   (b) C6597/31/18.   (c) C6632/31/18.   (d) C6633/31/18.   (e) C6634/31/18.   (f) C6632/31/18.   (g) C6633/31/18.   (h) C6661/31/18.   (j) C6389/5/18.

that, at midnight, M. Spaak and his Chef de Cabinet had come to the British Embassy to say that the Belgian and Dutch General Staffs had reported German activity since 9 p.m. along the whole of the German frontier from the Dutch province of Overyssel to Luxembourg. Although this activity might be no more than an exercise, the Belgian Government thought that the situation required very careful watching. Later the Chef de Cabinet telephoned Sir L. Oliphant that information had been received of orders for a general attack in the west on the morning of May 10. Sir L. Oliphant reported this message in a telegram of 2.35 a.m.[1]

At 3 a.m. on May 10 the Germans began their invasion of Belgium, the Netherlands and Luxembourg. The first news of this attack appears to have been received in London about 5 a.m. and to
(a) have referred only to the invasion of the Netherlands.[2] At 6 a.m. Mr. Churchill asked M. Corbin to enquire from the French Government whether the Allied armies would move into Belgium on the information already received. M. Corbin replied at 6.20 a.m. that Belgium had also been invaded and had asked for help. The Netherlands Minister, who had previously telephoned to Lord Halifax, reached the Foreign Office at 6.30 a.m. with a lengthy note
(b) asking for various forms of assistance. This note was at once communicated to the Chiefs of Staff.

At 6.55 a.m. the Belgian Ambassador brought to Lord Halifax at the Dorchester Hotel a copy of a communication made to Sir L. Oliphant at 5.50 a.m. announcing the German attack and asking for Allied help. Lord Halifax told the Ambassador that we would give to Belgium all the assistance in our power. He also asked the Ambassador to let him have early information about the bombing of civilians; we would wish to know whether such bombing had been deliberate or whether it could be excused in any way by the nearness of military objectives. At Lord Halifax's request, the Ambassador took the Belgian communication at once to the Foreign Office, where
(c) he arrived about 7.30 a.m. At 9.40 a.m. the Foreign Office were informed that the Belgian Government had declared Brussels an open city, and had said that no troops were stationed in the city or would pass through it. Later in the morning the Belgian Government also asked the British and French Governments to announce that they would regard the bombing of open towns in Belgium as on the same footing as the bombardment of such towns in France. The French

---

[1] Sir L. Oliphant did not telephone these telegrams. It will be seen that the two telegrams were dispatched about the same time. There is no evidence to show why the first telegram was not sent earlier.

[2] Mr. Makins, the first senior member of the Foreign Office staff to hear the news, was informed by telephone at his house by the Resident Clerk at the Foreign Office; he reached
(d) the Foreign Office at 5.30 a.m.

(a) WM(40)117.   (b) C6674/31/18.   (c) C6680/279/18.   (d) C6660/65/17.

Government proposed a broadcast statement which was accepted, with minor alterations, by the War Cabinet.[1]

The statement was as follows:

'His Majesty's Government in the United Kingdom, who in their reply of September 1 to the appeal of the President of the United States gave the assurance that their air forces had received orders prohibiting the bombing of civilian populations and limiting bombing to strictly military objectives, now publicly proclaim that they reserve to themselves the right to take any action which they consider appropriate in the event of bombing by the enemy of civil populations, whether in the United Kingdom, France, or in countries assisted by the United Kingdom.'

This declaration was of far-reaching importance, since it fore-shadowed the fateful retaliation which the Germans ultimately brought upon themselves by their employment of indiscriminate bombing as a 'terror weapon'. For the time, however, they were able to use this weapon to accelerate the surrender of the Dutch. They bombed Rotterdam on May 14, and threatened similar attacks upon the civilian population of Utrecht.

In any case the military capitulation of the Dutch could hardly have been long delayed. There had been no co-ordination between the Dutch and Belgian schemes of defence. The main Dutch defences were based, as in the past, on a 'water line' running from the south of the Zuider Zee across the widening estuaries of the great rivers and thus protecting the cities of Amsterdam, The Hague and Rotterdam. The Belgian line ran along the Albert Canal from the Meuse to Antwerp. There was thus a gap of over thirty miles between the two defence lines. The Germans passed through this gap and captured one of the bridges over the Maas (Meuse). They were thus able to send an armoured force against Rotterdam. In the north they broke through the Yssel defences and secured another bridgehead at Arnhem. No Allied reinforcements could reach the Dutch, and no hope of successful resistance remained for them.

Events in Belgium and France moved as quickly towards catas-trophe on a much larger scale. The first action of the British and French armies in the north was to advance from the Franco-Belgian frontier to the so-called Antwerp–Namur line. This move was made at once on May 10 in accordance with the plan of campaign pre-

---

[1] The War Cabinet met three times on May 10: at 8.0 a.m., 11.30 a.m. and 4.30 p.m. Mr. Chamberlain presided over the meetings. This broadcast statement was accepted upon the general authorisation of the War Cabinet at the second of the meetings. The German Government were told of the declaration by the United States Chargé d'Affaires at Berlin. The first action under the declaration took place with a raid of 100 British bombers mainly on the Ruhr on the night of May 15–16.

viously approved by General Gamelin and accepted by the Supreme War Council.[1] The British commanders had regarded the plan with some misgiving, but had agreed to it for political reasons because it seemed likely to encourage Belgian resistance; a plan based on the line of the Scheldt or the Franco-Belgian frontier would have exposed the greater part of the country to invasion if, as was likely, the Belgian army had been forced to retreat.

General Gamelin's plan, however, assumed that the Belgians would hold out at least for some time along the Albert Canal, and that they would have constructed adequate anti-tank fortifications along the Antwerp–Namur line, and especially in the open country—unprotected by any large river—between Louvain and Namur. Neither of these conditions was fulfilled. The Belgian army lost the line of the canal almost at once; the fortifications between Louvain and Namur were incomplete. This weakness was the more serious because the Maginot line on the French frontier did not extend along the southern flank of the Ardennes; the military reason for leaving the area without the strongest fortified works and protected by a relatively weak defence force was that the French High Command did not believe that the Germans could develop a large-scale offensive through the Ardennes.

Here also the French calculations were wrong. On May 14 the Germans crossed the Meuse and broke through the French lines north of Sedan. The German armour then began to spread rapidly westwards in open country. Three days later the gap in the French defences was nearly sixty miles wide and the head of the German armoured columns was approaching St. Quentin, some sixty miles from their crossing of the Meuse. The French were unable to stop these armoured columns, or to prevent the mass of the German infantry from following them in a westward advance which would reach the mouth of the Somme and cut off the Allied forces in the north.

At this point M. Reynaud took two steps which turned out to be disastrous. On May 18 be appointed Marshal Pétain Vice-President of the Council of Ministers; on May 19 he gave the supreme command of the French armies to General Weygand (whom he had recalled from Syria). Marshal Pétain proved to be completely defeatist; General Weygand failed to act with the speed and resolution which were essential if the northern armies were to avoid utter disaster. The German advance in northern Belgium, after the Belgians had been driven from the Albert Canal, was a serious danger; the break-through at Sedan made it necessary for the British and French to withdraw from their advanced positions. At midnight on May 19–20 the British forces were back again on the Scheldt just beyond the

[1] See above, Chapter I, Section (iii).

Franco-Belgian frontier. They could not stay there without being enveloped from the west. In order to avoid this envelopment, and in the hope of a French counter-attack from the south, they turned in a south-westerly direction towards the Somme.

At this point indeed the only hope of saving the situation was an advance northwards by the French armies south of the 'gap' made by the Germans; if this advance had succeeded, the German tanks and infantry might have been 'sealed off' by a junction between the northern and southern armies. General Weygand attempted to carry out this plan. The attempt failed.[1] Hence the German advance continued, with decreasing resistance from the French whose armies were bewildered by the new armoured tactics and by the suddenness, speed, and extent of the German attack. On May 20 the Germans reached Abbeville: their way was open to the Channel coast north of the Somme. The northern Allied armies were now not only cut off but also in danger of losing touch with the Channel ports. Since there was clearly no hope of a junction with the southern armies, the only hope of survival for the British Expeditionary Force, the Belgian army, and the French forces in this northern area was an escape by sea. Boulogne was lost on May 25; British forces held Calais with great determination until May 26 and thereby enabled the main body of the British Expeditionary Force and the French to fight their way to Dunkirk. Here their chances of escape were endangered by the surrender of the Belgian army on the night of May 27–8. After this surrender, there seemed little prospect of saving more than a very small part of the British and French forces.

The embarkation from the beaches and harbour of Dunkirk was thus the last stage in a series of fearful defeats. Nevertheless the rescue by sea of nearly 350,000 troops, even without their equipment, in the face of a powerful enemy, was so unexpected and so extraordinary a feat of arms that it took on the semblance of a victory. Moreover, from the British point of view, the political and military consequences of saving a trained army were far-reaching enough to justify a return of confidence at the moment when, in France, all hope had almost disappeared.

(ii)

The collapse of armed resistance in the Netherlands and in Belgium: refusal of the King of the Belgians to leave Belgium (May 10–28, 1940).

The part played by the British diplomatic representatives in France, the Netherlands and Belgium and, for that matter, by the

---

[1] The reasons for failure are outside the scope of this History.

Foreign Office in London, during these weeks of calamity was fragmentary and confused. In general, the diplomatic representatives could do little more than act as channels of military communication, and the Foreign Office could instruct them only as circumstances allowed. In the Netherlands these instructions were at first concerned with preventing as much material as possible from falling into enemy hands.

(a) At 9 a.m. on May 10 the British Military Attaché asked for an interview with the Dutch Commander-in-Chief in order to emphasise the importance of preventing oil stocks, especially at Rotterdam, from falling into German hands. The Commander-in-Chief said that the matter was receiving attention, but declined British help in preparing for the destruction of stocks. During the night of May

(b) 11–12 the Foreign Office, on the instructions of the War Cabinet, asked Sir N. Bland to impress again on the Dutch authorities how urgent it was to destroy or run off the oil. If measures to this end were delayed, there was a risk of large stocks falling into German hands. Sir N. Bland replied on May 12 that he had continued to make representations at the Ministry of Foreign Affairs. The Dutch Foreign Office were fully aware of the importance of the matter.[1] They thought, however, that the position at Rotterdam was improving.

(c) On the Dutch side Sir N. Bland was asked in the afternoon of May 10 to transmit a special appeal to Lord Halifax that British aircraft should bomb the aerodrome at Waalhaven where German parachutists were landing.[2] The Royal Air Force bombed Waalhaven on the night of May 10–11: at 1.25 p.m. on May 12 Sir N.

(d) Bland telephoned another message from the Air Attaché to the Air Ministry that the Dutch General Staff were 'seriously upset' at the refusal of the British authorities to bomb Waalhaven again. German troops were continuing to land there and the Dutch felt that their own forces were unlikely at present to recapture the aerodrome.

(e) Meanwhile at 10.30 a.m. on May 11 Sir N. Bland had telephoned an urgent request from the Dutch Council of Ministers for the despatch of British troops to the Netherlands. The Council of Ministers suggested two divisions; Sir N. Bland thought that two battalions would be 'better than nothing'. The Military Attaché had already telephoned on the subject to the War Office. Sir N. Bland

---

[1] On May 13 Lord Halifax raised the question with the Netherlands Foreign Minister,
(f) M. van Kleffens. M. van Kleffens said that, if necessary, the oils could be mixed in order to make them useless for aeroplanes. They could not be released into the tidal river without setting fire to every place between Rotterdam and the sea.

[2] The British Air Attaché at The Hague had already transmitted requests for the bombing of this aerodrome.

(a) C6990/6990/29. (b) C6728/31/18. (c) C6721/31/18. (d) C6745/31/18. (e) C6724/31/18. (f) C6788/5/18.

suggested that the Foreign Office should give the strongest support to the request.

Owing to the rapid development of the German attack elsewhere, it was impossible to meet this request. In any case, British assistance could not have arrived in time to save the military situation. The Dutch royal family left the Netherlands early in the morning of May (a) 13, and at 8.30 a.m. on this day the British Naval Attaché was told (b) that the Dutch Government had decided that they and the Corps Diplomatique must leave the country. At 1.15 Sir N. Bland asked at the Ministry of Foreign Affairs for confirmation of this report. On hearing that no decision had been taken Sir N. Bland decided to remain at The Hague. A few hours later, however, he was advised by the Ministry of Foreign Affairs to leave. He and most of his staff left the Legation at 5.15 p.m. The Military Attaché, who stayed on with members of a special Military Mission, was told at midnight on May 13-14 that the Ministry of Foreign Affairs had not been allowed to let Sir N. Bland know earlier in the day that the Dutch Government had already left, but that they had given him as broad a hint as possible that he should go.

The report from the Military Attaché gave the impression that Dutch resistance might be continuing. On the morning of May 14, M. Corbin told Lord Halifax of a message from the Queen of the (c) Netherlands to the French President that unless the Allies could send help at once, the Dutch Commander-in-Chief would have to do what he thought fit, in view of the position of the civilian population and the very considerable losses of the Dutch army. Later in the morning M. van Kleffens spoke in similar terms to Lord Halifax, and asked whether we could take off Dutch troops in order that they might continue to help the Allied cause. He had already enquired on (d) the previous day whether, if necessary, the Dutch Government could establish themselves in London.

On the morning of May 15 M. van Kleffens brought to Lord Halifax a communiqué issued on the previous night to the effect that (e) the Dutch Commander-in-Chief had ordered his troops to cease military resistance. Lord Halifax said that no one in Great Britain would wish to criticise the Commander-in-Chief or the Dutch people for this decision. It was, however, essential that a state of war should continue between the Netherlands and Germany; therefore the Commander-in-Chief must not negotiate or co-operate with the Germans, but merely accept their terms under protest. M. van Kleffens said that he and other members of the Netherlands Government agreed with this view.

(a) C6744/31/18. (b) C6990/6990/29. (c) C6724/31/18. (d) C6788/5/18. (e) C6724/31/18.

(a) The invasion of the Netherlands raised, incidentally, one minor question upon which a decision had to be taken. Mr. Churchill asked the Foreign Office on May 10 whether the ex-Emperor William II should be told that, if he wished to leave the Netherlands, he would be received with consideration and dignity in Great Britain. The possibility of offering the ex-Emperor an asylum in Great Britain had been discussed in November 1939, when a German attack on the Low Countries seemed likely. Sir N. Bland had then been instructed that he should try to get the ex-Emperor moved to Sweden or Denmark, and only in the last resort to Great Britain.

The Foreign Office now thought that we might say that, if the ex-Emperor asked to be allowed to come to England, he would be suitably received but that we should not go out of our way to invite him. Mr. Churchill considered that a more direct hint might be given. Lord Halifax agreed, and asked Sir A. Hardinge to enquire the views of His Majesty The King. Sir A. Hardinge replied that His Majesty agreed with the suggestion, but that he did not know where the ex-Emperor would live in England; he 'presumed, however, that someone would be glad to offer him shelter'. Sir N. Bland was there-fore instructed on May 11 to arrange for a message to be sent privately to the ex-Emperor. The message, which was sent through the Burgomaster of Doorn, was declined with thanks.[1]

Events in Belgium moved no less rapidly towards catastrophe, although the Germans had to meet the resistance of the three Allied armies. As in the Netherlands, His Majesty's Mission was used as a channel of military communication, but in the confusion which followed the removal of the Belgian Government from Brussels on May 16, and was constantly increased by the differences of view between the King of the Belgians and his Ministers, the Foreign Office could not easily keep in touch with events.[2] Late in the evening
(b) of May 11 Sir L. Oliphant reported that, according to M. Spaak, while the situation in the Netherlands was a trifle better, the position

---

[1] The ex-Emperor, in fact, greeted the arrival of German troops with pious enthusiasm, and also with a total lack of concern for his Dutch hosts whose territory was being invaded.

[2] The difficulty was greater owing to Sir L. Oliphant's premature move from Bruges, and subsequent disappearance (see below, p. 185), and the semi-independent position of Admiral Sir R. Keyes. Sir R. Keyes was appointed special liaison officer with the King of the Belgians on May 10, with diplomatic status as an additional Naval Attaché at His Majesty's Embassy. In these circumstances Sir R. Keyes was independent of the Ambassador but under the general orders of the Foreign Office. Sir R. Keyes submitted a report
(c) of his mission to Lord Halifax on July 1, 1940. The report was strongly polemical, and devoted mainly to a vindication of the King of the Belgians from the charge of treachery in surrendering to the Germans.

(a) C6726/1603/18.   (b) C6723/31/18.   (c) C7927/292/4.

in Belgium was very serious indeed. An important bridge over the Albert Canal had not been blown up because a shell had killed the officer in charge of demolition work and had cut telephone communications. German reinforcements were now using the bridge. M. Spaak asked that the British and French air forces should destroy it.[1] During the night of May 11–12 M. Spaak also raised the (a) question of the passage of British troops through Brussels on their way to the Antwerp–Namur line. He said that this passage was causing him the greatest anxiety owing to the Belgian declaration that Brussels was an open city. He must therefore insist upon the use of other routes by the troops. He was unable to suggest any other routes, but claimed that the Allies had previously agreed not to send troops through Brussels. The Foreign Office considered that nothing could be done to meet M. Spaak's objections and that it was impossible at this stage to alter the plan of campaign because the Belgians had given an assurance to the Germans without consulting us.

On the night of May 13 the Belgian Ambassador brought to the Foreign Office a memorandum on the question. The Ambassador said that the passage of troops was contrary to the declaration made by the Belgian Government after previous agreement with the British High Command; that it would expose Brussels to certain destruction and that orders should be given for the agreed route to be 'scrupulously and exclusively followed'. The Ambassador was told that the Foreign Office had no knowledge of any such agreement and that the object of our forces was to reach the best defensive line for the preservation of Belgium. The message was, however, transmitted to the Chiefs of Staff who replied during the early morning of May 14 that the use of roads through the outskirts of Brussels was essential for the transport of troops to their defence positions and for their maintenance while in these positions. The Foreign Office communicated this reply in writing to the Belgian Ambassador on May 14.

The King of the Belgians and General van Overstraeten also protested to Sir R. Keyes about the passage of troops. Sir R. Keyes (b) pointed out that he had seen as many Belgian as British troops in Brussels, that the British Military Attaché had not been given the information promised to him in connexion with the entry of British troops into Belgium,[2] and that he had been told that additional bridges would be built to provide the B.E.F. with an alternative route avoiding the passage through Brussels. General van Overstraeten admitted that there had been difficulty about providing the

---

[1] Sir L. Oliphant did not give the exact location of the bridge. He was instructed to state exactly where it was. After he had done so he was told that throughout the day of (c) May 12 the Royal Air Force would bomb the road on which it was situated.
[2] See above, p. 136.

(a) C6736/31/18. (b) C7970/40/41. (c) C6723/31/18.

bridges, but said that in any case there was no need for the B.E.F. to use the main boulevards of the city.

This controversy was ended on May 15 by an announcement from the Germans that they would no longer consider Brussels an open city. In any case the rapid advance of the German armies brought other questions into the foreground. At midday on May 14
(a) Sir L. Oliphant telephoned that the Belgian Government would probably move to Ostend, and that he would go with them. For the next thirty-six hours there was uncertainty about the intentions of the Belgian Government. The general impression was that the King of the Belgians wished the Government to stay in Brussels while the Ministers thought it necessary to move. In the early hours of May 16
(b) the Belgian Government and Sir L. Oliphant left for Ostend.

On May 17 Sir L. Oliphant telephoned that the Government
(c) were unable to decide whether they should stay in Ostend or, if they moved, where they should go. There seemed to be a difference of view between the King and the Ministers. A move to France by land would be difficult because the roads were blocked with traffic. The Government might make their decision suddenly; they would then almost certainly go to Dover. Sir L. Oliphant proposed to ask the Ministers what they intended to do. He therefore wanted to know what reply he should give if they made a request for transport to Dover.[1]

At 4 p.m. Sir L. Oliphant telephoned that, for the time, the
(d) Belgian Government had decided to stay at Ostend. If they left Ostend, they would go to France. According to M. Spaak, the situation was serious, but neither very critical nor catastrophic. Later in the evening Sir R. Campbell reported from Paris that the Belgian Government had lost touch with the King and had asked the French Government whether they could come to France.[2] The French Government had replied that, in their opinion, the withdrawal of the Belgian Government while the army was fighting would have a bad effect.

At 10 a.m. on May 18 Sir L. Oliphant reported that the Belgian
(e) Government were leaving Ostend and had asked the French Government to receive them, probably at Le Havre. The Foreign Office received a slightly different report from the Belgian Embassy in London. According to the Embassy M. Spaak had asked only for French hospitality for 'certain elements of the Government'. The

---

[1] This message was transmitted to the Admiralty who replied that their latest reports did not suggest that the situation at Ostend was very bad. Bombing was relatively light and ships were coming in and out of the port without much difficulty.

[2] The Belgian Government appeared to have made no arrangements in advance for a transfer of the Government or administration from Brussels in the event of an invasion.

(a) C6723/31/18. (b) C7818/243/4. (c) C6873/31/18. (d) C6850/243/4. (e) C6873/31/18.

main seat of Government would remain at Ostend as long as possible. At 7.15 p.m. Sir L. Oliphant, who had moved to Dunkirk, repeated the information which he had sent during the morning. He expected the Belgian Government to leave for Le Havre within the next two or three days, with the exception of two or three Ministers who would stay behind as a 'token Government' on Belgian territory. On the following day Sir L. Oliphant telephoned that, according to the French Ambassador, the Belgian Government had left for Le Havre, but that M. Spaak, the Prime Minister, and the Minister of National Defence had gone to Belgian Headquarters at Bruges. If the British and French Governments agreed, Sir L. Oliphant and the French Ambassador would leave at once for Le Havre.

The two Governments at first agreed on practical grounds with this proposal, but M. Daladier thought that the French Ambassador should stay with M. Spaak. Similar instructions were therefore sent to Sir L. Oliphant. On the morning of May 20 Sir L. Oliphant decided to leave Bruges and set out by road for Le Havre; he was unable to reach it and on June 2 had to give himself up to the (a) Germans.[1]

On May 22 the Belgian Ambassador and M. Gutt, Belgian Finance Minister, raised with the Foreign Office the question of the evacuation of the King and of those members of the Government who were still in Belgium. Lord Halifax brought the matter before (b) the War Cabinet. A message from Sir R. Keyes, however, said that the Belgian army wanted to maintain contact with the B.E.F. and that the King was determined to stay with the army and hoped that it might be re-formed in France.

In the afternoon of May 22 it became clear, from a telephone conversation between the Belgian Embassy and M. Spaak, that the (c) Ministers in Belgium had made the proposal for evacuation without consulting the King. M. Spaak agreed that the plans should be submitted to the King without telling him that the proposal came from the Ministers.

On May 24 the Foreign Office sent a message to the Belgian Ambassador that the British Government would have plans ready for (d) evacuation and that they were 'deeply impressed with the necessity, from an international point of view, of maintaining the King and the Belgian Government in a place of safety'.

'They would not, at this moment, wish to urge upon His Majesty the decision to leave his country and his army, which His Majesty would, of course, not wish to do, as long as it is possible for him to remain, and on the best military advice, do not think that this is

---

[1] The French Ambassador stayed at Bruges until May 23. On May 24 he crossed to (e) England from Dunkirk.

(a) C14412/14412/4 (1941). (b) WM(40)133; C6873/31/18; C7927/292/4. (c) C6873/31/18. (d) C6873/31/18. (e) C7010/5076/4.

immediately necessary tonight. But if and when the moment should come, His Majesty's Government will be ready, in good time, to make a representation to His Majesty which might make it easier for him to take a distasteful decision.'

In the afternoon of May 24 the Belgian Ambassador and M. Gutt

(a) asked Lord Halifax to send a message through Sir R. Keyes to the King that the British Government thought it of the utmost importance—from the point of view of winning the war—for him to avoid being taken prisoner by the Germans. The Foreign Office drafted a message, which was sent by the War Office to Sir R. Keyes as from the Prime Minister, repeating in slightly different terms the statement given earlier to the Ambassador.

At 11.50 a.m. on the following morning the Counsellor of the

(b) Belgian Embassy told the Foreign Office that he had been able to reach M. Spaak by telephone at Bruges and that he had arranged with the Admiralty for the evacuation to take place not from Ostend but from Dunkirk. The Belgian Ministers had left Bruges for La Panne on the night of May 24–5 and, after trying in vain to persuade the King to go with them, had decided to move to Dunkirk and thence to England. As far as the Counsellor knew, the King was remaining in Belgium.[1]

(c)   The War Cabinet agreed to make a further appeal to the King. The Foreign Office had no means of communication with him, but

(d) Sir R. Keyes had arranged to telephone to the Prime Minister at 5 p.m. It was therefore decided to use this opportunity to send the following message:

'We understand King of the Belgians refuses to leave his army. While respecting His Majesty's decision and the motives which led him to take it, we cannot doubt that, from the point of view of Belgium's political future and the future prosecution of the war, His Majesty should be strongly pressed to reconsider it and allow us to help him to withdraw from Belgium.'

(e)   Meanwhile, on May 25 the King of the Belgians had written a letter to His Majesty the King.[2] He said that Belgium had kept to

---

[1] M. Spaak stated to the British press on May 28 that at 5 a.m. on May 25 M. Pierlot, the Belgian Prime Minister, and other Ministers had told the King that he ought to be prepared to leave the country in order to avoid capture. The King had refused to leave Belgium. According to Sir R. Keyes, the Ministers spent most of the night in trying to persuade the King to go with them. Sir R. Keyes gave the King the message sent at the request of the Belgian Ambassador. The King answered that he had decided to stay in Belgium. Sir R. Keyes in a message back to the Prime Minister on May 25 supported the King's decision and suggested that we should not be 'unduly impressed' with the arguments of the Belgian Ministers.

[2] The letter (brought to England by General Dill) was sent by Sir A. Hardinge to the
(f) Foreign Office on May 26.

(a) C6873/31/18.   (b) C6873/31/18.   (c) WM(40)138.13, C.A.   (d) C6873/31/18.
(e) C6873/31/18.   (f) C7927/292/4; C6873/31/18.

her engagements, but that the Belgian means of resistance were now nearing their end. There was no possibility of further retreat, or of creating a new force, since the whole cadre of officers and staff were engaged in the present battle. The King felt that his duty compelled him to share the fate of his army and remain with his people.

'To act otherwise would amount to desertion. Whatever trials Belgium may have to face in future, I am convinced I can help my people better by remaining with them than by attempting to act from outside, especially with regard to the hardships of foreign occupation, the menace of forced labour, or deportations, and the difficulties of food supplies. By remaining in my country, I fully realise that my position will be very difficult, but my utmost concern will be to prevent my countrymen from being compelled to associate themselves with any action against the countries which have attempted to help Belgium in her plight. If I should fail in that endeavour, and only then would I give up the task I have set myself.'

On the morning of May 26 Lord Halifax saw MM. Spaak and Pierlot, who had reached England from Dunkirk. M. Pierlot said (a) that the military situation was very bad, and M. Spaak asked whether His Majesty the King would make an appeal to King Leopold. If the latter were taken prisoner, the Belgian Government would be without a Head, and the consequences would be very serious from the point of view of Belgian co-operation against Germany. Lord Halifax asked whether the Belgian Government could assume the constitutional powers vested in the King. M. Pierlot said that, if the King were a prisoner, there were obvious difficulties in the way of his action as a free agent in the political sphere. At best his capture and separation from the Government would be interpreted as a sign of division in the country.

After this interview Lord Halifax drafted a letter for submission to His Majesty the King and, if His Majesty approved, for despatch to King Leopold through Sir R. Keyes. The letter explained the extreme importance of preserving a united Belgian Government with full authority outside Belgian territory. If the King were able to remain at liberty and mix with his people and to act and speak for them, there might be great value in the establishment of such a rallying point for the Belgian nation. The King would, however, not be free to act in this way and might be taken as a prisoner to Germany. 'Such a position would leave your people bereft of their natural leader without . . . any compensating advantage.' Sir R. Keyes seems to have received this message at 6 a.m. on May 27. (b) He gave the message to the King who took it away for discussion with the Queen Mother. Later the King said that he and the Queen Mother had decided to stay in Belgium, at all events as long as they

(a) C6873/31/18. (b) C7927/292/4.

were allowed to do so. King Leopold thought that the message represented the views, not of His Majesty, but those of his Government.[1]

(a)   At 11.20 p.m. on May 27 Sir R. Campbell reported from Paris that he and General Spears[2] had been told by M. Reynaud and General Weygand that the King of the Belgians had asked the Germans for an armistice. In fact, the Belgian army, at the King's orders, ceased fighting on May 28 at 4 a.m. In the morning of May 28 the Belgian Ambassador and M. Gutt came to see Lord Halifax at the Foreign Office. They brought a message from M. Pierlot that the Belgian Government were fully determined to fight the war to the end with Great Britain and France. The position was very painful for the Government because the capitulation—although foreseen for some time[3]—and the King's decision to stay in Belgium forced them to choose between their King and their country. They could not do otherwise than choose their country. The Ambassador added that the King was a prisoner; the army had surrendered, and a Government inside Belgium could act only under duress. The existing Belgian Government was therefore the legal Government of the country.

Lord Halifax replied only that the King's motives were entirely honourable, but that his decision was, on a long view, a disaster for Belgium and for the Allies an immediate danger with consequences hard to measure.

---

[1] According to Sir R. Keyes, the Prime Minister instructed him, apparently on the evening of May 27, to try once again to persuade King Leopold and the Queen Mother to come to England.

[2] General Spears was appointed by the Prime Minister (as Minister of Defence) special liaison officer with M. Reynaud (in the latter's capacity of Minister of Defence). This appointment was intended to supplement, and not in any way to supersede, the functions of His Majesty's Ambassador in France.

[3] Mr. Aveling considered that the King had raised the question of capitulation with his Ministers on May 25 and that they had tried to dissuade him. Mr. Aveling also had (b) information suggesting that the King had tried to secure the signature of a Minister which would enable him to dismiss the Government and appoint a new Government, in German-occupied territory. The political acts of the King in relation to his own Government, and the question whether he was justified on military grounds in asking for an armistice, fall outside the scope of this *History*.

(a) C7124/243/4.   (b) C7816/243/4.

(iii)

The political situation in France before the opening of the German offensive: the German 'break-through' at Sedan: French appeals for fighter aircraft: the Prime Minister's visit to Paris, May 16: changes in the French Government and High Command (May 10–19, 1940).

As in the Netherlands and Belgium, the British Embassy in France became a channel of rapid communication for every kind of business during the period of German invasion leading to the French military collapse and surrender. Some weeks before the opening of the offensive, at the time of the fall of M. Daladier's administration, Sir R. Campbell had reported at length upon the political situation in (a) France. He thought that M. Daladier's fall was due partly to his failure to conciliate opposition. He had concentrated too much business in his own hands, and even his own party were discontented with his methods. The collapse of Finland and the apparent inaction of the Allies had brought this general discontent to a head. M. Laval and other opponents of M. Daladier were also using the opportunity given by the course of events. M. Laval was still biding his time. He favoured the conciliation of Germany and a policy of concessions to Italy, and was generally labelled as a defeatist. Sir R. Campbell could not be more definite about his policy because he (Sir R. Campbell) had considered it undesirable to renew contact with him. Sir R. Campbell thought that M. Laval would certainly 'seek an early accommodation with Germany', and that an attack which he had recently made on M. Daladier in the Senate was probably intended to mark his first important re-entry into politics.

Sir R. Campbell also regarded the disloyalty of some of M. Daladier's colleagues as among the causes of his fall. The reasons for this disloyalty were obscure and had to be looked for 'in the mire into which parliamentary government in France has fallen'. Sir R. Campbell expected M. Reynaud to be given a fair trial, and pointed out that he could not have formed a ministry if M. Daladier had not agreed, out of a sense of public duty, to support him. M. Reynaud had courage, resolution, adaptability and imagination. He was very friendly to Great Britain, and would press hard for more energy in the prosecution of the war. On balance, however, Sir R. Campbell did not welcome the change of ministers. The Foreign Office agreed with Sir R. Campbell's view. In mid-April they had further confirmation from neutral sources of (b) M. Laval's intentions, and of the existence of elements in France

---

(a) C4658/65/17. (b) C5839/6/18.

'which would be glad to accept a peace offensive'. M. Laval was 'very bitter against the English, and well-disposed towards Italy'.

(a) On the night of May 9–10 Sir R. Campbell telegraphed that the debate in the House of Commons on the conduct of the war and press speculation on the probable sequel (i.e. the resignation of Mr. Chamberlain) had precipitated a ministerial crisis in France which had been 'simmering for some days but which would otherwise probably not have come to the boil before the Chamber met again on May 16'. As far as Sir R. Campbell could discover, the crisis concerned the relations between M. Reynaud and M. Daladier. The final break had come over M. Reynaud's wish to make a change in the French High Command. M. Reynaud's resignation might take place 'at any moment'.

At 12.15 a.m. on May 10 Sir R. Campbell telegraphed that M. Reynaud and his Cabinet had resigned. The fact had not been made public owing to M. Herriot's absence from Paris. The President could not therefore consult M. Herriot before the morning of May 10. Sir R. Campbell repeated that the crisis had arisen over M. Reynaud's insistence on replacing General Gamelin by General Weygand. M. Reynaud could hardly succeed in forming a new Cabinet without M. Daladier's support. The only possible solution, therefore, lay between M. Herriot and M. Daladier, 'with odds . . . slightly in favour of the former'. Later on May 10 the Foreign Office was informed by telephone that M. Reynaud was unlikely to resign[1] but that he might enlarge his administration, possibly by the inclusion of MM. Blum and Marin and Marshal Pétain, in order to form a 'Government of National Union'. In the evening of

(b) May 10 Sir R. Campbell telephoned a communiqué in which M. Reynaud announced the reconstruction of his Cabinet to obtain the participation of all the political parties.

During the first few days of the German offensive Sir R. Campbell transmitted messages from M. Reynaud asking for more assistance in the air from Great Britain. M. Reynaud first made this appeal on the morning of May 13. He told Sir R. Campbell on the night of

(c) May 13–14 that he had done so at M. Daladier's request. On
(d) May 14 M. Reynaud renewed his appeal in a telephone message to the Prime Minister. He said that the Germans had broken through the French front at Sedan, and asked for the immediate despatch of ten additional fighter squadrons.[2] Without this support, the French could not be sure of stopping the Germans between Sedan and Paris. The War Cabinet agreed with the Prime Minister that until we had

---

[1] M. Reynaud withdrew his resignation after hearing the news of the German offensive.

[2] Ten squadrons were already operating in France.

(a) C6660/65/17. (b) C6689/65/17. (c) C6828/5/18. (d) WM(40)122.

more information we could take no decision which would mean a further weakening of our home forces.

Early on the morning of May 15 the Prime Minister told the War Cabinet of an alarmist message from M. Reynaud that as a (a) result of the break-through at Sedan, the battle was lost and the road was open to Paris. M. Reynaud appealed urgently for British help. The Prime Minister had refused to accept so gloomy a view of the situation and had pointed out that we could not send more divisions to France at present, and that in any case they could not arrive in time at the scene of action. The Prime Minister had then telephoned to General Georges, who had taken a calmer view of the situation, but had asked for more air assistance.

At 2 p.m. on May 15 Sir R. Campbell telephoned a further message from M. Reynaud. M. Reynaud thought that Mr. Churchill (b) might have misunderstood him. As head of the French Government he had felt bound to pass on the statement made to him by the Minister of Defence. He did not wish the Prime Minister to conclude that he was weakening. While any Frenchmen remained fighting, and while he was Prime Minister, there would be no weakening.

During the evening of May 15 M. Corbin went to see Sir A. Cadogan. He said that there appeared to have been some mis- (c) understanding earlier in the day, and that the British staff did not realise that the French needed more fighters at once. The mistake had been corrected during the afternoon by a message from Generals Gamelin and Vuillemin asking for more fighter assistance. M. Corbin understood our reply to have been that we could send only replacements, not additional squadrons. This would mean delay; new squadrons could go into action at once, but time would be taken in fitting reserve machines into existing squadrons. M. Corbin then talked at some length about German strategy. The Germans were throwing all their strength into a battle which might decide the war if there were a break-through at the point where the Maginot fortifications abutted on the less strongly fortified French line. Practically all the specialised material of the German army and air force was in use. If the French army were out of the war, the result would be fatal to Great Britain as well as to France. M. Corbin wondered whether we could ever win the war unless a man were found to direct the whole allied war effort as a single entity.

Sir A. Cadogan took M. Corbin to mean that some one should have authority to order our fighters to join in the battle. He said that he would tell the Prime Minister and Lord Halifax at once what M. Corbin had said. M. Corbin hoped that Sir A. Cadogan would represent his views as strongly as possible; he repeated once or twice

---

(a) WM(40)123. (b) C6828/5/18. (c) C6828/5/18.

that the future of what he called the whole coalition might depend on the outcome of the present battle.

The Prime Minister sent an answer to M. Reynaud through
(a) Sir R. Campbell at 6.40 a.m. on May 16.[1] The Prime Minister said that he had examined with the War Cabinet the requests which M. Reynaud had made for more fighter aircraft. He explained that it would be a short-sighted policy to squander 'bit by bit and day by day the fighter squadrons which are in effect our Maginot Line. The enemy can switch his bomber force on to these islands at a few hours' notice; and, if he should find them inadequately defended, he would be able to strike a blow at our war industry which might irretrievably damage the Allied cause.' We had sent more fighter squadrons to France than we had agreed to send and in so doing we had reduced our fighter strength to a minimum. We expected a German attack and would welcome it as diverting the enemy from France. We would consider carefully the latest French demands but we could not 'rupture our final line of defence'.

Sir R. Campbell reported by telephone at 11.15 a.m. on May 16 that he had delivered the Prime Minister's message. The situation was very bad. M. Reynaud's reply to the message had been that this war was not like the last war. The German armoured divisions were well on their way to Paris and might reach there 'tonight'. General Gamelin had telephoned that he had sent a fresh appeal by cypher telegram that help from British fighters was essential. The fighters could be based on the Lower Seine (which was not yet threatened) and could return thence rapidly to England in case of need.

(b) The War Cabinet met at 11.30 a.m. on May 16. They decided to send four more squadrons at once to France, and to prepare for sending two additional squadrons at short notice. The Prime Minister also decided, with the approval of his colleagues, to fly to Paris for consultations with the French. He left about 3 p.m.

(c) Meanwhile, at 2.15 p.m. Sir R. Campbell reported that, on the advice of the Ministry of Foreign Affairs, he was destroying the Embassy archives and that he was sending the women members of his staff away by train to Le Havre.

The Prime Minister saw MM. Reynaud and Daladier and General Gamelin about 5.30 p.m. at the Quai d'Orsay. General Gamelin explained the gravity of the military situation—the mass of German armour driving toward Amiens and Arras, with motorised divisions close behind them. He asked for more British help in the air. The Prime Minister made it clear that, unless the French made a

---

[1] The draft of this telegram is dated May 15 and is signed by the Prime Minister.

(a) C6828/5/18.   (b) WM(40)124.   (c) C6828/5/18.

supreme effort, we should not feel justified in accepting the grave risk to Great Britain entailed by the despatch of more fighters to France. After the meeting he decided to advise the War Cabinet to take this risk. He therefore gave Sir R. Campbell a message— (a) transmitted at 9 p.m.—for the urgent consideration of the War Cabinet. In this message the Prime Minister described the position as 'grave in the last degree'. The German thrust through Sedan had found the French armies ill-grouped. Many were in the north; others were in Alsace. At least four days were needed to cover Paris and to strike at the flanks of the 'bulge' now 50 km. wide. Three German armoured divisions, and two or three infantry divisions were advancing through the gap; large masses were behind them. Hence there were two dangers: the B.E.F. might be left largely 'in the air' as a result of taking no action to make a difficult disengagement and to retreat to the old line, or the German thrust might wear down French resistance before it could be 'fully gathered'. Orders had been given to defend Paris at all costs, but the archives at the Quai d'Orsay were already burning. The Prime Minister thought that the next two, three or four days would be decisive for Paris and probably for the French army. Therefore we must decide whether we could send more fighters in addition to the four squadrons; and whether most of our long-range bombers could be used on May 17 and the following nights against the German masses crossing the Meuse and flowing into the bulge. Even so the results could not be guaranteed, but, unless the 'battle of the bulge' were won, French resistance might be broken up as rapidly as the resistance of Poland. The Prime Minister thought that we ought to send on May 17 the additional six squadrons for which the French asked, and that all available French and British aircraft should be concentrated to dominate the 'bulge' for the next two or three days, not for local purposes, but to give the French a last chance of rallying. The position would not be good 'historically' if the French request were denied, and 'their ruin resulted'.

The Prime Minister considered the German tank and air forces to be fully extended. He pointed out that we should not underrate the difficulties of the German advance if it were strongly counter-attacked. If everything failed in France, we could move what remained of our own striking force to help the B.E.F. in the event of the latter being forced to withdraw. The Prime Minister again emphasised the 'mortal gravity' of the hour. He said that General Dill agreed with him, and that he must have an answer by midnight in order to encourage the French. The War Cabinet, which met at 11 p.m. on the night of May 16–17, accepted the Prime Minister's (b)

(a) C6828/5/18.   (b) C6828/5/18.

recommendations[1] and sent a formal reply through Sir R. Campbell at 1.11 a.m.[2] The Prime Minister gave the reply at once to MM. Reynaud and Daladier, and flew back to England in the morning of May 17.

(a) Twelve hours later (1.25 p.m.) Sir R. Campbell telephoned that he was waiting until the evening to see M. Reynaud, and that he had been told that MM. Reynaud and Daladier had been much heartened by the Prime Minister's visit, and that the morale of the French divisions which had been heavily engaged was much improved. At 11.10 p.m., however, Sir R. Campbell telephoned that M. Reynaud was depressed at the latest news of the military situation.

In the afternoon of May 18 Sir R. Campbell again reported an improvement in the morale of the French troops. Shortly afterwards
(b) he telephoned that Marshal Pétain had accepted the Vice-Presidency of the Council, and that the prestige of his name would reassure public opinion. M. Mandel had been appointed Minister of the Interior in order to secure a strong hand in dealing with 'fifth column' or latent communist activity. General Weygand was coming back from Syria and would either succeed General Gamelin or become some kind of 'super-adviser' and as such actually supersede him. M. Daladier's position was still uncertain.[3]

The Prime Minister sent a message to M. Reynaud through
(c) Sir R. Campbell at 1.45 p.m. on May 19 congratulating him on the 'strong, compact government' which he had formed. The Prime Minister added that there appeared to be a substantial improvement in the military situation, and that the danger was 'equal for both armies. A very rapid transformation in our favour would be possible. We must not be intimidated by a few hundred armoured vehicles pushing about here and there behind our lines. If they are behind us, we are behind them.'

Sir R. Campbell reported at 5.10 p.m. M. Reynaud's reply. He
(d) wished to assure the Prime Minister of his inflexible determination that France 'should fight on, come what may'. Sir R. Campbell

---

[1] The Chief of the Air Staff explained to the Cabinet that the bases in northern France could take only three more squadrons. He proposed to send six squadrons to Kentish aerodromes, and to send servicing parties to France. Three squadrons would thus be able to work in France from dawn until noon; they would then return to Kent and be replaced by the other three. With these six squadrons the number of British fighter squadrons to operate in or over France would total twenty, double the number provided for at the beginning of the western offensive. These reinforcements did not include the equivalent of two squadrons despatched on May 13, and incorporated into existing units.

[2] The Prime Minister had suggested that the reply should be telephoned in Hindustani to General Ismay at the British Embassy. The reply seems to have been telephoned in this way about 11.30 p.m., i.e. earlier than the despatch of the cyphered message to Sir R. Campbell. General Ismay had previously telephoned in Hindustani to the War Cabinet Office that the Prime Minister was sending an urgent message.

[3] Sir R. Campbell reported later in the day that M. Daladier had accepted the Ministry of Foreign Affairs. M. Reynaud himself took over the Ministry of National Defence and War.

(a) C6844/5/18.   (b) C6844/5/18.   (c) C6828/5/18.   (d) C6844/5/18.

thought M. Reynaud in better heart than he had been in the morning. M. Reynaud said that Marshal Pétain was very lucid, and that his advice would be of very great help and comfort. M. Reynaud had appointed General Weygand (who had now returned) Chief of the General Staff for National Defence. In this capacity he would co-ordinate the French military effort, but would not interfere with the detailed plans of each Commander-in-Chief. General Georges was now Commander-in-Chief in France;[1] General Gamelin was being relieved of his post. M. Reynaud asked whether Sir R. Campbell thought that these changes would be in any way displeasing to the Prime Minister. Sir R. Campbell said that he was sure that the Prime Minister would regard the changes as for the better if M. Reynaud himself took this view. Sir R. Campbell ended his report by saying that, from all that he had heard, he regarded the move as a good one.

Two hours later Sir R. Campbell reported that he had seen M. Daladier, and had found him calm but dejected. Sir R. Campbell (a) was taking the line in his conversations with French Ministers that, if the Allies could check the present onrush, they would be on the road towards winning the war, but he found the Ministers 'suffering under the unexpectedness of the blow in the same way as the French troops went down under the first shock of the German onslaught. Alas, there is no Clemenceau.'

Sir R. Campbell saw M. Mandel, and, for a few moments, M. Reynaud during the evening of May 19. He reported that M. Mandel was carrying out a number of drastic measures against cowardice and defeatism, and that he was a first-rate influence in the Government. M. Reynaud was 'much relieved' that he had persuaded General Weygand to take the post offered to him. Sir R. Campbell also spoke for a short time with General Weygand, (b) and regarded it as greatly to M. Reynaud's credit that he had acted so quickly in getting rid of General Gamelin.

(iv)

Consideration of measures to be taken in the event of a military collapse of France: M. Reynaud's proposal for an approach to Mussolini with a view to mediation: discussion and rejection of the proposal by the War Cabinet: President Roosevelt's approach to Mussolini (May 17–27, 1940).

In view of the news from France on May 16–17 about the extent

---

[1] This information was inaccurate. General Weygand succeeded General Gamelin as Chief of the General Staff and Commander-in-Chief of the French (and Allied) armies. General Georges was (and remained) Commander-in-Chief of the French armies of the North-East.

(a) C6844/5/18. (b) C6844/5/18.

of the German 'break-through', the possibility of a French military collapse had to be taken into consideration. A meeting, at which
(a) Lord Halifax was present, took place in London on May 17 to discuss what action might be necessary if this collapse should occur. Lord Hankey submitted to the Foreign Office a memorandum summarising the discussion. The Foreign Office had already found,
(b) on enquiry through Sir R. Campbell, that the French gold reserve had been distributed in safe areas in the south of France, and that the Belgian and Swiss gold reserves were also in France. Steps were also being taken to work out plans for the destruction of oil stocks in northern France, the removal of shipping, and the blocking of the northern French ports. It was suggested, among other proposals, that the French Government should be asked where they would go if Paris fell or if they were driven out of France; that no French warships should be allowed to fall into German hands; that a 'further desperate appeal' should be made to President Roosevelt to send aeroplanes and anti-aircraft guns at once,[1] and that the French Government should be asked to arrange forthwith for the destruction of factories which would otherwise fall into German hands. The Foreign Office thought it possible to approach the French Government only on the first and last of these proposals.
(c) Sir R. Campbell reported on May 19 that the first move would be to the neighbourhood of Tours.

In the afternoon of May 21 Sir R. Campbell reported that the general situation in Paris was 'depressed and depressing'. The city was calm, but the calmness was due less to fortitude than to stupefaction in view of the discovery that the French fortifications were not, as had been supposed, impregnable. Nine months of easy warfare, German threats, and subterranean communism had told on French morale, and this morale was being lowered by the flood of refugees. The air was full of rumours, and there seemed to be some fifth column activity. MM. Reynaud and Mandel were doing everything possible to restore the situation. They had had some success. The return of Marshal Pétain and of General Weygand was creating a certain amount of confidence, but it was 'late in the day'. Sir R. Campbell concluded with the words: 'People are not getting angry as I should like to see'.

The Prime Minister sent a message of general encouragement to
(d) M. Reynaud on May 21. Sir R. Campbell, who delivered the message, reported that M. Reynaud was pleased with it, and that he also

---

[1] See below, pp. 337–8 for the Prime Minister's message to the President asking for fighter aircraft.

(a) C6901/5/18.   (b) C6828/5/18.   (c) C6876, 6844/5/18.   (d) C6844/5/18.

found great comfort and support in Marshal Pétain, 'whose spirit was unshakeable and brain still very lucid'. At 1.10 a.m. on May 22 Sir R. Campbell was asked to tell M. Reynaud that Mr. Churchill would come to Paris at 11 a.m. to meet him (M. Reynaud) and General Weygand. At this meeting General Weygand expounded his (a) plan for effecting a junction between the British, French and Belgian forces to the north of the 'gap' and the French forces to the south of it. He also asked for the complete engagement of the Royal Air Force in the forthcoming battle.

There was, however, no improvement in the military situation on May 22. At 10.50 a.m. on May 23 Sir R. Campbell was instructed to give to M. Reynaud a message from the Prime Minister that strong (b) enemy armoured forces had cut the communications of the northern armies and that these armies could be saved only by the immediate execution of General Weygand's plan. The Prime Minister asked that the French commanders in the north and south and the Belgian general headquarters should be given the most stringent orders to carry out this plan.

Sir R. Campbell replied at 1.45 p.m. that he had delivered this message at once. M. Reynaud was aware of the situation, and said (c) that the plan was being carried out. Later in the day, after the Prime Minister had spoken by telephone to M. Reynaud and to General (d) Weygand, M. Reynaud sent for Sir R. Campbell in order to tell him that the Prime Minister's message had been passed to General Weygand. General Weygand had said that the operation agreed to on May 22 was being carried out in satisfactory conditions.

Sir R. Campbell transmitted further messages to and from the Prime Minister and General Weygand on the military situation on May 24 and 25; the last of these messages accepted M. Reynaud's suggestion that he should come to London for a meeting at noon on May 26. It was now clear to the British military authorities that General Weygand's plan would not succeed, and that if the northern armies—including the British Expeditionary Force—were not to be totally lost, the only course was to try to evacuate them by sea. The chances of carrying out this operation were most uncertain.

The War Cabinet thus met on the morning of May 26 (before M. Reynaud's arrival) at one of the most dangerous moments in the war. (e) The Prime Minister told the War Cabinet that M. Reynaud might say that the French could not carry on the fight. The Prime Minister would try to persuade M. Reynaud not to surrender and would point out that at least the French were bound in honour to do everything possible for the withdrawal of the British Expeditionary Force. The Prime Minister thought that there was a good chance of saving

---

(a) WM(40)134.1, C.A. (b) C6844/5/18. (c) C6844A/5/18.
(d) WM(40)136,C6844A/5/18. (e) WM(40)139.1, C.A.

a considerable portion of the British Expeditionary Force. In order to be prepared against all eventualities which would arise if the French did not continue the war, he had asked the Chiefs of Staff on May 19 to prepare an estimate of our prospects of fighting alone against Germany, and probably against Italy.[1]

Lord Halifax told the War Cabinet at this meeting of Signor Bastianini's 'soundings' to him on the previous evening about the possibility that His Majesty's Government might agree to a conference.[2] Signor Bastianini had said that Mussolini's principal wish was to secure peace in Europe'. Lord Halifax had replied that peace and security in Europe were equally our main object and that 'we should naturally be prepared to consider any proposals which might lead to this, provided our liberty and independence was assured'. Mr. Churchill's comment to the War Cabinet was that 'peace and security might be achieved under a German domination of Europe. That we could never accept.' Mr. Churchill was opposed to 'any negotiations which might lead to a derogation of our rights and power'.

At his meeting with the Prime Minister, M. Reynaud said that, if the battle of France were lost, they must reckon upon the possibility of a move by Marshal Pétain in favour of an armistice. The purpose of M. Reynaud's visit was thus primarily to obtain support from His Majesty's Government for concessions to Mussolini in the hope of keeping Italy out of the war, and to explore the larger possibility of securing mediation in some form by the Italian Government.

(a) The Prime Minister first saw M. Reynaud alone at Admiralty House.[3] The War Cabinet then met in the early afternoon and the Prime Minister gave an account of his discussion with M. Reynaud. M. Reynaud had made it clear that the French Ministers accepted General Weygand's view that, with 50 divisions against 150 German divisions, French resistance was unlikely to last very long. The French Ministers therefore concluded that the war could not be won on land. At sea we had good fleets which had established a superiority over Germany, but if the Germans had command of resources from Brest to Vladivostock it did not appear that the blockade would win the war. It was also clear that Great Britain would take a long time to build up an army and that we could not make a big effort on land in 1941. This left the air. If the Germans took Paris, they would have the air factories of the region, as well as those of Belgium and the Netherlands. There was little hope for the present from the United

---

[1] For this report, see *Grand Strategy*, II, ch. IX. The estimate was discussed by the War Cabinet on May 27.

[2] For Lord Halifax's conversation with Signor Bastianini, see also below, pp. 236–7.

[3] Mr. Churchill had not yet moved to No. 10 Downing Street from his official residence as First Lord of the Admiralty.

(a) WM(40)140, C.A.

States owing to the smallness of the munitions industry in that country.

Where then could France look? The suggestion had been made that she might approach Italy. Italy would probably ask for the neutralisation of Gibraltar and the Suez Canal, the demilitarisation of Malta, and the limitation of naval forces in the Mediterranean. She would also want a change in the status of Tunis, and the Dodecanese would have to be put right.[1]

The Prime Minister explained to the War Cabinet that apparently the French suggestion was that the offer of such terms might keep Italy out of the war. M. Reynaud realised that the Germans would probably not keep any terms to which they agreed. He had hinted that he would not himself sign peace terms imposed upon France, but that he might be forced to resign, or feel that he ought to resign.

The Prime Minister, after hearing M. Reynaud, had put the other side of the case, and suggested that, as soon as the situation in north-east France had been cleared up, the Germans would make no further attacks on the French line but would at once attack Great Britain. M. Reynaud thought that the dream of all Germans was to conquer Paris, and that they would march on the city.

The Prime Minister had said that we were not prepared to give in. We would rather go down fighting than be enslaved to Germany. In any case we were confident that we had a good chance of surviving the German attack. France, however, must stay in the war. If we could hold out for another three months, the position would be entirely different. The Prime Minister had asked M. Reynaud whether any peace terms had been offered to France. M. Reynaud said 'no', but added that the French Government knew that they could get an offer if they wanted one.

The Prime Minister suggested to the War Cabinet that Lord Halifax should see M. Reynaud at Admiralty House and that he (the Prime Minister) should come over a few minutes later with Mr. Chamberlain and Mr. Attlee.[2]

The War Cabinet then discussed shortly whether we should make an approach to Italy. Lord Halifax favoured this course on the ground that Mussolini did not want to see Hitler dominating Europe and that he would wish to persuade Hitler—if he could do so —to take a more reasonable attitude. The Prime Minister doubted whether anything would come of an approach to Italy, but said that the matter was one which the War Cabinet would have to consider.

---

[1] The Prime Minister told the War Cabinet that he did not understand what M. Reynaud meant by this point.

[2] I have been unable to trace any British record of a conversation between M. Reynaud, the Prime Minister, and Mr. Chamberlain and Mr. Attlee after the meeting of the War Cabinet, other than the summary in Lord Halifax's memorandum for the War Cabinet.

M. Reynaud explained to Lord Halifax his plans for a direct
(a) approach to Mussolini.[1] He proposed: (i) a frank explanation of the
position in which Mussolini would be placed if the Germans dominated Europe; (ii) a statement that Great Britain and France would
fight to the end for the preservation of their independence, and that
they would be helped by the resources of other nations as yet outside
the war; (iii) an undertaking that if Mussolini would co-operate in
obtaining a settlement of all European questions safeguarding the
independence and security of the Allies, and sufficient as a basis of
a just and durable peace for Europe, we would at once discuss, with a
desire to find solutions, the matters in which Mussolini was primarily
interested; (iv) a request that, since we understood that he wished the
solution of certain Mediterranean questions, Mussolini should state
in secrecy what these questions were. Great Britain and France
would then do their best to meet Mussolini's wishes on the basis of
the co-operation set out in (iii).

After M. Reynaud had left, an informal meeting of War Cabinet
(b) Ministers was held at Admiralty House. The Prime Minister said[2]
that our position was different from that of France. We still had
powers of resistance and attack; Germany was more likely to offer
acceptable terms to the French than to us. If France could not
defend herself, it was better that she should get out of the war rather
than that she should drag us into a settlement which involved
intolerable conditions. There was no limit to the terms Germany
would impose on us if she had her way. From one point of view, Mr.
Churchill would rather France was out of the war before she was
broken up, and while she might still be able to retain the position of a
strong neutral whose factories could not be used against us.

The Prime Minister hoped, however, that France would remain in
the war. At the same time we ought to take care not to be forced into
a weak position in which we invited Mussolini to go to Hitler and ask
him to 'treat us nicely'. We must not get entangled in a position of that
kind before we had been involved in any serious fighting.

Lord Halifax said that he did not disagree with this view, but that
he attached perhaps rather more importance than the Prime Minister
to the desirability of allowing France to try out the possibilities of European equilibrium. He was not quite convinced that it was in Hitler's
interest to insist on outrageous terms. We might say to Mussolini that,
if there were any suggestion of terms which affected our independence,
we should refuse to consider them. If, however, Mussolini were as

---

(c)   [1] The proposals appear to have been put into written form by Lord Halifax.
        [2] The record of this meeting is incomplete as the Secretary of the War Cabinet was not
present for the first quarter of an hour of the discussion.
   (a) WP(40)170; R6309/58/22.   (b) WM(40)140, C.A.   (c) WP(40)170; R6309/58/22.

alarmed as in our judgment he must be in regard to Hitler's power, and if he were prepared to look at matters from the point of view of the balance of power, then we might consider Italian claims. At any rate, there would be no harm in trying this line of approach.

After further discussion the Prime Minister said that he thought it best to decide nothing until we knew how much of the Army we could re-embark from France. The operation might be a great failure; on the other hand we might save a considerable portion of the force.[1]

Lord Halifax then explained the position with regard to Italy. He read out the Anglo-French communication to Mr. Roosevelt of May 25 and an account of his own interview of that day with the Italian Ambassador.[2] The Prime Minister's general comment was that the suggested approach to Mussolini implied that, if we were prepared to give Germany back her colonies and to make certain concessions in the Mediterranean, it was possible for us to get out of our present difficulties. He thought that no such option was open to us. For example, the German terms would certainly prevent us from completing our rearmament. Lord Halifax said that in such case we should refuse the terms; he was sure, however, that Mussolini must feel in a most uncomfortable position.

The Prime Minister said that Hitler thought he had the whip hand. The only thing to do was to show him that he could not conquer this country. If, on M. Reynaud's showing, France could not continue, we must part company. At the same time, the Prime Minister did not raise objection to some approach to Mussolini. Lord Halifax then read the draft which he had discussed with M. Reynaud.[3] During the consideration of this draft Mr. Chamberlain said that Mussolini was likely to say that he knew what he wanted, but that he was only prepared to deal as part of a general settlement. Lord Halifax thought that if we reached the point of discussing the terms of a general settlement and found that we could obtain terms which did not postulate the destruction of our independence, we should be foolish not to accept them.

The Ministers finally agreed that the draft of the proposed communication to Italy, together with a record of Lord Halifax's conversation with Signor Bastianini, should be circulated in a memorandum to the War Cabinet for discussion on May 27. Lord Halifax

---

[1] The evacuation of the B.E.F. from Dunkirk began during the night of May 26–27. Over 7,000 were brought away on May 27; nearly 18,000 were brought on May 28, nearly 50,000 on May 29, and over 60,000 on each of the next two days. The number of British and French troops evacuated in nine days was 338,226, of whom nearly 200,000 were British.

[2] See below, pp. 235–6 for the *démarche* to Mr. Roosevelt and pp. 236–7 for Lord Halifax's interview with Signor Bastianini.

[3] The draft thus circulated was the summary quoted above, p. 200.

said in his memorandum for the War Cabinet that the British Ministers had not given M. Reynaud a definite reply to his proposal, and that the proposal had only a very slender chance of success.[1] This chance indeed depended principally on the degree of discomfort which the prospect of a Europe dominated by Hitler might cause to Mussolini.

During the night of May 26–7 the Prime Minister sent a personal message to M. Reynaud that he could not send the formula for the approach to Mussolini until May 27, since he had to consult his colleagues. The Prime Minister said that he would do his best, but that he felt convinced that the only safety lay in our ability to fight.

At the meeting of the War Cabinet in the afternoon of May 27 (a) Lord Halifax reported that President Roosevelt had agreed to the Anglo-French suggestion of May 25 that he should make another approach to Mussolini, and that this approach was being made in the terms suggested by Lord Lothian and the French Ambassador at Washington. Lord Halifax also said that M. Corbin had given him during the morning a message from M. Reynaud. M. Reynaud's message was that he regarded it as 'a matter of great urgency' to give 'geographical precision' to the terms of the approach to Mussolini.

(b) Lord Halifax had told M. Corbin that the War Cabinet would certainly be opposed to this suggestion. M. Corbin had then said that at the present moment every opportunity should be tried. He added that 'he would not like it to be thought that, if certain action had been taken, France might have been able to continue the struggle'. Lord Halifax had replied that the difference between a general approach and an approach offering geographical precision could not possibly turn the scale as far as Mussolini was concerned, while an offer, not of general discussion but of definite concessions might have a lowering effect on Allied morale.[2]

The War Cabinet[3] discussed the French proposal at some length. They were in agreement that the approach to Mussolini was most unlikely to have any practical effect. Even if Mussolini stayed out of the war, the position of France would not be much improved. Most of the Ministers thought that the approach would be positively damaging to the interests of Great Britain. The Prime Minister felt

---

[1] M. Reynaud had the impression that Mr. Attlee and Mr. Chamberlain, like Mr. Churchill, did not favour an approach to Mussolini.

[2] Lord Halifax's comment to the War Cabinet on M. Corbin's communication was that 'it rather looked as though the French were preparing to put the blame on us'. Lord Halifax told the War Cabinet that he was not prepared to accept the French views on the question of 'geographical precision' in an approach to Italy.

[3] In addition to the five standing members of the War Cabinet, the only other Minister present was Sir A. Sinclair, Secretary of State for Air.

(a) WM(40)142, C.A.; R6309/58/22. (b) R6308/438/22.

strongly on the futility of an approach which Mussolini would regard with contempt and which would involve us in a deadly danger by ruining the integrity of our fighting position in Great Britain. Even if we mentioned no details in our approach, everyone would know what we had in mind. If the French were not prepared to go on with the struggle, let them give up, though the Prime Minister doubted whether they would do so. Our best help to M. Reynaud was to let him feel that, whatever happened to France, we were going to fight to the end. Our prestige in Europe was now low. The only way we could get it back was by showing the world that Germany had not beaten us. If, after two or three months, we could show that we were still unbeaten, our prestige would return. Even if we were beaten, we should be no worse off than if we were now to abandon the struggle. Let us therefore avoid being dragged down the slippery slope with France. The whole of the proposed manoeuvre was intended to get us so deeply involved in negotiations that we should be unable to turn back.

Finally, it was agreed that, although the proposed approach would not serve any useful purpose, we ought, from the point of view of our relations with the French, to avoid giving it a complete refusal. We had a good argument for delay since we now knew of President Roosevelt's approach and we could say that a simultaneous approach by Great Britain and France would only confuse the issue and create an impression of weakness.

During the discussion Lord Halifax pointed out that the Prime Minister had previously not been unwilling to discuss terms if they did not affect matters vital to the independence of the country but that he now seemed to suggest that under no conditions would he contemplate any course except fighting to a finish. Lord Halifax thought the issue was probably academic, since we were unlikely to be offered terms which we should regard as acceptable. If, however, we were offered such terms, Lord Halifax considered it doubtful whether we should be wise to refuse them.

The Prime Minister thought it unnecessary to widen the discussion by including an issue which was unreal and unlikely to arise. Thus it was most improbable that Hitler would offer to make peace on terms such as the return of the German colonies and the overlordship of central Europe. Lord Halifax said that, if France collapsed, and Hitler offered terms, the French might answer that they could not deal with an offer made to themselves alone but that Hitler must deal with France and Great Britain as Allies. If, in these circumstances, Hitler was anxious owing to internal weaknesses in Germany to end the war, and offered terms to France and Great Britain, would the Prime Minister be prepared to discuss them? The Prime Minister answered that he would not join France in asking for terms, but if he were told what the terms offered were, he would be prepared to consider them. Mr. Chamberlain thought that Hitler was more likely to offer terms to France and, when the French said that they had Allies, to reply that the British could send a delegate to Paris. The War Cabinet agreed that the answer to such an offer could only be 'No'.[1]

(a) Sir R. Campbell was instructed in the late evening of May 27 to give an answer to M. Reynaud on the lines accepted by the War Cabinet, i.e. that in view of Mr. Roosevelt's action and of the fact that Mussolini had taken Mr. Roosevelt's earlier warning badly, we might well produce an effect contrary to our intentions if we duplicated approaches. The Prime Minister therefore inclined to think that there were no advantages, and some danger, in a further approach on the lines which M. Reynaud had suggested. We did not exclude further consideration of the matter when we knew the result of Mr. Roosevelt's action.

---

[1] The memoirs, etc. of the Ministers present at this important meeting add little to the documentary record. Lord Birkenhead (*Life of Lord Halifax* (Hamish Hamilton, 1965), 458) prints an extract from Lord Halifax's diary about the meeting. 'At Cabinet we had a long and rather confused discussion about, nominally, the approach to Italy, but also largely about general policy in the event of things going really badly in France. I thought Winston talked the most frightful rot, also Greenwood, and after bearing it for some time I said exactly what I thought of them, adding that, if that was really their view, and if it came to the point, our ways must separate . . . I despair when he (Mr. Churchill) works himself up into a passion of emotion when he ought to make his brain think and reason.'

These differences of emphasis re-emerged three weeks later. On June 17, 1940, M. Prytz, Swedish Minister in London, telegraphed to the Swedish Foreign Office an account of an interview on that day with Mr. R. A. Butler. There is no contemporary record of the interview in the Foreign Office archives. According to a broadcast by M. Prytz on

(b) September 7, 1965, Mr. Butler said to him that 'no opportunity would be neglected for concluding a compromise peace if the chance offered on reasonable conditions', and that 'the so-called diehards would not be allowed to stand in the way of negotiations'. During the talk Mr. Butler was called away to see Lord Halifax. On his return Mr. Butler gave M. Prytz a message from Lord Halifax that 'common sense and not bravado would dictate the British Government's policy'. Lord Halifax said that he knew such an attitude would be welcomed by M. Prytz but that he must not interpret it to mean peace at any price. M. Prytz added in his report that in conversation with M.P.s it was possible to discern the hope that an opportunity for negotiations with Germany would show itself after June 28, and that Halifax could then be expected to replace Churchill.

(c) The Swedish Foreign Minister on June 19 asked Sir V. Mallet, British Minister at Stockholm, whether he could explain M. Prytz's account of the interview, and whether Mr. Butler's remarks were to be taken by the Swedish Government as a 'hint'. Sir V. Mallet referred the Foreign Minister to Mr. Churchill's broadcast on June 18 and to 'the determination therein expressed to continue the war with all our strength'.

(d) On June 20 (i) M. Prytz telegraphed to the Swedish Foreign Minister that his conversation with Mr. Butler should be regarded as representing his (Mr. Butler's) and Lord Halifax's personal views, and were not intended for report to the Swedish Government. Pending the results of the secret session of the House of Commons, the attitude of the British Government had not 'crystallised'. (ii) The Foreign Office telegraphed to Sir V.

(e) Mallet from Lord Halifax that 'certainly no hint was intended', and that M. Prytz might have exaggerated the importance of any 'polite messages' conveyed by Mr. Butler from Lord Halifax.

(a) R6308/438/22. (b) Report of M. Prytz's broadcast in the Swedish *Dagens Nyheter*, September 8, 1965. (c) N5848/112/42 (1940). (d) *Dagens Nyheter, ib.* (e) N5848/112/42 (1940).

Lord Lothian reported during the night of May 27–8 that Mussolini's answer to Mr. Roosevelt was 'entirely negative'. Sir A. Cadogan commented on this telegram:

'Of course Mussolini is not going to, and in fact, dare not make any separate agreement with the Allies, even if he wanted to. He is simply wondering how much of the general "share-out" he will be allowed by his "Ally" to take, and whether he will ultimately get more, or less, by spilling Italian blood for it. We can't tell which way he'll jump, but I hope we shan't delude ourselves into thinking that we shall do ourselves any good by making any more "offers" or "approaches".'

On the evening of May 28 Sir P. Loraine reported that (with (a) Lord Halifax's approval) he had asked Ciano whether there was any answer to the suggestion made by Lord Halifax to the Italian Ambassador on May 25. Ciano said that the subject fell under the general ban placed by Mussolini on any discussions whatever with the Allies.[1]

(v)

Renewal of French proposal for a direct approach to Mussolini: the Prime Minister's message of May 28 to M. Reynaud: comments of M. Reynaud and M. Daladier on the message (May 28–29, 1940).

At midday on May 28 Sir R. Campbell telegraphed that, in a panicky mood after the Belgian defection, the Council of Ministers (b) had discussed on the previous night the question of an 'immediate and firm offer of a very far-reaching character direct to Mussolini'. This plan had been stopped in the morning of May 28 by a message from M. François-Poncet that any offer would be badly received. A new proposal was being worked out for a direct approach to Mussolini on more general lines, and would be submitted later during the day through M. Corbin.

Before the meeting of the War Cabinet on May 28, at which the French proposals were again discussed, Lord Halifax had received (c) M. Reynaud's detailed suggestions. M. Reynaud said that the Council of Ministers wanted the British Government to re-examine as soon as possible the offer to Italy according to the formula drawn up by Lord Halifax in the presence of M. Reynaud on May 26. The Council of Ministers thought it necessary to introduce

---

[1] See below, p. 238.
(a) R6308/438/22. (b) R6308/438/22. (c) R6308/438/22.

'précisions' into the formula, as follows: (i) the cession of the coast of French Somaliland and the exploitation of the Addis Ababa Railway, with rights, and possibly a 'zone de relâche' in the port of Jibuti; (ii) a rectification of the frontiers of Tunis and Libya; (iii) the cession of a very large area ('d'une très grande amplitude') of territory between the hinterland of Libya and the Congo coast. If this last suggestion were not sufficient, the French Government would substitute a reform of the status ('statut') of Tunis which would allow Italo-French collaboration in the protectorate.

The Council of Ministers explained that, even if their chances of success were small, they ought not to neglect any means of avoiding a new 'aggravation' which might have a decisive influence on the issue of the war. They pointed out that an offer by one Ally in isolation would reduce still further any possibilities of success. With regard to procedure, they thought that the best method would be an approach through the Vatican.

(a)   The War Cabinet discussed on May 28 this further message from the French proposing a direct approach to Mussolini. The discussion differed little from that on May 26 and 27. It was taken for granted that, whatever the French might do, we should not capitulate. The general view, as before, was that an approach to Mussolini was most unlikely to produce terms which we could accept. Lord Halifax agreed with this view, but thought that we should not refuse the French suggestion to 'try out' the possibilities of Italian mediation. The Prime Minister regarded acceptance of the French proposal as dangerous, since we should find that the terms offered to us were unacceptable; there would then be a great risk that the very fact of entering a conference would have weakened the resolution to continue fighting. The War Cabinet finally agreed that the Prime Minister should tell M. Reynaud that we thought it useless to approach Mussolini; at the same time we should take care that our answer did not provide the French with any pretext for giving up the struggle at once. We should therefore explain that we had been considering the proposal from the point of view of French interests as well as our own.

Sir R. Campbell was therefore sent on the night of May 28–9 a (b) message from the Prime Minister to M. Reynaud. The Prime Minister explained that we had carefully examined M. Reynaud's proposal, 'fully realising the terrible situation with which we are both faced at this moment'.

> 'Since we last discussed this matter the new fact which has occurred, namely the capitulation of the Belgian army, has greatly changed our position for the worse, for it is evident that the chance of with-

---

(a) WM(40)145.1,C.A. (b) R6309/58/22.

drawing the armies of Generals Blanchard and Gort from the Channel ports has become very problematical. The first effect of such a disaster must be to make it impossible at such a moment for Germany to put forward any terms likely to be acceptable, and neither we nor you would be prepared to give up our independence without fighting for it to the end.

In the formula prepared last Sunday by Lord Halifax it was suggested that if Signor Mussolini would co-operate with us in securing a settlement of all European questions which would safeguard our independence and form the basis of a just and durable peace for Europe, we would be prepared to discuss his claims in the Mediterranean. You now propose to add certain specific offers, which I cannot suppose would have any chance of moving Signor Mussolini, and which once made could not be subsequently withdrawn, in order to induce him to undertake the rôle of mediator, which the formula discussed on Sunday contemplated.

I and my colleagues believe that Signor Mussolini has long had it in mind that he might eventually fill this rôle, no doubt counting upon substantial advantages for Italy in the process. But we are convinced that at this moment when Hitler is flushed with victory and certainly counts on early and complete collapse of Allied resistance, it would be impossible for Mussolini to put forward proposals for a conference with any success. I may remind you also that the President of the United States has received a wholly negative reply to the proposal which we jointly asked him to make, and that no response has been made to the approach of Lord Halifax made to the Italian Ambassador here last Saturday.

Therefore, without excluding the possibility of an approach to Signor Mussolini at some time, we cannot feel that this would be the right moment, and I am bound to add that in my opinion the effect on the morale of our people, which is now firm and resolute, would be extremely dangerous. You yourself can best judge what would be the effect in France.

You will ask, then, how is the situation to be improved? My reply is that by showing that after the loss of our two [Northern] armies and the loss of our Belgian Ally we still have stout hearts and confidence in ourselves, we shall at once strengthen our hands in negotiations, and draw to ourselves the admiration and perhaps the material help of the U.S.A. Moreover, we feel that as long as we stand together our undefeated Navy and our Air Force, which is daily destroying German fighters and bombers at a formidable rate, afford us the means of exercising in our common interest a continuous pressure upon Germany's internal life.

We have reason to believe that the Germans too are working to a timetable, and that their losses and the hardships imposed on them, together with the fear of our air raids, are undermining their courage. It would indeed be a tragedy if by too hasty an acceptance of defeat we threw away a chance that was almost within our grasp of securing an honourable issue from the struggle.

In my view, if we both stand out we may yet save ourselves from the fate of Denmark or Poland. Our success must depend first on our unity, then on our courage and endurance.'

(a) Sir R. Campbell reported in the afternoon of May 29 that he had discussed the Prime Minister's message briefly with M. Reynaud and subsequently with M. Daladier and M. Charles-Roux.[1] M. Reynaud inclined to the Prime Minister's view, but admitted that he was in a difficult position with his colleagues who thought the entry of Italy into the war would be almost a mortal blow for France and that it was therefore essential to try every possibility of preventing it.

M. Daladier began his conversation with 'his usual gloomy picture' of the result of Italian participation in the war. Sir R. Campbell said that these results were not in question. The point was whether there was any step which we could take with a sufficiently large chance of success to justify the risk, since, in case of failure, we should certainly have aggravated our situation. We had approached Mussolini through Signor Bastianini and Mr. Roosevelt without response: 'could we suppose that a direct approach would fare better?' Our best chance of 'making Signor Mussolini still hesitate' was to show him that we still had faith in ourselves. If we displayed lack of spirit now, we should prejudice our chances of help from the United States.

Sir R. Campbell found that the French proposal came from M. François-Poncet, who had thought of acting through the Pope, 'thus placing things rather on the religious plane'. The plan differed from the proposal made through Mr. Roosevelt only to the extent that it would be accompanied by specific offers.

M. Daladier said that he would study the Prime Minister's message. Sir R. Campbell pointed out the catastrophic effect of isolated action (i.e. by France). M. Daladier said that there could be no question of (b) such action. Later in the day Sir R. Campbell telegraphed that he had reason to believe that the French proposal would probably be dropped. M. Daladier, however, raised the matter again on May 30 and, in spite of Sir R. Campbell's arguments, insisted on making a direct appeal to Mussolini. The War Cabinet considered that they (c) could not prevent M. Daladier from taking action, but that the French Government should be told that any statement on their part to Mussolini would not engage Great Britain. M. Daladier, in fact, persuaded his colleagues to attempt an approach, but the Italian answer was an abrupt refusal.[2]

---

[1] M. Charles-Roux had taken M. Léger's place on May 18 as Secretary-general at the Ministry of Foreign Affairs.
[2] See Chapter VIII, section (iii).

(a) R6309/58/22.   (b) R6309/58/22.   (c) WM(40)148; R6309/58/22; R6308/438/22.

(vi)

Possibility of a separate peace offer to France: M. Reynaud's proposal for an appeal to the United States: views of the British Government on the undesirability of M. Reynaud's proposal: President Roosevelt's advice against an appeal.

The discussions at the Foreign Office on May 17[1] had not envisaged a situation in which France might make a separate peace with Germany.[2] It was assumed that, if driven from France, the French Government would establish themselves elsewhere, and probably in North Africa. After May 17, and before M. Reynaud's visit to London, the rapid advance of the Germans far behind the French lines of defence and the failure to deliver successful counter-attacks brought much nearer the possibility that within a short time the French might be out of the war. It was already obvious that the Germans would exploit their victory to the full, but in the first few days after the 'break-through' on the Meuse, the main military and political lines of this exploitation were uncertain. According to information received on the night of May 19–20 from a neutral (a) source, the Germans intended to make a peace offer similar to that put forward after the occupation of Poland. If the offer were rejected, Germany would open a ruthless attack on Great Britain.

On May 22 Sir P. Loraine reported (from a very reliable source) that (i) Mussolini would enter the war as soon as the Germans had (b) reached the Channel ports; (ii) Hitler intended to speak to the peoples of Great Britain and France over the Paris radio on June 15. He would say that he had now secured the objectives which he had announced for years past as his aim, and that the British and French peoples had been duped by their Governments; (iii) the German Ambassador in Italy was certain that the French would make a separate peace, and Mussolini believed that he could come to an agreement with them; (iv) the Germans had recalled all their submarines to prepare them for the transport of troops and equipment.

On May 23, however, Sir R. Campbell reported that, contrary to (c) rumour, the French had not received an offer of a separate peace, though they were expecting such an offer in the near future. Sir R. Campbell thought that there were 'a number of people here in high places who would be tempted', but that, with M. Reynaud

---

[1] See above, p. 196.

[2] It is hardly necessary to point out that during these critical days, as indeed at all times, the Foreign Office took for granted that Great Britain would fight the war to a finish.

(a) C6915/6/18. (b) C6915/6/18. (c) C6876/5/18.

B.F.P.—K

in control, and backed by Marshal Pétain and General Weygand, we need have no fears.

The Foreign Office were less confident of the French resistance to proposals for a separate peace if their armies were defeated. On (a) May 28 Sir R. Campbell reported that M. Reynaud was having difficulty with the 'more wobbly' members of his Administration, but that he seemed 'to be holding his own well'. Later in the day Sir R. Campbell telephoned that M. Mandel was satisfied with the spirit of the Government 'as a whole'. There were weak elements, but these elements consisted of those who always had been weak. M. Mandel was inclined to doubt the wisdom of defending Paris. The defence would cost large numbers of troops, and, after Paris had fallen, 'the wobblers would say "We are quite ready to go on with the struggle, but with what?"' M. Mandel thought that France generally was sound, but he was afraid of trouble from communists in the suburbs of Paris during the attack on the city.

On May 29 Sir R. Campbell reported that French working class morale had resisted satisfactorily the shock of the Belgian surrender, though the peasants might take longer to recover. French left-wing opinion expected a German peace offensive. M. Blum thought that at present this move would have no success among the masses, and that, as long as the line of the Somme were held, there would be no response to a peace offer. If the Germans broke through this line, and took or threatened Paris, M. Blum could not foretell the popular reaction.

Other indications came from Italy and Switzerland that the Germans intended to come to terms with France and to isolate Great Britain before delivering their grand attack. The attack could then be organised safely, and carried out before the United States would be able to intervene.

On May 29 Lord Halifax said to M. Corbin that he expected a (b) peace offer from Hitler. M. Corbin agreed, but thought that the offer would be made only to France. The crucial question for the French was whether they could continue to produce the necessary material. The 'main supply' of aircraft from the United States would not arrive until August. Lord Halifax said that 'it was vital, if and when Hitler offered peace to France, that the French Government should say that they were unable to consider any proposals except in conjunction with His Majesty's Government. Hitler was clearly conscious of the difficulties of his own position; he had thrown everything into the present battle, and it would be tragic if the Allies were to lose what might be an opportunity, if we stood firm,

(a) C6844A/5/18.   (b) A3310/1/51.

of encompassing his defeat.' M. Corbin answered that the French Government 'fully realised the danger of any acceptance by them of a German peace offer, but the effect on French morale of the loss of more and more territory, with factories closing down and French effectives dwindling, must not be left out of consideration'. For this reason M. Reynaud had taken a strong line in condemnation of the attitude of the King of the Belgians. At the same time M. Corbin 'had the impression that France would continue to resist, even if the Somme line were broken'. He wished only to 'explain the difficult position in which the French Government now found itself and the background against which French policy had to be shaped'.

During this conversation M. Corbin also spoke to Lord Halifax of the possibility of an appeal to the United States. Sir R. Campbell had telegraphed on May 28 that M. Reynaud had made this (a) suggestion to him. M. Reynaud admitted that for the present the United States could give no effective help, but he thought that the moral result of a favourable answer would be considerable both on Allied and on German public opinion. Moreover, if Mr. Roosevelt could send a fleet to European waters, his action would be an effective restraint upon Mussolini. The lines of the appeal might be that the Allies were fighting for the liberty of the world and that they had been stabbed in the back by the defection of Belgium. Sir R. Campbell had suggested that M. Reynaud should consult Mr. Bullitt. M. Reynaud had telephoned later that Mr. Bullitt approved of the idea and was in favour of a joint appeal.[1]

The Foreign Office thought the proposal wholly inexpedient. American opinion knew why we were fighting and wanted us to win. An appeal on M. Reynaud's lines would only suggest weakness or even panic. The War Cabinet agreed with this view, and considered that, if any action were taken, the best mode of approach (b) would be to follow a suggestion made by General Smuts to the United Kingdom High Commissioner in South Africa on May 27. General Smuts thought that we might appeal to the United States through diplomatic channels (followed, if necessary, by a public statement) on the basis that we were continuing the war in any circumstances. We wanted nothing for ourselves, but were concerned only with the defence of liberty in the world against Nazi domination. Would the United States help, or would they stand aside and take no action in defence of the rights of man?

Lord Lothian was therefore given an account on the night of May 28-9 of the proposals from M. Reynaud and General Smuts,

---

[1] M. Léger told Mr. Bullitt on May 18 that M. Reynaud was considering a personal appeal to Mr. Roosevelt to obtain a declaration of war from Congress. Mr. Bullitt explained that Congress would certainly not agree to a declaration of war. M. Reynaud raised the question again on May 22.

(a) A3310/1/51. (b) WM(40)145; A3310/1/51.

and of the opinion of the War Cabinet that an appeal on M. Reynaud's lines would be regarded as the result of despair, and would confirm American views of our weakness, and might even be exploited in this sense by Hitler. On the other hand, the declaration proposed by General Smuts might help Mr. Roosevelt in accelerating the evolution of opinion in the United States. Mr. Roosevelt, however, must be the judge of the matter.

(a)   In his conversation with M. Corbin on the morning of May 29 Lord Halifax explained the views of the War Cabinet on M. Reynaud's proposal and said that they were awaiting Lord Lothian's answer. M. Corbin asked whether Lord Lothian could be instructed to enquire whether Mr. Roosevelt would send the United States fleet to the Mediterranean. The French Government thought that the results would be good, especially in the Balkans. Lord Halifax promised to mention the suggestion to the War Cabinet, but did not think that there was the least chance that Mr. Roosevelt would agree to it. Shortly after midday Sir R. Campbell reported discussions with M. Daladier and M. Charles-Roux in which they also made the suggestion about the United States fleet.

Lord Lothian's reply was received late in the evening of May 29. His first impression was unfavourable to an appeal, but he suggested the possibility of an 'open letter' to the United States from the Prime Ministers of the Dominions and of the remaining European democracies if and when any part of the British or French forces in France had to surrender. Later in the night of May 29–30, Lord Lothian replied to a telegram reporting M. Corbin's request about the fleet. Lord Lothian said that he had not realised that the main concern of MM. Reynaud and Daladier was to secure a final effort on the part of the United States to keep Mussolini out of the war. Mr. Roosevelt had told him on May 29 that the United States could not send their fleet to the Mediterranean. The fleet must stay in the Pacific until any threat to the British fleet compelled some transfer of American ships to the Atlantic. Owing to the situation in South America, it was necessary for the United States to show their flag in Uruguay and Brazil.

Mr. Roosevelt did not regard an appeal as desirable for the present. Lord Lothian then suggested that, in view of Mussolini's rejection of Mr. Roosevelt's warning,[1] Mr. Roosevelt should say at once that Italian entry into the war would greatly prejudice United States nationals and the interests of the United States in the Mediterranean and elsewhere, and that the United States therefore could not be indifferent to the consideration of means—especially

---

[1] See below, p. 230, for this 'warning' sent by Mr. Roosevelt on May 14.
(a) A3310/1/51.

financial and economic means—of retaliation against Italy. Lord
Lothian also suggested that Mr. Roosevelt should announce that
American warships en route for Lisbon[1] would call at Cadiz,
Gibraltar and Algiers in order to protect American interests.
Mr. Roosevelt asked Mr. Welles to draft action on these two
suggestions for his consideration on the morning of May 30.

A meeting was held in the Foreign Office on the morning of
May 30 to consider Lord Lothian's first telegram. The second (a)
telegram does not appear to have been decyphered in time for this
meeting; the decision reached was that no further action could be
taken until Mr. Roosevelt's views were known. There was, however,
general agreement that anything in the nature of an appeal to the
United States would have an effect contrary to our intentions. The
Foreign Office also thought that Lord Lothian's suggestion of an
open letter would be bad tactics, and that a better plan might be a
broadcast by the Prime Minister.

In the evening of May 30 a reply was sent to Lord Lothian's
second telegram. It was explained that the French were concerned (b)
not only with keeping Mussolini out of the war but with heartening
their own people by a successful appeal to the United States. The
French Government would probably press us to support this appeal.
We did not think the plan tactically wise, since Mr. Roosevelt and
the United States Administration could not give a really encouraging
answer, and might not be able to give any answer. Hence we should
be in a much stronger position with the French if we knew
Mr. Roosevelt's views. Lord Lothian was then told the Foreign
Office view that the best plan would be a broadcast by the Prime
Minister showing the grounds for our 'reasoned optimism'.

Lord Lothian replied to this telegram during the night of
May 31–June 1 that the Under-Secretary of State had told him (c)
that Mr. Roosevelt had telegraphed to Mr. Bullitt his strong dis-
approval of the proposed appeal. Mr. Roosevelt thought that such
an appeal would hinder him in getting materials to the Allies and
would be an obstacle to the development of American opinion
because it would be taken as an attempt by foreigners to influence
the United States in the direction of war. On the other hand, a

---

[1] On May 22 Lord Lothian had been instructed that His Majesty's Government would
consider it useful if the two or three United States warships at Lisbon could remain there (d)
for the present. A 'deterioration in the situation in the Mediterranean' might be accompanied by 'fifth column' action in Spain and Portugal promoted by local Germans against
the régimes of General Franco and Dr. Salazar (both of whom wished to maintain
neutrality). The 'fifth column' action would aim at establishing régimes which would act
in concert with the Axis. The presence of United States warships would therefore have a
steadying effect.

It was announced on May 29 that the United States cruiser *Vincennes* and two destroyers
had been ordered to Lisbon.

(a) A3310/1/51. (b) A3310/1/51. (c) A3310/1/51. (d) A3255/1/51.

broadcast by the Prime Minister might be useful if it were addressed to the British Empire. Lord Lothian also said that he was making a speech on June 4 which would be broadcast throughout the United States. He proposed in this speech not to refer in detail to Allied needs but to assert our determination to go on fighting to the end.

(a) Lord Lothian was instructed on June 2 to emphasise not merely our resolve to go on fighting but also our complete confidence in victory if all lovers of freedom played their part. He was also told that the Prime Minister would probably be speaking in the House of Commons on June 4[1] and broadcasting on June 5.

Sir R. Campbell was informed on June 2 that, in view of Mr. Roosevelt's opposition, His Majesty's Government assumed that M. Reynaud would abandon the idea of an appeal in the form contemplated by him. Sir R. Campbell replied on June 3 that M. Reynaud had 'dropped the idea'.[2]

(vii)

The situation after Dunkirk: General Weygand's letter of May 29: tenth meeting of the Supreme War Council, May 31: Sir R. Campbell's reports, June 4–7: French demands for more fighter assistance, June 1–8.

The unexpected success in saving the personnel of the British Expeditionary Force had far-reaching effects on British morale. Resistance to a German invasion, which seemed likely, was not a 'forlorn hope'. There were good chances of success, and an obvious and immediate objective for work at the highest speed in re-equipping the army which had come back from France, and in thus providing the means once again to snatch victory from defeat. Moreover from a British viewpoint there were elements of real victory in the actual evacuation. This passage of so many thousands of men across the Channel showed the significance of sea-power, and also the fighting strength of the Royal Air Force. The land forces were carrying out a retreat after being involved in military disaster but the Air Force was attacking, and attacking with success an enemy superior in

---

[1] The Prime Minister's speech in the House of Commons on June 4 on the course of the war concluded with a statement of confidence that Great Britain could 'ride out the storm of war and outlive the menace of tyranny, if necessary for years, if necessary alone . . . We shall never surrender, and, even if, which I do not for a moment believe, this island, or a large part of it, were subjugated and starving, then our Empire beyond the seas, armed and guarded by the British Fleet, would carry on the struggle, until, in God's good time, the New World, with all its power and might, steps forth to the rescue and the liberation of the Old.' *H. of C. Deb.*, 5th ser. vol. 361, cols. 787–96.

[2] M. Reynaud later returned to the plan. See below, Chapter IX.

(a) A3310/1/51.

numbers. The Germans were not masters of the sea and air: unless they obtained this mastery they could not conquer England.

These considerations had no effect, or rather they had an opposite effect on the French. The British were alone, but they had withdrawn behind the 'moat defensive' of their house. The French were alone with the victorious German forces already in occupation of a great part of France and continuing their advance by means of tactics which the French army had been unable to withstand. To the French there seemed to be no motive left for resistance. They could do nothing to turn defeat into victory. French armies had fought and won campaigns against worse odds. They had done so under resolute leadership; this leadership was now wanting. General Weygand improvised a line along the Somme and the Aisne; the British troops still in France took part in this final defence. The French, however, in spite of heroic action at isolated points, failed to hold the German attack when it reopened in full force on June 5. Within four days the Germans had taken most of the area between Rouen, Beauvais and Compiègne. The way to Paris was open; there were no armies south or west of Paris to stop the German tanks. On June 10 the Germans crossed the Seine and, on June 11, the Marne. They then came on even more quickly as French resistance ebbed away. On June 14 the Germans were in Paris, and, to the east, approaching Chaumont. General Weygand now told General Brooke, commander of the British forces in France, that 'organised French resistance' had ceased. On the next day the Germans were at Sens and on June 16 on the line of the Loire between Orléans and Cosne; to the south-east they had passed Dijon and reached Besançon. The Italians had declared war on June 10,[1] but their entry made no difference to the issue; the French, although greatly outnumbered, maintained their positions against Italian attack. The fate of France was in the hands of the Germans, and the rate of the German advance henceforward depended not on the power of the French to delay it but on the calculation of Hitler whether it might be more politic to complete his military victory by a march on Bordeaux or to allow the defeatists in France time to surrender their government as well as their army.

The drift towards surrender was harder to resist because the counsels of despair came from a quarter where they might have been least expected. M. Reynaud had brought Marshal Pétain into his Government, and had given the highest military command to General Weygand because he had thought that these appointments would do much to restore confidence. He was right in the sense that parliamentary opinion and the press had approved his action, and that for a short time the French had recovered from the shock—in General Weygand's own words reminiscent of the *grande peur* of 1789

---

[1] The declaration took effect at midnight on June 10–11. See below, p. 244.

—which had followed the German break-through at Sedan. Unfortunately Marshal Pétain and General Weygand themselves took the lead in advocating political as well as military capitulation.

General Weygand had proposed on May 25 to the French Government an immediate consultation with Great Britain on the question of continuing the war. Marshal Pétain had supported his argument, but M. Reynaud had refused to accept the proposal. Four days later—after the Belgian surrender—General Weygand returned to the question.

During the night of May 29–30 Sir R. Campbell telegraphed that
(a) M. Reynaud had read to him a letter from General Weygand. M. Reynaud dictated passages of this letter (which he had not yet shown to anyone else)[1] to Sir R. Campbell. General Weygand wrote that he would carry out his orders to defend the Somme–Aisne–Maginot line to the last. In view of the immense superiority of the enemy's forces, the line might be broken, and the French army might not be able to stop a raid against Paris. If Paris were lost, and, with Paris, 75 per cent of the remaining French industries, France would no longer be able to carry on the struggle in a manner which would ensure a co-ordinated defence of her territory. General Weygand then contrasted the position with that in 1914–18 and advised that the British Government should be asked at once to send two or three divisions now in England, tank units, artillery and anti-aircraft weapons, and to provide assistance by Royal Air Force units based on England. General Weygand thought that the British Government should know that the moment might come when, notwithstanding her will, France might find herself unable to continue effectively the struggle to defend her soil. Such a time would come with a complete break-through ('rupture définitive') on the Somme–Aisne line upon which the French armies had been told to fight without thought of retirement.

In answer to questions from Sir R. Campbell, M. Reynaud said that, as long as he was in control, and there were troops left to fight, France would fight on.

(b)   The War Cabinet met on May 30 at 12.30 p.m. and again at 5.30 p.m. At the first meeting it was agreed that the Prime Minister should send a message to M. Reynaud drawing attention to the

---

[1] In his book *La France a sauvé l'Europe* (Paris, 1947), II, 182–4, M. Reynaud states that General Weygand had read to him a note, on the lines of this letter, on the morning of May 29, and that the note appeared to have been approved by Marshal Pétain.

(a) C7012/3/18.   (b) WP(40)147, 148.

number of encouraging features in the situation, i.e. the great successes of the Royal Air Force, and reports of very heavy German losses. At the second meeting, after hearing information given to the Prime Minister by General Spears about the position of the French army and French demands for assistance, the War Cabinet agreed that the Prime Minister, Mr. Attlee, and General Dill should go to Paris on May 31 for a meeting of the Supreme War Council. At 9.30 p.m. Sir R. Campbell was instructed that the Prime Minister would like an opportunity for an informal conversation with M. Reynaud during (a) the morning of May 31, before the meeting of the Council.

The Supreme War Council met at 2.30 p.m. on May 31, at the Ministère de la Guerre. On the French side M. Reynaud was the (b) only civilian Minister present; Marshal Pétain, General Weygand and Admiral Darlan attended the meeting. The discussion covered the whole field of military operations; the evacuation of Narvik; the position at Dunkirk; the question of further British air assistance in France; the action to be taken if Italy entered the war. At the conclusion of the meeting the Prime Minister stated the determination of Great Britain to go on with the war, if necessary, from the New World, and emphasised the vital importance of maintaining close contact between Great Britain and France. Mr. Attlee supported the Prime Minister's statement, and M. Reynaud agreed with it. M. Reynaud said that, if one country 'went under', the other must continue the struggle.

Four days after this meeting of the Supreme War Council Sir R. Campbell sent to the Foreign Office a despatch which he had (c) been writing on the general political situation. He explained that he was sending it without further delay because he thought that he ought to try to give some idea of the intentions of the French Government. After eight or nine months of easy warfare, in which German propaganda had gone far to undermine the fighting spirit present in France at the beginning of the war, the German break-through had stunned French opinion. The Government and officials were temporarily paralysed. Most of the latter failed either to give the necessary orders or, if they gave them, to see that they were carried out. For a week the French had been in the grip of a 'sort of mass fear' caused by German technique and increased by a panic spread by hordes of terror-stricken refugees.

The Government and the public were now 'reacting' and were in a more combative mood. Government departments were settling down again and preparations were being made in military and civilian spheres to organise resistance to a thrust against Paris. Although it had been decided to hold the Somme–Aisne line at all costs, there

---

(a) C6844A/5/18. (b) C7135/9/17. (c) C7121/5/18.

was a danger that a break-through on this line by armoured and mechanised forces might induce a fresh wave of despair and a new current of inertia. Good progress had been made in organising methods of dealing with German marauding columns but General Weygand was not too optimistic about a battle in which, in his own statement, the French would be inferior in material and outnumbered by three to one. It was therefore necessary to face the possibility—almost the probability—that the Germans would reach the Paris region and capture three-quarters of what remained of French industry. General Weygand had warned the French Government of the consequences of a break-through of this kind.

What would the French Government do if it were clear that further military resistance was hopeless? Sir R. Campbell thought that they had given up the idea of a move to Touraine, and that they intended to go to Bordeaux. They would probably carry out this plan and would not weaken until after that stage had been reached. What then? MM. Reynaud and Mandel maintained that France would never make terms, even if the Government had to move to North Africa. M. Reynaud tended to qualify this statement by adding 'so long as I am in control'. Sir R. Campbell could not say whether M. Reynaud would refuse to allow himself to be set aside. A situation might occur in which the forces in favour of composition with Germany were too strong. These forces existed inside and outside the Government. Sir R. Campbell regarded MM. Laval and Flandin as the most dangerous figures. If either broke the silence which both had observed since the opening of the German offensive, a number of politicians would come forward to acquiesce in compounding with the enemy.

An offer of a separate peace to France was expected soon; the Germans would then turn to the invasion of Great Britain. If the offer were made before the present battle had been decided, it would be refused. A refusal would be less certain with the Government at Bordeaux. There would be considerable confusion. The French armies would be incapable of further large-scale action; the Germans would be sweeping across France to the Atlantic coast and consolidating their position along the Channel.

Would the French Government go to North Africa or elsewhere, or would it surrender? Sir R. Campbell thought that the chances of the first alternative were not very high, especially if the Germans offered lenient terms. In any case the practical difference was not great from the point of view of French resistance.

On June 5 Sir R. Campbell wrote again that he had not much
(a) faith in the ability of the French to hold the Germans. He feared

---

(a) C7074/5/18.

that, with the Germans in Paris, French resistance would be 'as good as broken', and that, if the French Government reached Bordeaux, it would not last much longer. There was talk of a move to North Africa. French soil would obviously be the best place 'in which to keep the national spirit alive'. From all other points of view, such as distance, and lack of contact with His Majesty's Government, North Africa would be impracticable. Sir R. Campbell considered England to be the most suitable place. He also thought that an offer from His Majesty's Government to receive the French Government in London might be the determining factor in a decision against a separate peace. The question might therefore be considered in London. It was necessary to prepare for the worst, and to be ready for the worst 'to come more quickly than we expect'.

At the meeting of the Supreme War Council on May 31 the Prime Minister, in answer to the French request for more air assist- (a) ance, had reminded M. Reynaud of his statement of a fortnight earlier. He had then said that the ten additional squadrons[1] which had been sent to France were the last reserve with which Great Britain might have to defend her life. British air forces were very much inferior numerically to those of Germany. The ratio was not less unfavourable than $2\frac{1}{2}$ to 1. Very little was left of the ten squadrons.[2] Great Britain had now only twenty-nine squadrons left. The Prime Minister was not authorised, and would not be willing to let British aircraft factories run any greater risks; he promised, however, to see what further air support could be provided.

In the early days of June, however, M. Reynaud continued his requests for more squadrons. After making direct appeals to the Prime Minister, M. Reynaud sent for Sir R. Campbell on the (b) morning of June 4 in order to give him a letter from General Weygand in support of an appeal from General Vuillemin for the immediate despatch of ten more fighter squadrons, and of a further ten squadrons as soon as possible. All the squadrons were to be based upon aerodromes in France.

Sir R. Campbell, with General Spears's agreement, said that these requests would put the British Government in an impossible position. He asked M. Reynaud to imagine that the situation was reversed. Did M. Reynaud believe that any French Government would act as he was asking the British Government to act? M. Reynaud repeated again and again that the coming battle would decide the issue of the

---

[1] See above, p. 194, note (1).

[2] British losses in the air, May 15–31, were 430 aircraft.

(a) C7135/9/17. (b) C6828/5/18.

war, and that strong reinforcements of British aircraft would make the difference between victory and defeat.

(a)   During the evening of June 5 Sir R. Campbell telegraphed that, according to a statement by M. Reynaud, Marshal Pétain, on hearing that the British reply was unfavourable,[1] said: 'Well, there is nothing left but to make peace. If you do not want to do it, you can hand over to me.' M. Reynaud had repudiated the idea; he mentioned it only to show the gravity of the situation. He asked whether Sir R. Campbell thought that the British Government fully realised how serious the position was. Sir R. Campbell said that they were aware of the facts and were giving, and would continue to give as much help as possible. If they denuded the British Isles of the whole of their air defences on the eve of an invasion carried out by all of the enemy's devices, they would incur an 'unforgivable responsibility'.

In the early evening of June 6 Sir R. Campbell was sent another
(b) message for transmission by General Spears to M. Reynaud. This message gave an account of measures which were being taken to accelerate the despatch of troops to France. Bomber and fighter aircraft from Great Britain were again taking part in the Somme battle. The fighters were refuelling in France and were thus able to operate for longer periods. Considerable forces of bombers would also continue their attacks during the night of June 6–7 on objectives specified by the French High Command.

On the morning of June 7 Sir R. Campbell telegraphed a con-
(c) sidered statement of his views[2] for submission to the Prime Minister. He could not estimate the French chances of holding up the German attack long enough for a complete change to take place in the military situation. The French army was said to be fighting magnificently, but there was great depression in the High Command, from General Weygand downwards, owing to our failure to respond to 'their appeal to place a large and specified proportion of the Royal Air Force at their disposal'.

Sir R. Campbell knew that we could not agree to this demand. He did not suggest that we should agree to it, but he asked that we should send as powerful a force as we could spare, day by day, to operate after refuelling in France against objectives indicated by the French High Command. If we acted in this way, and if we kept on telling the French what we were doing, we should be taking the only possible measures to prevent them from giving way to despair. Apart from any material help which we could give, the moral factor was

---

[1] The reply appears to have been sent directly to General Spears.
[2] Sir R. Campbell said that General Spears agreed with his statement.
(a) C6828/5/18. (b) C6828/5/18. (c) C6828/5/18.

all-important. The French might not be far wrong in claiming that the vital battle of the war was now being fought, and that the Germans could turn to the British Isles only if the French army had been 'knocked out'. Sir R. Campbell asked: 'Is it fair to suggest that every German machine and pilot destroyed in France means one each less for use against the British Isles later?' M. Reynaud was receiving demands from the army and from the Foreign Affairs Commissions of the Senate and Chamber to be told what proportion of the Royal Air Force was co-operating in France. Sir R. Campbell and General Spears were asking him not to put the question in that form but to rely on the Prime Minister to keep a maximum strength day by day in operation. M. Reynaud described himself as being 'between the hammer and anvil' in the matter.

In the afternoon of June 7 M. Corbin made a personal appeal to Lord Halifax. He said that he could understand we did not wish to (a) give up the principle of keeping the Royal Air Force for the defence of the United Kingdom, but the result was that the whole of the French air force was in constant service—the pilots were in action two or three times a day—and the French armies had to abandon positions which they would otherwise have held. If we were afraid of being unprepared for raids, M. Corbin would argue that such raids would have to be on an enormous scale to achieve results at all comparable with the result of a German victory in the present battle in France. The recent raid (June 3) on Paris was important as far as numbers went, but it had done little damage. In any case the Royal Air Force could be brought back from France to meet raids in Great Britain. M. Corbin thought that there was a lamentable lack of co-ordination of Allied effort not merely in the air but in the whole conduct of the present battle. The German method was to attack one enemy at a time; therefore we ought to find where the greatest risks lay and to concentrate our efforts in order to prepare for them.

Lord Halifax said that he did not think we could get more complete co-ordination on the military side. On the political side we were slower than the enemy in taking decisions because we were two Allied Governments fighting a single dictator. As far as concerned air co-ordination, we had to distinguish between unity of resources and unity of objective. There was no difficulty about the latter; the real problem was the disposition of our fighter strength. We were making more fighters available, but, if Germany at any time were able to destroy British aircraft factories, the result would be fatal for Great Britain and France. There was no question of fear of air raids. We were not thinking of the effect of raids on public opinion. The sum of the matter was that, 'if our fighter squadrons were to be

---

(a) C6828/5/18.

completely disorganised or destroyed, the situation both of France and of Great Britain would be desperate'.

(a) Lord Halifax said that he would put M. Corbin's argument before the Prime Minister. At 11.15 p.m. Sir R. Campbell was given a message from the Prime Minister for M. Reynaud and General Weygand. This message described the increase in air assistance during the previous twenty-four hours and spoke of plans to send two more squadrons[1] to be based in France, and four squadrons based in England to operate daily from advanced fuelling grounds south of the Somme. Recent experience had shown that we could not at present maintain a greater number of squadrons at the high rate of battle casualties. The Prime Minister also referred to bombing co-operation and mentioned the German air attacks on objectives in Great Britain.

(b) The French Government continued their appeals on June 8. Sir R. Campbell saw M. Reynaud after the latter's morning conference with Marshal Pétain, General Weygand and Admiral Darlan. The news was bad, since the Germans had broken through at Forges-les-Eaux and were threatening Rouen and Le Havre. Although M. Reynaud was grateful for all the air help which was being sent, he was inclined 'to press for more and more'. General Weygand also described the Royal Air Force as 'co-operating splendidly', but he too 'emphasised the gravity of the hour'. M. Reynaud told Sir R. Campbell that he had 'won the day', and obtained a decision that the French would go on fighting as long as anything were left with which they could fight. He admitted that 'there had been a moment when he had been alone in feeling like that'.

(c) At 2 p.m. Sir R. Campbell transmitted a message to the Prime Minister from M. Reynaud in the following terms:

'Rouen and Le Havre are definitely threatened, and with them the supplies for Paris and for half of the army. I thank you for your effort, but the situation calls for a greater one, notably that fighter squadrons should be based in France in order that they can be employed to their full effectiveness.[2]

The nine fighter squadrons which you are good enough to promise us are only a quarter of the thirty-nine fighter squadrons which on May 31, according to your declaration at the last Supreme Council

---

[1] For this purpose three squadrons were being amalgamated into two. Three full squadrons were already based in France so that the total so based would become five.

[2] Sir R. Campbell sent a message to M. Reynaud that, in the opinion of the British Air Attaché, the effectiveness of British fighter squadrons would be reduced rather than increased by basing them in France where, among other difficulties, they would be subject to enemy action whilst on the ground. M. Reynaud, in reply, asked Sir R Campbell to add the words 'according to the opinion of my experts' to this sentence of his message. Sir R. Campbell telephoned this addition at once.

(a) C6828/5/18.   (b) C6828/5/18.   (c) C6828/5/18.

meeting, were being used in a proportion of twenty-nine for the defence of Great Britain and the remainder for the Flanders battle which has since ended.

I feel bound to ask you to throw all your forces into the battle as we are doing.

With friendly greetings.'

The Prime Minister decided at first to send a message explaining (a) once again that it would be a great strategic blunder to throw away in a battle depending mainly on troops and tanks the force with which Great Britain hoped to break Hitler's air weapon when he attempted an invasion.[1]

This message was cancelled, and, at 9.30 p.m. on June 8 Sir R. Campbell was instructed to give a short message to M. Reynaud as follows: 'We are giving you all the support we can in this great battle short of ruining the capacity of the country to continue the war. We have had very heavy and disproportionate loss in the air today, but we shall continue tomorrow.'

In the early afternoon of June 9 M. Reynaud sent another message through Sir R. Campbell asking that the promised reinforcements (b) of troops should be hastened. The Prime Minister replied at 11.40 p.m. that British forces were giving the maximum support. The Royal Air Force had been continuously engaged over the battle-fields. Within the last few days fresh British forces had landed in France and further reinforcements were being organised and would shortly be available.[2]

(viii)

Consideration of the future of the French fleet in the event of the surrender of France (May 27–June 11, 1940).

The possibility of a French surrender had already led to the con-sideration of the terms which the Germans might impose and of the importance of getting out of German reach material of high value for the conduct of the war. Obviously the most important question for Great Britain was the future of the French fleet. On May 27

---

[1] The draft of this first message contained the following sentence: 'There is no reason why you should give in if this battle goes against you, and certainly it must not be the end of the resistance of Great Britain, for then all hope of final victory would be gone.'

[2] The despatch of these troops was undertaken more as a political gesture than in the hope of successful resistance. On June 14, after General Brooke had been told by General Weygand that organised French resistance had ceased, the Prime Minister decided not to send any more troops. Nearly 150,000 British troops were brought back from ports in Normandy. See below, p. 267.

(a) C7182/5/18. (b) C7182/5/18.

(a) Lord Hankey in a private letter to Lord Halifax had assumed that, if the French asked to be released from their undertaking not to make a separate peace,[1] we were entitled to make conditions. We should ask for the removal to British ports of the whole of the French navy and mercantile marine. We should offer to accept the officers and men of the French navy as volunteers and to work the mercantile marine, as the Dutch merchant fleets were being worked, from Great Britain. Lord Hankey also referred to the French air force, oil stocks, supplies of arms, machine tools and other material, and to the French gold reserves.

The Foreign Office view was that the Germans would certainly demand these assets of military value, and that it was doubtful whether the French would agree to transfer them to us, since to do so would be to increase the severity of any armistice or peace terms. The attitude of the French Government would not be governed by a long-range view that in strengthening Great Britain they would be increasing the chances of a British victory and their own restoration. They would not ask for an armistice until they had lost all hope of ultimate victory. In any case we could not approach the French until they had decided to surrender.

Sir R. Campbell was asked his opinion on June 3. He replied on (b) June 4. He thought that, in the event of a collapse, the French air force would practically have ceased to exist. French military material would have been heavily reduced, and 80 per cent. of French industry would have fallen into German hands. Sir R. Campbell agreed that we could not yet mention the subject to the French Government. He thought also that the Germans would demand the surrender of the fleet, and that the French Government might agree to it. The only solution would be to persuade Admiral Darlan, in defiance of the French Government, to order the whole fleet to British waters and to take personal command of it. Sir R. Campbell could not be sure whether Admiral Darlan would agree to such a plan. He might agree if several British officers of high rank came to him secretly and urged him to act in this way.

In view of Sir R. Campbell's letter the Foreign Office suggested (c) that the First Sea Lord, Lord Hankey and Sir A. Cadogan should meet to consider the question of the fleet. This meeting was held on June 7. It was agreed that the Germans would insist upon obtaining the fleet intact and would continue to 'batter' the French until it was handed over to them. It was most unlikely that Admiral Darlan, or anyone else, would order the fleet to Great Britain or to the United States. Even if the fleet sailed to British waters, we should be in the

---

[1] See below, note to Chapter IX.

(a) C7074/5/18.   (b) C7074/5/18.   (c) C7074/5/18.

intolerable position of watching the continued devastation of French towns from the air, for which we should be regarded as responsible as long as we held the fleet.

On the other hand, the humiliation of handing over a fleet was so great that a naval commander would do his utmost to avoid it. We should aim, therefore, at getting the fleet scuttled. If the French would not scuttle it, we should do the work for them. In order to be able to act at short notice, the First Sea Lord decided to send an officer to discuss the question with Sir R. Campbell and, under the latter's guidance, to keep in touch with Admiral Darlan and any other naval officers with whom contact might be desirable.

On June 11 the Prime Minister asked the Foreign Office for a memorandum setting out 'the considerations which arise and the demands we should make' in the event of a French collapse. The Prime Minister added: 'there is I think no need to anticipate an immediate collapse, but the matter must be watched by someone from day to day who has access to Darlan and Reynaud'. The memorandum was prepared at once, with the help of Lord Hankey, and taken by the Prime Minister to France in the afternoon of June 11. (a)

The memorandum dealt with two hypotheses: (a) the French might refuse to come to terms with Germany and might move their Government to the United Kingdom, Algeria, or elsewhere; (b) the present French Government or a new government might make a separate peace.

We should try to induce the French Government to follow the example of the Dutch and the Belgians. Sir R. Campbell had been given discretion, when the time should come, to offer the French Government an asylum in Great Britain. If the French Government took refuge outside France, there would be no difficulty about securing the transfer of the fleet to British ports or to French colonial ports. If, on the other hand, the French asked for an armistice, the Germans would almost certainly demand the surrender of the fleet. If the fleet were not surrendered, France might be exposed to great sufferings until it was given up. In these circumstances there would be heavy pressure on the fleet to return. The best course would therefore be for the fleet to be sunk before a request was made for an armistice.[1]

---

[1] The memorandum also referred to aircraft, oil supplies, the mercantile marine, machine tools, and material on order for France in the United States. I have not dealt with the later history of these proposals or with the efforts made (in some cases most successfully, e.g. the removal of industrial diamonds) by British representatives to prevent valuable material from falling into German hands. I have also not dealt in detail with the attempt to secure the transfer to Great Britain of captured German airmen, many of whom had been shot down in France by the Royal Air Force. See, however, below, p. 258, note (3) and p. 403.

(a) C7074/5/18.

CHAPTER VIII

The entry of Italy into the war

(i)

Effect of the German successes on Mussolini, May 10–15: consideration of policy with regard to Italy: the Prime Minister's message of May 16 to Mussolini; and the latter's reply of May 18: Italian agreement to the resumption of negotiations on contraband control, May 18, 1940.

(a) ON the morning of the German invasion of Belgium and the Netherlands, Sir P. Loraine told Ciano that Great Britain was responding to the Belgian appeal for help. He asked Ciano whether the 'new developments' would bring any change in the Italian attitude. Ciano answered that there would be no immediate change, and that there was no more reason for a change than there had been at the time of the German attack on Norway and Denmark; he could not say anything about the future. Mussolini would fulfil his obligations to Germany, but 'non-belligerency' was compatible with them. During the conversation Sir P. Loraine thought that, although Ciano wanted the German attack in the west to fail, he believed that it was likely to succeed. At the end of the conversation Ciano walked to the door with Sir P. Loraine. He then took his (Sir P. Loraine's) hand affectionately in both his hands and said, 'One (b) day, though I hope not, I may have to tell you disagreeable things, but of one thing you can be absolutely certain. I shall never cheat you about anything I say.'[1]

It seemed probable, indeed, that Italian 'belligerency' would not (c) be long delayed. Information received through Prince Paul of Yugoslavia on May 10 and dating from a week earlier suggested that Mussolini was merely waiting for a favourable development in the military situation, and that he had decided for some time past to enter the war, but had been held back by the King of Italy, Marshals Badoglio and Graziani, Ciano and others. The King had threatened to abdicate and had pointed out the danger which this act might cause to the régime. Mussolini had been told that the whole nation was against war, and that there might even be disorders if Italy

---

[1] The German Ambassador in Rome reported on May 14 that Ciano 'had expressed himself for the first time favourably regarding active intervention by Italy'. They would not wait more than 10 to 14 days (*D.G.F.P.*, IX, No. 242). Mussolini had told Hitler on May 10 that Italian forces would be ready for action by the end of the month (*D.G.F.P.*, *ib.*, No. 232).

(a) R5952/58/22.   (b) R5954/60/22.   (c) R5997/58/22.

entered the war. Mussolini's reply had been that these considerations were nothing to him because he had given his word of honour to Hitler that he would intervene.

Sir P. Loraine reported on May 10 that the head of the Economic (a) War Department at the Ministry of Foreign Affairs had presented a long report to Mussolini on the 'very grave damage' done to Italian interests by the Allied blockade. This report was given great prominence in the Italian press on May 12; on the night of May 10–11 anti-British posters had appeared in Rome and there was evidence of deliberate anti-British propaganda among students and youth organisations. Sir P. Loraine thought that Hitler wanted the Allies (b) to be provoked into a declaration of war on Italy and that Mussolini had been told to 'trail his coat'. Our right course would be to wait for Mussolini's attack. The date of his decision would depend on the degree of success obtained by the Germans in their offensive. If the Germans had great success Mussolini might come in during the week. Sir P. Loraine thought that warnings or threats would be useless and that our policy should be to make it plain that the sole reason for Italian entry into the war had been the personal decision of Mussolini.

Mr. Osborne, Minister to the Holy See, also reported on the evening of May 12 an audience with the Pope. Mr. Osborne had (c) been instructed to support an appeal by the French Ambassador that the Pope should use his influence against Italian participation in the war. The Pope said that he had already written in this sense to Mussolini. Mussolini had sent a polite reply that there was no immediate prospect of an Italian entry into the war but that he could give no guarantee for the future.

On May 13 Ciano told Sir P. Loraine that there was no change in the Italian attitude and that he did not expect the balance of (d) advantage in the western battle to be apparent for another four weeks. Sir P. Loraine thought that Mussolini, if he had not already made up his mind, might wait three or four weeks longer. On the other hand, Ciano said to the American Ambassador in Rome on (e) May 14 that Mussolini had taken his decision; the information received from Hitler showed that Germany had won a complete victory in Belgium and the Netherlands, and the popular demonstrations in Italy showed that, except for a small minority, the Italian people were in favour of entry into the war.

The alternative policies open to the British Government in these circumstances were summed up in a Foreign Office memorandum of (f)

(a) R5972/51/22.   (b) R5995/58/22.   (c) R5979/58/22.   (d) R6000/58/22.
(e) R6048(II)/58/22. (f) R6067/58/22.

May 14. Mussolini had now begun a course of open provocation and had 'practically reached the point of declaring his enmity without having yet declared war'. Should we refuse to allow ourselves to be provoked into war or should we force the issue by provoking Mussolini? If we were strong enough, there would be great advantage in forcing Mussolini to declare himself, but unless the Chiefs of Staff were definitely in favour of this policy, we ought not to adopt it but to maintain our present policy of refusing to be provoked. Owing to our air weakness in the Mediterranean we needed to avoid war with Italy as long as possible; we also had to show that Italy was the aggressor if we were to bring Turkey into the war in accordance with our agreement. We were still trying to negotiate a trade agreement with Italy and were applying our contraband control lightly. If, however, Italian provocation increased, we might find it difficult to continue this course. We might have to make some more definite sacrifices, e.g. (i) in order to gain time we might offer to discuss Italian 'claims' with Mussolini and try to buy him off by offering him satisfaction in regard to certain of them—possibly a share in the control of the Suez Canal and a more privileged position for the Italian population in Tunisia. (ii) We might abandon our contraband control. As long as we applied this control we were supplying Mussolini with the best means of provoking us and at the same time arousing Italian indignation. Hitherto Mussolini had not taken measures directly to resist our control. He might do so by convoying his ships through the Straits of Gibraltar and the Suez Canal. In order to forestall anything of this kind we might offer to hold another review of the question and to discuss any aspects of the blockade which could definitely be considered detrimental to Italian interests. Either of these approaches would, however, now be taken by Mussolini as a sign that we were even weaker than he had supposed, and the result might be the reverse of what we had hoped if we did not at the same time increase our strength in the Mediterranean.

The War Cabinet discussed the position on May 14 and 15. On
(a) May 14 Lord Halifax said that Mussolini evidently wanted us to declare war and that, even if Italy invaded the Dalmatian coast, it was doubtful whether it would be to our advantage to go to war. At the same time there were obvious disadvantages in doing nothing. Lord Halifax suggested, as a middle course, that we should close the Suez Canal and stop Italian supplies. The Prime Minister thought that we must 'wait and see' what action Mussolini might take. The War Cabinet also considered the possibility that an Italian merchant vessel escorted by warships might try to evade contraband control at

---

(a) WM(40)122, R6067/58/22.

Gibraltar. Here also the Prime Minister thought that in the first (a) instance we should do nothing.

During the night of May 14–15 Sir P. Loraine was instructed to (b) tell Ciano that he had noted in the Italian press reports of a long memorandum on contraband control. We had not received this memorandum, but, when we had received it, we should be willing to discuss it with the Italian Government and to try to minimise the inconvenience caused by our administration of the control. There were a number of points upon which we thought that the administration could be simplified in a direction agreeable to the Italian Government and, if their response were favourable, we would send a member of the Ministry of Economic Warfare to Rome.

Lord Halifax reported these instructions to the War Cabinet on May 15. He also suggested that the Prime Minister—as he had (c) recently assumed office—might send a personal message to Mussolini. The Prime Minister said that he also had thought of this plan. He mentioned the general lines of a message, and said that he would draft the text and consult Lord Halifax about it.

Sir Percy Loraine had just received the text of the Prime Minister's message when he saw Ciano and explained that proposals for (d) simplifying contraband control had been under consideration by the British Government before the publication of the Italian report. Ciano said that he would submit the suggestion to Mussolini.

The Prime Minister's message to Mussolini was telegraphed to Sir P. Loraine on the morning of May 16. The message ran as (e) follows:

'Now that I have taken up my office as Prime Minister and Minister of Defence I look back to our meetings in Rome and feel a desire to speak words of goodwill to you as chief of the Italian nation across what seems to be a swiftly-widening gulf. Is it too late to stop a river of blood from flowing between the British and Italian peoples? We can no doubt inflict grievous injuries upon one another and maul each other cruelly, and darken the Mediterranean with our strife. If you so decree it must be so; but I declare that I have never been the enemy of Italian greatness, nor ever at heart the foe of the Italian law-giver. It is idle to predict the course of the great battles now raging in Europe, but I am sure that whatever may happen on the Continent, England will go on to the end, even quite alone, as we have done before, and I believe with some assurance that we shall be aided in increasing measure by the United States and indeed by all the Americas.

I beg you to believe that it is in no spirit of weakness or of fear that I make this solemn appeal which will remain on record. Down the

---

(a) WM(40)121, R6067/58/22. (b) R6000/58/22. (c) WM(40)123, R6081/58/22.
(d) R6094/58/22. (e) R6081/58/22.

ages above all other calls comes the cry that the joint heirs of Latin and Christian civilisation must not be ranged against one another in mortal strife. Hearken to it I beseech you in all honour and respect before the dread signal is given. It will never be given by us.'

There was little change in the situation on May 16. Sir P.
(a) Loraine reported that he had spoken to Ciano on the question of British subjects in Italy. He did not want to tell them to leave Italy, but felt that, if war broke out, his personal responsibility would be heavy. Ciano answered that he found it difficult to give advice. He promised that, if war broke out, everything possible would be done to provide facilities for the evacuation of British subjects.
(b) Lord Halifax told the War Cabinet on May 16 that President
(c) Roosevelt had sent another 'exceedingly strong' message[1] to Mussolini on May 14, and that, according to the American Ambassador in Rome, 'things were neither better nor worse'. The
(d) Italian Ambassador in London had said to Mr. Butler on the evening of May 15, during a discussion of the contraband control,[2] that the Italian attitude did not depend entirely upon the result of the battle of the Meuse, and that he did not despair of the position. He used the phrase 'Tout n'est pas fini entre nous'. During the night of
(e) May 15–16, however, Sir P. Loraine telegraphed that, according to Ciano, Mussolini had refused to receive President Roosevelt's message personally from the United States Ambassador. The message was therefore left with Ciano.[3] Mussolini's reply (on May 18) to the message was that there were in Italian policy two fundamental motives which 'could not escape' Mr. Roosevelt's 'spirit of political realism': Italy was and intended to remain allied to Germany and Italy could not 'remain absent' at the moment when the fate of Europe was at stake. Mussolini therefore reaffirmed the substance of his earlier reply.

On the morning of May 17 Lord Halifax told the War Cabinet that,
(f) on the latest evidence, he was inclined to think that Mussolini had very nearly reached the point of bringing Italy into the war. In the
(g) evening of this day Sir P. Loraine reported there were indications that Italy would not enter the war during the next ten days. Sir P. Loraine thought that Mussolini might be waiting for the fall of Paris.

---

[1] For President Roosevelt's earlier message, see above, p. 153, note 1.

[2] See below, p. 231.

[3] Ciano described President Roosevelt's second message derisively to the German Ambassador as 'an *opus* consisting of sentimental Christian observations' (*D.G.F.P.*, IX, No. 255). Later Ciano said that Mussolini's reply would have as its basis 'a Biblical quotation which seemed very appropriate for this purpose' (*D.G.F.P.*, *ib.*, No. 266).

(a) R6079/58/22. (b) WM(40)124, R6081/58/22. (c) A3258/1/51. (d) R5946/58/22. (e) R6086/58/22. (f) WM(40)126. (g) R6081/58/22.

Sir P. Loraine received Mussolini's reply to the Prime Minister's message in the afternoon of May 18.[1] Mussolini said that the Prime (a) Minister must be aware of 'grave reasons of a historical and contingent ('*contingente*') character which have ranged our two countries in opposite camps'.

'Without going back very far in time I remind you of the initiative taken in 1935 by your Government to organise at Geneva sanctions against Italy engaged in securing for herself a small space in the African sun without causing the slightest injury to your interests and territories or those of others. I remind you also of the real and actual state of servitude in which Italy finds herself in her own sea. If it was to honour your signature that your Government declared war on Germany, you will understand that the same sense of honour and respect for engagements assumed in the Italo-German treaty guides Italian policy today and tomorrow in the face of any event whatsoever.'

At his conversation with the Italian Ambassador on the evening of May 15 Mr. R. A. Butler said that 'if the Italian Government (b) showed a wish to discuss their difficulties in the matter of contraband control, His Majesty's Government for their part would be very ready to suggest means by which the inconveniences in this control could be minimised as far as possible'. The Ambassador said that the German invasion of Denmark and Norway and the Low Countries had altered the whole aspect of the blockade. Italy now appeared to be the 'principal target' of contraband control, and the situation seemed to be reverting to that prevailing during the sanctions period. Mr. Butler thought that we might be able to go 'a considerable way' towards meeting the Italian Government if the latter agreed to discuss the whole question. The Ambassador agreed to telephone to the Italian Government a report of the conversation.

On May 18 the Ambassador communicated a note to the Foreign Office that the Italian Government were ready to enter into negoti- (c) ations at Rome on the conditions that the purpose should be to reach 'a speedy, effective, radical, and definite solution'; that Italian Mediterranean traffic should be excluded from control, and that the discussions should begin with a 'clean slate'. Mr. Butler told the Ambassador that we were unable to accept the 'complete abandonment of any sort of control'. The Ambassador said that he 'would not rule out' the navicert system or the possibility of a State guarantee,[2]

---

[1] Ciano told the German Ambassador that 'perhaps the only point of interest' in the Prime Minister's letter was a reference to 'the possibility of an English defeat' (i.e. the statement that England would prevail in the end with the help of America). (*D.G.F.P.*, *ib.*, No. 266).

[2] i.e. against the re-export of goods to Germany. This proposal for a State guarantee had been discussed earlier in the year.

(a) R6081/58/22. (b) R5946/58/22. (c) R5946/58/22.

but that the Italian Government wanted to avoid the stoppage and
detention of ships at control points, and that by a 'clean slate' they
meant the 'complete liberation of stocks at present on "hold-back"
guarantees'.

Later on May 18 the Ambassador was given a note that the
(a) Master of the Rolls was going to Rome with full authority to negotiate
an agreement which would take into consideration 'the rights and
necessities of both parties', and that we were also ready to release
forthwith goods in Italian ports under 'hold-back' guarantee and
with an Italian destination. The Master of the Rolls left for Rome on
May 21.[1]

(ii)

*Proposed public statement on an Allied offer to Italy: French proposal to
approach Mussolini through President Roosevelt: instructions to Lord
Lothian: Lord Halifax's conversation of May 25 with the Italian
Ambassador.*

On May 17 the Foreign Office decided to consult the French
Government on the desirability of a public statement 'designed to
(b) reduce the propaganda value to Mussolini of the exploitation of
Italian grievances real and imaginary. Such a statement might be
made in the form of an interview with an Italian journalist in this
country or in some other more official manner.' The French Government agreed with this proposal and accepted the text of a draft
statement submitted to them through Sir R. Campbell. The text,
which was sent to Sir P. Loraine during the night of May 18–19,
was as follows:

'In view of the many rumours concerning the likelihood of a disturbance of the peace in the Mediterranean, it is well to establish
clearly the position of His Majesty's Government.

We have brought our Mediterranean fleet up to normal strength.
The naval victory we gained over the German fleet in the Norwegian
operations has enabled us to do so and at the same time to maintain
all the naval strength necessary for defence of our home waters and
for all other tasks allotted to the navy.

The Allied fleets in the Mediterranean threaten no one. They are
a defence and not a challenge, and when this war is over we shall be

---

[1] I have not dealt in detail with the resumption of negotiations on contraband control,
since they belong to the official history of the economic blockade, and had no political
repercussions. The negotiations were broken off within a week by Mussolini (see below,
p. 238).

(a) R5946/58/22.   (b) E6127/58/22.

happy to discuss with all interested nations the measures necessary to ensure to the Mediterranean area a period of lasting peace and prosperity based on mutual goodwill and benefit.

The Allied Governments are aware that the Italian Government have particular complaints as to the administration of Allied Contraband Control, and also certain grievances in regard to the Italian position in the Mediterranean.

The former the Allied Governments are prepared to examine at once, with every desire to minimise as far as possible the inconvenience caused by the administration to the Italian Government and people. They would further hope that at the peace conference which will follow the war Italy would participate with a status equal to that of the belligerents in order that her claims might be dealt with as part of the general settlement of Europe.'

In view of Mussolini's answer to his personal message, the Prime Minister said to the War Cabinet on May 21 that he thought it (a) undesirable to make the proposed statement. The French Government, however, took a different line. On May 20 Sir R. Campbell reported that M. Daladier had asked the American Ambassador (b) whether Mr. Roosevelt would try again with Mussolini. During the evening of May 21 Sir R. Campbell telegraphed that, after 'painting lurid pictures of what war with Italy would mean', M. Daladier had said that he was thinking over the possibility of opening negotiations with a view to immediate concessions to Italy. Sir R. Campbell replied that these negotiations would be 'almost certainly fruitless and possibly harmful'. M. Daladier answered that Sir R. Campbell might be right, but that the prospect of 2,000 Italian aircraft bombing all the vital spots within their reach made him consider any chance of averting war.

The Foreign Office considered that it would be 'hopeless' to make immediate concessions but that we might offer something (on the lines of the proposed public statement) about Italian participation in the peace conference on an equal footing with the Allies. The timing of the statement was of the greatest importance. Sir A. Cadogan considered that the moment was not opportune, but that we should concert a statement with the French for publication if an Allied counter-offensive were successful.

On May 23 Sir R. Campbell reported that M. Charles-Roux had suggested that we should offer the Italians a share in the control of (c) the Suez Canal, 'adjustments' at Jibuti, and a modification of the status of Italians in Tunis. Sir R. Campbell had said that he expected Mussolini now to ask a much heavier price, and that he doubted whether we could buy him off. In these circumstances a 'maximum' offer would only humiliate us. M. Charles-Roux thought that everything should be tried.

(a) WM(40)132, R6127/58/22. (b) R6086/58/22. (c) R6198/438/22.

Later on May 23 M. Daladier told Sir R. Campbell that he and M. Reynaud agreed that a last effort should be made with Mussolini, and that Mr. Roosevelt might be asked whether he would enquire from Mussolini why Italy was 'on the brink' of war against the Allies. If Mussolini stated his grievances, the United States Ambassador in Rome might reply that Mr. Roosevelt was prepared to tell the Allied Governments of the Italian claims, or the Ambassador might use 'some other words which would have a delaying action'. If Mussolini put forward 'absolute' claims, the Allied Governments might be able to 'make some capital with the Italian people of the fact that they had been ready to make concessions'. If Mussolini said that he was going to war because he had given his word to his ally, there was nothing to be done, but the Allies would not have lost anything by their enquiry. In any case they would have gained time. M. Daladier said that he would not put his request to Mr. Roosevelt until the British and French Governments were in agreement about it. Finally M. Daladier talked again about the 'appalling blow' for France if Mussolini entered the war within the next few days.

On May 24 the War Cabinet approved the instructions[1] which the Foreign Office wished to send to Sir R. Campbell to the effect that we agreed with M. Daladier's proposal for an approach to Mussolini through President Roosevelt and had indeed been considering such an approach. We would suggest that the President might tell Mussolini that the Allied Governments were aware that Italy felt certain grievances about her position in the Mediterranean. The Allied Governments were prepared to take reasonable Italian claims into account at the end of the war and would welcome Italian participation in the peace conference on a status equal to that of the belligerents. Since this offer would be more attractive if it were guaranteed by the United States, His Majesty's Government would suggest to President Roosevelt that he should offer such a guarantee and thus ensure that Italian claims would be dealt with as part of a general settlement of Europe, provided always that Italy had not joined in the war against the Allies.

Sir R. Campbell replied in the early afternoon of May 25 that the French agreed with the terms of the proposed approach to Mr. Roosevelt. Lord Lothian was therefore instructed to approach Mr. Roosevelt at once. Later in the evening of May 25 Sir R. Campbell telegraphed that the French Government proposed certain changes in the formula of approach, and that they had sent these changes to the French Ambassador at Washington. They wished Mr. Roosevelt to suggest that the Allies would consider Italian claims at once, and

---

[1] These instructions crossed a telegram from Sir R. Campbell that M. Daladier hoped soon to hear from His Majesty's Government. The news from Rome was getting worse and the French suggestion, in M. Daladier's opinion, was the only hope of restraining Mussolini or of gaining time. Sir P. Loraine also telegraphed urging the 'utmost rapidity of action'.

agreed upon a settlement which would come into force at the end of the war. They proposed this change because they thought it would be useless to offer merely a consideration of Italian claims after the war. They also dropped the suggestion that Mr. Roosevelt might go as far as guaranteeing the Allied offer. (Mr. Bullitt had explained to the French Ministers that a guarantee of this kind was not within the constitutional powers of the President.) They were therefore suggesting that Mr. Roosevelt should ask Mussolini to tell him his demands and say that he was ready to *prendre acte* (a) of any agreement which might be reached, (b) of a promise by the Allies to fulfil such an agreement and (c) of an assurance from Mussolini that the fulfilment of the agreement would satisfy Italian claims.

Lord Lothian telegraphed during the night of May 25–6 that he had seen Mr. Roosevelt. Mr. Roosevelt was disposed to agree with the French proposals and would consult Mr. Hull on May 26 with a view to action. Lord Lothian and the French Ambassador intended to submit the Allies' proposal in the following terms:[1]

'The Allied Governments suggest that the President on his own initiative should ask Signor Mussolini for the reasons which apparently induce him to contemplate an immediate entry into the war . . . and that he should further state that, if Signor Mussolini will inform him of his grievances or claims against the Allies he will immediately communicate them to the Allied Governments in order to leave nothing undone to prevent an extension of the war.

They suggest that the President should inform Signor Mussolini that he has reason to believe that the attitude of the Allies towards the Italian Government can be defined as follows:

(*a*) The Allied Governments are aware that the Italian Government entertains certain grievances in regard to the Italian position in the Mediterranean.

(*b*) The Allied Governments would welcome Italian participation at the Peace Conference with a status equal to that of the belligerents.

(*c*) Signor Mussolini would thus be invited by the President to notify him for transmission to the Allies the claims of Italy, the fulfilment of which would in his view ensure the establishment in the Mediterranean of a new order guaranteeing to Italy satisfaction of Italian legitimate aspirations in that sea. If the negotiations succeeded, the President would then formally record (*a*) the agreement thus arrived at; (*b*) the undertaking of the Allies to execute the agreement at the end of the war; (*c*) the assurance of Signor Mussolini that the claims of Italy would be satisfied by the execution of this agreement. The Agreement thus arrived at to be dependent of course on Italy not entering the war against the Allies.'

President Roosevelt sent a message in these terms to Mussolini on May 26 through the United States Ambassador in Rome.

---

[1] It will be seen that Lord Lothian and the French Ambassador had slightly different instructions and that they co-ordinated them without reference to London or Paris.

Lord Halifax spoke to the Italian Ambassador on May 25 in order to make it clear that the British Government were prepared to satisfy reasonable Italian demands and to accept Italian collaboration at the peace conference in securing the resettlement of Europe.[1] Lord Halifax explained to Signor Bastianini what we should have said and the reason—Mussolini's discouraging reply to the Prime Minister—why we had not made the statement. In view of a possible misunderstanding Lord Halifax wished to tell the Ambassador that, while recognising the special relations between Italy and Germany, we had always been ready to discuss questions with Italy, and would propose to do so at any time if we could be assured that we would not be rebuffed. We should also go into detail in our discussion. Lord Halifax thought that he ought to make this statement to Signor Bastianini in order that they might both feel that nothing had been left undone which might avoid 'misunderstanding or something worse'.

Signor Bastianini said that he knew nothing of the exchange of messages between the Prime Minister and Mussolini, but that he would pass on Lord Halifax's message. He knew that Mussolini had always thought that a settlement of questions between Italy and any other country should be a part of a general European settlement; could he say that His Majesty's Government also thought it opportune now to examine questions within the larger framework of a European settlement? Lord Halifax agreed about the desirability of an examination within this framework, but thought that the possibility of settling, during the war, the questions of particular anxiety to Italy must depend upon the issues raised and upon the course which any discussions might take.

Signor Bastianini then asked whether His Majesty's Government would consider it possible to discuss general questions involving other countries in addition to Great Britain and Italy. Lord Halifax said that it was difficult to 'visualise' such discussions while the war was being fought. Signor Bastianini said that once a discussion were begun war would be pointless. Mussolini was interested in European questions, e.g. Poland, and in a settlement that would not merely be an armistice, but would protect European peace for a century.

Lord Halifax said that His Majesty's Government had a similar purpose and that 'they would never be unwilling to consider any proposal made with authority that gave promise of the establishment of a secure and peaceful Europe'. Lord Halifax added that this was also the attitude of the French Government.

---

[1] The Italian Government appear to have become aware of the proposed public statement and the Foreign Office had received a hint from a member of the Italian Embassy that a private discussion might be useful.

Signor Bastianini asked whether he could tell Mussolini that 'His Majesty's Government did not exclude the possibility of some discussion of the wider problems of Europe in the event of the opportunity arising'. Lord Halifax answered that he could certainly do this since the 'secure peace in Europe' which we and Mussolini wanted could come only by finding, through frank discussion, solutions generally acceptable, and by the joint determination of the Great Powers to maintain these solutions.

In spite of the reopening of negotiations on contraband control, the general trend of information reaching the Foreign Office on May 23–5 did not suggest any change in Mussolini's intention to enter the war. The date on which this step would be taken was, obviously, unknown, but the Foreign Office was less inclined than the French Government to expect it at once. On the night of May 22–23 Sir P. Loraine telegraphed that, according to information received by Mr. Osborne, the Italians would not come in until (a) June 10. By this time Hitler expected to have broken French resistance and to have entered Paris. He would offer peace to France on generous terms, without an indemnity and without asking for the return of Alsace-Lorraine. Hitler would then have to deal only with Great Britain before establishing a lasting peace and a new order. At this point Mussolini would enter the war; meanwhile he was said to be watching with satisfaction the heavy German expenditure of men and material, since Germany would thus be exhausted after the war and incapable of giving further trouble, while Italy would be in good condition. Further information from the Vatican on May 24 and 25 (b) was to the effect that Mussolini had decided 'irrevocably' on war, and that the King of Italy had accepted this decision. There might still be some delay before the decision was put into effect, but neither the Pope nor Mr. Roosevelt could do anything to change it.

(iii)

Mussolini's refusal to continue negotiations on contraband control, May 28: renewal of French proposal for a direct approach to Mussolini, May 30: statement by the British Government on Anglo-Italian relations, June 1, 1940.

The Italian answer given on May 27 to President Roosevelt's *démarche* was entirely negative; Mussolini had refused even to see the (c)

(a) R5997/58/22. (b) R6145, 6270/58/22. (c) R6308/438/22; R6309/58/22.

United States Ambassador and Ciano had said that any attempt to prevent Italy from fulfilling her engagements was 'ill-regarded'.[1] There was also no response to Lord Halifax's approach through the Italian Ambassador on the possibility of discussing Italian claims. M. Reynaud had come to London on May 26 to secure British assent to a wider plan in which an offer of concessions to Mussolini was linked with a proposal for his mediation and support in securing a general settlement.[2] The War Cabinet were from the first most doubtful about M. Reynaud's plan and advised its postponement until the character of Mussolini's answer to Mr. Roosevelt's approach of May 26 was known. In spite of Mussolini's complete rejection of the President's proposal, M. Reynaud did not give up his plan. The War Cabinet, however, considered on May 28 that a direct approach to Mussolini would be useless.

It was indeed clear that Mussolini did not intend any discussions. His refusal to consider Lord Halifax's suggestions to the Italian Ambassador was not known in London until after the War Cabinet had definitely rejected the French plan, but it was already clear that no response was likely. Ciano said on May 28 that Mussolini had placed a general ban on 'any discussions whatever with the Allies'. The 'general ban' included the negotiations on contraband control.

(a) Ciano told Sir P. Loraine during their conversation on that day that 'five minutes earlier' Mussolini had telephoned that these negotiations must be broken off at once. According to Ciano, Mussolini had been provoked into this decision by reading a summary of the British press which quoted the headlines in half a dozen newspapers about the negotiations.[3] Mussolini resented what he called an attempt to make political capital out of purely economic matters. Sir P. Loraine protested at the decision and pointed out that His Majesty's Government would now have full freedom of action as regards contraband control. Ciano agreed, but 'as friend to friend' hoped that there would not be any 'incident' which might 'aggravate or precipitate' a situation already serious.

---

[1] On May 30 the President sent another message to Mussolini to the effect that the 'extension of the war as the result of Italian participation would at once result in an increase in the rearmament program of the United States itself, and in a redoubling of the efforts of the United States to facilitate in every practical way the securing within the United States by the Allied Powers of all the supplies and *matériel*' which they might require. *F.R.U.S.*, 1940, II, 713–4. Mussolini's answer was that he desired to fulfil his engagements with Germany and did not wish to receive any further pressure from the United States.

[2] See above, Chapter VII, section (iv) for M. Reynaud's proposals and the attitude of His Majesty's Government towards them.

[3] In fact the Foreign Office had taken particular care to ensure that the British press should avoid language which Mussolini might regard as provocative. The Foreign Office considered the attitude of the press as 'in general correct'.

(a) R6335/51/22.

Sir P. Loraine was now sure, from Ciano's statements, that Italy would enter the war; the only remaining doubt was the date on which (a) she would come in. This date might be a week, or more than a week ahead. Sir P. Loraine told Ciano that he was bound to take measures (b) for getting as many British subjects as possible out of Italy. After some discussion Ciano said that he had 'no good reason for trying to dissuade' Sir P. Loraine from this course. Ciano explained that Mussolini had refused President Roosevelt's proposals because he (c) thought it incompatible with his obligations to Germany to accept political discussions with Great Britain or France. Mussolini regarded such proposals as an attempt to make him break faith with Germany: 'Fascists did not break faith'. Ciano said that on the previous evening he had told M. François-Poncet that Mussolini would decline to discuss 'even an offer tomorrow to cede Tunis, Algeria and Morocco'.[1]

Sir P. Loraine said that Ciano and Mussolini must have no doubt that war would be met by war. Ciano answered that 'they understood this' and that he 'knew the strong fibre of the British race'. Sir P. Loraine then said that the responsibility would be solely with Mussolini. Ciano thought that the question was less one of responsibility than of rapid development in the gravity of the situation. Sir P. Loraine considered the meaning of this statement to be that Mussolini was waiting for the 'moment of maximum embarrassment of the Anglo-French allies' before making his attack.

During the afternoon of May 30 Sir R. Campbell telephoned to Sir O. Sargent from Paris that M. Daladier had again raised the (d) question of a direct approach to Mussolini. M. Daladier proposed to give the Italian Ambassador in Paris a document containing a declaration that the French Government did not regard the French and Italian régimes as 'incompatible', and an offer to contemplate measures which might reinforce and render lasting the mutual independence of the two régimes. These measures would include an immediate examination of all Mediterranean questions affecting Italian development. In the course of such negotiations, which would be 'direct' and have 'a general aim', France was resolved to repudiate neither her alliance nor her engagements, but would welcome all solutions likely to promote the establishment of a new *statut* of the Mediterranean.

Sir R. Campbell argued with M. Daladier about the expediency of this offer. M. Daladier, however, thought that a '1000 to 1' chance was worth trying, and that French public opinion would expect such

---

[1] Ciano said to the German Ambassador that he had told M. François-Poncet that 'even if he served him up Tunis, Algiers, Corsica and Nice on a platter, he could only say no, because there was only one thing for Italy now and that was war'. (*D.G.F.P.*, IX, No. 340).

(a) R6331/58/22. (b) W8023/8023/49. (c) R6331/58/22. (d) R6309/58/22.

an attempt. Sir R. Campbell said that he could not engage the British Government or hold out any hope of their agreement. Obviously a new order in the Mediterranean must affect Great Britain very closely, although there was no mention of Great Britain in the French document.

Sir R. Campbell suggested to Sir O. Sargent that we might perhaps let the French do as they wished in the matter, but that we should ensure that they did not engage us. M. Daladier had argued that Lord Halifax had approached Signor Bastianini without concerting his action with the French Government.

Lord Halifax told the War Cabinet on May 30 of Sir R. Campbell's
(a) telephone message. The War Cabinet agreed that it would be useless to try to stop the French, but that we should explain clearly that we must not be committed to any statement which the French Government made to Mussolini.

M. Daladier's approach had no success. Sir R. Campbell reported
(b) the failure of the *démarche* during the night of June 1–2. Later on June 2 he telegraphed that, according to M. Daladier, Ciano had communicated the Italian reply orally to M. François-Poncet, and had said that the French statement had not modified and could not modify the Italian attitude. Ciano added that there seemed no need for a more formal reply, since the French statement neither asked any 'specific questions' nor made any 'concrete proposals'. He then went on to say that the Italian decision to enter the war had been taken, and that only the date remained to be settled. M. Daladier agreed with Sir R. Campbell's assumption that the French Government would not attempt a further approach.

Sir O. Sargent's comment on the failure of the French *démarche* was that 'it was to be expected'. It had seemed possible that Mussolini might have decided not to attack France, but to isolate Great Britain in the Mediterranean. France could now escape from the Mediterranean war only if she agreed also 'to retire from the German war'.

At the end of May the British Government had no doubt that Mussolini was on the point of entering the war. They had tried every means of keeping Italy out of the war, and of gaining time. Henceforward they were concerned, apart from military measures,[1] only with strengthening public opinion in Great Britain and with 'isolating' Mussolini, as far as possible, from public opinion in Italy. They decided to draft a statement for the B.B.C., and also, more generally,
(c) for the guidance of the press during the few days before Italian intervention took place.

---

[1] These measures included steps to intercept Italian ships *en route* for Italy with important cargoes.

(a) WM(40)148, R6309/58/22.   (b) R6308/438/22.   (c) R6331/58/22.

The draft was sent for comment to Sir P. Loraine during the night of May 30–1. Sir P. Loraine suggested some additions, and the statement was issued on June 1 in the following terms:

'In the view of Great Britain the problem of Anglo-Italian relations may be defined as follows:

It is an unusual and unwelcome situation for Great Britain to stand in the expectation of hostile action on the part of a country whose position, influence, and recent territorial expansion she has recognised and with which she is not conscious of any differences that need recourse to armed force for their solution. But goodwill, however characteristic, is a plant which cannot be kept alive unless refreshed with a certain measure of reciprocity.

Great Britain has no desire to interfere with the position of Italy in the Mediterranean or in East Africa and the Anglo-Italian agreement concluded by Signor Mussolini and Mr. Chamberlain was inspired by this sentiment. The British and French Governments have for a long time past made known to the Italian Government both directly and indirectly their willingness to discuss and meet all legitimate Italian aspirations, but the Italian Government have never been willing to enter into any conversations on the subject.

On the other hand Great Britain is determined to resist German aspirations to hegemony, which, if realised, would reduce England, France, and Italy to the status of vassal States.

As regards our economic warfare against Germany, in so far as measures which we have adopted have affected Italian interests, Great Britain has always been anxious to meet Italian requirements, and the British Chairman of the Anglo-Italian Committee for dealing with economic differences was sent to Rome to propose a new method. The Italian Government, however, declined to co-operate in giving effect to this arrangement which the Italian experts had accepted as satisfactory.

Nevertheless the British Government, so far as it lies with them, are still giving effect to the new method devised to meet Italian complaints.

In a word the British Government are prepared to meet legitimate Italian political aspirations and complaints about contraband control. If the Italian Government nevertheless decide to choose the path of war, the responsibility will be theirs for the extension of hostilities, for the loss of life on both sides and for the further impoverishment of the peoples of Europe. Great Britain has always wished, and wishes, to form a friendship between the two peoples, a friendship which would rest on a real community of interests. But if Italy without cause attacks Great Britain, she will know how to defend herself, and the sword will be met by the sword.'

On June 3 Sir R. Campbell reported that M. Reynaud was thinking of a broadcast to influence French public opinion which (a)

(a) R6396/58/22.

did not understand why Italy was on the point of coming into the war. M. Reynaud also had Italian public opinion in mind. M. Reynaud wanted to know Sir R. Campbell's views on his proposal. Sir R. Campbell asked the opinion of the Foreign Office. He was told on
(a) June 4 that it was probably more important to prepare France for the shock of Italian intervention than to avoid a statement which might help Mussolini in getting Italian public opinion into line about the war. Hence we ought not to try to stop M. Reynaud from giving his broadcast, on condition that he did not make any appeal, offer concessions in the view that Italy could be bought off, give an impression that we were on the brink of war, or compromise Mr. Roosevelt or the United States Government.

Sir R. Campbell replied that M. Reynaud agreed with the points
(b) mentioned to him, but that he had wanted to refer to the *démarche* made through Mr. Roosevelt. M. Reynaud might, however, drop the idea of a broadcast. If Italy entered the war, he would 'tell the whole story'.

(iv)

Final evidence of Italian intentions, June 2–9: Italian declaration of war, June 10: statement by the British Government on June 19, 1940: Turkey and the entry of Italy into the war.

During the night of June 2–3 Sir P. Loraine telegraphed a report
(c) from an Italian source that, in a speech of May 16 to party leaders of the Trentino, Mussolini had displayed a map showing the Italian claims. France was required to give up to Italy Nice, Savoy, Corsica and Tunis. Italy would obtain also Malta and Cyprus, a protectorate over Egypt, Syria and Iraq, and a joint Italo-Egyptian protectorate over the Sudan. Gibraltar and Suez were to be internationalised and Morocco to be divided between Spain and Germany. Mussolini had said in his speech[1] that, as long as the war was confined to Poland or Norway, Italy could remain non-belligerent. The Italian position was bound to change when the war had reached Lyons and Toulon. Italy must now finally break her Mediterranean prison and honour her signature. 'It is inevitable that Italy should intervene. And she will intervene. This is not the moment to fix the date, but, when the hour comes, we will march.'

During his conversation of May 28 with Sir P. Loraine Ciano had said that he maintained his promise to give fair warning of Italy's

---

[1] This speech was not published, but copies of it were distributed. The recipients of these copies included, among others, the workmen employed on the construction of the buildings, etc., for the 1942 Exhibition in Rome.

(a) R6421/438/22. (b) R6421/438/22. (c) R6385/58/22.

entry into the war. On June 3 he told Sir P. Loraine that the decison would not be taken on June 4, but that it was imminent. The French (a) Government heard that an ultimatum, with a time-limit of 24 or 48 hours, would be presented on June 5. Mussolini made no move on June 5 or 6. On June 7 Sir P. Loraine asked Ciano at midday whether there was any change in the Italian position. Ciano replied that 'nothing would happen' on June 7 or 8. Sir P. Loraine then asked whether the change would come early in the following week. Ciano said that this might be so.

Ciano also said that M. Reynaud's allusion in his broadcast to 'peaceful solutions' sounded like a change in tone; the speech was in (b) a different key from the Prime Minister's last speech, and less forcible than this speech.[1] Sir P. Loraine replied that it had not even occurred to him that M. Reynaud's speech might indicate any weakening on the part of the French. The phrase in question might have been addressed to Italy; in such case it would be consistent with the general attitude of the French Government. It was necessary also to take into account generally the difference of régimes. In democratic countries people had to be told the news, however bad it might be; they would face any situation when they knew what it was.

Ciano asked what would happen if Paris were taken, and France were 'beaten to her knees', so that she could no longer resist. Sir P. Loraine said that, on such an unlikely hypothesis, the war would go on, and would be very long. Ciano asked how Great Britain could continue the war, if France were 'knocked out'. Sir P. Loraine said that he would put the question differently. 'My country had not got the habit of being beaten in war; we had no intention of surrendering, and, if we did not surrender, the war continued *ipso facto*. As regards means, we had command of the sea, limitless resources, and a magnificent Air Force.' If the enemy controlled France, we should have only another stretch of coast to blockade. The situation was not without precedent in Napoleon's control of the Continent.

Ciano said that Germany would be able to draw upon all the resources of the Continent. Sir P. Loraine answered that there was plenty of 'consumption capacity' for these resources outside Germany, and that the wastage of war was already cutting into them. Germany was still excluded from overseas resources, and, when Italy entered the war, the Italian channel of supply would also be blocked.

Those arguments made Ciano 'think a lot'.[2] He was silent for a few moments. Then he said 'Is that what you really think?' Sir P. Loraine answered: 'I am sure of it. You would be seriously miscalcu-

---

[1] The reference is to the Prime Minister's speech in the House of Commons of June 4.

[2] Ciano noted in his *Diary* (p. 262) Sir P. Loraine's 'imperturbable firmness' and confidence in victory.

(a) R6079/58/22.   (b) C7179/5/18.

lating the British character if you thought I was mistaken.' Towards the end of the conversation Ciano admired our feat of extricating 335,000 men from Flanders.

Sir P. Loraine thought that the idea of a long war made Ciano 'very thoughtful, and rather glum'.

In the afternoon of June 9 Sir P. Loraine sent two telegrams. In (a) the first telegram he said that it looked as though the rupture with Italy would not be long delayed. He therefore asked whether there was anything for him to say to Ciano if he should see him on leaving Rome. On the evening of June 10 Sir P. Loraine was given discretion to say what he thought fit. He might tell Ciano that the story of the past few weeks would certainly show that the responsibility for any disasters which might befall Italy would rest upon Mussolini.

In his second telegram Sir P. Loraine said that he still thought (b) Mussolini might make some peace proposals of a blackmailing character, probably in the hope of detaching France from Great Britain. Sir R. Campbell also reported on the night of June 9–10 a statement from M. Reynaud that M. Laval had told the President of the Republic of a message which he (M. Laval) had received from Signor Aloisi's secretary.[1] This message seemed to hold out hopes of negotiation. The President had telephoned to M. Reynaud and had also told M. Laval to see him. M. Reynaud left M. Laval in no doubt about his views. M. Laval appeared to accept the situation; he said that he would go home to Auvergne. M. Reynaud suspected that M. Laval's move was due to Italian political intrigue.

During the night of June 9–10 Sir P. Loraine telegraphed that (c) Ciano had told M. François-Poncet that the 'die was cast' and that the Allied Ambassadors would be leaving on June 11 or 12. At (d) 5.58 p.m. on June 10 Sir P. Loraine reported that, at 4.45 p.m. Ciano had told him that the King of Italy would consider himself in a state of war with the United Kingdom as from midnight on June 11. A similar communication had been made to the French Ambassador. At 7 p.m. Sir P. Loraine sent a further message that, in answer to a question, Ciano had said that his communication was a declaration of war, and not a pre-announcement of such a declaration. Ciano added that no similar communication was being made to His Majesty's Government through the Italian Embassy in London.

Beyond reserving to himself the delivery of any final communication which he might be instructed to deliver to the Italian Government, Sir P. Loraine made no observations to Ciano.

---

[1] Baron Aloisi had been Italian delegate to the League of Nations, 1933–37. In 1939 he became a member of the Italian Senate.

(a) R6436/58/22. (b) R6436/58/22. (c) R6079/58/22. (d) R6490/58/22.

Eleven days after the Italian entry into the war the Foreign Office sent a circular telegram to all His Majesty's Missions. The telegram called attention to a reply to questions in the House of Commons on (a) June 19 regarding the British attitude to the Italian position in Abyssinia and Albania. The reply stated that, in view of the un-pro voked entry of Italy into the war against this country, we held ourselves entitled to reserve full liberty of action in respect of any undertakings given by us in the past to the Italian Government concerning the Mediterranean, North or East African and Middle Eastern areas.

The object of this statement was described in the telegram as freeing us from commitments assumed in the past, particularly under the Anglo-Italian Agreement of 1938, without binding us as regards the future.

At the entry of Italy into the war Sir H. Knatchbull-Hugessen was instructed to enquire whether the Turkish Government were ready to take action in accordance with the tripartite Anglo-Franco-Turkish treaty. Lord Halifax saw the Turkish Ambassador on June 11. The Ambassador said that Turkey would have to act with (b) a certain prudence: if Lord Halifax approved, he would suggest to the Turkish Government that they should enquire of Bulgaria whether she would maintain neutrality, and, after an answer had been received, consult Yugoslavia and Greece about their attitude. Lord Halifax pointed out that these enquiries would take some time, and that meanwhile he would feel 'a certain anxiety lest the impression should be given in any quarter that there was any doubt at all about the Turkish attitude'. It appeared likely on June 12 and 13 that the Turkish Government would merely break off diplomatic relations with Italy and that they might claim that the tripartite treaty was invalidated if the French could not fulfil their part in the provision of mutual assistance. In any case the Italians would maintain that they did not intend to take hostile action against Turkey and were concerned only with helping Germany to defeat Great Britain and France.

On June 13 Sir H. Knatchbull-Hugessen reported that the Turkish Government considered 'the pure and simple application of Article 2[1] of the Tripartite Treaty would be likely to draw Turkey into armed conflict with the U.S.S.R.'. They had therefore decided to 'refer to the dispositions of Protocol 2 of the Treaty'.[2] The Turkish Prime Minister had shown Sir H. Knatchbull-Hugessen the text of a

---

[1] i.e. the article providing for mutual assistance.
[2] i.e. the provision that Turkey would not be required to take action likely to involve her in war with the U.S.S.R.

(a) R705/705/22 (1942).   (b) R6510/316/44.

declaration which he proposed to make to the effect that the Turkish Government had 'decided, in agreement with the Allied Governments, to adopt an attitude of non-belligerency'.

(a) Lord Halifax told the War Cabinet on June 14 that the probable explanation of the Turkish action—apart from the course of events in France—was that the Soviet Government, under German and Italian pressure, was threatening Turkey in order to drive her to an appeal to the Protocol. Lord Halifax thought that we could at least urge the Turkish Government to recall their Ambassador from Rome; we could also make clear that we could not accept the proposed declaration that Turkey was acting 'in agreement with' her Allies.

The War Cabinet accepted this suggestion. In the evening of June 14 Lord Halifax discussed the matter with the Prime Minister. They decided that it would be best to accept the declaration if the Turkish Government would alter the phrase about 'agreement' to 'in agreement *with its Allies* to adopt *for the present* an attitude of non-belligerency'.

(b) Sir H. Knatchbull-Hugessen was instructed to tell the Turkish Foreign Minister that we regarded these changes as essential. We also expected the recall of the Turkish Ambassador in Rome, the expulsion of the Italian Ambassador from Ankara, and the execution of other measures appropriate in the case of a breach of diplomatic relations. We regarded the stoppage of commerce with Italy as of more importance than the expulsion or internment of Italian nationals. We thought that the Turkish Government might also follow the example of Egypt in the enforcement of censorship, the enactment of legislation against trading with the enemy and the institution of exchange control.

The Turkish Government decided to adopt the suggestions of His Majesty's Government with regard to the wording of their proposed declaration, but on June 18 M. Saracoglu told Sir H. Knatchbull-
(c) Hugessen that when they were about to make the declaration they heard the news of Marshal Pétain's decision to ask for an armistice. They had therefore cancelled the declaration and were uncertain what to do. They could not now use the words 'in agreement with its Allies'. They were likely to make a declaration of their own (i.e. without reference to 'Allies') and were willing to keep the words 'to adopt for the present an attitude of non-belligerency'. They could not, however, break off diplomatic relations with Italy since this step would mean war. Similarly they were unable to take the detailed measures which we had suggested to them. They would do what they could by way of delays and obstructions to hamper Italian trade, as they had hampered German trade for months past. In any case Italy

---

(a) WM(40)166, R6538/316/44. (b) R6459/58/22. (c) R6510/316/44.

owed Turkey large sums and the sale of Turkish produce to her was thus impracticable.

Sir H. Knatchbull-Hugessen was instructed on June 21 to suggest (a) to the Turkish Government that they should make their declaration, possibly with the substitution of 'in agreement with Great Britain' for 'in agreement with its Allies'. The withdrawal of France from the war would not affect Turkish obligations under the treaty, and in fact the 'war in the Mediterranean' involving France and Great Britain which was envisaged under Article 2 of the treaty had broken out before the French defection. None the less it was clear that the Turkish attitude would not be determined by juridical considerations, and we did not wish to refer to them.

The declaration as finally made by the Turkish Prime Minister in the National Assembly on June 26 ran as follows:

'The Government of the Republic have considered the situation which has arisen from Italy's entry into the war and have decided on the application of the ruling of Protocol 2. The Government have made the necessary notification to this effect.

Consequently Turkey will preserve her present attitude of non-belligerency for the security and defence of our country. While continuing on the one side to perfect our military preparation, we have also to remain more vigilant than ever. We hope, by this position of watchfulness and by avoiding any provocation, we shall preserve the maintenance of peace for our own country and for those who are around us.'

This declaration thus omitted any reference to the agreement with Great Britain or a hint that Turkish non-belligerency was only provisional, and the paragraph on Turkish military preparations fell far short of a notice of mobilisation or anything likely to tie up Italian forces as the Italians before their entry into the war had tied up Allied forces. The general impression was that Turkey had moved towards strict neutrality. The British Government, however, did not press the Turkish Government for a more satisfactory statement.

(v)

The position of Egypt after the entry of Italy into the war.

At the time of the collapse of France, the strategic position of Egypt was precarious. Italian territory lay on the western frontier of the country, and on the south-east flank of the Anglo-Egyptian Sudan. After the French armistice some 200,000 Italian troops, or more, were free to move against the Nile Delta and Suez. The failure

(a) R6510/316/44.

of the Italians to use their opportunities on land and sea and the record of the British defence are matters for the military historian. The main concern of the Foreign Office during the two and a half years between June 1940 and November 1942, was to ensure that the attitude of the Egyptian Government and the 'atmosphere' of Egyptian public opinion were such as to allow the most favourable conditions for the conduct of military operations. In order to secure these conditions, it was necessary, especially in the summer of 1940, that the King of Egypt should give his confidence to Ministers who would carry out the terms of the Anglo-Egyptian treaty of 1936. The Foreign Office were anxious to obtain this co-operation without interference in the internal affairs of Egypt; the British representatives in Cairo who were responsible for the execution of policy thought at times that a stronger line should be taken against the risks of 'Palace' intrigue.

Under the treaty of 1936 (article 5) Egypt was pledged not to adopt in relation to foreign countries an attitude inconsistent with her alliance with Great Britain. She was also pledged (article 7) as an ally to come to the aid of Great Britain if the latter should unavoidably become engaged in war. In accordance with this obligation, the Egyptian Government, at the request of His Majesty's Government, broke off diplomatic relations with Germany on September 6, 1939. They had been asked at first to declare war on Germany. The Egyptian Prime Minister, Ali Maher Pasha, had appeared ready to do so, but within a few days drew back, and argued that, technically, a declaration of war would come within the category of 'aggression' and that under the Egyptian constitution the Government could not declare an 'aggressive' war without the consent of Parliament (which was not then in session). Ali Maher Pasha also maintained that Egypt had based her undertaking in the treaty on the assumption that Italy would be involved from the outset in a war against Great Britain and would attack British forces in Egypt. Finally, he considered that a declaration of war was unnecessary because the Egyptian Government had already taken all the measures required by the British Government, and intended to forbid trade with Germany and to sequestrate German goods.

The War Cabinet decided not to discuss the legal aspect of the question with the Egyptian Government or to press for a formal declaration of war. The military authorities were satisfied with the defence and other precautionary measures to which the Egyptian Prime Minister had referred. Egyptian neutrality had some value from the point of view of trade relations with other neutrals, and there was nothing to be gained by forcing the country into an unwilling declaration of war.

The situation changed, however, when Italian entry into the war

was imminent. On April 25 the War Cabinet, with the approval of
the Chiefs of Staff and (on May 2) of the French Government, (a)
decided that, if Italy came into the war, they would press the Egyptian Government to declare war on her. Instructions were sent
accordingly to Sir Miles Lampson, the British Ambassador. There
could be no grounds for arguing that such a declaration would be an
act of aggression. It was obvious that the Italian threat to Egyptian
independence was direct and could be met only by resisting force
with force. Nevertheless the Egyptian Government in office at this
time did not take a robust view of the situation. In the early days of
June, Sir Miles Lampson reported that the political situation was (b)
rapidly getting worse. Already during the winter there had been
signs of growing anti-British feeling, and actual friction over the
British representations for the removal of the Egyptian Chief of Staff
in view of his attitude towards Anglo-Egyptian military co-operation.
King Farouk and Ali Maher Pasha remained outwardly friendly, but
there was evidence (in particular, articles in the Arab press, and the
openly pro-Axis sympathies of the Egyptian Ambassador in Rome)
that their policy was less satisfactory. Although he had spoken very
plainly to the Prime Minister, Sir M. Lampson was not fully assured
of his good faith.

The War Cabinet discussed Sir M. Lampson's report on June 8. (c)
They approved his action, and told him that Ali Maher Pasha must
understand that any suggestion of Egyptian neutrality was misleading, since we should certainly have to make Egypt a base for
military operations. Three days later, at the suggestion of the Prime
Minister and Lord Halifax, the War Cabinet came to a different (d)
view. They decided that, as long as our military operations were not
hindered, it would be better that a state of war between Egypt and
Italy should result from Italian aggression rather than from British
pressure upon the Egyptian Government. We might even accede to
the Egyptian wish that Cairo should be declared an open town. Sir
M. Lampson was therefore instructed that he need not insist upon an (e)
immediate declaration of war if the Egyptian Government would
give us full facilities for the conduct of our operations, and would take
all essential measures to assist us—e.g. they must break off diplomatic
relations with Italy, prohibit trade with the enemy, and maintain
internal security.

Sir M. Lampson saw Ali Maher Pasha before receiving these (f)
second instructions. The interview was unsatisfactory, but on the
following day the Prime Minister was much more ready to meet the
requirements which did not include a declaration of war. The
Egyptian Government broke off diplomatic relations with Italy, and

---

(a) WM(40)103; J1321/418/16; J1239/12/16.   (b) J1491/37/16.   (c) WM(40)158,
J1491/37/16. (d) WM(40)162, J1491/37/16. (e) J1321/418/16. (f) J1491/37/16.

the Prime Minister told Parliament in a secret session that Egypt would fulfil her treaty obligations, although she would not declare war unless she were attacked.

Sir M. Lampson, however, still doubted the good faith of the Prime Minister. He complained of his slowness in taking measures against (a) Germans and Italians in the country, and in enforcing the departure of the Italian diplomatic staff. Sir M. Lampson also objected to the tone of the Government-inspired press. He said that Egyptian military co-operation was inadequate, and that the attitude of the Government was affecting the morale of the army. He regarded the Prime Minister as closely associated with the Palace, and thought that King Farouk was trying to reinsure himself against the consequences of a possible Italian victory. Sir M. Lampson, with the agreement of the Commander-in-Chief, General Wavell, recommended an immediate change of Government.

The Foreign Office agreed upon the need of change, and instructed Sir M. Lampson to tell King Farouk that the vacillation of Ali Maher Pasha was neither in accordance with the spirit of the Anglo-Egyptian treaty nor representative of the feelings of the Egyptian people, nor conducive to the ultimate interests of the country, and that another Government should be formed. Sir M. Lampson had to argue very strongly in Cairo, and Lord Halifax had to use equally firm language with the Egyptian Ambassador in London, before the King would agree to dismiss Ali Maher Pasha, or even to ensure that the Italian diplomatic staff left the country. On June 22, however, (b) the Italians were sent away, and two days later Ali Maher Pasha's resignation was announced. On June 28 the King invited a 'neutral' Prime Minister, Hassan Sabry Pasha, to form a new Government.

Hassan Sabry Pasha was entirely ready to fulfil the treaty obligations of Egypt to Great Britain. Anglo-Egyptian relations also improved after the negotiation of a bulk purchase of the 1940 cotton crop by Great Britain. For the rest of the year, although the repercussions of Egyptian internal politics caused frequent difficulties, relations in general were satisfactory. After Hassan Sabry Pasha's sudden death on November 14, 1940, Hussein Sirry Pasha formed a Government. The new Prime Minister was a man of great energy and determination, and continued the policy of friendly co-operation. The Greek successes in November 1940, and the Allied offensive in December, as well as the German failure to invade Great Britain restored confidence in Egypt. The British Government did not think it desirable to suggest that Egypt should declare war on Italy, since there would now be no political or military advantages in a formal declaration of war, and the Italians might reply by the bombing of Cairo.

(a) J1491/37/16; J1588/15/16; J1597/131/16. (b) J1604/3/16; J1607/12/16.

CHAPTER IX

The collapse of French military resistance : British offer of union with France : resignation of M. Reynaud

(i)

Move of the French Government to Touraine: the Prime Minister's visit to M. Reynaud at General Weygand's headquarters (June 9–12, 1940).

IN the afternoon of June 9 Sir R. Campbell reported that the French Government were beginning the evacuation of depart- (a) ments from Paris and that only a skeleton staff was remaining at the Ministry of Foreign Affairs. Less than twenty-four hours later— at noon on June 10—Sir R. Campbell was told that the French (b) Government were leaving Paris and that the Ministry of Foreign Affairs would move at 3 p.m. Sir R. Campbell decided to go with the Government and to hand over the care of the Embassy to the United States Ambassador. Before leaving Paris Sir R. Campbell telegraphed that he was more satisfied with the general situation than (c) he had expected. In spite of the German progress on the previous day, the French were putting up a better fight than had seemed possible. Morale was good everywhere, and there was general determination to fight to a finish. M. Reynaud had said that he ordered the preparation of defence lines in Brittany. General Weygand was calm and resolute; M. Reynaud was unlikely to be 'stampeded' easily by his colleagues.

During the afternoon Mr. Churchill suggested that he might come to France for consultation with M. Reynaud. M. Reynaud, however, (d) replied that a meeting would be difficult to arrange because he was leaving on June 11 to visit the battle zone, and might go on to Touraine, and General Weygand was moving his headquarters. M. Reynaud hoped that a meeting could be arranged in a few days' time.

At 9 p.m. Sir R. Campbell left Paris for Touraine. He reached at 4 a.m. on June 11 the Château de Champchevrier at Cléré which had (e) been allocated by the French Government to the Embassy. The French plan of evacuation to Touraine had been based on the assumption that heavy air attacks might compel the removal of government departments from Paris. As a precaution against similar attacks in

---

(a) C6876/5/18. (b) C7541/65/17. (c) C6876/5/18. (d) C7182/5/18. (e) C7541/65/17.

Touraine, the departments were dispersed over a wide area. Thus the Ministry of Foreign Affairs were at Langeais, 18 km. from Cléré, and the Air Ministry at Amboise. The Ministry of War was even further away from Cléré, and the Ministry of Supply had been sent to the central *massif*, some 125 miles from the Ministry of Foreign Affairs. In spite of these plans for dispersal nothing had been done to provide special telephone arrangements. The Ministries, and the British Embassy, had therefore to rely on the local telephone service.

(a)   In the morning of June 11, Sir R. Campbell saw M. Baudouin, Under-Secretary for Foreign Affairs, and M. Charles-Roux. M. Reynaud was a hundred miles away at General Weygand's head-quarters at Briare: neither M. Baudouin nor M. Charles-Roux had heard any news since leaving Paris on the previous afternoon. About 300 telegrams had reached the Post Office at Tours, but the cyphering clerks, after an all-night journey, were too tired to look at them. Sir R. Campbell came to the conclusion that the 'wiser heads' regarded the move to Tours merely as a stage on the road, and that the only question was whether the next move would be to Bordeaux or to Brittany.

Meanwhile Mr. Churchill, Mr. Eden and General Dill flew to General Weygand's headquarters in the afternoon of June 11 and stayed there until the morning of June 12.[1] Sir R. Campbell was not present at the meetings and did not know that they were to take place until after Mr. Churchill had arrived. In his account[2] of the meetings

(b) to the War Cabinet at 5 p.m. on June 12 Mr. Churchill said that it was clear that France was near to the end of organised resistance. General Weygand, whose report was corroborated by General

---

[1] Two meetings were held with M. Reynaud and the French military commanders: Marshal Pétain and General Weygand were present at both meetings. General de Gaulle, who had been appointed Under-Secretary for National Defence, and General Georges were present at the first meeting, and Admiral Darlan at the second meeting.

[2] This account is fuller, on the political side, than the minutes of the meetings. These minutes dealt more particularly with the military discussions, including the very strong French demands for more fighter aircraft and the Prime Minister's argument that the destruction of the British fighter force would end the last hope of Allied resistance. The Prime Minister said that the Germans would attack Great Britain and this attack would in all probability bring in the United States who were already near the point of intervention. American intervention, and the losses which we hoped to inflict on the German air force, might well turn the scales in favour of victory. Mr. Churchill has given further details of the meetings in *The Second World War*, II, Chapter VII.

During the evening of June 11 the British representatives heard that the French would not allow British bombers bound for Italy (in accordance with previously arranged Anglo-French plans for the bombing of Italian targets) to leave the aerodrome of Salon near Marseilles. As a result of strong British protests, M. Reynaud undertook to order that the bombers should be allowed to go on their mission. The French, however, prevented them from taking off by putting farm carts across the runways.

On the following day the British 51st Division was forced by the German advance to give up an attempt to escape by sea at St. Valéry. The division, which had not taken part in the retreat to Dunkirk, and had been assisting in the defence of the Somme line, had been instructed earlier from London to fall back if in danger of being cut off. The French Command refused until too late to allow the divisional commander to carry out his instructions and escape capture by falling back either to Rouen or to Le Havre.

(a) C7541/65/17. (b) Z7718/5/69 (1943), WM(40)163.

Georges, described the French army as now almost completely exhausted after fighting for six nights and days. The enemy out-numbered them and had outmatched and outwitted them. The French were on their last line; this line had already been penetrated, though not decisively, in two or three places. If resistance on the line collapsed, General Weygand would not be responsible for an attempt to carry on the struggle. General Weygand also expressed the opinion that the Allies had entered upon the war very lightly and without making the necessary preparations. On the other hand General de Gaulle, who was with General Weygand, was strongly in favour of carrying on a guerilla warfare. General de Gaulle was young and energetic and had made a very favourable impression. It seemed possible that, if the present line collapsed, M. Reynaud would turn to General de Gaulle to take command.

M. Reynaud had said that Marshal Pétain had made up his mind that France would have to ask for peace. His view was that the country was being systematically destroyed by the Germans and that it was his duty to save the rest of it from such a fate. He had gone so far as to write a memorandum on the subject. There could be no doubt that he was a dangerous man at this juncture. He had always been a defeatist, even in the last war.

The Prime Minister had asked whether the large built-up area of Paris—like Madrid—would not be a good centre of resistance to enemy tanks. General Weygand replied that he had already informed the Paris deputies that the city would be declared an open town and that no attempt at resistance would be made in it. It was full of defenceless people, and he could not see it destroyed by German bombardment.

In a further discussion of the military prospects, the Prime Minister had suggested that the French might be able to continue resistance by means of a 'war of columns'. This would force the Germans to expend a large number of troops and enable France to hold out until the United States came into the war on our side. General Weygand did not think that the French could hold out for so long, but he repeated a previous statement of his willingness to serve under any other general who would undertake the task of command.

The Prime Minister said that M. Reynaud seemed determined to fight on and that Admiral Darlan had declared emphatically that he would never surrender the French Navy to the enemy. In the last resort he would send it to Canada. Nevertheless there was a danger that he might be overruled by the politicians. The Prime Minister had emphasised to the French that, 'if there were any grave deterioration in the situation on which they had to take decisions of great moment, we must be informed immediately and given an opportunity to consult with them before such decisions were taken'.

After the Prime Minister had made his report to the War Cabinet Mr. Eden said that the effect of the Prime Minister's visit to the French Government had been remarkable. They had at first appeared as men who had abandoned hope, but they were now inspired to see what could be done if their line were broken. The chief dangers to the continuance of French resistance were Marshal Pétain's defeatism and the possibility that the French politicians in favour of coming to an understanding with the Germans might find themselves strong enough to overthrow M. Reynaud. The French had not reproached us, but they showed clearly that they regarded our military effort as small, and remarked that we had put only one-quarter to one-third of our fighter force into the battle. Out of such thoughts an anti-British feeling might easily be worked up. Mr. Eden considered that the one factor which might decide the French to continue to fight would be some decisive step by the United States such as breaking off diplomatic relations with Germany.

The Prime Minister said that he had promised to send a further message to President Roosevelt in order to place before him clearly the present situation. During a discussion in the War Cabinet of the part played by the air in the battles in France, the question was asked whether, if we had thrown in the whole of our fighter resources regardless of our own safety, the battle would thereby have been won. The Chief of the Imperial General Staff was emphatic that this would not have been so. The disparity in numbers after the loss of the armies of the north, and the German armoured divisions, would still have been too much for the French. It was pointed out that M. Reynaud and General Weygand had said that a great attack by the Allied air forces might even now turn the scale.

The Prime Minister did not believe this to be the case, but he had promised that the War Cabinet would earnestly consider what air support we could give and would not in any way lessen the amount which had hitherto been given.

The Prime Minister summed up the position by saying that a chapter in the war was now closing. The French might continue the struggle; there might even be two French Governments, one which made peace, and one which organised resistance in the colonies and with the fleet, and carried on a guerrilla warfare—it was too early yet to tell, but effective resistance as a great land Power was coming to an end. We must now concentrate everything on the defence of our island, though for a period we might still have to send a measure of support to France.

The Prime Minister viewed the new phase with confidence. A declaration that we were firmly resolved to continue the war in all circumstances would prove the best invitation to the United States of America to lend us their support. We should maintain the blockade, and win through, though at the cost of ruin and starvation throughout Europe. In the meanwhile, the flow of our forces to France must continue, and the Air Staff must consider how great an effort we could put in during the following two or three days to support the battle.

The War Cabinet agreed (i) to explain the situation fully and frankly to the Dominions through our High Commissioners, and also to President Roosevelt; (ii) to reinforce, through Sir R. Campbell, the Prime Minister's request to M. Reynaud—which M. Reynaud had accepted—that the French Government would inform us before taking any decisive action; (iii) to send a message—from the Prime Minister—to the French Government in order to sustain their determination and to assure them of our 'unwavering support in all circumstances'.

(ii)

Meeting of the Supreme War Council at Tours on June 13: M. Reynaud's question whether the British Government would release the French Government from their obligation not to conclude a separate armistice or peace: the Prime Minister's reply to M. Reynaud.

In the evening of June 12 M. Reynaud established himself at the Château de Clissay, two hours' drive from Cléré. Sir R. Campbell called on him during the morning of June 13. M. Reynaud said that (a) he had decided to send another appeal to President Roosevelt— following a message which he had sent on June 10.[1] He would make it clear that the salvation of France depended upon a declaration of war in the immediate future by the United States, and that France was in the position of a drowning man calling for help. M. Reynaud had also telephoned to the Prime Minister asking him to come to a meeting of the Supreme War Council on June 13.

---

[1] M. Reynaud's message of June 10 included the following passages:
'. . . Nous lutterons en avant de Paris, nous lutterons en arrière de Paris, nous nous enfermerons dans une de nos provinces, et, si nous en sommes chassés, nous irons en Afrique du Nord, et, au besoin, dans nos possessions en Amérique.

Une partie du Gouvernement a déjà quitté Paris. Moi-même, je m'apprête à partir aux armées. Ce sera pour intensifier la lutte avec toutes les forces qui nous restent, et non pour l'abandonner. Puis-je vous demander, Monsieur le Président, d'expliquer tout cela vous-même à votre peuple, à tous les citoyens des Etats-Unis, en leur disant que nous sommes résolus a nous sacrifier dans la lutte que nous menons pour tous les hommes libres . . .

En même temps que vous exposerez cette situation aux hommes et aux femmes d'Amérique, je vous conjure de déclarer publiquement que les Etats-Unis accordent aux Alliés leur appui moral et matériel par tous les moyens, sauf l'envoi d'un corps expéditionnaire. Je vous conjure de la faire pendant qu'il n'est pas trop tard. Je sais la gravité d'un tel geste. Sa gravité même fait qu'il ne doit pas intervenir trop tard . . .'

(a) C7541/65/17.

In the evening of June 12, after his return from France, the Prime
(a) Minister had sent a personal message to Mr. Roosevelt. He said that
Generals Weygand and Georges had explained the situation in the
gravest terms. The Prime Minister was therefore considering what
would happen 'when and if the French front breaks, Paris is taken,
and General Weygand reports formally to his government that
France can no longer continue what he calls "co-ordinated war".
The aged Marshal Pétain, who was none too good in April and July
1918, is, I fear, ready to lend his name and prestige to a treaty of
peace for France.' M. Reynaud was in favour of continuing to fight,
and had 'a young General de Gaulle, who believes much can be
done'. Admiral Darlan had said that he would send the French
fleet to Canada.

The Prime Minister thought that there must be many elements in
France who would wish to continue the struggle, either in France or
in the French colonies or in both, and that the moment had come for
Mr. Roosevelt to strengthen M. Reynaud. The Prime Minister had
told the French that, whatever happened, we would go on fighting,
and that 'we thought Hitler could not win the war or the mastery
of the world until he had disposed of us, which has not been found
easy in the past, and which perhaps will not be found easy now'.

In the morning of June 13, before leaving for Tours, the Prime
(b) Minister sent another message to Mr. Roosevelt that the French had
again asked for a meeting, and that this summons meant that a crisis
had arrived. Anything which Mr. Roosevelt could say or do to help
the French might 'make the difference'.

The meeting—the last of the meetings of the Supreme War Council
—was held at Tours. Lord Halifax, Sir A. Cadogan and Lord
Beaverbrook (Minister of Aircraft Production) went with
(c) Mr. Churchill. They reached Tours at 2 p.m. and left again at
5.30 p.m. On arrival at the aerodrome they found that they were
not expected. After some difficulty they were taken to the Prefecture,
where they found matters in complete chaos. The Prefect appeared
(again after some delay) and telephoned to M. Reynaud. A meeting
was then arranged for 3.45 p.m. The meeting appears actually to have
opened at 3.30 p.m. M. Reynaud and M. Baudouin were the only
French civilians present, and General de Gaulle, who attended at the
later stages of the meeting, the only French general officer.
M. Reynaud began by describing the situation as reported by
General Weygand. The French Armies were at their last gasp;
General Weygand had said that it would soon be necessary to ask
for an armistice to save the 'soil and structure of France'. M. Reynaud
had replied that he did not yet consider the situation to be desperate.

(a) A3261/1/51.   (b) A3261/1/51.   (c) C7541/65/17; Z7718/5/69 (1943); Z4124/
1053/17 (1949).

Great losses had been inflicted on the enemy, and, if the armies could fight on awhile, help would soon come from Great Britain and from the United States. 'What was imperative now was to have definite proof that America would come in with sufficient speed and force.' Mr. Roosevelt had suggested to M. Reynaud that the latter's message to him of June 10 should be published in France and in the United States and had promised an increase in the supply of aircraft and guns.

M. Reynaud then summarised the text of his message of June 10. He said that he proposed to send a further message to Mr. Roosevelt that 'the last hour had come' and that the fate of the Allied cause lay in the hands of America. He would be unable to persuade the French Government to carry on unless Mr. Roosevelt's reply contained a firm assurance of immediate aid. The Government itself could of course retreat elsewhere, but, if Hitler occupied the whole of France, the population would be systematically corrupted and 'France would cease to exist'.

Hence the Council of Ministers had asked M. Reynaud on the previous day to enquire what would be the attitude of Great Britain if France had to ask for an armistice. He was aware of the agreement not to make a separate peace,[1] but France had already sacrificed everything. In these circumstances it would be a shock if Great Britain failed to concede that France was physically unable to carry on, and if France were still expected to fight on and 'thus deliver up her people to the certainty of corruption and evil transformation at the hands of ruthless specialists in the art of bringing conquered peoples to heel'.

The Prime Minister said that Great Britain, whose turn would soon come, realised how much France had suffered and was suffering. Nevertheless the one thought of the British was to win the war and to destroy Hitlerism. Everything was subordinate to that aim. Hence they hoped that France would carry on fighting, south of Paris to the sea, and, if need be, from North Africa. At all costs time must be gained. The period of waiting was not limitless: a pledge from the United States would make it quite short.

The alternative course to fighting meant destruction for France quite as certainly, since Hitler would abide by no pledges. If France remained in the struggle, fighting a guerrilla war, and if Germany failed to destroy England, the whole hateful edifice of Nazidom would topple over. Given immediate help from America, perhaps even a declaration of war, victory was not so far off. At all events England would fight on. She had not altered and would not alter her resolve: no terms, no surrender.

M. Reynaud said that he had never doubted England's determin-

---

[1] For this agreement see note at end of chapter.

ation. The point was what the British Government would say if the present French Government, or another, saw no hopes of an early victory and could not count on American help,[1] and therefore had no choice other than to surrender, and to make a separate peace.

The Prime Minister said that in no case would Great Britain waste time in reproaches and recriminations. 'That . . . did not mean that she would consent to action contrary to the recent agreement.'[2] The Prime Minister thought that the first step should be M. Reynaud's further message to Mr. Roosevelt. Let them await the answer before considering anything else, and let M. Reynaud put the position in the strongest terms. Mr. Churchill would support the message by another, in continuation of recent despatches pleading for France. Meanwhile M. Reynaud could rest assured that there would be no reproaches, whatever happened; that England would continue to cherish the cause of France and that if she herself triumphed France would be restored in her dignity and in her greatness. Let Mr. Roosevelt's reply be awaited before anything was said regarding British consent to a departure from the solemn undertaking.

M. Reynaud agreed with this course and outlined the terms of his proposed message. Mr. Churchill then referred to other factors in the situation. The war would continue and the blockade would become increasingly effective. France, under German occupation, could not hope to be spared; there might thus arise bitter antagonism between the French and English peoples.

M. Reynaud said that he viewed with horror the prospect that Great Britain might inflict the immense suffering of an effective blockade upon the French people. Even if the worst came, he hoped that Great Britain would make some gesture which would obviate the risk of antagonism between the two peoples.

The meeting then adjourned, and the British representatives consulted together in the garden of the Prefecture. On the resumption of discussions Mr. Churchill said that his colleagues were in agreement with what he had said to M. Reynaud. M. Reynaud then mentioned again what he proposed to say to Mr. Roosevelt in asking for some sign of hope for the French people.

The Prime Minister said that he also would explain the position bluntly to the President and include a reference to M. Reynaud's question and to his own statement that His Majesty's Government could give no answer until they knew Mr. Roosevelt's reply. The Prime Minister then suggested,[3] and M. Reynaud agreed, that they

---

[1] M. Reynaud in this context used the phrase 'There is no light at the end of the tunnel' to which Mr. Churchill subsequently referred. See below, p. 262.

[2] i.e. not to make a separate peace.

[3] Before the meeting ended, the Prime Minister asked M. Reynaud whether he would arrange for the transfer to England of the several hundred German pilots who were prisoners of war in France. M. Reynaud agreed to do so (see also below, p. 270). After M. Reynaud's resignation, his order for the transfer of the prisoners was not carried out.

should meet again as soon as Mr. Roosevelt's reply had been received.[1]

(iii)

Mr. Roosevelt's message of June 13 to M. Reynaud: meeting of the War Cabinet on June 13 after the Prime Minister's return from Tours: messages to the French Government from the British Government: personal messages from the Prime Minister to M. Reynaud and to President Roosevelt, June 13: move of the French Government to Bordeaux, June 14; President Roosevelt's refusal to allow the publication of his message of June 10, 1940, to M. Reynaud.

On their return to London from Tours the British representatives found that the United States Ambassador had received the text of Mr. Roosevelt's reply to M. Reynaud's message of June 10. Mr. (a) Kennedy brought the reply to the Prime Minister. The President repeated his previous statement that the United States Government were doing everything possible to make available to the Allies the material so urgently required. Mr. Roosevelt said that he was 'personally, particularly impressed by your declaration that France will continue to fight on behalf of Democracy even if it means slow withdrawal, even to North Africa and the Atlantic. It is most important to remember that the French and British fleets continue in mastery of the Atlantic and other oceans; also to remember that vital materials from the outside world are necessary to maintain all armies.' The President concluded that he was 'also greatly heartened by what Prime Minister Churchill said a few days ago about the continued resistance of the British Empire and that determination would seem to apply to the great French Empire all over the world. Naval power in world affairs still carries the lessons of history, as Admiral Darlan well knows.'

A meeting of the War Cabinet was held at 10.15 p.m. The Prime Minister gave an account of the discussions with M. Reynaud and the (b) War Cabinet considered the interpretation of President Roosevelt's message. The President had not said definitely that the United States would declare war. On the other hand, no Head of a State would be likely to send such a message urging France to prolong her suffering unless he were certain that his country was coming to her aid. M.

---

[1] The Bordeaux Government, in a statement of June 25 to the United States Government (see below, p. 329), alleged that the Prime Minister had been expected to attend a meeting of the French Cabinet. The Prime Minister did not in fact receive an invitation to attend such a meeting.

(a) C7182/5/18.   (b) WM(40)165.

Reynaud could say, therefore, that France was going forward with the struggle in the sure and certain hope of the full support of the United States.

The War Cabinet considered, however, that, although the implications of the message might be clear to us, they might appear in rather a different light to the French, who would be looking for something more definite. It would be necessary to point out to them that the message contained two points which were tantamount to a declaration of war—first a promise of all material aid, which implied active assistance, and second, a call to go on fighting even if the Government were driven out of France.

The Prime Minister suggested that he should say to M. Reynaud that President Roosevelt's message fulfilled every hope and could mean only that the United States intended to enter the war on our side. If the French continued the struggle, Hitler would enter Paris within a day or so, but he would find the capital an empty shell. Although he might occupy much of her country, the soul of France would have gone beyond his reach. No doubt he would offer very specious terms to the French, but these we could not permit them to accept. When Hitler found that he could get no peace in this way, his only course would be to try to 'smash' Great Britain. He would probably make the attempt very quickly, perhaps within a fortnight; but before that time the United States of America would be in the war on our side.

The War Cabinet agreed that, in addition to the Prime Minister's message to M. Reynaud, a statement should be issued in the form of a message from the British Government to the French Government emphasising the solidarity and indissoluble union of 'our two peoples and of our two Empires', and that the Prime Minister should send a telegram to President Roosevelt asking for his consent to the publication of his (the President's) message and supporting the further appeal made by M. Reynaud.

The Prime Minister then left the Cabinet to speak to the American Ambassador. During his absence the War Cabinet was given a summary of a broadcast appeal from M. Reynaud to President Roosevelt. On his return the Prime Minister said that Mr. Kennedy had spoken to the President. The President was willing to allow the publication of his message but Mr. Hull was opposed to publication. The President had heard that the meeting at Tours had been very successful. It seemed that he did not realise how critical the situation was. Mr. Kennedy had gone back to the American Embassy in order to communicate to the President a full account of the meeting, based on notes supplied to him by the Prime Minister. He was then returning to No. 10 Downing Street.

The Prime Minister read to the War Cabinet the drafts of telegrams from himself to M. Reynaud and to President Roosevelt and of a message to the French Government. The War Cabinet accepted these drafts.

The message to the French Government was as follows:[1]

'In this solemn hour for the British and French nations and for the cause of Freedom and Democracy to which they have vowed themselves, His Majesty's Government desire to pay to the Government of the French Republic the tribute which is due to the heroic fortitude and constancy of the French armies in battle against enormous odds. Their effort is worthy of the most glorious traditions of France and has inflicted deep and long-lasting injury upon the enemy's strength. Great Britain will continue to give the utmost aid in her power. We take this opportunity of proclaiming the indissoluble union of our two peoples and of our two Empires. We cannot measure the various forms of tribulation which will fall upon our peoples in the near future. We are sure that the ordeal by fire will only fuse them together into one unconquerable whole. We renew to the French Republic our pledge and resolve to continue the struggle at all costs in France, in this Island, upon the oceans, and in the air, wherever it may lead us, using all our resources to the utmost limit and sharing together the burden of repairing the ravages of war. We shall never turn from the conflict until France stands safe and erect in all her grandeur, until the wronged and enslaved States and peoples have been liberated, and until civilisation is freed from the nightmare of Nazidom. That this day will dawn we are more sure than ever. It may dawn sooner than we now have the right to expect.'

The personal message for M. Reynaud was telegraphed at 1.35 a.m. on June 14 in the following terms:

'The Cabinet is united in considering this magnificent document [i.e. Mr. Roosevelt's reply] as decisive in favour of the continued resistance of France in accordance with your own declaration of June 10 about fighting before Paris, behind Paris, in a province, or, if necessary, in Africa or across the Atlantic. The promise of redoubled material aid is coupled with definite advice and exhortation to France to continue the struggle even under the grievous conditions which you mentioned. If France on this message of President Roosevelt's continues in the field and in the war we feel that the United States is committed beyond recall to take the only remaining step, namely, becoming a belligerent in form as she already has constituted herself in fact. The Constitution of the United States makes it impossible, as you foresaw, for the President to declare war himself, but, if you act on his reply now received, we sincerely believe that this must inevitably follow. We are asking the President to allow publication of the message, but even if he does not agree to this for a day or two, it is on the record and can afford the basis for your action. I do beg

(a)

---

[1] This message was published in the press on June 14.

(a) C7182/5/18.

you and your colleagues, whose resolution we so much admired today, not to miss this sovereign opportunity of bringing about the world-wide oceanic and economic coalition which must be fatal to Nazi domination. We see before us a definite plan of campaign and the light which you spoke of shines at the end of the tunnel.'

(a)   The Prime Minister's message to Mr. Roosevelt on the night of June 13–14 stated that Mr. Roosevelt would have been given details of the meeting at Tours by Mr. Kennedy. The critical character of the meeting could not be exaggerated. The French were 'very nearly gone'. General Weygand had advocated an armistice while he still had enough troops to prevent France from lapsing into anarchy. M. Reynaud had asked whether we would release France from her obligation not to conclude a separate peace. Although the fact that we had unavoidably been largely out of the battle in France weighed with us, we had refused to consent to an armistice or separate peace, and had urged that the question should not be discussed until M. Reynaud had made a further appeal to Mr. Roosevelt. The Prime Minister had undertaken to second this appeal. M. Reynaud had said that it was beyond his power to encourage the French to fight on without hope of ultimate victory. Such a hope could be kindled only by American intervention up to the extreme limit open to Mr. Roosevelt.

The Prime Minister then said that the War Cabinet were most grateful for Mr. Roosevelt's message to M. Reynaud. He added:

'I must tell you that it seems to me absolutely vital that this message should be published tomorrow (June 14) in order that it may play the decisive part in turning the course of world history. It will, I am sure, decide the French to deny Hitler a patched-up peace with France. He needs this peace in order to destroy us and take a long step forward to world mastery. All the far-reaching plans, strategic, economic, political and moral, which your message expounds may be still-born if the French cut out now. Therefore I urge that the message should be published now. We realise fully that the moment Hitler finds he cannot dictate a Nazi peace in Paris he will turn his fury on to us. We shall do our best to withstand it, and, if we succeed, wide new doors are opened upon the future and all will come out even at the end of the day.'

At 12.30 a.m. on June 14 Sir R. Campbell reported that German tanks had broken through at Evreux; the columns were moving southwards and might reach Tours during the day. Three hours
(b) later Sir R. Campbell telegraphed that some members of the staff of the Ministry of Foreign Affairs had been told to be ready at dawn for
(c) a probable move.[1] At 5.15 a.m. Sir R. Campbell telegraphed that the

---

[1] In his final report Sir R. Campbell wrote that he had heard about this move at 8 p.m. on June 13.

(a) A3261/1/51.   (b) C7541/65/17.   (c) C6876/5/18.

French Government had decided to leave for Bordeaux early in the morning. They did not expect to be able to stay there for more than a short time, and advised the early despatch of a British warship to take off the Embassy staff.

Sir R. Campbell thought that the political situation had deteri- (a) orated during June 13. After the British Ministers had left Tours rumours had begun to spread that, if the United States did not declare war, Great Britain would liberate France from her engagements. At 3.15 a.m. on June 14 Sir R. Campbell, after seeing M. Mandel, sent a message from himself and General Spears reporting these rumours and M. Mandel's private advice that the British Government should make clear, in documents which would have to be placed before the French Cabinet, that they did not intend to release the French Government from their engagements. On M. Mandel's recommendation Sir R. Campbell and General Spears suggested a blunt statement that the joint Anglo-French declaration had been made to cover cases such as that which had now arisen, and that the British Government trusted the French Government not to follow the surrender of the Netherlands and Belgium.[1] Since there had been much emphasis on the fact that only two British divisions were now engaged in the battle, the statement should also announce most clearly that Great Britain intended to fight on with all her strength. M. Mandel said that the statement ought to reach the French Cabinet on June 14. He also said that the French Cabinet had spent half an hour in discussing the fate of the navy in the event of an armistice. The discussion had been inconclusive, but the general opinion had been in favour of scuttling the fleet if Mr. Roosevelt rejected M. Reynaud's appeal. If a vote had been taken at the Cabinet meeting the majority would have favoured an armistice.

The War Cabinet discussed Sir R. Campbell's telegram on June 14. (b) The Prime Minister suggested that Lord Halifax should send a message by Sir R. Campbell pointing out that in our view President Roosevelt's message of June 13 gave M. Reynaud the assurance of further support which he considered essential. The telegram might deny the rumours of which Sir R. Campbell had spoken.

The Prime Minister also told the War Cabinet on June 14 that the American Ambassador had been informed that President Roosevelt was unwilling to allow the publication of his message of June 13. Mr. Kennedy had asked the Prime Minister whether he would explain the position to M. Reynaud. The Prime Minister had refused and had emphasised strongly the disastrous effect on French resistance of any

---

[1] The text of the telegram was corrupt at this point. In fact neither the Dutch nor the Belgian Government had surrendered.

(a) C7541/65/17; C7182/5/18. (b) WM(40)166, C7263/65/17.

sign that the President was now holding back. On June 15 the Prime

(a) Minister gave the War Cabinet the substance of a message from President Roosevelt that his message of June 13 had not been intended to commit the United States to military participation in the war. This could be done only by Congress. Hence the President could not agree to the publication of his message, since he had to avoid any chance of misunderstanding.

The War Cabinet approved on June 15 a draft reply by the Prime

(b) Minister expressing disappointment that the President had not seen his way to agree to publication of the message. He pointed out that events were now moving 'downward' very fast. A declaration that 'the United States will, if necessary, enter the war', might save France; otherwise French resistance might come to an end within a few days.[1]

Sir R. Campbell was instructed at 4.22 p.m. on June 14 to inform

(c) M. Reynaud of the rumours that the British Government had released the French Government from their obligation, and to invite him to help in denying them. M. Reynaud knew that the Prime Minister had been careful on June 13 not to say anything which might imply acquiescence in the negotiation by France of a separate armistice or peace. We were convinced that any such action would be the gravest mistake. The rumours, in the form reported, were plainly incorrect since M. Reynaud himself had let it be understood that he did not expect the United States to declare war.

(d) Lord Halifax had already seen M. Corbin and had given him an account of the sequence of events from the Prime Minister's visit to M. Reynaud at French Headquarters on June 11–12 to the publication of the statement by the British Government of the night of June 13–14.[2] M. Corbin thought that there was nothing more to be done as far as the United States were concerned, but that there might be scope for further action in the field of Anglo-French relations. He had the impression that everything done by Great Britain was considered as 'the British contribution to the cause of France'. The press was trying to show that Great Britain was making a contribution to a common cause, yet it was doubtful whether public opinion in the two countries understood the fact. Would it be possible to find means of emphasising that the cause was common and of softening the impression that France was bearing all the burden? It was well known in France that Great Britain was short of equipment. In these circumstances a message to the French Government about giving the utmost possible aid was not enough. His Majesty's

---

[1] For the full text of this message see below, pp. 346–7.

[2] See above, p. 261.

(a) WM(40)167. (b) C7294/65/17. (c) C7182/5/18. (d) C7263/65/17.

Government should come forward, for example, with suggestions for the defence of certain parts of France and of their own country.

Lord Halifax said that we had thought that M. Reynaud once had the idea of defending Brittany, but that he had now given up the plan. General de Gaulle, on the other hand, seemed to think guerilla warfare a possibility in certain parts of France. A suggestion had also been made that the Cherbourg peninsula might be held as a bridge-head.

M. Corbin regretted M. Reynaud's request to the Prime Minister that France might be released from her obligations. Lord Halifax said that in his opinion M. Reynaud had put the question in order to get a negative reply, and thereby to strengthen his hand, but that General Weygand himself had asked to be allowed to seek an armistice. M. Corbin thought General Weygand's attitude 'an immense mistake'.

M. Corbin enquired whether Great Britain could transport to Great Britain or Canada 2–3 million of the 6–7 million refugees (including 2 million Belgians) in southern France. In this matter Great Britain could show that she was willing to share the burdens of the French people. Lord Halifax said that he would consider the question, but that the problem of food supplies (upon which our resistance depended) would arise with any large transfer of refugees to Great Britain. M. Corbin thought that Germany could not starve us out and that our fears in this respect were 'an insular reflex'.

Note to section (iii). The question of refugees in France.

The Foreign Office had instructed Lord Lothian on May 23 to raise (a) with the United States Government the question of the refugees from areas of fighting in the Low Countries. Owing to the employment of all our available shipping on military purposes, we could not bring the refugees in large numbers to Great Britain: we had, however, taken 10,000 of them. Would the United States Government offer help if they were approached by the Belgian and Dutch Governments? On grounds of humanity the United States might be willing to receive and maintain large numbers for the duration of the war. We realised the legal difficulties, but thought that these difficulties might be overcome in view of the extent and immediacy of the problem.

Lord Lothian reported on May 25 that he had given this message to Mr. Hull. Mr. Hull said that the United States Government was urgently considering the question and that he would give an answer as soon as possible. On May 30 Lord Lothian transmitted a message from Mr. Hull that the United States Government could not take the action suggested without making changes in their immigration laws. They felt it undesirable, at the moment, to propose these changes.

(a) W7986/771/48.

Existing quotas for some of the countries concerned were not full, and a limited number of refugees could thus enter under their national quotas, but all cases would have to be considered individually.

Lord Lothian recommended the British Government not to press the matter. He knew that the Administration was giving a great deal of thought to refugee problems and hoped that 'something more practical' might emerge.

(iv)

Instructions of June 15 to Sir R. Campbell: Sir R. Campbell's reports from Bordeaux: M. Reynaud's 'final appeal' to Mr. Roosevelt: the Prime Minister's message on the evening of June 14 to Mr. Roosevelt: Lord Lothian's interview of June 15 with Mr. Roosevelt.

(a) Sir R. Campbell left Cléré at 10 a.m. on June 14 and reached Bordeaux at 7 p.m. Here he found that the accommodation provided for the Embassy was 50 km. from the city. He therefore appealed to M. Mandel who secured him ten rooms in a hotel in Bordeaux. After dinner Sir R. Campbell went with General Spears to see M. Reynaud (whom he could not find earlier) in order to give him the full text of the Prime Minister's message of which he had telephoned the substance from Cléré.[1]

(b) Sir R. Campbell reported that M. Reynaud had received only a fragmentary version of Mr. Roosevelt's answer to his appeal of June 10. M. Reynaud was disappointed with the answer because it contained no promise of the declaration of war which France needed as an encouragement. M. Reynaud had sent his second message during the morning of June 14. He seemed worn out and made no response to Sir R. Campbell's remarks that he (Sir R. Campbell) did not think that the British Government would willingly accept the idea of a French surrender.

M. Reynaud said that the British Government must realise the difficulty of his position. He was faced with the possibility that Marshal Pétain and General Weygand might resign. Sir R. Campbell thought that 'the only bright spot' was M. Reynaud's indication that his Government would withdraw to North Africa and his statement that he had sent General de Gaulle to London in order to enquire about the transport of war material.

During the conversation M. Reynaud said that when on June 13

---

[1] Sir R. Campbell does not appear to have received at the time of this interview the telegram despatched to him at 4.22 p.m. See above, p. 264.

(a) C7541/65/17.   (b) C7263/65/17.

he had asked what would be the British attitude in the event of a French surrender, he was speaking on behalf of the French Cabinet, and that his words did not necessarily represent his own views. Sir R. Campbell was afraid that most of M. Reynaud's colleagues, who were continually pressing for Cabinet meetings, were working on him in a defeatist sense, and that he was swaying 'backwards and forwards'. In order to strengthen his position with his colleagues, Sir R. Campbell proposed to try once more on June 15 to make it plain that the British Government would be unable to condone a breach of the agreement not to conclude a separate peace. M. Mandel continued to advise us not to leave the French Government in any doubt on the subject. Sir R. Campbell intended to emphasise the point with other members of the Government, and especially with M. Baudouin.

On the evening of June 14–15 General Brooke reported to the Chief (a) of the Imperial General Staff that, according to General Weygand, the French army was no longer capable of organised resistance or concerted action. After telephoning to General Brooke, the Prime Minister sent a message through Sir R. Campbell to M. Reynaud, informing him of General Weygand's statement and continuing as follows: 'In these circumstances I feel sure that you will agree that the Allied cause would best be served by our stopping the disembarkation of any further British forces in France till the situation is more clear.' Sir R. Campbell gave this message to M. Reynaud at 4 p.m. on (b) June 15.[1]

An answer to Sir R. Campbell's telegram asking for a statement (c) was sent to him at 2.45 p.m. on June 15. He was instructed that, whatever the military situation might be, the British Government felt very strongly, and would impress upon the French Government the 'absolute necessity of refusing to take any action by way of negotiation with Hitler for a separate peace. M. Reynaud will be under no illusion as to what must be our attitude on this matter.' The situation might come in which the military commander found it necessary to ask for an armistice. 'That is entirely different from the Government formally consenting to negotiate a peace or surrender. We have the example in Holland of the army surrendering while the Government yet survives and provides a rallying-point for the national life of Holland and of her overseas Empire.'

We did not know the precise intentions of the French Government with regard to their future movements and course of action. M. Reynaud had said that, after a retreat into the provinces, the Government would retire, if necessary, overseas. We hoped that, in making their ultimate decision, the French Government would 'take into

---

[1] See below, p. 269. The message was despatched by the Foreign Office at 9.35 p.m. on June 14.

(a) C7263/65/17. (b) C7263, 7541/65/17. (c) C7263/65/17.

account the alternative of seeking asylum in the United Kingdom', where we should be most glad to receive them. In many ways a withdrawal to the United Kingdom would be a good solution, since it would assure 'the intimate and indissoluble partnership between our two Governments and thus facilitate the devotion of all our resources to the common cause'. It was of vital importance, if the worst should come, that the French Government should be resolved to keep 'all the resources they can in being, to be continuously employed for the purpose on which French restoration depends. In particular it would be vital to retain the French Fleet and Air Force in the service of the Allies.'

(a)   Sir R. Campbell did not receive this telegram in time for use on June 15. Indeed his first knowledge of its despatch came in a reference to it in a telephone conversation of 11.50 p.m.[1] At 2 a.m. on June 16 it had not arrived. He was then given the text in cypher over the telephone from the Foreign Office, but owing to the delays in cyphering and decyphering the instructions were not available to him at 3.40 a.m. when he telephoned again to London.[2] This cyphering work, carried on under great difficulty by a small staff at Bordeaux, made it necessary for Sir R. Campbell to shorten his telegrams as far as possible. In addition, the actual transmission service was overburdened and there were delays and uncertainties about whether telegrams had been transmitted. During the afternoon of

(b)   June 15 Sir R. Campbell[3] again asked that a British warship should be sent to Bordeaux. In the improbable event of the ship arriving before it was needed for the evacuation of the Embassy staff, it could be used for the transmission of telegrams. In fact, on the night of June 14–15 a telegram had been sent to him that a small cruiser would arrive on June 16, but this telegram also was delayed.

Nevertheless, Sir R. Campbell was able to send a certain number of messages in the afternoon and evening of June 15 dealing with the changes in the situation at Bordeaux. At 1.30 p.m. he reported that

(c)   the text of M. Reynaud's 'final appeal' (i.e. his message of June 14) to President Roosevelt was too long to send; the general sense of the message was that the decision of France to continue the war depended on the receipt of an assurance from the President that the United States would enter the war at a very early date. The President had not yet answered the message. Sir R. Campbell thought that, if no assurance were received, the French Government would come very rapidly to a decision to ask for an armistice. In this event he and

---

[1] See below, p. 272.

[2] See below, p. 273.

(d)   [3] Sir R. Campbell also telegraphed during this afternoon that all telegrams were being sent jointly by General Spears and himself.

(a) C7263/65/17.   (b) C7263/65/17.   (c) C7263/65/17.   (d) C7263/65/17.

General Spears would do their utmost to secure the scuttling of the fleet, but they had 'little confidence now in anything'.

At 2.45 p.m. Sir R. Campbell telegraphed his impression that (a) 'things are slipping fast'. As the situation grew worse, it was increasingly difficult to get a straight answer to a plain question or indeed any definite expression of opinion. The French Ministers took refuge in talking about the impossibility of the troops standing firm in their present state of fatigue, and of the necessity of putting an end to present conditions and of preventing anarchy.

At 4 p.m. Sir R. Campbell reported that Marshal Pétain was (b) determined to resign unless the French Government asked for an armistice or the United States declared war. General Weygand was of the same opinion. The military view seemed to be that the Germans 'could be induced to stop' and that there was danger of bolshevism if an armistice were not concluded. The present tendency seemed to be to favour two Governments, one of which would remain in France to negotiate with the Germans, while the other would continue the war from North Africa. Marshal Pétain would be head of the former and M. Reynaud head of the latter Government. This plan was unlikely to be carried out if the United States did not declare war.

General Spears had suggested to M. Reynaud that, after the French Government had left France, a declaration could be made by wireless that any abuse of power by the Germans in France would be visited instantly by a special bombardment of Germany. This proposal had appealed to M. Reynaud, but he thought that England alone could make such a declaration. General Spears said that he was certain that the Prime Minister would agree to make it.

At 6.5 p.m. Sir R. Campbell telegraphed that M. Reynaud had (c) said that he was holding a Cabinet meeting at 4 p.m. The time had come for a clear understanding with his colleagues, since he could not withstand their steady pressure on him. He would tell them, that whatever might be the German terms or promises, France, if she failed her ally and made a dishonourable peace, would share sooner or later the fate of all countries which had fallen under the Nazis. Peace in such circumstances would mean centuries of servitude, and the reduction of France to the status of Slovakia. M. Reynaud would resign if he failed to get enough support. At the least he expected four or five Ministers, including Marshal Pétain, to resign. During the conversation M. Reynaud said that he would never be a party to the surrender of the fleet or allow it to be used against a loyal ally. Sir R. Campbell assumed from this remark that some of M. Reynaud's colleagues might agree to a surrender of the fleet.

At this interview Sir R. Campbell told M. Reynaud of the message sent to him on the previous night that, in view of the end of organised

---

(a) C7263/65/17. (b) C7263/65/17. (c) C7263/65/17.

(a) French resistance, orders were being given to stop the disembarkation of British troops. He and General Spears also gave M. Reynaud a

(b) written reminder of his promise to send captured German air pilots to England and asked him to let them know as soon as possible the ports from which these prisoners would be sent.

After receiving Sir R. Campbell's telegram reporting M. Reynaud's 'final appeal' of June 14 to Mr. Roosevelt, the Prime Minister

(c) telegraphed (10.45 p.m.) to the President that at the time of his earlier message on June 15[1] he had not known the terms of the 'final appeal'. The Prime Minister considered that there was 'no getting away from the fact' that, as Sir R. Campbell had reported, if Mr. Roosevelt's reply 'did not contain the assurance asked for, the French will very quickly ask for an armistice'. In such an event the Prime Minister doubted whether it would be possible to keep the French fleet out of German hands. The message concluded: 'When I speak of the United States entering the war I am, of course, not thinking in terms of an expeditionary force, which I know is out of the question. What I have in mind is the tremendous moral effect that such an American decision would produce, not merely in France but also in all the democratic countries of the world, and, in the opposite sense, on the German and Italian peoples.'

(d)   Lord Lothian and the French Ambassador also saw Mr. Roosevelt and Mr. Hull on June 15. Lord Lothian asked what answer Mr. Roosevelt felt able to make to M. Reynaud's last appeal. Mr. Hull read a reply about material and supplies which had been despatched in the morning[2] of June 15 and was published during the afternoon. Mr. Roosevelt then said that the question of entering the war rested with Congress and that it would be useless to initiate a campaign by radio and platform in favour of a declaration of war with the certainty that the immediate result would be the political destruction of the authority of his Government. Mr. Hull confirmed this view. The President then said to the French Ambassador that it was very difficult in the circumstances even to suggest giving advice to France, but that, in his opinion, the French would be no worse off if they allowed Germany to occupy the whole of their country and if the Government, part of the army and the fleet then moved across the seas than if they asked for an armistice now and came to terms. Mr. Roosevelt emphasised particularly the importance of not allowing Hitler and Mussolini to get hold of the French fleet, since the possibility (which was otherwise 'quite good') of an Allied victory, and the restoration of France would then be much less likely. Germany could not go on

---

[1] For this earlier message, see above, p. 264 and below, pp. 346–7.

[2] Washington time.

(a) C7263, 7541/65/17.   (b) C7263/65/17.   (c) C7294/65/17.   (d) C7294/65/17.

fighting on all fronts for ever. As long as Great Britain, France and the United States controlled the oceans, the blockade would eventually be effectual. The French Ambassador said that this argument was cold comfort for France at a time when she was confronted by a terrible decision and wanted immediate aid and a real prospect of victory.

Lord Lothian said to Mr. Roosevelt that, while the case of France was most urgent, that of Great Britain might soon be analogous. Great Britain would fight desperately, but the ultimate decision about peace and the destiny of the British fleet, like that of France, might depend on the possibility, for either country, of seeing 'light at the end of the tunnel'; in other words, the issue was 'whether by the time when the decision was necessary, the United States had thrown its heart and soul into the business of resisting Hitler's aggression or not'. If 'Yes', the chances of eventual victory were quite good; otherwise they were very poor. 'What were the chances of the United States being at war with Hitler before these final and critical decisions had to be made?'

The President said that no one could answer the question, since the answer depended on the movement of American opinion, and, even more, 'on whether before that time the Dictators had taken some action which compelled the United States to go to war in self-defence'. The President implied that he believed this latter would be the case as far as Great Britain was concerned, but again the answer could be only conjectured. Lord Lothian then said that he hoped that the United States would now realise the possibilities. If Great Britain were overrun, and the United States were not in the war, and if Hitler 'threatened torture' unless the British fleet were surrendered, the British fleet would sink itself either at sea or in a hopeless attack on Germany. If, on the other hand, the United States were in the war, France, Belgium, the Netherlands and Great Britain might be willing to submit to a period of violent repression by Germany in the hope of ultimate victory. Congress had therefore to decide whether it could grapple with this issue in time or drift to disaster.

Lord Lothian's impression was that the United States Government realised that it could do nothing beyond sending supplies as quickly as possible to help France and Great Britain at the moment; on the other hand it had not yet 'faced the fact that the only way in which it can save itself from being confronted by totalitarian navies and air forces three or four times as powerful as its own in the near future is by setting the situation in all its stark brutality in front of Congress without delay and inviting it to go to war with all its resources in the hope of saving Britain and France while there is still time'.

(v)

M. Reynaud's second appeal to the British Government for the release of the French Government from their engagement: proposed meeting between the Prime Minister and M. Reynaud: meeting of the War Cabinet on the morning of June 16: instructions to Sir R. Campbell to inform M. Reynaud of the conditional assent of the British Government to the French request.

(a) Between 11.50 p.m. and 12.50 a.m. on the night of June 15–16 Sir R. Campbell was able to telephone directly to London. The conversation had to be conducted in veiled language owing to the danger of tapping. Sir R. Campbell said that the question put by M. Reynaud at his last meeting with the Prime Minister had now been put again in a 'brutal form' since the reply received from the United States was unsatisfactory. Lord Halifax, to whom this message was repeated, instructed Sir R. Campbell to resist the French proposal as strongly as possible on the lines suggested in the telegram sent to him at 2.45 p.m. on June 15. Sir R. Campbell should remind the French of the understanding on which the last conversation had ended, and should impress on them on no account to come to a final decision before a personal exchange of views had taken place with us. If these arguments failed, Sir R. Campbell should urge the French Government to follow the example of the Dutch and to leave France with him. They should not, however, in any circumstances, come to a decision hostile to the British Government before they left France.

(b) Sir R. Campbell said that he was sending by telephone three cyphered telegrams. The first of these telegrams reached the Foreign Office at 1.5 a.m. on June 16. The telegram stated that it would be followed by another telegram with a message from M. Reynaud to the Prime Minister. M. Reynaud asked 'insistently' for an answer early in the morning of June 16. A third telegram would give Sir R. Campbell's own observations, but would in no way affect the sense of M. Reynaud's message. This message represented a formal decision taken after a meeting presided over by the President of the Republic.

Sir R. Campbell's second telegram arrived at 1.20 a.m. M. Reynaud's message was as follows:

'1. The Council of Ministers at their meeting this afternoon held that the departure of the Government from France, thus abandoning the French people at a moment when the enemy is about to occupy whole of national territory and to impose cruel privations and sufferings, might give rise to a violent reaction on the part of public opinion if it is not established that peace conditions imposed by Herr Hitler and Signor Mussolini were unacceptable as being contrary to honourable and vital interests of France.

(a) C7263/65/17. (b) C7263/65/17.

2. The Council does not doubt that these conditions would in effect be unacceptable but considers it indispensable that this should be proved beyond doubt, in default of which Government would break up, a large number of its members refusing to leave the soil of France.

3. In order to learn German and Italian conditions the Council decided to seek the British Government's authorisation to enquire through United States Government what armistice conditions would be offered to France by German and Italian Governments.

4. If British Government authorises French Government to take this step the President of the Council is authorised to declare to British Government that surrender of French fleet to Germany would be considered an unacceptable condition.

5. In the event of British Government withholding its consent to this step, it seems probable in the light of opinions expressed at today's Cabinet meeting that the President of the Council would have no alternative but to resign.

6. The President of the Council has just received answer[1] of President Roosevelt who declares himself unable to give Allies the military help asked of him.

7. At meeting held in Tours last Thursday it was agreed at your suggestion that question of authorising a request for an armistice would be reconsidered if President Roosevelt's reply was negative. This eventuality having materialised the question must now be put afresh.'

At 2 a.m. Sir R. Campbell again telephoned to London. He asked (a) whether he could assume that a further personal exchange of views between the two Governments would be practicable. On being told that an exchange could probably be arranged he suggested that a meeting place 'farther north in France' might be convenient, but that he could not say whether the plan was practicable. He telephoned again at 3.40 a.m. that he would give the message from Lord Halifax to M. Reynaud at the earliest possible hour at which he could see him; he would also take up the question of a meeting.

The Foreign Office received Sir R. Campbell's third telegram at (b) 4 a.m. Sir R. Campbell reported M. Reynaud's explanation that, according to a majority of Ministers, the French Government would be regarded as having run away, and would therefore lose authority, if they moved overseas without having previously ascertained that the armistice terms were unacceptable. M. Reynaud seemed to have put up a good fight, but to have been overwhelmed by numbers. He had made it clear that, if the British Government refused to authorise the French Government to enquire about the German terms, he would resign, since in no circumstances would he repudiate a document which he had signed. In this event he could not guarantee that

---

[1] The exact time at which this message was received is not clear from Sir R. Campbell's reports. It had not been received at 4 p.m.

(a) C7263/65/17. (b) C7263/65/17.

his successor would maintain the decision that the surrender of the fleet would be an unacceptable condition of an armistice.

Sir R. Campbell and General Spears had argued that the German terms, whatever they might be, would be broken as soon as it might suit Germany to reduce France to vassalage, and that the fate of the French people would be the same (or worse) after surrender as it would be if they did not surrender. M. Reynaud said that he had used this argument again and again, but had not convinced his colleagues. General Weygand had exercised great pressure, and had said that the French army might break up at any moment.

M. Reynaud pointed out to Sir R. Campbell that the German armoured divisions might very soon reach Bordeaux. The removal of the Government would then be impossible. Hence he asked for an answer in terms of 'yes' or 'no' from the British Government on June 16 and, if possible, by telephone.

Sir R. Campbell reported that M. Mandel had given a different account of the meeting of Ministers. M. Mandel said that a majority had not been in favour of asking for an armistice, but that, faced with the actual crisis, the majority had favoured a compromise in the form of the solution finally recommended. M. Mandel 'emphatically' recommended the British Government to point out that Poland, Norway and the Netherlands did not give up the struggle in similar circumstances, and that we expected no less determination from France. M. Mandel said that condonation of a request for an armistice would result in abject surrender. Finally Sir R. Campbell reported that, according to several sources, Admiral Darlan had said that in no circumstances would the French navy submit to surrender.

(a)   At 11 a.m. on June 16 Sir R. Campbell telephoned that M. Reynaud welcomed the idea of a meeting and suggested Nantes as a place. Sir R. Campbell was told that the War Cabinet was in session and that he would be given an answer to M. Reynaud's request as soon as possible and that the question of a meeting would be con-

(b) sidered later. Sir R. Campbell telegraphed again at 11.50 a.m. that M. Reynaud could leave Bordeaux for Nantes at 1 p.m.

(c)   The War Cabinet met at 10.15 a.m. on June 16 to consider M. Reynaud's request. The Prime Minister explained that the issue was plain. The French Government were insisting that before they left French soil they must at least find out what the enemy's terms for an armistice would be. This seemed to imply that, if the terms were too harsh, the French Government might be willing to carry on the struggle from outside France. We now had to decide whether we should release them from their obligations to us not to enter into any discussion of terms. The question of their acceptance or refusal of such terms would arise later when the terms themselves were known.

(a) C7263/65/17.   (b) C7263/65/17.   (c) WM(40)168.1, C.A.

The War Cabinet agreed to send a short message stating our readiness to release the French Government from their engagement to the limited extent necessary for an enquiry about the German terms, but only on condition that the French fleet was immediately ordered to a British harbour. The main argument used in the War Cabinet for acquiescence in the French request was that, if we sent a refusal, M. Reynaud's Government would resign, and would be succeeded by a Government which might not keep the fleet out of German hands.

During the discussion it was suggested that, if the French Government invited President Roosevelt to act as intermediary for them, they might find it easier to save their fleet. The Prime Minister, however, pointed out the danger that Mr. Roosevelt might give advice which was applicable to Great Britain as well as to France. He might, for example, appeal to the belligerents to call the war off. At the present juncture all thoughts of coming to terms with the enemy must be dismissed as far as Great Britain was concerned. The War Cabinet therefore decided to put the question in a negative form, i.e. express to the President a hope that, if he were asked by the French Government to act as an intermediary, he would say to them that he could not do so unless he were assured that the French fleet had been moved to British ports. The President agreed on the night of June (a) 16–17 to speak in this sense if he were asked to act as intermediary.[1]

The reply[2] to M. Reynaud's message asking for the release of (b) France from her engagement was sent to Sir R. Campbell at 12.35 p.m. on June 16 in the following terms:

'You should deliver the following message which has been approved by the Cabinet to M. Reynaud.

Our agreement forbidding separate negotiations, whether for armistice or peace, was made with the French Republic and not with any particular French administration or statesman. It therefore involves the honour of France. Nevertheless provided, but only provided, that the French Fleet is sailed forthwith for British harbours pending negotiations, His Majesty's Government give their full consent to enquiry by the French Government to ascertain the terms of an armistice for France. His Majesty's Government, being resolved to continue the war, wholly exclude themselves from all part in the above-mentioned enquiry concerning an armistice.'

At 3.10 p.m. a second message[3] was sent to Sir R. Campbell as (c) follows:

---

[1] See also below, p. 348. Lord Lothian did not see the President until after the news of M. Reynaud's resignation had reached Washington.

[2] Telegram No. 368. Mr. Hopkinson informed Sir R. Campbell by telephone at 11.50 a.m. that this reply was on its way.

[3] Telegram No. 369.

(a) C7263, 7294/65/17. (b) C7263/65/17. (c) C7263/65/17.

'You should, in continuation of my message contained in my telegram No. 368, inform M. Reynaud as follows:

We expect to be consulted as soon as any armistice terms are received. This is necessary not merely in virtue of Treaty forbidding separate peace or armistice but also in view of vital consequences of any armistice to ourselves, having regard especially to the fact that British troops are fighting with French army.

You should impress on French Government that in stipulating for removal of French Fleet to British ports we have in mind French interests as well as our own and are convinced that it will strengthen the hands of the French Government in any armistice discussions if they can show that the French Navy is out of reach of the German forces.

As regards the French Air Force we assume that every effort will be made to fly it to North Africa, unless indeed the French Government would prefer to send it to this country.

We count on the French Government doing all they can both before and during any armistice discussions to extricate the Polish, Belgian and Czech troops at present in France, and to send them to North Africa.

Arrangements are being made to receive Polish and Belgian Governments in this country.'

(vi)

Meeting of the War Cabinet in the afternoon of June 16: proposal by the British Government for an Anglo-French Declaration of Union[1]: resignation of M. Reynaud, June 16: formation of Marshal Pétain's Government: French enquiry about armistice terms.

(a)   At 3.10 p.m. a telegram was sent *en clair* to Sir R. Campbell telling him to ask M. Reynaud to delay action on the telegram (No. 368) of 12.35 p.m. until he had received a further and most important communication from the Prime Minister. This communication would arrive during the afternoon. At 4.45 p.m. Sir R. Campbell was instructed to suspend action on the telegram (No. 369) of 3.10 p.m. giving the continuation of the message of 12.35 p.m.

(b)   Sir R. Campbell was told at 8 p.m. on June 16 that he had been asked to suspend action on the instructions sent to him because, after consultation with General de Gaulle, the Prime Minister had decided to ask M. Reynaud to meet him on June 17 in Brittany in order to make a further attempt to dissuade the French Government from

---

[1] For an examination of the antecedents of this project and of the circumstances in which it was drawn up, see essay by M. Beloff in *Mélanges Pierre Renouvin. Etudes d'histoire des relations internationales* (Presses Universitaires de France, 1966).

(a) C7263/65/17. (b) C7294/65/17.

asking for an armistice. On General de Gaulle's advice, the Prime Minister intended to offer to join with M. Reynaud forthwith in a declaration announcing the immediate constitution of the closest Anglo-French union in all spheres in order to carry on the war. The proposed text of the joint declaration was being sent to Sir R. Campbell at once for submission to M. Reynaud. General de Gaulle had already telephoned the terms in outline to M. Reynaud. M. Reynaud had replied that such a declaration by the two Governments would make all the difference to the decision of the French Government with regard to an armistice. General de Gaulle was returning to Bordeaux during the evening with a copy of the text.

This telegram summarised a series of rapid decisions taken during the morning and afternoon of June 16.

At a meeting of the War Cabinet held at 3 p.m. the Prime Minister (a) recalled that at the conclusion of the previous day's meeting there had been some discussion on a proposal for the issue of a further declaration of closer union between the countries of France and Great Britain.[1] The Prime Minister had also seen General de Gaulle who had impressed on him that some very dramatic move was essential to give M. Reynaud the support necessary to keep his Government in the war. General de Gaulle had suggested that a proclamation of the indissoluble union of the French and British peoples would serve the purpose. General de Gaulle and M. Corbin had been concerned at the decision reached by the War Cabinet at their first (10.15 a.m.) meeting on June 16 and embodied in telegram No. 368. The Prime Minister had then heard that a new declaration had been drafted for consideration, and General de Gaulle had telephoned to M. Reynaud. The Prime Minister had therefore thought it desirable to suspend action for the moment on the earlier decision taken by the War Cabinet, and had sent a telegram to Sir R. Campbell to this effect.[2]

Lord Halifax said that, after the morning meeting of the War Cabinet, he had seen Sir R. Vansittart. He had previously asked Sir R. Vansittart to draft some dramatic announcement which might strengthen M. Reynaud's hand. Sir R. Vansittart had been in consultation with General de Gaulle, M. Monnet and M. Pleven and, with them, had drafted a declaration. General de Gaulle had insisted upon the need for publishing the document as quickly as

---

[1] Mr. Chamberlain had brought to the attention of the War Cabinet on the morning of June 15 a memorandum which had been shown to him and other Ministers proposing some dramatic expression of Anglo-French unity. Mr. Chamberlain said that the form of (b) unity proposed—joint Parliaments and a joint Cabinet—did not seem to have been very fully thought out, and that he was doubtful about the proposal. The War Cabinet inclined to think that frequent meetings of the Supreme War Council, if the French Government came to Great Britain, would provide adequate machinery for very close co-operation. Sir A. Cadogan was also doubtful about the feasibility of the proposals in the memorandum. (Sir A. Cadogan was out of London from the afternoon of June 15 until after the War Cabinet meeting at 3 p.m. on June 16.)

[2] This telegram was actually despatched at 3.10 p.m. See above, p. 276.

(a) WM(40)169. (b) WM(40)167.6, C.A.

possible, and had proposed to take the draft back with him to France during the night of June 16–17.

The War Cabinet then considered the draft declaration. The draft was in the following terms:

'At the most fateful moment in the history of the modern world, the Governments of the United Kingdom and of the French Republic desire to make this declaration of indissoluble union and unyielding resolution in defence of liberty and freedom against subjection to a system which reduces mankind to a life of robots and slaves.

The two Governments declare that France and Great Britain shall no longer be two nations but one.

There will thus be created a Franco-British Union.

Every citizen of France will enjoy immediately citizenship of Great Britain; every British subject will become a citizen of France.

The devastation of war, wherever it occurs, shall be the common responsibility of both countries and the resources of both shall be equally, and as one, applied to its restoration.

All customs are abolished between Britain and France.

There shall not be two currencies, but one.

During the war there shall be one single War Cabinet. It will govern from wherever it best can. The two Parliaments will unite. A constitution of the Union will be written providing for joint organs of defence and economic policies.

Britain is raising at once a new army of several million men, and the Union appeals to the United States to mobilise their industrial power to assist the prompt equipment of this new army.

All the forces of Britain and France, whether on land, sea or in the air, are placed under a supreme command.

This unity, this union, will concentrate the whole of its strength against the concentrated strength of the enemy, no matter where the battle may be.

And thus we shall conquer.'

In discussing the draft the War Cabinet recognised that such a proclamation raised some very large questions with which it was difficult to deal at such short notice. The various clauses were then discussed *seriatim*:

(i) Common Citizenship. The proposal for common citizenship was felt to be acceptable.

(ii) Restoration of War Damage. Both nations would be faced with similar problems after the Germans had turned their whole offensive power on to Great Britain, and there would therefore appear to be no objection to common responsibility and pooling of resources.

(iii) Customs and Currency. The abolition of customs would raise extremely difficult problems. Not only would the Ottawa agreements and other commercial treaties have to be taken into account, but tariffs were also a fundamental part of the economy of several Dominions. A fusion of the two currencies would not be a practical proposition, and the same result could be achieved by a stabilisation of the rate of exchange. It was agreed that it would be better to delete any specific reference to these matters in the proclamation.

(iv) System of Government. Although the proclamation might declare that there should be a single War Cabinet, it would be necessary to maintain the two existing Cabinets with a 'Super Cabinet'. The result would be very similar to present arrangements, but the use of the phrase 'War Cabinet' instead of 'Supreme War Council' would emphasise the closeness of the union. It would be impracticable for the two Parliaments to legislate as one body, but some arrangement for occasional joint sessions might be worked out. A written Constitution of the Union providing for joint organs of defence and economic policies could no doubt be drafted, and provided it was kept on very broad lines would seem to present no insuperable objection.

(v) The sentence about the raising of a new army was drafted in more general terms.

(vi) In existing circumstances the British would be predominant, especially at sea and in the air, in any 'unified command'.

After Liberal and Labour support had been given to the declaration, it was pointed out that, if the proposal were meant to cover the peace after the war, as well as the period of the war, it raised issues upon which an opinion could not be given at short notice, e.g. the constitutional difficulties would be very complex (including the position of the Crown), and would take a generation to solve. It seemed likely that the Dominions would assent to any decision taken by the Government of the United Kingdom, but that the proposal might provoke very grave criticism in Great Britain. The matter would be different, however, if it related merely to the war and the period immediately following it.

Lord Halifax thought we should be prepared to take some risks but that there was nothing in the document which raised really fundamental issues except the phrase that 'France and Great Britain shall no longer be two nations but one'.

The Prime Minister said that his first instinct had been against the idea, but in this grave crisis we must not let ourselves be accused of a lack of imagination. Some dramatic announcement was clearly necessary to keep the French going. The proposal could not be lightly brushed aside; he was encouraged to find such a body of opinion in the War Cabinet in favour of it.

At 3.55 p.m. news was received of an announcement on the French wireless that the Council of Ministers would meet at 5 p.m. to decide whether further resistance was possible, and of a telephone message to General de Gaulle from M. Reynaud that, if a favourable answer on the proposed proclamation of union were received by 5 p.m., M. Reynaud felt that he could hold the position.

The War Cabinet then discussed in detail several amendments to the draft proclamation. After further discussion, the War Cabinet reached the conclusion that the draft as amended did not present any insuperable difficulties, and that the right course was to proceed with the proposal, since it gave the resolute elements in France a chance to hold their own.

The War Cabinet therefore approved the draft as finally amended, and authorised its despatch by the hand of General de Gaulle to M. Reynaud.

They also authorised a message to be sent by telephone to M. Reynaud informing him of the draft in time for the meeting of the Council of Ministers at 5 p.m., and invited the Prime Minister, Mr. Attlee and Sir A. Sinclair to meet M. Reynaud at the earliest possible moment to discuss the draft Proclamation and related questions.

The final text of the draft declaration was as follows:

(a)
THE DECLARATION OF UNION

'At this most fateful moment in the history of the modern world, the Governments of the United Kingdom and the French Republic make this declaration of indissoluble union and unyielding resolution in their common defence of justice and freedom, against subjection to a system which reduces mankind to a life of robots and slaves.

The two Governments declare that France and Great Britain shall no longer be two nations but one Franco-British Union.

The constitution of the Union will provide for joint organs of defence, foreign, financial and economic policies.

Every citizen of France will enjoy immediately citizenship of Great Britain, every British subject will become a citizen of France.

Both countries will share responsibility for the repair of the devastation of war, wherever it occurs in their territories, and the resources of both shall be equally, and as one, applied to that purpose.

During the war there shall be a single War Cabinet, and all the forces of Britain and France, whether on land, sea or in the air, will be placed under its direction. It will govern from wherever it best can. The two Parliaments will be formally associated.

The Nations of the British Empire are already forming new armies. France will keep her available forces in the field, on the sea, and in the air. The Union appeals to the United States to fortify the economic resources of the Allies, and to bring her powerful material aid to the common cause.

The Union will concentrate its whole energy against the power of the enemy no matter where the battle may be.

And thus we shall conquer.'

(a) C7294/65/17.

General de Gaulle's message reached M. Reynaud while he was discussing the earlier messages (i.e. telegrams 368 and 369) with Sir (a) R. Campbell and General Spears. Sir R. Campbell reported as follows on this discussion:

'We delivered the messages. M. Reynaud who was in dejected mood as he had this morning with difficulty induced Marshal Pétain to return his written resignation to his pocket, did not take them well and at once remarked that withdrawal of French Mediterranean fleet to British ports would invite immediate seizure of Tunis by Italy as well as create difficulties for British fleet.

2. He had got no further than this when Prime Minister's message telephoned by General de Gaulle came through. It acted like a tonic on M. Reynaud who said that for a document like that he would fight to the last. We were joined for a moment by M. Mandel and M. Marin who obviously were equally relieved.

3. M. Reynaud then left with a light step to read the document to the President of the Republic.

4. Immediately after he had gone we were able to send a messenger after him to say that the two earlier messages should be considered as cancelled.[1]

5. M. Reynaud is much worried by Marshal Pétain's attitude from point of view of public opinion. We suggested as public at large would not know of his resignation if accepted, there being no longer any newspapers, it could not have very serious consequences. M. Reynaud took the point.'

In view of M. Reynaud's reception of the proposal telephoned to him by General de Gaulle, the Prime Minister made preparations for (b) a meeting in Brittany on June 17. Sir R. Campbell was instructed at 6.45 p.m. that the Prime Minister, Mr. Attlee, the Secretary of State for Air, and the three Chiefs of Staff would arrive at Concarneau in a cruiser at noon on June 17. General de Gaulle thought the time and place would suit M. Reynaud, and the Prime Minister suggested that the meeting should be held on board ship.

The Prime Minister had already gone to the train for the port of embarkation when Sir R. Campbell reported (10.10 p.m.) that a (c) ministerial crisis had opened, and that the President of the Republic was consulting the Presidents of the Senate and the Chamber. Sir R. Campbell hoped to have news by midnight. Meanwhile the meeting arranged for June 17 could not be held. Shortly afterwards Sir R. Campbell telephoned the news of M. Reynaud's resignation and at 11.30 p.m. a French wireless announcement stated that the Cabinet had resigned, and that Marshal Pétain had been asked to form a new

---

[1] The instructions sent to Sir R. Campbell used the words 'delay' and 'suspend', not 'cancel'.

(a) C7294/65/17. (b) C7294/65/17. (c) C7294/65/17.

administration in which General Weygand would be Vice-President of the Council.

(a)   After the Cabinet meeting at which he resigned, M. Reynaud saw Sir R. Campbell and General Spears. Sir R. Campbell's report of the course of events was received at 4.5 a.m. on June 17. Although M. Reynaud had been much heartened during the afternoon by the Prime Minister's message (i.e. about the proposed joint declaration), he told Sir R. Campbell later that the forces in favour of ascertaining the terms of an armistice had become too strong for him. He had read the Prime Minister's message twice to the Council of Ministers. He had explained to them the importance of the message, and the hope which it held out for the future, but he had not persuaded them. Sir R. Campbell and General Spears attempted for half an hour to encourage M. Reynaud to try to get rid of the evil influences among his colleagues. They then saw M. Mandel for a moment before calling— for the second time during the day—on the President of the Senate, in the hope that he might be able to persuade M. Lebrun to insist that M. Reynaud should form a new administration. They begged M. Jeanneney to make it clear to M. Lebrun that the Prime Minister's offer could not be extended to a Government which entered into negotiations with the enemy.

An hour or so later M. Reynaud told Sir R. Campbell and General Spears that he was beaten, and that he had handed in his resignation. Marshal Pétain and General Weygand were 'living in another world, and imagined that they could sit round a green table discussing armistice terms in the old manner', but their combination had been 'too much for the weaker members of the Cabinet upon whom they had worked by waving the spectre of revolution'.

M. Reynaud had not told the Council of Ministers of the two earlier messages of June 16;[1] he had said that he asssumed that the Council would still consider the surrender of the fleet—a stab in the back of a loyal Ally—an unacceptable condition. To this statement there had been general assent.

The first act of the new French Cabinet[2] was to ask, through the Spanish Government, for the terms under which Germany would agree to an armistice. Sir R. Campbell was told of this decision by M. Baudouin at 1 a.m. on June 17. He reported the interview as (b)   follows at 4.40 a.m.:—

---

[1] It should be noted that the Council of Ministers had thus not received any formal release from His Majesty's Government from their agreement not to negotiate an armistice except by mutual agreement

[2] The leading members of Marshal Pétain's Government were M. Chautemps (Vice-President of the Council), General Weygand (Defence), General Colson (War), Admiral Darlan (Marine), General Pujot (Air), and M. Baudouin (Foreign Affairs).

    (a) C7294/65/17. (b) C7294/65/17.

'M. Baudouin, Minister for Foreign Affairs of new Government, sent for me at 1.0 a.m. this morning. He asserted that decision to ask for armistice conditions had been inspired solely by the fact that French armies surrounded and broken up were no longer able to stand up to enemy. France was militarily beaten and it was only the matter of very few days before German armies would have become masters of the whole country. General Weygand had been warning Government for several days that he could no longer guarantee that men would not turn on their officers. Sufferings also of civilian population, many of whom had been stranded on the roads starving and destitute, were appalling. No Government could have left France at this moment [? under] appearance of abandoning people to their fate. The new Government had therefore felt compelled to ask through Spanish Government (this choice being due to Marshal Pétain's friendship with General Franco) for cessation of hostilities and to be informed on what conditions armistice would be granted. If conditions were such that their acceptance would be a stain on the honour of France they would be refused. But people would then know that their sufferings could not have been avoided. Among such conditions most dishonouring would be surrender of the fleet and he was authorised to give me Government's [? formal] assurance that although they expected this to be one of the conditions it would in no circumstances be accepted. The appointment of Admiral Darlan as Minister of Marine should afford His Majesty's Government additional guarantee if it were needed. The change of Government, continued M. Baudouin, implied no change of heart towards their Ally. The generous words spoken by the Prime Minister at Tours encouraged them to hope that although His Majesty's Government could not approve of the French Government's action they would at least understand it.

Whenever M. Baudouin repeated the assurance about the fleet, which he did several times, I said that I took formal note of his words on behalf of my Government. Apart from expressing great distress that a French Government should have gone back on the signature of an agreement expressly designed to prevent such a thing happening (whichever of the two Allies had first been afflicted), I thought it well to restrain myself from indulging in any severe recrimination such as might create an impression that His Majesty's Government will henceforward wash their hands of France, and thereby give any who would be ready to grasp at it the shameless pretext to the claim that the Government was released from its understanding about the fleet to which it is essential to hold them.

I will see Marshal Pétain as soon as possible and will appeal to him as a soldier to accept no armistice terms such as which [? will] jeopardize[1] . . .'

Sir R. Campbell sent two other messages with this report. He said that the new French Government did not intend to make any pro- (a)

---

[1] The text of the last words of the telegram is uncertain.

(a) C7294/65/17.

nouncement until midday, when Marshal Pétain would broadcast to the French people, and that he (Sir R. Campbell) had seen Admiral Darlan a few hours earlier, and had said a few words 'intended to provoke some personal assurance' about the fleet. Armiral Darlan had answered at once :'So long as I can issue orders to [the fleet], you have nothing to fear'.

Note to Chapter IX. The Anglo-French declaration not to conclude a separate armistice or peace treaty.

This declaration arose out of a wish on the British side to counter German propaganda aimed at dividing Great Britain and France. One possible way of meeting such propaganda was by means of a joint Anglo-French declaration that neither country would make a separate peace with Germany. A declaration of this kind, however, implied a previous agreement upon war aims.

On their side the French Government regarded an agreement on war aims as desirable, since they were afraid that British opinion might not allow the British Government to go far enough to satisfy French demands for material guarantees against the possibility of a renewal of German aggression. French nervousness on this point was not lessened by the concentration of British propaganda against Hitler and National Socialism, and the consequent tendency to assume that, if National Socialism and its leaders were removed, Germany would cease to be a potential danger to European peace.

(a)   On October 23, 1939, the French Ambassador gave Lord Halifax a memorandum suggesting a discussion of war aims. The memorandum proposed that, in addition to securing reparation for German aggression and violation of rights, the Allies should render it impossible for Germany again to disturb the peace of Europe. A change of government at Berlin was not sufficient, since we could not depend upon German goodwill. Our principal war aim should therefore be the creation of effective material guarantees. It might be useful for tactical purposes—i.e. in order to hasten the disaffection of the German people—to name Hitler as the principal obstacle to the re-establishment of peace, but we should take care to avoid defining our objections in such a way as to put all the Germans behind Hitler. Hence M. Daladier wanted a careful study of the whole question, and, in the first place, a study of the necessary guarantees. M. Daladier thought that at first this study should be carried out by exchange of correspondence. The British Government therefore replied by a memorandum of their own. Their reply could not be given at once because they had to consult the Governments of the Dominions. A final draft of the

(b)   reply was approved by the War Cabinet on December 20 in the following terms:—

'Before receiving the memorandum of the French Government, His Majesty's Government had already given some preliminary consideration to the question of war aims. They had been prompted to

---

(a) C17105/13669/62.   (b) WM(39)120, C20801/13669/62; WP(G)(39)150, C20438/13669/62.

consider this matter not only in order that some guidance might be given at a suitable opportunity to certain sections of British public opinion, but in order that the cause in whose defence His Majesty's Government stood united with the French Government might gain a wider and more intelligent support.

2. The cause for which the Allied Governments of France and Great Britain have taken up arms is to stop acts of aggression on the part of the German Government in the present and to ensure against their repetition in the future. Two wars imposed on Britain and France in a single generation by the action of German Governments, differing in outward complexion but inspired by the same aggressive and dominating spirit, are a solemn warning that this spirit, if it be not extinguished and laid to rest by the Germans themselves, must be rendered harmless by those whom it threatens.

3. His Majesty's Government are therefore in agreement with the French Government in desiring to find the surest and most enduring guarantees against any further repetition of German aggression. They are convinced that such guarantees can only be based on close and continued co-operation between the French Government and His Majesty's Government during the period which will follow after the defeat of Germany. That co-operation, which during the war will have covered economic as well as military and political problems, should be extended after the war had ended, and should, as His Majesty's Government would hope, be inspired by a common purpose and outlook on the machinery required to enable the nations of Europe to regain or maintain their liberties, and to strengthen their political, social, and economic structures.

4. To achieve this common purpose His Majesty's Government and the French Government must, unless a German Government can be found which is willing and able voluntarily to accept their terms, secure the defeat of Germany, and this, in the opinion of His Majesty's Government, constitutes the primary war aim of the two Governments. It is only in the light of the circumstances prevailing at the time when their object is achieved that the lines of any territorial settlement can be profitably considered. It would therefore be premature to enter into detailed discussion of territorial questions. For this reason His Majesty's Government have been careful not to define in precise terms what they imply by the restoration of independence to Poland and Czechoslovakia, and to limit themselves to referring in general terms to the recovery by the Polish, Czech and Slovak peoples of their liberties. His Majesty's Government trust that the French Government will adopt a similar attitude. It should, however, be pointed out that while it is hoped to secure independence for all European peoples, one of the weaknesses of the post-war settlement was the establishment of a number of small national States which were "viable" neither in the military nor economic sense. The settlement was therefore highly unstable, and proved an ineffective barrier to the expansionist ambitions of Great Powers either in the West or in the East. Accordingly, it may be necessary to contemplate

some form of closer association, at the least a system of financial and economic co-operation in Central and South-Eastern Europe.

5. For this purpose His Majesty's Government suggest that it would be wise to encourage at once closer co-operation between the Balkan States and closer co-operation between the various refugee groups of Poles, Czechs, Slovaks and Austrians.

6. As regards the future of the German Reich, His Majesty's Government agree that the removal of Herr Hitler and his entourage will not of itself be a sufficient remedy against the re-emergence of German militarist and expansionist ideas, but it is not at present possible to tell in what conditions the defeat or surrender of Germany will take place, and any suggestion that it was the intention of His Majesty's Government and the French Government to seek the political dismemberment of Germany or to disrupt German unity, whatever arguments might be adduced on one side or the other in any discussion on these matters, would have the immediate effect of rallying the German people behind their present leaders. His Majesty's Government therefore consider it wiser to watch the course of events and to arrange for further consultation as soon as it is possible more closely to forecast the course of internal political developments in Germany.

7. As regards material guarantees, the first must evidently be that Germany shall never again be allowed to build up a preponderance of armed force to menace the peace of European nations and of the world. The methods of establishing this guarantee may perhaps be left for further consideration and in view of what has been said above it would seem premature to make any public statement of war aims in precise terms. His Majesty's Government would prefer that the two Governments in agreement should limit their public declarations to the general principles on which their common policy is, and will continue to be, based, and that, while protecting the world, so far as is humanly possible, from a recurrence of war, they should emphasise their common desire to secure a post-war settlement, which would be satisfactory not only to themselves but to all other peoples whose collaboration will be essential in the work of reconstruction.

8. These are the preliminary comments of His Majesty's Government on the approach made by the French Government. His Majesty's Government will welcome a further exchange of views with the French Government, and will be glad to consider any proposals which the French Government have to make both in regard to the terms on which peace should be concluded with Germany, and the wider European settlement which might follow the termination of hostilities.'

(a) This memorandum was given to M. Corbin on December 22. Meanwhile Mr. Chamberlain raised the question of a 'no separate peace'
(b) declaration at the third meeting of the Supreme War Council (December

---

(a) C316/7/62 (1940).   (b) C941/9/17 (1940).

19). M. Daladier agreed upon the importance of countering German propaganda but repeated his view that the form of the declaration would need careful study, since it involved the problem of Allied peace terms. French opinion did not want 'illusory solutions' such as the dismemberment of Germany, but the removal of Hitler would not be sufficient. In M. Daladier's view, no guarantee could replace a strategic and military (but not a territorial) frontier on the left bank of the Rhine.

Mr. Chamberlain said that His Majesty's Government also wanted lasting guarantees. He then referred to the British memorandum which would be communicated to the French Government, and might serve as a basis of discussion.

After the meeting of the Supreme War Council the text of a draft declaration was prepared in the Foreign Office. This text, which was (a) limited to an agreement not to conclude a separate peace, was shown to the Dominion Governments and to the Government of India. From the replies received it became clear that it would not be possible to associate all the Dominions with the declaration. Hence it was desirable that the declaration should be made only by the Governments of the United Kingdom and of France. This course was also open to some objection, since it might lead to questions about the attitude of the Dominions and might give an opening to German propaganda.

Sir R. Campbell therefore explained the position to the French Government and asked whether they would like to drop the proposal or to accept a declaration with the United Kingdom alone. The French Foreign Office were strongly in favour of the latter plan. It was then suggested that the declaration would have a greater effect if it included a reference to economic and military co-operation after the war. An addition in this sense would also help to avoid the difficulty about leaving out the Dominions. The Dominions were not parties to the Anglo-French Financial Agreement or to the economic arrangements in force between the two countries. Hence it would appear logical that a declaration covering financial and economic co-operation should be limited to the United Kingdom and France.

The Dominions agreed with this suggestion, and on March 26, 1940, the Foreign Office proposed that the French Government should be (b) invited to approve a text for publication. On the following day the War (c) Cabinet approved of a draft in the following terms:

> The two Governments 'being equally determined to carry on the war with the utmost vigour until the purposes for which it was undertaken are attained, mutually undertake that during the present war they will neither negotiate nor conclude an armistice or treaty of peace except by mutual agreement.
>
> The two Governments further declare their intention to continue the closest co-operation in their financial, economic and defence policy after the conclusion of peace.'

At the meeting of the Supreme War Council on March 28 Mr. Chamberlain referred to the draft declaration. He said that the declaration would (d)

(a) C20760/281/17; C1864, 3894, 3929, 4359, 4489/9/17 (1940); C2051, 2986/9/17. (b) C4616/9/17. (c) WM(40)76, C4621/9/17. (d) C5988/9/17.

have a good effect on public opinion, although the two Governments were not in need of it to ensure their close co-operation and mutual understanding. If the declaration not to conclude a separate peace were accompanied by an affirmation to continue co-operation in the fields of policy, finance, and defence after the conclusion of peace, a valuable feeling of security and continuity would be conveyed to all those who hoped for a new Europe on the ruins of the old.

M. Reynaud agreed with Mr. Chamberlain's proposal, and asked only that, as a matter of drafting, a formula might be found to cover the question of post-war security. M. Reynaud suggested a French text. Mr. Chamberlain accepted this text as an improvement on the British draft. The final text published on March 28 therefore read as follows:

> [The French and British Governments] 'mutually undertake that during the present war they will neither negotiate nor conclude an armistice or treaty of peace except by mutual agreement.
>
> They undertake not to discuss peace terms before reaching complete agreement on the conditions necessary to ensure to each of them an effective and lasting guarantee of their security.
>
> Finally, they undertake to maintain, after the conclusion of peace, a community of action in all spheres for so long as may be necessary to safeguard their security, and to effect the reconstruction, with the assistance of other nations, of an international order which will ensure the liberty of peoples, respect for law, and the maintenance of peace in Europe.'

CHAPTER X

The Franco-German Armistice: the recognition of General de Gaulle as the leader of 'Free Frenchmen'

(i)

The situation on June 17: the question of the French fleet: instructions to Sir R. Campbell and to Lord Lothian.

THE immediate concern of the War Cabinet, on hearing the news of Marshal Pétain's request to the Germans for the terms of an armistice, was the fate of the French fleet. The change of government could not affect the military situation to any appreciable extent in metropolitan France since the French armies were already broken beyond recovery. Even if, as still seemed possible, though unlikely, the new French Government were to continue resistance in North Africa or elsewhere, the burden of war would fall almost entirely upon Great Britain. From the British point of view, therefore, the importance of the French fleet could not be exaggerated. The importance of this fleet was indeed so very obvious that the Germans also would not overlook it. The Foreign Office had assumed that the Germans might be expected to refuse an armistice until the French fleet were in their hands; the only feasible plan for keeping the fleet out of German hands was to ensure either that it sailed to British (or American) ports or that it was scuttled.[1]

The actual demands made by the German Government appear to have taken the Foreign Office—and Sir R. Campbell—by surprise. The memoranda and notes of discussions in London and the instructions sent to Sir R. Campbell assumed a German demand for the surrender of the fleet. There was, however, a good reason why the

---

[1] The disposition and movements of the larger vessels of the French fleet were at this time as follows:

Brest: *Richelieu* (battleship near completion) left June 18, originally for Casablanca; arrived Dakar, June 23: *Courbet* (old battleship) arrived Plymouth, June 18.
St. Nazaire: *Jean Bart* (battleship, unfinished and without guns) left for Casablanca, June 19.
Cherbourg: *Paris* (old battleship) arrived Portsmouth, June 18.
Toulon: 4 8-inch gun cruisers, 4 6-inch gun cruisers.
Algiers: 3 8-inch gun cruisers, 4 6-inch gun cruisers.
Oran (and the adjacent naval port of Mers-el-Kebir): *Provence, Bretagne* (battleships), *Dunkerque, Strasbourg* (battle cruisers), 1 aircraft transport.
Alexandria: *Lorraine* (battleship), 3 8-inch gun cruisers, 1 light cruiser.
West Indies: *Béarn* (aircraft carrier), 2 light cruisers.
Far East: 1 light cruiser.

Germans should hesitate to make this demand. A similar demand had been made to them in 1918. They had replied by scuttling their ships at the moment of surrender. They might well fear that the French would follow this precedent. In order to avoid such a risk the Germans adopted the method of allowing the French to keep nominal possession of a dismantled fleet in ports mainly within German and Italian reach. This offer allowed the French to claim, speciously, that they were keeping their pledge to Great Britain. It also left the Germans every chance of persuading or compelling the French later on to give them direct possession of the ships.[1]

On June 17 the decisions taken in London and the instructions sent to Sir R. Campbell were based on the view that the British Government should attempt to get the fleet away from metropolitan French ports or scuttled before the Germans asked for it.

(a)   Lord Halifax reported to the War Cabinet at 11 a.m. on June 17 the constitution of the new French Government. He pointed out that MM. Flandin, Laval[2] and Bonnet were not among the Ministers. He also mentioned Admiral Darlan's statement to Sir R. Campbell about the fleet. Lord Halifax explained that M. Reynaud had received the message giving the terms under which the British Government would release the French Government from their engagement not to ask separately for an armistice but that, as he had been told to suspend action on this message,[3] it was uncertain whether he had shown it to other Ministers. Sir R. Campbell had therefore been instructed to give the message to Marshal Pétain.

(b)   These instructions were sent to Sir R. Campbell at 11 a.m. He was told to tell the new French Government (if he had not already done so) of telegram No. 368 and to make the communication in telegram No. 369.[4] Two hours later Sir R. Campbell received further instruc-

(c)   tions[5] that a 'necessary pre-condition' of our assent to the French application for an armistice had been that the French fleet should sail to British ports. It appeared from Sir R. Campbell's telegram[6] of 4.40 a.m. that the French Government had now asked for an armistice, but there was no news that the fleet had sailed. In these

---

[1] According to Ciano (*Diary*, pp. 266–7), Mussolini wanted the surrender of the French fleet. Hitler told Ciano four days after the fighting at Oran (see below, pp. 403–4) how fortunate it was that he and Mussolini had not insisted on the surrender of the French fleet: 'one would never get the French fleet that way', whereas owing to their [the Axis] intelligent handling of the matter, England and France had been made mutual enemies. (*D.G.F.P.*, X, No. 129.)

[2] Laval had refused to join the Ministry unless he was given the office of Minister of Foreign Affairs. On June 23 he came in as Minister of State, and Vice-President of the Council.

[3] i.e. in view of the later offer of an Anglo-French union.

[4] See above, pp. 275–6.

[5] At the Prime Minister's suggestion the War Cabinet had authorised the despatch of these further instructions in order to ensure that Marshal Pétain and his Government should be absolutely clear about the British position.

[6] See above, p. 283.

(a) WM(40)170, C7301/65/17. (b) C7294/65/17. (c) C7294/65/17.

circumstances 'the French Government must understand that the vital condition on which the assent of His Majesty's Government was given has not been fulfilled'. Sir R. Campbell was therefore instructed not to cease from urging the French Government, if they persisted in seeking an armistice, to sail the fleet at once.

This telegram crossed a message from Sir R. Campbell (received at (a) 4 p.m.) that during the morning the French Government had asked the Nuncio to transmit to the Italian Government through the Vatican an intimation of their desire to seek the basis of a lasting peace.[1] M. Baudouin had told Sir R. Campbell that he had no doubt that the terms offered in response to this approach to the Italian Government would be wholly unacceptable.

Shortly afterwards (4.25 p.m.) a telegram was received by wireless (b) from Sir R. Campbell that he had seen Marshal Pétain immediately before a meeting of the Council of Ministers. He had told the Marshal that he came to him not only as President of the Council but as a soldier upon whom he (Sir R. Campbell) could count to do everything possible not to make the situation of an Ally worse than it was. Sir R. Campbell had gladly received Marshal Pétain's solemn assurance that in no circumstances would the fleet be handed over to the Germans, but had insisted it was 'absolutely essential' that, when the Germans asked for it, the fleet should be in British control and no longer at the disposal of the French Government. Otherwise we and the French would be in an intolerable position. From our point of view this action with regard to the fleet was the least that we could expect. Marshal Pétain said that his own idea was that the fleet should be scuttled.

Sir R. Campbell also raised the question of the French ports. These ports must not be handed over intact to the Germans. Marshal Pétain said that unfortunately the Germans would soon be able to take them at will, but that he would see that they were made unusable.

Sir R. Campbell then asked Marshal Pétain whether the French Government would go to North Africa if, as he presumed, the German terms were unacceptable. Marshal Pétain said that he would stay in France, but he supposed that a small government might go overseas. Sir R. Campbell pointed out that this latter step was of vital importance since if offered the last hope of ensuring the future restoration of France. Sir R. Campbell reported that Marshal Pétain was most dispirited: that he was thinking mainly of the sufferings of the people, and that conversation with him was fruitless.

Meanwhile at noon Marshal Pétain had broadcast an announce-

---

[1] Mr. Makins commented on this telegram: 'I do not understand how this fits in with the initiative through the glorious General Franco. The French can hardly expect to get one set of terms from Italy and another set from Germany.'

(a) C7301/65/17. (b) C7301/65/17.

ment[1] that he had assumed direction of the government and had applied 'to our opponent to ask him if he is ready to sign with us, as between soldiers after the fight, and in honour, a means to put an end
(a) to hostilities'. At 5.45 p.m. Sir R. Campbell was instructed that he had been authorised in telegram No. 368 to tell M. Reynaud that we would not object to an enquiry by the French Government about German peace-terms 'on the strict and explicit condition' that the French fleet 'was out of harm's way' before the enquiry was made. We had now heard from Marshal Pétain's broadcast that he had already entered into pourparlers with the enemy.[2] We had taken it for granted that Marshal Pétain would wish to be scrupulous on any point of honour, but we did not yet know that our express and vitally important stipulation had been fulfilled. It was unnecessary to remind Marshal Pétain that this agreement[3] had been concluded, not on behalf of any particular French Government, but on behalf of the French Republic. His Majesty's Government were sure that Marshal Pétain had already taken full account of this fact.

Sir R. Campbell was instructed to see Marshal Pétain at once, and to explain that the fundamental reason for our insistence upon the question of the fleet was that failure to implement our condition 'would compromise the successful continuance of the struggle here— which we are determined to continue in any case and at any cost— and on which now depend the salvation and liberation of France'.

(b)   At 6.45 p.m. a telegram was received from Sir R. Campbell reporting that, according to M. Baudouin, the German terms had not arrived. Sir R. Campbell was insisting that we should be consulted before the terms were accepted, but he was doubtful whether the French would consult us. The new French Government had already broken their word by violating their agreement with us not to ask separately for an armistice; they were unlikely to hesitate before a second violation.

(c)   At 8.10 p.m. the Foreign Office received a telegram by wireless which seems to have been drafted before 6.45 p.m. but to have been delayed in transmission. In this telegram Sir R. Campbell replied to the message of instructions sent to him at 11 a.m. He said that in all his conversations he had spoken 'in the terms contained in your telegrams 368 and 369' and about bringing the fleet within British

---

[1] Owing to the disorganisation of the French press, most Frenchmen heard the news of Marshal Pétain's action from this broadcast. Sir R. Campbell heard at this time that the French as well as the Germans were trying to 'jam' broadcasts in French from Great
(d) Britain. 'Jamming' interfered with Sir R. Campbell's own wireless communication with London.

[2] In this broadcast, which was reported to the War Cabinet before the end of their morning meeting, Marshal Pétain used the phrase: 'il faut cesser le combat'. In the version of the broadcast given to the forces the words used were 'il faut *tenter* cesser'.

[3] i.e. the agreement not to conclude a separate armistice or peace.

(a) C7301/65/17. (b) C7301/65/17. (c) C7301/65/17. (d) C7541/65/17.

control; the only answer given was that in no circumstances would the French Government surrender the fleet to Germany. The Naval Attaché had been told that the French Mediterranean fleet had been in action off the Italian coasts. He thought that the fighting spirit of the fleet was high; that senior officers considered that the men would refuse to abandon France and to become part of the British navy, but there were hints that the fleet would be scuttled as an alternative to surrender.

At 11.45 p.m. Sir R. Campbell telegraphed[1] that, in order to be (a) absolutely certain that no member of Marshal Pétain's Government was in doubt about the attitude of His Majesty's Government, he had asked the Secretary-General to bring, formally and in writing, the contents of telegrams 368 and 369—the messages of the previous day to M. Reynaud—before the notice of the Council of Ministers. The Secretary-General had promised to do this.

During the evening of June 17 Sir R. Campbell also saw M. Chautemps. M. Chautemps had led the movement for asking the (b) terms of an armistice on the ground that the Government could not leave France to carry on the war overseas until they had evidence that the German terms were dishonouring. He now told Sir R. Campbell that he and his supporters were as strongly determined as ever to reject dishonourable terms. He added that the new Government contained elements whose opinions he could not guarantee beyond all doubt. His own view was that the surrender of the fleet would be the most dishonourable of all conditions.

Sir R. Campbell said very forcibly to M. Chautemps that the British Government expected to be consulted before a reply was sent to the Germans and that they also expected the fleet to be sent forthwith to British waters. M. Chautemps agreed, but thought that there might be no time for consultation; on the question of the fleet he would say no more than that it would in no case be surrendered. Sir R. Campbell concluded his telegram by saying that M. Baudouin had given a formal undertaking to tell him when the German terms had been received.

During the night of June 17–18 the Prime Minister sent a personal message through Sir R. Campbell to Marshal Pétain and General (c) Weygand in the following terms:[2]

'I wish to repeat to you my profound conviction that the illustrious Marshal Pétain and the famous General Weygand, our comrades in

---

[1] This message was received at 2.10 a.m. on June 18.

[2] Earlier in the day Sir R. Vansittart had suggested a message to Marshal Pétain. Sir R. Vansittart's draft was shown to the Prime Minister who thought it better to send the (d) message in shorter terms. Sir A. Cadogan also thought it desirable to 'tone down' the message.

(a) C7301/65/17. (b) C7301/65/17. (c) C7301/65/17. (d) C7301/65/17.

two great wars against the Germans, will not injure their Ally by delivering over to the enemy the fine French fleet. Such an act would scarify their names for a thousand years of history. Yet this result may easily come by frittering away these few precious hours when the fleet can be sailed to safety in British or American ports carrying with it the hope and the future and the honour of France.'[1]

(a)   Sir R. Campbell was also instructed that the French Government seemed to assume that they could first ascertain the German terms and, if these terms were found to include a demand for the surrender of the fleet, decline them and retain control over the movements of the fleet. The terms, however, would be so framed that, unless the fleet were out of German control, the Germans would 'use it as a lever for extracting ultimate concessions'. The only means of avoiding this danger would be for the French Government to place the fleet where it would be beyond their power of reach. 'This necessarily means sending it to British ports forthwith. This step would not for a moment mean that the French fleet would be abandoning France. On the contrary, this is the only way in which the French navy can continue to serve France. There would further be no question of the fleet becoming part of the British navy. It would continue as hitherto on a basis of free co-operation.'[2]

Another message was sent to Sir R. Campbell at 2.40 a.m. on June 18 to the effect that we realised that, under stress of emotion, Marshal Pétain was contemplating a course which, in his opinion, would spare the French army and people from suffering. Nevertheless we remained convinced that Marshal Pétain was misguided in his choice. Did he think that he would obtain terms allowing a future independent existence for France, or that, if he were able to get such terms on paper, they would be observed by Hitler? Did he think that, by throwing himself on Hitler's 'mercy', he would be providing the French people with a better fate than by asking them to continue the struggle? The French Government would be confronted with terms such as France could not accept without adding shame to disaster. Other nations had been defeated, but had not capitulated. They sought refuge in Great Britain and their presence was yet another reason for continuing the struggle for their ultimate liberation. 'We invite the French Government to join with us here in England. They would not thereby be running away; they would be rejoining their friends and concentrating their forces.'

---

[1] Sir R. Campbell was instructed to give copies of this message to the President of the Republic and to Admiral Darlan. On the morning of June 17 M. Cambon had told Sir
(b) O. Sargent that the new French Government would 'behave worse than King Leopold' and that we ought not to put too much trust in Admiral Darlan.

[2] The First Sea Lord had asked the Prime Minister that a message in these terms should be sent to the French Government.

(a) C7301/65/17. (b) C7301/65/17.

The United States Government had also tried to persuade Marshal Pétain to send the French fleet out of German reach. At 1.30 p.m. on June 16 Lord Lothian had been instructed to tell President (a) Roosevelt of the Prime Minister's message to M. Reynaud about the conditional assent of the British Government to the French request for release from their obligations. Lord Lothian was also instructed to suggest that, if the President were asked by the French Government to act as an intermediary with the Germans, he should reply that he must first be assured that, in accordance with the British request, the French fleet had been moved to British ports. The Prime Minister also hoped that Mr. Roosevelt would make it clear, if necessary, to the Germans that the United States would not allow a demand for the surrender of the French fleet.

In view of the later proposal for Anglo-French union, Lord Lothian (b) was asked to suspend action on these instructions. He was given a short account of the new proposal, and repeated it during the evening (c) of June 16 to the President. Mr. Roosevelt had then heard of the resignation of M. Reynaud and the formation of a new government by (d) Marshal Pétain. He approved strongly of the Prime Minister's proposals to M. Reynaud and agreed that, if he were asked to act as intermediary, he would make the transfer of the French fleet to Great Britain a condition of his mediation.

During the night of June 17–18 Lord Lothian was sent further instructions. He was told that he would have realised from Marshal (e) Pétain's broadcast how fast things were moving. Lord Halifax hoped that Mr. Roosevelt would now put immediate pressure upon the French Government to send the fleet to British ports before the conclusion of an armistice. Marshal Pétain had acted in complete disregard of our stipulations; we could have no confidence in anything else he might do unless he were 'stiffened' to act in accordance with the principal condition upon which we had been willing to release the French from their obligation.

Lord Lothian replied that he had asked Mr. Roosevelt and Mr. (f) Hull during the afternoon to act as Lord Halifax had suggested. Mr. Roosevelt agreed to telegraph at once in the strongest terms to Marshal Pétain, and to point out that the surrender or sinking of the fleet would produce a deplorable effect on American opinion and greatly weaken the possibility of the eventual liberation of France. Mr. Roosevelt also said that he would send a private message to Admiral Darlan urging him to put the fleet at once under British control.

(a) C7263/65/17. (b) C7263/65/17. (c) C7294/65/17. (d) C7294/65/17. (e) C7301/65/17. (f) C7301/65/17.

(ii)

The situation on June 18–19: assurances from Marshal Pétain and Admiral Darlan about the fleet: visits of Mr. Alexander and Admiral Sir D. Pound and of Lord Lloyd to France.

(a)   On the morning of June 18 Sir R. Campbell telegraphed that he expected the Council of Ministers to take a 'satisfactory decision' about the fleet. At 1.50 p.m., however, he reported that this decision had not been ratified, but had been replaced by a unanimous decision to refuse terms involving the surrender of the fleet.

Shortly afterwards the Foreign Office received from Sir R. Camp-
(b) bell a more detailed account of the course of events.[1] On receiving the Prime Minister's message Marshal Pétain had said that he would be seeing General Weygand shortly before the meeting of the Council of
(c) Ministers and would repeat the message to him. General Weygand afterwards told Sir R. Campbell, in terms of great indignation, that he could not allow anyone to use such language to him. Marshal Pétain, however, had assured Sir R. Campbell that he need have no misgivings about the fleet. Sir R. Campbell answered that this assurance did not satisfy him, and that the decision which he had been constantly urging must be taken within the next few hours. M. Baudouin, who came into the room at this point, said that the decision about the fleet had been taken, and remained only to be confirmed by the Council of Ministers. M. Baudouin had no doubt that it would be confirmed. He said that His Majesty's Government could set their minds at rest.

(d)   While the Council of Ministers was in session Sir R. Campbell was told that the decision had been changed because the Ministers thought that, as a point of honour, France should receive the German terms while her fleet and army were still fighting. The new decision, which was unanimous and engaged the honour of Marshal Pétain, General Weygand and Admiral Darlan, confirmed the view that any terms involving the surrender of the fleet should be rejected, and that, if such terms were put forward, France should continue to fight as long as possible. Before the land forces surrendered the fleet would join up with the British navy or, in the last resort, carry out pre-arranged scuttling orders. Sir R. Campbell was assured that General Weygand would be given formal instructions not to discuss armistice terms involving the surrender of the fleet.

Sir R. Campbell thought that the new decision was due to the reluctance of Admiral Darlan to give up the fleet while fighting continued, and to a slightly stiffer attitude of the Government as a

---

[1] This account was despatched an hour later than the telegram despatched at 1.50 p.m.
(a) C7301/65/17. (b) C7301/65/17. (c) C7541/65/17. (d) C7301/65/17.

whole. From this latter point of view the change—although Sir R. Campbell regretted it—might be considered a healthy sign.

On June 18 the War Cabinet decided to ask Mr. Alexander, the First Lord of the Admiralty, and the First Sea Lord, who had already (a) gone to Bordeaux, to stay there for the time. On the same day M. Monnet, a member of the Anglo-French Co-ordination Committee (b) in London, suggested to the Prime Minister that another member of the Cabinet should fly to Bordeaux. M. Corbin strongly supported this suggestion. With the Prime Minister's consent Lord Lloyd left for Bordeaux on the morning of June 19. The choice of Lord Lloyd (c) was determined partly by the fact that, as Secretary of State for the Colonies, he was concerned directly with questions affecting the continuance of French resistance overseas. Lord Lloyd also had many contacts in France, and had been an outstanding supporter of the Entente with France and of resistance to Germany.

During the night of June 18–19 Sir R. Campbell transmitted a (d) message for the Prime Minister from Mr. Alexander and Admiral Pound. Their report was optimistic. They found the situation with regard to the fleet 'completely different' from their expectations. Fighting was still continuing at sea, and would go on until the armistice terms were known. If these terms contained, as might be expected, demands for the surrender of the fleet, they would be rejected as dishonourable. The conference with the Germans would come to an end; fighting would be resumed and would continue until further resistance was impossible. Before they capitulated the French would sail their fleet to friendly ports or, in the last resort, destroy it. Steps had already been taken to send the *Richelieu* for 'working up' to Dakar, to divert the *Béarn* to Martinique and to prepare for the destruction of the unfinished *Jean Bart* if the ship could not be got away. Ships in French ports would go to their war stations before the ports fell into German hands. All other ships capable of steaming would go to Dakar, and those which could not reach Dakar would be destroyed. All merchant ships would be sailed to British ports as soon as the French ports were cleared of magnetic mines. Mr. Alexander and Admiral Pound were impressed with Admiral Darlan's sincerity and determination. They found him 'very friendly' and convinced that the French fleet would obey any order which he might give to them.

Sir R. Campbell's view, telegraphed during the early hours of the (e) morning of June 19, was less hopeful. He said that the French Government were 'very indignant' at a message communicated to

---

(a) WM(40)171.   (b) WM(40)172, C7352/65/17.   (c) C7301/65/17.   (d) C7301/65/17.
(e) C7301/65/17.

them on the morning of June 18 by the American Ambassador that they would lose the friendship and goodwill of the United States if they did not put their fleet in a place of safety before negotiating an armistice. The French Government considered this message an 'intolerable interference' on the part of a neutral country and especially on the part of a country which had 'failed to come up to their expectations'.

(a)   Sir R. Campbell also telegraphed a short résumé of the situation. He thought that 'the rot was originally started by General Weygand' who had told the French Government each day in more pressing terms that, as the French army was beaten, it would be useless to allow further carnage. Marshal Pétain had supported General Weygand. M. Reynaud had stood for fighting to the last and then moving the Government to carry on the war overseas, but he had been overridden by a faction which had grown up within the Government under the leadership of M. Chautemps. Marshal Pétain had put weaklings into the places of the firmer elements of M. Reynaud's Government. Sir R. Campbell thought that the new Cabinet were undecided whether to move to French colonial territory and that they were much embarrassed by the declared intention of Marshal Pétain and General Weygand to remain in France. Meanwhile 'the sands were running out'. The German advance continued, and the reply to the request for an armistice had not yet come, although, according to the Spanish Ambassador, it might arrive 'shortly'. The Ministers talked of refusing dishonouring terms, and of leaving France when the army had to capitulate, but they evaded every question put to them on the subject. Much political manoeuvring was going on, and, except for Marshal Pétain, who would talk only 'generalities', mainly about the sufferings of the people, Sir R. Campbell felt that he could not 'believe anyone implicitly'.

The War Cabinet met during the morning of June 19. The Prime
(b) Minister summarised the message from Mr. Alexander and Admiral Pound, and described this message as encouraging. Admiral Pound, who had come back from Bordeaux during the night, then gave the War Cabinet the latest information. The Germans were said to be 120 km. from Bordeaux. There seemed to be no signs of preparations to defend the city. The Government had a system of warnings of any German approach, and intended to 'slip out' before the Germans arrived. Admiral Darlan had seemed very calm and determined, and, in conversation, had steadfastly maintained that the fleet would not be surrendered. It would not be possible at present to send it to British ports because it could not desert the country while French

---

(a) C7301/65/17.   (b) WM(40)172, C7352/65/17.

troops were still fighting; it must remain in French waters until France surrendered. There would be time to get it away while the negotiations were being conducted.

Lord Halifax told the War Cabinet that the position in the French and Belgian colonies was, on the whole, satisfactory. Most of the local authorities seemed likely to co-operate with Great Britain whatever the French Government might do.[1]

In the afternoon of June 19 Sir R. Campbell reported that he and (a) Mr. Alexander had been told by Marshal Pétain and M. Baudouin of a message received during the morning from the Spanish Ambassador that, if the French Government would nominate plenipotentiaries, the Germans would indicate a time and place of meeting for negotiating the terms of an armistice. The French had nominated delegates without plenipotentiary powers and had thus reserved a final decision on the terms. The Council of Ministers had also decided that, on the approach of the Germans to Bordeaux, the President of the Republic and the Presidents of the Senate and Chamber of Deputies (MM. Jeanneney and Herriot) would go overseas, probably to Algiers, in order to carry on the government. M. Lebrun would nominate the Ministers for this purpose; they would leave with a written order signed by himself and countersigned by Marshal Pétain. General Weygand was also likely to go to North Africa where he could co-ordinate the French war effort overseas. M. Baudouin explained that steps had already been taken to send aeroplanes and stores to North Africa.

On Lord Lloyd's arrival at Bordeaux Sir R. Campbell and Mr. (b) Alexander discussed with him a message which he had brought for the French Government. In this message the British Government undertook to put transport at the disposal of the French for the evacuation to North Africa of as many men and as much material as possible, and also to take off from Bordeaux such persons as the French Government might designate. The British Government promised collaboration in the defence of North Africa and confirmed their offer to transform the Anglo-French alliance into a complete union.[2]

---

[1] For the approaches by His Majesty's Government to French colonial authorities during this period, see below, section (v) of this Chapter. The War Cabinet instructed Lord Halifax at this meeting once again to draw the attention of the French Government to their responsibility, as a matter of honour, for the security of Allied troops (i.e. Polish and Czech) who had been fighting on French soil.

[2] The envoys appear also to have been instructed to state the satisfaction of the British Government at the French decision to refuse dishonouring terms, and to repeat the (c) arguments in favour of the establishment of a French Government overseas. In view of the French decision in this matter and of the reassuring accounts of Admiral Darlan's attitude, Sir R. Campbell and Mr. Alexander and Lord Lloyd decided not to put these arguments but to give the assurances about the provision of transport as a response to the French statement of intentions.

(a) C7301/65/17.   (b) C7541/65/17;   WM(40)173,   C7352/65/17;   C7342/839/17.
(c) WM(40)173, C7352/65/17.

(a)   Sir R. Campbell sent in the early morning of June 20 an account of Lord Lloyd's meetings with the President of the Republic and the French Ministers.[1] Lord Lloyd, with Sir R. Campbell and Mr. Alexander, delivered to M. Lebrun the message from the British Government at 7.30 p.m. M. Lebrun was clearly unable to cope with the situation and nothing had emerged from the conversation. At 10 p.m. the Ambassador and the two British Ministers saw Marshal Pétain and M. Baudouin. Lord Lloyd repeated his message, and, after making an offer of transport, raised the question of the fleet. Marshal Pétain gave the strongest assurances that the fleet would not be handed over to the Germans, but said that it might be scuttled. M. Baudouin explained that Marshal Pétain was considering the highly improbable hypothesis that, apart from a demand for the fleet, the armistice terms might prove acceptable. In this case the fleet could be scuttled rather than surrendered to the Germans. If the armistice terms were generally unacceptable, the fleet would go on fighting. Mr. Alexander told the War Cabinet that he asked the

(b)   French Ministers not to have the destroyers scuttled but to hand them over to Great Britain. Marshal Pétain, who had taken the view that Great Britain would have no difficulty in resisting invasion, thought it unlikely that the French Government would agree to Mr. Alexander's proposal.

(c)   Sir R. Campbell reported that Marshal Pétain was 'indefinite' when Lord Lloyd raised the question of the departure of the French Government. M. Baudouin said that the question had been decided in principle; it would be settled finally, and the time of departure fixed, on the following morning. M. Baudouin was reminded of his statement earlier in the day that the matter had already been settled. He answered that the principle had been accepted, but that the decision remained to be ratified finally on June 20. Sir R. Campbell and the British Ministers pointed out the dangers of delay, but M. Baudouin hoped that the party leaving France might go in the early afternoon of June 20.

(d)   In his report to the War Cabinet Mr. Alexander said that the withdrawal of the Government from France had been complicated by the unwillingness of M. Lebrun to leave the country, and that Lord Lloyd had spoken again to M. Baudouin, after the meeting with Marshal Pétain, of the danger of delay. The French plenipotentiaries had not left Bordeaux; the German terms might not be

---

[1] This telegram was drafted by Sir R. Campbell and Lord Lloyd by candlelight during
(e)   a German air raid on Bordeaux. It was received in London by wireless at 6.50 a.m. on June 20 but delayed for checking. Mr. Alexander came back to London during the night of June 19–20 and gave to the War Cabinet on June 20 an account of the discussions up to the time at which he had left Bordeaux.

(a) C7301, 7541/65/17. (b) WM(40)173, C7352/65/17. (c) C7301/65/17. (d) WM(40) 173, C7352/65/17. (e) C7541, 7301/65/17.

received for several days, and meanwhile the Germans were rapidly approaching the city.[1]

After Mr. Alexander had left Bordeaux Sir R. Campbell and Lord (a) Lloyd called on MM. Jeanneney and Herriot who said that they had not ceased to advocate the withdrawal of the Government overseas and that they were perplexed and distressed at the delay. They asked that a British ship might be sent to Bayonne to take off 50 French officers who wished to place their services at the disposal of His Majesty's Government and a number of active politicians who were 'marked men'. As it seemed possible that considerable numbers of French officers would respond to General de Gaulle's broadcast[2] from London, Sir R. Campbell asked that this ship, or two ships (b) should be sent.

(iii)

The situation on June 20–21: decision of the French Government to move to Perpignan: reversal of this decision: uncertainty of the situation at Bordeaux.

During the night of June 19–20 the Germans bombed Bordeaux. The bombardment was not heavy, but the French Government decided on June 20 to move to Perpignan. Sir R. Campbell reported this decision in four telegrams despatched between 3 p.m. and 4 p.m. (c) on June 20. He explained that the purpose of the move was to enable the Ministers to hold in safety another meeting at which they could take cognisance of the German terms. French representatives were receiving these terms at Tours on the night of June 20–1. After the meeting of the Council of Ministers at Perpignan, M. Lebrun, with MM. Jeanneney and Herriot and more Ministers than had been previously contemplated, would leave from Port Vendres for North Africa. Sir R. Campbell reported that Admiral Darlan had shown to him and to Lord Lloyd written instructions that the fleet was to go on

---

[1] It should be noticed that on the British side there does not seem at this time to have been a realisation that the German tactics might be to halt their advance, and thereby to avoid driving the French Government overseas.

[2] General de Gaulle had left France on June 17. On June 18 he broadcast from London a message to the French nation appealing to all Frenchmen who were in Great Britain or might arrive there, to get into touch with him in order to maintain French resistance. The War Cabinet on June 18 were at first opposed to this broadcast not on account of its (d) contents, but because General de Gaulle, as a strong opponent of the policy of surrender, was known to be *persona non grata* to Marshal Pétain's Government. It was therefore considered undesirable that he should broadcast as long as it was still possible that the French Government would act in a way conformable to the interests of the Anglo-French alliance. Later on June 18 the members of the War Cabinet were consulted individually on the question and agreed that General de Gaulle should give the broadcast. See also below, p. 321.

(a) C7301, 7541/65/17. (b) C7342/839/17. (c) C7352/65/17. (d) WM(40)171.

fighting fiercely ('farouchement') unless it received orders to the contrary from a properly constituted government outside enemy control.

Until a late hour during the evening of June 20 Sir R. Campbell expected the move to Perpignan to take place. The reports received (a) in London from him between 4 a.m. and 5.30 a.m. on June 21 (though drafted before midnight) were to the effect that there had been a 'last minute' change of plan. The Germans had offered to reinstate the telephone line between Tours and Bordeaux, and the French Government had decided to remain in Bordeaux to receive the terms. They expected to receive them during the night. Sir R. Campbell was assured that the terms would be rejected if they contained 'dishonouring clauses'; he was, however, unable to discover whether those Ministers who were going overseas would leave from Bordeaux or from Port Vendres.[1] At 12.15 a.m. Sir R. Campbell (b) knew only that the armistice conditions had not been received, but that fighting in the Tours area had ceased in order to allow the passage of the French delegation. At 8 a.m.[2] Sir R. Campbell heard (c) that the delegation had been delayed by the destruction of a bridge, and that they had reached Tours only at 4 a.m.; consequently the French Government were still without information about the terms.

At 10.32 a.m. Sir R. Campbell sent a more detailed account of the (d) position. He had reminded the French Ministers that we expected to be consulted about the German terms. These terms would probably contain a short time-limit. It was therefore to be anticipated that no effective consultation, and possibly no consultation of any kind, would be feasible. The Germans had halted their advance but there was nothing to prevent them from reaching Bordeaux in a very short time. Sir R. Campbell believed that the instructions issued on June 20 had safeguarded the question of the fleet. He proposed to repeat to the French Government that, 'apart from French interests', the establishment of the Government overseas would alone 'encourage His Majesty's Government to stand by France to the end'. He had no reason to suppose that there had been any weakening on the subject, but he would not feel satisfied until the Government had left France. Although he had impressed the point many times on Marshal Pétain in the bluntest language, the Marshal seemed unable to grasp its significance, and thought only of staying in France in order to stand by the people and to do what he could to mitigate their sufferings under German occupation.

(e)   At 11.05 a.m. Sir R. Campbell telegraphed[3] that, in reply to his

---

[1] i.e. in the case of a previous move to Perpignan.

[2] This telegram was not received in London until 5.05 p.m. on June 21.

[3] This telegram did not reach London until 2.20 a.m. on June 22.

(a) C7352/65/17.   (b) C7541, 7352/65/17.   (c) C7352/65/17.   (d) C7352/65/17.
(e) C7352/65/17.

written communication about consultation with us, M. Baudouin had sent him a note that it had not been thought necessary to inform him that the Council of Ministers intended to have an exchange of views with His Majesty's Government as soon as they knew the armistice terms. They did not expect to hear the terms until late in the afternoon. Sir R. Campbell thought it satisfactory to have received an acknowledgment of his communication; on the other hand this did not alter his view that, if the time-limit were short, there could be no effective consultation.

At 12.30 p.m. Sir R. Campbell drafted[1] another report on the situation. After the decision to move to Perpignan had been cancelled, (a) M. Herriot had arranged for a ship at Bordeaux to take off a number of Deputies. This ship was now waiting at the mouth of the Garonne.[2] Unfortunately the Deputies on board were those who stood for resistance. Their weaker colleagues were still in Bordeaux. M. Laval and his friends were also active. Although M. Herriot had been told that among the civilians in the Cabinet there was still a majority in favour of resistance, Sir R. Campbell thought it significant that they were no longer unanimous. He feared that the majority might dwindle, and that, after the abandonment of the plan of a move to Perpignan, the next step might be to give up the idea of sending M. Lebrun and a nucleus of the Government overseas.

The situation was thus changing from hour to hour. M. Herriot had told Sir R. Campbell that, if dishonouring terms were accepted, he would be prepared to notify M. Lebrun and Marshal Pétain that a cession of territory made without consent of Parliament was constitutionally invalid. Sir R. Campbell intended, if the decision to send a small Government overseas were abandoned, to try to persuade MM. Lebrun, Herriot and Jeanneney, and 'any other right-minded parliamentarians' whom he could reach, to come to England.[3]

At 2.30 p.m. Sir R. Campbell drafted another telegram[4] that the (b) Germans had taken the French delegation to Paris.[5] The delegates

---

[1] This report was not despatched until 5 p.m.; it was received in London at 8.40 p.m.

[2] This ship, the *Massilia*, sailed on the afternoon of June 21 and reached Casablanca on June 24. Among the passengers were MM. Daladier, Mandel and Campinchi. M. Mandel attempted without success to proclaim a 'resistance administration' in North Africa. He and the other passengers were subsequently held on board the *Massilia* and forbidden communication with the shore. One of the reasons for the decision of the War Cabinet (see below, p. 327) to send Mr. Duff Cooper, Minister of Information, and Lord Gort to Casablanca and Rabat was that they might get in touch with the Ministers; but the French authorities refused to allow any contact. On July 1 the Prime Minister gave orders to the Admiralty that an attempt should be made, if possible, to take the passengers off the ship, but these orders could not be carried out since for three weeks the *Massilia* remained under the shelter of the shore batteries of Casablanca.

[3] At one point during this time Marshal Pétain told Sir R. Campbell that, if the British torpedoed a ship taking the French Government overseas, he would have no regrets.

[4] This telegram was despatched at 4 p.m. and received in London at 8 p.m.

[5] The French delegation met Hitler at Rethondes in the Forest of Compiègne at 2.45 p.m. on June 21.

(a) C7352/65/17. (b) C7352/65/17.

would ask that the French Government should be allowed to examine the terms in peace, i.e. free from bombing. A similar message had been sent through the Spanish Ambassador and the Germans had been given a hint that otherwise the French Government would have to move 'elsewhere'. Sir R. Campbell thought that if, as was likely, this hint was intended to suggest a move overseas, it was a bad sign, since it implied that, unless there were interference with their deliberations, the Government would not move. Furthermore, although an order instructing French colonial governors to take independent action was being discussed, this order had not yet been sent. The situation, therefore, was not improving. The German conditions were not expected until the night of June 21–22: meanwhile a German armoured division had passed Valence with the obvious intention of cutting off the retreat of the French Government to Perpignan.[1]

(a) Sir R. Campbell saw M. Baudouin again at 4 p.m.[2] M. Baudouin said that as yet there had been no contact with the French delegation. The intentions of the French Government were unchanged: M. Lebrun and a small Government would be sent overseas. Admiral Darlan had been instructed to provide a warship for them at St. Jean de Luz. Sir R. Campbell reported that, even if these assurances were true at the moment, 'evil influences' were at work.

(b) After seeing M. Baudouin, Sir R. Campbell had a talk with M. Chautemps. M. Chautemp's ideas were still 'variable' on the subject of rejecting dishonouring or severe terms and of establishing a government overseas. He confirmed the intrigues and the 'kaleidoscopic character of the situation', and described as a 'lamentable influence' General Weygand's 'mystical, disinterested mood which leads him to hold that France, having made mistakes, deserves to suffer'. Sir R. Campbell also reported that M. Reynaud saw Marshal (c) Pétain once or twice a day, and was doing his best, although without much success, to stiffen him.

Owing to the difficulties of communication, the rapid changes in the situation at Bordeaux were not known in London in time to take immediate action on them. In any case, the War Cabinet had full confidence in Sir R. Campbell and did not send him too many instructions. On the morning of June 21, M. Corbin suggested to (d) Lord Halifax that, in order to encourage the French and to counteract

---

[1] The record of an interview between Hitler and Mussolini at Munich on June 18, 1940, shows the importance which they put on preventing the French fleet from falling into British hands and the French Government from leaving France for North Africa. It is of interest that Hitler admitted to Mussolini that it was 'doubtful whether France would put any faith in a guarantee by the Führer [about the fleet]. She would perhaps be more ready to trust the Duce.' (D.G.F.P., IX, No. 479.)

[2] The telegram reporting this interview was drafted at 6 p.m. and despatched at 6.43 p.m. It was received in the Foreign Office at 2.25 p.m. on June 22.

(a) C7352, 7541/65/17.   (b) C7352/65/17.   (c) C7352/65/17.   (d) WM(40)171, C7352/65/17.

German propaganda that we were treating France as an enemy or as a colony, we should send aircraft to drop food for the French troops still fighting in eastern France, and allow French ships with cargoes of food to enter French metropolitan ports not occupied by the Germans. M. Corbin also suggested that the French cruiser *Emile Bertin* now at Halifax with a cargo of bullion should be allowed to go to Martinique.

The War Cabinet discussed these suggestions on June 21. The first proposal had already been considered but was regarded as impracticable, or rather as involving risks entirely disproportionate to the results. The second suggestion was not accepted. There was in fact no evidence that food ships were being held up; most of the ships which were being detained temporarily in British ports were colliers. The third proposal offered considerable difficulties. The *Emile Bertin* had on board 300,000,000 dollars' worth of bullion consigned by the Bank of France to the Bank of Ottawa. It was not known why the French Government now wanted the ship to go to Martinique. The Senior Naval Officer at Halifax had been told to use persuasion and obstruction in order to hold up the ship, but not to take any warlike action. The War Cabinet agreed to continue this procedure. Later in the day M. Corbin again raised his three questions. The Prime Minister was inclined to allow the release of the gold from (a) Halifax, but the matter was settled by the ship leaving the port[1].

(iv)

The situation on June 22: the reception of the German terms: French refusal to consult the British Government: Sir R. Campbell's protests to Marshal Pétain and M. Baudouin: further protests by Sir R. Campbell: signature of the armistice: Sir R. Campbell leaves Bordeaux.

The French Government received the German terms[2] about mid-

---

[1] The *Emile Bertin* reached Martinique on June 26; two British cruisers were instructed to watch her movements. The French Admiral landed the gold on the island, giving assurances that it would not be allowed to fall into German hands.

[2] For the terms, see note at end of this Chapter.

D.G.F.P., IX, Nos. 512, 513–5, 521–2, contain a summary of the negotiations at Rethondes and of intercepted telephone conversations between General Huntziger and General Weygand and later General Weygand's adjutant. It appears from these documents that when General Huntziger was able to telephone the armistice terms to General Weygand the latter answered that there was no one in his office to take them down since all the secretaries had gone home. A secretary was, however, found to write down the terms at General Weygand's dictation. General Huntziger began by saying that he was unable to learn the German peace terms since the Germans refused to discuss them; he had only the terms of an armistice treaty of twenty-four clauses. General Huntziger said little about article 8 except to call General Weygand's attention to the mention of the French colonial empire and to the statement that in the peace treaty Germany did not intend to make any demands for the French navy.

(a) C7455/65/17.

night on June 21–22. After they had replied to them and received a counter-reply from the Germans, they accepted the terms. Their delegation signed the armistice at 6.36 p.m. (German summer time) on June 22. The Germans broadcast an account of the ceremony, but did not state the terms.

During the interval between the reception of the German terms at Bordeaux and the final French surrender Sir R. Campbell sent frequent reports on the situation but owing mainly to the difficulties of transmission there was again considerable delay in the arrival of some of these messages. The instructions sent to Sir R. Campbell therefore were based upon an incomplete view of the situation and also took a long time to reach him. The delays were of little practical importance. As the Prime Minister said to the War Cabinet on June 21 in regard to M. Corbin's suggestions, the policy of the French Government depended not on any action which we might take but upon the terms offered by the Germans.

(a) Sir R. Campbell's first telegram on June 22[1] reported that the French Government had received the armistice terms at 4.0 a.m., and were required to send their reply to them by 9 a.m. on that day. The Franco-German armistice convention would come into force as soon as the French Government had concluded an armistice with Italy, and hostilities would cease six hours after the Italian Government had announced to the German Government the conclusion of the Franco-Italian armistice. No Italian representatives were present at the Franco-German meeting, and the Germans refused to disclose the Italian terms. They stated that they would notify the French Government by wireless of the time at which hostilities would cease.

Sir R. Campbell said that he was sending in his next telegram a translation of the conditions with regard to the French fleet, and that a summary of the rest of the terms would follow as soon as it could be cyphered. It was impossible to send the full text verbatim, since it covered nine pages of typescript.

(b) Sir R. Campbell's second telegram, despatched at 10.9 a.m., and received at 2.40 p.m., reported that Article 8 (in the armistice convention) proposed that the French fleet, except ships left free for the safeguard of French interests in the colonial Empire, was to be collected in ports to be specified; the fleet would be demobilised and disarmed in these ports under German or Italian control. The normal peace-time ports would be taken for purposes of this specification.

The German Government solemnly declared that they had no intention of using for their own purposes during the war the French

---

[1] This telegram was despatched at 8.50 a.m., but appears to have been drafted at 4 a.m. It was received at 10.40 a.m.

(a) C7375/7362/17. (b) C7375/7362/17.

fleet stationed in ports under German control except those units necessary for coast surveillance and mine-sweeping. The German Government also declared, under this formula, their intention of not making claims in respect of the French fleet at the time of the negotiation of peace terms. Except for that part (to be determined) of the fleet destined for the protection of colonial interests all ships outside French territorial waters were to be recalled to France. Sir (a) R. Campbell's third telegram, received (by wireless) at 12.45 p.m., gave an account of his action after he had heard by telephone (about midnight on June 21–22) from the Ministry of Foreign Affairs that the armistice conditions had been telephoned to the French Government, and that the Council of Ministers would consider the terms at 1 a.m. as soon as copies of them had been made. M. Baudouin said that he would see Sir R. Campbell after the meeting of the Council.

Sir R. Campbell went at once to the Presidency of the Council where M. Charles-Roux gave him a broad outline of the conditions. On hearing of the condition about the fleet Sir R. Campbell hastily wrote a note calling attention to the insidious character of the terms, and to the folly of placing any reliance upon the German word which had been so many times broken. He asked that this note should be taken into the Council of Ministers. The Council was now in session in the Presidency of the Republic. Sir R. Campbell went to the building, and was joined there at his invitation by the Canadian and South African Ministers.

After the Council meeting M. Baudouin came up to Sir R. Campbell and said that he was going away to draft a reply in accordance with the decision of the Council. Sir R. Campbell answered that he and the Canadian and South African Ministers must be received, and that they must be told of the German conditions and the proposed reply. M. Baudouin answered rudely that 'what interested us was the condition about the fleet'. The French Government were making, on Admiral Darlan's suggestion, a counter-proposal that the fleet should be sent to ports in North Africa, where it could be dismantled. Sir R. Campbell said that the fleet should go to more distant waters, since there was a risk that in the Mediterranean it might fall into Italian hands. M. Baudouin answered that, if there were any such danger, the fleet would be scuttled in accordance with the decision already taken. M. Baudouin then moved away. Sir R. Campbell said that he must protest formally against this procedure. He insisted that he and his Canadian and South African colleagues should be received 'somewhere where we could talk quietly'. M. Baudouin showed them, with bad grace, into the Council room. Here they found M. Lebrun. 'Much the same scene occurred', and Sir R. Campbell renewed his protest in the presence

(a) C7375/7362/17; C7541/65/17.

of M. Lebrun, who merely made some irrelevant remark. At one stage in the conversation Sir R. Campbell reminded M. Baudouin of the notes exchanged between them, and requested at least that he should be given a copy of the German terms. M. Baudouin said at first that he had no spare copy. He produced a copy only after Sir R. Campbell's continued insistence. He also said that the French reply would not be 'définitive', but would 'put questions'. Sir R. Campbell ended his telegram with the words: 'The French have completely lost their heads as witnessed by the shameful scene as above described, and are totally unmanageable.'

(a)   Before leaving his hotel at 7.45 a.m. on June 22 to see Marshal Pétain Sir R. Campbell drafted a short telegram as follows:

(b)   'Diabolically clever German terms have evidently destroyed the last remnants of French courage. If, as I presume to be certain, Germans reject French counter-proposal as regards the fleet, I do not believe for a moment that the French, in their present state of collapse, would hold out against original German condition to recall the fleet to French ports, and might even reverse scuttling order. They could still square their conscience by saying ships could not be used against us. We are thus thrown back on Darlan's pathetic assurances to First Lord of the Admiralty.'

Sir R. Campbell said that he would get into touch with Admiral Darlan as soon as possible.

Sir R. Campbell saw Marshal Pétain and M. Baudouin just before
(c)   the meeting of the Council of Ministers to consider the draft French reply to the German terms. He said to Marshal Pétain that 'at an hour when France had laid down her arms and her Ally was about to plunge into a life and death struggle' he came to the Marshal, 'whose name throughout the world was synonymous with honour, to beg him on behalf of His Majesty's Government to see to it that France kept a solemn engagement, binding the honour of France and renewed more than once in recent days, not to allow the fleet to fall into German hands and thus strike a mortal blow at an Ally who had always been loyal and with whom France had had a "no separate peace" obligation'. If France were no longer able to uphold this latter obligation, she could still keep to her engagement about the fleet. The recall of the fleet to French ports to be disarmed under German control was equivalent to surrender.

At this point Marshal Pétain interrupted Sir R. Campbell to say that, as he had already explained, the British Government need have no qualms about the fleet. The French Government hoped to get the fleet away to African ports. Marshal Pétain spoke of Dakar or Madagascar. The fleet would sink itself if it were ever in danger of falling into enemy hands. The interview took place while the

(a) C7541/65/17.   (b) C7375/7362/17.   (c) C7375/7362/17; C7541/65/17.

Ministers, who were standing round, were waiting to go into the Council. Marshal Pétain said that he could not keep them waiting any longer.

Sir R. Campbell reported that he was unable to explain the discrepancy between Marshal Pétain's statement about the fleet and M. Baudouin's statement that it was being sent to Mediterranean ports. The change might possibly be due to Sir R. Campbell's own representations about the danger of the Mediterranean; a more likely explanation was that the Ministers were confused. At the previous Council meeting they might have talked merely of African ports. The Ministers were distraught, with the exception of Marshal Pétain who was becoming increasingly difficult to approach and, in spite of Sir R. Campbell's 'utmost insistence', more and more silent.

Sir R. Campbell added that the French were asking for other modifications, e.g. a reduction in the area under German occu- (a) pation. He hoped to get a copy of the French reply after the Council had adopted it, but he was 'being kept more and more at arm's length', and was 'becoming the object of hostile looks from the rank and file' of Ministers.

While this interview with Marshal Pétain was taking place, the Naval Attaché was assured by Admiral Auphan, the Naval Chief of (b) Staff, that no unit of the fleet would be handed over to the Germans, and that the French Government hoped to arrange internment away from the metropolitan ports. Admiral Auphan mentioned Dakar, the French Congo, and Madagascar as possible places. He said 'categorically' that the ships would remain under the French flag, and with orders that the crews should sink them at once if the Germans or Italians attempted to interfere with them in any way or at any time.

After the meeting of the Council of Ministers, Sir R. Campbell reported that, 'with the utmost difficulty', he had at last obtained a (c) copy of the French reply to the German terms. The clause dealing with the fleet in the French counter-proposals ran as follows:[1]

'La flotte de guerre française (à l'exception de la partie qui est laissée à la disposition du Gouvernement français pour la sauvegarde des intérêts français dans son empire colonial), après avoir été démobilisée et après avoir débarqué ses munitions sous le contrôle de l'Allemagne ou respectivement de l'Italie, sera basée dans les ports français de l'Afrique. Les effectifs de chaque navire ne devront pas dépasser la moitié des effectifs normaux du temps de paix.'[2]

---

[1] General Huntziger gave as the reason for this counter-proposal that French warships, if laid up in Atlantic or Channel ports, would be exposed to British air attack and that the French were therefore trying to bring them to safety by directing them to African ports. The German answer was that the safeguarding of the demobilised French fleet was a matter for the Armistice Commission.

[2] The two remaining paragraphs remained unchanged.

(a) C7375/7362/17. (b) C7375/7362/17; C7541/65/17. (c) C7375/7362/17; C7541/65/17.

Sir R. Campbell considered this clause wholly unsatisfactory. As soon as he had seen the text, he 'forced his way' into M. Baudouin's house and asked to be received at once. He argued that, if the fleet fell into German hands for purposes of control no ship would ever be allowed to leave. M. Baudouin said that most of the ships were away from their base ports, and the Germans would be invited to send commissions to them. In other cases the scuttling order would be carried out if any attempt were made to remove or otherwise inter- fere with French crews. Sir R. Campbell insisted that these proposals would lead to a breach of faith on the part of France. M. Baudouin continued to argue that the scuttling order was the key to the situa- tion. He offered to ask Admiral Darlan to explain in detail how this order would be carried out.

Sir R. Campbell thought that we were now confronted with deliberate bad faith; his only hope was an approach to Admiral Darlan whom he would see as soon as possible. There was much anglophobia amongst Ministers and parliamentarians as a result of 'clever and successful fifth column work'. Sir R. Campbell added, with bitterness, that he had to deal 'mainly with a crook who is now the leading spirit in the Government and an old dotard whose word of honour nevertheless remains our only hope'.[1]

(a) At 6 p.m. M. Charles-Roux told Sir R. Campbell that he had been instructed to let him know secretly that Admiral Darlan's dispositions were such that 'no ship would be utilisable, were the attempt to use it to be made'. M. Charles-Roux argued that the French decisions gave Great Britain complete satisfaction. Sir R. Campbell rejected this argument in very strong terms and pointed out that the terms might well mean 'just the difference for us between victory and defeat' and might thereby 'jeopardise also all hope of a future for France'.

At the end of his talk with M. Charles-Roux Sir R. Campbell said that he intended to leave with his staff as soon as the armistice had been signed. M. Charles-Roux 'affected surprise' and asked for Sir R. Campbell's reasons. Sir R. Campbell said that he had been accredited to a free and Allied Government. He did not think that his Sovereign or his Government would wish him to stay with a French Government which in a few hours might be under enemy control. Furthermore it would be futile to suppose that in these circumstances the Germans would allow him to communicate with the French Government. Since he could be of no further use in France, he ought in any case to go home for consultation and report.

---

[1] In his Report on the events of his Mission from June 9 to his return to England Sir R. Campbell stated that, in the last stages, he had begun to have doubts of Admiral Darlan's
(b) good faith. He did not think, however, that the French collapse could be explained by treachery. He was not sure of M. Laval or M. Baudouin, but he had no reason to suppose that M. Baudouin, whose dominant motives were fear and a desire to stand in well with the conqueror, would have acted as he did if there had been no military collapse.
(a) C7375/7362/17; C7541/65/17. (b) C7541/65/17.

Sir R. Campbell added this 'rider' in order to avoid giving the impression that we might abandon France altogether, or encouraging the French Government to think that they were now free from further obligation to us and, in particular, free from their undertaking to scuttle the fleet rather than allow it to be used against us.

Later in the evening of June 22 Sir R. Campbell and the two Dominion Ministers went to call on General Weygand. General (a) Weygand said that the armistice had been signed. Sir R. Campbell then spoke to him on the lines of the conversation with M. Charles-Roux. General Weygand at first seemed to be surprised at Sir R. Campbell's decision to leave France, but later realised the force of his argument. At one point in the interview General Weygand said that, although they had paused for a time in their advance on Bordeaux, the Germans might well reach the city on June 23. If they decided to move on, there was nothing to stop them.

About 10 p.m. Sir R. Campbell called on M. Baudouin. M. Baudouin also affected surprise at Sir R. Campbell's decision, but accepted it on hearing the reasons. Sir R. Campbell asked whether he could see Marshal Pétain. M. Baudouin said that the Marshal was in bed, and must not be disturbed, but that he (M. Baudouin) would be responsible for giving him a message.

Finally Sir R. Campbell went to see M. Lebrun. M. Lebrun also (b) was in bed, and Sir R. Campbell was received by M. Magre, head of the civilian household of the President. Sir R. Campbell said he had not come to ask for a farewell audience, and therefore did not think it necessary to disturb M. Lebrun.

Sir R. Campbell, with the Dominions Ministers and his staff, left at midnight for Arcachon. Here, early in the morning of June 23, they went on board a small boat from which they were transferred in the open sea to the Canadian destroyer H.M.C.S. *Fraser*. This ship took them to St. Jean de Luz, whence they sailed to England in H.M.S. *Galatea*.

(v)

Meetings of the War Cabinet on June 22: the Prime Minister's appeal of June 23 to Frenchmen: appeals to the French colonial authorities, June 15–23, 1940.

The action taken in London during the morning and afternoon of June 22 was affected by the 'time-lag' in the information from Bordeaux. Thus the War Cabinet met in the morning without (c) knowledge of the German terms, and even the news (from Sir R.

(a) C7541/65/17. (b) C7541/65/17. (c) WM(40)175, C7375/7362/17.

Campbell's telegram of 8.50 a.m.)[1] of the presentation of the terms reached them only at the end of their meeting. Mr. Alexander reported that Admiral Odend'hal at Portsmouth had received orders for French warships in British ports to leave for African ports (apparently for Dakar). The War Cabinet thought it undesirable to risk upsetting Admiral Darlan by making difficulties about French warships leaving British ports. During this discussion Lord Halifax was called away to speak on the telephone to Mr. Churchill who was at Chequers. On his return to the War Cabinet Lord Halifax said that the Prime Minister wanted to send another message to the French Government reminding them that we were entitled to be taken fully into their confidence at this critical moment. The War
(a) Cabinet agreed upon the terms of a message as follows:

'In this critical hour, when France is faced with a fateful decision, His Majesty's Government, who are resolved in all circumstances to continue the struggle with all the means at their command, must recall once more that they have never released the French Government from their solemn obligation not to sign a separate armistice or peace, and that the French Government themselves have only lately reaffirmed that they will at least consult with His Majesty's Government before proceeding to any such signature. His Majesty's Government do not doubt that the French Government, in the interests of all that we together stand for, will insist on sufficient latitude to permit of this undertaking being made effective.

His Majesty's Government feel the deepest sympathy with the French Government at this moment when the latter are exposed to the full brutality of Germany. As His Majesty's Government have repeatedly intimated, they are prepared to make every possible effort to assist France to continue the struggle, whether in France itself or in French overseas territories, where wide resources exist, if the French Government, as His Majesty's Government earnestly hope they will, prefer that alternative to surrender to a foe without honour from whom no mercy can be expected.'

The Prime Minister approved of this text. A telegram was therefore sent to Sir R. Campbell but did not reach him until several hours after the signature of the armistice.[2]
(b)   The War Cabinet met again in the evening of June 22. The German conditions about the French fleet were now known to them[3]

---

[1] See above, p. 306.

[2] After the receipt of Sir R. Campbell's telegrams giving an account of his interviews in the early morning of June 22 a telegram was sent to him (at 5.50 p.m.) to the effect that the
(c) French Government were apparently helpless; and that the only hope seemed to rest with Admiral Darlan, from whom the French fleet might take orders. If the fleet could not be transferred to British or to United States ports it should be scuttled. There is no evidence that Sir R. Campbell received this telegram.

[3] See above, pp. 306–7. In addition to the telegram of 10.9 a.m. Sir R. Campbell sent
(d) another telegram, which was received at 4.45 p.m., giving a brief summary of the armistice terms. Two further summaries, of articles 1–9 and of the remaining articles (10–24), arrived respectively at 5.50 p.m. and 10.35 p.m.

(a) C7375/7362/17. (b) WM(40)176. (c) C7375/7362/17. (d) C7375/7362/17.

and the Prime Minister had now returned from Chequers. Sir R. Campbell's account of his interviews with Marshal Pétain and M. Baudouin before the meeting of the Council of Ministers had been received, but the general attitude of the War Cabinet would appear to be summed up in Mr. Alexander's view that we did not yet know that we had been betrayed by the French as it appeared that Marshal Pétain had renewed his assurances regarding the safety of the fleet. The War Cabinet decided, with a view to the vital need for obtaining control of the French fleet, to address a further appeal to Admiral Darlan as a personal message from Mr. Alexander and Admiral Pound and to appeal also to Admiral Esteva at Oran. For this purpose it was agreed that Lord Lloyd and the Vice-Chief of Naval Staff should fly to Oran.

At this point news was brought to the War Cabinet that the Germans were broadcasting an account of the signing of the armistice. The War Cabinet then agreed that the Admiralty should ensure that the *Richelieu* and the *Jean Bart* did not leave Dakar and Casablanca, and that 'procrastinating tactics' should be continued with regard to the detention of French warships in British ports.

After the meeting of the War Cabinet the Prime Minister and Lord Halifax decided that it would be wiser to postpone Lord Lloyd's visit to Oran, at all events for twenty-four hours until more was known of the situation.[1]

At this meeting of the War Cabinet the Prime Minister also suggested that as soon as possible a broadcast should be delivered on (a) the German terms. These terms could be described as drawn up with the intention of using the French Government as a tool of the enemy in striking down the late Ally of France. The broadcast should also make clear that, in accepting the terms, the Bordeaux Government had negotiated under duress, and had been deprived of all liberty.

On June 23 the Prime Minister issued the following statement:

'H.M. Government have heard with grief and amazement that the terms dictated by the Germans have been accepted by the French Government at Bordeaux. They cannot feel that such or similar terms could have been submitted to by any French Government which possessed freedom, independence and constitutional authority. Such terms if accepted by all Frenchmen would place not only France

---

[1] At 8.40 p.m. Sir R. Campbell was instructed to deliver a message from His Majesty The King to the President of the Republic pointing out the danger of leaving the French (b) fleet in ports where it might fall into enemy hands. This message did not reach Sir R. Campbell until he was about to set sail for England in H.M.S. *Galatea*. He forwarded the message by telegraph from St. Jean de Luz. M. Lebrun replied to the message, but on June 24 the War Cabinet agreed to advise His Majesty The King not to make a further communication to M. Lebrun.

(a) WM(40)176; C7380/7327/17.   (b) C7375/7362/17; C7541/65/17; C7146/9/17; WM(40)179.

but the French Empire entirely at the mercy and in the power of the German and Italian Dictators. Not only would the French people be held down and forced to work against their Ally, not only would the soil of France be used with the approval of the Bordeaux Government as the means of attacking their Ally, but the whole resources of the French Empire and of the French Navy would speedily pass into the hands of the adversary for the fulfilment of his purpose.

His Majesty's Government firmly believe that whatever happens they will be able to carry the war wherever it may lead on the seas, in the air, and upon land to a successful conclusion. When Great Britain is victorious she will in spite of the action of the Bordeaux Government cherish the cause of the French people and a British victory is the only possible hope for the restoration of the greatness of France and the freedom of its people. Brave men from other countries overrun by Nazi invasion are steadfastly fighting in the ranks of freedom. Accordingly His Majesty's Government call upon all Frenchmen outside the power of the enemy to aid them in their task and thereby render its accomplishment more sure and more swift. They appeal to all Frenchmen, wherever they may be, to aid to the utmost of their strength the forces of liberation which are enormous and which faithfully and resolutely used will assuredly prevail.'

The Prime Minister's statement of June 23 showed that the British Government had some hope that, in spite of the refusal of Marshal Pétain's Government to continue the war from French overseas territory, the military and civil authorities in the French colonial empire might withhold obedience from the home Government and maintain resistance, and that large numbers of French officers and men in metropolitan France would wish to go on fighting at the side of the British forces. Neither hope was entirely fulfilled or entirely disappointed.

The movement to continue resistance on French colonial territory was encouraged by Great Britain before the armistice; the establishment of a military, naval, and air force of 'Free Frenchmen' was the work of General de Gaulle. General de Gaulle's appeal to his countrymen in France and throughout the French Empire very soon made him the centre of a continued French resistance. His Majesty's Government recognised General de Gaulle's leadership, and the two currents of resistance in metropolitan and overseas territory were thus brought together.

It is necessary, therefore, to distinguish three stages in the encouragement and organisation of a continued French resistance: (i) the period between June 14 and June 18, i.e. before General de Gaulle made his first broadcast[1] from Great Britain, (ii) the period between June 18 and June 23, i.e. before General de Gaulle announced the formation of a French National Committee, (iii) the period, after June 23, during which a number of Frenchmen from metropolitan

---

[1] See above, p. 301, note (2).

France, and a number of the French colonies joined General de Gaulle. The first of these three periods was one of tentative and exploratory action by the British Government; the second period was one of hesitation and confusion, due, at first, to uncertainty about the action of Marshal Pétain's Government, to doubts about the expediency of allowing a second broadcast which General de Gaulle proposed to make from Great Britain, and also to a certain lack of co-ordination in British policy. The third period was one of considerable disappointment. The authorities in French North Africa and Syria, after some vacillation, accepted the armistice terms, and continued to obey the orders of Marshal Pétain's Government. The response from French officers and men in Great Britain was also on a smaller scale than had been expected. Finally, the refusal of the French naval commander at Oran to reject the terms of surrender accepted by the French Government (which included Admiral Darlan) and to send his ships out of German and Italian reach resulted in the naval action which brought Frenchmen into battle with their former Allies.

After the first appeal by M. Reynaud for the release of France from her engagement not to make a separate demand for an armistice the British Government considered it necessary to take preliminary steps to ensure the support of the French colonies for the continuance of the war. On June 14 the Chiefs of Staff drew up a memorandum (a) reviewing the situation brought about by the French collapse. The memorandum assumed that the German terms would include the cessation of hostilities in all French colonies, the use of bases for themselves and the Italians, and possibly a demand that the economic resources of France and her overseas possessions should be put at the disposal of Germany and Italy.

The Chiefs of Staff considered that, after the collapse of France, our ability to defeat Germany would depend upon our power to control the essential external supplies of Europe, and particularly the supplies of tropical and colonial produce and non-ferrous metals, and upon our retention of key strategic points from which we could exert a blockade of all Europe. We therefore needed to control French colonial products and to deny French air and naval bases such as Dakar, Syria and Madagascar to Germany and Italy. We also required the use of such bases, e.g. Casablanca[1], as we might need, and the refusal of the use of French territory for military operations or subversive activities against our own possessions. Without the French fleet we could not control the western Mediterranean or prevent the enemy from using the resources and bases of French North Africa. Elsewhere the colonial position would depend

---

[1] Casablanca would be specially important if we lost the use of Gibraltar.
(a) C7278/65/17.

largely upon the attitude of the French local administration. There could be no question of taking over French possessions.

The main recommendations of the Chiefs of Staff were as follows: (i) We should try, at the right moment, to get the French Government to send a secret message urging their local authorities overseas to co-operate with British forces in spite of the terms to which the central Government might have to agree under duress. (ii) The Foreign Office should explain our policy and plans to all British consular representatives in French overseas territories. (iii) At the time of the French surrender we should offer to do everything possible to help the French in overseas territories to defend themselves. (iv) We should prepare plans for economic pressure on territories refusing to co-operate. (v) We should try to persuade the United States to declare that they would regard as a *casus belli* any change in the *status quo* in the Far East or the Pacific.

The first step taken by the Foreign Office in an approach to the (a) French colonial authorities was the despatch of a telegram of June 15 to British consular representatives in French colonial territory.[1] This telegram informed the Consuls of the policy of the British Government in the event of a French collapse, but warned them not to discuss the situation with the French authorities until they had received further instructions.

On June 17 the Consuls were told to approach the French authori- (b) ties and to explain our policy to them.[2] They were authorised to make the following communication:

> 'His Majesty's Government recognise that the French Government has been compelled to capitulate under duress, and in spite of the heroic resistance of the French armies supported by their Allies. The British people, knowing that the French army has laid down its arms against its will and that of the French people, intend to continue the struggle. The greater part of France is now in enemy occupation, but her overseas territories retain their freedom. The British forces will therefore do all in their power to assist these territories to defend themselves against the enemy, and the British people are confident that their co-operation will be forthcoming.'[3]

The response of the French colonial authorities to this communi- (c) cation from the British Government was uncertain. Mr. Knight,

---

[1] This telegram was sent to Algiers, Bangkok (for Saigon), Beirut, Dakar, Damascus, Jibuti, Léopoldville (for Brazzaville), Rabat and Tunis. Indo-China, Syria and the territories under French rule in Africa were of the greatest immediate importance. The telegram was to have been sent also to Madagascar, but seems to have been delayed through cyphering difficulties.

[2] These instructions were sent in view of Marshal Pétain's broadcast. See above, pp. 291-2.

[3] The Consuls were also authorised to state that His Majesty's Government would provide economic and financial assistance.

(a) C7278/65/17. (b) C7278/65/17. (c) C7316/65/17.

Consul at Tunis, delivered the communication to M. Peyrouton, the newly-appointed Resident-General, on the morning of June 18. M. Peyrouton said that he had come to Tunis 'to make war', and was convinced that a French Government would be established in North Africa and would continue the war. He thought it inconceivable that the Government would accept the 'crushing terms' which the Germans would impose. On the other hand he ruled out a local separatist movement on a large scale. In the evening of June 18 M. Peyrouton told Mr. Knight that he was sending a strongly worded telegram to the French Government in support of Mr. Knight's representations and containing a summary of the communication which he had made.

The attitude of General Blanc, military commander in Tunis, was also satisfactory. General Blanc explained, however, that he was under (a) the orders of General Noguès. Mr. Knight thought that he would not take independent action, but that, as in the case of the air force, a good many officers would try to reach British or neutral territory in the event of a complete French surrender. The General commanding the air force in Tunis also said that the necessary preparations were being made to continue the war, and that no other eventuality was even envisaged, but he 'would not be drawn' on the question of independent local action. The Admiral commanding the French naval forces said that in no circumstances would the ships under his command be surrendered. He was 'firmly convinced' that the French fleet would join the British fleet: he did not say that he would act on these lines against orders from Admiral Darlan.

Mr. Hurst, Consul at Rabat, reported on June 18 that, after the first shock, morale in the French zone of Morocco was stiffening, but (b) that there was still no frank declaration of an intention to fight on in North Africa. On June 19 Mr. Hurst was told that the heads of the French ex-combatant groups in Morocco had telegraphed to Marshal (c) Pétain in favour of continuing resistance in North Africa. They had also told General Noguès of their intention to fight on and had received a reply that he shared their views. They asked that General de Gaulle should be informed in answer to his broadcast of June 18 that the great majority of Frenchmen in Morocco and North Africa intended to continue the fight. The Resident-General asked Mr. Hurst to regard these facts as most confidential and, for the time, not to let General de Gaulle know of them. On June 20 Mr. Hurst reported that the senior Residency officials continued to await events in France and would give no frank indication of their intentions or say anything more than reminders that they were subordinate to General Noguès. Very many Frenchmen in the zone were becoming increasingly perplexed at the attitude of their Government.

(a) C7343/7327/17. (b) C7316/65/17. (c) C7343/7327/17.

(a)   Mr. Jakins, Consul at Jibuti, reported that the Governor of the French Somali Coast had said on June 17 that he had no official news from France, but that, if he were instructed by the French Government to surrender Jibuti, he would obey his orders. The General in command said that, in such case, he would use force against the Governor, and that he would continue to fight under General

(b) Wavell's orders. On June 19 the Governor was 'shifting his ground', but there might be a danger that, if they were given time to reflect, the French officers would come to realise that they could continue to fight only as rebels against their own Government, while other ranks would be open to the propaganda cry 'Why fight for the English?' In order to close these loopholes, it appeared essential that, if the French Government surrendered, a new Government should be found in order to give the colonial Governors a basis of loyalty for going on fighting. The General Commanding had suggested M. Reynaud, in preference to a soldier, as head of this government.

Mr. Havard, Consul-General at Beirut, reported that the French

(c) High Commissioner, in agreement with General Mittelhauser, had said that he would go on fighting, whatever orders he might

(d) receive. The Governor-General at Hanoi stated that, in his view, whatever might happen in Europe, the Anglo-French alliance must continue in Indo-China and that he relied on British military co-operation in the event of the Japanese attack with which he was

(e) now threatened. In French West Africa the Governor-General was hesitating; the armed forces and the local population were strongly in favour of continuing resistance. The local authorities in the Cameroons were also anxious to continue resistance and had asked for British support. The Governor of French Equatorial Africa said that he would resist if French West Africa resisted. Otherwise, and if he could not get British protection, he and his general officer commanding would withdraw on their own responsibility to British territory and would be followed by nine-tenths of their troops and of the civil population.

The communication of the message from the British Government to the Governor-General of Algeria had an immediate sequel which showed the weakness of the colonial position. During the night of

(f) June 18–19 Sir R. Campbell reported that M. Charles-Roux had spoken to him officially on the subject, and had 'deplored' the effect of the message at a time when the French troops were still fighting and the Government had decided to continue resistance if the German terms were 'excessive'. M. Charles-Roux asked the British Government not to 'render more difficult the task of those here who were working in the direction we should wish them to go'. On the

(a) C7316/65/17.   (b) C7343/7327/17.   (c) C7316/65/17.   (d) C7343/7327/17.
(e) C7316/65/17. (f) C7316/65/17.

night of June 19 Sir R. Campbell was instructed to tell M. Charles-Roux that the instructions to deliver the message had been sent after the formal declaration by Marshal Pétain that French resistance had ceased and that he had asked for an armistice. We could not then foresee that the French Government would again rally.

Lord Halifax mentioned M. Charles-Roux's protest to the War (a) Cabinet on June 19 as a warning of the need for caution. He repeated his warning on June 21, and the War Cabinet agreed that it should (b) be passed to the British representatives in the French colonial territories. Meanwhile the reports from these representatives suggested little change in the position. The attitude of the authorities at Algiers was still uncertain. In the evening of June 20 the Consul-General reported information that, after pressure from his Financial (c) Council, the Governor-General, with several delegates, had visited General Noguès on June 19, and had urged him to go on fighting. General Noguès's answer had been non-commital, but might be considered as a qualified acceptance. No steps for separation from France would be taken openly until after the publication of the peace terms, and until it was certain that, under these terms, North Africa would be handed over to the enemy. Twenty-four hours later the Consul-General reported that the situation was unchanged, and (d) would probably remain unchanged until the German terms were known. General Noguès had issued a proclamation on June 20 that, for the time, there was no question of ceasing to fight. On the other hand the proclamation asked for full confidence in the French Government.

Mr. Knight asked on June 20 whether he could give unofficial publicity to the British promise of support to French overseas (e) territory.[1] The effect would be very great, although the military authorities would almost certainly forbid an official announcement of the promise. On the next day Mr. Knight reported that numbers of French officers and men had called on him on behalf of their comrades to say how much they wished to fight on in North Africa, and to join the British forces in the event of a French surrender. About three-quarters of the reserve officers held these views. Feeling among regular officers was less strong or less freely expressed. Owing to the lack of co-ordination among discontented officers the local troops and air force would probably obey orders even to surrender. Everything appeared to depend on the attitude of General Noguès.

The Consul-General at Dakar also reported on the evening of

---

[1] Mr. Knight was told on June 21 that we were considering a public declaration about the French colonial empire, but that for the time no publicity should be given to the promises in our communication (of June 17). Even unofficial publicity might have adverse results in view of the fact that the French were still undecided what to do.

(a) WM(40)172, C7352/65/17. (b) WM(40)174, C7343/7327/17. (c) C7343/7327/17. (d) C7366/5/18. (e) C7343/7327/17.

(a) June 21 that, in spite of fervent protestations from various branches of the administration, the armed forces, and the population in general, the local attitude would not be clear until the decision of the French Government was known. The attitude of the Governor-General at

(b) Brazzaville was similar. The Governor-General had said that the 'desire' of French West Africa to continue resistance did not imply a 'determination' to resist, and that, while a French Government existed, he must decline a declaration of policy, and regard decision as premature until the situation in Europe was more clear.

The most favourable news came on June 22 from Saigon where

(c) General Catroux as the Governor-General had issued a proclamation in the following terms: 'As long as the destiny of Indo-China is confided in me, this country will remain French, and I will not lower my flag which is that of France.'

On the evening of June 22 when it was clear that Marshal Pétain's

(d) Government intended to accept the German terms, the War Cabinet, at the suggestion of Lord Halifax, agreed to make an appeal to the French colonies as soon as the acceptance was a *fait accompli*. Instructions were therefore sent during the early hours of June 23 to all British consular representatives in French colonial territory in the following terms:

> 'French Government have accepted enemy's conditions for an armistice, and you should immediately make following communications to French authorities:
>
> The present French Government, in accepting under duress the enemy's conditions for an armistice have been prevented from making good the solemn pledge of France to her British Allies. They have resigned themselves to the accomplished fact of the German occupation of metropolitan France. But this occupation does not extend to the vast territories of the French Overseas Empire, which remains with its frontiers, its defences and its huge economic resources intact.
>
> The French Overseas Empire has still a vital part to play in the struggle for civilisation, the successful outcome of which alone can restore the liberty of France. We, the British Government and British people, are resolved to continue this struggle to the end, and our victory will mean the restoration of the greatness of France. We call upon the civil and military authorities of all French overseas territories to stand by our side and fight hand in hand with us until victory is reached, and thus redeem the pledge of the French Republic.
>
> We appeal to them to do this even if they receive orders from the Government in France to surrender to the enemy, for that Government are already under the control of the enemy and can no longer be regarded as representatives of France. Moreover the Government have no constitutional mandate to surrender French territory.

(a) C7343/7327/17.   (b) C7343/7327/17.   (c) C7380/7327/17.   (d) WM(40)176, C7380/7327/17.

Until such time as a free, independent, and constitutional authority has been re-established on free French soil we shall do everything in our power to maintain the integrity and economic stability of all French overseas territories provided they stand by us. We further guarantee that these territories will be provided with funds to cover the payment of the salaries and pensions of all civil and military officials throughout the French Overseas Empire who are prepared to co-operate with us.'

(vi)

Decision to postpone broadcasts by General de Gaulle on June 19 and 20: General de Gaulle's broadcast of June 22: proposal for the formation of a French National Committee, June 23: General de Gaulle's broadcast of June 23: British recognition of General de Gaulle as the leader of 'Free Frenchmen', June 28, 1940.

General de Gaulle's broadcast from London on June 18 to which British Ministers had agreed after a first refusal,[1] was an appeal to Frenchmen to get into touch with him in London in order to organise continued French resistance. The appeal was not addressed to French colonial authorities and did not suggest the establishment of a French Government in opposition to that of Marshal Pétain. General de Gaulle had become known to the Prime Minister and, more closely, to General Spears, through his spirited advocacy of 'new methods' of countering German tactics and through his refusal to associate himself with the defeatism of Marshal Pétain and General Weygand. The General had come to London only when it was impossible for him to do anything more in France. There were no political reasons on the British side for inviting him, and no plans for asking him to undertake any political activities. It was obvious that weight would be attached to his advice; he was, in fact, one of the promoters of the Declaration of Union proposed to M. Reynaud immediately before the latter's resignation.

After his broadcast of June 18 General de Gaulle and other (a) Frenchmen in London thought it desirable to go a stage further in the organisation of French resistance. They suggested on June 19 a draft statement as follows:

'Le Gouvernement de la France ayant capitulé est au pouvoir de l'ennemi. Il ne représente donc plus la Nation française. Tout, cependant, n'est pas perdu. Un nouveau gouvernement, composé d'hommes libres, dignes représentants du peuple français, a été

---

[1] See above, p. 301, note 2.
(a) C7389/7389/17.

constitué immédiatement à Londres (?)[1] en toute indépendance. Il va prendre en mains la destinée du Pays.

Français!

D'énormes ressources sont encore à notre disposition dans notre Afrique du Nord, et dans nos colonies. Nous avons des Alliés puissants. Nous lutterons. Nous triompherons.

Dès sa constitution, le nouveau gouvernement fera une déclaration.'

The Foreign Office view of this draft, and of a longer broadcast[2] which General de Gaulle proposed to make in the evening of June 19, was that 'we ought to be careful not to ride two horses at the same time'. General de Gaulle's broadcast of June 18 (which Sir R. Vansittart had regarded as inexpedient at the time) had the appearance of a challenge to the Government at Bordeaux. This Government had already taken offence at our communication to the French colonial authorities and at President Roosevelt's message about the French navy. In view of the information received that the President of the Republic, General Weygand and other Ministers might go to North Africa to organise French resistance, it would be a mistake for General de Gaulle to issue from Great Britain an appeal to Frenchmen to rally under him.

General de Gaulle was therefore asked for the present not to (a) broadcast either the shorter or the longer statement. On June 20 General Spears sent a memorandum to the Prime Minister suggesting as a matter of 'utmost urgency' that General de Gaulle should broadcast on the night of June 20–1. General Spears argued, from the response to General de Gaulle's appeal of June 18, that he was reviving hopes in men who were previously in despair, and providing a 'focal point' for thousands of individuals who otherwise, however great their desire to resist, 'did not know where to make for'. General de Gaulle intended to make it entirely clear that he held himself, and all those who rallied to his call, at the disposition of any French Government ready to carry on resistance.

In the afternoon of June 20 General de Gaulle came to the (b) Foreign Office. The Foreign Office had already heard that a statement had been issued on the midday French wireless disowning the General. The Foreign Office view was that it was still inopportune for the broadcast to be delivered. Sir A. Cadogan told General de Gaulle of the possibility that General Weygand might go to Africa and suggested that, in these circumstances, it might be better for

---

[1] This query is in the copy of the text in the Foreign Office archives.

[2] The text of this broadcast, which had the approval of Mr. Duff Cooper, the Minister of Information, was in the name of Frenchmen in London. The broadcast appealed ('au nom du Peuple français, nous, conscients d'être les représentants du peuple, donnons l'ordre à nos généraux, à nos amiraux, à tous ceux qui ne sont pas sous la botte allemande, de continuer à se battre') to General Noguès and General Mittelhauser by name and to 'l'Amiral commandant la flotte'.

(a) C7389/7389/17.   (b) C7389/7389/17.

General de Gaulle to hold his hand until the situation became clearer. General de Gaulle seemed fully to accept the point that there might be a risk of giving an impression of divided counsels; he said that, if General Weygand were shown to be organising resistance in French overseas territory, he would at once offer his own services to him.

General de Gaulle did not broadcast on June 20 or 21. On June 21, apparently at the suggestion of the Foreign Office, a Cabinet committee was set up to examine and co-ordinate plans for the continued resistance of France.[1] The committee decided, for the time being, that no broadcasts should be given by 'eminent Frenchmen arriving from France' and that public indications of lack of confidence in the French Government should be avoided. At the same time the Committee wished the B.B.C. to repeat at frequent intervals the statement already broadcast that all Frenchmen coming to Great Britain would be welcomed.

At their midday meeting on June 22 the Committee discussed the question of a direct appeal to French troops to come to Great (a) Britain. They thought that the French Government would give no help in the matter and that little help would come from other French authorities in France. Hence the best plan would be for a broadcast to be given by General de Gaulle or another French general in London. The Committee agreed therefore to seek immediate authority from Lord Halifax for such a broadcast.

In the evening of June 22 the Minister of Information gave the War Cabinet the draft of a proclamation which General de Gaulle (b) proposed to broadcast at 10 p.m. The War Cabinet had some doubts about the desirability of a broadcast, but Lord Halifax considered that His Majesty's Government would not be compromised in any way if they allowed a distinguished French officer to use the British wireless for a message to his own countrymen. General de Gaulle would not be 'the mouthpiece of the British Government'. Lord Lloyd said that, while he was in Bordeaux, he had been told by many French officers that they had heard only through General de Gaulle's previous broadcast of the opportunity offered to them to continue resistance on the side of Great Britain. The War Cabinet therefore consented to the delivery of General de Gaulle's broadcast at 10 p.m. on June 22. They also agreed to the Prime Minister's suggestion that as soon as possible a broadcast should be delivered on the German terms. As a result of this suggestion the Prime Minister issued his statement of June 23.[2]

---

[1] This committee, which included representatives from the Foreign Office, continued to sit until the middle of August 1940, when its terms of reference were extended to cover Allied resistance generally and it was renamed the Committee on Foreign (Allied) Resistance.

[2] See above, pp. 313–4.

(a) C7456/7389/17.   (b) WM(40)176, C7389/7389/17.

(a)   In the morning of June 23 the War Cabinet considered a proposal by General de Gaulle for the formation of a French National Committee. Lord Halifax gave the names of a number of Frenchmen for whom Sir R. Campbell was trying to arrange embarkation from Bordeaux. These Frenchmen would form a nucleus for the continuation of the struggle in the French Empire, and General de Gaulle might well be the centre around which some of the more resolute French statesmen might rally. The Prime Minister read to the War Cabinet a letter from General de Gaulle outlining his proposal for a Council of Liberation (Comité National Français). General de Gaulle asked the British Government to recognise this committee.

The Prime Minister said that General de Gaulle was a good fighting soldier, with a good reputation and a strong personality who might well be the right man to set up such a Council. It would be desirable, however, before approving or recognising the Council, to find out what Frenchmen were available to serve on it and whom, in particular, General de Gaulle had in mind.

The War Cabinet agreed in principle upon the recognition of the (b) Committee. The Prime Minister, Lord Halifax, and Sir A. Cadogan then saw General de Gaulle. The General proposed various names, including that of M. Reynaud whom he suggested as head of a provisional government. He explained that the committee would merely assist in the formation of this Government.

The Prime Minister explained the views of the War Cabinet to General de Gaulle and, after discussion of details, left the General to go on with his plan, and promised that His Majesty's Government would prepare a draft announcing the committee and their own readiness to support it.

General de Gaulle broadcast his statement on the evening of June 23. After stating that in the situation brought about by the capitulation of the Bordeaux Government, the political institutions of France could not function freely and the French people were without means of expressing their true will, the General announced the formation of a French National Committee, 'in agreement with the British Government'.

> 'The French National Committee will account for its acts either to the legal and established French Government, as soon as such a one exists, or to the representatives of the people as soon as circumstances allow them to assemble in conditions compatible with liberty, dignity and security.
>
> The French National Committee will take under its jurisdiction all French citizens at present in British territory and will assume the direction of all military and administrative bodies who are now, or may in the future be, in Great Britain. The French National Com-

---

(a) WM(40)177, C7389/7389/17. (b) C7389/7389/17.

mittee will get into touch with such bodies in order to call for their participation in its formation.

The war is not lost, the country is not dead, hope is not extinct. Vive la France.'

At the conclusion of General de Gaulle's broadcast a statement was also broadcast in French on the authority of the British Government. This statement affirmed that the terms of the armistice signed in contravention of the solemn agreements between the Allied Governments would reduce the Bordeaux Government to a state of complete subjection and deprive it of all right to represent free French citizens. The British Government therefore could not recognise the Bordeaux Government as that of an independent country. At the same time the British Government took note of the formation of a Provisional French National Committee, fully representing independent French elements, and declared that they would recognise such a Committee and deal with it on all matters concerning the prosecution of the war as long as it continued to represent all French elements resolved to fight the common enemy.

During June 22 and 23 the information reaching the Foreign Office showed little change in the attitude of the French colonies. Opinion in Indo-China was strongly in favour of resistance. The (a) Governor-General of French West Africa had been in touch with other colonial governors and was convinced that a government would be formed to represent the will of the French Empire to continue resistance. According to the French Military Attaché at Tangier, General Noguès seemed likely to declare himself in favour of continuing the war.

On the other hand General de Gaulle's optimism about the reception of his proposals by Frenchmen was not borne out by M. Corbin and M. Léger. M. Corbin told Lord Halifax before General de Gaulle's broadcast on June 23 that he and M. Léger felt grave concern over the support which we were giving to the General's (b) movement. M. Corbin had asked that we should not allow the General to broadcast.[1] After the delivery of the broadcast M. Corbin telephoned his alarm at its terms and at the statement by His Majesty's Government recognising the committee. M. Corbin said that we were making a wrong approach to the question of continuing French resistance. He asked that the British statement should not be mentioned in the press. Lord Halifax thought that, as the statement had been broadcast, the question of publication in the press was not of

---

[1] M. Corbin and M. Léger were at Sir R. Vansittart's house at Denham on the evening of June 23. At 9.15 p.m. Sir R. Vansittart telephoned on M. Corbin's behalf to Sir A. Cadogan asking that the broadcast should be altered. Sir A. Cadogan consulted Lord Halifax who agreed that it was too late to change it.

(a) C7380/7327/17. (b) WM(40)178, C7389/7389/17.

much importance, but in view of M. Corbin's insistence, Lord Halifax 'reluctantly agreed' to do his best to withhold publication.

(a) On the morning of June 24 M. Corbin again discussed the question with Lord Halifax. He said that we were giving support to a National Committee which had not yet been formed. In French eyes this Committee constituted on British soil with British support would not appear any more independent than the Bordeaux Government. The establishment of a Government in North Africa would be a different matter, but one formed in Great Britain, without representative interests, would fail, and no one would pay attention to it.

M. Corbin thought that the reaction of Frenchmen who wanted to maintain the independence of France would be unfavourable. They would ask how the British Government could expect them to condemn their own Government and to continue a resistance which was already impossible. They might feel the armistice to be shameful, but they would resent any statement by the British Government about breaking off relations with the Bordeaux Government. Lord Halifax argued with M. Corbin that General de Gaulle's Committee would at least provide a nucleus without which it was difficult to see how French opinion could ever rally; M. Corbin said that, if we wanted an organisation to serve as a nucleus of resistance, this organisation must have the appearance of an independent body. Otherwise even those in France with friendly feelings towards Great Britain would have nothing to do with it.

At a meeting of the War Cabinet on June 24 the Prime Minister (b) read a message which M. Reynaud[1] had sent to him through M. Corbin. M. Reynaud tried to argue that, notwithstanding the terms of the armistice, we should be safeguarded against the risk of an attempt by the enemy to get possession of the French fleet. The Prime Minister considered that no more reliance could be put upon M. Reynaud than upon other members of the French Government. This Government had broken their treaty obligations and were under German control. They would allow all their resources to fall into the hands of the enemy and to be used against their former allies. There was grave danger that 'the rot would spread from the top' through the fleet, army and air force and through all the French colonies. The Germans would put every form of pressure upon the French Government to act to our detriment. The French Government would be drawn more and more into making common cause with Germany, and we must soon expect to be the object of the deepest hate in France. As long as the possession of the French warships was unsecured, these ships could be used as a blackmailing threat against us.

---

[1] M. Reynaud was still in Bordeaux and had not gone to Morocco with other French politicians who had left Bordeaux in the *Massilia*. See above, p. 303, note (2).

(a) C7389/7389/17.   (b) WM(40)178, C7389/7389/17.

At all costs we must secure that the ships came under our control or were put out of action for good. In the near future we should have to solve the problem of our future relations with the French Government. If this Government were located in an enclave surrounded by enemy territory, we could not keep our Ambassador there, since we should be unable to communicate with him. In such a case it was difficult to see how we could receive a French Ambassador in London. Our relations with France might therefore approach very closely to those of two nations at war with each other.

The War Cabinet was informed of a message from M. Herriot to the Prime Minister pleading for no recriminations against Marshal Pétain. M. Herriot and others favourable to us intended to stay in France, where, in their opinion, they could do more good than by leaving for one of the colonies. Lord Halifax then gave an account of his conversation with M. Corbin. He said it was disturbing to find M. Corbin in opposition to General de Gaulle who had mentioned him as the first of his backers. Lord Halifax agreed with the Prime Minister's statement about the problem of our relations with the Bordeaux Government but thought that for the present we should go rather slow in withdrawing recognition from Marshal Pétain.

The Prime Minister said that he would explain the position to M. Reynaud. He would make it clear that no trust could be put in German promises and that there was no limit to the pressure which Germany could exercise on France. The question was not one of recrimination, but of things which to us were matters of life and death. It was pointed out that, for the moment, we had no further step to take in relation to General de Gaulle whom we had recognised as the head, not of an independent government, but of a committee established to facilitate the co-operation of those Frenchmen who were determined to go on fighting the common enemy.

The War Cabinet also agreed later on the same day to a proposal by the Committee on French resistance that special steps should be taken to send a representative to see General Noguès. Mr. Duff Cooper, and Lord Gort, as a military representative, were authorised to go to Morocco for this purpose and to urge M. Reynaud, and the members of his administration now at Rabat, to set up a government in North Africa or Syria, or, if these places were not possible, in Great Britain.

During the afternoon of June 24 M. Cambon came to the Foreign Office (where he saw Mr. Strang) with a series of communications (a) from the French Government. The French Government complained that General de Gaulle, whom they had recalled to France for disciplinary reasons, was allowed to make a public broadcast. They also complained of communications made by British Consular

(a) WM(40)179.

Representatives at Rabat, Algiers and Tunis to the effect that the French Government, having been obliged to sign an armistice, no longer had any powers in territory occupied by the enemy, and that the British Government therefore appealed to all French territories overseas to abandon their own Government and to continue the struggle with Great Britain.[1] The French Government wished to say that these communications were 'inadmissible' and appeared to show that we did not intend to continue our relations with them. They asked whether this was the case and suggested that the consular representatives in question should be recalled. The French Government also wished to state that in their view they had not agreed in the armistice terms to any condition likely to make France an instrument which might be directly used against Great Britain; in particular they thought it certain that in any event such use could not be made of the French fleet. They protested therefore against the language used on the subject by the Prime Minister.[2] They also claimed that they were not the 'Government of Bordeaux'[3] but the Government of France which had the full support of Frenchmen.

The War Cabinet were told of this communication on the evening of June 24, but did not consider it desirable to send a reply.

The reports received late on June 24 and on June 25 showed a decline in the will to resistance throughout the French colonies and a disappointing reaction to General de Gaulle's appeal. It appeared increasingly unlikely that (with the exception of Indo-China) any of the larger French colonies would break with Marshal Pétain's Government and continue resistance. At the same time there was more evidence of the completeness with which the French Government had broken with Great Britain. Lord Halifax read to the War Cabinet on the morning of June 25 a statement in which the French (a) had presented their case to the United States Government. According to this statement, the French Government regretted the critical attitude of the British Government and, in a summary of events, alleged the failure of Great Britain to mobilise her manpower and to despatch to France 26 divisions which had been promised. A delegation from the French press had visited England, and had reported on the unsatisfactory state of war production. It was obvious that the

---

[1] Mr. Strang pointed out that this was an inaccurate summary of our communications.

[2] In making this communication, M. Cambon said that M. Corbin, who was unlikely to remain Ambassador much longer, was unwilling to deliver it, and that he had asked him (M. Cambon) to do so. M. Cambon himself doubted whether, if there were many such communications to make, he would be able to continue to come to us with them. At the same time M. Cambon thought we should take care in our reply to avoid giving the French Government the chance of saying that they had wished to remain on friendly terms with us, and that we had rejected their offer.

[3] For the use of this term, see below, p. 401, note 1.

(a) WM(40)181, C7294/65/17.

British believed more in the blockade than in the provision of material assistance to their Ally. The Prime Minister, on his last visit to France, had been expected to attend a Council of Ministers, but had failed to do so. The British Government had been asked what they would do if France felt obliged to sue for peace. The British reply had been that they intended to go on fighting but would not reproach France for her default. Subsequently, owing to intervention by M. Mandel and others, the British Government had adopted a different attitude.

The Prime Minister said to the War Cabinet that this statement was entirely false. He explained the points which he proposed to make in a speech in the House of Commons later on in the day.[1] He would say that in our future relations with the Bordeaux Government we should take such action as we might think necessary for our own security and the future prosecution of the war.

The attitude of Admiral Darlan was shown on June 25 in a (a) message received from Admiral Odend'hal by the Admiralty and transmitted to the Foreign Office. Admiral Darlan had telegraphed in the afternoon of June 24 that France had accepted the dispositions of the armistice on condition that the French fleet must definitely remain French, under the French flag, and with a reduced French complement. Admiral Darlan thought that these dispositions were not in any way contrary to British interests. He therefore regretted that we should have found it necessary to detain French ships in British ports. This detention was almost an unfriendly act, and Admiral Darlan asked for the release of the ships.

The Foreign Office pointed out to the Admiralty that Admiral Darlan's statement about the safeguarding of the French fleet was 'quite contrary' to their information, and that the last part of the message was ominous, since Admiral Darlan might say that, since we had taken matters into our own hands, he was released from all obligations to us.

The attitude of General Mittelhauser was also uncertain. On June 25 the General said to the head of the British Military Mission (b) in Syria that he had not changed in his determination to go on fighting, but that he felt 'an enormous weight of responsibility for his decision'. General Mittelhauser also asked for assurances that the British Government did not intend to take Syria after the war.

General Noguès refused to see Mr. Duff Cooper and General Gort, and, on the night of June 26–7, ordered out of the country a British (c) officer on special mission at Casablanca. On June 28 it was clear, from French sources, that there was no chance of winning over (d)

---

[1] For this speech, see *Parl. Deb.*, 5th Ser., H. of C., Vol. 362, Cols. 301–05.

(a) C7375/7362/17. (b) C7380/7327/17. (c) C7366/5/18. (d) C7445/7389/17; C7497/5/18.

General Noguès. Naval opinion at Casablanca and Rabat was hostile to Great Britain and opinion in the Air Force was also hostile. The Admiral at Casablanca had said that he would fire on any British ships trying to enter the port.

(a) On June 28 His Majesty's Government decided finally to announce their official recognition of General de Gaulle. The recognition was given in a short statement at the time of a broadcast by General de Gaulle on the evening of June 28. The formula agreed by the War Cabinet was in the following terms: 'His Majesty's Government recognise General de Gaulle as the leader of all free Frenchmen, wherever they may be, who rally to him in support of the Allied cause'.

Note 1 to Chapter X.

(i)

Article 8 of the Franco-German Armistice of June 22, 1940. (French Version).

Article 8

La flotte de guerre française (à l'exception de la partie qui est laissée à la disposition du Gouvernement français pour la sauvegarde des intérêts français dans son empire colonial) sera rassemblée dans des ports à déterminer et devra être démobilisée et désarmée sous le contrôle de l'Allemagne ou respectivement de l'Italie. Les ports d'attaché du temps de paix de ces navires serviront pour la désignation de ces ports.

Le Gouvernement allemand déclare solennellement au Gouvernement français qu'il n'a pas l'intention d'utiliser pendant la guerre à ses propres fins, la flotte de guerre française stationnée dans les ports sous contrôle allemand, sauf les unités nécessaires à la surveillance des côtes et au dragage des mines. Il déclare en outre solennellement et formellement qu'il n'a pas l'intention de formuler des revendications à l'égard de la flotte de guerre française lors de la conclusion de la paix.

Exception faite de la partie de la flotte de guerre française à déterminer qui sera affectée à la sauvegarde des intérêts français dans l'empire colonial, tous les navires de guerre se trouvant en dehors des eaux territoriales françaises doivent être rappelés en France.

(a) WM(40)186, C7389/7389/17.

(ii)

Text (a) of the French proposed amendment to article 8 and (b) of the German reply to the French proposal.

(a) *Article 8.*—Modification du premier paragraphe.

La flotte de guerre française (à l'exception de la partie qui est laissée à la disposition du Gouvernement français pour la sauvegarde des intérêts français dans son empire colonial), après avoir été démobilisée et après débarqué ses munitions sous le contrôle de l'Allemagne ou respectivement de l'Italie, sera basée dans les ports français de l'Afrique. Les effectifs de chaque navire ne devront pas dépasser la moité des effectifs normaux du temps de paix.

Les deux autres paragraphes, sans changement.

(b) *Article 8* (Fleet).—The proposed modification is not accepted for insertion in the convention. The Germans do not refuse to contemplate acceptance of the proposal made, but they consider that it is a measure of application falling within the competence of the Armistice Commission.

Note 2 to Chapter X. German plans for the invasion of Great Britain.

After the collapse of France the Prime Minister and his Service advisers expected a German attempt at invasion within a short time. It seemed unlikely, in view of the well-laid German plans for the occupation of Norway, Denmark, and the Low Countries, and for their western offensive, that Hitler would not have prepared plans for the exploitation of victory by a final blow against Great Britain. The Germans, in fact, had no plans for an invasion, and found it difficult to improvise them when the opportunity came suddenly to them. They showed a surprising amount of confusion and indecision. Hitler did not issue a directive on preparations for an invasion until July 16. The preparations were to be completed by the middle of August. On July 31 he ordered the opening of a concentrated air attack which might of itself force a British surrender or at least enable the Germans to land without much co-ordinated opposition. He hoped for the success of this attack within a month. No date was fixed for invasion if the air attack did not bring the hoped for surrender, but the invading force was to be ready by September 15. The Germans planned to land 120,000 men with their equipment between Folkestone and Brighton within three days and to have increased their invading force to twenty-three divisions within six weeks.

For a short time—until mid-September—Hitler believed that the air attack would be sufficient, and that he could cancel the proposed landing operations; on September 14 he gave orders for the invasion but still did not name a definite date. Within a few days, since the air attacks had obviously not brought the needed superiority, Hitler ordered a postponement. The operation was not cancelled but the chance of carrying it out in 1940 became less with every week of delay. On October 12 the operation was called off at least for the year 1940.

It is not within the scope of this History to ask whether Hitler ever really intended an invasion. The question cannot be answered with any certainty. Nevertheless the evidence does not suggest that the elaborate preparations of the late summer were either a 'blind' or a bluff. The final abandonment of the plan for 1940 did not mean that Hitler was less confident that he could ultimately carry it out. On the other hand it is necessary to take into account not only Hitler's realisation of the practical difficulties— amply pointed out by his naval advisers—of a successful landing in the face of superior British sea-power, especially while the German Air Force had not won its expected victory. Hitler's own attitude was not fixed. He seems to have been surprised and, indeed, taken aback by the refusal of Great Britain to come to terms. He wanted to break, once for all, British power in relation to Germany, and thus make the British Empire sub-servient to German demands; he did not want the complete destruction of the British Empire, since he could not be certain of collecting all the prizes for Germany. He was set more upon obtaining physical control of a great deal of Russian territory and resources. This aim would be realised after full victory in the west, but, when the British refusal to surrender and their surprising resistance to air attack showed that there was no chance of winning this victory at once, Hitler began to think that he might postpone his final assault on Great Britain until he had defeated the U.S.S.R. He seems to have believed that one reason for the stubborness of British resistance was a hope of action against Germany by Russia (in fact, British 'hope' was not directed towards Russia but towards the United States). If he defeated Russia—as he expected to do without much difficulty—success against Great Britain would be doubly assured.

Hitler first told his generals at the end of July about the new plan to attack Russia. The generals did not like the proposal but could not resist Hitler at the height of his power and success. Hitler was not yet committed to the plan, but became more determined to carry it out after the failure against England, and with the increasing signs of Russian hostility to his Balkan moves, in spite of the continued willingness of the U.S.S.R. to fulfil and even increase their economic commitments to Germany. Mean-while General Franco's obstinacy ruled out an attack on Gibraltar. For the evolution of Hitler's plans, see below, pp. 494, note 1, and *Grand Strategy*, vol. II, chs. XII and XXIII.

CHAPTER XI

Anglo-American relations during the period of the collapse of France[1] : proposals for the grant of bases to the United States and for the transfer to Great Britain of American destroyers

(i)

Introduction

THE success of the German offensive in the Low Countries and France obviously had a bewildering effect on American opinion. Hitherto Americans had regarded it as possible and desirable to avoid participation in the war. They had assumed freedom of choice in the matter, and had not envisaged a sudden and complete German victory. In other words they had not asked, or had not asked seriously, what would happen if there were no longer a British fleet, and if the whole European coast, and the west coast of Africa were under German control.

In the opening phase of the offensive, American opinion was more concerned with the possible repercussions of British action to protect the valuable Dutch West Indian islands than with the ominous facts of the German advance. As the full extent of the French catastrophe became known, a section of American opinion assumed that Great Britain also was lost and could be 'written off'. The United States Government were bound at least to face this possibility. They were very much less prepared for war than the Allies a year or two years earlier, and unless they could count on Great Britain maintaining her resistance, they might be unwise to risk sending material which would either be lost *en route* or would fall into the hands of the Germans after they had compelled a British surrender.

As the position was viewed from the United States, there was at this stage no question of America coming into the war as a belligerent. Apart from the danger that Japan might take the chance of attacking in the Pacific if the American fleet were concentrated in the Atlantic, military argument was in favour of avoiding a war which the country was not ready to fight. Domestic political considerations added to the difficulty of a decision likely to lead to belligerency. The presidential

---

[1] Some aspects of the relations between the Allies and the United States (e.g. M. Reynaud's appeals to Mr. Roosevelt, and the joint Anglo-French *démarche* of May 25 to President Roosevelt with regard to an offer to Mussolini) have been dealt with in chapters VII–X of this volume. This chapter has therefore been limited as far as possible to Anglo-American relations.

333

election was approaching; a party which advocated American entry into the war would be heavily defeated.

On the European side of the Atlantic the perspective was different. Here the moment of decision was at hand, and the issues could not be avoided. In such circumstances it might not seem unreasonable to suppose that the United States, in spite of American unpreparedness, would declare war on Germany. Such a declaration, even though it could not be followed at once by acts of war on land, might well have led to a different political development in France. With the Germans at the Channel ports, and the French armies in confusion, Englishmen and, even more urgently, Frenchmen had some excuse for anticipating the evolution of American opinion and exaggerating the immediacy of the risks to American security. Demands which in Washington took on an appearance almost of absurdity looked sensible and prudent in the time-scale suddenly revealed by the advance of the German armies, when four weeks had seen the collapse of France.

In retrospect one may regard Mr. Roosevelt's decision—announced in a speech of June 10, 1940—to continue assistance to Great Britain (in his own words 'to extend to the opponents of force the material resources of this nation') as all that he could have done. He added a second assurance that production would be increased in the United States so that—again in his own words—'we in the Americas may have equipment and training equal to the task of any emergency and every defence'. The significance of these promises was only slowly realised because at first they could not be fulfilled on a large scale. Moreover Mr. Roosevelt himself did not at once understand that, in the event of a German occupation of Great Britain, it would hardly have been practicable—in spite of Mr. Churchill's splendid words—for the British fleet to have continued the war across the seas.

On the British side one may also notice in retrospect the very great importance of Mr. Churchill's own clear expositions in the form of personal messages to the President.[1] Mr. Churchill insisted, in

---

(a)

[1] While Mr. Churchill was First Lord of the Admiralty he had begun, with the Prime Minister's approval, a series of direct messages to Mr. Roosevelt. These messages were sent under the style of 'Naval Person' through the United States Embassy in London. On October 19, 1939, Lord Lothian reported that Mr. Welles had shown him a message (of which he had not previously heard) from Mr. Churchill to President Roosevelt on the subject of the American plan for a 'security zone'. The Foreign Office made enquiries at the Admiralty, and obtained copies of two messages, dated October 5 and 16, both of which had been seen by Lord Halifax before they were sent to the United States Ambassador. Copies of the messages were sent to Lord Lothian by bag on November 15, but before they reached him he telegraphed again (November 16) that he had been considerably embarrassed to hear from Mr. Welles of the message of October 5, since this message appeared to conflict to some extent with his own instructions from the Foreign Office.

The American Department of the Foreign Office thought this duplication of channels undesirable, and suggested that Mr. Churchill should be asked not to discuss with the President matters actually under negotiation between the two Governments, or at least that

(a) A8146, 9127/5992/51 (1939); A434/434/45 (1940).

particular, on the determination of the British Government and people to continue the war. He also showed that the United States could not count upon reinforcement by the British fleet in the event of a complete defeat and invasion of Great Britain. As early as June 18, he gave the President a reasoned statement of the chances of British survival, and of the immediate assistance required from the United States if the position were to be held. At this stage, in his practical demands, Mr. Churchill did not and could not look far beyond the immediate future—that is to say, survival—towards ultimate victory, just as Mr. Roosevelt could not promise American participation in the war. Nevertheless on each side there was no doubt of the facts, though they were stated and conveyed indirectly; Mr. Churchill understood that without American entry into the war, victory was hardly possible. He expected that the United States would come into

he should show his messages to the Foreign Office. Lord Halifax thought that there were some advantages in the direct correspondence, subject to the knowledge and concurrence of the Foreign Office. He therefore wrote to Mr. Churchill on December 8 that Lord Lothian ought to be kept informed of any messages. Lord Halifax asked Mr. Churchill to send in advance to the Foreign Office drafts of his messages, so that Lord Lothian could be told of them and the Foreign Office could ensure that the messages were consistent with their own instructions. A copy of this letter was sent to Lord Lothian on December 12.

On December 25 the Admiralty gave the Foreign Office a copy of a message sent on that day to the President through the United States Embassy. Lord Lothian had already heard of the message from the Argentine Ambassador in Washington (who had been told of it by Mr. Welles) before the Foreign Office telegraphed it to him on December 26. Lord Halifax therefore wrote to Mr. Churchill again on January 6, 1940, asking that the messages should be sent through the Foreign Office and Lord Lothian rather than through the United States Embassy and the State Department. Mr. Churchill replied on January 12 that he thought it a mistake to close down the Embassy channel, and that he had assumed that the Foreign Office had informed Lord Lothian at once of his message of December 25. He suggested that the messages should be sent to Lord Lothian simultaneously with their despatch through the United States Embassy. Lord Halifax agreed with this proposal and asked that two copies (one for himself and one for despatch to Lord Lothian) should be sent to the Foreign Office, if possible before, or at least simultaneously with their transmission to the United States Embassy.

Mr. Churchill continued this interchange (under the style of 'Former Naval Person') after he became Prime Minister. It will be seen from the text that in many cases, though not always, Mr. Churchill consulted the Foreign Office or the Secretary of State before the despatch of the messages dealing with what would have been Foreign Office business. On May 21, 1940, and on the advice of Mr. Welles, Lord Lothian suggested that for security reasons the best means of transmission would be through the British Embassy in Washington. The Foreign Office also considered that, owing to Mr. Kennedy's openly expressed defeatism, the United States Embassy was an undesirable channel. On May 27 the Foreign Office were informed that Mr. Churchill agreed with this suggestion, but on June 12 he again sent a message through the United States Embassy. On June 14 Lord Lothian telegraphed that Mr. Roosevelt was so much overworked that he (Lord Lothian) could not easily see him unless he had a message to deliver. Lord Lothian suggested that, whenever the Foreign Office might wish him to reinforce by personal argument a message from the Prime Minister to Mr. Roosevelt, this message should be sent through the Embassy in Washington. Lord Lothian was told in reply on June 17 that the American Ambassador was anxious that the messages should go through him, and that it was thought desirable to agree to his wishes. Lord Lothian, however, repeated his argument. On June 30 Lord Halifax arranged to discuss the matter with the Prime Minister. An arrangement was reached on July 3, and communicated to the Foreign Office on July 9, whereby the method of transmission would be raised in every case, if possible, with the Prime Minister.

From May 19, 1940, onwards the daily telegrams of information on naval, military and air operations sent through the Dominions Office to the Commonwealth Prime Ministers were also sent to Mr. Roosevelt for his personal information.

(a) A3261/1/51.

the war, and that in this way victory would be attained. Mr. Roosevelt also realised that, sooner or later, the United States was likely to enter the war.

These are the facts which emerge from the diplomatic record beginning with enquiries about the status of the Dutch West Indies and reaching a new stage, only four weeks later, with a proposal from Washington for Anglo-American staff talks on naval and air questions.

(ii)

The opening of the German offensive: Mr. Churchill's exchange of messages with Mr. Roosevelt and statement of Allied requirements, May 15–23: Lord Lothian's proposal for an offer to the United States of the lease of sites for defence purposes in the West Indies, May 24–5: consideration of the proposal by the War Cabinet, and reply to Lord Lothian, June 2, 1940.

One of the first indirect consequences of the German invasion of the Netherlands was the despatch of a small Allied force to the two Dutch West Indian islands of Curaçao and Aruba. These islands had little strategic value in themselves in relation to the war with Germany, but important oil refineries were situated on them. In view of German action elsewhere there was a danger of sabotage against which the small Dutch forces might be insufficient protection. On the other hand, the occupation of the islands by Allied forces was likely to bring protests from Venezuela and other Latin American States, and might be taken as a precedent by the Japanese for similar action by themselves in the Dutch East Indies. For this latter reason and also from the point of view of opinion in Central and South America the United States Government were unwilling to send forces of their own to the islands.

The matter was settled—not without some preliminary confusion and misunderstanding—when the British Government made it clear that British forces[1] were not 'occupying' the islands but were merely providing, at Dutch request, reinforcements for the maintenance of security under Dutch authority. There was thus no question of changing the status of the islands. The Netherlands Minister at Washington also informed the United States Government that the Netherlands Government were satisfied with the action taken, and had no fear of any alteration in the political or economic status of the Dutch East or West Indies and that they also felt confident about the attitude of the Japanese Government.

---

[1] French troops were landed at Aruba on the night of May 10–11. British troops arrived at Curaçao on May 12.

Within a few days the progress of the German offensive over-shadowed other questions. On the night of May 13–14 Lord Lothian (a) reported a discussion of the Italian situation with Mr. Roosevelt. Mr. Roosevelt described the representations which he had made to Mussolini and explained that the state of American opinion did not allow him to do more. Lord Lothian telegraphed that it would be a mistake to press for further action: Mr. Roosevelt was as anxious as the British Government to keep Italy out of the war. Lord Lothian thought however, that it would be desirable to let Mr. Roosevelt know any British requirements which could be met within the limits set by the Neutrality legislation and by American public opinion.

On May 15 the Prime Minister sent a personal message to Mr. (b) Roosevelt as follows:

'. . . The scene has darkened swiftly. The enemy have a marked pre-ponderance in the air, and their new technique is making a deep impression upon the French. I think myself the battle on land has only just begun, and I should like to see the masses engage. Up to the present, Hitler is working with specialized units in tanks and air. The small countries are simply smashed up, one by one, like matchwood. We must expect, though it is not yet certain, that Mussolini will hurry in to share the loot of civilisation. We expect to be attacked here our-selves, both from the air and by parachute and air-borne troops in the near future, and are getting ready for them. If necessary, we shall continue the war alone, and we are not afraid of that.

But I trust you realise, Mr. President, that the voice and force of the United States may count for nothing if they are withheld too long. You may have a completely subjugated, Nazified Europe established with astonishing swiftness, and the weight may be more than we can bear. All I ask now is that you should proclaim non-belligerency, which would mean that you would help us with everything short of actually engaging armed forces.'

Mr. Churchill went on to state the most urgent British needs. He asked whether the United States could lend Great Britain forty or fifty of their older destroyers to tide over the period before the ships under construction were completed. He pointed out that in the near future we might have to deal with a hundred Italian submarines. Mr. Churchill's second request was for several hundred of the latest type of aircraft, of which the United States were now getting de-livery.[1] He mentioned other requirements—anti-aircraft equipment and ammunition, and steel—and also suggested, in view of reports of possible German attacks on Ireland, a prolonged visit of a United

---

[1] Mr. Churchill suggested that they could be replaced by the aircraft under construction for the British Government in the United States. He also said that Great Britain would go on paying for material as long as she had the dollar resources, but that he would 'like to feel reasonably sure that when we can pay no more' the United States would none the less continue to supply the material.

(a) A3255/1/51. (b) A3261/1/51.

States squadron to Irish ports. Finally he said that we reckoned on American action to keep Japan out of the war; for this purpose Great Britain could offer the facilities of Singapore to the United States navy. Mr. Roosevelt replied at once to Mr. Churchill's message.

(a) He said that he was most happy to continue his private correspondence and that he was giving every possible consideration to Mr. Churchill's suggestions. He could not lend any destroyers without authorisation of Congress and doubted whether at the moment it would be wise to ask for it. He also doubted whether, from the standpoint of their own defences, the United States could give up the destroyers even temporarily. In any case they would not be ready for service under the British flag at least for six or seven weeks. The President made detailed suggestions about other British requirements but said nothing about aircraft or the question of dollar payments.

(b) Mr. Churchill repeated his warning about the gravity of the situation in a message of May 18 to Mr. Roosevelt. He said that Great Britain would 'persevere to the very end', whatever might be the result of the battle in France. We expected to be attacked 'on the Dutch model before very long' and hoped to 'give a good account of ourselves. But if American assistance is to play any part it must be available soon.'

(c) On the evening of May 18 Lord Lothian reported a conversation in which he had given Mr. Roosevelt figures about the engagement of British air forces in the fighting. Mr. Roosevelt had said that two days earlier the French had been 'very critical' on the subject, but that they were now 'far better satisfied'. Mr. Roosevelt referred to the question of the sale of United States destroyers in terms similar to his reply to Mr. Churchill.

Mr. Roosevelt said that he was doing everything possible to keep Mussolini out of the war; the United States air programme was designed to deter both Mussolini and Japan. He also said that the size and efficiency of the American Atlantic patrol was increasing, and implied that we could leave the protection of our West Indian interests to the United States navy, and that, if a German ship appeared in West Indian waters, the United States navy would not hesitate to deal with it.

Lord Lothian asked what Mr. Roosevelt thought about the situation if we were left to stand alone and were subjected to continuous bombardment from the south and east. It was imperative for American security, as well as for the security of the British Empire, that the British navy should keep a dominant position in the Atlantic, with bases in Great Britain and control over the Straits of Gibraltar. If the United States navy were held in the Pacific, Germany and Italy could establish themselves in Brazil with the help of German

---

(a) A3261/1/51. (b) A3261/1/51. (c) A3261/1/51.

and Italian 'fifth columns' already in the country, and rapidly developing. They would then be within bombing distance of the Panama Canal. If, on the other hand, the United States navy had to remain in the Atlantic, the Japanese could menace Alaska and Hawaii. If the navy were divided, the United States might be in a position of inferiority in both the Atlantic and in the Pacific. For these reasons, Lord Lothian thought it of vital importance that the United States should do everything possible by supplying food, destroyers and aeroplanes, and by putting pressure on Spain not to enter the war, to help the British navy to maintain command of the Atlantic, and thus allow the United States navy to retain its predominance in the Pacific.

Mr. Roosevelt agreed with this view, but said that he could not move beyond the point at which Congress would agree with his policy, and that public opinion had not yet grasped the strategic situation. He thought that, owing to the exhaustion of German supplies in the present war, Hitler would not lightheartedly take on the United States. If the worst came to the worst, the British fleet might cross the Atlantic to Canada or to the United States. Lord Lothian said that such a move would depend on the entry of the United States into the war. He doubted whether British public opinion would entrust the fleet to a neutral United States. Mr. Roosevelt 'seemed impressed by this possibility'.

On May 20 the Prime Minister sent a further message through Mr. Kennedy to Mr. Roosevelt. He said that Lord Lothian had (a) reported his conversation with Mr. Roosevelt. The Prime Minister said that he understood the difficulties, but was very sorry about the destroyers. If the ships were here within six weeks, they would be invaluable. The battle of France was full of dangers to both sides. The Germans had numerical superiority in the air. Our most vital need was therefore the diversion to us, at the earliest possible moment, of the largest possible number of Curtiss P 40 fighters now in course of delivery to the United States army.

'Our intention is, whatever happens, to fight on to the end in this Island and, provided we can get the help for which we ask, we hope to run [the Germans] very close in the air battles in view of individual superiority. Members of the present Administration would [be] likely [to] go down during this process, should it result adversely, but in no conceivable circumstances will we consent to surrender. If members of the present Administration were finished, and others came in to parley amid the ruins, you must not be blind to the fact that the sole remaining bargaining counter with Germany would be the fleet, and, if this country was left by the United States to its fate, no one would have the right to blame those then responsible if they made the best

(a) A3261/1/51.

terms they could for the surviving inhabitants. Excuse me, Mr. President, putting this nightmare bluntly. Evidently I could not answer for my successors, who, in utter despair and helplessness, might well have to accommodate themselves to the German will. However, there is happily no need at present to dwell upon such ideas. Once more thanking you for your goodwill.'

Mr. Roosevelt does not appear to have sent any direct answer to this message, but Lord Lothian telegraphed on the night of May 23–4 (a) that the Under-Secretary of State had told him that urgent consideration was being given to all our requests. The extent of American action would depend on the willingness of Congress to make a 'radical departure' from the policy embodied in the Neutrality Act, and from their interpretation of international law. Lord Lothian thought that a favourable decision on these points appeared likely, but that there would be great difficulty in getting the agreement of Congress for the transfer of destroyers.

At the request of the United States Government the British Government had agreed in September 1939, to negotiations between the United States Government and the colonial authorities concerned for the use of ports and waters, and for the lease of sites to the United States naval authorities, in Trinidad, Bermuda and St. Lucia. The American request was made ostensibly with a view to facilitating American naval manoeuvres; it arose in fact out of proposals for a 'neutrality patrol'.[1] The leases were still current in May and June 1940, but for reasons of domestic policy[2] the United States had made no use of them.

During the night of May 24–5 Lord Lothian telegraphed a sug- (b) gestion that we might offer to allow the United States Government to construct aerodromes and naval stations on British islands of importance to American security. Lord Lothian put forward this suggestion because public anxiety about the security of the United States had brought into the foreground of discussion the question of the future of British and French islands off the east coast of America. Proposals were being made that these islands should be ceded to the United States in part payment of war debts. Mr. Roosevelt had always discouraged the discussion of such proposals, and Lord Lothian had said privately the matter could not be raised at present. Nevertheless he thought that the time had come for him to be authorised to inform the President that we recognised the seriousness of the new threat to American security, and that, while we could not discuss modifications of sovereignty, we should be prepared to consider immediate leases of areas to the United States for the construction of airfields or naval

---

[1] See above, p. 158.
[2] See below, p. 360.
(a) W8002/79/49.   (b) A3297/2961/45.

stations on any of the islands which the United States regarded as important from the point of view of their defence.

Lord Lothian thought the United States were concerned mainly with Trinidad and Newfoundland. An air base at Trinidad would enable the United States to deal with possible German and Italian air threats through Brazil to the Panama Canal. A base in New-foundland would be useful against a German attack on Iceland which was at present undefended.[1] Lord Lothian said that his proposal was only an extension of the arrangement made in 1939, and never carried out. He did not suggest that the offer should be connected with the question of war debts, but he thought that a public announce-ment of our readiness to help the United States in organising their defence would make a deep impression, and would add to our own security and involve active co-operation in naval and air defence between the British Commonwealth and the United States. An immediate offer would have the advantage of spontaneity, and was also necessary in order that, if the proposals were to have full effect, Congress might vote the requisite financial appropriations before their adjournment early in June.

The War Cabinet considered this proposal on May 27 and 29. (a) They saw serious difficulties in the way of the plan (although the Chiefs of Staff were in favour of it) and decided to ask Lord Lothian what advantages he expected from it. Meanwhile they considered that the matter should not be mentioned to Mr. Roosevelt. The Foreign Office therefore telegraphed to Lord Lothian on June 2 (b) pointing out that (i) if we made a formal offer, the question of sovereignty could hardly fail to arise. The United States would be spending, at our invitation, large sums of money on fixtures in the islands, and would naturally want security of tenure. In particular, leases on a large scale at Trinidad, with its vital oil fields, would mean the investment of a great deal of American plant and capital; the United States Government would thereby tend to obtain a controlling interest in the island. (ii) The only facilities in New-foundland likely to interest the United States would be those of the airport. This airport had just been completed at a cost of £750,000, and negotiations were in progress for the assumption of responsibility for the port during the war by the Canadian Government. His Majesty's Government in the United Kingdom were at present trustees for the people of Newfoundland, and the transfer of the airport to the United States might well cause resentment in the

---

[1] A small British force had been landed in Iceland on May 10, 1940. See above, p. 119, note 1.

(a) WM(40)141; WM(40)146. (b) A3297/2961/45.

island. In any case it would be necessary to consult Newfoundland and Canada, owing to the intimate connexion of Canadian defence with that of Newfoundland, and to the arrangement about the airport. (iii) Once the question had been raised with Mr. Roosevelt it would be difficult to draw back, even if the political objections under (i) and (ii) proved insuperable. (iv) Isolationists might well misrepresent any offer which came from our side as an attempt to involve the United States in the war or as a sign that we were in despair. (v) 'A definite assurance of concrete results sufficiently advantageous to us should be a prerequisite for concession on our part.'

In these circumstances Lord Lothian was asked what were his reasons for thinking that, if the political objections were overcome, we should obtain really substantial advantages from an offer. Moreover, although no use had been made of them, the United States Government did not appear to have given up the rights granted to them at Trinidad, Bermuda and St. Lucia. Therefore, if they wished to do so, they could take at least some action without any further offer on our part. The fact that they had not taken action suggested that at present they had no wish to do so.

Lord Lothian did not reply to this telegram until the night of June 22–3; the consideration of the proposals which he then made belongs to a later phase of Anglo-American relations.[1]

(iii)

Further messages from the Prime Minister to Mr. Roosevelt: the British need of destroyers (May 24—June 12, 1940).

(a) On May 26 Lord Lothian reported a conversation of the previous evening with Mr. Roosevelt. Mr. Roosevelt had said that he was 'merely thinking aloud, and making no representations of any kind to His Majesty's Government'. He had been considering his conversation of May 17 with Lord Lothian about the British navy and the Prime Minister's telegram on the matter. He thought that, if things came to the worst, the British fleet, and as many partly finished ships as possible, should be treated, not as British, but as Empire possessions, and transferred to Canada or Australia before they could be captured or surrendered. The British, French, Dutch and Belgian overseas empires constituted very formidable resources for prosecuting the war. If the navy were surrendered, the whole edifice

---

[1] See below, Chapter XII, section (ii).

(a) A3261/1/51.

would collapse, whatever promises Hitler might make. Lord Lothian asked Mr. Roosevelt whether the United States would be in the war on our side 'if such a catastrophe impended, because that fact could probably exercise a profound influence on the British decision'. Mr. Roosevelt answered that the American decision did not rest with himself, but with Congress. He could therefore give no definite answer, but he thought it probable. 'As things were going, it seemed likely that Germany would challenge some vital American interest in the near future, which was the condition necessary to make the United States enter the war with the necessary popular support.' Opinion was changing rapidly on the subject of the vital interests of the United States. Mr. Roosevelt added that, if it became necessary for His Majesty The King to leave Great Britain and for the Imperial as distinct from the Home Departments of His Majesty's Government to be moved out of the country, it might be better to establish a temporary capital at Bermuda, and not in Canada. The Canadians might find difficulties about the transfer of Downing Street to Toronto, and American republicans might be 'restless at monarchy being based on the American continent'.

During the few days following this conversation, the situation in France grew rapidly worse. At this time Lord Lothian was primarily concerned with M. Reynaud's proposal, which the British Government accepted, for an approach by Mr. Roosevelt to Mussolini, and with the later French proposal, which His Majesty's Government could not accept, for an Anglo-French appeal to the United States.[1]

It was evident from Lord Lothian's conversations with Mr. Roosevelt that the President was inclined to assume that, in the event **(a)** of a successful German attack on Great Britain, the British fleet would certainly be transferred to Canadian or Australian waters. The Prime Minister had made it clear in his message of May 20 to the President that this assumption ought not to be made: Lord Lothian described it as Mr. Roosevelt's 'paralysing illusion'.

Mr. Casey, Australian Minister in Washington, also discussed the situation with Mr. Welles on May 31. Mr. Casey told Mr. Welles that undoubtedly Great Britain had no hope that the United States would come into the war. Mr. Welles asked what would happen to the British fleet if Great Britain were defeated. Mr. Casey thought that a German landing in Great Britain was a possibility; he said that the fleet would never surrender, and would probably destroy itself in an attack on German naval ports. Mr. Welles considered this plan unwise and illogical, since as long as the fleet existed, there was always a chance of retrieving the situation. Mr. Casey answered that, if it were thought in Great Britain that there was a chance of American entry

[1] See above, Chapters VII and VIII.
(a) A3261/1/51.

into the war, the fleet might be kept in being, but that Mr. Roosevelt alone could save the British, French and Dutch Empires. Mr. Welles's view was that the disappearance of the British fleet would be against the vital interests of the Dominions. Mr. Casey agreed but pointed out that in the terrible conditions which Germany probably could and would bring about in Great Britain, logic was unlikely to be uppermost in British minds. The only question would be whether the United States would be in the war 'in not too remote a time'.

Mr. Welles said that the picture was 'much graver than he had thought'. Mr. Casey replied that he had not exaggerated the situation. Moreover the time was passing when American help in material would be of use; political assistance in the form of a declaration (of war)[1] by the United States would soon be the only thing which could save the world. Mr. Welles said that he would speak at once to the President in the light of Mr. Casey's statement.

After the unexpectedly successful evacuation of the B.E.F. from Dunkirk, the situation changed. The need of immediate American help in material of war was even greater, especially in the matter of destroyers and other small craft; the total military collapse of France could also be foreseen even more closely, but the chances of successful resistance by Great Britain had increased.

In the afternoon of May 31 Lord Halifax asked the American (a) Ambassador whether there was a possibility of obtaining the destroyers about which the Prime Minister had spoken to Mr. Roosevelt. The War Cabinet had indeed considered on May 27 the question (b) of sending a special mission to the United States in order to supplement the efforts which were being made through diplomatic channels to obtain the release of destroyers, and other material. The Foreign Office thought this plan inopportune, since the arrival of a new mission would be given wide publicity and might be interpreted as a sign of panic and as a despairing effort by the Allies to involve the United States in the war.

Mr. Kennedy, in answer to Lord Halifax's question, said that he intended to tell Mr. Roosevelt 'very shortly' that the psychological moment had now arrived, and that any assistance which the United States could give 'within the next week would be worth ten times as much as similar assistance in a month's time'. Mr. Kennedy thought that if legislation were needed for the release of the destroyers, Mr. Roosevelt would be 'able to make the necessary arrangements'.

Lord Halifax told Mr. Kennedy of M. Reynaud's suggestion for an appeal to the United States, and of the view of the British Government that 'a despairing appeal might well have the opposite effect to that which we desired'. Mr. Kennedy agreed with this view, and

---

[1] These two words do not appear in the text of the telegram summarising the conversation, but the meaning is clear.
(a) W8124/79/49. (b) WM(40)141.

said that, from the point of view of public opinion in the United States, 'what we had been doing at Dunkirk was worth forty appeals by M. Reynaud'.

On June 1 Lord Halifax wrote to Mr. Kennedy that there might be 'one step at least that the President might be ready to take immedi- (a) ately, namely, the putting in hand of the reconditioning of the older destroyers'. Two days later Mr. Kennedy told Lord Halifax that, although he had received no reply from his Government on the question of the destroyers, he was inclined to think that the absence of a reply was an encouraging sign. Thirty or forty United States destroyers were at present being recommissioned; Mr. Roosevelt 'might be waiting for the entry of Italy into the war to serve as the final pretext for sending us the assistance which we needed'.

Lord Lothian was a little concerned that the peroration[1] of Mr. Churchill's speech in the House of Commons on June 4 might be taken by American opinion as supporting the view that the United States could count on getting the British fleet even if Great Britain were defeated.

Mr. Churchill explained to Lord Lothian that his speech was intended primarily for Germany and Italy, 'to whom the idea of a war of continents, and a long war are at present obnoxious' and for the Dominions, for whom we were trustees, but that he had always kept in mind the point about the fleet. Mr. Churchill wished Lord Lothian to talk to the President and to discourage any 'complacent assumption' on the part of the United States that they would be able to 'pick up the débris of the British fleet by their present policy. On the contrary they run the terrible risk that their sea-power will be completely over-matched.' If Great Britain were defeated, a pro-German Government might be set up, and surrender the fleet in order to obtain better terms from Hitler. Germany and Japan would then be masters of the New World.

On June 10 Mr. Roosevelt referred in a public speech at Charlottesville to Mussolini's rejection of the proposals which he (Mr. Roosevelt) had made to him and to the entry of Italy into the war. Mr. Roosevelt spoke in plain terms of the danger threatening the United States, and promised that the United States would 'extend to the opponents of force the material resources of this nation, and harness and speed up the use of those resources in order that we ourselves may have the equipment and training equal to the task in any emergency'.

---

[1] See above, p. 214, note 1.
(a) W8124/79/49.

(a)   In the afternoon of June 11 the Prime Minister sent a personal message through Lord Lothian to Mr. Roosevelt that everything must be done to keep France in the fight, and to ensure that the fall of Paris—if this event should occur—did not become the occasion of any kind of parley. Hitler would soon turn on Great Britain. We were preparing to resist him. We had saved the B.E.F., and therefore did not lack troops at home. As soon as our divisions could be equipped on the much larger scale needed for Continental service, they would be sent to France. For the campaign of 1941 we intended to have a strong army fighting in France. The Prime Minister said that he had already cabled to Mr. Roosevelt on the subject of aeroplanes and flying boats. The need for destroyers was even more pressing, especially since the entry of Italy into the war. We could fit 30–40 reconditioned old United States destroyers very quickly with asdics. These ships would bridge the gap of six months (i.e. before our new ships were ready). We could return the United States ships or their equivalent at six months' notice, but, if in the coming six months a new and heavy German-Italian submarine attack were launched against our commerce, the strain might be beyond our resources, and our ocean traffic might be strangled.

(iv)

Further messages to Mr. Roosevelt on the general position and on the British need of destroyers, June 15–17: statement of June 18 to Mr. Roosevelt on the situation brought about by the French collapse and on the prospects of the war: agreement to hold staff talks with the United States, June 18—July 1, 1940.

On the days following this appeal to Mr. Roosevelt the Prime Minister was occupied with the situation in France. He kept Mr. Roosevelt in close touch with the rapid movement of events and tried to obtain his (Mr. Roosevelt's) consent to the publication of his message of June 13 to M. Reynaud.[1] After it was clear that the President would not agree to publication, and that the French were likely to ask for an armistice, the Prime Minister once again put the whole situation in messages to Mr. Roosevelt. The Prime Minister sent these messages during the afternoon and late evening of June 15. The first

(b) message was as follows:

'I am grateful to you for your telegram and I have reported its operative passages to Reynaud to whom I had imparted a rather more sanguine view. He will, I am sure, be disappointed at non-publication.

---

[1] See above, pp. 259–64.

(a) A3261/1/51. (b) C7294/65/17.

I understand all your difficulties with American public opinion and Congress but events are moving downward at a pace where they will pass beyond the control of American public opinion when at last it is ripened. Have you considered what offers Hitler may choose to make to France? He may say: "Surrender the Fleet intact and I will leave you Alsace-Lorraine", or alternatively: "If you do not give me your ships I will destroy your towns". I am personally convinced that America will in the end go to all lengths, but this moment is supremely critical for France. A declaration that the United States will if necessary enter the war might save France. Failing that in a few days French resistance may have crumbled and we shall be left alone.

Although the present Government and I personally would never fail to send the Fleet across the Atlantic if resistance was beaten down here, a point may be reached in the struggle where the present Ministers no longer have control of affairs and when very easy terms could be obtained for the British Islands by their becoming a vassal state of the Hitler empire. A pro-German Government would certainly be called into being to make peace and might present to a shattered or a starving nation an almost irresistible case for entire submission to the Nazi will. The fate of the British Fleet, as I have already mentioned to you, would be decisive on the future of the United States because, if it were joined to the fleets of Japan, France, and Italy and the great resources of German industry, overwhelming sea-power would be in Hitler's hands. He might, of course, use it with a merciful moderation. On the other hand he might not. This revolution in sea-power might happen very quickly, and certainly long before the United States would be able to prepare against it. If we go down, you may have a United State of Europe under the Nazi command far more numerous, far stronger, far better armed than the New World.

I know well, Mr. President, that your eye will already have searched these depths, but I feel I have the right to place on record the vital manner in which American interests are at stake in our battle and that of France.

I am sending you through Ambassador Kennedy a paper on destroyer strength prepared by the Naval Staff for your information. If we have to keep, as we shall, the bulk of our destroyers on the East Coast to guard against invasion, how shall we be able to cope with a German-Italian attack on the food and trade by which we live? The sending of the thirty-five destroyers as I have already described will bridge the gap until our new construction comes in at the end of the year. Here is a definite, practical, and possibly decisive step which can be taken at once, and I urge most earnestly that you will weigh my words.'

The second message referred to M. Reynaud's urgent appeal[1] for a (a) declaration that the United States would enter the war. The third message gave an account of our losses in destroyers, and stated that (b)

---

[1] See above, pp. 266 and 268.

(a) C7294/65/17.   (b) A3582/131/45.

out of 133 destroyers in home waters only 68 were actually fit for service. This was the lowest level since the outbreak of war. (In 1918 some 433 destroyers were in service). The Prime Minister pointed out that the critical situation in relation to land operations had made less apparent our grave difficulties at sea. Owing to the seizure of the Channel ports we had to concentrate our shipping in our western ports. Hence the Germans could also concentrate their attacks within a more limited area, while the entry of Italy into the war had added 100 to the German total (on a conservative estimate) of 55 submarines. We had to face the possibility of invasion, in view of the German control of the whole of the European coastline from Norway. It was necessary to counter this danger by means of patrols; we might also be forced to divert further destroyer forces to the Mediterranean.

> 'We are now faced with the imminent collapse of French resistance. If this occurs, the successful defence of this island will be the only hope of averting the collapse of civilisation as we define it. We must ask therefore, as a matter of life and death, to be reinforced with these destroyers. We will carry on the struggle, whatever the odds, but it may well be beyond our resources unless we receive every reinforcement, and particularly do we need this reinforcement on the sea.'

(a) During the night of June 15–16 Lord Lothian telegraphed his impression that, although the delivery of munitions was being speeded up, the United States Government felt almost helpless to do anything at the moment to affect the French decision. Lord Lothian still thought that the United States were drifting towards war; that public opinion was almost unanimously pro-Ally, but that, owing to the constitution, nothing save a direct challenge to American vital interests and honour would drive the United States 'across the Rubicon'. Lord Lothian also repeated to Mr. Roosevelt on June 15

(b) his opinion that, unless the United States were in the war, the British fleet would sink itself in the event of a successful German invasion of Great Britain.[1]

Lord Lothian was given full information in the afternoon of June 16 about the messages to M. Reynaud on the British conditions for releasing France from the 'no separate peace' agreement,[2] and the

(c) offer of Anglo-French union. Lord Lothian saw Mr. Roosevelt in the evening of June 16 after the President had heard of M. Reynaud's resignation and the formation of a government by Marshal Pétain. The President approved of the Prime Minister's telegrams to M. Reynaud and said that, if he were asked to act as intermediary, he

---

[1] See above, p. 271.
[2] See above, pp. 275–80.
(a) C7294/65/17. (b) C7294/65/17. (c) C7263, 7294/65/17.

would make the transfer of the French fleet to Great Britain a condition of his mediation. He hoped that as many French airmen as
possible (and others) could continue the war in Algeria or in Great
Britain, and that, if ever a similar crisis arose in Great Britain, the
war would be carried on overseas, and that the British fleet would
not be given up.

Lord Lothian repeated the views he had stated on the previous
evening. He pointed out that Great Britain could not be expected to
send her fleet across the seas and to associate it with any country not
intending to use the fleet and its own resources to the limit in order
to rescue Great Britain from conquest. Mr. Roosevelt said that, as
far as he had been able to think out the position, the British fleet
should go to Capetown, Singapore, Aden, and Sydney, if Great
Britain were rendered useless as a naval base, while the main
American navy would control[1] the Atlantic and undertake the defence
of Canada and other British possessions.

Lord Lothian's report of this conversation crossed a message to him
from the Prime Minister for transmission to Mr. Roosevelt. The
Prime Minister said that he was deeply sensible of Mr. Roosevelt's (a)
desire to help us. 'The most effective thing he can do is to let us have
destroyers immediately. Our need of them is vital, and their addition
to our fleet might be decisive. It is most important that not a day
should be lost.'

Lord Lothian gave this message to Mr. Roosevelt on June 17, and
supported it with the arguments in the message of June 15 about our (b)
need for more destroyers. Mr. Roosevelt said that he was already
having the greatest difficulty in persuading the Naval Affairs
Committee of the Senate to release the motor boats,[2] and that, in the
present anxiety about American defence, it was impossible to get
Congress to release the destroyers. Lord Lothian asked whether the
time had not come for Mr. Roosevelt to make a completely frank
statement to Congress about the gravity of the naval position, and
the consequences to the United States of the defeat of Great Britain.
Hitherto the 'realities' of the situation had not been brought home to
the United States public. The proposed statement might enable this

---

[1] The text of the telegram is uncertain, but the correct word seems to be 'control'.

[2] On May 28 the Admiralty made enquiries about buying some or all of 23 motor
torpedo-boats which they understood to be in course of construction for the United States
Navy (the first of these MTBs would be ready in July). On May 31 the Anglo-French
Purchasing Commission in New York replied that we should be allowed to buy 20 of them.
The Navy Department approved of the sale but when it became known in Washington
there were objections in Congress, partly on the ground that the boats were needed for the
defence of the United States, and partly because the Navy Department was alleged to have
acted without the knowledge of the Senate Naval Affairs Committee. On June 24 the
President announced that he had instructed the Navy Department to terminate the
negotiations, in view of a ruling by the Attorney-General that the sale or delivery of any
vessel of war to a belligerent was contrary to an Act of 1917.

(a) A3582/131/45. (b) A3582/131/45.

public to see that assistance in every possible way to Great Britain was their own best mode of defence.

Mr. Roosevelt said that he would consider a press statement on June 18. Lord Lothian also asked him whether he did not think that staff talks should take place to consider how the British and American fleets and, if necessary, air forces should deal with the various situations which might arise in the near future. Mr. Roosevelt approved of this proposal and suggested that the talks should take place at once.

(a)   On the morning of June 18 Lord Lothian was sent a full statement of the views of the British Government on the situation brought about by the French collapse, and the future prospects of the war. This statement followed the text of a memorandum drawn up (for Lord Lothian's use) on June 13 by the Chiefs of Staff on instructions from the War Cabinet, and approved, with minor alterations, by the War Cabinet on June 14.

The statement was in these terms:

'In the event of a complete capitulation by France we intend to continue the struggle. The military situation which would confront us would be as follows:

General Situation

All French European and Northern African territory and resources would become available to the enemy in due course, though elements of the fleet and certain forces in the French Empire might be denied to the enemy. It is by no means improbable, however, that the French might be forced to hand over their fleet, and our enemies would thereby gain a considerable accession of naval strength. All existing European neutrals, with the possible exception of Turkey, would eventually fall under German or Italian military or economic domination, and our position in the Mediterranean and the Middle East might be ultimately reduced to denying the Suez Canal to the enemy. The attitude of India might be doubtful, but, with the possible exception of Eire, the whole Empire would increase their efforts in our support. Japan might attempt a more actively opportunist policy in the Far East. Russia would probably become alarmed at Germany's success and cease to assist her.

Ability to Defeat Germany

We consider that in these circumstances the defeat of Germany could still be achieved but only by a combination of economic pressure, air attack on economic objectives in Germany, with its resultant effect on German morale, and the creation of widespread revolt in the conquered territories.

It would be essential to secure the British Isles as the main base

(a) C7278/65/17; WP(40)203, WM(40)166.

for the operation of naval and air forces since we could not maintain our air offensive against Germany from the American Continent nor employ our fleet effectively unsupported by the naval resources of this country.

The final issue will therefore hang at first on our ability to withstand the great effort which the enemy is likely to make against Great Britain in the *immediate* future. If we can withstand the effects of large scale air attack against our industry, our ports and centres of population by denying to the enemy air superiority over this country and its approaches, and so long as we maintain command of the sea, we hope to resist invasion successfully. In this connexion the direct danger is the extreme vulnerability of our aircraft industry.

At the same time, we shall have to withstand intensified naval and air attacks against our seaborne trade, to meet which there is an acute shortage of destroyers and flying boats.

We should be in a good position to control the economic resources of the Allied Overseas Empires, and we could exercise Naval Control of the wider oceans and focal points leading to the blockaded areas. This pressure would not, of itself, bring about the defeat of our enemies. To achieve this, full Pan-American co-operation is essential so that raw materials of the world may be controlled at source.

In effect, our ability to defeat Germany would ultimately depend on a complete blockade of Europe, which must include the cutting off of supplies via Russia. Any relief to populations in territory occupied by the enemy would only serve to prolong the struggle.

Without the full economic and financial co-operation of the whole of the American Continent the task might in the event prove too great for the British Empire single-handed. Nevertheless, even if the hope of victory in these circumstances appeared remote, we should continue to fight as long as it was humanly possible to do so.

It has been suggested that, in the event of the United Kingdom being overrun by the enemy, the struggle could be continued by the British Fleet from the American Continent. In resisting invasion, however, the whole of our naval resources in home waters would be thrown into the defence and a successful invasion would automatically imply the loss of a large proportion of our fleet. The remaining forces, operating from America, would be faced with considerable problems of maintenance, supply and manning, and the combined German and Italian fleets, possibly strengthened by captured units of the French navy, might extend their activities well beyond the confines of Europe. Without our air weapon and with our ability to exert economic pressure through sea-power considerably reduced, our chances of victory would be virtually at an end, even with the full military and economic assistance of the American Continent.

Far East

The collapse of France would provide Japan with the temptation to take action against French, British or Dutch interests in the Far East. We see no hope of being able to despatch a fleet to Singapore. It will therefore be vital that the United States of America should publicly declare her intention to regard any alteration of the *status quo* in the Far East and the Pacific as a *casus belli*.

West Indies and South America

We regard the maintenance of the *status quo* in the West Indies as of military importance, but we believe this to be assured by United States Administration's approval of resolutions recently submitted to Congress reaffirming the Monroe doctrine in which it was stated that the United States could not recognise transfer or acquiesce in an attempt to transfer any region of Western hemisphere from one non-American Power to another.[1]

Assistance we would require from the Americas

Our full requirements from the American Continent are clearly a matter for detailed examination but, in broad terms, they would be as follows:—

(*a*) The immediate and vital requirement would be the provision at once of first line aircraft (including flying-boats), destroyers, light naval craft, military equipment and supplies necessary to maintain our defence forces in being, whilst our own production is being disorganised by the enemy offensive and our reserves expended. Personnel, possibly on a voluntary basis, to assist in manning ships and aircraft, are also needed.

(*b*) For the further prosecution of the war we should require arrangements to ensure:—

(i) the stoppage at source of all supplies to enemy countries and territory in enemy occupation, and full co-operation in our contraband control against the remaining European neutrals, including Asiatic Russia.

(ii) the supplies of food, munitions, and raw materials, if necessary on a credit basis.

(iii) the provision of merchant shipping to ply between the Americas and the United Kingdom.

(*c*) The Government of the United States of America should add to their declaration regarding the West Indies a further declaration to the effect that any alteration to the *status quo* in the Far East and the Pacific would be regarded by them as a *casus belli*.'

In the report of his discussion with Mr. Roosevelt on June 17 about (a) the desirability of Anglo-American staff conversations on future naval plans Lord Lothian had said that the President had asked whether such talks should take place in London or in Washington.

---

[1] These resolutions were passed by the Senate on June 17 and by the House of Representatives on June 18. On June 17 Mr. Kennedy gave the Prime Minister a copy of a warning sent to the French Government on these lines, together with a statement that the (b) United States Government would be ready, if in their judgment such a step were necessary, to undertake to constitute, in conjunction with the other American republics, an inter-American trusteeship for the French possessions in the Western Hemisphere. Such a trusteeship would be of a temporary character, and would continue only until such time as the complete autonomy and independence of France were fully established. The Prime Minister told Mr. Kennedy that he had no comment to make on this communication.

(a) A3582/131/45. (b) A3373/131/45.

On the night of June 22–3 Lord Lothian telegraphed that he would be glad to have an early answer to his question. The Prime Minister sent a minute to Lord Halifax that he was doubtful about the (a) expediency of Lord Lothian's proposal because he was afraid that the Americans might bring the discussions round to the question of the transfer of the British fleet to transatlantic bases if Great Britain were overrun: any discussion of this possibility would weaken confidence at home at a moment when all should brace themselves for the supreme struggle.

The Prime Minister brought before the War Cabinet the draft of a telegram to the Prime Minister of Canada in reply to a question from (b) the latter about the possibility of a transfer of the fleet in the event of a British defeat. The Prime Minister considered that there could be no question of a bargain with the United States for the transfer of the fleet in return for a declaration of war by the United States. He deprecated 'dwelling on' the 'contingency' of a defeat. 'I have good confidence in our ability to defend this Island and I see no reason to make preparations for or give any countenance to the transfer of the British fleet. I shall myself never enter into any peace negotiations with Hitler, but obviously I cannot bind a future Government which, if we were deserted by the United States and beaten down here, might very easily be a kind of Quisling affair ready to accept German overlordship and protection.' Mr. Mackenzie King was therefore asked to impress this danger upon Mr. Roosevelt.

The War Cabinet accepted this draft. The question of staff talks, however, remained for decision. Lord Lothian reported on the night of June 24–5 that Mr. Hull had said that the question of British naval policy was entirely a matter for Great Britain and the Dominions just as American naval policy was a matter for the United States. Mr. Hull therefore inclined to think that, owing to the danger of leakage in the press, it would be better to hold discussions through diplomatic rather than service channels. Lord Lothian asked whether he should discuss the questions with Mr. Hull.[1]

The Prime Minister's comment on his telegram was to repeat his view that it was undesirable to hold immediate staff talks, since they would turn only upon the transference of our fleet to America. Lord (c) Halifax, however, submitted to the Prime Minister that, although the

---

[1] On June 26 Lord Lothian reported that a wave of pessimism was passing over the United States to the effect that the defeat of Great Britain was inevitable. Lord Lothian suggested a 'resolute and cheering broadcast' by the Prime Minister. The Prime Minister instructed Lord Lothian, who thought the President was affected by the prevailing mood, to repeat the argument that, in the event of a British defeat, the United States would not be able to secure the safe removal of the British fleet, since a Quisling government might well buy terms with it. Mr. Churchill said that he would broadcast 'presently', but that for the time being words did not count for much and that too much attention should not be paid to 'eddies of United States opinion'. Mr. Churchill concluded: 'Your mood should be bland and phlegmatic. No one is downhearted here.'

(a) A3582/131/45. (b) WM(40)171. (c) A3582/131/45.

United States representatives might insist on discussing the question of a possible transfer of the fleet to transatlantic waters, some answer had to be given to Mr. Roosevelt about the talks. It was sound policy to fall in with any 'reasonably practical suggestion' made by the President and, if we failed to take up this particular suggestion, we might never have another chance of obtaining staff talks; Mr. Hull was indeed already raising doubts about them. The 'increasingly menacing attitude' of Japan[1] made it desirable to decide upon the talks, at all events about the Pacific.

The Prime Minister accepted these arguments. Lord Lothian was

(a) therefore instructed on June 30 to say that we agreed with the proposal, but that we thought that the talks should take place in London.

(b) Lord Lothian replied on the night of July 1–2 that Mr. Roosevelt agreed upon the importance of holding technical discussions on the situation in the event (a) of a British withdrawal from Gibraltar, (b) of the Germans securing the French fleet, (c) of the Germans and Italians basing their blockade on the French Channel and Atlantic ports. Mr. Roosevelt considered it essential, in view of the presidential election, that there should be no publicity about the discussions. He was consulting Mr. Hull and the United States Chiefs of Staff about the best method of holding the discussions in London.[2]

---

[1] See Volume II, Chapter XXII.

[2] An American Mission arrived in London for exploratory talks in the middle of August. In order to maintain secrecy, the name 'Standardisation of Arms Committee' was used for the proceedings of the committee.

(a) A3583/131/45. (b) A3583/131/45.

CHAPTER XII

Anglo-American relations from the collapse of France to the end of 1940: the transfer of American destroyers to Great Britain and the lease of sites to the United States in Newfoundland and British Colonial Territories: Lord Lothian's visit to England in October: the Prime Minister's letter of December 7 to Mr. Roosevelt: Mr. Roosevelt's statements of December 17 and 29, 1940[1]

(i)

Introduction.

FROM the collapse of France at least until the early winter of 1940–1 Great Britain was fighting for survival. This primary fact limited the scope of British diplomatic action in two ways. Some countries thought a British collapse so certain that they would not listen to any suggestions from the Government of Great Britain; others were less sure of a German victory but through fear of German retaliation against themselves dared not give Great Britain the support which they might otherwise have afforded.

The Government of Marshal Pétain took an entirely defeatist view of British chances; their own surrender had been due, in part at least, to the belief that Great Britain could not hold out for more than a few weeks after the military surrender of France,[2] and that the French might perhaps obtain slightly less harsh treatment from Hitler if they came to terms with him at once. Marshal Pétain and his Ministers persisted in this defeatist course long after the facts had shown that a British defeat would certainly not be immediate and very possibly might not take place at all. Moreover one inevitable corollary of French defeatism was a mood of sullen resentment against the British Government based on the assumption that they had recklessly dragged France into a war for which neither country was prepared and in which the French armies had received inadequate

---

[1] For Anglo-American discussions with regard to the Far East, see Volume II, Chapter XXII.

[2] The French generals, in particular, could not allow themselves to believe that after the French army, which they regarded as the finest in the world, had been completely defeated, the small British army could hold out against the Germans. See R. Aron, *Histoire de Vichy* (Paris, 1954), p. 91, n.1.

help from their Ally. In this mood the 'men of Vichy' were even more indignant at the British support of General de Gaulle whose movement frustrated their own chances of compounding with the Germans. In any case, if they had shown less ill-will to Great Britain, the Government of Marshal Pétain after the conclusion of the armistice were in the power of the Germans and could have done little or nothing to help their former Ally, except to send out of the reach of the Germans and Italians the units of the fleet which were already outside French metropolitan waters. They were unwilling even to connive at a measure of this kind. From the British point of view their refusal was a matter of great danger and might well have led to the ruin of British hopes of victory.

If France under the control of Marshal Pétain was only a sinister factor during these months of the British struggle for survival, everything depended on the degree of American confidence in a successful defence of the British Isles. In the first days of astonishment at the German victories, American opinion was hardly more hopeful than opinion in France. As the summer went by, and the Germans had not invaded Great Britain, there was a more solid basis for confidence; anyhow the United States Government did not withhold assistance until they were certain at least that a German invasion would be postponed. The amount of material aid provided during the most critical months of July and August, though valuable in itself, was not great; the important consideration was that the supply did not cease and that preparations were made for increasing it. The American attitude towards the blockade had also become less unfriendly. From August 1, 1940, Great Britain introduced new and more stringent methods of economic warfare based on 'control at source', and making the use of navicerts compulsory. Without the acquiescence and informal co-operation of the State Department the new policy could not have been employed with effect.

The British Government had been urging upon the United States the importance of setting up a system of export licensing control in order to prevent the depletion of American stocks of strategic materials for the benefit of the Axis Powers and Japan. The American Defence Act of July 2, 1940, secured the beginnings of this control, and already in June and July the State Department had limited to navicerted cargoes the chartering of oil tankers to Europe.

After the great air battles of August and September the situation changed. The Germans had planned an invasion, and had not been able to carry it out. If they had failed at a time of British weakness, their future chances of success were not too high. It was therefore possible to envisage a long war in which American material assistance might decide the issue. Henceforward the question was not whether it was a mistake to give this assistance; the discussions over 'Lend-Lease' which began at the end of December 1940, took American help for granted, and dealt only with ways and means whereby it could be provided, in spite of the inability of Great Britain to pay for it in dollars. Furthermore by this time there was more evidence of British chances of survival. The Germans had turned to indiscriminate night bombing in order to break British morale and to destroy British factories and communications. Their air attacks had not weakened the national will to resist and had not done irreparable material harm to British industry. The gravest danger came from attacks on shipping. Here the British were compelled to use mainly their northern and western ports; they were also cut off, by the neutrality of Eire, from harbours and bases on the southern and western Irish coast which would have been invaluable for defence. The situation was serious, but it was not desperate. American production could help to make good the shipping losses and also to increase the means of defence against attack. There was indeed reason to expect that these means of defence would be greatly increased in and after the spring of 1941, and the experience of the first war—as well as the action against the magnetic mine in 1939—had shown that a vigorous counter-offensive had an important moral as well as material effect upon the enemy; in other words, as more submarines were sunk, with their skilled crews and commanders, the German attack was likely to become less daring.

Finally, the offensive in Libya at the end of the year and the successes against the Italian navy were as heartening to American as to British opinion. In six weeks General Wavell had captured Tobruk and had taken 113,000 prisoners and 700 guns. In addition the Italian fleet had suffered heavily in an air attack on Taranto Harbour on November 11. The Italian ships, in the few encounters where British ships had found them, had already made a feeble showing. Italian military prestige had everywhere fallen; the attack on Greece had failed, and the Greeks were carrying out a successful counter-offensive. In the Sudan, where they had greatly superior numbers, the Italians had made no attempt to use their opportunities until it was too late.

The signs of American confidence, fortified by the Presidential election which had returned Mr. Roosevelt to office, were among the most hopeful results of these months of British endurance and action. There was indeed a reverse to the picture; although Americans were willing to send material in increasingly large quantities to the assistance of Great Britain, their determination to keep out of the war seemed as firm as ever, and their belief that they would be able to keep out of it was strengthened by the evidence that the immediate threat to American security was receding. Nonetheless to most British observers the situation seemed not unlike that of the first stages of the war of 1914–18. Sooner or later American intervention would come. Meanwhile the fact that this intervention appeared a long way off was of less moment since from a military point of view the Americans were still unprepared for war and their best immediate contribution to it was by the provision of supplies.

There was one qualification to this judgment. If Japan came into the war on the German side, America alone could save the situation. The general British view was, however, not only that the entry of Japan into the war would mean the participation of the United States but that the Japanese themselves drew this conclusion, and that, if they had not seized the chance at the time of greatest British weakness, they would not actually go to war until they were more certain of a German victory in Europe.

In these circumstances, as the autumn of 1940 turned to winter, there was a little more scope for British political action, or perhaps it would be better to say that in the fields where such action was at all possible, it could be on a slightly bolder scale. The field of action was in fact narrow. In the Far East the British Government reopened the Burma Road; they could not do more either to support China or to check the 'step by step' methods of Japanese aggression. There was little to be done in Europe: General Franco's desire to keep Spain out of the war was not due to friendly feelings towards Great Britain, and with the Germans already at the frontier the only counter-pressure which British policy could exercise on Spain was through offers to relieve the desperate economic position of the country.

The importance of keeping General Franco neutral, even if his neutrality were mainly malevolent, lay in the position of Spain at the western end of the Mediterranean and on the road to Africa. At the other end of the Mediterranean, and especially after the bold resistance of Greece to Italian aggression, Turkey was even more important, but the Turkish Government could not be expected to risk the anger of Germany and Russia at a time when they could get little or no military help from Great Britain. In the Balkans and Near East generally British policy had temporarily lost the initiative; the main hope of warding off another German advance was that Russia would not allow it. It was however impossible to know whether the Russian reaction to the collapse of France would show itself in greater or less subservience to Germany. In June 1940, the Soviet Government had ousted the Governments of Lithuania, Latvia and Estonia and established garrisons in these States; in July the parliaments of the three countries voted for incorporation into the Soviet Union. At the end of June also the Russians had compelled the Roumanian Government to surrender northern Bessarabia and Bukovina. These acts might well be directed against the increased risks of German aggression now that the Soviet Union had brought upon themselves by their policy since August, 1939, the possibility of a 'single-front' war from which they had manoeuvred to escape. The Russians had not envisaged the destruction of the French army, but no one outside the Kremlin could guess whether they would try to buy safety by more concessions. A tentative British approach to the Soviet Government at the end of June had no result, except to show that, however much the Soviet leaders who had favoured a pact with Germany might be alarmed at the results of their action, they would not do anything likely to provoke Germany to attack. They would probably try to gain time by promises of closer collaboration and, meanwhile, partly to satisfy Germany, their propaganda would continue to show ill-will to Great Britain and, as far as it had any results, would continue also to hamper the British productive effort. At the turn of the year, the Russian attitude seemed unchanged. There was no reason to suppose that this attitude would be changed. The conception of a 'second front' which was argued so strongly by Soviet leaders not many months later did not arise out of any willingness to help Great Britain in the crisis of British fortunes.

(ii)

Renewal of Lord Lothian's proposals for meeting American defence requirements in Newfoundland and British colonial territories: the Prime Minister's appeal for American destroyers (June 22—July 30, 1940).

Lord Lothian had suggested before the end of May 1940, that His Majesty's Government should consider making a formal offer to allow the United States Government to construct aerodromes and naval stations on British islands of strategic importance to American security.[1] Lord Lothian thought that the United States Government were concerned chiefly with Newfoundland and Trinidad.

The War Cabinet considered, however, that it would be undesirable to make an offer unless we were assured of substantial advantages from it. On the night of June 22-3 Lord Lothian reported that, in view of the opinion expressed by the War Cabinet, he did not wish to (a) press his suggestion, but that he knew the immediate requirements of the American Army and Air Forces for purposes of national defence. These requirements were the right to land aircraft at Trinidad, Georgetown (British Guiana) and Jamaica, and the lease to Pan-American Airways of areas in these places.

Eleven days later Lord Lothian repeated his suggestion. He (b) reported that there was a popular demand in the United States in

---

[1] See above, pp.340–2.
(a) A3297/2961/45.   (b) A3297/2961/45.

favour of taking over all the Caribbean Islands in the interest of American defence. The demand was gaining in force as the Americans realised the risk to themselves from the French collapse and the impending attack on Great Britain. The best answer therefore would be to make the offer which he (Lord Lothian) had outlined.

(a) An interim reply was sent to Lord Lothian on July 6 that, in the view of His Majesty's Government, an offer to the United States could be profitably discussed only in connexion with the wider issue of general Anglo-American strategic co-operation, but that a reply to Lord Lothian's proposal would be sent as soon as possible.

Two days later Lord Lothian reported that he was anxious for an early reply in view of the Pan-American Conference to be held at Havana on July 20. Mr. Hull was afraid that the United States representatives at the Havana Conference might want the Caribbean islands to be placed under American control for purposes of defence. Lord Lothian wished to forestall any demands of this kind. He added

(b) on July 10 that Colonel Knox, who had recently been appointed Secretary of the Navy, had asked him whether it would be possible to arrange for the transfer of the British West Indian islands in return for the cancellation of the British war debt to the United States. Lord Lothian answered that opinion in the United States and in Great Britain took very different views of the war debt and that the defence problem could not be handled in this way.

Meanwhile Lord Lothian's proposals had been under consideration

(c) in London. Lord Lothian was asked on July 11 to explain why the United States had not availed themselves of the leasehold rights granted to them in 1939 at Trinidad, Bermuda and St. Lucia. He

(d) answered that the rights had not been used because the struggle with Congress over the amendment of the Neutrality Act had made Mr. Roosevelt very unwilling to do anything that could be interpreted by the isolationists as entangling the United States in the European war and because the United States navy had been short of flying-boats suitable for the Atlantic patrol. The United States navy had also been able to organise an Atlantic patrol from bases outside British territory. The situation had now changed. American public opinion and the Administration were deeply pre-occupied with the question of defence and anxious to organise communication with South America in order to be able to intervene there in the event of 'fifth column' or other German action in Brazil.

(e) The Foreign Office were strongly in favour of Lord Lothian's proposals, and, at Lord Halifax's request, drew up a memorandum

---

(a) A3297/2961/45. (b) A3297/2961/45. (c) A3297/2961/45. (d) A3297/2961/45. (e) A3600/2961/45, WP(40)276.

for the War Cabinet. The memorandum summed up the enquiries already made. The Chiefs of Staff had agreed that it was desirable to meet the American requirements. The Governors of Jamaica, Trinidad and British Guiana had given their approval; so also, with the assent of the Canadian Government, had the Government of Newfoundland. The main argument for the proposals was our immediate need of American help, but it could also be said that the future of our Empire depended upon an enduring Anglo-American collaboration. This fact might be obvious to us; to American opinion it was a new and startling doctrine. We ought therefore to try to assist the United States in taking up the 'new and heavy responsibility for which so little in her tradition and history has prepared her'. On our part we should recognise that a responsibility involved a right to the means for discharging it. Until late in the last war Great Britain had been almost alone for nearly a century in guarding the English-speaking peoples by sea, and the British Empire rather than the United States was still in possession of the naval and air facilities (actual and potential) protecting the American continents. In future we might be unable to perform these functions unaided; we could not hope for the cordial co-operation of the United States unless we shared with them the strategic facilities which these duties required. If Great Britain were defeated, Americans would have to defend their shores without any prepared bases in the Atlantic under their control. American opinion was bound to feel bitterness if we failed to recognise the facts.

We could make a free offer or suggest a bargain. A bargain would be open to the difficulty that we were already in debt to the United States after the last war and would be more in debt as a condition of winning this present war, and that we could not repay these debts. The United States were being generous to us, since, if they wished, they could break our blockade. Hence we should offer the facilities mentioned in Lord Lothian's telegram of June 22–3 without suggesting a *quid pro quo*.

The War Cabinet discussed this memorandum on July 29. Meanwhile the Prime Minister was considering another appeal to Mr. Roosevelt on the subject of destroyers. Lord Lothian had telegraphed a message to the Prime Minister on July 5 that American opinion (a) had at last begun to realise that the United States might lose the British fleet if they remained neutral and the war went against us. A number of influential people were thinking of demanding that the United States should enter the war at once in order to give more effective help during the next critical months. They thought that it would be hard to get public opinion to consider this argument

(a) A3582/131/45.

without an assurance that, in the event of America coming into the war, the British fleet or what was left of it would cross the Atlantic if Great Britain were overrun. Lord Lothian's view was that, if we were formally asked, we should give such an assurance because the problem of winning the war would take a new aspect with American participation.

(a) Lord Lothian referred to this message in a telegram of July 22 to the Prime Minister. He said that, with the end of the Conventions for the presidential election, public attention was again concentrated on the war. Lord Lothian had been asked by Americans what action the United States should take. He had replied privately that the United States should send 100 destroyers and some flying-boats manned by Americans (who, if necessary, would be volunteers). Assistance of this kind would be decisive against attacks on the fleet and on merchant shipping, and would enable us to maintain indefinitely a fleet based on Great Britain as well as to hold Gibraltar and Suez. The American fleet could then be kept in the Pacific, and the United States could carry on its rapid production of armaments behind the shield of the two navies. A refusal to send these reinforcements to us at once would risk the betrayal of vital American interests. If Great Britain were defeated in the autumn, the United States would be unable to defend South America or to complete their rearmament because Hitler would control resources for building ships and aeroplanes on a scale three times greater than the resources of the United States.

(b) Lord Lothian telegraphed on July 25 that he had broadcast a statement referring to our need of about 100 destroyers and some seaplanes. These facts were becoming understood, but unfortunately the American press had quoted an Admiralty statement that we had as many destroyers as at the outbreak of war and had thereby given the impression that we were not worrying about the problem.[1] Lord Lothian asked whether the Prime Minister could state at once (i) whether we should like 50–100 destroyers, and, if so, with or without crews; (ii) whether these destroyers would make a decisive difference to the battle in progress. A similar statement should be made about seaplanes; (iii) what other supplies would make a vital difference during the autumn.

(c) The Prime Minister asked the Admiralty for an immediate answer to these questions and said that he might be sending a personal message on the subject to Mr. Roosevelt. On the night of July 27 the Prime Minister replied to Lord Lothian that our need of destroyers was more urgent than ever. There could be no greater help from the United States than the despatch of 50 destroyers to bridge the gap

---

[1] The reference here is to an article in the *Daily Express*. This article was based partly on material supplied on request by the Admiralty.

(a) A3582/131/45. (b) A3582/131/45. (c) A3582/131/45.

until our new production was available; 100 destroyers would be even better. Mr. Churchill added a note from the Admiralty to the effect that the article in the *Daily Express* had given a wrong view of the situation. Very few new destroyers would be ready in 1940. We began the war with fewer destroyers than we needed but we had powerful French help which we had now lost. The Naval Staff thought the destroyer question was vital to us. Hence the answers to Lord Lothian's questions were as follows: (i) We should like 50–100 destroyers. We had already asked for and could man 48. If we were given 100, so much the better. We should like most of all to get them with American crews, but we realised that this was more than we could expect because it would mean the entry of the United States into the war. The next best thing would be for the Americans to bring the destroyers to us; otherwise we would fetch them. (ii) This number of American destroyers, sent quickly, might make a decisive difference to the future of the war. We wanted flying-boats rather than seaplanes. The American PBY type suited us, and we had a number of them on order. If we could get 100 now, the difference to the future of the war would be 'tremendous'. (iii) We needed anti-aircraft guns and ammunition.

On July 30 the Prime Minister drafted a personal message to Mr. Roosevelt in the following terms:[1]

'It is some time since I ventured to cable personally to you, and many things both good and bad have happened in between. It has now become most urgent for you to let us have the destroyers, motor-boats and flying-boats for which we have asked. The Germans have the whole French coastline from which to launch U-boat and dive-bomber attacks upon our trade and food, and in addition we must be constantly prepared to repel by sea action threatened invasion in the narrow waters and also to deal with break-outs from Norway towards Ireland, Iceland, the Shetlands and Faroes. Besides this we have to keep control of the exits from the Mediterranean and, if possible, the command of that inland sea itself and thus to prevent the war spreading seriously into Africa. We have a large construction of destroyers and anti-U-boat craft coming forward, but the next three or four months open the gap of which I have previously told you. Latterly the air attack on our shipping has become injurious.' Four destroyers had been sunk and seven damaged in the last ten days. 'Destroyers are frightfully vulnerable to air bombing and yet they must be held in the air-bombing area to prevent seaborne invasion. We could not sustain the present rate of casualties for long, and, if we cannot get a substantial reinforcement, the whole fate of the war may be decided by this minor and easily remediable factor.'

The Prime Minister explained that we could fit 50–60 of the oldest American destroyers with asdics and use them at once against

---

[1] This message was despatched on July 31.

U-boats in the Western Approaches, and thus keep our modern and better gunned craft for the narrow seas. 'Mr. President, with great respect I must tell you that in the long history of the world this is a thing to do *now*.' If we were given the destroyers, 'the motor-boats and flying-boats, which would be invaluable, could surely come in behind them'.

Mr. Churchill's summary of the position was: 'I am beginning to feel very hopeful about this war if we can get round the next three or four months.'

(iii)

Decision to offer the facilities required by the United States, July 29: Mr. Roosevelt's proposals for the sale of destroyers in exchange for colonial bases and for a declaration with regard to the British fleet: reply of August 8 to Mr. Roosevelt's proposals.

(a)   After discussing the Foreign Office memorandum the War Cabinet agreed on July 29 to offer to meet the requirements of the United States Government. While the conditions of the offer were being considered, Lord Lothian telegraphed on the night of August 1–2
(b) that Mr. Roosevelt's principal advisers wanted to sell to us 50–60 destroyers but that legislation was necessary for the transfer of the ships. This legislation would be opposed by the isolationists of both parties in a Congress which did not understand the strategic dangers of the present situation. Hence the issue might be brought into the election campaign and so cause 'complete paralysis'. Another difficulty was the increasing reluctance of the military and naval authorities to part with any of the totally inadequate defence equipment of the United States.

Efforts had been made to persuade Mr. Willkie[1] to agree not to oppose the sale of the destroyers. Although Mr. Willkie would not commit himself, he was said not to be unfriendly to the proposal if Mr. Roosevelt would take the responsibility of initiating it. According to report Mr. Roosevelt thought that Congress would agree to the sale if the transaction could be presented as an exchange beneficial to the defences of the United States and not carrying with it the risk of involving the United States in the European war.

Lord Lothian said that two possible ways out of the difficulty were under consideration: (i) The United States might sell the destroyers

---

[1] Mr. Wendell Willkie was Republican candidate in the 1940 presidential election.
(a) WM(40)214, A3600/2961/45. (b) A3582/131/45.

to Canada and in return for sending them to European waters the Canadian Government might be given a lien on some of the larger British cruisers which, in the event of our defeat, would then form part of the Canadian contribution to the defence of North America. (ii) The destroyers might be sold in exchange for the sale to the United States of defence bases in Newfoundland, Bermuda, Trinidad and possibly one or two smaller islands.

Colonel Knox considered that Congress would accept only the second alternative. Lord Lothian also favoured this alternative if the destroyers and flying-boats were made available without delay because he thought that we had everything to gain by treating the defence of the Atlantic coast of the United States as a joint Anglo-American co-operative interest.

An answer was given to Lord Lothian at once that the War Cabinet had decided in favour of meeting the American require- (a) ments as set out in Lord Lothian's telegram of June 22. Further instructions were sent to Lord Lothian on August 3 that we would accept the second alternative, i.e. an exchange of destroyers for bases, (b) though we should prefer an indefinite lease to a sale of territory. We did not think the suggestion about cruisers to be practicable. The question of bases, however, was not wholly within the competence of His Majesty's Government in the United Kingdom, but we would consult the Dominions and Colonial Governments as soon as we knew details.

On the night of August 3–4 Lord Lothian telegraphed that Mr. Roosevelt, who was leaving Washington for several days, had told (c) him the outcome of the Cabinet discussions. Mr. Roosevelt said that it was quite clear that there was no way of carrying out the sale of the destroyers except by legislation in Congress. This would be possible only by giving Congress 'molasses' in the form of a public assurance from the present British Government that, if things went badly for us, the British fleet, or what was left of it, would not be given in any circumstances to the Germans but would leave British waters, if necessary, and continue to fight for the British Empire overseas. Mr. Roosevelt thought that public opinion would be favourably impressed by such a declaration, although everyone knew that it could not bind a successor to the existing British Government. Mr. Roosevelt also wanted some kind of arrangement whereby we would give air and naval facilities to the United States for hemispheric defence. This would imply that if any of our possessions in the Western Hemisphere were likely to fall into the hands of the enemy,

(a) A3600/2961/45. (b) A3600/2961/45. (c) A3670/131/45.

the United States would be able to assume protection over them until the end of the war.

Lord Lothian reported that Mr. Roosevelt was frightened of filibustering by fifteen or twenty determined isolationists in the Senate. There was no way of enforcing the closure; hence the project might be wrecked until after the election. Mr. Roosevelt realised the urgency of our need and was working to introduce the bill into the Senate by August 7–10. The passage of the bill would take about a fortnight. Lord Lothian asked for authorisation to tell Mr. Roosevelt that, on the understanding that the destroyers would be speedily available, he could inform Congress of our willingness to provide the facilities and to give an assurance about the future of the fleet.

On the night of August 4–5 Lord Lothian reported that he had (a) seen Mr. Hull and Mr. Welles. They had agreed with Mr. Roosevelt's view. They explained also that the declaration about the British fleet should be unilateral.[1] Mr. Hull thought, however, that the chances against the passing of the bill were four to one.

(b)   The War Cabinet considered the American proposals on August 6 and invited Lord Halifax, in consultation with the Prime Minister, to draw up a reply. The Prime Minister gave Lord Halifax to understand that he would be prepared to make the declaration about the fleet only if it were clearly understood that His Majesty's Government must be the sole judge when, if ever, the moment had come for the fleet to leave Great Britain. A draft reply to Lord Lothian was submitted to the Prime Minister who then drew up another draft in the form of a message from himself to Lord Lothian. The Prime Minister also sent a note to Lord Halifax to the effect that only a war alliance with the United States would justify any stipulation about the fleet. The declaration suggested by Lord Lothian would have a disastrous effect on British morale and was not warranted by the situation. The colonial leases were more than enough to give for 50 or 60 old destroyers.

On the morning of August 7 a message was received from Lord Lothian that Mr. Roosevelt wanted an immediate answer to the (c) question about the fleet. He wished to be assured that, if Great Britain were overrun, the fleet would continue to fight for the Empire overseas and would not be surrendered or voluntarily sunk. This argument would have the greatest effect on Congress. Lord Lothian

---

[1] Later on August 5 Lord Lothian reported that Mr. Welles had said that His Majesty's (d) Government need do no more than inform him (Lord Lothian) privately of their willingness to make a declaration that the British fleet would go on fighting for the Empire 'even if it is compelled to evacuate Great Britain if and when the President asks for it'. The last sentence of this telegram was ambiguous. The Prime Minister appears to have taken it to mean, not that the declaration should be made, but that the fleet would be handed over if and when Mr. Roosevelt asked for it.

(a) A3670/131/45. (b) WM(40)220. (c) A3670/131/45. (d) A3670/131/45.

asked whether a reply could be telephoned as early as possible on August 7. He added that the prospects of legislative action were steadily increasing.

An interim reply was sent to Lord Lothian promising an answer (a) within twenty-four hours. Meanwhile the Prime Minister held up his message and on August 7 wrote to Lord Halifax that in his view the position was clear.

'We have no intention of surrendering the British fleet or sinking it voluntarily. Indeed such a fate is more likely to overtake the German fleet or what is left of it. The nation would not tolerate any discussion of what we should do if our island were overrun. Such a discussion, perhaps on the eve of an invasion, would be injurious to public morale, now so high. Moreover we must never get into a position when the United States Government may say "We think the time has come for you to send your fleet across the Atlantic in accordance with our understanding of the agreement when we gave you the destroyers". We must refuse any declaration such as is suggested and confine the deal solely to the Colonial bases.'

Lord Halifax now drafted an alternative telegram to be sent as a message from the Prime Minister to Lord Lothian. The Prime Minister, however, preferred that the telegram should take the form of a message from Lord Halifax rather than from himself. This telegram was sent in the afternoon of August 8. Lord Lothian was (b) instructed that we found great difficulty even in giving a simple assurance of the kind desired by Mr. Roosevelt. If Great Britain were overrun, the position of the fleet, as far as concerned the present British Government, would be as described in the Prime Minister's speech of June 4[1] but a declaration on the matter would provoke discussion and involve great risk, here and among our enemies, of an impression that we thought of the collapse of Great Britain as a possible contingency. Lord Lothian was asked whether he could suggest any way round this difficulty. There was also a risk that Congress might be less anxious to go on helping us if they were less anxious about the security of the United States.

Lord Lothian was instructed to authorise Mr. Roosevelt to inform (c) Congress that as soon as we received the destroyers we would provide the facilities which Lord Lothian had mentioned with regard to the lease of naval and air bases. For his own information he was told that we should prefer leases to sales, and that 'obviously the fewer concessions, even in the form of leases, the better'.

---

[1] See above, p. 214, note 1.

(a) A3670/131/45. (b) A3670/131/45. (c) A3670/131/45.

(iv)

Mr. Roosevelt's message of August 13 to the Prime Minister: discussion in the War Cabinet on August 14: the Prime Minister's reply of August 15 to Mr. Roosevelt: American proposal for an exchange of letters with regard to the transfer of destroyers and the grant of bases, August 19–20, 1940.

(a)   Lord Lothian replied on the night of August 8–9 that he had carried out his instructions. He had confined himself to the offer of a lease of bases to Pan American Airways, since the United States authorities did not revert to their own proposal that the bases should be sold to the United States Government. In return for our offer he had asked for 12 flotillas of 8 destroyers, 20 motor torpedo-boats, 50 flying-boats, some dive-bombers, and 250,000 rifles. In conversation with Lord Lothian Mr. Roosevelt had not gone beyond 50–60 destroyers.

(b)   Lord Lothian telegraphed on August 14 that Mr. Roosevelt had told him of a message which he had sent to the Prime Minister through Mr. Kennedy to the effect that he might be able to provide the destroyers without going to Congress. He thought, however, the legislation would be necessary, and that it would take about a month. As soon as the bill had been passed the destroyers would be available.

(c)   Mr. Roosevelt's message was that he thought it would be possible to give at least 50 destroyers, some motor torpedo boats and 5 aircraft of each of the categories concerned. The United States would want (i) an assurance from the Prime Minister that, if the waters of Great Britain should become untenable for British ships of war, the ships would not be turned over to the Germans, but would be sent to other parts of the Empire 'for [the] continued defence of the Empire'; (ii) an agreement by Great Britain authorising the use by the United States of Newfoundland, Bermuda, the Bahamas, Jamaica, St. Lucia, Trinidad and British Guiana as naval and air bases in the event of an attack on the American hemisphere by a non-American nation, and the immediate acquisition by the United States and the employment for purposes of training and exercise, of bases in these areas—the necessary lands to be acquired by purchase or on a 99 years lease. Mr. Roosevelt thought it unnecessary to consider at once specific details under (ii). He also had in mind, not a public statement about the fleet, but a personal assurance to himself on the lines which he had indicated, e.g. a repetition to him of Mr. Churchill's statement of June 4.

(d)   The War Cabinet considered Lord Lothian's telegram and Mr. Roosevelt's message on August 14. The Prime Minister thought that,

---

(a) A3670/131/45.   (b) A3793/131/45.   (c) A3793/131/45.   (d) WM(40)227; A3793/131/45.

if the proposal went through, the United States would have taken a long step towards coming into the war on our side. The sale of destroyers to a belligerent Power was not a neutral action. The 50 destroyers would be of enormous value and the fact of their sale would have an immense effect in Germany.

The crucial point, however, was what Mr. Roosevelt would say publicly about the assurance for which he had asked. The Prime Minister reminded the War Cabinet of his statement of June 4. This statement had been made partly in order to reassure public opinion immediately after the collapse of France. Nothing must be said now which would disturb morale or lead people to think that we would not 'fight it out here'.

The War Cabinet agreed that it was of the highest importance to make absolutely clear our firm resolve to continue to the utmost our resistance in Great Britain, and that, even if, contrary to our expectation, we should feel ourselves overwhelmed, we should retain entirely unfettered the right to decide when (if ever) we should send the fleet away to defend our kith and kin overseas.

The general view of the War Cabinet was also that, although, from the point of view of tangible assets, the terms of the bargain were not very favourable to us, it was impossible to look at the matter merely as an exchange. It might be the first step in the constitution of an Anglo-Saxon *bloc* or indeed a decisive point in history. Mr. Roosevelt's proposed action was very different from the line taken by the U.S.S.R. and Japan, and the effect would be all the greater if the transaction went through before the Germans had attempted invasion. The War Cabinet therefore agreed in principle on an affirmative answer.

On August 15 Lord Lothian was sent a copy of a reply from the (a) Prime Minister to Mr. Roosevelt's message. The Prime Minister, after thanking Mr. Roosevelt, said that we also needed motor torpedo-boats and that we had a million men waiting for rifles. We could meet both Mr. Roosevelt's points if we were assured that there would be no delay in the provision of the destroyers and the flying-boats. The Prime Minister accepted the proposals for the lease (not sale) of bases, but explained that it would be necessary to consult the Governments of Canada and Newfoundland. The Prime Minister could repeat what he had said in Parliament on June 4; he asked Mr. Roosevelt, if he should use the statement, to remember 'the disastrous effect from our point of view, and perhaps also from yours, of allowing any impression to grow that we regard the conquest of the British Isles and its naval bases as any other than an impossible contingency. The spirit of our people is splendid. Never have they been so determined. Their confidence in the issue has been enormously

(a) A3793/131/45.

and legitimately strengthened by the severe air fighting of the past week.'

(a)   On August 18 Mr. Mackenzie King telegraphed that he had met Mr. Roosevelt by invitation on August 17,[1] and that he had Mr. Roosevelt's authority to say that he (Mr. Roosevelt) hoped before the week was out to begin sending the destroyers. He would send 50 in all and hoped that he would not need special authorisation from Congress. He would also send 20 motor torpedo-boats, 10 flying-boats, and 250,000 rifles (without ammunition), and 150–200 aircraft. Mr. Roosevelt was quite satisfied with the statement which Mr. Churchill proposed to make on the lines of the statement of June 4.

(b)   The Prime Minister told the War Cabinet on August 19 that he proposed to deal with the 'assurance' about the fleet in a speech on August 20. On the night of August 19–20, however, Lord Lothian

(c)   reported that Mr. Welles had told him that all difficulties about the destroyers and other material would be overcome if there were an exchange of letters signed by him (Lord Lothian) and Mr. Hull. This method was essential because it was legally impossible for Mr. Roosevelt to send the destroyers without legislation except in exchange for a definite consideration and unless under the legislation of June, 1940, the Chief of Naval Staff would certify that they were not essential to the national defence of the United States.

Mr. Welles had drafted the text of the letters to be exchanged. Lord Lothian proposed a number of changes in the text. The most important of these changes was the omission of a reference to the Prime Minister's statement of June 4 about the British fleet. Lord Lothian pointed out that the Prime Minister could not make a statement about the British fleet in a letter intended for publication. Mr. Welles understood the reasons why such a statement could not be made. He suggested that the Prime Minister might send a private letter or statement marked 'not for publication'. He also agreed to the omission of a reference to the fleet in the letters to be exchanged.

Lord Lothian also said that we should object strongly to the treatment of the transaction 'as a deal in which we made these far-reaching and tremendous concessions' in exchange for 50 old destroyers. From the British point of view it was essential that our part of the transaction should be represented as a contribution, which had long been under consideration, to the security of North America, including Canada. Otherwise British public opinion, and possibly opinion in the United States, would think that the United

---

[1] At this meeting the President and Mr. Mackenzie King agreed upon the establishment of a Permanent Joint Board of Defence to 'consider in a broad sense' the defence of the northern half of the western hemisphere.

(a) A3893/131/45.   (b) WM(40)230; A3893/131/45.   (c) A3917/3742/45.

States had driven an intolerably hard bargain at the moment of our greatest difficulty.

The final text proposed by Lord Lothian for the letter on behalf of His Majesty's Government ran as follows:—

'I am instructed by His Britannic Majesty's Government to transmit in its name to the Government of the United States the following declaration:[1]

His Majesty's Government in the United Kingdom, in consultation with the Government of Canada, has for some time had under consideration that they should offer to the United States certain aircraft bases and naval stations off the Atlantic coast of America with the object of enabling them greatly to strengthen their ability to co-operate effectively with other nations in North, Central and South America in defence of the Western Hemisphere. His Majesty's Government therefore hereby formally declare to the Government of the United States that they are willing to make available to them immediately, the use of naval and aircraft bases in Newfoundland, Bermuda, the Bahamas, Jamaica, Santa Lucia, Trinidad and British Guiana, such bases to be leased by the United States for a period of 99 years.

The two Governments will immediately determine by common agreement the exact location of such bases within the colonies above-mentioned as may be required in the judgment of the United States for purposes of defence as well as for peace-time training.

The British Government, in the terms of the leases to be agreed upon, will grant to the United States for the period of the leases all rights, power and authority within the bases leased, and within the limits of the territorial waters adjacent to such bases, which the United States would possess and exercise if it were sovereign of the territory and the waters above-mentioned.[2] However, individuals, other than citizens of the United States, who may be charged within the area of the bases leased with crimes or misdemeanours amenable to the laws of the British colonies within which such bases are located, shall be delivered by the appropriate United States authorities to the duly authorised authorities of the colonies in question.'[3]

The final text proposed by Lord Lothian for Mr. Hull's reply was as follows:—

'I have received your communication of (date) of which the text is as follows:—

(Here followed the text of the proposed letter from Lord Lothian).

---

[1] The American draft here read 'commitments'.

[2] In the American draft there followed after 'above-mentioned' the phrase 'to the entire exclusion of the exercise by the British Government and its agents of such sovereign rights, power or authority'.

[3] The American draft concluded with the words:—
'The British Government will accept as in full compensation for the leases referred to . . . above . . . the following naval and military materials:—'

Inasmuch as in the opinion of the Government of the United States the declaration[1] on the part of the British Government contained in your communication is destined to enhance the national security of the United States and greatly to strengthen its ability to co-operate effectively with other nations of the Americas in the defence of the Western Hemisphere, it is gladly received and accepted.

The Government of the United States will immediately designate commissioners to meet with the commissioners designated by the British Government to determine upon the exact location of the naval and aircraft bases mentioned in paragraph 2 of your communication under acknowledgment.

In consideration of the declaration of His Majesty's Government in the United Kingdom that it is prepared to lease to the United States for 99 years the aircraft and naval bases abovementioned,[2] the Government of the United States will immediately transfer to the British Government 50 destroyers, 20 motor torpedo-boats, 5 of the latest model military aeroplanes and 5 of the latest model naval flying-boats.'[3]

(v)

Objections of His Majesty's Government to the proposal for an exchange of letters: the Prime Minister's message of August 22 to Mr. Roosevelt: Lord Lothian's conversation of August 22 with Mr. Welles: the Prime Minister's message of August 25, 1940, to Mr. Roosevelt.

(a) The War Cabinet discussed this new American proposal on August 21. They considered that Lord Lothian's amendments had improved the letters, but that, according to previous understanding of the matter, Mr. Roosevelt had not intended to establish any open connexion between the measures which the two Governments were to take.

The War Cabinet thought that a formal bargain on the lines proposed was out of the question. No monetary relationship could be established between the benefits to be conferred by either side. From our point of view we were offering facilities worth far more than 50 old destroyers and other war material the chief value of which to us lay in our urgent need of it. It would be asked why we were not obtaining a more valuable consideration such as the cancellation of

---

[1] The original text submitted to Lord Lothian read 'commitments'.

[2] The original text read 'In full payment for 99 years lease for such bases'.

[3] The original text read 'transfer to the British Government the naval and military material listed in your communication above quoted, and which is as follows: 50 destroyers', etc.

(a) WM(40)231; A3917/3742/45.

our debt to the United States. Criticism of such a bargain might well embitter Anglo-American relations. The exchange of letters had doubtless been proposed for reasons connected with politics in the United States. We had also been told that it was legally impossible for Mr. Roosevelt to part with the destroyers without legislation except for a definite consideration unless it were certified that they were not essential to the defence of the United States.

The Prime Minister reminded the War Cabinet of his speech of the previous day.[1] He thought that our own and the American attitude in the matter should be that each of us as friends was prepared to do what was possible to help the other to gain added security without receiving any *quid pro quo*. If we now made it plain that we would provide without payment the facilities wanted by the United States, the United States would find it possible to send us the destroyers. If the United States wished to link the two transactions, they could do so, but we could not link them.

The War Cabinet thought that the Prime Minister's speech might increase confidence in the United States and dispose the Administration towards less rigorous terms. Hence it might be better to wait a day or two before sending a reply. The War Cabinet accepted on (a) August 22 the draft of a message from the Prime Minister to Mr. Roosevelt in the following terms:

'I am most grateful for all you are doing on our behalf. I had not contemplated anything in the nature of a contract, bargain or sale (b) between us. It is the fact that we had decided in Cabinet to offer you naval and air facilities off the Atlantic Coast quite independently of destroyers or any other aid. Our view is that we are two friends in danger helping each other as far as we can. We should therefore like to give you the facilities mentioned without stipulating for any return and, even if tomorrow you found it too difficult to transfer the destroyers etc., our offer still remains open because we think it is in the general good.

2. I see difficulties and even risks in the exchange of letters now suggested or in admitting in any way that the munitions which you

---

[1] In this speech Mr. Churchill gave the House of Commons a review of the situation at the end of the first year of the war. He referred indirectly to the future of the fleet, saying: 'If we had been put in the terrible position of France, a contingency now happily impossible, although, of course, it would have been the duty of all war leaders to fight on here to the end, it would also have been their duty, as I indicated in my speech of 4th June, to provide as far as possible for the Naval security of Canada and our Dominions and to make sure they had the means to carry on the struggle from beyond the oceans'. Mr. Churchill stated the decision of His Majesty's Government that the interests of the United States and of the British Empire required that the United States should have facilities for the naval and air defence of the Western Hemisphere against the attack of a Nazi power which might have acquired temporary but lengthy control of a large part of Western Europe. 'We had therefore decided spontaneously, and without being asked or offered any inducement, to inform the Government of the United States that we would be glad to place such defence facilities at their disposal by leasing suitable sites in our transatlantic possessions.' *Parl. Deb., 5th Ser., H. of C.*, Vol. 364, cols. 1168, 1170.

(a) WM(40)232. (b) A3917/3742/45.

send us are a payment for the facilities. Once this idea is accepted people will contrast on each side what is given and received. The money value of the armaments would be computed and set against the facilities and some would think one thing about it and some another.

3. Moreover, Mr. President, as you well know, each island or location is a case by itself. If, for instance, there were only one harbour or site, how is it to be divided and its advantages shared? In such a case we should like to make you an offer of what we think is best for both rather than to embark upon a close-cut argument as to what ought to be delivered in return for value received.

4. What we want is that you shall feel safe on your Atlantic seaboard so far as any facilities in possessions of ours can make you safe, and naturally, if you put in money and make large developments, you must have the effective security of a long lease. Therefore I would rather rest at this moment upon the general declaration made by me in the House of Commons yesterday, both on this point and as regards the future of the Fleet. Then if you will set out in greater detail what you want, we will at once tell you what we can do and thereafter the necessary arrangements, technical and legal, can be worked out by our experts. Meanwhile we are quite content to trust entirely to your judgment and the sentiments of the people of the United States about any aid in munitions, etc., you feel able to give us. But this would be entirely a separate, spontaneous act on the part of the United States arising out of their view of the world struggle and how their own interests stand in relation to it and the causes it involves.

5. Although the air attack has slackened in the last few days and our strength is growing in many ways I do not think that bad man has yet struck his full blow. We are having considerable losses in merchant ships on the north-western approaches, now our only channel of regular communication with the oceans, and your fifty destroyers, if they came along at once, would be a precious help.'

This message was sent to the President at once on August 22. The (a) text was also telegraphed to Lord Lothian. Lord Lothian was instructed that it was open to Mr. Roosevelt to present the matter to Congress as he might choose, and that we should not object if he felt justified in regarding the facilities which we had given spontaneously as an adequate *quid pro quo* for the destroyers which he had subsequently made available to us. This was entirely his affair and did not risk committing us to the idea of a bargain. We could maintain the position that we had made of our own free will concessions to the United States which we believed to be in the common interest of both countries, and that we had later found ourselves the beneficiaries of a similar spontaneous and generous act on the part of the Government of the United States.

(a) A3917/3742/45.

Lord Lothian saw Mr. Welles in the afternoon of August 22.[1] (a)
Mr. Welles said that Mr. Roosevelt had received the Prime Minister's
message, but that he regretted that an exchange of letters still
seemed to him the only way of dealing with the matter. Mr. Roosevelt
had referred again to the necessity of giving 'molasses' to Congress.
The constitutional position made it impossible to send the destroyers
as a free gift. Under existing legislation by Congress the Chief of
Staff and the General Board of the Navy could not give a certificate
that the ships were not essential to the defence of the United States.
Without such a certificate the transfer could not be made legally
except in return for a definite consideration which could be certified
as adding to the security of the United States. For this reason it was
necessary to include a reference to the exercise by the United States
of rights, power, and authority within the bases and territorial
waters as though they were sovereign territory of the United States.

Mr. Welles said that Mr. Roosevelt was much exercised about the
question. He had worked hard to make it possible to send the
destroyers at once. Unless he acted promptly, isolationists—and
others—would have a chance to undermine the position. Mr. Roosevelt therefore hoped that the Prime Minister would agree with his
proposals.

Lord Lothian, in his telegram, considered that Mr. Welles's view
represented 'realities'. The United States legal officers had tried to
find a way out of the difficulty. Lord Lothian thought that his drafts
avoided the idea of a bargain. He had now persuaded Mr. Welles to
include a reference to the Prime Minister's speech. The plain truth
was that everyone in the United States realised that the questions of
the bases and the destroyers were connected, especially from the
American point of view. The Prime Minister's speech had made
public the fact that we had long been considering the question of
giving naval and air bases to the United States; the exchange of
letters could be regarded more or less as a legal appendage.

Lord Lothian also hoped that the Prime Minister would agree,
since otherwise we should probably lose the destroyers. Moreover in
the long run the important facts were that we and the United States
were now beginning to organise the joint defence of North America,
and that the United States were helping in the defence of Great
Britain by the transfer of destroyers, although such a transfer was
technically an act of war, because they realised the vital significance
of Great Britain to them. The surrender to the United States of the
equivalent of sovereign rights in any naval bases upon which large
sums of money might be spent was the sole condition under which
Admiral Stark felt able to certify that the security of the United

[1] As elsewhere in these chapters, it is necessary to keep in mind the difference between
Washington and London time.
(a) A3917/3742/45.

States would be enhanced and that the destroyers could therefore be transferred without risk.

(a) Lord Lothian telephoned to Sir A. Cadogan in the afternoon (London time) of August 23 that he saw no alternative to Mr. Roosevelt's proposed method of procedure. If we could not adopt this method, or even if we delayed acceptance of it, we should probably lose the destroyers. Sir A. Cadogan therefore went to see the Prime Minister.

The Prime Minister disliked the procedure. He was afraid that serious difficulties would arise under it, since the United States would give definite value, i.e. 50 destroyers, while our offer would be in general terms, and discussions would thus follow on its exact scope. The Americans might put upon the offer a larger interpretation than we had intended and an acrimonious controversy might take place between the two Governments. The Prime Minister thought that, if necessary, we could do without the destroyers. Our own construction would put us in a safe position by the end of the year; meanwhile even without the American destroyers we were unlikely to lose so much tonnage as to cripple our war effort. The Prime Minister wished to make the most generous offer at once, and in the fullest detail. He believed that, in the face of our offer, the Administration would give us the destroyers.

(b) These considerations were put to Lord Lothian with instructions to make no reply to the United States Government until he had received a message which the Prime Minister was drafting for Mr. Roosevelt. The Prime Minister sent this draft to the Foreign Office on the morning of August 24. The Foreign Office agreed with the terms, but the Admiralty informed them that the Prime Minister appeared to have read 'January' for 'June' in an Admiralty statement about destroyers and that the figure of new constructions was thus smaller than he had calculated. The message was therefore delayed for checking, and was sent to Mr. Roosevelt on August 25. The final text was as follows:

(c) 'I fully understand the legal and constitutional difficulties which make you wish for a formal contract embodied in letters, but I venture to put before you the difficulties and even dangers which I foresee in this procedure. For the sake of the precise list of instrumentalities mentioned, which in our sore need we greatly desire, we are asked to pay undefined concessions in all the islands and places mentioned from Newfoundland to British Guiana "as may be required in the judgment of the United States". Suppose we could not agree to all your experts asked for, should we not be exposed to a charge of breaking our contract for which we had already received value? Your commitment is definite, ours unlimited. Much though we need the destroyers we should not wish to have them at the risk of a mis-

---

(a) A3917/3742/45.   (b) A3917/3742/45.   (c) A3917/3742/45.

understanding with the United States or indeed any serious argument. If the matter is to be represented as a contract, both sides must be defined with far more precision on our side than has hitherto been possible. But this might easily take some time. As I have several times pointed out, we need the destroyers chiefly to bridge the gap between now and the arrival of our new construction which I set on foot on the outbreak of war. This construction is very considerable. For instance we shall receive by the end of February new destroyers and new medium destroyers, 20: corvettes, which are a handy type of submarine-hunter adapted to ocean work, 60: M.T.B.s, 37: motor anti-submarine boats, 25: Fairmiles (a wooden anti-submarine patrol-boat), 104: 72-foot motor launches, 29. An even greater inflow will arrive in the following six months. It is just in the gap from September to February inclusive while this new crop is coming in and working-up that your 50 destroyers would be invaluable. With them we could minimise shipping losses in the North-Western Approaches and also take a stronger line against Mussolini in the Mediterranean. Therefore time is all-important. We should not however be justified, in the circumstances, if we gave a blank cheque on the whole of our Transatlantic possessions merely to bridge this gap through which anyhow we hope to make our way, though with added risk and suffering. This I am sure you will see sets forth our difficulties plainly.

2. Would not the following procedure be acceptable? I would offer at once certain fairly well-defined facilities which will show you the kind of gift we have in mind, and your experts could then discuss these or any variants of them with ours—we remaining the final judge of what we can give. All this we will do freely, trusting entirely to the generosity and goodwill of the American people as to whether they on their part would like to do something for us. But anyhow it is the settled policy of His Majesty's Government to offer you and make available to you when desired solid and effective means of protecting your Atlantic seaboard. I have already asked the Admiralty and the Air Ministry to draw up in outline what we are prepared to offer, leaving your experts to suggest alternatives. I propose to send you this outline in two or three days and to publish in due course. In this way there can be no possible dispute, and the American people will feel more warmly towards us because they will see we are playing the game by the world's cause and that their safety and interests are dear to us.

3. If your law or your Admiral[1] requires that any help you may choose to give us must be presented as a *quid pro quo*, I do not see why the British Government have to come into that at all. Could you not say that you do not feel able to accept this fine offer which we make unless the United States matched it in some way and that therefore the Admiral would be able to link the one with the other?

4. I am so very grateful to you for all the trouble you have been taking and I am sorry to add to your burdens knowing what a good friend you have been to us.'

---

[1] i.e. Admiral Stark.

(vi)

Further discussions with regard to the form of the announcement of the grant of bases and the transfer of destroyers: exchange of notes of September 2, 1940.

(a) Lord Lothian discussed the problem with Mr. Roosevelt and Mr. Hull on August 25. They continued to regard an exchange of letters between Lord Lothian and Mr. Hull as a satisfactory mode of procedure. The President, however, considered that Congress would raise objections, if there were not something more detailed than a 'bare declaration' by His Majesty's Government of their intention to make available air and naval facilities to the United States.

Lord Lothian had already drafted two letters, which he might send to Mr. Hull. He now altered the draft of the first letter to include the President's requirements, i.e. an 'outline' enumeration of the 'facilities', and an arrangement whereby a Board appointed by the two Governments should determine them in detail as soon as possible. The draft of the second letter was a confirmation of the Prime Minister's statements of June 4 and August 20[1] with regard to the fleet.

In transmitting the drafts to London (with the additions to meet the President's wishes) Lord Lothian explained that they did not meet the difficulty that the President could not dispose of Government property, i.e. the destroyers, without some consideration in return. Lord Lothian agreed with the Prime Minister that this particular difficulty concerned the United States Government. He expected that the President would have to relate in some way the transfer of the destroyers to the naval and air facilities. He said that the President and Mr. Hull were discussing this problem in the light of the Prime Minister's message.

These drafts which Lord Lothian had submitted were considered by the War Cabinet on August 27. The Prime Minister had
(b) already sent—on the morning of August 27—a message to Mr.
(c) Roosevelt accepting in general outline the requirements which the United States Government had listed. The Prime Minister made an additional offer of a base at Antigua for flying-boats. He agreed with the terms of the draft letters, but said that he did not wish the second to be published because he thought it 'much more likely that the German Government will be the one to surrender or scuttle its fleet or what is left of it. In this, as you are aware, they have already had some practice.' He added: 'If you felt able after our offer had been made to let us have the instrumentalities which have been mentioned or anything else you think proper, this could be expressed

---

[1] See above, p. 373, note 1.

(a) A3980/3742/45. (b) WM(40)235. (c) A3980/3742/45.

as an act not in payment or consideration for, but in recognition of, what we had done for the security of the United States.' The War Cabinet approved of the Prime Minister's telegram and agreed to the terms of the formal offer to the United States.

During the night of August 27–8 Lord Lothian telegraphed a new draft of a proposed letter to Mr. Hull. He again explained that the (a) American view was that there must be an agreement for an exchange. The generosity of the Prime Minister's public offer of August 20 had complicated the position, since we had now offered the facilities as a free gift, and the President had no power to make a free gift of the destroyers. The new proposal was that part of the facilities should be regarded as a free gift and the balance as an exchange. Mr. Roosevelt also suggested that the question of the future of the navy should be dealt with apart from the exchange of letters. Mr. Roosevelt would send the Prime Minister a telegram assuming that the declarations of June 4 and August 20 were valid, and the Prime Minister would answer 'yes'.

On August 28 Mr. Hull asked Lord Lothian to report how much (b) he (Mr. Hull) regretted the constitutional difficulties. Mr. Roosevelt's decision to transfer the destroyers without seeking the approval of Congress meant that he and the Administration were risking their political existence. Even in the form of an exchange of letters the transaction was of 'arguable legality'.

The War Cabinet decided on August 29 to accept the American (c) plan. Lord Lothian was therefore instructed on the evening of August 29 that we understood the difficulties on the American side and greatly appreciated the efforts made by the Administration to meet our point of view. We should have preferred a transaction on the 'no deal' basis, but we would accept the American proposals. Lord Lothian was also told that the Prime Minister agreed to an exchange of telegrams about the British fleet, but that, in his opinion 'such a contingency is much more likely to affect the German fleet than the British'. Lord Lothian replied during the night of August 29–30 that Mr. Roosevelt proposed to telegraph as follows: (d)

'The Prime Minister of Great Britain is reported to have stated on June 4, 1940, to Parliament, in effect that, if, during the course of the present war in which Great Britain and [the] British Commonwealth are engaged, the waters surrounding [the] British Isles should become untenable for British ships of war, the British fleet would in no event be surrendered or sunk, but would be sent overseas for the defence of other parts of the Empire.

The Government of the United States would respectfully enquire

(a) A3980/3742/45.   (b) A3980/3742/45.   (c) WM(40)236, 237; A3980/3742/45.
(d) A4022/3742/45.

whether the foregoing statement represents the settled policy of the British Government.'

(a)   Lord Lothian was instructed during the night of August 30–1 that the Prime Minister proposed to reply as follows:

'You ask, Mr. President, whether my statement in Parliament on June 4 about Great Britain never surrendering or scuttling her Fleet "represents the settled policy of His Majesty's Government". It certainly does. I must however observe that these hypothetical contingencies seem more likely to concern the German Fleet or what is left of it than our own.'

(b)   During the night of August 29–30 Lord Lothian reported that the final texts of the letters had been agreed and that he was signing them on August 30. Mr. Roosevelt wanted to present them to Congress on its reassembly at 12 noon (Washington time) on September 3. In the

(c)   evening of August 31, Lord Lothian reported that Mr. Hull thought it best to deal with the question of the fleet by an exchange of *aides-mémoire* (which could be published) between the State Department and His Majesty's Embassy.

The Prime Minister accepted this change of method. Lord Lothian

(d)   had also transmitted, during the night of August 30–1, a message from Mr. Hull hoping that, in explaining the agreement, the Prime Minister would keep in mind the difficulties of the Administration. Lord Lothian pointed out that any mishandling of the matter might affect the presidential election. The agreement would be violently attacked in the United States on two grounds: (i) that Mr. Roosevelt had acted without obtaining the consent of Congress; (ii) that the transfer of the destroyers was an act of war calculated to involve the United States in the European war. The Prime Minister, therefore, should not say that he intended the transfer of bases to be a free gesture of goodwill because this statement would start Congress on the line that the delivery of the destroyers had never been necessary in order to secure the bases.

(e)   Lord Lothian was instructed on September 2 that the Prime Minister would doubtless wish to have all possible regard for Mr. Roosevelt's difficulties, but that he (Lord Lothian) should remind Mr. Hull as soon as possible that the Prime Minister had already made in Parliament the statement to which Mr. Hull found objection, and that we also had difficulties with that section of public opinion which thought that we had the worst of the bargain.

The notes were finally exchanged on September 2.[1]

---

[1] For the text see Annex at the end of this chapter.
(a) A4022/3742/45.   (b) A4022/3742/45.   (c) A4022/3742/45.   (d) A4031/3742/45.
(e) A4031/3742/45.

On September 5 the Prime Minister, in a note to Lord Halifax, suggested that a telegram might be sent to Lord Lothian expressing (a) on behalf of the War Cabinet approval of the manner in which he had 'handled the whole destroyer question'. The Prime Minister asked at the same time 'what is being done about getting our 20 motor torpedo-boats, the 5 P.B.Y., the 150–200 aircraft and 250,000 rifles, also anything else that is going? I consider we were promised all the above and more too. Not an hour should be lost in raising these questions. "Beg while the iron is hot".'[1]

Messages on the lines suggested by the Prime Minister were sent to Lord Lothian on September 6. In reply to the message of thanks Lord Lothian telegraphed his own appreciation of the willingness of the War Cabinet to make allowances for 'the exigencies of the American political and constitutional situation when pressure on themselves was so incomparably greater'. To the telegram about the M.T.B.s, etc., Lord Lothian replied on the night of September 6 that he had (b) already asked Mr. Roosevelt when we could expect delivery. Mr. Roosevelt had answered that the rifles were ready but that, owing to the Attorney-General's opinion, he could not deliver any of the M.T.B.s before January. He agreed however that an alternative programme (e.g. additional flying-boats) could be discussed.

Lord Lothian reported on September 14 that these negotiations (c) were taking place. He was asked again on September 18 what progress had been made, and told that it was assumed that he was 'maintaining pressure on the United States Government to obtain our full *desiderata*'. The news of the bombing of London 'should have produced an atmosphere conducive to our receiving complete satisfaction, and we count on you to achieve the necessary very early results'.

On September 20, at the Prime Minister's instructions, Sir A. (d) Cadogan telephoned to Lord Lothian to ask where we stood in relation to the 'other *desiderata* promised to us at the time of the grant of naval bases and the transfer of destroyers'. Sir A. Cadogan repeated that the Prime Minister attached the greatest importance to the matter. He had been assured that this material was promised to us and could not but feel growing disappointment at its failure to materialise.

Lord Lothian referred to the ruling of the Attorney-General which made it impossible for the transfer of the motor torpedo-boats to take

---

[1] Lord Lothian had explained on August 28 that the draft American reply referred only to destroyers, and that M.T.B.s, flying-boats and rifles would have to be dealt with separately. He was pressing for a definite statement about these further transfers on August (e) 28 on the ground that Mr. Roosevelt was already committed to them. On the same day Mr. Hull asked Lord Lothian to assure Lord Halifax that the transfers would be dealt with 'in the same spirit and at the earliest possible moment'.

(a) A4123/3742/45.   (b) A3980/3742/45.   (c) A4123/3742/45.   (d) A4123/3742/45.
(e) A3980/3742/45.

place before January 1941. After further discussion Sir A. Cadogan again said that the Prime Minister regarded the matter as of the greatest urgency and importance.

On receiving a report of this conversation the Prime Minister gave instructions for the enquiry to be repeated to Lord Lothian on

(a) September 22. Meanwhile Lord Lothian had telegraphed a summary of the position. He explained that the question of material which the United States could supply had been under discussion throughout the summer with constant changes of detail. About the time of the negotiations on the destroyers and bases Mr. Roosevelt said that he expected that the United States would be able to provide twenty M.T.B.s, five Flying Fortresses, five P.B.Y.5 flying-boats and (he hoped) 250,000 rifles. Partly owing to the Attorney-General's opinion that the transfer of the M.T.B.s was illegal, the destroyers alone had been mentioned in the exchange of letters. In fact Mr. Welles, when he went on holiday, had not told Mr. Hull of the *desiderata* other than destroyers, and Mr. Roosevelt had not told the Navy Department about the flying-boats. When, at the end of the negotiations, Lord Lothian had pointed out this omission, he was informed that in due course the supplies asked for or their equivalent would be provided 'in some other way'.

Lord Lothian had been doing his utmost to get this promise fulfilled, but, as he had explained, Mr. Roosevelt could not give the M.T.B.s before January at the earliest. Lord Lothian doubted whether, 'owing to the perversities of the legal position', the boats would be supplied. Mr. Roosevelt fully admitted his obligation, and the Administration was trying to work out a scheme for early delivery which would be as good or even better than the original plan. Mr. Roosevelt also thought that it would be a mistake to tell Congress that these additional items had been attached to the 'destroyer deal'. It might therefore be necessary for His Majesty's Government to pay for them, but Mr. Roosevelt had 'personally undertaken' that a way would be found for repaying or 'off-setting' the amount before the exhaustion of our dollar assets came in sight.

The actual terms of agreement over the allocation of bases etc. were settled only after long negotiations.[1] These negotiations were not easy, partly owing to the large demands made on the American side, partly owing to the strength of local feeling in the areas concerned.

Furthermore, the detailed negotiations were not smoothed by the fact that, owing to their age and condition, the American destroyers were found to need an unexpected amount of repairs, etc. and were therefore of less use than had been hoped in the critical months

---

[1] The leases were signed on March 27, 1941.

(a) A4123/3742/45.

before the new British construction was available. Nine only of the destroyers were in service at the end of December 1940.[1]

(vii)

Correspondence between the Prime Minister and Mr. Roosevelt on the general position with regard to the war and the need of American supplies: Lord Lothian's visit to England (October 4—December 31, 1940).

During the months of October and November 1940, His Majesty's Government felt great anxiety over the possibility of the surrender of French ships and bases to Germany and Italy by the Vichy Government. The representations made by the United States Government, at the request of the Prime Minister, to Marshal Pétain on this matter are described in a later chapter.[2] The question of the reopening of the Burma Road, and, in general, of Anglo-American policy after the German-Italian-Japanese agreement of September 27 has also been dealt with in its Far Eastern context.[3]

In addition to these urgent political questions His Majesty's Government were also concerned with their plans for the year 1941 and with the increase of American supplies essential to the fulfilment of these plans. In a message of October 4 to Mr. Roosevelt on the (a) subject of the Burma Road, Mr. Churchill had said that, whereas we had previously spoken in terms of pilots, our need of aircraft had now increased and might be the limiting factor in the immediate future.

In this telegram Mr. Churchill did not mention any future plans. He did not feel that the danger of invasion was over. In Mr. Churchill's words ,'the gent has taken off his clothes and put on his bathing suit, but the water is getting colder and there is an autumn nip in the air. We are maintaining the utmost vigilance.' On October 26 Mr. Churchill told Mr. Roosevelt that, although the invasion (b) danger was not yet at an end, we were increasing our transports to the East. The strain was very great in both theatres of war and 'all contributions will be thankfully received'.

In his message of October 27 on the dangers of a French surrender (c) of bases and ships Mr. Churchill was more explicit. He said that we

---

[1] It should, however, be mentioned that there was a certain feeling on the American side, which to the Foreign Office did not seem altogether unjustified, that on the British side the execution of the agreement about the bases was unnecessarily slow and at times hampered by departmental obstructiveness. I have not dealt with the details of the execution of the agreement or with subsequent negotiations about the motor torpedo-boats, etc.

[2] See below, Chapter XIII, section (iii).

[3] See Volume II, Chapter XXII.

(a) A4437/131/45. (b) A4437/131/45. (c) A4437/131/45.

were trying to assemble a very large army in the Middle East and that the campaign there in the New Year might involve Turkey and Greece and would make demands on our shipping and munitions which we could fulfil only with American help to a point which would secure victory. We had to continue our provisions for the defence of Great Britain against an invasion for which sixty of the best German divisions and a superior air force were in readiness. The U-boat attacks on our only remaining life-line—the North-Western Approaches—would be repelled only by the strongest concentration of our flotillas.

Mr. Roosevelt would therefore see the greatness of our dangers. 'We feel, however, confident of our ability, if we are given the necessary supplies, to carry the war to a successful conclusion, and anyhow we are going to try our best. You will however allow me to impress upon you the extreme urgency of accelerating the delivery of the programme of aircraft and other munitions which has already been laid before you.' The Prime Minister referred to a technical memorandum which was being prepared for Mr. Roosevelt and concluded with the words 'The world cause is in your hands'.

(a)   On November 6, in a message of congratulation to Mr. Roosevelt on his re-election, the Prime Minister said:

'We are entering upon a sombre phase of what must evidently be a protracted and broadening war, and I look forward to being able to interchange my thoughts with you in all that confidence and goodwill which has grown up between us since I went to the Admiralty at the outbreak. Things are afoot which will be remembered as long as the English language is spoken in any quarter of the globe, and in expressing the comfort I feel that the people of the United States have once again cast these great burdens upon you, I must avow my sure faith that the lights by which we steer will bring us all safely to anchor.'

The general subject of American assistance to Great Britain was discussed with Lord Lothian during a visit by him to England from October 20 until November 11. There was indeed a prior question which the British Government was bound to consider. Was it of
(b)   greater advantage to us for the United States to enter the war or should we obtain more supplies at a quicker rate if the United States remained out of the war, and merely accelerated the policy of benevolent neutrality? The only argument in favour of the maintenance of technical neutrality by the United States was that an American declaration of war would result in a diminution in the supply of munitions to Great Britain, partly owing to American war needs, and because the United States would wish to be adequately armed against any eventuality.

(a) A4437/131/45. (b) A4453/131/45.

The reply to this argument was that, if the United States were to declare war, the declaration would most probably be against Japan and that at least at first belligerent action would be confined to the navy and would make little demand on the types of munitions which we hoped to obtain from American sources. Moreover, although the United States Government had allocated very large sums for the building up of American defences, American industry was not likely to be put on a war footing as long as the United States were neutral. Thus a declaration of war might bring about such an increase in American output of munitions that our share might be larger.

American entry into the war would also have a moral effect on ourselves and on our enemies. It was widely believed outside Great Britain that we were in imminent danger of defeat, while few people thought that we could hope for more than a stalemate. This latter view appeared to be held by the 'more disillusioned elements' in Germany. In fact, as long as enemy morale held, it seemed hardly possible for us to defeat Germany by direct action on the Continent. On the other hand, if America entered the war, and if we could increasingly enforce our blockade of foodstuffs and raw materials, our enemies were likely to reflect that, however long they held out, the situation would grow worse for them, whereas we and our Allies (and the French) would be correspondingly encouraged.

There was another consideration. Could we be sure that, if America remained neutral, she would continue to act in a sense most favourable to us? We should require a very great deal from the United States in the near future not merely in the allocation of a large part of the American industrial output but also in the form of financial assistance. This latter demand was likely to meet with serious obstacles, e.g. it would bring up the 'sore subject' of our indebtedness to the United States. Legislation would be required in Congress before we could receive any substantial help. This would give a chance to the isolationists. Furthermore the United States might threaten to break our food blockade of Europe as a result of ill-considered humanitarian sentiments.

The greatest danger was the possibility of the war lasting a long time or, even worse, of a serious reverse to us in the Mediterranean or elsewhere. A great part of American support might then be withdrawn at a time when we were in most need of it. The United States had in fact acted in this way at first during the collapse of France. As an emotional people, far removed from the theatre of war, Americans would almost certainly jump to the conclusion that we were being beaten whenever things were going badly for us. The only way to be sure that America would give us all the help in her power until we achieved victory would be for her to burn her bridges behind her and throw in her lot with us. Hence on those few occasions in which our policy might influence an American decision to enter the war, we should always so act as to influence her towards the more vigorous course.

Hitherto it had seemed likely that, if America had gone to war, she would have fought Japan alone, and that her energies might have been diverted from assistance to us. The Axis Powers had now stated in effect that, if America found herself at war with Japan, she would 'automatically also be at war with themselves'.[1] The result had been not, as the Axis Powers desired, to alarm American public opinion, but to strengthen the resolve to aid Great Britain and to protect the interests of the United States in the Far East. America might there-fore well reach the position in which she would concentrate her main energies less on the prosecution of a war with Japan than on meeting Japan's 'far more powerful co-belligerents in Europe'.

(a)   Lord Lothian was strongly in favour of doing everything possible to encourage American entry into the war and did not attach much weight to the view that the effect might be a diminution in the supply of munitions to Great Britain. Lord Lothian thought that Mr. Roosevelt would be able to convince American opinion that, if we were defeated as a result of losing American supplies, the United States would not have time to make adequate preparations to meet a German attack. Lord Lothian believed, however, that our supplies would suffer if the Americans waged an offensive war against Japan but that there would be no diminution if they waged a defensive war. Lord Lothian's view was that, if the Americans sent a fleet to Singa-pore, they could reduce their force at Hawaii to a defensive basis and at the same time prevent the Japanese from striking at the Dutch East Indies or the Philippines and also protect the west coast of America.

The most important general discussion of American aid took place
(b)   on November 9. On this day Lord Lothian met Mr. Alexander and the Naval Staff. The question was raised whether the United States might give naval protection to our convoys without a formal declara-tion of war on Germany. Lord Lothian asked whether, in the event of such a move, we could tell the United States that we felt no further serious anxieties about the protection of our sea-borne trade and that Germany and Japan would be bound to feel that they had lost the war at sea.

The naval representatives agreed that we could make such a state-ment to the United States, but were doubtful whether we could get the naval protection which we desired unless the United States formally entered the war. Lord Lothian thought that mainly owing to the constitutional requirement of a decision by Congress, a formal

---

[1] See Volume II, Chapter XXII, section (v).
    (a) A4666/131/45.   (b) A4848/131/45.

declaration of war would be difficult to obtain, but that short of it the United States would help us the full extent of their power.

Mr. Alexander suggested that the United States might be persuaded to take an active part, not merely with destroyers but with cruisers, in the defence of the trade routes on the excuse of protecting the material which they were sending to us. The Vice-Chief of Naval Staff pointed out that we should be careful not to establish any precedent at variance with the principle that a neutral had no right to escort convoys in such a way as to frustrate the rights of a belligerent Power at sea. We might avoid this difficulty if the United States acted not on grounds designed to stultify German belligerent rights, but to defend their own trade against the illegal methods adopted by the Germans in defiance of the accepted rules of war at sea.

The meeting then discussed the shipping position and the possibility of getting more American destroyers. In answer to a question from Lord Lothian, the naval representatives said that we should be glad to secure another 50 destroyers, and, in particular, new destroyers which were fitted with excellent anti-aircraft defences.

The Vice-Chief of Naval Staff explained the great anxieties which the shipping position was causing us. The Americans might help in three ways. They could repeal or get round the restrictions arising out of the Neutrality Act on the entry of United States ships into belligerent ports. They could turn over to us ships building to American order in the United States. Our shipbuilding capacity had fallen so very seriously in recent months that early reinforcements of this kind were as important as a long-term building programme. They could also help us to lay down a really large programme of merchant shipbuilding in the United States. Our own programme did not now keep up with our losses.

Lord Lothian said that the way to get American help was to convince the United States that without such help we might lose the war and that their last remaining line of defence would thereby be overrun. Thus we should say that without their help we and they would lose the shipping war and that, if they did not want to see their material aid rendered useless, they must help us to provide ships to carry supplies and to protect them *en route*. On these lines we could ask for an American flying-boat service based on Ireland and also explain that it was vital to us to hold Suez and therefore advantageous for them to use their great naval strength in such a way as to release some of our warships for a greater concentration in the Mediterranean and some of their merchant shipping in order to speed up the arrival of supplies and reinforcements in the Middle East.

The naval representatives then spoke of the serious consequences of our lack of bases in Eire and suggested that we might ask the United States to put pressure on Eire to allow us the use of bases. Lord

Lothian agreed that we might make this approach, but thought that we should first convince the people of the United States that the refusal of the Irish bases amounted to the sabotage of the American policy of giving all material aid to Great Britain, i.e. the war aims of the United States were being ruined by the intransigence of Mr. De Valera. The naval representatives proposed that as an interim stage we might persuade the United States to send a cruiser squadron on a visit to Eire.

(a) On the night of November 21–2 Mr. Butler[1] reported from Washington that the release of any more destroyers seemed out of the question. The Foreign Office considered that it was therefore desirable to give Mr. Roosevelt as soon as possible a full picture of our position and needs. The Prime Minister and Lord Lothian had already been discussing a plan of this kind. Lord Halifax raised the matter with the Prime Minister on November 27 and the Prime Minister agreed to hasten the consideration of a letter which he had begun to draft.

(viii)

The Prime Minister's letter of December 8 to Mr. Roosevelt: Mr. Roosevelt's statements of December 17 and December 29: the initiation of 'Lend-Lease' proposals.

(b) The Prime Minister sent a letter to Mr. Roosevelt in the following terms:[2]

'My dear Mr. President,
As we reach the end of this year, I feel that you will expect me to lay before you the prospects for 1941. I do so with candour and confidence, because it seems to me that the vast majority of American citizens have recorded their conviction that the safety of the United States as well as the future of our two democracies and the kind of civilization for which they stand, are bound up with the survival and independence of the British Commonwealth of Nations. Only thus can those bastions of sea-power, upon which the control of the Atlantic and

---

[1] Mr. Nevile Butler was Chargé d'Affaires in Washington during Lord Lothian's absence.

[2] This letter was given to Mr. Hull in Washington on December 8 for delivery to Mr. Roosevelt. Some minor changes in the text were subsequently telegraphed from the Foreign Office. At the same time a memorandum on shipping losses and replacements was given to Mr. Hopkins and to the Secretary of the Treasury.

(a) A4790/131/45. (b) WP(40)466 (Final Revise).

Indian Oceans depend, be preserved in faithful and friendly hands. The control of the Pacific by the United States Navy and of the Atlantic by the British Navy, is indispensable to the security and the trade routes of both our countries, and the surest means of preventing war from reaching the shores of the United States.

2. There is another aspect. It takes between three and four years to convert the industries of a modern state to war purposes. Saturation point is reached when the maximum industrial effort that can be spared from civilian needs has been applied to war production. Germany certainly reached this point by the end of 1939. We in the British Empire are now only about half-way through the second year. The United States, I should suppose, was by no means so far advanced as we. Moreover, I understand that immense programmes of naval, military and air defence are now on foot in the United States, to complete which certainly two years are needed. It is our British duty in the common interest, as also for our own survival, to hold the front and grapple with Nazi power until the preparations of the United States are complete. Victory may come before two years are out; but we have no right to count upon it to the extent of relaxing any effort that is humanly possible. Therefore, I submit with very great respect for your good and friendly consideration that there is a solid identity of interest between the British Empire and the United States while these conditions last. It is upon this footing that I venture to address you.

3. The form which this war has taken, and seems likely to hold, does not enable us to match the immense armies of Germany in any theatre where their main power can be brought to bear. We can, however, by the use of sea power and air power, meet the German armies in regions where only comparatively small forces can be brought into action. We must do our best to prevent the German domination of Europe spreading into Africa and into Southern Asia. We have also to maintain in constant readiness in this Island armies strong enough to make the problem of an overseas invasion insoluble. For these purposes we are forming as fast as possible, as you are already aware, between 50 and 60 divisions. Even if the United States were our Ally, instead of our friend and indispensable partner, we should not ask for a large American expeditionary army. Shipping, not men, is the limiting factor, and the power to transport munitions and supplies claims priority over the movement by sea of large numbers of soldiers.

4. The first half of 1940 was a period of disaster for the Allies and for the Empire. The last five months have witnessed a strong and perhaps unexpected recovery by Great Britain fighting alone, but with the invaluable aid in munitions and in destroyers placed at our disposal by the great Republic of which you are for the third time chosen chief.

5. The danger of Great Britain being destroyed by a swift, overwhelming blow, has for the time being very greatly receded. In its place, there is a long, gradually maturing danger, less sudden and less

spectacular, but equally deadly. This mortal danger is the steady and increasing diminution of sea tonnage. We can endure the shattering of our dwellings and the slaughter of our civil population by indiscriminate air attacks, and we hope to parry these increasingly as our science develops, and to repay them upon military objectives in Germany as our Air Force more nearly approaches the strength of the enemy. The decision for 1941 lies upon the seas. Unless we can establish our ability to feed this Island, to import the munitions of all kinds which we need, unless we can move our armies to the various theatres where Hitler and his confederate, Mussolini, must be met, and maintain them there, and do all this with the assurance of being able to carry it on till the spirit of the Continental Dictators is broken, we may fall by the way, and the time needed by the United States to complete her defensive preparations may not be forthcoming. It is therefore in shipping and in the power to transport across the oceans, particularly the Atlantic Ocean, that in 1941 the crunch[1] of the whole war will be found. If, on the other hand, we are able to move the necessary tonnage to and fro across the salt water indefinitely, it may well be that the application of superior air power to the German homeland and the rising anger of the German and other Nazi-gripped populations will bring the agony of civilization to a merciful and glorious end. But do not let us underrate the task.

6. Our shipping losses, the figures for which in recent months are appended,[2] have been on a scale almost comparable to that of the worst year of the last war. In the five weeks ending the 3rd November losses reached a total of 420,300 tons. Our estimate of annual tonnage which ought to be imported in order to maintain our effort at full strength is 43 million tons; the tonnage entering in September was only at the rate of 37 million tons and in October at 38 million tons. Were diminution to continue at this rate it would be fatal, unless indeed immensely greater replenishment than anything at present in sight could be achieved in time. Although we are doing all we can to meet this situation by new methods, the difficulty of limiting losses is obviously much greater than in the last war. We lack the assistance of the French Navy, the Italian Navy and the Japanese Navy, and above all of the United States Navy, which was of such vital help to us during the culminating years. The enemy commands the ports all around the northern and western coast of France. He is increasingly basing his submarines, flying-boats and combat planes on these ports and on the islands off the French coast. We are denied the use of the ports or territory of Eire in which to organise our coastal patrols by air and sea. In fact, we have now only one effective route of entry to the British Isles, namely, the Northern approaches, against which the enemy is increasingly concentrating, reaching ever farther out by U-boat action and long-distance bombing. In addition, there have for some months been merchant ship raiders, both in the Atlantic and Indian Oceans. And now we have the powerful warship-raiders to

---

[1] The Foreign Office printed text here reads 'crux'.
[2] I have not included the detailed list of losses.

contend with as well. We need ships both to hunt down and to escort. Large as are our resources and preparations, we do not possess enough.

7. The next six or seven months [will] bring relative battleship strength in home waters to a smaller margin than is satisfactory. *Bismarck* and *Tirpitz* will certainly be in service in January. We have already *King George V*, and hope to have *Prince of Wales* in the line at the same time. These modern ships are of course far better armoured, especially against air attack, than vessels like *Rodney* and *Nelson* designed twenty years ago. We have recently had to use *Rodney* on trans-Atlantic escort, and at any time when numbers are so small a mine or a torpedo may alter decisively the strength of the line of battle. We get relief in June, when *Duke of York* will be ready, and will be still better off at the end of 1941, when *Anson* also will have joined. But these two first-class modern 35,000-tons, 15-in.-gun German battleships force us to maintain a concentration never previously necessary in this war.

8. We hope that the two Italian *Littorios* will be out of action for a while, and anyway they are not so dangerous as if they were manned by the Germans. Perhaps they might be! We are indebted to you for your help about the *Richelieu* and *Jean Bart*, and I daresay that will be all right. But, Mr. President, as no one will see more clearly than you, we have during these months to consider for the first time in this war a fleet action, in which the enemy will have two ships at least as good as our two best and only two modern ones. It will be impossible to reduce our strength in the Mediterranean, because the attitude of Turkey, and indeed the whole position in the Eastern basin depends upon our having a strong fleet there. The older, unmodernised battleships will have to go for convoy. Thus even in the battleship class we are at full extension.

9. There is a second field of danger: the Vichy Government may either by joining Hitler's New Order in Europe or through some manoeuvre, such as forcing us to attack an expedition despatched by sea against the Free French Colonies, find an excuse for ranging with the Axis Powers the very considerable undamaged naval forces still under its control. If the French Navy were to join the Axis, the control of West Africa would pass immediately into their hands, with the gravest consequences to our communications between the Northern and Southern Atlantic, and also affecting Dakar and, of course, thereafter South America.

10. A third sphere of danger is in the Far East. Here it seems clear that Japan is thrusting southward through Indo-China to Saigon and other naval air bases, thus bringing them within a comparatively short distance of Singapore and the Dutch East Indies. It is reported that the Japanese are preparing five good divisions for possible use as an overseas expeditionary force. We have today no forces in the Far East capable of dealing with this situation should it develop.

11. In the face of these dangers we must try to use the year 1941 to build up such a supply of weapons, particularly of aircraft, both by

increased output at home in spite of bombardment, and through ocean-borne supplies, as will lay the foundations of victory. In view of the difficulty and magnitude of this task, as outlined by all the facts I have set forth, to which many others could be added, I feel entitled, nay bound, to lay before you the various ways in which the United States could give supreme and decisive help to what is, in certain aspects, the common cause.

12. The prime need is to check or limit the loss of tonnage on the Atlantic approaches to our Island. This may be achieved both by increasing the naval forces which cope with attacks, and by adding to the number of merchant ships on which we depend. For the first purpose there would seem to be the following alternatives:—

(1) The reassertion by the United States of the doctrine of the freedom of the seas from illegal and barbarous warfare, in accordance with the decisions reached after the late Great War, and as freely accepted and defined by Germany in 1935.[1] From this, the United States ships should be free to trade with countries against which there is not an effective legal blockade.

(2) It would, I suggest, follow that protection should be given to this lawful trading by United States forces, i.e., escorting battleships, cruisers, destroyers and air flotillas. The protection would be immensely more effective if you were able to obtain bases in Eire for the duration of the war. I think it is improbable that such protection would provoke a declaration of war by Germany upon the United States, though probably sea incidents of a dangerous character would from time to time occur. Herr Hitler has shown himself inclined to avoid the Kaiser's mistake. He does not wish to be drawn into war with the United States until he has gravely undermined the power of Great Britain. His maxim is "one at a time". The policy I have ventured to outline, or something like it, would constitute a decisive act of constructive non-belligerency by the United States, and more than any other measure, would make it certain that British resistance could be effectively prolonged for the desired period and victory gained.

(3) Failing the above, the gift, loan or supply of a large number of American vessels of war, above all destroyers, already in the Atlantic is indispensable to the maintenance of the Atlantic route. Further, could not the United States naval forces extend their sea control of the American side of the Atlantic, so as to prevent molestation by enemy vessels of the approaches to the new line of naval and air bases which the United States is establishing in British islands in the Western Hemisphere? The strength of the United States naval forces is such that the assistance in the Atlantic that they could afford us, as described above, would not jeopardise the control over the Pacific.

(4) We should also then need the good offices of the United States and the whole influence of its Government, continually exerted, to procure for Great Britain the necessary facilities upon the southern

---

[1] i.e. in the naval agreement of that year with Great Britain.

and western shores of Eire for our flotillas, and still more important, for our aircraft, working to the westward into the Atlantic. If it were proclaimed an American interest that the resistance of Great Britain should be prolonged and the Atlantic route kept open for the important armaments now being prepared for Great Britain in North America, the Irish in the United States might be willing to point out to the Government of Eire the dangers which its present policy is creating for the United States itself.

His Majesty's Government would of course take the most effective measures beforehand to protect Ireland if Irish action exposed it to German attack. It is not possible for us to compel the people of Northern Ireland against their will to leave the United Kingdom and join Southern Ireland. But I do not doubt that if the Government of Eire would show its solidarity with the democracies of the English-speaking world at this crisis, a Council for Defence of all Ireland could be set up out of which the unity of the Island would probably in some form or other emerge after the war.

13. The object of the foregoing measures is to reduce to manageable proportions the present destructive losses at sea. In addition, it is indispensable that the merchant tonnage available for supplying Great Britain and for the waging of the war by Great Britain with all vigour, should be substantially increased beyond the $1\frac{1}{4}$ million tons per annum which is the utmost we can now build. The convoy system, the *détours*, the zig-zags, the great distances from which we now have to bring our imports, and the congestion of our western harbours, have reduced by about one third the fruitfulness of our existing tonnage. To ensure final victory, not less than 3 million tons of additional merchant shipbuilding capacity will be required. Only the United States can supply this need. Looking to the future it would seem that production on a scale comparable with that of the Hog Island scheme of the last war ought to be faced for 1942. In the meanwhile, we ask that in 1941 the United States should make available for us every ton of merchant shipping, surplus to its own requirements, which it possesses or controls, and should find some means of putting into our service a large proportion of merchant shipping now under construction for the National Maritime Board.

14. Moreover, we look to the industrial energy of the Republic for a reinforcement of our domestic capacity to manufacture combat aircraft. Without that reinforcement reaching us in substantial measure, we shall not achieve the massive preponderance in the air on which we must rely to loosen and disintegrate the German grip on Europe. We are at present engaged in a programme designed to increase our strength to 7,000 first-line aircraft by the spring of 1942. But it is abundantly clear that this programme will not suffice to give us the weight of superiority which will force open the doors of victory. In order to achieve such superiority it is plain that we shall need the greatest production of aircraft which United States of America are capable of sending us. It is our anxious hope that in the teeth of continuing bombardment we shall realise the greater part of

the production which we have planned in this country. But not even with the addition to our squadrons of all the aircraft which, under present arrangements, we may derive from planned output in the United States can we hope to achieve the necessary ascendancy. May I invite you then, Mr. President, to give earnest consideration to an immediate order on joint account for a further 2,000 combat aircraft a month? Of these aircraft, I would submit, the highest possible proportion should be heavy bombers, the weapons on which, above all others, we depend to shatter the foundations of German military power. I am aware of the formidable task which this would impose upon the industrial organisations of the United States. Yet, in our heavy need, we call with confidence to the most resourceful and ingenious technicians in the world. We ask for an unexampled effort, believing that it can be made.

15. You have also received information about the needs of our armies. In the munitions sphere, in spite of enemy bombing, we are making steady progress here. Without your continued assistance in the supply of machine tools and in the further release from stock of certain articles, we could not hope to equip as many as 50 divisions in 1941. I am grateful for the arrangements, already practically completed, for your aid in the equipment of the army which we have already planned, and for the provision of the American type of weapons for an additional 10 divisions in time for the campaign of 1942. But when the tide of dictatorship begins to recede, many countries trying to regain their freedom may be asking for arms, and there is no source to which they can look except to the factories of the United States. I must therefore also urge the importance of expanding to the utmost American productive capacity for small arms, artillery and tanks.

16. I am arranging to present you with a complete programme of munitions of all kinds which we seek to obtain from you, the greater part of which is, of course, already agreed. An important economy of time and effort will be produced if the types selected for the United States services should, whenever possible, conform to those which have proved their merit under the actual conditions of war. In this way reserves of guns and ammunition and of aeroplanes become interchangeable, and are by that very fact augmented. This is, however, a sphere so highly technical that I do not enlarge upon it.

17. Last of all, I come to the question of finance. The more rapid and abundant the flow of munitions and ships which you are able to send us, the sooner will our dollar credits be exhausted. They are already, as you know, very heavily drawn upon by the payments we have made to date. Indeed, as you know, orders already placed or under negotiation, including the expenditure settled or pending for creating munitions factories in the United States, many times exceed the total exchange resources remaining at the disposal of Great Britain. The moment approaches when we shall no longer be able to pay cash for shipping and other supplies. While we will do our utmost, and shrink from no proper sacrifice to make payments across

the Exchange, I believe you will agree that it would be wrong in principle and mutually disadvantageous in effect if, at the height of this struggle, Great Britain were to be divested of all saleable assets, so that after the victory was won with our blood, civilisation saved, and the time gained for the United States to be fully armed against all eventualities, we should stand stripped to the bone. Such a course would not be in the moral or economic interests of either of our countries. We here would be unable, after the war, to purchase the large balance of imports from the United States over and above the volume of our exports which is agreeable to your tariffs and industrial economy. Not only should we in Great Britain suffer cruel privations but widespread unemployment in the United States would follow the curtailment of American exporting power.

18. Moreover, I do not believe the Government and people of the United States would find it in accordance with the principles which guide them, to confine the help which they have so generously promised only to such munitions of war and commodities as could be immediately paid for. You may be certain that we shall prove ourselves ready to suffer and sacrifice to the utmost for the Cause, and that we glory in being its champion. The rest we leave with confidence to you and to your people, being sure that ways and means will be found which future generations on both sides of the Atlantic will approve and admire.

19. If, as I believe, you are convinced, Mr. President, that the defeat of the Nazi and Fascist tyranny is a matter of high consequence to the people of the United States and to the Western Hemisphere, you will regard this letter not as an appeal for aid, but as a statement of the minimum action necessary to the achievement of our common purpose.

I remain, etc.

WINSTON S. CHURCHILL'

This letter reached Mr. Roosevelt while he was cruising in an American warship in the Caribbean. On December 17—the day after his return—his response was to make an open reference to the idea of 'leasing' material to Great Britain. Mr. Roosevelt said that some people had suggested gifts to Great Britain, and that although this might be necessary, there were other ways of building up American production facilities and continuing the flow of munitions to Great Britain. The United States might take over British orders, since they were for the commodities required also for American needs, and might then sell or lease the products to Great Britain. On the view that the best defence of Great Britain was also the best defence of the United States, the materials would be more valuable in use than 'if kept in storage' in America. Mr. Roosevelt said that he wanted to get rid of the dollar sign in the relations between the two countries and to substitute a gentlemen's agreement.

The Foreign Office does not appear to have recognised at once the
(a) immense significance of these words. Mr. Butler[1] did not suggest
until the night of December 18–19 that the Prime Minister might
make a public acknowledgment of the President's statement. The
Foreign Office thought it unwise to make a special occasion of such
an acknowledgment, but that a general reference to American help
and to Mr. Roosevelt's plan and also to our determination and
capacity to win the war if we had the necessary supplies might be
brought into any statement given to the House of Commons on the
military situation.

In any case it was thought desirable to consult the Treasury
before taking action. The Treasury view was that the appropriate
time had not yet come for a public acknowledgment of Mr. Roosevelt's
declaration about increased assistance. The Prime Minister had made
no arrangements for a speech and Parliament had adjourned until
January 21.

Meanwhile Mr. Roosevelt spoke even more frankly in a broadcast
'fireside' talk of December 29 to the American people. The theme of
his talk was the national security of the United States. Mr. Roosevelt
concluded:

'The British people are conducting an active war against [the] unholy
alliance [of the Axis Powers]. Our own future security is greatly
dependent on the outcome of that fight. Thinking in terms of today
and tomorrow, I make the direct statement to the American people
that there is far less chance of the United States getting into [the war]
if we do all we can now to support the nations defending themselves
against attack by the Axis than if we acquiesce in their defeat, submit
tamely to an Axis victory, and wait our turn to be the object of
attack in another war later. . . . there is risk in any course we may
take, but . . . the course that I advocate involves the least risk now
and the greatest hope for world peace in the future. The people of
Europe who are fighting to defend themselves do not ask us to do
their fighting. They ask for the implements of war, the planes, tanks,
guns, freighters which will enable them to fight for their liberty and
security. . . . Emphatically we must get these weapons to them in
sufficient volume and quickly enough so that we and our children
will be saved the agony and suffering of war which others have had to
endure.'

Before this broadcast was delivered Mr. Butler had reported that
(b) Mr. Roosevelt would probably say that American interests required
the United States to ensure the victory of the Democracies, but that
the 'real battle' would be engaged when Mr. Roosevelt's proposals
were under discussion by Congress.

---

[1] Lord Lothian died on December 12 after a short illness. Lord Halifax was appointed as
his successor on January 24, 1941, and Mr. Eden succeeded Lord Halifax as Secretary of
State for Foreign Affairs on December 23, 1940.
(a) A5171/131/45. (b) A5251/131/45.

The form which these proposals would take was not yet known to the British Government. Mr. Churchill in a message of thanks to the President on December 31, raised some of the immediate questions which were of deep concern to the War Cabinet, e.g. how long would Congress debate the proposals, and how could we pay for our orders in the meantime? The answers to these questions became clear after the introduction of the Lend-Lease Bill to Congress on January 10, 1941.[1]

ANNEX TO CHAPTER XII

Exchange of notes between Lord Lothian and Mr. Hull, September 2, 1940.[2]

(1)

Note from Lord Lothian to Mr. Hull.

'Sir,

1. I have the honour, under instructions from His Majesty's Principal Secretary of State for Foreign Affairs, to inform you that in view of the basis of friendly and sympathetic interest of His Majesty's Government in the United Kingdom in the national security of the United States and their desire to strengthen the ability of the United States to co-operate effectively with other nations of the Americas in the defence of the Western Hemisphere, His Majesty's Government will secure the grant to the Government of the United States, freely and without consideration, of the lease for immediate establishment and use of naval and air bases and facilities for entrance thereto and the operation and protection thereof, on the Avalon Peninsula and on the southern coast of Newfoundland, and on the east coast and on the Great Bay of Bermuda.

2. Furthermore, in view of the above and in view of the desire of the United States to acquire additional air and naval bases in the Caribbean and in British Guiana, and without endeavouring to place a monetary or commercial value upon the many tangible and intangible rights and properties involved, His Majesty's Government will make available to the United States for immediate establishment and use of naval and air bases and facilities for entrance thereto and

---

[1] The Anglo-American financial discussions arising out of the problem of the exhaustion of British gold and dollar reserves fall outside the scope of this *History*. The Foreign Office and the British Embassy in Washington acted as channels of communication throughout the discussions, but, for obvious reasons, the conduct of the negotiations was in the hands of representatives of the Treasury. See R. A. Sayers, *Finance, 1939–45* (H.M.S.O., 1956), and W. K. Hancock and M. M. Gowing, *British War Economy* (H.M.S.O., 1949) (both in the Official History of the Second World War, United Kingdom Civil Series). The Lend-Lease Act was passed by Congress on March 11, 1941.

[2] Cmd. 6224, Treaty Series No. 21, 1940.

the operation and protection thereof, on the eastern side of the Bahamas, the southern coast of Jamaica, the western coast of St. Lucia, the west coast of Trinidad, in the Gulf of Paria, in the island of Antigua and in British Guiana within fifty miles of Georgetown in exchange for naval and military equipment and material which the United States will transfer to His Majesty's Government.

3. All the bases and facilities referred to in the preceding paragraphs will be leased to the United States for a period of ninety-nine years, free from all rent and charges other than such compensation to be mutually agreed on to be paid by the United States in order to compensate the owners of private property for loss by expropriation or damage arising out of the establishment of the bases and facilities in question.

4. His Majesty's Government, in the leases to be agreed upon, will grant to the United States for the period of the leases all the rights, power and authority within the bases leased, and within the limits of territorial waters and air spaces adjacent to or in the vicinity of such bases, necessary to provide access to and defence of such bases, and appropriate provisions for their control.

5. Without prejudice to the above-mentioned rights of the United States authorities and their jurisdiction within the leased areas, the adjustment and reconciliation between the jurisdiction of the authorities of the United States within these areas and the jurisdiction of the authorities of the territories in which these areas are situated, shall be determined by common agreement.

6. The exact location and bounds of the aforesaid bases, the necessary seaward, coast and anti-aircraft defences, the location of sufficient military garrisons, stores and other necessary auxiliary facilities shall be determined by common agreement.

7. His Majesty's Government are prepared to designate immediately experts to meet with experts of the United States for these purposes. Should these experts be unable to agree in any particular situation except in the case of Newfoundland and Bermuda, the matter shall be settled by the Secretary of State for Foreign Affairs.

I have the honour etc.,

LOTHIAN'

(2)

Note from Mr. Hull to Lord Lothian.

Mr. Hull's reply began with a repetition of Lord Lothian's note and continued as follows:—

'I am directed by the President to reply to your note as follows:

The Government of the United States appreciates the declarations and the generous action of His Majesty's Government as contained in your communication, which are destined to enhance the national security of the United States and greatly to strengthen its ability to co-operate effectively with the other nations of the Americas in the defence of the Western hemisphere. It therefore gladly accepts the proposals.

The Government of the United States will immediately designate experts to meet with experts designated by His Majesty's Government to determine upon the exact location of the naval and air bases mentioned in your communication under acknowledgment.

In consideration of the declarations above quoted, the Government of the United States will immediately transfer to His Majesty's Government 50 United States Navy Destroyers generally referred to as the 1,200-tons type.

Accept, etc.

CORDELL HULL'

CHAPTER XIII

Anglo-French relations from the Franco-German Armistice to the end of January 1941

(i)

Relations with the Government of Marshal Pétain from the Franco-German Armistice to August 10, 1940.

MR. Roosevelt's proposals for Lend-Lease meant that within the limits set by their own national requirements the productive resources of the United States would be assured to Great Britain for the defeat of Germany. Wars are not won merely by a superiority in material but they may well be lost without it. Henceforward, on the British side, there could now be confidence not merely in survival but in victory. If Marshal Pétain and his associates had taken a different line at the time of the collapse of French armed resistance on the metropolitan territory of France, they might have avoided the humiliating position into which they fell more deeply during the months when Great Britain was slowly enabled—in M. Reynaud's phrase—to see light at the end of the tunnel. Since, however, they had put themselves in the power of Hitler, the French Ministers could not avoid the consequences of national surrender. A section of French opinion—represented in the most influential quarters by Laval (and, after the engagement at Oran, by Admiral Darlan)—had indeed no idea of avoiding those consequences. Laval was ready to accept the fact of German supremacy in Europe and to make the best of it. In a strange way his policy, and that of other full collaborationists, was a grotesque parody of French policy nearly fifty years earlier. After Fashoda French statesmen had realised that, if France could not go to war with Great Britain, the best plan would be to come to a friendly arrangement with her on the most advantageous terms, and at least to get the most out of a situation in which France gained nothing by stubborn opposition. Laval took the same view in very different circumstances about French relations with Germany.

Other members and supporters of the defeatist Ministry which had taken over the government of France did not go so far in applying to their situation the strict logic of Laval, but the practical results of their efforts to evade the consequences of their surrender were not very different. The Bordeaux Government,[1] while they were still under the delusion that the surrender of Great Britain was only a matter of weeks, did not regard themselves as having betrayed an ally. Their view was rather that Great Britain had dragged France into war and had then failed to take an adequate part in the fighting. Their resentment and bitterness increased after the destruction of the French ships at Oran. They failed to see that this action was taken by Great Britain in view of the French refusal to put their fleet out of German reach. It may be that the British Government under-rated the successful possibility of 'passive resistance' by the French to German pressure after the armistice, just as the French under-rated the possibility of successful active resistance by Great Britain to German attack. Nevertheless, taking every factor into account, a nation determined as the British were to fight to the last could not shrink from desperate remedies to meet a desperate situation and could not be expected to share the French delusion that the armistice terms really safeguarded the fleet.

The bitterness of the 'men of Vichy' was deepened by the British support of General de Gaulle. Frenchmen indeed understood—the French of Vichy understood more clearly perhaps than Englishmen—the moral importance of General de Gaulle's movement. In any case, from a practical point of view, General de Gaulle weakened such little bargaining power as the French possessed since in Hitler's eyes the resistance of any Frenchmen deprived the French Govern-ment even of the despicable credit of surrender.

As the months passed, and events showed how wrong Marshal Pétain and his colleagues had been in their assumption of a rapid and easy German victory over Great Britain, the psychological and practical aspects of the attitude of the Vichy Government did not change. The full collaborators—Laval and his friends—were more anxious for a British defeat, and the Germans put more pressure upon the French to serve them now that they had more need of French collaboration. The moderate supporters of Vichy were still hoping, like Marshal Pétain, that they could obtain a reasonable settlement with Hitler. They had gone too far both in their domestic policy and

---

[1] This term was used in Great Britain until Marshal Pétain's Government was estab-lished at Vichy. At the end of June Clermont-Ferrand was expected to be the seat of Government in unoccupied France.

Mr. Bullitt, United States Ambassador in France, reported to Washington on July 1, 1940, that after long conversations with Marshal Pétain, Admiral Darlan, General Weygand, and other French Ministers, his impression was 'the extraordinary one that the French leaders desire to cut loose from all that France has represented during the past two generations; that their physical and moral defeat has been so absolute that they have accepted completely for France the fate of becoming a province of Nazi Germany. Moreover, in order that they may have as many companions in misery as possible, they hope that England will be rapidly and completely defeated by Germany and that the Italians will suffer the same fate. Their hope is that France may become Germany's favourite province.' (*F.R.U.S.*, 1940, II, 462–9.)

in their attitude towards the war to allow even the possibility of a reconciliation with General de Gaulle, and their self-esteem was more wounded than elated at the remarkable British recovery, since they were now shown to have misjudged the situation at the time of their surrender. In any case they could do nothing, or rather they remained defeatist and were unwilling to face the risks involved in doing anything, which would bring once more the full fury of Hitler against them.

Thus, while Anglo-American relations became more clearly defined, and began slowly to take the pattern of a military alliance, the relations between Great Britain and France remained uncertain and angry. The lack of direct contacts, the knowledge on each side that the French Government had lost its freedom, British suspicion that the feeble Marshal Pétain would be driven by his entourage to further surrender, including the surrender of the fleet, French *amour-propre* and exasperation at the support given to General de Gaulle, all these factors made even a tacit understanding between the two countries impossible.

The absence of mutual confidence between Great Britain and France was symbolised by the breaking off of regular diplomatic intercourse between the British and French Governments after the armistice. The gulf between them was too wide to be bridged by formal diplomatic contacts. For a time in the view of the Foreign Office it was impossible and indeed undesirable to raise the question (a) of future British representation in unoccupied France. We were supporting General de Gaulle and recognising him as the rallying-point of French resistance to the enemy. General de Gaulle hoped to recruit a French force which he would take to North Africa and there act in defiance of the Bordeaux Government.[1] We were also considering how we could prevent the French fleet from falling into enemy hands. We were treating the whole of France, from the point of view of contraband control, as enemy-occupied territory. In such circumstances the Foreign Office thought it impossible to send an

---

[1] Attacks were made on the 'men of Bordeaux' and the 'men of Vichy' in the British press and wireless, although, especially after August, 1940, care was taken not to attack Marshal Pétain or General Weygand.

About the end of 1940 information reached the Foreign Office that the use of the term 'Vichy Government' in official documents and by the B.B.C. was causing offence in France. Hence it was decided as a general rule to substitute in public statements the term 'Government of Marshal Pétain', but in practice references to the Vichy Government continued.

His Majesty's Government never contested the legality of Marshal Pétain's Government (the Free French maintained, on good legal authority, that it was not a legal Government). The Foreign Office used the term 'French Government' in official communications with the Vichy Government; they did not wish, however, this term to be accepted generally, since it carried the implication that the Government at Vichy was free and independent, whereas it was known to be under German control in all vital matters. There were special reasons e.g. connected with the control of French ships and cargoes, why it was important not to give the impression that the British Government regarded the Government at Vichy as 'independent'.

(a) C7652/9/17.

ambassador to France; it was also unlikely that the Germans would allow the French Government to give him the usual diplomatic rights of communication by cypher, etc.

On the other hand the Bordeaux Government had said that they did not want to break with Great Britain. It was possible that sooner or later there might be a development in French opinion favourable to ourselves, but the converse seemed equally likely, i.e. the Germans might turn the French actively against us. The action of the Bordeaux Government in returning to the Germans 400 German air force prisoners whom M. Reynaud had promised to send to England showed what we might expect from the defeatist régime which, under Hitler, now controlled France. The gravest danger, however, as we had repeatedly protested to the Bordeaux Government, lay in the terms of the armistice with regard to the French fleet. The measures which His Majesty's Government felt compelled to take on July 3 at Oran were a direct consequence of these terms. In spite of their promise to us not to allow the risk of their fleet falling into German hands, the French had agreed with Germany to recall to French ports all French ships of war, except those allowed for the protection of French colonial interests, for demilitarisation under German and Italian control. Hence there was only the shadowy safeguard of a German promise that, once in French ports, these ships would not be seized for their own use by the Germans, with the most serious consequences to the balance of naval strength in the Mediterranean, and therefore to the attitude of Turkey, Egypt and Iraq. Moreover, the Germans could denounce the armistice with France, and would therefore be absolved from any undertaking to the French Government if the latter, in the German view, failed to fulfil the whole of their obligations.

There were ships—mostly small craft—of the French fleet at British home ports[1] and a stronger detachment at Alexandria. These ships were prevented from leaving port, and offers were made to repatriate officers and men who did not wish to continue the war against Germany. A more powerful French squadron was at Oran. On the morning of July 3 the French Admiral Gensoul, who was in command at Oran, was sent a statement.[2] This statement, after promising the restoration of France, in the event of an Allied victory, offered the Admiral the choice between (i) joining the British fleet and continuing the war, (ii) sailing to a British port, or (iii) sailing to a French port in the West Indies for demilitarisation. If no one of these choices were accepted, the Admiral would be required to sink his ships within six hours: otherwise the British navy had instructions

---

[1] For the distribution of the French units in British ports, see above, p. 289, note 1.

[2] Captain Holland, R.N., formerly Naval Attaché at Paris, brought the communication in person, but Admiral Gensoul refused to see him.

to use whatever force might be necessary to prevent the ships from falling into German or Italian hands. The Admiral refused the offers made to him; the consequence was an action in which four French ships were heavily damaged and nearly 1,300 of their crews lost their lives.

The decision in this matter was taken for naval and military reasons, and was therefore outside the sphere of the Foreign Office.[1] The War Cabinet, however, were aware at all events of the immediate political risk, including the possibility of a declaration of war by the French Government, and had concluded that these risks had to be taken. M. Cambon, French Chargé d'Affaires, sent a formal protest to the Foreign Office on the morning of July 3 about the treatment of (a) the French ships in British ports. A full explanation was given to him later in the day of the reasons why action was being taken at Oran. M. Cambon replied on July 4 that the events at Oran had created so serious a situation between the two countries that he could not foresee what decision the Government of the Republic would have to take in the matter. On the following morning M. Cambon said that he felt compelled to resign his post as Chargé d'Affaires.[2]

On July 7, the Marquis de Castellane[3] told the Foreign Office informally that within a few days he would be making a communication that the French Government could no longer continue unilateral diplomatic relations with His Majesty's Government. The War Cabinet decided on July 7 to answer the communication by a (b) reply asking for the elucidation of a number of points: e.g. what would be the position of consular officers? We could say that we had

---

[1] The later controversies—British and French—over the action are outside the scope of this history. The best accounts of it are in the official histories, S. W. Roskill, *The War at Sea*, I, pp. 241–5, and I. S. O. Playfair, *The Mediterranean and Middle East*, I (H.M.S.O., 1954), pp. 131–8.

It is only fair, however, to mention (1) that Admiral Gensoul did not inform the French Admiralty of the alternative courses offered to him: he merely reported that he had been ordered to sink his ships within six hours, and (2) that Admiral Darlan, on June 24, had in fact issued a secret order that all French ships were to sail for the United States or to be scuttled if there were a danger of their falling into enemy hands; the British Government had been told only in general terms of these instructions, and, in view of the failure of the French to fulfil so many of their engagements, could not be sure that this particular order had been given, or that, if given, it would be carried out by a French authority which was under German control or that the Germans would not employ some trick to foil the French intentions.

[2] M. Corbin, on his own initiative, had resigned his post as Ambassador on June 26. The Bordeaux Government, while claiming that the departure of Sir R. Campbell, and the broadcast recognition of General de Gaulle, constituted a breach of diplomatic relations on the part of the British Government, had continued up to this date to be represented by M. Cambon as Chargé d'Affaires. M. Cambon gave as his own reason for resigning his fear that he might have to make a communication from the French Government which he would not wish to make.

[3] M. Cambon's place as Chargé d'Affaires was taken temporarily by the Marquis de Castellane.

(a) C7483/839/17.   (b) WM(40)196, C7652/9/17.

withdrawn our Ambassador in order to prevent his capture by the Germans and that, if suitable arrangements could be made, we were ready to appoint a Chargé d'Affaires. We could also refer to the desirability of maintaining contact over colonial questions.

M. de Castellane, who had delivered the formal French com- (a) munication on July 8, was handed a note in reply on July 9. On July 11 Lord Halifax told the War Cabinet of an answer from the French (b) Government that they could not alter their general decision about the withdrawal of representatives, but that they proposed to appoint a representative for the liquidation of economic and other matters between the two Governments. The Foreign Office took this step to mean that the French Government did not intend to close down entirely their representation in Great Britain. The War Cabinet therefore accepted the suggestion of the Foreign Office for the appointment of a Consul-General at Vichy in order to balance the French representation in Great Britain, while M. Chartier, French Consul-General in London, stayed on as Acting French Agent.[1] On July 12, however, there was a report that the French Government intended to move to Paris or Versailles. It was therefore necessary to (c) include in a communication to the French a reservation that His Majesty's Government would have to reconsider the matter of representation if the French Government should move to enemy-occupied territory.

His Majesty's Government designated Sir N. Bland as British (d) Agent at Vichy, and the French Government let it be understood that this appointment was acceptable to them. On July 25, however, M. (e) Chartier brought a statement to the Foreign Office that, since the conclusion of the agreement to exchange agents, His Majesty's Government had detained in the United Kingdom a number of officers belonging to the French missions and had also dropped leaflets in Morocco. Until these two incidents had been disposed of, the French Government could not receive Sir N. Bland.[2]

The Foreign Office view of this communication was that the two points were of minor importance, and that an answer might be given in conciliatory terms which would allow the French, if they wished, to withdraw their refusal. At this time the Foreign Office were beginning to doubt whether it would be possible to maintain diplomatic relations of any kind with the Vichy Government. From the British

---

[1] See also Volume II, Chapter XXI, note to section (i).
[2] At the end of September, 1940, the Foreign Office obtained information which they (f) regarded as reliable that these two reasons were only pretexts and that the French refusal was due in fact to German pressure.
(a) C7700/9/17. (b) WM(40)200, C7652, 7700/9/17. (c) WM(40)201, C7652/9/17.
(d) C7923/9/17. (e) C7652/9/17. (f) C10510/9/17.

point of view some contact was desirable, in order to know what was happening in France and what were the aims and policy of the Vichy Government. On the other hand we were about to make an agreement with General de Gaulle which would certainly result in violent protests from Vichy. We were applying contraband control to the whole of France and French North Africa. We had seized and requisitioned French ships and were making propaganda against Vichy. The Germans were using occupied France as a base of operations against us, particularly from the air, and the French were closing down all our consulates. Thus there were likely to be recurrent crises in our relations, and in the end we might have to withdraw our Agent.

The War Cabinet decided, on balance, and with the approval of

(a) General de Gaulle, to 'keep the door open', but the French answer[1] on August 10 to a British note of August 4 was unsatisfactory. The French Government wanted an assurance that we would refrain from action hostile to the French Government in France and throughout French territories overseas. The Foreign Office replied to this note that they were unable to find in it 'any indication that the French Government desire the maintenance of contact between the two Governments in the manner which had been agreed'. His Majesty's Government for their part, continued 'to attach importance to the exchange of Agents and they would be happy to know that this view [was] still shared by the French Government'.

(ii)

Exchange of letters with General de Gaulle, August 1940 : further exchanges with the Vichy Government : the Dakar episode (July 30—October 19, 1940).

The British Government received the French note of August 10 after they had taken a further step in recognising the position of

(b) General de Gaulle. On July 30 General de Gaulle wrote to the Prime Minister that he considered it desirable to set up a 'Conseil de Défense de la France d'Outre-mer' as an organising and directing

---

[1] This correspondence was exchanged through the British and French Ambassadors in Madrid. M. Chartier communicated 'for information' on August 2 a note of protest against the British blockade. M. Chartier said the note would be transmitted officially through the United States Government, and that he was not authorised to discuss the questions raised in it. No copy was received from the United States Government: hence no reply was sent to the note, but the Prime Minister explained in the House of Commons on August 20 the attitude of the British Government towards the blockade. In fact, owing to the shortage of naval craft, the blockade of French North Africa was hardly more than nominal. (See also sections (iv) and (v) of this chapter). M. Chartier later communicated a note in which the

(c) French Government were prepared to agree to the British proposals for the establishment of four Consuls in unoccupied France.

(a) WP(40)218, C7920/7559/17; C7652, 8834/9/17.   (b) C8172/8172/17.
(c) C9258/9/17.

body for the revival of French resistance. He hoped that the British Government would recognise the Council as competent to treat with them on all matters concerning common action in the war. He also thought, in view of the Prime Minister's broadcast of July 14,[1] that we should make a public statement about the measures of economic assistance which we proposed to grant to such parts of the French Empire as might rally to the Council of Defence. With the agreement (a) of the War Cabinet the Prime Minister replied on August 5 that His Majesty's Government approved in principle the formation at a (b) suitable time of a Council composed of the authorities in the French colonies which decided to join General de Gaulle in pursuing the war; they would be prepared to discuss with such a Council all matters involving collaboration in the defence of these colonies or affecting their economic interests.

Two days later the Prime Minister sent General de Gaulle an agreed memorandum on the organisation, employment and conditions of service of the French volunteer movement under his command. The terms of this memorandum allowed General de Gaulle to recruit and maintain armed forces in Great Britain and to set up a civil establishment for the organisation of these forces. The memorandum, and the covering letters exchanged between the Prime Minister and General de Gaulle were published. The memorandum included the phrase 'this force will never be required to take up arms against France' ('Cette force ne pourra jamais porter les armes contre la France'). The Prime Minister ended his letter with the words: 'I would take this opportunity of stating that it is the determination of His Majesty's Government, when victory has been gained by the Allied arms, to secure the full restoration of the independence and greatness of France' ('la restauration intégrale de l'indépendance et de la grandeur de la France').

In an unpublished letter of August 7 the Prime Minister explained these phrases more fully. He thought it necessary to put on record that the expression 'full restoration of the independence and greatness of France' had 'no precise relation to territorial frontiers. We have not been able to guarantee such frontiers in respect of any nation now acting with us, but, of course, we shall do our best.' The Prime Minister added: 'The Article which specifies that your troops will not have to "take up arms against France" must be interpreted as meaning a France free to choose her course without being under direct or indirect duress from Germany. For instance, a declaration of

---

[1] In this broadcast the Prime Minister said: 'So long as our path to victory is not impeded we are ready to discharge such offices of good will towards the French Government as may be possible, and to foster the trade of those parts of the French Empire which are now cut off from captive France but which maintain their freedom'.

(a) WM(40)219.   (b) C8172/8172/17.

war by the Government of Vichy against the United Kingdom would not constitute a declaration of war by France, and there may be other cases of the same kind.'

In a reply of August 7 General de Gaulle accepted these qualifications with the hope that 'les circonstances permetteront un jour au gouvernement Brittannique de considérer ces questions avec moins de réserve'.

The next important stage in the development of General de Gaulle's organisation came with his assumption at the end of August of the administration of the Chad territory and the Cameroons under French mandate. General de Gaulle was thus in a position to change his title from 'leader of Free Frenchmen' to 'leader of Free France'. His Majesty's Government recognised General de Gaulle's action. At the same time, in an exchange of letters, the Prime Minister promised economic assistance to the Free French territories 'until such time as an independent and constitutional authority has been re-established on Free French soil'. The Prime Minister also gave an undertaking to defend from invasion or attack by sea any French colonies which rallied to General de Gaulle. Our policy was to regard the Free French territories as being administered in trust for a Free France of the future. We should prefer to deal with the administration through a Council of Defence rather than through an individual, but we were prepared to continue our arrangement with General de Gaulle or with General Catroux, if General de Gaulle came to some arrangement with him.

M. Chartier communicated to the Foreign Office on August 31 a protest from the Vichy Government against the Prime Minister's
(a) letter of August 27 to General de Gaulle. The French note (i) stated that the words used by the Prime Minister were an indirect attack upon the constitutional authority of the Government of Marshal Pétain and (ii) objected to the promise of economic assistance to French colonies which 'rebelled' against France. An answer was given to M. Chartier (i) that the Prime Minister's words were 'until such time as an independent and constitutional authority' had been 're-established on Free French soil' and that these words did not bear the meaning attributed to the Prime Minister in the note,[1] (ii) that His Majesty's Government would not have expected the French Government to object to the grant of assistance to those colonies which were cut off from the Mother Country and had 'freely declared their desire to assist in securing the retention of the French Overseas Empire for France'.

[1] The term 'independent' was omitted from the French reference to Mr. Churchill's phrase.

(a) C9367/7327/17.

Meanwhile on September 1 Sir S. Hoare, British Ambassador in (a) Madrid, had received from the French Embassy a communication from Vichy to the effect that contact might be maintained through the French and British Embassies in Madrid, but that such contact would be pointless if the British Government did not renounce for the future interference with French overseas possessions and activities embarrassing to the French Government. Sir S. Hoare considered that the French authorities in Madrid seemed increasingly anxious to work with us, and that some kind of relationship with the Vichy Government would be of help in dealing with Spain, since the Spanish Government regarded Marshal Pétain as the only hope against a France totally occupied by Germany. We also needed a channel of communication to settle questions of British refugees and prisoners. On September 6 Sir S. Hoare was instructed to reply that we would agree to continue discussions in Madrid, but could not accept the French use of the term 'interference'. The decisions to join the Allied cause had been taken freely by the authorities and populations of the territories concerned and it was natural that we should wish to give economic help to them.

On September 3 M. de la Baume, the French Ambassador at (b) Madrid, gave to Sir S. Hoare a personal message from M. Baudouin to Lord Halifax. M. Baudouin wanted the British Government to consider the dangerous situation which was being created in Africa by the encouragement of General de Gaulle's movement. This movement was unlikely to get much support, but, if it succeeded, it would bring the Germans and Italians into Morocco and also draw Spain into the war. An answer to this message was sent to Sir S. Hoare on (c) September 10 repeating the facts about the Free French movement, i.e. that the movements in Africa were spontaneous in origin, that we had given certain undertakings to General de Gaulle and did not intend to withdraw from them, and that we had publicly expressed our determination, after victory had been won, to secure the full restoration of the independence and greatness of France.

A second message, which was despatched on September 6, but did not reach the Foreign Office until September 17, was brought by the (d) French Naval Attaché at Madrid on his return from a visit to Vichy. The French Naval Attaché said that this message came from M. Baudouin and Admiral Darlan, with the knowledge of Marshal Pétain. The French Government wanted to retain contact with the British Government and ultimately to take up arms against Germany. In order to develop their resistance, it was essential that the French people should be fed. Hence the Government were asking unofficially that some food ships should be allowed to reach French ports, i.e.

(a) C9390/9/17.   (b) C9825/7327/17.   (c) C9825/7327/17.   (d) C9679/9/17.

there would be no ostensible raising of the blockade, but the ships would in practice not be stopped.

In view of the acts of the Vichy Government, it was impossible on the British side to judge how far this appeal was merely a trick to secure the lifting of the blockade or a genuine change of feeling due to the fact that, contrary to French expectations, the Germans had not broken British resistance. No answer was therefore sent to the message.

(a)   Sir S. Hoare transmitted yet another message from M. Baudouin on September 13. M. Baudouin wanted 'a colonial *modus vivendi*' and, according to the French Ambassador, Marshal Pétain was prepared to dismiss M. Laval and other pro-German Ministers in order to prepare for a united French movement of resistance in the future. The Ambassador also asked most strongly that there should be no attempt at a *coup* in Morocco. An answer was sent to Sir S. Hoare on September 15, to the effect that we were most anxious to avoid disorder in French Morocco and would do nothing to promote it, but the French Government would understand that we could not go back on our promises to General de Gaulle or refrain from assisting any French territories overseas which might follow his leadership and declare for Free France. Subject to these considerations, we should be glad to know what M. Baudouin meant by a colonial *modus vivendi*.

Before the middle of September the French Cameroons, and the greater part of French Equatorial Africa, New Caledonia, the French Government in the Condominium of the New Hebrides and the French establishments in India had come over to the side of Free France. The movement then received a temporary set-back. General de Gaulle's information led him to think (wrongly) that, if he appeared off Dakar with French troops, he could secure Senegal. The British Government were the more ready to support General de Gaulle's plan because they had reports of the spread of German influence towards Dakar. There were, however, delays in the sailing of General de Gaulle's expedition and changes in the plan of operations. Meanwhile the Vichy Government sent three French cruisers and three destroyers to Dakar from Toulon through the Straits of Gibraltar. Owing to mischance, information about their sailing and probable destination was delayed. In any case our general policy since the engagement at Oran had been not to interfere with the movements of French warships if they were not sailing to ports under enemy control. Hence these ships from Toulon were allowed to pass through the Straits of Gibraltar and to turn southwards to Dakar. Some of them left Dakar and again turned south. Since they might

(a) C9849/9849/28.

be intending to interfere with the situation in French Equatorial Africa, they were now intercepted by ships of the Royal Navy. Two of the cruisers were able to get back to Dakar; the third was diverted to Casablanca.

On the morning of September 23 emissaries of General de Gaulle, including a grandson of Marshal Foch, attempted to land at Dakar. Their boat flew the tricolour and the white flag in order to show both their French nationality and their peaceful intentions. They were fired upon from the shore, and the French batteries and warships opened fire on General de Gaulle's ships and ships of the Royal Navy which were standing by to give assistance if necessary. This fire—after warning by signal—was returned. General de Gaulle's forces also attempted a landing, but it became clear that the place could be taken only after a serious military operation. Hence on September 25 the British and French forces withdrew, since neither the British Government nor General de Gaulle wished to undertake operations against French supporters of the Vichy Government.

The British Government had assured the Spanish Government that (a) a success at Dakar would not be followed by a similar *coup* against French Morocco. They also realised that their action, whatever its success or failure, might bring a declaration of war from Vichy. This latter risk was lessened by a promise[1] from President Roosevelt to let (b) the Vichy Government know that a declaration of war against Great Britain would be 'derogatory to Franco-American relations' and would mean the loss to Vichy of French possessions in the West Indies and the Pacific.

The uncertainty about the attitude of the Vichy Government continued after General de Gaulle's repulse at Dakar. Once again His Majesty's Government received messages through the French Ambassador at Madrid and also through the French Naval Attaché. The latter's message, which came from the French Admiralty, (c) described the Dakar affair as an attack on a French colony in violation of our undertakings. The French Navy would retaliate against any further attack (as they had retaliated after the attempted landing at Dakar by the bombing of Gibraltar) and would make the Mediterranean untenable for us, if we did not suspend all attacks, renounce propaganda for a civil war, and allow the passage of food supplies to unoccupied France.

The message from M. Baudouin was more conciliatory. He said (d) that, if the French Government were not to be driven entirely into

---

[1] President Roosevelt gave this promise at Lord Lothian's suggestion when the latter delivered to him a message from the Prime Minister on the night of September 22–3 about the Dakar plan.

(a) C10236/7327/17. (b) C10236/7327/17. (c) C9679/9/17. (d) C9679/9/17.

German hands, Great Britain must allow supplies to reach unoccupied France from the French colonies. The French Government would guarantee that these supplies, or their equivalent, would not get into German hands. If the Germans tried to seize them, the French Government would move to Morocco, and France would be united again with Great Britain against Germany. This message did not contain any threat and made no reference to propaganda.

No reply was sent to the message from the French Admiralty, but

(a) on October 3 Sir S. Hoare was authorised to deliver an answer to the message from M. Baudouin. The answer began by a reference to the reply to M. Baudouin's previous question about a colonial *modus vivendi*, and pointed out that, since a reply had been sent, French forces had fired on British ships at Dakar when invited to parley and French aeroplanes had bombed Gibraltar without warning. Any further attack would be met by immediate retaliation against French colonial ports and territory. Furthermore, we could not withdraw our support of General de Gaulle's movement. Subject to these conditions, we were willing to consider a discussion on the proposals for trade between the French colonies and unoccupied France. It would be necessary to ensure that those parts of the French Empire not 'now or hereafter' controlled by General de Gaulle should not come under German or Italian influence, and that ships of the French navy should not fall into German or Italian hands. At the same time we intended to employ the weapon of blockade fully against the enemy, and could relax it in favour of unoccupied France only if we were assured that the French Government were able and willing to act in regard to their overseas territories 'independently of German and Italian dictation', and were also 'ready to adopt a more co-operative attitude than they have hitherto shown in their dealings with His Majesty's Government'.

During this time an exchange of views was also taking place

(b) between General Smuts and the French Minister to the Union of South Africa. General Smuts explained to the Minister on September 30 our anxiety lest the Germans might use their rights under the armistice to seize bases like Dakar; he asked whether the French Government could give some assurance, possibly an undertaking to inform a third party, in the event of such a danger. The Minister later answered that the French Government would act in this way.

(c) On October 14 the French Ambassador at Madrid brought another message. The French Government maintained that they had not taken and would not take the initiative in attack but would reply to attacks on French ships or territory. They recognised neither the 'cause' nor the 'authority' of General de Gaulle. There was only one French Government charged with the defence of the French Empire

(a) C9679/9/17.   (b) C10647/9/17.   (c) C9679/9/17.

and its eventual restoration. British recognition of any other authority or support of attempts to detach French possessions from the authority of the French Government would make Anglo-French reconciliation impossible. The French Government considered themselves the injured party, but hoped to reap the fruits of their policy of patience. They 'earnestly' desired the establishment of an 'economic *modus vivendi*' with regard to trade between France and the colonies.

(iii)

Attitude of His Majesty's Government towards the negotiations of the Vichy Government with Germany; representations from the United States Government to the Vichy Government (October 20–November 30, 1940).

The War Cabinet thought that this reply was disappointing, but (a) that it was intended to keep open the possibility of negotiation. Sir S. Hoare was therefore instructed on the night of October 18–19 to give a verbal answer maintaining our previous statements and suggesting discussions at Madrid.

On the following day the Prime Minister instructed Sir S. Hoare that he should make clear to the Vichy Government through the (b) French Ambassador at Madrid that we were still ready to collaborate with the French Government against the common enemy; that we were confident of victory and could not understand why some of the French leaders did not now go to North Africa and make common cause with us there. In giving the message to the Ambassador, (c) Sir S. Hoare therefore let it be understood that the Prime Minister wished his hint to reach Generals Weygand and Noguès who were already in Africa.[1]

At this stage news reached the Foreign Office that M. Laval had told the Vichy Government of a peace offer from the Germans. The terms of this offer, which appeared to have been made a few days after a meeting between Hitler and Mussolini on October 15, were said to be as follows: (i) France would participate with Germany and Italy in the 'new World Order' not as a Great Power, but as an 'Associated Power'; (ii) France would cede Alsace-Lorraine to Germany and Nice to Italy, and allow Germany and Italy the use of all her air and naval bases in Africa and the Mediterranean; (iii) French troops in Africa would take part in the offensive against the British Empire in Egypt, Syria and Palestine; (iv) the French fleet

---

[1] General Weygand was appointed Delegate-General of the Vichy Government in North Africa on September 9. See also note at the end of this section.
   (a) WM(40)273, C11099/7327/17.   (b) C11099/7327/17.   (c) C11099/7327/17.

(a) and air force would also co-operate in this offensive; (v) France would keep Algeria; Tunis would be divided between France and Italy and Morocco between France and Spain. Germany would receive back her former colonies and all other French colonies would become a German-Italian-French condominium.

M. Laval, Admiral Darlan and M. Baudouin were said to favour acceptance of these terms: Marshal Pétain, with the strong support of General Weygand, had refused to sign them. The other Ministers had rejected the terms without otherwise defining their position.

Later reports received by the Foreign Office suggested a considerable modification of these demands, but it was clearly necessary to try to impress upon French opinion the enormity of the commitments which M. Laval was trying to force upon his country. The

(b) Prime Minister broadcast an address to the French nation on October 21 warning them that they could expect from Hitler only the complete obliteration of France and appealing to all Frenchmen at least not to hinder, if they could not yet help, the British in their struggle for victory. This address would obviously have no influence upon Marshal Pétain and his Ministers; the only effective means of pressure on the Vichy Government was action by the United States.

(c) Hence on October 21 the Prime Minister sent a message to Mr. Roosevelt suggesting that the French Ambassador in Washington should be warned that the United States would disapprove very strongly of anything like the surrender of the Toulon fleet to Germany.

On October 22 M. Laval saw Hitler and Ribbentrop; two days later Marshal Pétain went with M. Laval to meet Hitler, Ribbentrop, and General Keitel.[1] Further reports reached the Foreign Office that M. Laval and Admiral Darlan were urging agreement with the Germans over the transfer of the fleet and the use of bases.[2]

(d) On October 25 Mr. Butler was instructed to give another message to Mr. Roosevelt about the reports of French intentions and to say that there appeared to be a desperate struggle going on between Marshal Pétain and Laval. If the French fleet and African bases were

---

[1] Between these two meetings (at Montoire in occupied France) Hitler had seen Franco at Hendaye, and had been disappointed and exasperated at the very large demands which Franco had put forward as the condition of Spanish collaboration. Hitler tried to get Marshal Pétain to agree to full collaboration, but the Marshal would not go beyond general affirmations accompanied by appeals for immediate concessions. According to the German report of the meeting, Marshal Pétain said to Hitler that the English were providing the best opportunity for Franco-German co-operation; their behaviour towards their French Ally since the armistice had been 'exceedingly bad'. (*D.G.F.P.*, XI, No. 227.)

[2] Sir S. Hoare reported on the night of October 23–4 that the French Ambassador at
(e) Madrid thought it essential—in view of the struggle between Laval and his colleagues—that the information communicated to him (the Ambassador) about our attitude to the Vichy Government should reach General Weygand. The Ambassador suggested that a Frenchman (not a Gaullist) should transmit a message to General Weygand from Egypt.

(a) C11182/89/18. (b) C11710/11304/17. (c) A4437/131/45. (d) C11099/7327/17.
(e) C11099/7327/17.

betrayed to the Germans, our task would be 'vastly more difficult' and the danger to the United States would be greater. The Prime Minister 'had the feeling that things are hanging in the balance at Vichy' and that a message from Mr. Roosevelt to Marshal Pétain might persuade him to resist the German demands. The matter was urgent because 'a very disastrous turn may very easily be given to the war by the Vichy Government committing another act of shame'.

This telegram crossed a message from Mr. Roosevelt delivered to the Prime Minister through Mr. Kennedy on October 25. Mr. (a) Roosevelt said that very strong representations had already been made to the French Ambassador, and that the Ambassador had now been given a personal message for immediate communication to his Government. This communication was to the effect that, in the opinion of the United States, the plea of the French Government that it was under duress and could act only to a very limited extent as a free agent did not in any sense justify the provision of assistance to Germany and her Allies in the war against the British Empire. The fact that a Government was a prisoner of war of another Power did not justify such a prisoner in serving its conqueror in opposition to its former Ally. The United States Government had received the most solemn assurances at the time of the formation of Marshal Pétain's Government that the French fleet would not be surrendered. If the French Government now allowed the Germans to use the French fleet in hostile operations against the British fleet, such action would constitute a flagrant and deliberate breach of faith with the United States Government. Any Franco-German agreement to this end would 'most definitely wreck' the traditional friendship between the French and American peoples and 'permanently remove' any chance of help from the United States to France in her distress and also create a wave of bitter indignation in American public opinion. Finally, Mr. Roosevelt stated that, if France took such action with regard to the fleet, the United States Government would make no effort when the appropriate time came to exercise influence in favour of the retention by France of her overseas possessions.

Mr. Roosevelt sent another message to the Prime Minister on (b) October 25 in reply to the message given to him by Mr. Butler. He thought that the Prime Minister would agree that his personal communication to Marshal Pétain through the French Ambassador at Washington met the case, but that he had also told the United States Chargé d'Affaires at Vichy to get an audience with Marshal Pétain and to repeat the contents of the message to him.

The Prime Minister telegraphed on October 26 his full agreement (c) with Mr. Roosevelt's message. In a second telegram to Mr. Roosevelt

(a) C11416/7327/17.   (b) A4437/131/45.   (c) A4437/131/45.

he thanked him for his action, but pointed out that 'everything [was] still in the balance'.[1] The President had already been told the German terms which Marshal Pétain was said to be resisting. The surrender of French bases in Africa for air and U-boat attacks would be as bad as the surrender of the French ships. In particular the Atlantic bases 'in bad hands' would be a menace to the United States and a 'grievous embarrassment 'to Great Britain. Mr. Churchill therefore hoped that Mr. Roosevelt would make it clear that this statement about the French ships applied also to the bases.

(a) On October 27 the Prime Minister sent another message to Mr. Roosevelt in the following terms:

'We have not yet heard what Vichy has agreed to. If they have betrayed warships and African and other colonial harbours to Hitler, our already heavy task will be grievously aggravated. If Oran and Bizerta become German-Italian air and submarine bases, our hopes of stopping or impeding the reinforcement of the hostile army now attacking Egypt will be destroyed, and the heaviest forms of German-organised Italian attack must be expected. The situation in the Western Mediterranean will also be gravely worsened. If Dakar is betrayed, very great dangers will arise in the Atlantic unless we are able to rectify the position, which will not be easy. On the other hand, the announcement of the Vichy terms may lead to the desired revolt in the French Empire, which we should have to aid and foster with further drains upon our slowly expanding resources. Either way, therefore, immense exertions will be required from us in the Mediterranean during the next year . . .'

(b) Meanwhile the French Ambassador at Madrid had suggested that it would be a good thing to reinforce the Prime Minister's message by a personal appeal to Marshal Pétain from His Majesty The King.

(c) The War Cabinet accepted this suggestion and agreed on a draft message for His Majesty's approval. The message was sent during the afternoon of October 25. After an expression of sympathy and a repetition of our resolve to restore the freedom and greatness of France, the message referred to the reported attempts of the Germans to secure peace terms far beyond the provisions of the armistice. The message mentioned Marshal Pétain's declaration that he would reject dishonourable terms, and hoped that he would now refuse proposals bringing dishonour to France and grave damage to Great Britain.

The French Ambassador gave Sir S. Hoare a reply from Marshal
(d) Pétain to His Majesty's message on November 2. The reply stated

---

[1] On October 26 the *Moniteur* published an article (attributed to Laval) suggesting that 'durable security' for France could be found only in collaboration with Germany. Laval's appointment as Foreign Minister, which had been rumoured on October 26, was announced on October 28, and on this day Laval and General Huntziger went to confer with the Germans in Paris.

(a) A4437/131/45. (b) C11099/7327/17. (c) WM(40)277. (d) C11949/9/17; C11461/7362/17.

that the French nation felt deeply the aggressions suffered from the British fleet and the support given to Frenchmen who were rebels. The French Government had tried to avoid action which could have aggravated the situation; they would not make any unjustified attack, but would know how 'honourably to respect the essential interests of the French nation'. The reply to President Roosevelt (a) repeated these charges against Great Britain and said that the French Government had already given a pledge that the fleet would not be handed over to others.[1]

The French Ambassador in giving Marshal Pétain's reply asked (b) Sir S. Hoare to add that the disappointing character of the reply was due to fear of the Germans and that the solid fact to be taken into account was the growing anti-German feeling in France. The Ambassador was sure that Marshal Pétain had not entered into new commitments with Hitler.

Before this message was received the Foreign Office had considered an important broadcast given by Marshal Pétain on October 30. According to this broadcast, the principles of Franco-German (c) collaboration had been accepted, and their application left for later discussion. There was nothing to show what price the French would have to pay for the 'alleviations' which they hoped to obtain from Hitler in matters such as the return of prisoners of war, the expenses of occupation, the line of demarcation or the provisioning of unoccupied France. From our point of view it might have been better if Marshal Pétain had either accepted the most humiliating terms or had rejected them entirely. In the former case, the French people might have overthrown their government and the French Empire might have rallied to us. As things were, there was no revulsion of feeling in France owing to the enormity of the terms, while we were still uncertain whether to take action to strengthen General de Gaulle's position and to bring increased pressure to bear on those parts of the French Empire which remained loyal to Vichy.

With the approval of the Prime Minister, Sir S. Hoare was (d) instructed on November 1 to tell the French Ambassador that we had had no answer to our message of October 19 but that meanwhile the Vichy Government appeared to have begun negotiations with the Germans on matters which must effect our own security and the conduct of the war. We had no reliable information about these

---

[1] The United States Chargé d'Affaires at Vichy reported that a less brusque reply drafted by the French Foreign Office had been set aside in favour of a draft by Marshal (e) Pétain and M. Laval. The Chargé d'Affaires thought that Mr. Roosevelt's message had caused resentment, but that it had given a 'wholesome shock' to Vichy opinion, and had restrained the Vichy Government from going further along the path of collaboration with Germany. *F.R.U.S.* 1940, II, 480.

(a) C11461/7362/17.   (b) C11461/7362/17.   (c) C11713/9/17.   (d) C11713/9/17.
(e) C11461/7362/17.

negotiations. We therefore had a right to ask the Vichy Government to explain the position to us and to let us know what agreement they had reached with the Germans. It was not enough for them to protest that they would not allow the Germans to use their bases. We had to make up our minds whether the Germans would not succeed in taking these bases for themselves. If we had not been continuing our resistance to the Germans, the French would not have been able to make any sort of bargain with them. Sir S. Hoare was authorised to repeat that if the French should force us into hostilities and attack us, we should take reprisals against unoccupied France and possibly against Vichy itself.

(a)   Sir S. Hoare carried out his instructions on November 4. He found the French Ambassador greatly depressed. The Ambassador had heard nothing from Vichy, but feared that Laval intended to sign a peace treaty on November 11 and, with the approval of the German Government, to use the French fleet and certain military units for the recovery of those French colonies which had declared for General de Gaulle.[1] If the French fleet then came into conflict with the British fleet, Laval would say that the British fleet had committed an act of aggression in preventing the French from restoring order in their own Empire.

(b)   On the night of November 6–7 Mr. Butler reported that Mr. Hull had spoken very strongly to the French Ambassador on November 4. The Ambassador said that Marshal Pétain had been hurt by the brusque tone of Mr. Roosevelt's message and by the attitude of the United States Government. Mr. Hull had replied that the French Government had joined the small number of States which had tried to withhold information from the United States representatives. The Ambassador said that he assumed this complaint to be directed against Laval. Mr. Hull did not deny this. He said that the United States did not complain that France was implementing all the conditions of the armistice agreement with Germany, but Laval was trying to 'appease the Germans, which would get him nowhere at all'. The Ambassador referred to the 'extreme pressure' exercised by the German Government on Vichy in relation to the prisoners of war. Mr. Hull repeated that the French Government should do nothing to help Hitler's war effort against Great Britain and that the United States Government regarded this matter as their vital concern in view of Hitler's 'patent ambitions'. France could expect nothing from the United States 'if her Government played with Hitler'.

---

[1] On November 3 Sir S. Hoare was instructed to tell the Ambassador that His Majesty's
(c) Government had heard that the battleships *Richelieu* and *Jean Bart* were to be moved from Dakar and Casablanca to other French ports for repair and completion. His Majesty's Government 'earnestly hoped' that this step would not be taken, since they wished to avoid a clash between French and British naval forces. The French reply was that the French Admiralty would move these ships if they wished but that they did not propose to do so.

(a) C11713/9/17.   (b) C11923/1101/17.   (c) C11779/839/17.

Further reports of Laval's plans reached the Foreign Office from another source. There were also indications that a French force was being concentrated at Dakar, possibly for an attack on the colonies. Hence, with the approval of the Prime Minister, Sir S. Hoare was given on November 7 an analysis of the situation. There was a (a) 'certain duality' in our relations with the Vichy Government. We had been compelled to take action against them at Oran. We had accepted General de Gaulle as the leader of all Free Frenchmen who rallied to him and supported the Allied cause at a time when he was the sole French focus of resistance to Germany and Italy. We had supported General de Gaulle's action in certain French colonies with the object of organising resistance in France and the French Empire to German and Italian pressure. On the other hand, we had not wished for a complete break with Vichy and 'the twilight which has characterised our relationship' had been maintained. It could hardly survive an operation by Vichy to eliminate General de Gaulle from Africa.

On the French side there was a similar duality; that is to say, the Vichy Government were leaning toward an arrangement with Germany but the French people were coming to realise the evils of German supremacy and the possibility of a British victory. At the time of the armistice the Bordeaux Government had expected our surrender in a matter of weeks. They might not yet be sure of our final victory; they probably wished to reinsure themselves with us.[1] They were, however, also negotiating with the Germans on terms of which we had no precise knowledge. The result of these negotiations would probably hamper our prosecution of the war.

Sir S. Hoare was therefore asked to make the following points 'very frankly' with the French Ambassador:

'In the dark days which followed the armistice His Majesty's Government contracted certain obligations to General de Gaulle. Their sole object in doing so was to prevent German and Italian infiltration into the French Empire at a moment when the French Government appeared not to have sufficiently recovered from the shock of defeat to organise an adequate defence of the Empire. We have of late been much impressed by the growing strength of French feeling in favour of resistance to Germany and Italy, particularly in the Empire, and we recognise that so far no part of the French Empire has passed into the hands of the enemy and that enemy infiltration has not, so far as our information goes, reached alarming proportions.

---

[1] On November 16, 1940, Marshal Pétain said to Mr. Matthews, United States Chargé d'Affaires at Vichy, that he did not believe the British would give in, but obviously they could not invade Germany. He therefore expected 'after much destruction, a drawn peace, and the sooner the better'. F.R.U.S., 1940, II, 412–3. A month later Marshal Pétain spoke in similar terms to Mr. Murphy. id.ib., 418.

(a) C11713/9/17.

We cannot see the future at all clearly, but, if the Vichy Government can satisfy us that they are resolved and are able to defend French overseas territory against the Germans and the Italians and to take all measures to prevent its absorption by the enemy by subterranean means, no conflict need arise between us.

If we could be satisfied on this point, we should for our part be prepared to facilitate the task of the Vichy Government in organising such defence of the Empire. If the French Government would refrain from attacking those territories which have in the main declared for de Gaulle (a course which must almost inevitably lead to direct conflict with ourselves), we would on our side refrain from undertaking any operation against Dakar so long as the French Government undertake not to allow it to fall into enemy hands, and we are prepared to give the French Government formal assurances in this sense, which we should hold binding unless any action of the French Government obliged us to give notice of a change of attitude.

We would repeat that our aim is and always has been, when victory has been won, to ensure the restoration of France and the unity of her Empire, including those territories which at present look to the Free French Movement. We covet no inch of French territory for ourselves.'

Sir S. Hoare reported on November 10 that he had had three long talks with the French Chargé d'Affaires; the Ambassador[1] had excused himself on the ground that he had not presented his credentials. The Chargé d'Affaires argued that the French Government could not give up their right to recover the 'mutinied' colonies, and that an undertaking to do so could be exploited by the Germans as a breach of the armistice terms. He also said that, if the sole reason for the British support of General de Gaulle had been to prevent German infiltration into the French Empire, there was no reason to continue this support since in fact no infiltration had taken place. Although Sir S. Hoare failed to convince the Chargé d'Affaires that the British Government could not repudiate General de Gaulle, he finally persuaded him to put the points made to him to the Vichy Government as a 'verbal communication'. Sir S. Hoare suggested that the best policy would be to try to begin conversations on economic matters.

(a) The War Cabinet agreed with this view: they also thought it expedient to continue, at least for a short time, to allow French ships to pass through the Straits of Gibraltar. Sir S. Hoare was therefore
(b) told on November 12 that we would welcome the opening of economic

---

[1] M. Piétri succeeded M. de la Baume as French Ambassador at Madrid on November
(c) 6. M. Piétri did not present his credentials until December 7. He came with M. de la Baume to see Sir S. Hoare on November 7. On November 10 and 30 Laval gave the Germans an account of Sir S. Hoare's conversations with M. de la Baume (*D.G.F.P.*, XI, No. 343).

(a) WM(40)286. (b) C11713/9/17. (c) C11938/9/17.

talks, but that we should want a reply to our question where the Vichy Government stood in relation to Germany. We were not asking the Vichy Government to abandon any right over the colonies or to give a formal undertaking to recognise the position established in Equatorial Africa. All we required was that the Vichy Government should not attack these colonies, since an attack on General de Gaulle would almost certainly cause war with us and thus bring the Germans and Italians into the French Empire.

These instructions crossed a telegram from Sir S. Hoare that on November 11 he had received a note from the French Chargé (a) d'Affaires. In this note the Vichy Government said that they had never taken the initiative in an attack against Great Britain and did not intend to do so. They must repeat their protest against British assistance to Frenchmen who were rebels against their own country. They must also state that they would try to safeguard the unity of their Empire by every means in their power. Their conversations with the Germans had not affected their independence and liberty of action. Finally they hoped that the British Government would not hinder their shipping which only served the provisioning of the civil population. The French Chargé d'Affaires suggested that the British Government should not take this note 'too tragically'. The Vichy Government were in a very difficult position; their intentions were better than their words. The United States Government also informed the Foreign Office that Marshal Pétain had said to the (b) United States Chargé d'Affaires at Vichy that the *Richelieu* and *Jean Bart* were not being moved and that there was no intention of allowing the French fleet to fall into German hands.[1]

Note to section (iii). Professor Rougier's visit to England, October 1940.

On October 22, a Professor Louis Rougier arrived in London, not as an official agent sent by the Vichy Government, but with the approval of Marshal Pétain and the Vichy Foreign Office. M. Rougier had started on his journey to England via Lisbon when the Dakar

---

[1] The Prime Minister sent a message to Mr. Roosevelt on the night of November 10 asking whether the United States Government could give a further warning at Vichy (c) about the possible grave consequences of an attempt to move these ships to Toulon. On November 14 the Prime Minister heard in reply that Mr. Roosevelt had given instructions accordingly to the American Chargé d'Affaires at Vichy. Mr. Roosevelt said that he was also offering, on behalf of the United States Government, to buy the two ships. Marshal Pétain repeated that the ships would never be allowed to fall into German hands, but that they could not be sold, since their sale would be contrary to the terms of the armistice, and in any case the Germans would not permit it. On November 23 Mr. Roosevelt told the Prime Minister that Marshal Pétain had undertaken not to move the two ships without first informing the United States Government.

(a) C12183/9/17.   (b) C11779/839/17.   (c) C11779, 13144/839/17.

incident took place; the Vichy Government, however, were willing that he should continue his journey.

On October 24 M. Rougier saw Lord Halifax, and made a number of suggestions for improving British relations with Vichy. He proposed that we should restrain General de Gaulle's activities at least during the coming six months; that we should relax our blockade, and modify our anti-Vichy broadcasts. On the following day the Prime Minister and Lord Halifax together saw M. Rougier. They explained (a) to him the points which we wished to make clear to the Vichy Government. M. Rougier asked that a message should be sent through Madrid to Vichy urging Marshal Pétain and the Government to take no irrevocable step until his (M. Rougier's) return.

M. Rougier was certain that Marshal Pétain would not accept the reported German terms with regard to the cession of bases. On (b) October 28, however, M. Rougier suggested that, as he could not get back to Vichy in time to be of any service (i.e. before an 'irrevocable' decision had been taken), he might more usefully go to Tangier in order to see Generals Weygand and Noguès. In view of the general situation, and of the advice of the French Ambassador at Madrid, M. Rougier's suggestion was accepted. Lord Halifax told him that we would be prepared to receive any accredited persons whom General Weygand cared to send to us, and to give them all the help in our power.

M. Rougier went to Tangier, but there was no sequel to his interview with General Weygand, since the General refused contact with British representatives on the ground that the Germans would hear of it, and compel the Vichy Government to dismiss him. In any case General Weygand thought that for the time no purpose would be served by a meeting. M. Rougier returned to Vichy but in the later part of November left again for another interview with General (c) Weygand. On December 6 M. Rougier sailed for the United States from Lisbon, apparently on a private visit, though he had a somewhat larger view of the services which he might render in America. Before leaving Europe, he drew up an account of his activities. He wrote, in a letter to the Prime Minister and Lord Halifax, that he had the following assurances from Marshal Pétain: (i) France would not sign (d) a separate peace with the Axis before the end of hostilities between Great Britain and Germany. (ii) France would not cede naval or air bases or the fleet to the Axis and would resist any attempt by Spain, Germany, or Italy to seize the French colonies in North Africa. (iii) France accepted the submission of French Equatorial Africa to General de Gaulle as a *fait accompli* to the end of the war on the understanding that the territories would then be restored to France and that meanwhile no attack would be directed against French West Africa, North Africa or Morocco. M. Rougier submitted other (e) information and suggestions which were laid before the War Cabinet in a Foreign Office memorandum of December 19, but no action was

---

(a) C11442/11442/17. (b) WM(40)278. (c) C13080/11442/17; C13289/7328/17.
(d) C13251/11442/17. (e) WP(40)486; Z2766/255/17 (1945).

taken on them, or indeed could be taken, through M. Rougier himself, since he remained in the United States.[1]

(iv)

Consideration of British policy towards the Vichy Government: discussions with General de Gaulle, November 1940.

During this exchange of notes with the Vichy Government, General de Gaulle was in Equatorial Africa. He issued a statement at (a) Brazzaville on October 27 that he was organising a Council of Defence of the Empire; this Council, in the name of France and of all French territories which were fighting or which would join in fighting, would exercise the powers of a war government.[2] The Foreign Office kept General de Gaulle in touch with their negotiations. General de Gaulle had previously decided to establish his headquarters at Brazzaville or Duala, but on October 29 the Foreign Office heard that he proposed to come back to London towards the end of November and to remain there. General de Gaulle had in fact

[1] Professor Rougier's account of his talks in London shows that he had the wrong impression that he was being offered the text of a secret 'gentleman's agreement' which, if accepted by Marshal Pétain, would henceforward be binding on the two Governments. This was not the intention of the British Ministers; the discussions were understood by them and by the Foreign Office merely as an exchange of views on the possible basis of an agreement for the implementation of which the British Government would obviously require practical evidence of sincerity on the French side. A certain amount of confusion was bound to arise in these tentative approaches by individuals, especially when the purposes on each side were very different. The British aim was primarily to prevent increased French collaboration with Germany and to secure contact with General Weygand with a view to French military co-operation in North Africa, while the French were concerned not with the revival of resistance, but with the lifting of the British blockade and with preventing any further loss of colonies to General de Gaulle. Similar considerations apply to the correspondence early in December between Lord Halifax and a personal friend in France, M. Jacques Chevalier. The confusion was not lessened by Marshal Pétain's vagueness in negotiation, and his ill-defined but persistent assumption that France could arrange with each of the belligerents to 'contract out' of the war on terms favourable to herself. In the latter part of June, 1941, a Colonel Groussard came to London with the knowledge of Marshal Pétain and General Huntziger. The main purpose of his visit seemed to be to obtain information which would enable the Vichy authorities to assess the chances of a British victory. He did not suggest any hope of French assistance to the Allied cause, or any readiness on the side of Vichy to make sacrifices in order to bring about the defeat of Germany. For a good summary of Professor Rougier's misconceptions, see Aron, *op. cit.*, 283–4 and 299–303.

[2] See above, pp. 406–8. In a letter of December 24, 1940, the Prime Minister informed General de Gaulle that His Majesty's Government in the United Kingdom would be 'happy to treat with you, in the capacity of Leader of Free Frenchmen in which they have (b) recognised you, and with the Council of Defence established by the decrees of October 27, 1940, on all questions involving their collaboration with the French overseas territories which place themselves under your authority', both in matters affecting the association of Free French and British forces, and in 'those affecting the political and economic interests of those territories'. The Prime Minister added a *caveat* that his communication expressed no views on the 'constitutional and juridical considerations' contained in General de Gaulle's decrees and declarations regarding the Council.

(a) C12411/7328/17. (b) Z11/11/17 (1941).

become nervous of the British attitude towards the Vichy Government. He submitted a memorandum on November 2 pointing out that he and the members of the Council of Defence of the Empire must take a different attitude. As Frenchmen they regarded the betrayal of French honour by the Vichy Government as an offence which rendered impossible any indulgence towards those responsible for it. They thought also that a policy of conciliation would have bad practical results in strengthening the Vichy Government both in France and in the Empire. The Council did not object to the policy of encouraging certain Frenchmen, such as Generals Weygand and Noguès, to break away from Vichy, but they would wish to be consulted before any agreement were made with such 'repentant' leaders.

Before receiving this note, the British Government had considered the proposed change in General de Gaulle's plans. They thought that General de Gaulle should come to London to discuss the situation and also to reorganise his London office, but that it was probably undesirable for him to stay in London, since we should thus be too closely associated with his actions and less able to refute enemy propaganda that he was merely a British puppet. On the other hand, if we wanted to support the candidature of General de Gaulle as head of a French Government in place of the Vichy Government, London would be the best headquarters until a more convenient centre than Brazzaville or Duala could be provided on French soil.

After discussion with the Prime Minister, a personal message was sent to General de Gaulle on November 9 suggesting that he should come to London as soon as possible instead of carrying out his plan of paying a visit to Cairo. The Prime Minister sent a second message on November 10 explaining shortly the situation with regard to the Vichy Government. Before receiving this second message General de Gaulle replied that he would come to London for consultation but that he would have to return to Africa and that he was certain of attack from Vichy and wanted to be sure of full British support. On November 13 the Free French forces entered Libreville; two days later the whole of the Gaboon became part of the Free French territory.

After receiving from Sir S. Hoare the French note of November 11, the Foreign Office again reviewed the situation. It appeared that the Vichy Government had begun to realise that they had a certain freedom of manoeuvre due above all to the continued resistance of Great Britain and also to German difficulties with Italy and Spain. The Italians would not allow a peace settlement with France to be made at the expense of their claims; Spain would not give up claims

(a) C11852/9/17.   (b) C12183/9/17.

to French Morocco. The Germans had failed to get an interim settlement with France which would place French resources at their disposal and the Vichy Government would still attempt to keep their fleet and Empire out of Axis control. We ought therefore to try to bring about a *rapprochement* between Generals de Gaulle, Weygand and Catroux. It would be impossible to reconcile General de Gaulle and Vichy, but we should make it clear to Vichy that we were working for the reconciliation of the whole French Empire, and that meanwhile the *status quo* must be maintained. General de Gaulle would make no more attacks if Vichy did not attack him or any French territories which might spontaneously come over to him. We were carrying an economic burden for the French Government, at some difficulty and cost, in the Free French territories and our successes against Germany and Italy were helping Vichy to resist German demands. The stronger their resistance, the less likelihood was there that General de Gaulle's movement would spread. This movement arose out of exasperation at the spirit of surrender shown by the Vichy Government. We naturally supported the movement, and should continue to support General de Gaulle in the territories now administered by him, but there was no reason why there should be trouble between General de Gaulle or ourselves and Vichy if the French overseas territories showed that they intended to keep out the Germans and Italians.

We should try to bring these general considerations into a discussion which might begin on economic questions. On the latter we should repeat our statement that we did not want to establish our control in the French territories—our object was to restore them to a free France after the war—but that we could not continue indefinitely our present indulgent treatment of French commerce. We were now interfering only with unescorted merchant ships. We should consider whether we should not bring convoyed vessels into port for examination, if we could do so without a naval engagement on a large scale.

The War Cabinet discussed the question of contraband control on (a) November 18. The situation was that French West African trade was being carried on almost without interference, and that a transatlantic trade was being developed from Martinique to Dakar and thence along the West African coast. An Italian ship was unloading at Port Lyautey a cargo which was being sent overland to Libya, presumably for shipment thence to Italy. There was information of a plan to organise escorted homeward convoys of French ships at present at Buenos Aires. Traffic from North Africa to France was proceeding almost normally.

Lord Halifax explained that much of this traffic into unoccupied France went on into enemy territory. The French had not answered

---

our approaches for a *modus vivendi* and were probably using them as a lever in their negotiations with Germany, while at the same time they were benefiting from the fact that we were not interfering with their trade.

We had not the naval forces to maintain a full blockade, but, at the Prime Minister's suggestion, the War Cabinet decided to take some (a) action at the first opportunity. They agreed on November 19 that orders should be given to stop escorted French convoys passing through the Straits of Gibraltar. After November 22 the ships used in this control were required to escort a British convoy to the central Mediterranean, and the contraband control measures were not resumed until December 12.

(b) On the night of November 22–3 Sir S. Hoare was sent instructions in the general sense suggested by the Foreign Office. He was told that the French replies to us had been 'tardy and equivocal' but that they had assured us that they would make no 'unjustified' attack on us, and would retain control of their colonial empire and fleet. All we asked of them was that for the time being they should tacitly adopt a policy of refraining from active operations against the Free French colonies, and resist German and Italian attack on, or infiltration into, other French colonies, and that they should also prevent their ports or territories from being used as bases for air or submarine attacks on us.

On our part we declared that we did not seek to acquire any French territory, and would indeed help to the utmost of our power French resistance to German or Italian designs. It was, however, necessary for us to state that, if any part of the French Empire should declare for General de Gaulle, we should recognise such accession, and apply to it our declaration to defend from the sea territory under General de Gaulle's control.

Finally, Sir S. Hoare was asked to repeat our previous statement of intention to restore the greatness and independence of France and to say that this declaration covered those parts of the French Empire which had declared or might declare for General de Gaulle.

These conditions were a provisional arrangement for holding the situation while we were seeking means for reaching a *modus vivendi*. On this understanding we were prepared to begin economic discussions, and to start with a review of the question of trade between French North Africa and ports in unoccupied France. We suggested that the Vichy Government should send a representative to Madrid to discuss economic matters. Sir S. Hoare was also told (for his own information only) that His Majesty's Government had decided to apply contraband control measures to French escorted convoys passing through the Straits of Gibraltar.

(a) WM(40)291.   (b) C12183/9/17.

Sir S. Hoare carried out his instructions on November 29. Meanwhile General de Gaulle, who had arrived in London on November 20, had seen the Prime Minister on November 25 and Lord Halifax three days later. The Prime Minister spoke to him of General Weygand, but General de Gaulle did not regard General Weygand or General Noguès as of much importance for the future. He warned (a) the Prime Minister and Lord Halifax of the dangerous and persistent opposition to be expected from Admiral Darlan. Lord Halifax asked General de Gaulle whether he thought us wrong in trying to establish a *modus vivendi* with the Vichy Government. General de Gaulle's answer was that on a short view we might not be wrong. We might delay, by small concessions, an irrevocable decision on the part of Vichy, but we could not make more than small concessions and these could have only a delaying effect, while, if we were evidently trying to improve our relations with Vichy, we might offend the majority of Frenchmen, who were coming to realise that the Vichy Government was wholly bad and entirely under German orders.

(v)

Mr. Dupuy's interviews with Marshal Pétain and Admiral Darlan, November 24 and December 6, 1940: proposals in January 1941 for economic discussions.

At the beginning of November the Government of Canada agreed (b) with a suggestion made by the Foreign Office that Mr. Dupuy, Canadian Chargé d'Affaires designate at Vichy, should pay a short visit to France, where he had a wide circle of acquaintance. The Foreign Office considered that Mr. Dupuy might be able to explain the British point of view, and to find out the attitude of French opinion towards Laval's policy of collaboration with Germany. Mr. Dupuy was instructed to say that events had falsified the two main assumptions upon which the French Government had concluded the armistice. The French Government had not obtained honourable terms from Germany: Great Britain had not been forced into capitulation. The sole hope of France was a British victory. If France would do what she could to help us, or at least would refrain from aiding our enemies, we should ensure the restoration of French independence and greatness. If France helped our enemies, we should not be answerable for her future.

We understood the French feeling of resentment against us. We appeared as a former Ally who (they wrongly thought) had 'let them

(a) C12865/7328/17. (b) C11885/1101/17.

down' or not helped them adequately and was now taking action against their naval forces and colonies. We wanted the French to understand that we were fighting for their lives as well as our own and that our acts of which they complained were due not to doubt of their good faith or pledged word, but to fear that in their situation they could not resist pressure or trickery by the Germans to obtain the use of French resources against us.

(a)   Mr. Dupuy asked the Foreign Office whether we could tell him— for communication to Marshal Pétain or Admiral Darlan—what guarantees we required in order to be reassured about the French fleet. Mr. Dupuy thought that, although Admiral Darlan was now incensed against us, he would in the end work with us again if the interests of France required it. Mr. Dupuy also asked if he could say to Marshal Pétain that we would allow a shipment of drugs and of milk for children to reach France. Distribution of this shipment would take place under the control of the International Red Cross and the British Red Cross would participate in the control.

(b)   The Foreign Office consulted the Ministry of Economic Warfare on this latter question. The Ministry replied that the French knew that we were not interfering with the import of genuine medical supplies; such supplies were in fact not contraband. We could not allow the import of food to France without making similar concessions to other German-occupied countries and therefore without weakening our blockade. In any case there was no reason to suppose that the French were short of food. Our blockade at Gibraltar was a blockade in name only; more than 200,000 tons of goods from North and West Africa had reached France between September 15 and October 15. The War Cabinet accepted this view.[1] They also considered that it

(c)   would be unwise to commit themselves to any statement about the French fleet. Mr. Dupuy was therefore instructed, if Admiral Darlan raised the question, to reply that he must refer the matter to His Majesty's Government.

(d)   On November 24 Mr. Dupuy had an interview with Marshal Pétain. The Marshal (who looked very tired)[2] was 'rather well disposed' towards Great Britain and considered General de Gaulle as the greatest obstacle. If the General's activities could be curtailed in Africa, the French Government would be in a better position to resist the German pressure for action against the Free French colonies. There was no question of using the fleet to reconquer these colonies.

---

[1] For the question of relief to unoccupied France, see Volume II, Chapter XXI.

[2] Mr. Dupuy's words were:—'He [Marshal Pétain] looked tired and sleepy—in fact he

(e) nearly fell asleep three times at the beginning of our conversation—and I succeeded in rousing him only by loudly repeating the name of General de Gaulle. I must say the reaction was immediate . . .'

(a) C11885/1101/17.   (b) C11885/1101/17.   (c) WM(40)287.   (d) C11885/1101/17.
(e) Z727/16/17 (1941).

In reply to this message Mr. Dupuy was asked to repeat the message to the Vichy Government sent to Sir S. Hoare on November 22–3.[1] On December 1 another message from Mr. Dupuy reached London. He had found Marshal Pétain so tired that he had wanted to confirm (a) one statement in the conversation of November 24. Marshal Pétain had said that the French Mediterranean naval bases would be defended against any attack. Mr. Dupuy asked whether this meant that France would not cede these bases to Germany. Marshal Pétain replied that he might have to cede bases if in the course of negotiations he were offered satisfactory compensation. Mr. Dupuy pointed out that actions of this kind meant intervention on the side of Germany against England. Marshal Pétain considered that the intervention would be passive and not active; he wanted a British victory and would never do anything against the British cause.

In view of the contradictory character of Marshal Pétain's statements, Mr. Dupuy made enquiries from one of his private advisers. He was told that the Marshal's reference to a possible surrender was not surprising; that it represented further success for Laval, but that this success would probably not be lasting. Mr. Dupuy was less sure that Laval could be removed. Laval not only hoped for a German victory but was willing to give active assistance to bring it about. There was a growing feeling in favour of Great Britain, but Laval might none the less secure concessions dangerous to us. Mr. Dupuy thought that Marshal Pétain might regard the release of a large number of prisoners as satisfactory compensation for the surrender of bases.

In reply to this message Mr. Dupuy was told that such a surrender (b) would be a dishonourable act and that we should be obliged to take counter-measures with the utmost vigour not only against the enemy but against those who abetted him[2]. Lord Lothian was also asked on December 7 to call the attention of the State Department (Mr. Roosevelt was away from Washington) to Mr. Dupuy's report. We had received independent confirmation that the Vichy Government were contemplating a deal over bases. It would therefore be helpful if the United States Government could address a strong warning to the Vichy Government, and perhaps suspend the departure of Admiral Leahy until satisfactory assurances had been received.[3]

Mr. Dupuy left Vichy on December 7 for Madrid on his return to London. He reported that he had seen Marshal Pétain and Admiral (c) Darlan on December 6. Admiral Darlan said that the French Government would resist, at all events until February, and possibly longer,

---

[1] See above, p. 426.

[2] Owing to Mr. Dupuy's departure from Vichy for Madrid this message was not transmitted.

[3] Admiral Leahy had been appointed United States Ambassador to the Vichy Government. He reached Vichy in January, 1941.

(a) C11885/1101/17.   (b) C11885/1101/17.   (c) C11885,13299/1101/17.

German pressure on them to attack the Free French colonies. He added that there was now no question of a surrender of metropolitan or African bases. If German pressure became irresistible, the French would invite us in time to take the bases. He was sure that the French ships would have time to leave the metropolitan bases. Otherwise the ships would be scuttled. Marshal Pétain agreed with these views.

The announcement of M. Laval's dismissal on December 13 and the appointment of M. Flandin in his place thus seemed on the whole favourable news, although there was some danger that M. Flandin, as a more 'respectable' politician in French eyes, might be more effective in persuading his colleagues to co-operate with Germany.

At the end of December Mr. Dupuy was trying to arrange to go
(a) back to Vichy, and, if possible, on his return journey from Vichy to visit North Africa and to see General Weygand. The Prime Minister authorised him to tell General Weygand that if he were willing to begin resistance in North Africa, we would support him to the extent of six divisions, with naval and air support, to assist in the defence of Morocco, Algiers, and Tunis. The Chiefs of Staff thought that we could spare these forces from the reinforcements which would otherwise go to the Middle East. Mr. Dupuy was also instructed to say that we were ready to hold staff talks of the most secret character, and that we regarded delay as dangerous. The Germans might come through Spain, close the Straits by taking over the batteries on each side and establish themselves on the Moroccan coast. Unless Anglo-French action took place quickly, the chances of success might pass.

The Prime Minister had also authorised Mr. Dupuy to give this information to Marshal Pétain, since we had heard that he needed support in his resistance to German demands. Marshal Pétain was told that we would provide our expeditionary force if at any time in the near future the French Government decided to cross to North Africa or to resume the war against Germany and Italy. Mr. Dupuy did not in fact return to Vichy until the end of January and did not go to North Africa. The message was sent to Marshal Pétain in the last week of January through the United States Chargé d'Affaires at Vichy, and to General Weygand about the same time by a French emissary.[1] Neither Marshal Pétain nor General Weygand answered these messages.[2]

Meanwhile on January 10, 1941, the Counsellor of the French Embassy at Madrid brought to the British Embassy a memorandum

---

[1] General Catroux, after consultation with Mr. Eden at Cairo, had also—in the previous November—sent a letter to General Weygand.

(b) [2] On January 21 the Prime Minister sent a message to Mr. Roosevelt asking that Admiral Leahy should tell Marshal Pétain that in the event of the resumption of hostilities against the Axis Powers by the French Empire in North Africa, we would give every facility for the mobilisation of the ships of the French fleet in Alexandria and for the departure of these ships to rejoin the French fleet elsewhere.

(a) Z21/16/17 (1941); also Z10741/255/17 (1945).　(b) C12626/7327/17.

covering the points on which the Vichy Government wished to open (a)
economic discussions. Before this memorandum was received it was
known that M. Flandin had told the Germans that economic discussions would be taking place with His Majesty's Government. M.
Flandin's reason for giving the Germans this information was that in
any case they would come to hear about the negotiations. The memorandum asked that navicerts should be granted for the import of
600,000 tons of wheat and 200,000 tons of maize into unoccupied
France from the United States or South America. The Vichy Government offered guarantees that these imports would be consumed only
in unoccupied France and that they would not serve to release a
similar quantity of home-grown cereals for export. They also asked
for a discussion of other imports into unoccupied France.

It was pointed out at once to the French Counsellor that His
Majesty's Government would be unlikely to agree to these proposals.
The Germans were using French bases from which to attack Great
Britain and had to feed their troops. If supplies had to be sent from
occupied France or elsewhere to unoccupied France, the difficulties of
providing for the German armies in the country were increased. We
had allowed the feeding of children under the supervision of the
American Red Cross,[1] and we should probably want to see the
results of this experiment before allowing further imports.

Sir S. Hoare was instructed on January 24 to give a written (b)
answer to the French memorandum. He was told to use the arguments
already put to the Counsellor and to add that, since there was
normally a surplus of cereals in occupied France, we could not
accept arrangements by which this surplus was left at the disposal of
the Germans. Similarly we could not discuss the question of other
imports into unoccupied France, since the French would presumably
be unwilling and unable to put an end to all economic exchanges
with occupied France, while we had to regard France as a single
economic unit for purposes of contraband control. We could not
therefore discuss an arrangement which would give more favourable
treatment to France than to Belgium and the Netherlands. Any
prospect of liberating France depended on our war effort. If the
French could not help this effort, they might at least abstain from
hindering it, e.g. by attempting to run the blockade and by protesting against the interception of their ships.[2]

These instructions to Sir S. Hoare crossed a telegram from him (c)
that he had received another memorandum from the Vichy Govern-

---

[1] See Volume II, Chapter XXI, section (i).

[2] On January 16 the French Ambassador left with Sir S. Hoare a protest against the (d)
interception by a British cruiser of a French ship with a cargo of wheat and meat from
South America.

(a) Z252/87/17.   (b) Z252/87/17.   (c) Z525/87/17.   (d) Z252/87/17.

ment giving detailed proposals for the control by American representatives of all overseas imports. The French Ambassador brought two more notes on January 30 about recent seizures of French ships (a) and repeated an appeal which he had previously made that His Majesty's Government should 'go slow' about interference with French shipping and open negotiations at once with regard to the import of foodstuffs.

CHAPTER XIV

Spanish 'non-belligerency' to the summer of 1941

(i)

Spanish 'non-belligerency', September 1939–October 1940.[1]

THE disintegration brought about by the collapse of France and the entry of Italy into the war had less effect than might have been expected on the two countries, Spain and Turkey, which were of the greatest strategic importance to the British position in the Mediterranean. If the Germans obtained control of Turkey, they could reach Egypt by land. If they secured a right of passage through Spain they could make Gibraltar untenable as a harbour, cross to the French ports on the Atlantic coast of Morocco, and gain control of the whole of French North Africa.

For the first seven months of the war, the danger of Spanish participation on the German side had not been great. General Franco wanted a German victory, or at all events, did not want the defeat of the Fascist Powers; he would also have welcomed a chance of increasing his domestic prestige by the recovery of Gibraltar and by gains in Morocco at the expense of France. On the other hand, he wished to maintain Spanish independence, and therefore had no particular interest in helping to bring about an overwhelming German victory—still less a victory in which Italy would also put forward claims in the Mediterranean. After the German Agreement with Russia, and the Russian attack on Finland, General Franco had no reason to suppose that an Allied victory would mean the encouragement of Communist revolution in Spain. Indeed Russian propaganda addressed to Communists abroad was hardly less hostile to democratic France and Great Britain than to Fascist Spain. In any case, whatever his inclination might be, General Franco knew that Spain had not the means to fight a war and that Germany could not provide them.

The Spanish people depended on the goodwill of the Allies and of the United States for the imports of wheat and oil required to maintain an economy which had not recovered from the effects of the civil

---

[1] Anglo-Spanish relations, especially after the collapse of France, turned so much upon the question of supplies to Spain that they cannot be described adequately without reference to the long and intricate negotiations which were conducted primarily by representatives of the Ministry of Economic Warfare. The reader is therefore referred to Medlicott, *The Economic Blockade*, I, chapter XV.

war.[1] The Allies could reply to a Spanish declaration of war by seizing the Spanish Atlantic islands and attacking Spanish Morocco even if they did not invade the Spanish mainland and overthrow General Franco's Government. General Franco realised these facts. As long as Italy remained neutral, and as long as the Germans were not winning great victories, he was therefore likely to maintain the neutrality of Spain.

The situation, however, appeared more doubtful with the German invasion of Scandinavia. General Franco was not inclined to alter his policy, but the Germans might alter it for him. In other words, they might apply to Spain the methods of infiltration and disguised entry which they had used in Norway, and, possibly after over-throwing General Franco himself, instal a government which would declare war on the Allies. To a very considerable extent the Germans had already prepared the way for seizing power in Spain. There were said to be 80,000 Germans in the country; 12,000 of them were believ-ed to hold Spanish papers without having renounced German nation-ality. The personnel of the German Embassy and of German con-sulates in the provinces was suspiciously large. German intelligence agents were active throughout the country and Germans were employed in the Spanish secret police and the censorship. Other Germans, including agents of the Gestapo, came and went without interference from the Spanish Government.

On April 22, 1940, Sir M. Peterson, British Ambassador at
(a) Madrid, spoke to the Spanish Foreign Minister, Colonel Beigbeder, of the British concern over the number of Germans in Spain. Colonel Beigbeder contested these figures and maintained that the Spanish Government kept watch on all German activities and had taken precautionary measures against a *coup* at any one of the three danger points, the Balearic Islands, Morocco, and the hinterland of Gibraltar. His attempts to explain away German activities were unsatisfactory, but he repeated the reasons why Spain was bound to remain neutral. He was known to support a policy of neutrality, and to take a good view of the chances of an Allied victory. On the other hand the Falangist party, with the influential support of Señor Suñer, General Franco's brother-in-law, was in favour of bringing Spain into the war. At the time of the opening of the German western offensive there were reports of a change in Spanish policy and of further German infiltration with a view to an attack on Portugal.

---

[1] In March, 1940, the British Government concluded a war trade agreement with Spain: the agreement provided a credit of £2,000,000 for purchases in the sterling area. The Spanish authorities produced by June, 1940, a detailed list of commodities which they wished to purchase. On July 24, 1940, credits were also provided for the purchase of Portuguese colonial produce.

(a) C6050, 6271/113/41.

The German successes in France, and the evidence that Mussolini had decided to enter the war, increased the danger that General Franco would give way to the arguments of the party in Spain which favoured intervention. The Duke of Alba, Spanish Ambassador in London, continued his assurances that Spain would remain neutral. Nevertheless, the War Cabinet thought it desirable to send to Madrid a Cabinet Minister whose status would enable him to insist upon direct access to General Franco. Sir S. Hoare was therefore appointed on May 20 Special Ambassador to Spain. He arrived at Madrid on June 1 and presented his credentials to General Franco on June 8, that is to say, two days before the Italian declaration of war, and at a time when it was almost certain that the French could not prevent the German armies from reaching the Pyrenees. If Hitler decided upon an advance into Spain, with or without General Franco's consent, the British Government could do nothing to stop him.

(a)

(b)

It must remain a matter of speculation whether the Germans would have moved into Spain if the French had continued their resistance in North Africa, and also what would have been the consequences of an advance so strangely similar in reverse to the campaign of Hannibal centuries earlier. As events turned out, the Germans did not enter Spain after the surrender of France, and did not regard Spanish belligerency as essential. General Franco thus remained free to decide on purely Spanish considerations whether he would or would not enter the war. On the invasion of the Low Countries he had re-affirmed the neutrality of Spain; with the Italian entry into the war he defined the Spanish attitude as one of 'non-belligerency', but the change of phrase had no practical consequences.

The Foreign Office did not think that General Franco—unless he were sure of the imminent defeat of Great Britain—would decide on war. At this time it was easier in Spain than in Germany to realise the significance of British sea-power and of the material support promised to Great Britain by the United States. On the other hand, if the Spanish interventionists could not persuade General Franco to declare war, they might well put pressure on him to raise demands about Gibraltar or other matters affecting British interests. On June 15 a Spanish force was sent to occupy Tangier. This occupation meant little in itself since the British and French Governments had agreed that, in the event of war with Italy, they would invite Spain to occupy the city of Tangier[1] and the surrounding territory. The

(c)

---

[1] Tangier and a zone of territory in its neighbourhood had been neutralised in the Tangier Statute signed in Paris on December 18, 1923, though they remained part of the dominions of the Sultan of Morocco. If Italy entered the war against France, the area of hostilities would include the French Protectorate of Morocco. Hence the Sultan of Morocco would be involved in war with Italy. From the Allied point of view, therefore, a Spanish occupation of the international zone, which was an enclave in Spanish Morocco, was the most desirable plan, since Spain would not have agreed to an Anglo-French occupation.

(a) C6729/113/41. (b) WM(40)127, C6881/113/41. (c) C7262/5847/28.

(a) Foreign Office considered, after the French collapse, that the question of Morocco was one between France and Spain and that, if Spain attacked or occupied a part of the French Protectorate, we should not treat such action as a *casus belli*. We could not, however, avoid an answer to demands which General Franco might make about

(b) Gibraltar. In fact, Sir S. Hoare asked on June 17 what he should say if such demands were made to him.

The War Cabinet discussed the matter on June 18. They decided

(c) to tell Sir S. Hoare that, if any question were put to him, he should say that he must refer to London for instructions. The reply would probably be '(i) that, for reasons which the Spanish Government would readily comprehend, we could not discuss the question of Gibraltar during the war; (ii) that we should be prepared to discuss any question of common interest to ourselves and Spain after the conclusion of hostilities; (iii) that we should regard this discussion and any settlement as matters primarily, if not exclusively, concerning ourselves and Spain'.[1]

The Spanish Government, in fact, made no demands during the critical days of the collapse of France. Colonel Beigbeder assured

(d) Sir S. Hoare on June 18 that General Franco was determined to keep out of the war, and to resist aggression of any kind. General Franco himself repeated these assurances of non-belligerency to

(e) Sir S. Hoare on June 22. He showed that what he mainly wanted was an end to the war and thereby a means of escape from his own economic difficulties. He refused to allow even the temporary entry of German troops into Spain for the ostensible purpose of holding 'fraternal' parades with their Spanish comrades in arms.

The situation remained unchanged for the next three weeks. On

(f) July 17 Sir S. Hoare telegraphed a report (which he considered reliable) that a few days earlier Mussolini had sent a messenger to Madrid with a private letter for General Franco. Mussolini was thought to have appealed to General Franco to enter the war at once; his strongest argument was that, with Gibraltar in British hands, it was impossible for Italy to operate successfully in the Mediterranean.

With the letter the messenger delivered verbally something like a threat that, although Mussolini appreciated Spanish difficulties, Hitler 'might not understand so well' why General Franco refused

---

[1] The War Cabinet also considered about this time the position of Dr. Negrin and other Spanish Socialists or Communists who had escaped from France and taken refuge in Great Britain. Sir S. Hoare thought it most undesirable in the interest of Anglo-Spanish relations that Dr. Negrin should be allowed to remain in Great Britain. The Foreign Office supported Sir S. Hoare's view, though they did not feel very strongly in the matter. The War Cabinet decided that Dr. Negrin should be invited to agree to pay a visit to the United States or Canada, but neither of these countries would admit him. Hence the matter was dropped, and Dr. Negrin remained in Great Britain.

(a) C7120/113/41.   (b) C7305/113/41.   (c) WM(40)171; C7305/113/41.   (d) C7281/113/41.   (e) C7281/113/41.   (f) C7942/113/41.

to enter the war. Sir S. Hoare believed that General Franco intended to wait for a few days and then to reply that Spain was not in a position to come into the war. On the night of July 19–20 Sir S. Hoare telegraphed that an answer had been given in this sense.   (a

During the next two months Spanish opinion remained divided. Señor Suñer and the Falangist party continued to favour active intervention on the German side; Colonel Beigbeder and the army supported a policy of neutrality. This balance between interventionists and non-interventionists was precarious, and there was always a danger that the Germans would force the issue. Towards the end of September it appeared likely that they might do so if they had to abandon for the time their plans to invade the United Kingdom. The Foreign Office therefore drew up a memorandum for the War Cabinet on the means of countering a German move towards the (b) Iberian peninsula.[1] A march through Spain, an attack on Gibraltar, the occupation of points on the Atlantic coast, and perhaps an advance into Morocco might be a fairly easy task for the German army and would provide a spectacular success to carry the German people through the winter. The Germans might therefore put great pressure on Spain to allow the passage of troops to Portugal and Gibraltar.

Our efforts to counter a plan of this kind would have to be more political and economic than military. The interventionists in Spain would be able to use the arguments about the part which Spain would play in Hitler's 'New Europe', and the consequent economic benefits to the Spanish people as well as the prospects of expansion in Africa. Señor Suñer was known to be on a visit to Berlin whence he might well come back with attractive promises.

We could meet this interventionist programme by a public statement with regard to Gibraltar on the lines of the instructions already sent on June 18 to Sir S. Hoare. In view of the Spanish interest in the matter we could also repeat our assurance that we did not desire trouble in Morocco and that we regarded the Spanish claims there under the Conventions of 1904 and 1912 as matters to be settled between France and Spain.[2] Our main method of persuasion, however, was in the economic sphere. We could 'offer Spain a livelihood'

---

[1] The Foreign Office noted two other possibilities: (i) a German attempt to reach Egypt through the Balkans, Turkey, Syria and Palestine; (ii)—more likely than (i)—co-operation with the Italians in Egypt. The Foreign Office pointed out that the diplomatic consequences of defeat under (ii) would be so very serious that we should 'proceed steadily with the reinforcement of Egypt on as large a scale as the prospects of an attack on the United Kingdom may permit'.

[2] The Franco-Spanish Convention of 1904 defined the boundary between the French and Spanish zones of Morocco. The French Government subsequently asked for a modification of this boundary, and their claims were largely met in the Convention of 1912. The Spanish Government were dissatisfied with this later settlement and also claimed that the French had occupied territory in excess of that assigned to them by the terms of the Convention.

(a) C7942/113/41.   (b) WP(40)394, C10480/75/41.

and apply the policy that, as long as a Government 'remained relatively independent of the Axis, its people could be sure of bread and a measure of economic security'.

Before the Foreign Office memorandum was discussed by the War
(a) Cabinet, Sir S. Hoare had sent an account of a long conversation with Colonel Beigbeder. Colonel Beigbeder had said that there seemed to be a good chance of success for his own policy, which was based upon the idea that the war would last a long time and would not end in a complete German victory. Señor Suñer, on the other hand, and the Falange had anticipated a short war with a complete German victory.

Colonel Beigbeder said that a long war would be unpopular in Spain and might be disastrous to the country. The Germans would put out propaganda that, when all the Continent wanted peace, Great Britain was continuing the war; that Spain would thus be ruined, and Great Britain, if she won the war, would bring back the Government of the 'Reds'. As a means of forestalling this propaganda, Colonel Beigbeder suggested that we should at once broadcast talks on our economic help to Spain and that at the right moment we should make a statement of a sympathetic kind about our political relations with Spain. It was clear to Sir S. Hoare that Colonel Beigbeder was more interested in Morocco than in Gibraltar. Colonel Beigbeder's view was that we could strengthen the forces in Spain which believed in a Spanish future outside the proposed German continental *bloc*. The Spanish Government might then be able to stand up to German demands or at least, if the Government were too weak to resist a demand for right of passage, there would be a great body of national resentment against the Germans, and their entry into Spain might result ultimately in another Peninsular War.

The War Cabinet agreed in principle to a public statement (which
(b) would include a reference to Spanish interests in Morocco), but considered it unwise to make any reference to Gibraltar. They accepted a suggestion from the Foreign Office that, in order to avoid irritating delays over particular questions in regard to the blockade, Sir S. Hoare should be given special authority to settle without reference to London matters of detail affecting ships and cargoes.
(c) The proposed general statement was discussed with Sir S. Hoare, but before the time came at which it was to be issued, the situation had again changed. From information available to the Foreign Office, it appeared that Señor Suñer had gone to Berlin in the hope of getting
(d) from Hitler a promise of Oran and Morocco from a line south of Fez to the Atlantic. Señor Suñer hoped for this 'concession' without a promise on his own part that Spain would come into the war on the

---

(a) C10480/75/41.   (b) WM(40)264, C10480/75/41.   (c) C10486/75/41.   (d) C10395/113/41.

Axis side.[1] The Germans gave a cold reception to his proposal and at the same time alarmed Suñer by their plans for a continental *bloc* in which Spanish trade would be largely controlled from Berlin. They also wanted Spain to enter the war, but in a note to Hitler, General Franco refused politely to alter his policy.

(ii)

Spanish 'non-belligerency' and Señor Suñer: offer of economic assistance to Spain (October–December 1940).

On Señor Suñer's return it seemed that, although General Franco might have to make some more 'face-saving' concessions to German and Italian demands, there was no immediate danger that Spain would become a belligerent or allow the Germans a right of passage. According to one source of information, the Germans had asked for the dismissal of Colonel Beigbeder, but General Franco was unlikely to remove him at once. Suddenly, on October 17, Colonel Beigbeder was dismissed. Señor Suñer became Foreign Minister; General Franco himself took over the Ministry of the Interior and a Falangist was appointed to the important Ministry of Industry and Commerce. These appointments were a defeat for the anti-German party; even so, they did not necessarily imply that Spain would come into the war. At an interview with Sir S. Hoare on October 19 General (a) Franco said that the ministerial changes did not mean a change in policy and would in fact make negotiations easier. The view of the Foreign Office was that Sir S. Hoare should show the proposed statement to Señor Suñer and tell him that it assumed the success of our economic negotiations with Spain, and the continued resistance of Spain to German and Italian pressure. Sir S. Hoare, however, thought it better to wait for a time before approaching Señor Suñer.

One good reason for delay was that Hitler had invited General Franco to meet him on the Franco-Spanish frontier on October 23. (b) Sir S. Hoare had already reported that Señor Suñer, while in Berlin, had suggested a meeting of this kind in order to avoid committing himself to the demands made to him, and that General Franco had not wanted the invitation but could not refuse it. Before the meeting took place Sir S. Hoare telegraphed that, according to Colonel (c) Beigbeder, the anti-German party in Spain expected a German

---

[1] According to one report, General Franco and Señor Suñer believed that the German air attacks would compel Great Britain to make peace: the Spanish claim therefore had to be made at once.

(a) C11166/30/41; C11492/113/41. (b) C11489/6013/41; C10395/113/41. (c) C11460/40/41.

request for right of passage some time within the next few months. The Germans were unlikely to move before 1941 since road and railway communications in Spain needed a good deal of improvement before they could take large forces. It was uncertain whether General Franco would accept the German demands. If he accepted them, there would be very strong anti-German feeling in Spain. We ought therefore to be prepared to support an anti-German movement, and for this purpose we should base our policy on the Spanish army and not on the 'Reds' or on the Basque and Catalan separatists. Sir S. Hoare thought that we should consider organising and assisting Spanish resistance, after a national rising had begun in Spain, by landings at Cadiz or in Portugal and also by sending munitions to Gibraltar for Spanish use. He suggested that the Chiefs of Staff should be asked their opinion on these possibilities.

(a) The Foreign Office submitted these questions to the Chiefs of Staff Committee with the comment that a landing in Spain would seem a 'rather ambitious' project. The Germans were hardly likely to move into Spain unless they knew that General Franco and the Spanish army would give them active help or at the least a right of passage. There was more to be said for a landing in Portugal. The Foreign Office had raised the question early in May in relation to the possibility of a German-sponsored *coup* in Portugal or a Spanish invasion of the country. The Chiefs of Staff had been consulted on the matter, but had given an unfavourable answer on May 29; the arguments against it at that time were that we had no troops to spare and that we had more to lose by a Spanish invasion of Portugal than by the continuance of Portuguese neutrality. The general military position was now better and the question of Portuguese neutrality was not relevant because we should land only to assist national movements of resistance which had already begun in Portugal and Spain.

(b) Sir S. Hoare heard later from a reliable source that General Franco at his meeting with Hitler refused to allow Germany or Italy the use of bases on Spanish territory or the right of passage and that he made very large territorial demands. Sir S. Hoare saw Señor Suñer on October 30 and found him more willing to take action to safeguard the interests of British subjects and, in general, better disposed towards Great Britain.[1] A visit by Señor Suñer to Berchtesgaden in November again brought no change.

(c) The position early in November thus appeared to be that for the time there was little danger of a German military advance into Spain, but that Spanish resistance might be weakened by increasing German

---

[1] Ribbentrop let Ciano know on October 25 that the negotiations with Franco were 'in part very difficult' (*D.G.F.P.*, XI, No. 228).

(a) C11460/40/41.   (b) C11573/40/41.   (c) C11573/40/41.

penetration into the economic life and administration of the country. In these circumstances the Foreign Office thought that two courses were open to us: (i) We could continue to be fairly generous in supplies, and carry through our proposals for credits to Spain on the assumption that, with the co-operation of the United States, we could provide a counter-attraction in the economic sphere to Germany and strengthen resistance to German pressure; (ii) We could refuse supplies or credits except in return for assurances to us and to the United States that Spain would remain out of the war, and would not give facilities or help of any kind to the Germans and Italians. We could also require the Spanish press and propaganda services to be less hostile and ask for proper treatment of British subjects in Spain.

Sir S. Hoare did not feel these two courses to be incompatible. A generous treatment with regard to supplies need not mean giving (a) up control. On the other hand, owing to the failure of the harvest and the exhaustion of Spanish sources of foreign exchange, the food situation was so very critical that we could not delay a decision while we were negotiating about assurances. Moreover we already had assurances that there would be no change in the policy of non-belligerency. We should therefore ask the United States to send a shipload of wheat at once, and open discussions on credits and on further supplies of wheat. Sir S. Hoare did not think it advisable to issue the proposed statement because it would have no effect until we had completed further economic agreements.

The War Cabinet accepted Sir S. Hoare's suggestions. On November 7 Mr. N. Butler was instructed to tell the United States (b) Government that we proposed to continue negotiations for supplies to Spain on a programme involving additional credits up to £2,000,000 by the end of March 1941. We should go on rationing these supplies in order to prevent an accumulation of stocks in Spain. We therefore hoped that the United States Government would send a wheat ship to Spain and negotiate an American loan for wheat and possibly other commodities. We also wished to keep closely in touch with the United States Government in all questions of supply and credit to Spain.

The Prime Minister telegraphed to President Roosevelt on the night of November 23–4 that an American offer to 'dole out food month by month so long as [the Spaniards] keep out of the war might be decisive. Small things do not count now, and this is a time for very plain talk to them.' Mr. Churchill pointed out the danger of the occupation of both sides of the Straits by the Germans. 'The Rock of Gibraltar will stand a long siege, but what is the good of that if we cannot use the harbour or pass the Straits? Once in Morocco the Germans will work south, and U-boats and aircraft will soon be

---

(a) C11573/40/41.   (b) C11573/40/41.

operating freely from Casablanca and Dakar. I need not, Mr. President, enlarge upon the trouble this will cause to us or the approach of trouble to the Western Hemisphere. We must gain as much time as possible.'

The United States Government were inclined to insist upon a
(a) public declaration of non-belligerency from General Franco in return for a gift of 100,000 tons of wheat. With the approval of the War Cabinet Lord Lothian was instructed to suggest that a private assurance would be sufficient. He replied on November 26 that the United States Government accepted this view. The situation indeed was such that the Foreign Office felt it undesirable to wait for the negotiation of political guarantees by the United States. The Spanish Government had to solve the problem of food supplies at once. If they did not get assistance from Great Britain with or without further credits from America, they would be compelled to accept help from Germany and thereby to allow their absorption into a German 'continental *bloc*'. They did not want German aid on these terms, while, from the British point of view, it was of the utmost importance to prevent them from accepting it. The Chiefs of Staff had reported in
(b) this sense on November 23, and the Foreign Office continued to hold that, if Spain were given sufficient economic help to justify a refusal of German offers, the forces of resistance in the Government and Army and among the Spanish people generally would be strong enough to make a German invasion too risky an undertaking.

(c)   On December 1 Sir S. Hoare was instructed to tell the Spanish Government that, in view of the serious economic distress in Spain, we were prepared to grant an immediate credit up to £2,000,000 and that, 'if the political situation developed favourably', we would increase the total to £4,000,000 up to June 1941. We would provide navicerts for wheat imports up to a million tons for the next twelve months and do what we could to arrange for these supplies if Spanish shipping were available. We wished at the same time to make it clear that we were prepared to give the policy of increased economic assistance a trial in spite of the unfriendly attitude of the Spanish press, the public manifestations of sympathy with our enemies, and the cases of persecution of British subjects in Spain. We were making this exceptional offer to a government which had been 'less than friendly' to us, and showing our desire to help the Spanish people in their difficulties. If at any time Spain should give assistance to our enemies, we should at once withdraw all help. If our confidence were justified, we might well try to do more. One method of increasing our confidence would be the cessation of unilateral action in the Tangier Zone. We also hoped that the Spanish Government would try to improve their relations with the United States. We attached

---

    (a) C11913, 12249, 12745/112/41.   (b) C12866/40/41.   (c) C12939/30/49.

only one condition to our offer; full publicity should be given to it in the Spanish press and broadcasts. We also relied on the Spanish Government to do everything possible to supply us with the Spanish products we required.

Sir S. Hoare carried out these instructions on December 3. (a)

(iii)

Consideration of measures to forestall a German occupation of the Spanish and Portuguese Atlantic islands (September—December 1940).[1]

Throughout this period the question of the Spanish and Portuguese islands was hardly of less strategic importance than that of the mainland of the peninsula. If Spain entered the war, the Allies, even before the collapse of France, did not regard the capture of the (b) Balearic Islands as practicable. After the collapse of France, and the loss of the French ports on the Atlantic coast of Morocco, the Canaries would have been of great value if Great Britain had also been deprived of the use of Gibraltar, but it would not have been possible at this time to spare the considerable force necessary to capture and hold them against heavy air attack from the mainland.

The Cape Verde Islands and the Azores, in enemy hands, would have provided bases for very serious interference with shipping and would have deprived us of the use of the transatlantic cable stations. Hence the Chiefs of Staff wanted to occupy the islands if Portugal were attacked or if Spain showed signs of entering the war. The Chiefs of Staff realised that an occupation of the islands in order to forestall the Germans might expose the Portuguese mainland to attack by Spain and that we could not give Portugal any direct help. Our action might also give the Japanese a pretext for seizing Portuguese Timor. On the other hand, the continued existence of Portugal or at least her existence as a colonial Power, depended upon a British victory and the German attacks on small States had made it impossible for Great Britain to go on risking her own existence in the observation of the territorial rights of the remaining European neutrals, all of whom were potential victims of German aggression.

The Foreign Office was most anxious that action should not be (c) taken unless it was clear beyond doubt that an occupation of the islands was necessary to forestall enemy action. Otherwise we should lose the goodwill of Portugal (whose loyalty and help had been of great value) and might well damage our good name in North and South

---

[1] For Anglo-Portuguese relations see Volume IV, Chapter XLVIII.
(a) C13002/30/41. (b) C7429/113/41. (c) C7429/113/41.

America and, consequently, our chances of help from the New World. The Prime Minister was more inclined to take the risks of

(a) preventive action, but the Foreign Office maintained their view that the result would be to turn Spanish and Portuguese opinion to the German side. Hence nothing more was done than to propose plans to meet an emergency. For the next few months, indeed, the danger of a German *coup* receded. Towards the end of September, 1940,

(b) President Roosevelt mentioned that, if the Germans invaded Portugal, the arrival of a British and an American warship would suffice to secure a movement separating the islands from the mainland. The Foreign Office thought it desirable to tell President Roosevelt of the emergency plan.

(c) At the beginning of October the Admiralty wished to establish a close patrol off the Azores, since there seemed some evidence of a revival of German plans to seize the islands as a preliminary to an

(d) advance into Spain. On October 31 the Chiefs of Staff asked the Foreign Office whether the seizure of the Azores in anticipation of German aggression in Spain would have the same effect on Spanish opinion as the seizure of ports on the Portuguese mainland. The

(e) Foreign Office answer was that both Spain and Portugal would regard our action as an attack on the neutrality of the Peninsula. The result would be to bring Spain into the war against us and to give the Germans bases of operations in Spain and Portugal. In Portugal an operation undertaken without provocation and without warning against the possessions of our oldest Ally would create bitter and lasting resentment. Opinion in the United States was less easy to predict, since the Administration was showing itself more aware of American interests in the eastern Atlantic. We should get American support only if we had good grounds for our action and if we were completely successful in carrying it out.

The Chiefs of Staff, however, thought it necessary to reconsider the matter at the end of November. They had found it impossible to maintain an effective naval patrol off the Azores. They also thought that the Germans had a fair chance of reaching the Azores from French or Scandinavian ports without our knowledge, and that, once they occupied the islands, they could not easily be dislodged. At the same time the Chiefs of Staff were most anxious to avoid bringing Spain into the war against us. They therefore had to decide whether to take the risk of Spanish and Portuguese hostility by acting before the Germans or of losing the chance of occupying the islands without bringing Spain and Portugal into the war on the German side.

(a) C7429/113/41.　　(b) C8361/75/41.　　(c) C10637/4066/36.　　(d) C10637/4066/36.
(e) C10637/4066/36.

They therefore again consulted the Foreign Office. Sir S. Hoare (a) was asked on November 29 to give his opinion on the following questions: (i) Would the Spanish Government regard our sudden occupation of the Azores and Cape Verde Islands as an attack on the Iberian Peninsula, and would they regard the Spanish-Portuguese protocol[1] as operative if Portugal should invoke it? (ii) If we did not occupy the islands, and if the Germans demanded passage for their troops through Spain, would the Spaniards resist, and, if so, how effective was their resistance likely to be? Would they accept our help and give us bases in the Canaries?

Sir S. Hoare replied on the night of December 3-4 that the effect (b) of a British landing in the Azores would be thoroughly bad, and would go far to destroy the chances of Spanish resistance to a German invasion of the Peninsula. The Spanish Government would regard our action as an attack on the Iberian peninsula, and even our best friends would feel that we had given the Germans an excuse for bringing Spain into the war. There might be no technical breach of the Spanish-Portuguese protocol, but Dr. Salazar would certainly regard it as a breach, and the Germans would certainly invade Portugal.

Sir S. Hoare had already reported upon the growing Spanish feeling in favour of resisting the Germans. He thought that at all events there would be a sufficient nucleus of resistance from which we should receive an invitation to interfere. The invitation would cover the Canaries and other Spanish islands. If, however, we occupied the Azores before a German move into Spain, the Spanish Government would be likely to invite the Germans into the Canaries. Sir W. Selby, His Majesty's Ambassador at Lisbon, agreed with these (c) views.

(iv)

Spanish action against the international administration in Tangier.

At the time of the occupation of the International Zone at Tangier (d) by Spanish troops, the Spanish Government gave assurances that the International Administration would be maintained. Nevertheless, after Señor Suñer's appointment as Foreign Minister, they began to encroach upon its functions and, in spite of British protests against

---

[1] A protocol was annexed on July 29, 1940, to the Spanish-Portuguese Treaty of March 17, 1939, which was solely a 'non-aggression' agreement, without reference to mutual consultation. The protocol provided for mutual consultation in the event of a threat to the independence of either country. See also Volume IV, Chapter XLVIII, section (i).

(a) C10637/4066/36. (b) C13107/4066/36. (c) C13107/4066/36. (d) C12943/5847/28.

their unilateral action, published on December 1 a law incorporating the International Zone in Spanish Morocco.

(a)   On December 11 Sir S. Hoare left an *aide-mémoire* with the Spanish Minister for Foreign Affairs protesting against this refusal to recognise British rights and stating that we should have to reconsider the proposed shipments of wheat to Spain unless the Spanish Government respected the rights of British subjects—including the maintenance in their posts of all British officials employed in the zone.

(b)   Two days later the Spanish Government announced that they were taking over forthwith the administration of the zone and were therefore dismissing the British subjects employed in it. The Foreign Office thought it desirable to make it very plain to Señor Suñer that we could not accept treatment of this kind and that, if the Spanish Government joined our enemies, we should deal with them as we were dealing with the Italians. We should say that we were now suspending our offer of economic assistance, including our credit proposals.

(c)   Sir S. Hoare was therefore told on the night of December 13–14 to speak in the strongest terms to Señor Suñer and to make it plain that we might find it impossible to secure approval for our offers of economic assistance and to implement the arrangements for the delivery of wheat unless the Spanish Government showed goodwill in the matter of Tangier.

(d)   Sir S. Hoare, who had already asked for an interview with Señor Suñer, carried out these instructions on December 14. He reported that in his opinion there was no chance of the withdrawal of the law of December 1, and that public opinion in Spain wholly supported Señor Suñer's action. The pro-British party in the army believed this action to be in our interest since it would side-track claims to Gibraltar or French Morocco. Sir S. Hoare considered that, if we pressed even our just demands, and cut off the proposed wheat supplies, we should raise an outcry that we were starving Spain and trying to dictate policy to her.

(e)   An answer was sent to Sir S. Hoare on December 15 that we could not hand over 1,700 British subjects in Tangier to a Spanish administration without safeguarding their interests in every possible way. We were, however, prepared to accept a reasonable compromise. Sir S. Hoare was asked to suggest to Señor Suñer that he should submit in writing the Spanish proposals about Tangier. We would then consider the proposals and decide whether or not to maintain our offer of wheat and credit. We did not want a breach with Spain, but we could not be sure that Señor Suñer was not trying to blackmail us with the idea of choosing an opportune moment to enter the war against us.

(a) C13056, 13205/5847/28. (b) C13372/75/41. (c) C13372/75/41. (d) C13428/75/41. (e) C13428/75/41.

Sir S. Hoare saw Señor Suñer again on December 20 and left with (a)
him another *aide-mémoire* with the request for specific proposals from
the Spanish side, and a suggestion that the Spanish Government
would do well to observe what was happening to the Italians. Since
it was clearly impossible for the parties to the Tangier Convention to
meet, Sir S. Hoare was authorised to negotiate a provisional arrange- (b)
ment with the Spanish Government. These negotiations were carried (c)
out with the assistance of the British Consul-General at Tangier and
a delegation from the British community. The points raised in the
negotiations were (i) the maintenance of the existing rights of
British subjects and institutions in the Zone; (ii) full compensation
for displaced officials; (iii) no fortification of the Zone; (iv) the
reintroduction of the Capitulations if the Mixed Tribunal were
abolished; (v) consultation before any more changes were made.

The Spanish Government appeared to accept all the British (d)
demands, but Señor Suñer subsequently tried to wriggle out of some of
them. On February 3 Mr. Eden submitted a memorandum to the
War Cabinet on the state of the negotiations; he suggested that we (e)
should regard the Spanish assurances as sufficient, and thereby
fulfilling our condition that we would continue economic and financial
assistance to Spain only if we were satisfied with regard to Tangier.

The War Cabinet agreed that, although the wording of the (f)
assurances to us was unsatisfactory, we should accept them even if we
could not obtain the amendments which we desired.

(v)

General Franco's policy of 'waiting on events', January—July 1941.

In the first week of January 1941, the Foreign Office received (g)
information that Hitler had sent a letter to General Franco on
January 2 asking Spain to declare war upon Great Britain and undertaking to provide air assistance in closing the Straits. After delaying
for a day and a half General Franco was said to have replied with his
usual argument that, while he would have liked to help Germany,
the economic condition of Spain (whose needs Germany could not
adequately supply) made it impossible for him to accept Hitler's
invitation. Sir S. Hoare thought that in these circumstances—when a
renewal of German pressure was likely—we should act quickly with

---

(a) C13428/75/41.   (b) C13/13/41   (1941).   (c) C303, 588/13/41.   (d) C913/13/41.
(e) WP(41)21, C919/919/41.   (f)WM(41)13, C1232/109/41; C1088, 1716, 2097/13/41.
(g) C232/222/41.

(a) our wheat and loan proposals if we could get satisfactory assurances over Tangier. On January 23 Sir S. Hoare reported that Hitler had asked on January 12 for a right of passage for German troops through Spain. Once again General Franco had refused.[1]

The situation changed little in February, and for some time, owing to the diversion of German resources to the Balkans, there seemed little immediate danger of an attempted drive through Spain. After the Tangier negotiations had been concluded an agreement was made to allow the import of 200,000 tons of wheat a month during February and March and also to provide 60,000 tons from British stocks. Full execution of this import programme was considered impossible owing to shipping difficulties but the most urgent requirements could be met. Señor Suñer, however, continued to delay the signature of a proposed loan agreement.

It appeared at this time to the Chiefs of Staff that, although the Spanish Government and people might wish to resist a German invasion, the army was not sufficiently well equipped or organised to do much more than delay the Germans in their advance. There were, however, large possibilities of guerrilla warfare against the German lines of communication and occupying forces. It would thus be good policy for us, on receiving a Spanish invitation, to land troops in the south of the country and thus incidentally keep the maximum control over Gibraltar.[2]

At the beginning of March Sir S. Hoare gave his opinion that the crisis over the German demands would come in about two months. Señor Suñer was still working for intervention on the German side. He was counting upon a British defeat in the Near East and of taking

---

[1] On December 31, 1940, Hitler told Mussolini that, owing to General Franco's refusal to co-operate, Axis plans for entering Spain in January (see below, pp. 488 and 494) and attacking Gibraltar in February could not be carried out (*D.G.F.P.*, XI, No. 586). Hitler, in fact, definitely countermanded on January 10 his earlier directive (of November) for the capture of Gibraltar. On January 21, 1941, Ribbentrop complained to the German Ambassador in Spain of General Franco's 'equivocal and vacillating' attitude. The Ambassador was instructed to tell General Franco that unless he decided immediately to join the war on the Axis side, the Reich Government could 'foresee the end of Nationalist Spain' (*ib.*, No. 682). After receiving General Franco's reply that Germany, owing to her failure to meet the country's economic needs, was responsible for the inability of Spain to enter the war (*ib.*, No. 695), Ribbentrop told the Ambassador on January 24 to repeat the demand that Spain must come into the war, and to ask for a 'final, clear answer' (*ib.*, No. 702). On February 28, 1941, Hitler wrote to Mussolini that General Franco did not wish to enter the war and would not do so. This refusal was regrettable because, for the time, there was no possibility of striking at Gibraltar (*id.*, XII, No. 110). According to the German record of a meeting between Hitler and Mussolini at German G.H.Q. on August 25–28, Hitler spoke 'in bitter terms' about his 'genuine and profound disappointment' with Spain. If General Franco had made up his mind in January or February, 1941, to enter the war, special heavy 620-mm mortars, and a German force which had been specially trained on a rock in the Jura resembling Gibraltar, could have been used to capture the fortress (*id.*, XIII, No. 242).

[2] In February a small delegation of representatives of the three services was sent to Gibraltar in order to be available in the event of a request by the Spanish authorities for co-operation in resistance to a German occupation of Spain.

(a) C232/222/41.

this opportunity to force Spain into the war. Señor Suñer was most (a) unpopular, but he controlled the governmental machine and, in the exhausted state of the country, could bring Spain into the war against the wishes of 90 per cent of the population. In any case, it was impossible for us to give a positive assurance of military help to the anti-German party, since we had been unable to do so in the case of Portugal.

The British reverses in the Balkans and North Africa in April brought fresh reports of German demands and a greater likelihood that Spain would give way to them. On April 22–3 Sir S. Hoare (b) reported that, according to a personal friend of Señor Suñer, the latter had said that the Germans expected to take Suez in a month's time and that General Franco would then change his policy.

On April 25 the Foreign Office asked the opinion of the Chiefs of (c) Staff upon the line of action to be adopted if Spain should join or seem to be on the point of joining the Axis. Hitherto the diplomatic action of the Foreign Office had been based on the recommendation of the Chiefs of Staff that Spain should be kept out of the war as long as possible. If this recommendation were still valid, we should probably decide to do no more than inform the Spanish Government that their policy had made it impossible for us to continue active economic assistance to Spain, and that what we did must depend upon the acts of the Spanish Government.

On the other hand, if Spanish belligerency had become of less moment to us, or if we wished to take some offensive action against Spanish territory we could adapt our diplomacy accordingly. Three courses were open to us: we could declare Spain and the Spanish colonies to be under enemy control. In consequence we should break off diplomatic relations, blockade Spain, and seize Spanish shipping; we could establish ourselves in the Canaries; we might even forestall Spanish adhesion to the Axis by picking a quarrel with the Spanish Government.

The Foreign Office pointed out that, if we were to take a drastic line with Spain, a very serious situation would arise with regard to Portugal, since, if we did anything likely to involve ourselves in war with Spain, we should in effect be abandoning our Portuguese ally who would then be exposed to the full force of the Axis, and whom we should not be able to defend. Such a course on our part might well have the most adverse reactions not only in Portugal but in the Portuguese possessions overseas, whereas, if Germany took the first step in the Iberian Peninsula, Portuguese opinion would probably be favourable to us. There was also the question of the supplies (mostly iron ore, pyrites and mercury) which we were drawing from Spain and from Spanish Morocco. Finally, a breach with Spain would

---

(a) C2065, 2420, 2997/306/41; C2328/222/41. (b) C4121/306/41. (c) C4505/306/41.

threaten our communications with America and Africa through Lisbon.

The Chiefs of Staff replied on April 29 that we should still aim at keeping Spain out of the war, and hope to stave off active Spanish assistance to Germany as long as possible.

(a) The Spanish Ambassador told Mr. Eden on May 8 that, as long as we held Suez, General Franco would be able to resist German requests for a right of passage through Spain, since he could say that it was useless to close the western end of the Mediterranean while the eastern end remained open. If, on the other hand, we were to lose the Canal, General Franco might still resist German demands, but resistance would be ineffective and short-lived, since Spain had no modern armaments. General Franco might therefore give way under protest to the Germans, or welcome them and provide them with all facilities. In any event the result of German occupation would be the hostility of the Spanish people, although, as in the Peninsular War, this hostility might take time to develop. A month later the Spanish Ambassador repeated his view that, as long as we held Egypt, General Franco would find it easier to resist German pressure.

Until the German attack on Russia there was not much change in the position. The Foreign Office did not think that the Germans would make a move into Spain until they were ready to deal with the (b) western Mediterranean situation as a whole. The problem from their point of view was not simple. They had to decide (i) whether they were prepared to occupy the whole of France, (ii) what would be the reaction in French North Africa, (iii) whether the Spaniards would resist them, (iv) whether the British would occupy the Portuguese and Spanish islands in the Atlantic in the event of a German entry into Spain, (v) whether the German action would hasten the entry of the United States into the war, and (vi) whether the British or Americans would occupy Dakar. It was unlikely that, if the Germans decided to enter Spain, we should get any political indications of their plans. On the other hand, except in the case of Norway, we almost always had military indications of impending German moves. Hence it was desirable to keep careful watch by air reconnaissance on the area of unoccupied France bordering Spain.

(c) On July 11—and two days before the party of three contingents of Spanish 'volunteers' left to fight against Russia—Sir S. Hoare sent a despatch summarising the results of his year's mission in Spain and estimating the general position and prospects. He agreed with the general view that, as long as we held Egypt, the will to resist German pressure would gather force in Spain. If we lost Egypt, this German pressure would be irresistible. General Franco was still waiting on

_____

(a) C4918/222/41. (b) C6874/306/41. (c) C7991/46/41.

events; he did not want to enter the war, but was determined that, if he entered it, he would come in on the winning side.

The German attack on Russia had altered the situation to the extent that General Franco and the majority of Spaniards saw in it not only a chance to avenge Russian participation in the Civil War but also to secure European peace. Spanish opinion was convinced that by the end of the summer the Germans would have occupied the key points in European Russia and that Hitler would then launch a 'peace offensive'. Since we should certainly refuse Hitler's offers, the Spaniards would be especially critical of us as standing in the way of the peace which they desired. The Germanophil party would then take the opportunity to try to bring Spain into the war on the German side.

Sir S. Hoare thought that the best preventive against these moves would be the entry of the United States into the war. There would then be no hope in Spain of an immediate peace and we should not appear as the one country in the way of European pacification. There was among Spaniards a good deal of talk, possibly instigated by the Germans, of a German entry into Spain in September. The Germans appeared to have pressed the Spanish Government to complete the gun emplacements in the Straits and to make certain preparations for the passage of trains through Spain. Sir S. Hoare could not give an opinion about these rumours, but he was sure that British policy should continue to ignore provocation on the Spanish side and to carry out the plan of wisely controlled economic help.

On July 17 General Franco delivered a speech in commemoration of his insurrection of July 18, 1936. The speech was mainly anti-communist rhetoric, but it contained an attack on the United States (a) and a statement that the Allies had lost the war. The Foreign Office considered that this speech committed General Franco to a German victory, and therefore to the Falangist party. The speech was not followed by new threats to British subjects or British interests in Spain, and the purpose of the General's oratory seemed to be mainly to stimulate the flagging enthusiasm of the Spanish people for the régime. The implications appeared serious in view of the general estimate at this time that the Russians might not hold out very long. If Hitler then decided to enter Spain, the chances of Spanish resistance were likely to be greatly reduced. On the other hand there were no advantages in provoking Spain to war. Spanish iron-ore was still being imported at about 60,000 tons a month, and the Spaniards could make it difficult or impossible for us to use Gibraltar as a naval base and a stage in the delivery of aircraft to the Middle East. War with Spain would also affect the position of Portugal.

(a) C8194/46/41, WP(41)174.

The Prime Minister was less inclined than the Foreign Office to
(a) regard General Franco's speech as of major importance. The War
Cabinet on July 21 therefore considered it inadvisable to take any
positive action as a result of the speech. On the other hand they
decided that they would not press the United States to continue against
their will to provide special facilities for Spain, and that in the event
of parliamentary enquiries, they would say that the unfriendly
attitude of General Franco made it extremely difficult for us to go on
sending economic assistance to Spain.

(a) WM(41)72, C8342/46/41.

CHAPTER XV

Anglo-Russian relations from the opening of the German offensive in Scandinavia to the end of 1940

(i)

Exchange of notes with the Soviet Government on the possibility of an Anglo-Russian trade agreement: decision to send Sir S. Cripps on a special mission to Moscow: Soviet refusal to accept a special mission: appointment of Sir S. Cripps as Ambassador to Moscow (April–June, 1940).

A T the time of the opening of the German offensive in Scandinavia, British policy towards the U.S.S.R. had been based—inevitably—on the acts of the Soviet Government since their agreement with Germany. 'Unfriendly neutrality' might be a correct legal or political term to describe the Soviet attitude (in an age which gave odd shades of meaning to the word 'neutral'), but their behaviour, whatever the reasons for it, was nearer to 'non-belligerent' enmity. The Russians were supplying Germany with materials which enabled her to mitigate the effects of the Allied blockade. These supplies were on a relatively small scale but the Russians at least talked about increasing them, and seemed likely, under German pressure, to fulfil their promises. Russian propaganda in Allied countries was directed at weakening the war effort of these countries—and thus promoting a German victory—by attempts, through the local communist organisations, to convince the working class that the Allies were fighting solely for imperialist reasons and that, from the point of view of working class interests, there was no difference between them and the Germans. The Soviet Government, after giving up all pretence of aiming at a common front against fascism, had shared in the destruction of Poland, and had then supported the German proposals for peace on terms which would have secured for Hitler the mastery of Europe. Soviet policy, in accelerating the end of Polish resistance, as well as in the attack on Finland, had followed lines of ruthless self-interest in disregard of the rights of small States for which Great Britain and France were fighting as well as for themselves, and which indeed the Soviet Government had pretended to support in their negotiations with the British and French Governments before the outbreak of war.

On their side the Allies had had to consider whether they might not be compelled, in the prosecution of the war against Germany, to try to cut off Russian supplies, and especially oil supplies, at the source, even though this attempt might bring the U.S.S.R. into the war against them. If it were not possible to defeat Germany without also fighting the U.S.S.R., the risks might well appear justified. The French Government had inclined to underrate these risks and to exaggerate the possibility of breaking German resistance, by depriving her of Russian oil, without the fearful losses of a direct assault on the German fortified lines in the west. The British Government held back from the French proposals, not owing to any sense of obligation to Russia—obviously no such obligation existed when the U.S.S.R. was assisting the enemy—but owing to a higher evaluation of the risks and a lower estimate of the results of our action against Russian oil supplies. Furthermore, Great Britain was less directly affected than France by the disruptive efforts of Russian propaganda and more inclined to think that the Soviet Government were unlikely to increase their collaboration with Germany.

Sir S. Cripps had been one of the leading political figures in Great Britain who regarded a *rapprochement* with the Soviet Government as practicable in spite of the general character of Russian policy. He (a) had seen M. Molotov in Moscow in mid-February 1940, and had come away with the impression that we could at least negotiate an (b) Anglo-Russian trade agreement. A month later M. Maisky had made a direct offer of trade discussions. The Foreign Office were inclined to doubt the genuineness of the Russian offer; the British Embassy in Moscow regarded it as part of a propaganda drive to give the British public the impression that the U.S.S.R. could be detached from the German side. The Russians also wanted to secure themselves against Allied attack and to cause dissension between Great Britain and France.

The Supreme War Council in March had discussed the relations between the Allies and Russia:[1] the British representatives had been much more hesitant than the French and less willing to engage in operations in the Caucasus which would have brought the U.S.S.R. into the war. They had agreed only to study the question of bombing Baku, without committing themselves to the operation. They had also said that they wished to explore the possibility of a trade agreement. M. Reynaud had accepted the latter plan, but had suggested that we might 'spin out' the negotiations in order to gain time and to test the sincerity of the Russian offer.

Shortly after the meeting of the Supreme War Council Sir S. Cripps, (c) while in Washington on his return from the Far East, sent a message to the Foreign Office through Lord Lothian that the Russians were considering a trade agreement with Great Britain, not because they

---

[1] See above, pp. 110 ff.
(a) N2779/40/38. (b) N3706/5/38. (c) N4114/5/38.

were modifying their general policy towards Germany but because they did not want a German monopoly of Russian imports and exports. M. Molotov had suggested that, if Great Britain were not prepared to negotiate by the end of the month (i.e. April), Russia was likely to take a 'decision highly unfavourable to us'. Sir S. Cripps took this to mean that the Soviet Government might make a military alliance with Germany.

In view of the decisions of the Supreme War Council, the Foreign (a) Office waited until April 19 to answer M. Maisky's offer of March 27. The answer (which had been considered and accepted by the War Cabinet) pointed out that His Majesty's Government had to shape their economic policy in accordance with their general war effort, and to adapt to war conditions any trade agreement with a neutral State. They would therefore have to be reassured about the amount of Russian goods exported to Germany and the destination of goods imported into the U.S.S.R., i.e. they would have to be satisfied that imports under a trade agreement with Great Britain were used in the U.S.S.R. and not re-exported to Germany. With this proviso they would be glad to learn 'what concrete proposals the Soviet Government would . . . make for a trade agreement'.

The Soviet Government answered these enquiries on April 29. (b) They stated that:

'(1) The U.S.S.R., as a neutral Power, has traded, and will continue to trade, with both belligerent and neutral countries, according to its own requirements in imports and exports.

(2) The Soviet Government has a trade agreement with Germany which it is carrying out, and intends to carry out in the future. The Soviet Government considers this agreement its internal affair, which cannot be made the subject of negotiations with third countries. The Soviet Government does not contemplate making any trade agreement which the British Government may have concluded with other countries the subject of negotiations between the U.S.S.R. and Great Britain.

(3) With regard to trade between the U.S.S.R. and Great Britain, the Soviet Government contemplates negotiations for a barter trade agreement with a view to importing goods for its own consumption, and not for re-exporting to other countries.

(4) The U.S.S.R. has always fulfilled, and is fulfilling, all obligations it has undertaken to abide by, and, in return, expects the other contracting party to observe a similar attitude in regard to its obligations towards the U.S.S.R. At this point it may be permitted to mention that Great Britain has infringed the "Temporary Commercial Agreement between the U.S.S.R. and His Majesty's Government

---

(a) WM(40)97, N4767/5/38; N4625, 4749/5/38. (b) N5273/5/38.

in the United Kingdom" of 1934[1] in some respects, thereby disturbing trading relations of the U.S.S.R. with foreign countries. Such infringements include the prohibition to export to the U.S.S.R. in the autumn of 1939 certain equipment purchased in Great Britain, and the detention by British authorities in Far Eastern waters of the Soviet steamships *Selenga* and *Mayakovsky*, which were both loaded with cargo destined for the internal use of the U.S.S.R.

(5) The Soviet Government is ready to re-establish trading relations with Great Britain in commodities which are of interest to both sides, on the basis of reciprocity, and providing that any agreement which may be concluded will not demand from either side the violation of its trading obligations *vis-à-vis* other countries.

(6) At the same time the Soviet Government is of the opinion that the release of the Soviet steamships *Selenga* and *Mayakovsky* at present detained by the British authorities would constitute the best possible condition enabling trade negotiations to be commenced and an adequate agreement concluded.'

(a) On May 6 Lord Halifax asked the War Cabinet for authority to complete, in consultation with the Ministers concerned (and particularly with the President of the Board of Trade), the draft reply to the memorandum of April 29 from the Soviet Government. Lord Halifax said that the matter was somewhat urgent and that it would be necessary to consult the French and also to state the terms of the reply in Parliament on May 8. Subject to the approval of the French Government, our reply would be that, if the Soviet Government were willing to give an assurance on certain points of interest to the Ministry of Economic Warfare, we should be prepared to enter into negotiations for a trade agreement.

(b) The War Cabinet accepted Lord Halifax's proposal. Lord Halifax therefore gave the reply to M. Maisky on May 8. The reply pointed out that the Soviet Government had not put forward any concrete proposals covering the *desiderata* laid down in the British note of April 19. His Majesty's Government therefore wanted to be sure that goods imported under an agreement would in fact be consumed within the Soviet Union, and that no equivalent quantities of such goods would be exported to Germany. They also asked whether the Soviet Government could suggest means by which the ultimate destination and utilisation of imports from the United Kingdom could be established.

In answer to the Soviet statement about their agreement with Germany, the note of reply commented that, since we did not know

---

[1] This Agreement, signed on February 16, 1934, provided for 'most favoured nation' treatment between the two countries and for other general measures intended to facilitate Anglo-Soviet trade, including the extension thereto of any export guarantee scheme financed by His Majesty's Government, and the establishment of a Soviet Trade Delegation in London.

(a) WM(40)113, N5449/5/38. (b) N5524/5/38.

the detailed provisions of this agreement, we could not judge whether the terms precluded a trade agreement with Great Britain.

'It would therefore be helpful if His Majesty's Government could be given further information showing the amount and nature of the goods which the Soviet Government have undertaken to supply to Germany under the Soviet-German Agreement, and over what period these goods are to be supplied; whether the Soviet Government are in a position to impose limitation on the supply to Germany of essential war materials, and whether they are prepared to supply similar materials to the United Kingdom; and whether the agreement precludes them from agreeing to restrict transit traffic to and from Germany or German-occupied territory across the Soviet Union. His Majesty's Government have declared their intention to prosecute the economic war against Germany to the utmost of their power, and, in the circumstances, they are not unconcerned with the amount of goods which are being sent from neutral countries to Germany or German-occupied territory.' If they could be reassured on the question of supplies to Germany, His Majesty's Government would consider 'what supplies from the United Kingdom or from British sources can be made available to the Soviet Government for their own domestic consumption, and to what extent they could supply the Soviet Government with an alternative market for the produce which might otherwise go to Germany'.

The reply then dealt with the Russian complaints. The restrictions of which the Soviet Government complained were imposed as a necessary measure on all exports from the United Kingdom, and therefore did not infringe the Temporary Commercial Agreement of 1934. As regards the *Selenga* and *Mayakovsky*, the French Government were detaining the ships and making enquiries about the destination of their cargoes; hence any representations should be made to the French, and not to the British Government. In general, however, since the interception of neutral vessels carrying contraband was a recognised instrument of maritime warfare which the Allied Governments could not be expected to forgo, difficulties were bound to arise if a neutral country allowed its territory to be used as a channel of supply to Germany. If, therefore, the Soviet Government wished to avoid incidents such as those of the *Selenga* and the *Mayakovsky*, their best method would be to reach agreement with the British Government regarding contraband control.

In giving this note to M. Maisky Lord Halifax said that he hoped that it would be possible to proceed with the discussions. M. Maisky, after reading the note, said that he did not feel hopeful of results. Our note mainly repeated in a more elaborate form the arguments put forward in the note of April 19. 'In other words, we still sought to control Soviet foreign trade, and this was absolutely unacceptable to the Soviet Government. We must understand that the only guarantee which we should receive was the word of the Soviet Government.' M. Maisky felt that no progress could be made without an increase in confidence between the two Governments. 'Altogether he considered the attitude of His Majesty's Government to be most unreasonable.'

Lord Halifax said that M. Maisky had misunderstood our attitude. We merely wanted to know what were the possibilities of Anglo-Russian trade in the light of the Russo-German agreement. M. Maisky answered that, if the Soviet Government had made a proposal for trade negotiations, we might assume that possibilities of trade existed. The best way of finding out these possibilities would be to open negotiations. Six weeks had now passed since the original Soviet approach and various documents had been exchanged, but we were still no nearer to an agreement.

Lord Halifax said that we considered it essential, before starting talks, to establish our respective positions. If the Soviet Government thought that this could best be done by means of negotiations, there was nothing to prevent them from suggesting negotiations. Lord Halifax added that he was as anxious as M. Maisky for an improvement in Anglo-Russian relations, but that, in his view 'it was through no fault of ours that those relations were at present so unsatisfactory. We appreciated the position of the Soviet Union as a neutral, and we expected the Soviet Union to appreciate our position as a belligerent.'

M. Maisky replied that he did not agree that the responsibility for the unsatisfactory state of Anglo-Russian relations 'lay elsewhere than with His Majesty's Government. If there was to be improvement in relations, it would certainly not be achieved by any such exchanges as these. His Majesty's Government would have to follow a straighter course, and their attitude would require to be considerably more frank.'

M. Maisky delivered the official reply of the Soviet Government (a) on May 22.[1] The Soviet Government reasserted their view that they had a right to trade with belligerent and neutral countries without the 'subordination' of their foreign trade to the 'war aims' of one or other of the belligerents. They refused to discuss with the British Government detailed questions of their trade relations with Germany, and rejected the British replies to their complaints. Their reply ended with the words:

'The Soviet Government cannot but remark that the very fact that the British Government put forward for consideration questions which rest exclusively in the competence of the Soviet Government, as well

---

[1] The Soviet Government gave the terms of this reply to the press two days before it was presented officially to the Foreign Office.

(a) N5661/5/38.

as the British reply in regard to the Soviet steamships *Selenga* and *Mayakovsky* contained in point (6) of the British memorandum, does not indicate that the British Government has a real desire "to facilitate trade between the United Kingdom and the Soviet Union", as it is so stated in the memorandum quoted above.

In conclusion the Soviet Government considers it necessary once more to underline that it is quite prepared to conduct trade negotiations on the principle of equality and reciprocal obligations without any direct or indirect subordination of the trade negotiations to the war aims which are in contradiction to the policy of neutrality pursued by the U.S.S.R.'

The success of the German western offensive had affected the Soviet attitude as well as that of the British Government towards the proposed negotiations. Lord Halifax told the War Cabinet on May 14 (a) of his interview of May 8 with M. Maisky. Lord Halifax thought that we should examine the Soviet reply to our note in the light of the general situation. For the present the only possibility seemed to be a barter agreement not related to our contraband control arrangements. In any case it was very desirable to avoid protracted negotiations and delays for which the Soviet Government would hold us responsible. On May 15 Mr. Attlee suggested to the War Cabinet that we might send a Minister on a special mission to Russia as well (b) as to Spain. Lord Halifax thought that we had better wait for an answer to our note. Three days later Lord Halifax told the War (c) Cabinet that he felt that the Soviet Government were uneasy at the German advance, and that we might be able to come to some arrangement with them. We should at least find out whether this were possible. Lord Halifax had thought that we ought to wait until we had received an answer to our note of May 8, but on May 16 M. Maisky had told Mr. Butler that he doubted whether we should get an answer to the note, and that the best way to pursue the negotiations would be by word of mouth.

Lord Halifax had therefore talked to Sir S. Cripps, who considered that we had handled the negotiations wrongly, and that we could get an agreement on trade, and possibly also on political questions. Sir S. Cripps said that he was willing to go to Moscow in order to explore the possibilities. After consulting the Prime Minister Lord Halifax had discussed the question with Mr. Dalton, Minister of Economic Warfare. They had agreed that Sir S. Cripps should be invited to go to Moscow on the understanding that he went merely to investigate the situation. Lord Halifax thought that, if Sir S. Cripps agreed to go, we should announce at the same time that we proposed shortly to send an ambassador again to Moscow. The French Government in present circumstances were unlikely to object, and the United

(a) WM(40)121, N5499/5/38. (b) WM(40)123, N5499/5/38. (c) WM(40)127, N5499/5/38.

States and Japan would probably be satisfied with the assurance that we were trying to find out whether, in view of the general situation, an Anglo-Russian agreement was possible.

The War Cabinet agreed with the proposal to invite Sir S. Cripps to go to Moscow, but the Prime Minister doubted whether we should announce at the same time Sir S. Cripps's mission and our intention to send an ambassador to Moscow. Lord Halifax, with Mr. Dalton
(a) and Mr. Butler, saw Sir S. Cripps in the afternoon of May 20. Sir S. Cripps agreed to undertake an 'exploratory' mission. Lord Halifax then told M. Maisky of the proposal. M. Maisky was very much pleased, and said that he expected an answer from the Soviet Government in two or three days.

The Foreign Office, however, considered that it would be desirable to make the double announcement. The Soviet Government might resent a special mission if they thought it a substitute for a permanent ambassador. It would also be more difficult for us, in the event of the failure of Sir S. Cripps's mission, to announce the appointment of a
(b) new ambassador. Lord Halifax put this view to the War Cabinet on May 25. He said that everything ought to be done to give the Cripps mission a chance of success, and that the Soviet Government now seemed in a mood to welcome a friendly gesture from us.

The War Cabinet accepted Lord Halifax's argument, and authorised the despatch of a telegram forthwith to the British Embassy at Moscow announcing the mission and also our intention to appoint a new ambassador to the Soviet Union.

This double announcement made to the Soviet Government did not have the desired result. On the afternoon of May 26 M. Maisky
(c) told Lord Halifax that the Soviet Government had no objection to a visit by Sir S. Cripps or any one else whom we might send but they wished the representative thus sent to be a regular ambassador and not a special envoy.

Lord Halifax said to M. Maisky that although we intended to appoint a new ambassador, our choice would not be Sir S. Cripps. Would the Soviet Government be satisfied if we were to inform them, simultaneously with Sir S. Cripps's departure on a special mission, that we intended to appoint a new ambassador, whose name would be notified within the next few days? M. Maisky answered that, since the Soviet Government had not been aware of our intention to appoint a regular ambassador at the time when they had sent him his instructions, he could not say whether this explanation would satisfy them.

Lord Halifax suggested to the War Cabinet on May 27 that
(d) Sir S. Cripps might be appointed ambassador on special mission,

---

(a) WM(40)132. (b) WM(40)138, N5689/40/38. (c) N5661/5/38. (d) WM(40)141, N5689/40/38.

and that we should announce—before Sir S. Cripps reached Moscow —our intention to appoint an ambassador. Sir S. Cripps, who had left for Athens on May 27, had agreed to serve as special ambassador if necessary. Lord Halifax hoped, however, that the Soviet Government would accept the solution which he had suggested.

The Soviet Government did not accept this solution. On May 30 a Tass communiqué announced that M. Maisky had been instructed to tell His Majesty's Government that the Soviet Government would not receive anyone 'in the capacity of special and extraordinary plenipotentiary. If the English Government really wishes to conduct negotiations on trade, and not simply to confine itself to talks about some non-existent turn in the relations between England and the U.S.S.R., it can do this through its ambassador in Moscow, Seeds, or some other person occupying the post of ambassador in Moscow should Seeds be replaced by another person.'

Lord Halifax told the War Cabinet on May 31 that he was not clear about the relation between this communiqué and our latest (a) offer which, according to M. Maisky, was likely to meet the objections of the Soviet Government.[1] We might have to agree to appoint Sir S. Cripps as ambassador.

The War Cabinet left the decision to Lord Halifax. Meanwhile on May 31 M. Molotov told Mr. Le Rougetel of the British Embassy (b) that the Soviet Government were prepared to take Sir S. Cripps as ambassador, if he were not described as on special mission. M. Molotov added that, if the British Ambassador were entirely in the confidence of His Majesty's Government, his political views were of no interest to the Soviet Government.

In view of the insistence of the Soviet Government, His Majesty's Government decided to appoint Sir S. Cripps as ambassador in succession to Sir W. Seeds.

(ii)

Sir S. Cripps's interview with M. Molotov, June 14: the Prime Minister's message of June 24 to Stalin, and instructions to Sir S. Cripps: Sir S. Cripps's interview of July 1 with Stalin: decision not to take action on Sir S. Cripps's proposal with regard to Russo-Turkish relations.

Sir S. Cripps arrived in Moscow on June 12 when the Soviet

---

[1] There is no record of any conversation with M. Maisky between May 26 and 31. Lord Halifax's statement therefore seems to have been somewhat optimistic.

(a) WM(40)149, N5689/40/38.   (b) N5689/40/38.

Government were faced with an entirely unexpected situation. The main assumption behind their policy had disappeared with the collapse of the Allied front in western Europe. Whatever motives had influenced their decision in August, 1939, to break off negotiations with the 'anti-fascist' Powers and to come to an agreement with Germany, the Russians had certainly thought that they had extricated themselves from participation in a war in which they might have to fight the German armies without much help from Great Britain and France. They had not reckoned upon an early and complete collapse of French resistance and the enforced withdrawal of British forces from the western front. They now had to take into account the possibility that Germany might make demands on them of a kind to which they could not safely agree. If they refused these demands, they would have to fight, at all events for a long time, the single-front war which they had tried to avoid.

Two courses of action, therefore, were open to them. There was indeed a third course: they might declare war immediately, in the hope of saving from destruction what remained of the French armies and of striking at the Germans before the latter could turn in strength to the east. The Russians were, however, not likely to consider this line of action. They were not ready for war, and the French defeat had gone so far that Russian intervention could not have saved France (though it might have prevented a political surrender) and would have committed the U.S.S.R. to the 'single front war', with the risk, if Japan entered the war, of other heavy commitments in the Far East. If, therefore, the Russians would not fight Germany, they might either increase their help to her (at a price), or merely try by delaying tactics to gain time and meanwhile to do what they could to avoid using their own resources to strengthen the German war machine.

The policy of gaining time and of reducing their supplies to Germany was clearly in Russian interests, but it could be carried out only with the greatest caution, and without much hope of ultimate success. The time would come when Hitler would make demands incompatible with the continued independence of the U.S.S.R. On either ground—whether they decided, as a form of appeasement, to increase their co-operation with Germany or to try to stave off German demands—the Soviet Government was unable to be more forthcoming to Great Britain. They were the prisoners of their own policy and could not, for example, call off their propaganda in foreign countries even if they had wanted to do so.

On their side the British Government had now much greater reason to try to improve their relations with the U.S.S.R. They realised that they could not expect Russian intervention, but they might at least try to prevent an increase in the Russian support of

Germany of a kind which might well have a fatal effect on the chances of British survival. Hence Sir S. Cripps's mission to Moscow, which the Russians had accepted, at all events ostensibly, with bad grace, now had a new and immense importance. His first practical business was the negotiation of a trade agreement, but within a fortnight of his arrival, he was authorised to deliver a message in which the Prime Minister stated to Stalin the general aim of British policy, and offered to discuss with the Soviet Government the problem presented by Hitler's success in Europe.

Sir S. Cripps saw M. Molotov on June 14. He expressed the wish of His Majesty's Government to improve Anglo-Russian relations (a) and their belief that the best method would be to start upon economic matters. M. Molotov agreed and hoped that there would be no delays. He suggested that Sir S. Cripps should see M. Mikoyan.[1] Sir S. Cripps then said that there were political questions upon which discussion might be useful but that, if M. Molotov wished, these discussions could be postponed until the economic negotiations were under way. M. Molotov asked what questions Sir S. Cripps had in mind. Sir S. Cripps mentioned 'generally' the Balkans and the Far East. The British Government wanted to maintain the independence of the Balkan States against German and Italian aggression and therefore had 'common cause with the U.S.S.R. who might assist in bringing the Balkan countries together for this purpose'.

M. Molotov was 'interested' in Sir S. Cripps's suggestion of a Balkan *bloc*, and said that Soviet policy in the Balkans was well known. He added that the U.S.S.R. had a special interest in Roumania. At the end of the conversation M. Molotov said that, owing to an appointment with the French Ambassador, he had little time to discuss the Far East, but he indicated that the attitude of the United States was unsympathetic and unlikely to be in accordance with that of Russia. Sir S. Cripps said that we wanted to prevent further hostilities in the Far East and that the Soviet Government probably shared our view.

Finally Sir S. Cripps stated that, whatever happened in France, Great Britain would continue the war. We should thus engage the naval and air forces of Germany, but if French military resistance collapsed, Germany would be free to turn to the east and, according to our information, intended to do so. While we hoped for their sake that the U.S.S.R. would not be involved in war, we might be able, if

---

[1] Sir S. Cripps saw M. Mikoyan on June 15. He outlined the terms on which trade talks might be held, and mentioned the commodities which we needed and those which we might have to offer. He asked M. Mikoyan for a corresponding statement on the Soviet side. M. Mikoyan merely said that he would let Sir S. Cripps know as soon as possible the views of the Soviet Government.

(a) N5840/5/38.

such an event occurred, to give economic assistance with certain raw minerals.[1]

Sir S. Cripps's remarks on the general situation arose out of a conversation of June 12 with M. Labonne, French Ambassador in
(a) Moscow. M. Labonne had told Sir S. Cripps that he proposed, in his interview of June 13 with M. Molotov, to say that the German successes in the west were upsetting the 'military equilibrium' in Europe. M. Labonne wanted to 'compel' the Soviet Government to decide whether they would take—or threaten to take—action which would draw German forces away from France.

Sir S. Cripps asked for instructions whether he should speak on similar lines. An answer was sent to him on June 13 that, if the
(b) Soviet Government were able to create a diversion, the situation in the west would obviously be much relieved, but that they could not be expected to decide at once upon a policy 'the implications of which they [had] always dreaded'. Sir S. Cripps was therefore told to do what he could in broaching the question from the point of view of the general European equilibrium.

On the evening of June 14 Sir S. Cripps was given further instruc-
(c) tions that, according to our information, Stalin and—especially— M. Molotov were alarmed at the German victories but were comforting themselves by the hope that these victories would be followed by revolution in Germany, or at least by revolution in Europe which the Germans would be unable to suppress. Sir S. Cripps should therefore tell 'prominent Soviet personalities' that Germany would be victorious 'now or never', since she would not face a long war. If she were victorious 'now', she would be strong enough to suppress revolution in Germany or elsewhere and also to menace the U.S.S.R., while an Allied victory would not be a threat of this kind. An early German victory could not therefore be in Russian interests.

Sir S. Cripps telegraphed on the night of June 17–18 that the only
(d) consideration which might induce the Soviet Government to make a stand would be a clear authoritative assurance of United States collaboration and support. If Lord Lothian could persuade Mr. Roosevelt to give this assurance, Russia might even yet be drawn into a common front against Germany.

Lord Halifax instructed Lord Lothian to raise the point with Mr. Hull but did not expect a favourable answer. In any case the term 'collaboration and support' seemed too vague to put to Mr. Roose-

---

[1] Sir S. Cripps telegraphed on June 14 that, on the occasion of the King's official
(e) birthday, cards were sent to the British Embassy—for the first time—by M. Molotov, his two deputies, the Secretary-General and other members of the People's Commissariat for Foreign Affairs.

(a) N5808/30/38.   (b) N5808/30/38.   (c) N5808/30/38.   (d) N5808/30/38.   (e) T5803/5803/373.

velt. The Soviet Government were unlikely to change their attitude towards Germany. They had been caught unawares by the rapidity of the German advance, but the *fait accompli* would make them more careful to keep on friendly terms with Germany, whatever their fears or hopes. Germany could now send up to 40 divisions to Russia within a fortnight. Hence instead of quarrelling with the Germans, Stalin was 'mopping up' the Baltic States[1] in order to secure a strong strategic frontier against the time when Russia might have to defend herself against German aggression. It might seem strange that Hitler should allow Stalin to strengthen the Russian position in the Baltic, but there might also be some comprehensive bargain enabling Russo-German collaboration to continue for the time or Hitler might think the Russian army and navy so ineffective that he need not trouble about the strategic balance in the Baltic.

Meanwhile the Foreign Office had further evidence of the Russian policy of using the European situation in order to secure strategic and economic advantages. Sir S. Cripps reported on June 19 that on the previous day the Turkish Ambassador in Moscow had told him (a) that in his view there was no danger of Russia making war supplies available to Germany. The Russians were, in fact, doing everything possible to sabotage their own agreements with the Germans and there was tension on both sides. The Russians might forestall Germany by occupying Bessarabia within the next few days. Sir H. Knatchbull-Hugessen reported on June 20 similar information from M. Saracoglu.[2]

In view of the general situation Lord Halifax suggested that the Prime Minister should send a message through Sir S. Cripps to (b) Stalin. The delivery of this message would also give Sir S. Cripps an opportunity to secure an interview with Stalin. The text of the Prime Minister's message was sent to Sir S. Cripps on the night of June 24–5 with instructions that our one chance of bringing about a change in Russian policy was through an approach to Stalin. Stalin would presumably not refuse an audience if Sir S. Cripps stated that he wished to deliver a special message from the Prime Minister. At this audience Stalin, if he wished, could speak about

---

[1] On June 14 the U.S.S.R. presented an ultimatum to the Lithuanian Government demanding the latter's resignation and the formation of a new government which would enjoy the confidence of the U.S.S.R. On the following day Russian troops occupied Lithuania. On June 16 the Latvian and Estonian Governments accepted similar demands for a change of government and the free passage of Soviet troops. The entry of Soviet troops into the two countries took place on June 17. For subsequent Russian action in the Baltic States, see below, p. 475.

[2] On the night of June 26–7 the Soviet Government delivered an ultimatum to the Roumanian Government demanding the cession of Bessarabia and northern Bukovina. The Roumanian Government accepted the ultimatum on June 28 under protest that they were yielding to force. Germany, having recognised in the Soviet-German pact that south-east Europe fell within Russian political interests, had unwillingly to advise the Roumanians to give way. For later German action, see below, p. 488.

(a) N5853/30/38. (b) N5888, 5853/30/38.

Soviet views and intentions in the face of the sudden overthrow of the military and political equilibrium in Europe. Sir S. Cripps was warned not to let Stalin think that we were running after him in order that he should pull our chestnuts out of the fire.[1] On the other hand, if Stalin made any approach, Sir S. Cripps could express our willingness for consultation and co-operation. He could also say that we realised that the Russians had a powerful weapon in their ability to grant or withhold supplies to Germany. The use of this weapon must affect the negotiation of a mutually profitable Anglo-Russian trade agreement.

Sir S. Cripps was instructed to avoid a discussion of Bessarabia; if necessary, he could say that our attitude was largely conditioned by that of Turkey. If the Baltic States were mentioned, Sir S. Cripps should 'affect to believe' that the recent action of the Soviet Government was dictated by the 'imminence and magnitude' of the German danger now threatening Russia and that the Soviet Government might well have been justified in taking, for reasons of self-defence, measures otherwise open to criticism.[2]

The Prime Minister's message contained no reference to the Far East. The reason for this omission was that the Foreign Office were considering the possibility of a joint Anglo-American offer to Japan in order to prevent Japanese entry into the war on the German side.[3] We could not make this offer in co-operation with Russia: it was therefore inadvisable for Sir S. Cripps to discuss the Far East with Stalin. We could then tell the Japanese Government that the question had not been mentioned in our approach to the Soviet Government.

The final text of the Prime Minister's message was as follows:

'At this time, when the face of Europe is changing hourly, I should like to take the opportunity of your receiving His Majesty's new Ambassador to ask the latter to convey to you a message from myself.

Geographically our two countries lie at the opposite extremities of Europe, and from the point of view of systems of government it may be said that they stand for widely differing systems of political thought. But I trust that these facts need not prevent the relations between our two countries in the international sphere from being harmonious and mutually beneficial.

In the past—indeed in the recent past—our relations have, it must be acknowledged, been hampered by mutual suspicions; and last August the Soviet Government decided that the interests of the Soviet

---

[1] Stalin himself had used this time-worn cliché of diplomacy in his speech of March 10, 1939, to the 18th Communist Party Congress.

(a) [2] In an earlier telegram of June 24 Sir S. Cripps was told that we had good reason for thinking that Stalin still considered collaboration with Germany to be in Russian interests, and that the Germans favoured an improvement in Anglo-Russian trade relations as a means of weakening the Allied blockade.

[3] See Volume II, Chapter XXII.

(a) N5757/283/38

Union required that they should break off negotiations with us and enter into a close relation with Germany. Thus Germany became your friend almost at the same moment as she became our enemy.

But since then a new factor has arisen which I venture to think makes it desirable that both our countries should re-establish our previous contact, so that if necessary we may be able to consult together as regards those affairs in Europe which must necessarily interest us both. At the present moment the problem before all Europe —our two countries included—is how the States and peoples of Europe are going to react towards the prospect of Germany establishing a hegemony over the Continent.

The fact that both our countries lie not in Europe but on her extremities puts them in a special position. We are better enabled than others less fortunately placed to resist Germany's hegemony, and as you know the British Government certainly intend to use their geographical position and their great resources to this end.

In fact, Great Britain's policy is concentrated on two objects—one, to save herself from German domination, which the Nazi Government wishes to impose, and two, to free the rest of Europe from the domination which Germany is now in process of imposing on it.

The Soviet Union is alone in a position to judge whether Germany's present bid for the hegemony of Europe threatens the interests of the Soviet Union, and if so, how best those interests can be safeguarded. But I have felt that the crisis through which Europe, and indeed the world is passing is so grave as to warrant my laying before you frankly the position as it presents itself to the British Government. This I hope will ensure that in any discussion that the Soviet Government may have with Sir S. Cripps there should be no misunderstanding as to the policy of His Majesty's Government or of their readiness to discuss fully with the Soviet Government any of the vast problems created by Germany's present attempt to pursue in Europe a methodical process by successive stages of conquest and absorption.'

The telegrams to Sir S. Cripps crossed a message from him that he had received no reply from M. Molotov to a request for an early (a) chance of continuing the discussion begun on June 14. On June 22 Sir S. Cripps sent a second request and was told that, owing to unusual pressure of work, M. Molotov would be unable to see him for another two or three days. In view of the reference to Russo-German relations in a Tass communiqué[1] of June 23, Sir S. Cripps

---

[1] This communiqué denied exaggerated reports of the number of Russian divisions in the Baltic States and rumours that Russian forces had been sent to those States in order to exert pressure on Germany. The communiqué concluded as follows: 'It is considered in responsible Soviet circles that those who spread those absurd rumours do so with the (b) particular object of casting a shadow on Soviet-German relations. Actually, however, they are only indulging in wishful thinking, being incapable of grasping the obvious fact that the good-neighbourly relations between the U.S.S.R. and Germany established as a result of the conclusion of a Non-Aggression Pact cannot be shaken by idle rumour or frivolous propaganda, for these relations are based not on transitory motives, which may change from day to day, but on the essential interests of the German and Soviet States.'

(a) N5853/30/38. (b) N5827/283/38.

inclined to think that the Soviet Government had decided to maintain their present show of benevolent neutrality towards Germany temporarily, or until this neutrality had been compromised by German action. In such case, an agreement would probably be reached with Germany about the Balkans, probably with a view to exerting pressure on Turkey to remain neutral, and later, to permit the passage of the Germans to the oil in Iraq or Iran. Russia might be attacked subsequently by the Germans, but not early enough to save the situation in the Balkans.

Sir S. Cripps intended to tell M. Molotov frankly that our attitude on the question of a trade agreement must be determined by the political intentions of the Soviet Government. Sir S. Cripps had received no further communication from M. Mikoyan since his interview on June 15, and found it 'increasingly difficult' to get information about Russian views and policy.

(a) Sir S. Cripps presented the Prime Minister's message to Stalin on July 1. The interview lasted from 6.30 p.m. to 9.15 p.m. Sir S. Cripps had given M. Molotov a copy of the message (with a Russian translation) at 5 p.m. so that Stalin and M. Molotov could have a preliminary discussion.

Stalin's main points at the interview were that (i) Germany could not dominate Europe without command of the seas. In any case she was not strong enough to dominate the whole of Europe. Stalin did not believe that she intended to do so. (ii) 'Whoever dominates Europe will dominate the world.' (iii) Russia would not go further into Roumania or the Balkans. She did not wish to become embroiled in the Balkans and was afraid that this would be the fate of any country which attempted to stabilise matters there. In any case the Balkan question was primarily one for Turkey. (iv) Russo-Turkish relations might be improved. The Soviet Government would welcome the help of the British Government in bringing about an improvement of these relations, since they were nervous of sudden action by Turkey. Russia had no thought of doing anything hostile in the Bosphorus or Black Sea, but the question of the control of the Straits should be dealt with, and all Black Sea Powers should have a say in it. Until this question had been settled, Russian relations with Turkey could not be wholly satisfactory. (v) Germany's desire for Roumanian oil was dangerous, but she was unlikely to attack Roumania since, with the Mediterranean closed, she would be getting all the Roumanian output. Germany was also unlikely to attack Turkey.[1] (vi)

---

[1] Sir S. Cripps reported that 'Stalin was distinctly sceptical about the imminence of a German offensive in the Balkans'.

(a) N5937/30/38.

The Soviet Government would not break their trade agreement with Germany. One of the terms of this agreement was that they supplied a part of the non-ferrous metals for goods manufactured for them in Germany. 'It was of no service not to state frankly that some of the imported metals [i.e. metals to be imported under an Anglo-Russian Agreement] would be so used, and if this was an impediment to an agreement with us, [Stalin] was sorry, but it could not be helped.' (vii) Russia did not intend to use her trade agreement with Germany against Great Britain.

Sir S. Cripps thought that the general tenor of the talk was 'friendly and severely frank', and that trade negotiations might start shortly. He also sent, in six other telegrams, more details about the conversations. Two of these telegrams referred to Stalin's remarks about Turkey. From this longer account of the conversation it is clear that, (a) while Stalin accepted the idea that the British Government might assist in improving Russo-Turkish relations, the actual suggestion came from Sir S. Cripps himself. On the question of the Balkans Stalin said that any Great Power which 'embarked on adventures in the Balkans would be drawn into the rôle of a "super-arbitrator" and obliged to maintain "an army of pacification"'. The U.S.S.R. certainly had no such intention.

Stalin's explanation of the export of non-ferrous metals to Germany had been given in answer to a question from Sir S. Cripps whether (b) Anglo-Russian relations were friendly enough to allow the assumption that goods exported by us to Russia would not be re-exported to Germany. Stalin said that, in making the Russo-German agreement, the Soviet Government had taken into account only the disposal of Russian surplus products and not the question of goods of which they were importers. Since the war there had been a shortage of non-ferrous metals, e.g. nickel and copper. Russia was also in urgent need of natural rubber, tin, machine tools and machinery. She had not undertaken to deliver any non-ferrous metals to Germany except a part of those required for the execution of Soviet contracts. The Germans had delivered to Russia a partly-finished cruiser, a number of 3-axle lorries and certain aircraft; as more contracts were executed, the Russians would send further supplies of non-ferrous metals to Germany.

Sir S. Cripps said that, although he had no specific instructions on the matter, he thought that we wanted to prevent the export to Germany of such metals for German use, and that the supplies to which Stalin had referred would not be an insuperable obstacle to an agreement.

The two remaining telegrams gave Sir S. Cripps's general impression of the conversations. He thought that Stalin was professing to (c)

(a) N5937/30/38. (b) N5937/30/38. (c) N5937/30/38.

accept German protestations at their face value in order to excuse himself from acting in concert with us against Germany. Stalin probably felt that Russia was not ready for war and that he could 'stall off' the Germans until it was too late for an attack before the winter.

Sir S. Cripps was particularly satisfied with Stalin's welcome to his offer to help in the improvement of Russo-Turkish relations. He also thought that Stalin took the view that America was 'substantially an ally of ours' and that 'when a peace comes to be worked out, it would be important for the U.S.S.R. to have a good basis of understanding with Germany's opponents' in order to guard against German domination.

Sir S. Cripps did not mention either the Far East or the question of territories occupied by the U.S.S.R. since the war. He concluded that the best approach to closer relations would be achieved by 'some measure of substantial agreement in regard to Turkey and the Straits rather than the prior conclusion of a trade agreement'. If we were to develop a closer political contact with the U.S.S.R. we must make up our minds about the nature of the 'equilibrium' for which we were working. 'Presumably it must be one in which [Russia] plays an important part, and it is on this point above all that the Soviet Government will require reassuring.'[1]

The general view of the Foreign Office was that at all events Stalin's remarks to Sir S. Cripps were an authoritative statement of Russian policy. Stalin had made it clear that, whatever his real feelings might be, he was not prepared to agree with us that the possibility of a German domination of Russia constituted a threat or called for Russian intervention on the side of the Allies. Stalin had said that Russo-German co-operation would continue, and Sir S. Cripps had implied that the U.S.S.R. could not meet a German attack before the summer of 1941.

The one positive result of Sir S. Cripps's interview was Stalin's approval of the suggestion that we might assist in the improvement of Russo-Turkish relations. Even here, the Foreign Office thought it unlikely that the Soviet Government were sincere or that they would accept anything less than a modification of the Montreux Convention on terms which would give them control of the Straits. It was, however, undesirable to refuse to take up Sir S. Cripps's suggestion once Stalin had accepted it; in any case we had already been sounding the Turkish Government on the possibility of a Russo-

---

[1] Stalin said that the U.S.S.R. had nothing but a non-aggression pact with Germany, and that this pact was not directed against Great Britain. The basis of the pact had been a common desire to get rid of the 'old equilibrium' in Europe which, before the war, Great Britain and France had tried to preserve. 'If the Prime Minister wishes to restore the old equilibrium', Stalin added, 'we cannot agree with him.'

On July 13 Molotov gave the German Ambassador in Moscow an account of Stalin's interview with Sir S. Cripps (D.G.F.P., X, No. 164).

Turkish *rapprochement*. There was an obvious danger that if the Russians continued their policy of annexing territory, or otherwise increasing their spheres of influence, they might make demands on Turkey which would drive the Turks to the German side as the lesser of two evils. If the Russians were acting solely from motives of self-preservation, they had more to gain by collaboration with Turkey to keep the Germans out of the Balkans and the Black Sea.

Lord Halifax therefore instructed Sir H. Knatchbull-Hugessen to enquire whether the Turkish Government would agree that the (a) British Government should ask Stalin to define more precisely what the Russians wanted. The Foreign Office considered that an enquiry of this kind would do no harm: it would enable us to test the sincerity of the Soviet Government without committing us or the Turks to any concessions on the Straits. Sir H. Knatchbull-Hugessen, however, (b) did not think that it would be possible for Turkey and Russia to reach a general settlement about the Straits, though he did not rule out some *ad hoc* agreement to meet the common danger of a German advance.

Sir S. Cripps's view was that it would be impossible to get Russia (c) to accept an agreement with Turkey unless it contained some modification of the Montreux Convention. He thought also that we should not approach the Russian Government without a definite proposal, otherwise they might make demands which would bring the negotiations to a standstill. The Turkish Government were not unwilling that we should make the approach, if we took care not to commit them to any concessions. M. Saracoglu did not regard an *ad hoc* arrangement as out of the question, but the Foreign Office came to the conclusion that there was little chance of getting the Soviet Government to agree except on terms which Turkey would be unable to accept. Sir S. Cripps was therefore instructed not to raise the matter with the Soviet Government and, if they should raise it with him, to ask them to define what they wanted.[1]

(iii)

Instructions to Sir S. Cripps with regard to a trade agreement, July 16–17: M. Molotov's unwillingness to see Sir S. Cripps.

After his conversation of July 1 with Stalin Sir S. Cripps had been most hopeful of the prospects of an Anglo-Russian trade

---

[1] For a fuller account of these negotiations, see below, Chapter XVI, section (i).
(a) N5969/30/38. (b) R6776/203/44. (c) R6776, 6830, 6987, 7048/203/44.

(a) agreement. He was instructed on July 16 that we did not find it easy to decide upon our attitude with regard to the Russian intention to supply imported raw materials to Germany for manufacture and re-export to the U.S.S.R. We required to know more about the extent and importance of this traffic, e.g. what were the raw materials in question, and how far they were under British control. Sir S. Cripps had mentioned only non-ferrous metals, but the Soviet Government might have in mind other raw materials such as rubber. We had thought of supplying the U.S.S.R. with tin, and, in spite of special difficulties, we might have to supply nickel if a refusal were likely to jeopardise the negotiations. If tin were the only non-ferrous metal to be supplied, we need not object to the Russian plan, but Stalin probably intended to send to Germany other metals, e.g. nickel and copper, obtained from us. We had also to decide whether we could trust the Russians to send only those quantities necessary for the fulfilment of their own orders. There could be no sure guarantee that substantial quantities would not remain in Germany, perhaps as part payment for German deliveries. On the other hand the Russians would probably not act voluntarily as a channel of supply to Germany. We also wished to know whether the materials were sent to Germany before manufacture, or whether they were refunded later.

If the subject were raised, Sir S. Cripps was authorised to say that we did not like the arrangement, but that, as long as small quantities were involved, we should not make it a question of principle. Sir S. Cripps was also warned not to commit himself with regard to particular commodities, since, even if we decided to acquiesce in the arrangement, we should be cautious before giving away important bargaining points.

Meanwhile Sir S. Cripps had telegraphed on July 15 that he
(b) proposed to ask for an interview with M. Molotov at the end of the week in order to test the attitude of the Soviet Government. He suggested that he should be given authority to say that five weeks had passed since he had made his proposals to M. Mikoyan for a barter agreement. His Majesty's Government therefore wanted to know whether the Soviet Government wished to proceed with the negotiations. His Majesty's Government could dispose at once of some of the principal commodities to other countries, e.g. tin and rubber to the United States. They were, however, unwilling to disappoint the Soviet Government, and still wished to give them a first refusal, but they must ask for an early reply.

Sir S. Cripps thought that M. Molotov would decline to see him. If M. Molotov suggested an interview with M. Lozovsky,[1]

---

[1] M. Lozovsky was Deputy People's Commissar for Foreign Affairs.
(a) N5969/30/38. (b) N5840/5/38.

Sir S. Cripps would say that he preferred to wait to be received by M. Molotov, because he had instructions to put to him (M. Molotov) personally a definite and important question.

A reply was sent (after consultation with the Ministry of Economic Warfare[1] and the Board of Trade) to Sir S. Cripps on July 17 that he (a) could usefully speak to M. Molotov on the lines proposed by him, but that he should avoid a reference to tin and rubber or a suggestion that we wished to give the Soviet Government the first refusal of these commodities.

Sir O. Sargent drew up a memorandum on July 17 which represented the general view of the Foreign Office at this time. He thought that Stalin might well consider that he could do nothing—short of active intervention—likely to have an immediate and decisive effect on the course of the war in the West. Active intervention was unlikely to recommend itself to the Russians, partly because they were afraid of Germany, partly because—for internal reasons—they wanted to avoid war with a great Power; they would also think that Germany would be unable to attack them at least until after 1940. Furthermore, although from the Russian point of view the ideal solution would be a long Anglo-German war exhausting both belligerents, the collapse of Great Britain would offer the Soviet Union considerable opportunities for expansion in Asia.

The Russo-German Pact of 1939 had not worked out as either of the contracting parties had hoped. Stalin had not expected to be left alone in Europe owing to the collapse of France; Hitler had not avoided war with Great Britain and France, and had not gained all the economic advantages which he had expected from the pact. The Russians, also, had seized more territory than Hitler had intended to allow them. On the other hand neither Stalin nor Hitler could risk denouncing the partnership. Stalin was in the weaker position, and was trying to strengthen his bargaining case by threatening Hitler with an Anglo-Russian *rapprochement*, but there was no reason to suppose that Hitler would drive him to this course. Hitler and Stalin regarded the British Empire as the ultimate enemy; on this basis, and in view of their increasing appetite for more territorial conquests, they might continue their collaboration in areas outside Europe. Stalin might hope to divert Hitler from the Ukraine to the Turkish route to the Middle East; Hitler might hope to check Russia's westward expansion by encouraging her to move in the direction of Persia and Afghanistan. The Straits would be a difficulty, but the Russians and Germans needed them for different purposes which were not necessarily irreconcilable.

---

[1] The Ministry of Economic Warfare at this time considered that the Foreign Office were inclined to go too far in concessions to the U.S.S.R.

(a) N5840/5/38.

With these possibilities in view we ought to continue our policy of trying to separate the Soviet Government from Germany and bringing them into closer relations with Turkey. Our chances of success were not good, and we must face the risk that, far from abandoning his policy of collaboration with Germany, Stalin might be willing to co-operate with Hitler in the Near and Middle East. We ought therefore to regard Turkey as the chief obstacle—apart from ourselves—to the path of the Dictators.

(a) On the night of July 30–1 Sir S. Cripps reported that, in spite of his requests to see M. Molotov, he was always being given a refusal. Sir S. Cripps thought that the time had come to make it clear through M. Maisky that we were beginning to doubt the utility of keeping an ambassador with a Government of which the Minister for Foreign Affairs refused to receive him. A reply was sent to
(b) Sir S. Cripps on August 2 that Lord Halifax would talk to M. Maisky but that it would be inadvisable to threaten to withdraw our ambassador. If M. Molotov persisted in refusing to see Sir S. Cripps we should then have to carry out our threat, and thereby admit publicly that we had failed in our attempt to drive a wedge between Berlin and Moscow.

A change in the war situation might still cause a change in the Soviet outlook. It would then be essential for us to be represented at Moscow by an active and sympathetic ambassador who would take immediate advantage of the new situation. Meanwhile Sir S. Cripps should ask to see M. Mikoyan in order to enquire from him the views of the Soviet Government on the suggestions put to him on June 15. He was also authorised to mention to the Soviet Government that we had been receiving peace-feelers from Hitler through unofficial channels.[1] We had ignored these overtures, but we suspected Hitler of putting them forward in order to free himself for action against Russia before the winter.

On August 1 M. Molotov referred to Anglo-Russian and Russo-German relations in a speech at the opening of the seventh session of the Supreme Council of the U.S.S.R. He said that after the hostile acts of England towards the U.S.S.R. it was difficult to expect a favourable development of Anglo-Soviet relations, although Sir S. Cripps's appointment might be a sign of a desire on the part of Great Britain to improve these relations. He gave the usual favourable description of the effects of the Russo-German Agreement, and spoke of the 'attempts to frighten us with the prospect of an

[1] See Volume II, Chapter XXV.

(a) N6072/30/38.   (b) N6072/30/38.

increase in German strength'. At the same time he made it clear that Germany's victories did not bring the end of the war in sight and had not induced Great Britain to listen to Hitler's peace proposals of July 19. In the final passage of his speech M. Molotov spoke of 'serious reverberations resulting from the weakening of one side in the war', and exhorted his hearers to 'increased military preparedness'.

Lord Halifax spoke to M. Maisky in the afternoon of August 2 (a) on the impossibility of making progress unless Sir S. Cripps were able to see M. Molotov.

(iv)

British attitude towards the incorporation of the Baltic States into the U.S.S.R.: Sir S. Cripps's arguments in favour of de facto *recognition (July 23–August 9, 1940).*

Meanwhile the question of the Baltic States had become a matter of acute controversy between His Majesty's Government and the U.S.S.R. The Russian military occupation of these States had been followed by general elections, and on July 21 the new parliaments had voted for the incorporation of their respective countries in the U.S.S.R. The Soviet Government had accepted these applications and had begun to enforce large-scale measures of nationalisation. It was obviously impossible for the British Government to regard the elections or the demands for incorporation as free decisions of the peoples concerned, and on July 23, in answer to notes[1] of protest at the Russian action presented by the Lithuanian and Latvian Ministers in London, Lord Halifax said that he was personally inclined to refuse to recognise 'the results of proceedings which (b) were so clearly fraudulent'.

On July 26 Lord Halifax submitted to the War Cabinet a memo- (c) randum on the question. He pointed out that reports from British representatives in the three countries confirmed the statements of the Ministers in London about the methods of force and fraud used by the Soviet Government. The incorporation of the three States into the U.S.S.R. was against the will of their peoples and was a 'conquest, of the same nature as the German conquests of Austria and Czecho-slovakia and the Italian conquest of Albania'. From the moral point of view there was everything to be said against recognition. It was

---

[1] The Estonian Minister left a similar note at the Foreign Office.

(a) N6105/40/38. (b) N6039, 6045/1224/59. (c) WP(40)287, N6081/1224/59.

true that in ordinary circumstances a refusal to recognise a *fait accompli* of this kind usually did no good in the long run either to the victim or to British interests, but these Baltic annexations had taken place during a European war, for reasons connected with the war, and there was no certainty that they would be permanent. There was also reason to believe that the Germans strongly resented the annexations and that Hitler was resolved to expel Soviet forces from the Baltic as soon as he had an opportunity. Hence premature recognition of the annexations by us would give Hitler a chance of posing as the champion of small nations and of damaging our reputation in neutral countries, especially in Sweden and Finland, where the Russian advance was being watched with increasing anxiety. The United States Government were also entirely opposed to the recognition of Russian aggression. Mr. Welles had issued a strong denunciation of the Russian action, and the American people as well as the Government would feel resentment if we took an opposite line without practical reasons of a convincing kind for doing so.

Were there any advantages in recognition which would outweigh these disadvantages? We were not likely to secure change in the general Russian attitude by 'throwing in' an offer of recognition as an added inducement. On the other hand it was doubtful whether refusal of recognition would make Russian policy towards Great Britain appreciably less forthcoming.

There were considerable British interests and property in the Baltic States—£1,000,000 in Estonia alone. Decrees had been issued for the nationalisation of private property, and our experience in Russian-controlled Poland showed that the U.S.S.R. did not recognise right to compensation even in the case of the property of foreigners. We had put an embargo on considerable Baltic funds in Great Britain and might use these funds for the protection of our interests, but the Soviet Government had already approached us[1] with a demand for the gold belonging to the Baltic States Banks now deposited with the Bank of England. If we recognised the validity of the Russian proceedings in the Baltic States, we should have no legal ground for detaining those assets. Non-recognition might also make it possible for us to use Baltic shipping in British ports. In short, 'expediency . . . recommends the same course as morality'. Lord Halifax therefore proposed that for the time we should refuse

---

[1] On July 23 M. Lozovsky gave Sir S. Cripps an *aide-mémoire* complaining that an order of July 13 from the Baltic State Banks for the transfer to the Soviet State Bank of gold in the custody of the Bank of England was ignored until July 20 and then not carried out owing to a Treasury Order of that date. The Soviet Government maintained that they had acquired the gold by purchase from the three Baltic Banks and that the action of the Bank of England and the Treasury was illegal. They asked for the immediate transfer of the gold to the Soviet State Bank.

(a) N6042/2039/59.

recognition and, without expressing views about the future of the Baltic States, say to the Baltic Ministers that, in our opinion, the circumstances attending recent political changes in their States were not such as to cause us to cease treating them as accredited representatives of their respective countries.

The War Cabinet discussed this memorandum on July 29. They considered that Sir S. Cripps should be asked whether our proposed (a) reply to the notes from the Baltic Ministers would prejudice our chances of bringing about a Russo-Turkish *rapprochement*. They also thought that it would be imprudent to hand over the Baltic gold until we had obtained compensation for British property and interests in the Baltic States, and that we should defer recognition of the Soviet absorption of the Baltic States until we could secure a *quid pro quo*.

Sir S. Cripps was asked for his views about our proposed reply on the night of August 2–3. The Foreign Office put to him in general terms the question whether the reply would be likely to prejudice our chances of improving Anglo-Soviet relations, and in particular, of obtaining a satisfactory trade agreement. They also mentioned that the Polish Government had pointed out that from their point of view our recognition of the incorporation of the Baltic States would create a serious precedent. A further telegram was sent to him on August 3 that renewed threats of a Soviet attack on Finland provided another argument in favour of non-recognition, since recognition would be interpreted in Finland and elsewhere as indicating that we should also recognise a Russian conquest of Finland.

Sir S. Cripps replied on August 4 that he was sending his comments by bag on August 5. He suggested that meanwhile no answer should (b) be given to the Baltic Ministers. On August 6 Sir S. Cripps was told that the bag would not arrive before August 11 or 12. The Baltic Ministers had already been kept waiting for a fortnight, and the uncertainty of their position was inconvenient both to them and to us. In any case it was becoming increasingly difficult to avoid giving a reply on the lines proposed since British property in the Baltic States had been nationalised and Baltic shipping ordered to leave British ports, while we on our side were holding the shipping and other Baltic assets.

Sir S. Cripps then replied that he saw serious objections to our proposed answer. The *de facto* absorption of the Baltic States could not be ignored and was indeed being recognised by the impending withdrawal of our Missions and the requests already made for (c)

(a) WM(40)214, N6081/1224/59. (b) N6081/1224/59. (c) N6081/1224/59.

facilities with regard to this withdrawal. We could justify the with-holding of recognition only by a vague accusation that the absorption of the Baltic States had been brought about by force. The Soviet Government would greatly resent this accusation since they had carefully observed all the legal formalities and there had been an outward appearance of spontaneity about the proceedings.

Our continued recognition of the Baltic Ministers (who, unlike the Polish Ambassador, represented 'nobody' and had in fact ceased to represent the Baltic Governments some time before the incorpor-ation of their countries into the U.S.S.R.) would cause equal resentment since it would be tantamount to non-recognition of the new situation and an incitement to the formation of governments in exile or national committees hostile to the U.S.S.R. We should be acting in a manner inconsistent with the withdrawal of our Ministers. There was no analogy with the hypothetical case of Finland since a Soviet advance there could be achieved only by an open use of force. The United States could afford to take a stronger line, but even they could hardly avoid recognising incorporation *de facto* or blame us for according such recognition. Sir S. Cripps thought that the Soviet Government would not press us for recognition *de jure* if it was accorded *de facto*. He therefore suggested that we should tell the Baltic Ministers that they had become *de facto* private citizens and that, if we refrained—as we wished to do—from granting *de jure* recognition to the incorporation, they must avoid raising embar-rassing questions which might force our hand.

Sir S. Cripps saw no legal justification for our retention of the Baltic assets or for their use as part of a bargain over recognition. These assets had been blocked before the incorporation of the Baltic States and their transfer had been ordered with due regard for legal formalities while the States were still independent. We might be able to hold on to them without legal justification but such action would gravely prejudice Anglo-Soviet relations. In any case the proposed bargain would not attract the Soviet Government since they had already secured *de facto* recognition in large and sufficient measure.

The Foreign Office considered that it would be better not to give an official reply to the Baltic Ministers, but to tell them verbally and privately that they had better not press for an official ruling and that, if they took no action, their names would remain in the Diplomatic List, i.e. they would continue for the present to enjoy diplomatic immunities. At the same time we should grant *de facto* recognition to the claim of the Soviet Government that the Baltic States were legally incorporated into the U.S.S.R. We should withdraw our Missions, but make no announcement on the subject until we were asked to do so by Parliament or by the Soviet Government. Our answer would then be that the facts had compelled us to grant *de facto* recognition, but that we did not propose to grant *de jure* recognition to any transfers of sovereignty or territory which had taken place during and as a result of the war, since we must reserve our full liberty of decision for the peace settlement. We should put in at once a formal claim for compensation on behalf of British interests and subjects whose property in the Baltic States had been nationalised and therefore confiscated by the Soviet Government. We should tell the Soviet Government that we would pay this compensation out of the Baltic gold and discuss with them the disposal of the balance. Finally, we ought to offer to discuss the ultimate ownership of the Baltic ships as part of a general settlement which would include a new trade agreement.

On August 8, however, the War Cabinet decided to defer a (a) decision on the whole question. On August 9 Lord Halifax told the (b) War Cabinet that he could not yet make a recommendation on the subject, and that there seemed little prospect of getting the Soviet Government to agree to provide compensation.

(v)

Sir S. Cripps's interview of August 7 with M. Molotov and proposals to His Majesty's Government for an approach to the Soviet Government: reply to Sir S. Cripps's proposals: Sir S. Cripps's objections to His Majesty's Government's suggestions with regard to the Baltic question (August 7–20, 1940).

On August 7 Sir S. Cripps was at last able to secure an interview with M. Molotov. He carried out the instructions sent to him on (c) August 2, and said that the contrast between the Soviet attitude towards Germany and their attitude towards Great Britain showed neither a strict neutrality nor an encouragement to Great Britain to improve Anglo-Soviet relations. If the Soviet Government desired such improvement, they should take steps to demonstrate the fact. Sir S. Cripps then dealt with the trade negotiations on the lines of his instructions. He spoke of the eight weeks of silence and delay on the part of the Soviet Government and asked whether they wanted to proceed with negotiations.

M. Molotov in reply said that Anglo-Soviet relations had been discussed with Stalin and that on the general question he had nothing to add. With regard to the 'inequality' of Soviet neutrality towards

(a) WM(40)222. (b) WM(40)223, N5081/4220/15. (c) N6105/40/38.

Germany and Great Britain he pointed out (i) that the Soviet Government had a non-aggression pact with Germany and no pact with Great Britain. This fact was of great importance. (ii) The discussions with Great Britain in 1939 had been 'abortive'. (iii) Other Russo-German agreements were of vital importance to Soviet foreign policy, e.g. the U.S.S.R. had been able to secure their interests in the Western Ukraine and White Russia, and to adjust their relations with the Baltic States. (iv) The Russo-German Trade Agreement was of great importance in securing machinery and military supplies in return for goods which the U.S.S.R. could spare. (v) The commercial transactions entered into with Great Britain in 1939 had not been fulfilled. (vi) Relations with Germany were more favourable, partly for geographical reasons. The U.S.S.R. had a long frontier with Germany but there was a geographical barrier between the U.S.S.R. and Great Britain.

There was certainly a difference between the attitude of the U.S.S.R. to Germany and to Great Britain, but this difference 'lay within the limits of Soviet neutrality', and the Soviet Government recognised the possibility of improving relations with Great Britain. An improvement in economic relations would be the means of improving political relations. Great Britain, however, had again 'entered on the path of injuring Soviet interests in the matter of the gold of the Baltic States'. This hostility had been met in other cases, e.g. the 'two ships'.[1] Such obstacles did not occur in Russo-German relations.

No one could expect the U.S.S.R. to violate the non-aggression pact with Germany, but, if Great Britain would try 'to preserve relations on acceptable conditions, this will be fully capable of being realised'. M. Molotov said that he would ask M. Mikoyan to meet Sir S. Cripps: 'If no questions crop up like that of the gold, it will help matters'. On the other hand, the Soviet Government could hardly be expected to make the first gesture towards better relations since they were the injured party in the matter of the gold.

During the conversation Sir S. Cripps asked whether the Soviet Government would be willing to conclude a non-aggression pact with Great Britain. M. Molotov made no direct reply. He also gave no answer to a remark from Sir S. Cripps that the Soviet Government had delayed the trade negotiations for six weeks before any question had arisen about the Baltic gold.

Sir S. Cripps's view of the conversation was that it confirmed his estimate that for the present Russo-German relations could not be shaken, but there might ultimately be a change and, even earlier, a diminution of Soviet help to Germany. We must therefore decide whether 'to go all out for better Anglo-Soviet relations with the object

---

[1] The reference here is probably to the s.s. *Selenga* and *Mayakovsky*.

of gradually divorcing Russia from Germany or to leave these relations to get along as best they can. No middle course would be worth while, since its adoption would not achieve the desired object and would only embarrass British policy in other spheres.'

The first alternative, which Sir S. Cripps strongly recommended, meant 'some sacrifice and a thoroughness equal to that of Germany'. The Soviet Government were not yet convinced of the genuineness of our professed desire for better relations and our action with regard to the Baltic assets and ships was a stumbling-block. Therefore, unless we decided that it was not worth while trying to influence the Soviet Government, we should approach them as follows:

(i) We concluded from Sir S. Cripps's interviews with MM. Stalin and Molotov that the Soviet Government shared our desire for a better understanding. For this purpose, and on the definite assumption that it would remove all existing causes of misunderstanding, we were ready to transfer forthwith the Baltic gold and release the Baltic ships.

(ii) Since the Soviet Government had indicated that they attached importance to non-aggression pacts as the basis of friendly relations between the U.S.S.R. and other countries, we should welcome such a pact, and proposed that it should be negotiated forthwith.

(iii) We should assume that the Soviet Government would regard this pact as inaugurating a new era in Anglo-Russian relations, and would henceforth conduct their dealings with us in as friendly a spirit of neutrality as that governing their relations with Germany. On this basis we should expect to be allowed such free access to surplus Russian commodities as was consistent with existing arrangements, and to enter at once into negotiations for a barter agreement. We should also expect the Soviet Government to afford to British subjects in the U.S.S.R. the same facilities and advantages, and to British diplomatic and consular representatives the same privileges as were enjoyed by Germany. We should accord corresponding facilities to the U.S.S.R. in Great Britain.

With the approval of the War Cabinet, the Foreign Office replied to Sir S. Cripps on August 13 that we wished to give him the fullest (a) support in the task of improving Anglo-Russian relations, although we expected the Soviet Government to be extremely cautious *vis-à-vis* Germany at least as long as they were doubtful whether we could maintain and improve our position at home and in the Mediterranean. We saw, however, great difficulty in giving *de jure* recognition to the incorporation of the Baltic States into the U.S.S.R. In addition to the reasons already mentioned to Sir S. Cripps, we could not allow ourselves to be driven into a position from which we should find it hard to refuse recognition of every *fait accompli* by countries

---

(a) WM(40)225, N6081/1224/59; N6105/40/38.

like Russia or Japan. It was also necessary to avoid giving precedents for the recognition of German *faits accomplis* by other countries: e.g. Sweden was being tempted to recognise a German-controlled régime in Norway. Hence our only safe course was to adhere to the logically defensible proposition that political changes brought about during the war ought not to be recognised *de jure* pending a general peace settlement.

Nevertheless, in deference to Sir S. Cripps's views, we were informing the Baltic Ministers orally and privately that no official answer would be returned to their Notes (though their names would remain on the diplomatic list).[1] We would also hold up the decision to requisition the Baltic ships. Furthermore Sir S. Cripps could tell the Soviet Government that we were prepared to recognise them as *de facto* in administrative control of the Baltic States and to deal with them on that basis in matters affecting those States. The Soviet Government must not, however, use this statement as the basis of a legal claim in the English courts to Baltic assets while refusing to pay compensation for seizure of British property in the Baltic States.

We were bound to do our best to secure this compensation and must retain the Baltic gold and ships for the purpose, but, if the Soviet Government refused direct payment, we might agree to recognise their claim for the gold and the ships (thus incidentally according *de facto* recognition) in return for a separate and, possibly, unofficial understanding that we should use the gold and ships to recoup ourselves for the loss of British property in the Baltic States. We should not in any circumstances hand over the gold until we had received satisfactory compensation for British interests. The Soviet Government would receive the balance in full settlement of their claims.

On general grounds we doubted the value of a major concession at this stage. Evidence of our determination to defend our interests might be as valuable as a gesture of unilateral generosity in preparing the way for a future improvement of Anglo-Soviet relations. Finally, Sir S. Cripps was instructed not to speak to M. Molotov on the lines suggested by him until we had given further consideration to his proposals.

(a)   On August 14 Sir S. Cripps was informed[2] that we did not feel able to commit ourselves to an arrangement involving the Baltic assets without consulting the United States Government; Sir S. Cripps might therefore prefer to suspend action for the time being on his instructions of August 13.

(b)   [1] This verbal answer was given to the three Ministers on August 14.

[2] On August 15, Sir S. Cripps was informed that, from the intercepted correspondence of a German firm, Russo-German negotiations appeared to be taking place with regard to
(c)   German property in the Baltic States.

(a) N6105/40/38. (b) N6325/1224/59. (c) N6105/40/38.

This telegram crossed a reply from Sir S. Cripps that it would be impossible to induce the Soviet Government to agree not to use our (a) proposed statement to them as the basis of a claim in the English Courts for the return of the Baltic assets. In any case our *de facto* recognition would be manifest even without a statement, and we could not deny it if the point were raised by an English court to which such a claim was addressed. Sir S. Cripps also thought that, in view of the far-reaching questions of principle and precedent involved in the matter, the Soviet Government would not agree to a deal on the lines suggested by us. Even the most 'unofficial' understanding about the retention of the Baltic assets would be generally known and would prejudice the Soviet position in principle. Hence as a tactical move there was no advantage in lodging an immediate claim to compensation. Perhaps 'for form's sake', we might have to lodge a claim, but our action would irritate the Soviet Government. We should therefore be wise to delay it until we had obtained the necessary facilities for the evacuation of the British Missions from the Baltic States.

Sir S. Cripps repeated his view that it was not too early to prepare the ground for an improvement in Anglo-Soviet relations 'which is admittedly not likely to crystallise'. From our point of view the release of the Baltic assets might be a major concession, but from the Russian point of view, our retention of these assets as a bargaining counter was an illegal act, and hence 'a gesture of defiance'. If the Soviet Government were not open to a bargain on the subject, and if they did not attempt, or failed to secure, their object by recourse to the English courts, the impasse would still be a cause of Soviet ill-will when other factors in the international situation might be conducive to a real improvement in our relations with them. Sir S. Cripps felt that he could not create a general psychological improvement in the atmosphere unless he were given practical means of doing so. His proposals had been put forward as part of a general bargain. If the Baltic question were settled by a separate deal, the whole scheme would appear less attractive to the Soviet Government. If the question were not eliminated, Soviet resentment would remain and it would be less worth while putting forward the scheme.

On August 20 Sir S. Cripps was told that, for the time, he need not attempt any negotiations with the Soviet Government but that, as (b) soon as agreement had been reached about a time limit for the closing down of our Missions, he should make a general reservation of our rights with regard to British property in the Baltic States on the same terms as our reservation with regard to British property in Soviet-occupied Poland. M. Maisky, in conversation with Lord Halifax, had (c) not ruled out the possibility of a bargain and Lord Halifax would

---

(a) N6263/40/38.   (b) N6263/40/38.   (c) N6250/1224/59.

sound him on the matter as soon as we knew the attitude of the
United States.

(vi)

*Proposal from the U.S.S.R. for a limited barter deal: exchange of views with
the United States on the question of the Baltic assets: proposal to the U.S.S.R.
for the abandonment by them and by His Majesty's Government of their
respective claims (August 22—September 29, 1940).*

(a) On August 22, M. Mikoyan proposed to Sir S. Cripps a limited
barter deal of 5,000 tons of flax in exchange for rubber. Sir S. Cripps
said that circumstances had probably altered during the ten weeks'
delay since his first discussion with M. Mikoyan, and that we wanted
an 'all in' barter agreement and would probably not be attracted by
a limited deal. M. Mikoyan objected that the time was unsuitable for
a general agreement. We were detaining the Baltic gold and shipping
and there was no guarantee that we would not seize other goods in an
equally illegal manner. Sir S. Cripps asked whether the Baltic
questions were the only obstacle to an agreement. M. Mikoyan at
first said that there were other questions too numerous to mention: later
he admitted, grudgingly, that there were no other real obstacles. Sir
S. Cripps thought it clear that M. Mikoyan had been instructed to
take a 'general line' on the unreliability of the British Government.

Sir S. Cripps said that we had a counter-claim, exceeding[1] the
value of the gold, in respect of confiscated British property. M.
Mikoyan finally agreed that it would be best to attempt a settlement
of the political questions before entering on the general trade talks.
He repeated, however, that the Soviet Government were ready to
conclude the limited deal which he had proposed.

Sir S. Cripps thought that the Soviet Government were particularly
anxious to obtain supplies of rubber and that, if our need of flax were
urgent,[2] we could negotiate the deal. Otherwise he recommended
'a certain coolness and detachment, refusing to deal with trade

---

(b) [1] Sir S. Cripps was informed on August 17 that the British claim was likely to amount at
least to £6,000,000 (property and investments, £4,000,000: British holdings in State and
municipal loans, £1,500,000: trade debts, guaranteed by the Export Credits Guarantee
Department, nearly £500,000).

(c) [2] A reply was sent to this telegram on September 19, after discussion with the Departments concerned, that we had no urgent need of flax for domestic use, but that we needed
it for our export trade in linen manufacture to dollar countries. Sir S. Cripps was therefore
asked to use his judgment whether to accept the offer. He could point out that boasts in
the Soviet press that the U.S.S.R. was helping Germany to defeat our blockade did not
increase our readiness to supply the Soviet Government with rubber. The Russian
'limited offer' was indeed unattractive because rubber was a 'dangerous commodity' from
the point of view of the blockade and because M. Mikoyan's remarks made it very clear
that the proposal was intended to frustrate rather than facilitate wider discussions.

(a) N6372/5/38.   (b) N6105/40/38.   (c) N6372/5/38.

questions piecemeal'. He also thought that British air successes had slightly influenced the Soviet Government and that there might now be a possibility of reaching an agreement on the political side.

The Foreign Office was unable to send further instructions to Sir S. Cripps on the Baltic questions for some time owing to delay caused by consideration of the attitude of the United States. Lord Lothian had been instructed on August 16 to explain the situation to Mr. Hull (a) and to ensure that action on our part would not lead the United States Government to modify their policy with regard to blocked foreign assets and, above all, the French gold in the United States.

Lord Lothian replied on August 28 that the release of the Baltic assets in London would cause the United States considerable (b) embarrassment. Before speaking to Mr. Hull, he wished to put forward certain considerations: (i) The United States Government had frozen, ostensibly for juridical reasons, but also on moral grounds, the assets of territories occupied by Germany and Russia. We had welcomed this action and had asked for the freezing of all German and Italian assets. The United States Government believed that their action was of help to us, and any breach in the principle would discourage them. (ii) The United States Government had recently rejected a Russian protest against the extension of their freezing order. Our release of the Baltic assets would greatly weaken their position. If the Soviet Ambassador in Washington asked them for similar treatment, they might be embarrassed in their negotiations with him on the improvement of Russo-American relations with a view to common pressure on Japan. (iii) We had provided for the postponement until the end of the war of a decision about the disposal of blocked assets. We wished the United States to adopt the same course, but the Vichy Government might ask for the release of assets belonging to unoccupied France. In any case the United States would find it difficult to resist this demand, and our action would increase the difficulty.

An answer to this telegram was sent on September 1. Lord Lothian was asked to explain that we did not propose to give back the gold (c) and the ships unconditionally, but only as part of an arrangement which would secure compensation for confiscated British property. We hoped that an arrangement of this kind might facilitate the con- clusion of a trade agreement and remove one of the obstacles in the way of an improvement in Anglo-Russian relations when the inter- national situation had changed in our favour. Hence we wanted to avoid a 'continuous deadlock' over the Baltic gold and ships.

Lord Lothian answered on September 6 that, before seeing Mr. (d) Hull, he had thought it best to arrange an informal discussion between two members of His Majesty's Embassy and Mr. Atherton and Mr.

(a) N6105/40/38. (b) N6454/2039/59. (c) N6454/2039/59. (d) N6454/2039/59.

Henderson[1] of the State Department. The American representatives made it very clear that they did not expect us to be able to reach a comprehensive agreement with the U.S.S.R. The Soviet Government would merely continue indefinitely their method of raising one detailed question after another as a 'pre-condition' of wider discussions. On the particular question of Baltic assets the United States Government would probably not relax their own freezing measures, or change their policy with regard to French assets as a result of action by us. Nevertheless Lord Lothian repeated his view that, if we released the Baltic assets, we should find it difficult to urge the United States Government to maintain their restrictions on French assets when pressure was put upon them by the Vichy Government.

In view of Lord Lothian's advice, Lord Halifax told M. Maisky on
(a) September 10 that we must give up the idea of a 'deal' on the Baltic questions unless the Soviet Government were willing to renounce their claim to the gold in return for the abandonment of our claim to compensation. If the Soviet Government would not agree to the arrangement, the situation could continue as at present (i.e. we should hold the gold and the Soviet Government would enjoy the use of the confiscated property) without prejudice to our mutual good relations in other respects and particularly with regard to the negotiations for a trade agreement.

M. Maisky asked what we proposed to do about the Baltic ships. Lord Halifax suggested that we might hire the ships during the war and pay for the hire to the Soviet Government after the war, since in English Law the ownership of ships could depend in some cases on *de facto* occupation of territory rather than *de jure* sovereignty. M. Maisky then enquired whether we should hand over to the U.S.S.R. the Baltic Legations in London as part of a general settlement. Lord Halifax explained that this question raised the same difficulties of principle as the surrender of the gold. He therefore advised M. Maisky not to press the matter.

Sir S. Cripps discussed the question with M. Vyshinsky[2] on
(b) September 14. M. Vyshinsky gave the impression that the Soviet Government would accept a 'deal' in the matter, but Sir S. Cripps had made it clear that we could not give way on the question of principle. M. Vyshinsky said that in this case it would be impossible to take up the subject of improved or wider trade relations. Sir S. Cripps said that we should then have to base our economic policy on the assumption that we should have no trade with Russia.

---

[1] Mr. Atherton was Head of the European Division and Mr. Henderson a Russian expert in the State Department.

[2] M. Vyshinsky's appointment as Deputy Commissar for Foreign Affairs was announced on September 8. M. Vyshinsky had previously been State Prosecutor.

(a) N6454/2039/59.   (b) N6594/2039/59.

After M. Vyshinsky had answered unfavourably the suggestion that for the duration of the war both sides should leave their claims standing, Sir S. Cripps proposed that the claims might be put aside for a limited period, e.g. six months. The German offensive against Great Britain might then be defeated and conditions might be more favourable to a settlement. M. Vyshinsky promised to submit this suggestion to his colleagues, but no answer was received about it.[1]

(vii)

The Brenner meeting between Hitler and Mussolini, October 4: Sir S. Cripps's suggestion for an Anglo-Soviet agreement: instructions to Sir S. Cripps, October 13–16: Sir S. Cripps's interview of October 22 with M. Vyshinsky: visit of M. Molotov to Berlin: Sir S. Cripps's interview of November 11 with M. Vyshinsky: question of the withdrawal of the British offer of an economic agreement (October–December 1940).

At the beginning of October, 1940, Anglo-Russian relations showed no obvious improvement. No trade agreement had been reached; the questions arising out of the Russian annexation of the Baltic States were not within sight of settlement. The attempts to secure a Russo-Turkish *rapprochement* had also not brought tangible results. If Russian co-operation with Germany was not, in fact, very close, every public reference in the U.S.S.R. to this co-operation was cordial. M. Maisky indeed told Mr. Butler on October 3 that a dramatic turn in Soviet policy was unlikely 'at the present time', and that there was (a) not enough background of confidence between Great Britain and the Soviet Union to allow any 'big change' in Anglo-Soviet relations.[2]

Behind the façade of co-operation the Soviet Government might be preparing to meet a German attack, but in this case their fear of Germany was likely to prevent them, even if they had wished to do so, from accepting offers of co-operation or even of close political discussion with the British Government. Sir S. Cripps had thought, in the third week of August, that the Russian authorities were impressed with British resistance to German air attack,[3] but he had also expressed the view that they would continue to act on the assumption that this resistance would be maintained without gestures on their part.

---

[1] See below, Chapter XVIII, section (1).

[2] On the anniversary of the Russo-German pact of August 23, 1939, the Russian press contained articles enthusiastically praising the pact and attacking the 'war-mongering western democracies' and their attempts to separate the U.S.S.R. from Germany. *Izvestiya* stated that the Russo-German economic agreements enabled Germany to receive raw materials which she needed as a result of the British blockade.

[3] Articles in the Russian press during September and October emphasised this resistance. M. Maisky also spoke of it to Mr. Butler on October 3.

(a) N6783/30/38.

On October 4 Hitler and Mussolini held a meeting at the Brenner Pass. Three days later the Roumanian Government announced that German troops, including motorised units, had arrived in the country to assist in the reorganisation of the army.

On October 12 an estimate of the situation was sent to Sir H.
(a) Knatchbull-Hugessen. According to our information about 2,500 German troops would arrive in Roumania towards the middle of the month nominally as 'instructors'. These troops should be considered as the first instalment of a German force for the defence of Roumania against the U.S.S.R.[1] War material to be imported from Germany would be sufficient to equip two motorised divisions and one armoured division.

We had also learned that the decisions taken at the Brenner meeting included the postponement of the invasion of Great Britain until the spring of 1941.[2] Meanwhile Germany and Italy would attack us in the Mediterranean area and at Suez and Gibraltar. The plan of attack in the east would be the seizure of Roumania and the Black Sea ports, the neutralisation of Russia, and operations against Turkey and Greece. These latter operations would be 'political' in the first instance, but also, if necessary, military. The role of Germany would be mainly in the Balkans and in the attack on Suez; the principal task of Italy would be naval action in the Mediterranean; she would be an 'accessory' in Africa and give 'symbolical' co-operation in the Balkans. The conditions necessary for success included the neutralisation of the United States by Japan. We could not check this information, but it did not seem improbable.

The Germans had already begun political preparations for a move into the Balkans. They had supported Bulgaria in her claim for the return of the Southern Dobrudja from Roumania. The Roumanians accepted this claim on August 22, 1940, and were compelled almost at once to agree to the arbitration of Germany and Italy on the demands made by Hungary for the return of Transylvanian territory surrendered to Roumania after the First World War. The 'arbitration' award gave two-fifths of the area to Hungary, and, in consequence of Roumanian dissatisfaction, King Carol of Roumania abdicated in favour of his son Michael and the pro-Axis General Antonescu became Prime Minister with dictatorial powers. The new moves were therefore a continuation of a policy which appeared to be directed towards setting the Balkan States against

---

[1] This information was correct. Hitler's own directive stated that the real (and secret) reason for this German 'aid' was to protect the oilfields and to prepare for German-Roumanian action in the event of war with the U.S.S.R. The first German troops to be sent into Roumania were to consist of a motorised division with tanks. (*D.G.F.P.*, XI, No. 84.)

[2] Hitler told Mussolini at the meeting that he was not without hope of getting the French to join in the attack on Great Britain (*D.G.F.P.*, XI, No. 149).

(a) R7849/5/67.

one another in order to make it easier to absorb them piece-meal into the Axis system.

If we were to counter these plans we needed, primarily, the co-operation of Turkey, but this co-operation would be affected by the view taken by the Turkish Government of Russian intentions, and the decisive factor therefore was the extent to which the Soviet Government would acquiesce in the German plans or give them active support.[1]

This review of the situation was also sent to Sir S. Cripps. He (a) replied on the night of October 13–14 that, if our forecast of German plans were correct, we were probably faced with our last chance of moving Russian policy in our direction, since an increase in Axis activity or a success in the Balkans or Middle East would add to Russian fears and difficulties. The German Ambassador might be returning from Berlin with attractive offers in return for the hostile neutrality of Russia towards Great Britain and Turkey or for Russian participation in action against Turkey. The Soviet Government would suspect and fear these offers but would also calculate the advantages and disadvantages of the alternative policy open to them. At present neither we nor Turkey would make concessions; at the same time we were wanting the U.S.S.R. to risk antagonising the Axis and Japan, with the possible result that the U.S.S.R. might be invaded from two sides. We were also still not prepared to give way on the question of the Baltic States.

Sir S. Cripps thought that the Russians did not want the Germans to win the war and that they would accept some definite risk in order to prevent a German victory. They might rely on postponing the German danger by 'coming in with the Axis Powers until they were strong enough to defeat them'. In these circumstances we should not move the Soviet Government unless we could make them at least some attractive offer with regard to their post-war position. From a short-term point of view the Germans obviously were able to make a better offer; we could interest and attract Russia only by a long-term offer. It was therefore 'completely idle' for Sir S. Cripps to tell M. Molotov of the danger to Russia from a German-Japanese combination. The Soviet Government were fully alive to this danger, and were asking how they could avert it with the 'maximum safety to themselves', and what would be their position after the war if they helped us to win. At the moment they knew only that we refused to acknowledge their territorial acquisitions since the outbreak of war, and that we were pledged to our Polish allies. This attitude was unlikely to attract them to our side.

They were also afraid that after our victory we should form an

---

[1] For the Turkish view of the situation, see below, pp. 514–7.
(a) N6675/176/38.

anti-Russian alliance with the rest of the world and hence be more dangerous to them than a victorious and war-weakened Germany. Sir S. Cripps asked whether we could not make a real effort to change the policy of the Soviet Government by telling them that, if they behaved to us in as friendly a way as they behaved to Germany, and if they were at least 'benevolently neutral' to Turkey and Iran (should either of these States be attacked), we would promise (a) to consult them fully on the post-war settlement of Europe and Asia in association with the other victorious Powers, (b) not to form or enter any anti-Russian alliance after the war, (c) to recognise, until the end of the war, their *de facto* sovereignty of the Baltic States and of those parts of Poland, Bessarabia, and Bukovina in their occupation, (d) to supply them with commodities which we could spare and which they required for arming themselves against possible Axis attack, (e) to guarantee them against attack from Turkey or Iran and, particularly, against an attack on Baku by us or any of our Allies.

We should ask them to 'evidence' this secret arrangement by concluding a trade agreement with us to cover materials supplied under (d) and, if the trade agreement produced no dangerous reactions from the Axis, to enter into a non-aggression pact with us on lines similar to their pact with Germany. We should also say that, unless they were prepared to enter into some such arrangement with us, they must understand that after the war we would not undertake (a), (b) or (c) or even help them with supplies in the event of attack. Sir S. Cripps repeated his view that we should do ' something really bold and imaginative' to counteract the Russian fears of Germany and Japan. If the United States would support our offer, their help would be of great value.

The War Cabinet considered this telegram and a draft reply on
(a) October 15.[1] Lord Halifax said that at first he had thought that we should ask whether the United States Government agreed with our proposed action, but it seemed enough to let them know what we were doing.[2] The War Cabinet agreed with this view, and considered an American commitment unlikely until after the presidential election. They also thought that we should compromise our present and post-war position if we made a statement implying *de jure* recognition of Russian aggression in eastern Europe. There was, however, a case for recognising a *de facto* situation which we could not alter at least until the end of the war. It would be imprudent to build on any result of our approach to the Soviet Government. Russian policy was influenced mainly by fear of Germany, but we

[1] On the previous day Lord Halifax had submitted Sir S. Cripps's telegram to the War
(b) Cabinet with a view to discussion on October 15.
[2] Lord Lothian was instructed on the night of October 15–16 to explain our action to
(c) Mr. Hull.

(a) WM(40)271; N6875/30/38. (b) WM(40)270. (c) N6875/30/38.

ought to make an approach, and have it on record that we had made it.

The Foreign Office therefore authorised Sir S. Cripps on the night of October 15–16 to approach the Soviet Government on the lines (a) suggested by him. He was asked to keep in mind the following points: (i) The Soviet Government should give some practical proof of 'benevolent neutrality' to Turkey or Iran before a German attack on Turkey, i.e. they should facilitate Turkish defence by all means consistent with technical neutrality as the United States had acted with regard to us and the Soviet Government themselves had acted with regard to China. It would also be very undesirable for the Soviet Government to make a pact with Japan involving the cessation or diminution of supplies to China and thus leave Japan free to press down on us and the Dutch in the South. If 'benevolent neutrality' took no account of our requirements in these matters, we might be giving far-reaching undertakings to the Soviet Government in return for nothing more than a promise not to fight against us—a course which in any case they were unlikely to take. (ii) Guarantees of post-war consultation would not imply readiness to accept Russian views on the future of Europe or Asia, and an undertaking not to form an anti-Russian alliance must be conditional on the Soviet Government undertaking nothing against our interests, either directly, or indirectly through revolutionary agitation. (iii) We already recognised *de facto* Russian control of the Baltic States and of occupied parts of Poland and Roumania, but we could not agree to *de jure* recognition. We had accepted in substance Sir S. Cripps's suggestion for dealing with the Baltic ships on a basis involving *de facto* recognition of the Russian occupation of the Baltic States, and we had offered to set off British claims to confiscated property against the gold. Sir S. Cripps's implication that we had shown intransigence on the Baltic questions was therefore not well-founded. (iv) If the articles required by the U.S.S.R. included material of war such as non-ferrous metals, we could supply them as part of a trade agreement; the quantities must obviously be a matter of careful discussion. (v) A guarantee against attack by Turkey could doubtless be given with the consent of the Turkish Government. Obviously neither we nor our Allies would attack Baku as long as the Soviet Government gave no ground for such action.

Sir S. Cripps was told that it was difficult to accept his suggestion that the U.S.S.R. was really more afraid of our post-war attitude than of that of a victorious Germany or that they believed that by postponing a German attack they would ultimately be strong enough to meet it. The reason for their present attitude was more likely to be fear of the immediate consequences of opposition to a

(a) N6875/30/38.

German-Japanese combination. We could not hope at present to remove their fear of Germany, but with American help we might go far to remove their fear of Japan. It was therefore important that the United States Ambassador at Moscow should impress upon the Soviet Government the determination of his country to prevent Japan from indulging in further adventures. Lord Lothian was being asked to make representations at Washington in this sense.

(a) Sir S. Cripps gave[1] M. Vyshinsky in the afternoon of October 22 a Russian translation of a document summarising proposals for an Anglo-Russian agreement. The preamble to this document referred to the success of the British air defence and the postponement of a German invasion, and estimated the probable results of attempts by the Axis Powers to extend the area of hostilities. The fate of countries still neutral was bound up with the success or failure of the British defence. We therefore regarded it as essential to define our attitude to the more important neutrals, particularly, in the European and Asiatic sphere, to the U.S.S.R., and to obtain from these neutrals a more precise definition of their attitude towards us.

We believed that these Powers had a major interest in safeguarding their position at the end of the war. The quality of their neutrality was of vital importance to us since a hostile neutrality might prolong the difficulties and dangers of the war and might almost amount to hostility, while a benevolent neutrality might be nearly as valuable as armed assistance in shortening the war. Hence it was 'not unnatural that His Majesty's Government, firm in their conviction of ultimate victory, should desire to ascertain the degree of benevolence or hostility' with which the 'great neutrals' intended to treat them so that they (His Majesty's Government) might 'recognise at the end of the war those who have been of help to their cause and ask them to share actively in the task of reconstruction'.

We felt it hardly necessary to point out that recent events made clear what would be the position of the U.S.S.R. in the event of a German victory, and that neither Germany nor her partners showed the slightest intention of consulting the U.S.S.R. upon the reconstruction of Europe or Asia. We realised that, in the present circumstances, we could not ask the U.S.S.R. to add to their dangers by

---

[1] On October 22 Sir S. Cripps telegraphed that he had asked on October 17 to see M. Molotov. He had received no answer on the night of October 21–22, and had then said that, if M. Molotov would not see him, he must see someone else. M. Molotov's secretary
(b) telephoned in the afternoon of October 22 asking Sir S. Cripps to see M. Vyshinsky. Sir S. Cripps said in his telegram that he would speak strongly to M. Vyshinsky on M. Molotov's refusal to receive him. He thought that M. Molotov's personal pro-German and anti-British sympathies and policy made him try to avoid closer contact which might call in question the soundness of this policy or influence Stalin in a direction opposed to his (M. Molotov's) wishes.
(a) N6875/30/38.   (b) N6875/30/38.

making an avowed change of policy; hence a closer Anglo-Russian understanding, 'not merely for the moment but for the future as well, once arrived at, should remain for the present confidential and unpublished'. We wished to offer to the U.S.S.R. co-operation in the post-war period, and, in return, to obtain some reciprocal contribution helpful to us in the present most difficult period. Once these present difficulties were past, Soviet assistance would become of far less value.

The terms of the proposed agreement were as follows:

(1) The Soviet Government would undertake (a) to apply to His Majesty's Government a neutrality as benevolent as that adopted towards Germany;

(b) to maintain a benevolent neutrality toward Turkey and Iran, especially if those States were involved in war with either or both of the Axis Powers, and to assist them in their defence by measures similar to those adopted by the U.S.S.R. in the past toward China;

(c) to continue undiminished their assistance to China, and to abstain from entering into any agreement with Japan which would prevent such assistance or encourage Japanese aggression against any British possession;

(d) in the event of a trade or barter agreement (see 2 (d)) provoking no dangerous reaction from the Axis Powers or Japan, to conclude with His Majesty's Government a non-aggression pact on the lines of the pact concluded with Germany.

(2) His Majesty's Government would undertake (a) to consult with the Soviet Government in regard to a post-war settlement in Europe and Asia. This undertaking would bind neither party in advance to agree with any particular views of the other, but would 'guarantee that the opinions of the Soviet Government would be taken fully into account on the basis of friendly association with the other Powers concerned';

(b) not to form or enter into any anti-Russian alliance after the war, as long as the Soviet Government abstained from any hostile action against the interest of His Majesty's Government, 'either directly or indirectly through the medium of internal agitation';

(c) to recognise, until consultations under 2 (a) took place, the *de facto* sovereignty of the U.S.S.R. in Estonia, Latvia, Lithuania, Bessarabia and Northern Bukovina and those parts of the former Polish State[1] now under Soviet control;

---

[1] Sir S. Cripps used this phrase on his own authority. The Foreign Office instructed him on October 30 that the Soviet Government might claim that the phrase implied recognition by His Majesty's Government that the Polish State had ceased to exist. In view of our agreement with Poland we could not accept this view. In reply to these instructions, Sir S. Cripps defended his use of the term. The Foreign Office then pointed out that a State did not cease to exist because its territories had been overrun. The Polish Government existed, and the armed forces of the Polish State were fighting against one of the invaders. The case of Poland was thus analogous to that of Belgium, the Netherlands and Norway. (a)

(a) N6875, 7046/30/38.

(d) to supply to the Soviet Government any available commodities or expert assistance required for the defence of Russia against any future attack by her neighbours;

(e) to guarantee that no attack should be made on the territory of Russia by way of Turkey or Iran, either by His Majesty's Government or by existing or future Allies.

Sir S. Cripps saw M. Vyshinsky again on October 26. M. Vyshinsky (a) put various questions, and said that the Soviet Government regarded the proposals as of the greatest importance and that he would (b) probably ask to see Sir S. Cripps again about them. On November 2 he repeated his talk about another meeting, but before the next interview a communiqué was issued (November 10) in Moscow announcing that, at the invitation of the German Government and in response to Ribbentrop's journey in the previous year to Moscow, M. Molotov would visit Berlin 'in the near future to extend and deepen, by the renewal of personal contact, current exchanges of views within the framework of the friendly relations existing between the two countries'.[1]

Sir S. Cripps's first views on the significance of this announcement (c) were that some Russo-German agreement had been reached, since M. Molotov would not otherwise go to Berlin. In this case the Soviet

---

[1] Ribbentrop had sent a letter to Stalin on October 13, 1940, inviting Molotov to Berlin. The letter gave a reassuring account of the Tripartite Pact (see Volume II, chapter XXII), and of the German action in Roumania, and spoke of the war against England. The German offensive against the Netherlands and Belgium was described as a move 'at the eleventh hour to prevent the contemplated thrust of the Anglo-French armies against the Ruhr' (*D.G.F.P.*, XI, No. 176).

Molotov's visit took place on November 12–14. Hitler and Ribbentrop assured Molotov that the Tripartite Pact signed on September 27, 1940, was not directed against Russia, and that Germany had no interest in the Balkans. They gave Molotov a typical account of their plan for a partition of British overseas possessions in which the German sphere of interest would be in Central Africa, the Italian sphere in North and East Africa, the Japanese sphere in East Asia, and the Russian in the Persian Gulf and Arabia, and a special position in the Straits. Molotov tried to bring the discussion to hard facts. He enquired why Hitler claimed that Great Britain was already defeated, and at the same time that he was fighting a deadly struggle against her. He asked whether the Germans would object to Russia giving Bulgaria the same kind of guarantee which Germany had given to Roumania, and when the Germans would stop sending troops through Finland to Norway. (*D.G.F.P.*, XI, Nos. 325–6, 328–9.)

In fact, on November 12 Hitler issued a general directive on the war in which he said that, whatever the outcome of the political discussions with Russia, preparation must continue for the event of an attack on her. Hitler had been considering this possibility since July. He had never given up his belief that war with Russia was inevitable. He continued to be as suspicious of Russian intrigues with Great Britain as the British Government was suspicious of closer Russo-German collaboration. He also realised from Molotov's attitude that the Russians would not accept the German and Italian plans for the Balkans.

By December Hitler was more convinced of the need to attack Russia, though he still did not commit himself completely to the attack. He settled his military plans in early December for the spring of 1940. He intended before the end of 1940 to open an air assault on Great Britain in the Eastern Mediterranean. Meanwhile, in February, if he could persuade General Franco to enter the war, an attack would be made on Gibraltar; Greece would be invaded in March. Hitler would then be free to move against Russia in mid-May. Hitler held to this decision in spite of very strong opposition from Admiral Raeder, who argued that Germany should concentrate against Great Britain, and in spite of the misgivings of the Army Command. See *Grand Strategy*, II, ch. XXIII, and III, pt. I, and *D.G.F.P.*, X, pp. 373–4, XI, Nos. 323 and 532.

(a) N6984/40/38. (b) N7089/40/38. (c) N7163/283/38.

Government had probably secured new concessions of real value owing to the difficulties of Germany's situation, and, possibly, to the disclosure to the Germans of the offer made by His Majesty's Government. This arrangement was probably opportunist in character, but Sir S. Cripps felt fairly sure that the Russians had decided temporarily 'to go with the Axis' as the safest policy for themselves, although they might try 'to keep His Majesty's Government in play'. M. Molotov's visit was 'a very important temporary diplomatic success for the Axis', but no irremediable damage was likely; in the long run, probably next year, the fundamental Russo-German hostility would reassert itself.

Sir S. Cripps saw M. Vyshinsky on the evening of November 11. He spoke strongly about M. Molotov's attitude and about his pro- (a) jected visit to Berlin. Sir S. Cripps said that M. Molotov's treatment of himself and his 'non-Axis colleagues' was unprecedented and showed unmistakably his completely un-neutral attitude. Our offer could not remain open indefinitely, and a friendly neutrality at a later stage would not have the same value as it now possessed. We had twice put forward proposals for an economic agreement without receiving even the courtesy of an answer. We should therefore have to make other arrangements for our surplus commodities and to regard closer contact between the Soviet Government and our enemies as a warning against the danger of indirect supplies to Germany via Russia.

Sir S. Cripps put two questions to M. Vyshinsky: had the Soviet Government decided not to proceed with the proposals made to them by us, and was he (Sir S. Cripps) to impress upon His Majesty's Government that M. Molotov's visit showed the unwillingness of the Soviet Government to improve Anglo-Russian relations?

M. Vyshinsky, after protesting against Sir S. Cripps's interpretation of M. Molotov's 'lack of neutrality', answered—as his personal view —that a reply to our proposals would be given in a few days, and that there was no connexion between the reception of these proposals and M. Molotov's visit to Berlin. This visit was not an unfriendly act towards His Majesty's Government. M. Vyshinsky's references to the British proposals were confused. He said that they had caused 'great stir' in the Soviet Government, but that the latter were uncertain why they had been made; that the proposals were not clear; that he did not know whether M. Molotov would discuss the proposals with Sir S. Cripps before an answer was given; that he could not discuss this point with Sir S. Cripps; and that a decision would be given when his report was submitted to the Soviet Government. Sir S. Cripps thought that M. Vyshinsky wanted to temporise, perhaps until the publication of reports of the Berlin meeting. He referred

(a) N7173, 7165, 7166/40/38.

constantly to the Baltic question, and said that, if smaller matters were settled, the larger questions might be decided. Sir S. Cripps replied that a settlement of the smaller questions was not possible until the 'fundamental attitude between the two countries' had been decided, and that a promise to deal with the larger matters 'would not influence His Majesty's Government to give in on the smaller ones'. Finally Sir S. Cripps asked whether there was any truth in the rumour that the U.S.S.R. intended to allow a German hegemony in the Balkans. M. Vyshinsky answered that it was not the habit of the Soviet Government to give away anything, especially if such action were in conflict with their interests.

The Foreign Office doubted whether the line taken by Sir S. Cripps was good tactics, since it might give the impression that we were very much frightened at the new Soviet move. It would be wiser to assume that, since the Russian and German Governments were allied, they must consult together when occasion required. Such an occasion had arisen owing to Hitler's manifest embarrassments which made it necessary for him to turn for help to his ally. The Russians would doubtless know what price to put on their help and what value to attach to Hitler's promises.

In fact, the Soviet Government made no further reference to the British proposals. On November 19 Sir S. Cripps suggested to the (a) Foreign Office that he should be given authority to withdraw the suggestions for an economic agreement if at any time he should feel it wise to do so. He thought that we should keep up pressure upon the Soviet Government until they had taken some step in our direction.

The Foreign Office disagreed with this view. The withdrawal of the proposals would not put pressure on the Soviet Government since the latter had shown so little interest in them for months past. On the other hand the Soviet Government would certainly announce our action as evidence of the insincerity of our approaches to them. After consultation with Mr. Dalton, Sir S. Cripps was instructed on December 2 that there were reasons against the withdrawal of the economic proposals. In addition to the arguments already suggested by the Foreign Office, our offer of a trade agreement was made on the assumption that the Soviet Government would continue their economic support of Germany and that the flax, chrome, and lubricating oil which we hoped to obtain would outweigh any possible disadvantages. We had not regarded the conclusion of the agreement as dependent upon the state of our political relations with the U.S.S.R.

(a) N7233/40/38.

Sir S. Cripps was given a summary of our information about the Hitler-Molotov meeting. We concluded that the result of this meeting (a) had been negative and that the Soviet Government wanted to keep their independence of action and to avoid involving themselves too deeply with the Axis Powers. They had not responded to Hitler's efforts to get their support and co-operation in a German move against Allied interests in the Near and Middle East. Their policy in the Balkans appeared to run counter to German designs, and they were maintaining their support of China. In these circumstances our attitude to the Soviet Government should continue, wherever possible, to be forthcoming and helpful, and, while leaving them to make the next move, we should abstain from any action which might suggest impatience, suspicion or irritation.

Sir S. Cripps was not altogether convinced by these arguments. He proposed to the Foreign Office that he should send a letter to (b) M. Mikoyan recounting the history of our attempt over the last six months to get a reply to our proposals for a trade agreement and indicating that, as we had to dispose of our surplus commodities, we must withdraw the proposals, though the Soviet Government, if they wished, could put forward counter-proposals. The Foreign Office asked Sir S. Cripps to send a draft of his letter. They considered that (c) the terms were too contentious and that it would be better to inform the Soviet Government that we could not leave open our offer indefinitely, and that, subject to any observations which M. Mikoyan might wish to make, we regarded the offer as withdrawn.

Sir S. Cripps, however, replied in strong terms that he would prefer not to send any letter than to send the amended draft. The (d) draft was therefore reconsidered by the Foreign Office in consultation with the Ministry of Economic Warfare. Meanwhile on December 23 Mr. Eden succeeded Lord Halifax as Secretary of State for Foreign Affairs. Sir A. Cadogan showed the new draft to Mr. Eden, but said that Sir S. Cripps had produced good arguments against the changes suggested to his letter. Mr. Eden, however, considered that, if the letter were sent at the moment of his assumption of office, the Soviet Government might conclude that he had introduced a new policy with regard to Anglo-Soviet relations. M. Maisky had appealed for his help in an attempt to improve these relations and had frequently stated that he (Mr. Eden) had tried to do this during his earlier period of office. For this reason the Soviet Government might take the letter as an even sharper rebuff.

These considerations were put to Sir S. Cripps on December 28. It was also pointed out to him that there was not much difference between his point of view and that of the Foreign Office. Sir S. Cripps wanted to withdraw our offer, but to add that, if the Soviet

---

(a) N7354/40/38.   (b) N7366/40/38.   (c) N7387/40/38.   (d) N7500/40/38.

Government wished to make an offer on their part, we would con-sider it. The Foreign Office had proposed to say that the offer must be regarded as withdrawn subject to anything which the Soviet Government might have to suggest. In each case the initiative would be left to the Russians.

Sir S. Cripps replied on the night of December 29–30 that he agreed with Mr. Eden's view and that he would not send the letter.

Note to Section (vii). Sir S. Cripps's letter of October 10 to Lord Halifax and Lord Halifax's reply.

A letter written by Sir S. Cripps to Lord Halifax on October 10 and Lord Halifax's reply of November 27 provides interesting material for a general view of the attitude of the Foreign Office at this period towards the U.S.S.R. and the possibility of an Anglo-Russian *rapprochement*.

(a) Sir S. Cripps began his letter by pointing out the damaging effect of the publicity given by the English press and the B.B.C. to any hopeful signs in Moscow. The facts were often stated inaccurately and with exaggeration so that the Soviet Government became con-vinced of our wish to embroil them with Germany and Japan. The last twenty years had taught the Soviet Government to look on British Governments led by Ministers now in the Cabinet as fundamentally hostile to the U.S.S.R. Hence they examined the present situation against this background of continued hostility. In this examination there were two main factors: (i) the general manner in which we dealt with the Soviet Government, e.g., did we treat them as equals, and (ii) day to day dealings, especially in matters where British interests were not the same, or not obviously the same as those of the U.S.S.R.

With regard to (i) the Soviet Government thought—with justifica-tion in so far as the past was concerned—that we were not prepared to acknowledge their influence or importance in a measure cor-responding to the facts. Their exclusion from the Munich meeting and from all consultation or exchange of views on the Far East were two examples of this refusal.

With regard to (ii) the questions affecting the Baltic States had been of importance. The Soviet Government thought that we were prepared to be friendly only when we hoped to gain some immediate advantage for ourselves and that we were unwilling to put ourselves out in any way to cultivate friendship or better relations for the value which these improved relations might bring. Against this background our actions since the war had done nothing to convince the Soviet Government of any fundamental change in our approach. They considered that we wanted to detach them from the Axis Powers merely for our convenience, and they asked themselves whether we were likely thereafter to be better or more useful friends to them. Our

(a) N7323/40/38.

attitude with regard to the Baltic States, our failure to consult the Soviet Government over the Far East until we felt the shoe pinching very hard or to do anything effective with regard to a Russo-Turkish understanding over the Straits showed that our fundamental attitude had not changed. A last-moment effort to draw the Soviet Government to our side increased their suspicions, especially when we were unwilling to settle the Baltic questions. They thought that the Baltic questions had become another 'special case' in which we were looking for advantages for ourselves. Another difficulty was the Russian fear of Germany, and, at present, of Germany and Japan. It was probably necessary to be at Moscow to realise how great and ever-present was this fear. The Soviet Government could not yet meet a German attack, and the German occupation of Roumania, which was likely to be followed soon by that of Bulgaria, increased Russian difficulties. Hence they were bound so to conduct their foreign policy as to avoid all danger of immediate attack. An open indication that they were moving away from the Axis would at once expose them to such danger. Nevertheless they knew that, unless we defeated Germany and the United States defeated Japan, they would have to meet a German-Japanese combination.

The question of the Dardanelles was another factor. The Russians were doubtless extremely alarmed at the danger of a German attack on Turkey, resulting in the closing of the Black Sea, and they relied in this respect on Turkish help.

The Germans could not object to the continuance of Russian help to China and, in a modified degree, to Turkey. The United States were neutral and a long way off, and hitherto uninterested in friendly relations with the U.S.S.R. The Germans therefore up to the present had not concerned themselves with Russo-American relations. Our position was different; for this reason the Germans paid the greatest attention to Anglo-Russian relations. The Soviet Government were most anxious not to antagonise us irreparably, but they dared not appear too friendly, especially since they did not trust the discretion of His Majesty's Government or of Sir S. Cripps himself.

We had therefore to convince the Soviet Government that, if and as far as they were prepared to 'go in' with us, the United States, and 'the others', our reception of them would not be merely a temporary expedient to suit our immediate dangers and convenience, but something of a permanent nature which would recognize them as full partners in world reconstruction after our victory. Finally the only way to work with them must be to avoid all publicity which would embarrass them. Sir S. Cripps repeated his view that 'if you want to win over this country, it has got to be on the basis of recognising a continuing friendship and a partnership in post-war reconstruction and not merely upon the basis of getting them to help us out of our awkward hole after which we might desert them and even join the enemies who now surround them'.

The Northern Department of the Foreign Office commented (October 24) on Sir S. Cripps's letter that, on the particular question of publicity, Sir S. Cripps's own friends and M. Maisky's confidants in Great Britain were the worst offenders. With regard to our general attitude, Sir S. Cripps's account of the Russian view of our policy described what we thought of Russian policy. The Soviet Government did not want 'a continuing friendship and partnership in post-war reconstruction' with a capitalist country. They might well desire assurances, which we could give them, that we should not interfere with them after the war; they would interpret any counter-assurances of non-interference with us in an entirely 'realistic manner' according to the convenience of the moment. The Soviet Government were far more 'realist' than Sir S. Cripps supposed; their reluctance to join us was not due to fear that we might join their enemies, but to their own fears of the same enemies, and to their desire to keep their hands free for the future.

Sir A. Cadogan doubted whether it was necessary to answer Sir S. Cripps's letter, but Lord Halifax replied to it on November 27. He wrote that we were doing everything possible to discourage tact-less comment in the press. We were not always successful and our task was complicated by the continued indiscretions of M. Maisky and of those sections of the press in closest contact with the Soviet Embassy. The obstacles in the way of Anglo-Russian understanding were, however, deeper. The Russians were realists, and not disposed to fight our battles for us or to help us to fight their own battles. Their attitude was understandable, if not admirable. They saw that Germany had little chance of coming out of the war strong enough to be a menace to Russia; hence, as long as we were wearing down German strength and, incidentally, placing a great strain on our-selves, they had no reason to undertake this arduous task.[1] They looked forward to the collapse of Germany and of Great Britain, and to a time when they would be able to impose their will on a Europe ripe for revolution. 'Even if they felt that their intervention was necessary to prevent a final German victory, it seems more than doubtful whether in the present state of the Red Army and of their economic and industrial system, they would be in a fit state to take preventive action against Germany.'

For the rest, the attitude of the Soviet Government continued to be dictated by fear of the German fighting machine and by a desire to appease the Germans. This might have been the motive of Molotov's visit to Berlin. On the other hand they felt that they could ignore Great Britain and rebuff her with impunity. Their realism disregarded everything except their own interests; even if this were not so, it would surely be a mistake to suppose that their sympathies were on

---

[1] On December 15 Sir S. Cripps was informed that, according to a neutral source in London, M. Maisky had recently told the Turkish Ambassador that Soviet policy was one
(a) of complete reserve. The Russians had not sufficient military strength and were content to see the two belligerent groups exhausting themselves. M. Maisky reckoned up daily the military damage and loss on each side not in two columns but in one, i.e. showing the total loss to non-Soviet belligerents.

(a) N7448/30/48.

the side of Great Britain. Our Empire and our system appeared to stand for a good many things which they were anxious to destroy.

In present circumstances we could only await the outcome of Molotov's visit to Berlin. If it became clear that the Soviet Government had committed themselves to a policy of large-scale economic co-operation with Germany and of facilitating or even taking part in a German move against our interests and those of our Allies in the Near East, there would clearly be little hope of establishing Anglo-Russian relations on a more satisfactory basis. On the other hand, if the Berlin visit were mere window-dressing, there was no reason why these relations should not remain undisturbed or even take a turn for the better.

Above all, it was essential that the Russians, as realists, should be convinced that we, and not the Germans, were going to win, and that those who had been on our side would fare better than those who had been against us. If they were persuaded of this they might show themselves more amenable over minor issues, e.g. Baltic questions, and readier than hitherto for consultation and even for co-operation on Far Eastern and other matters.

CHAPTER XVI

Turkey and the Balkans from the collapse of France to the British withdrawal from Greece

(i)

Anglo-Turkish relations after the collapse of France: suggestions for British mediation with a view to the improvement of Russo-Turkish relations (July 1– November 7, 1940).

THE whole of British policy in the Balkans and the Middle East from the entry of Italy into the war to the battle of El Alamein turned on the decision of the War Cabinet to keep a strong British fleet in the Mediterranean—eastern as well as western—and to reinforce the army and air force in Egypt even, in the twelve months after June 1940, at considerable risk to the defence of the United Kingdom. The determining factor in preventing defeat from turning to disaster, and in exploiting and confirming victory on land, was sea-power, or rather sea-power used with great courage and skill. Without sea-power Egypt would have been lost, and, after the loss of Egypt, Turkey could hardly have held out against German attack. The Middle East in the stricter geographical sense of the term, Iraq, Iran, Syria and Arabia, would have fallen under Axis control, and Japan could have joined up with the Axis forces from Europe.

The first effect of the maintenance of British power in Egypt and in the eastern Mediterranean was the strengthening of Turkey. Turkish territory lay across the land route from central Europe, and to a large extent also from Russia to the Middle East. Turkey was a leading member of the Balkan Entente as well as of the Saadabad Pact.[1] Turkish neutrality, therefore, was of great strategic value in the period immediately after the collapse of France. Even a formal entry of Turkey into the war at this time would have invited German and Italian attack and Russian 'precautionary' annexations. Great Britain could have given Turkey little active assistance, and a Turkish collapse would have had serious moral as well as strategic consequences.

The importance of Turkish neutrality between June and November 1940, was increased by the fact that Great Britain no longer had the means to develop a strong neutral *bloc* in the Balkans. In the early part of the war the attempt to secure such a *bloc* had depended not

---

[1] A pact of mutual guarantee signed in 1937 by Turkey, Iran, Iraq, and Afghanistan.

only on joint Anglo-French backing but also on the acquiescence of Italy. About the time of the Italian declaration of war suggestions (a) were made that we might try to persuade Yugoslavia and Greece as well as Turkey to come into the war while there was still some chance of holding the Axis Powers, and thus to save themselves from probable attack later on. Germany was clearly trying to win a decisive victory quickly, and a diversion in the Balkans might relieve the situation on the western front, upset German plans, and allow time for the preparation of a counter-attack.

The Foreign Office had not regarded this proposal as practicable, and the War Cabinet had decided on June 13 not to take any steps in (b) the matter until they heard more about the attitude of Turkey. In the event the rapidity of the German advance in France soon ruled out the proposal, even if the Balkan States had been willing to consider it. Within a few weeks the problem was very different. France was out of the war; Italy had entered it. The Balkan States could not have resisted attack and clearly would not provoke it. For reasons which the British Government could not easily dispute Turkey had not fulfilled the terms of the treaty which she had made on the assumption that, in the event of war with Italy, the Turks would have a full measure of Anglo-French assistance.[1]

The Turkish Government had explained that in any case they could not fulfil their engagement under their treaty with Great Britain without grave risk of war with the U.S.S.R. They had therefore invoked Protocol 2 of the treaty, i.e. the stipulation that the obligations undertaken by Turkey should not require her to take action which would involve her in war with the U.S.S.R. The British Ambassador believed that the Turkish fears were genuine; i.e. that M. Molotov had in fact made it clear that the Soviet Government disapproved of Turkish intervention, and that the Turkish attitude would change if these fears of Russia could be removed. At the end of June the Russian demands on Roumania for the cession of Bessarabia, and the Roumanian surrender to these demands and repudiation of the British guarantee, brought about yet another change in the political situation. There was reason to believe that the Soviet Government had acted without consulting Germany and Italy, and that their action was defensive, and a sign that they were themselves uneasy about the possibilities of an advance by the Axis Powers into the Balkans. On the other hand, the fact that Russia was using the opportunity to improve her own military position and was reviving her 'historic' movement southwards was bound to cause alarm in Turkey, and might even lead the Turks to look to the Axis Powers for protection which Great Britain could not give them.

---

[1] For the attitude of Turkey on this question, see above, pp. 245–7.
(a) R6476/58/22. (b) WM(40)164.

(a) At the same time the British Government heard from Sir S. Cripps that Stalin had told him on July 1 that the Soviet Government did not themselves intend any further move in the Balkans but were afraid of action by Turkey. Stalin wanted to improve Russo-Turkish relations, and would welcome British help in the matter. He had said, however, that a condition of improvement must be a change in the regulations controlling the Straits, i.e. in the terms of the Montreux Convention.[1]

The British Government could not easily refuse this invitation, although they doubted whether Stalin seriously wished for an agreement with Turkey. His remark that the U.S.S.R. was nervous of sudden attack by Turkey had at least an insincere ring about it. The only basis for a real agreement would be the common interest of the U.S.S.R. and Turkey in preventing Germany from reaching the Black Sea. It was unlikely that Stalin would commit himself to an agreement on these lines; he probably aimed solely at a modification of the Montreux Convention in the sense of depriving the Turks of their control of the Straits, and thus excluding us from them, while leaving Russia free to use them in all circumstances. We could not allow ourselves to become involved in negotiations initiated by Russia to this end. Nevertheless we were bound to do what we could to improve Russo-Turkish relations, and, indirectly, our own relations with the U.S.S.R. The discussion would allow us to gain time during which the situation in the Mediterranean might improve. We should also test the sincerity of the Russian Government and discover whether Russia and Turkey could co-operate against the danger of German penetration in the Balkans and the Black Sea. Such co-operation, though unlikely, would be of the greatest value to us, and would avoid the risk that the Russians, in their policy of 'self-protection', might make demands on Turkey which would drive the Turks to the German side for protection which we could not give. Moreover the Foreign Office had already been considering whether they could do anything to remove Turkish fears of Russian designs against the Straits or the Black Sea coast. Sir H. Knatchbull-Hugessen had been instructed on June 22 to sound the Turkish Government on the possibility of Russo-Turkish collaboration. He had replied on June 24 that the Turkish Government agreed that they had a common interest with the Russians in keeping Germany and Italy out of the Balkans and the Black Sea, but they could not trust the U.S.S.R. and, like ourselves, did not know the real nature of Russo-German relations. They could not approach the Soviet Government, but they would consider an approach from the Russian side.

---

[1] See above, p. 468.
(a) N5969/30/38.

Hence, on July 11, Sir H. Knatchbull-Hugessen was instructed to ask the Turkish Government whether they would agree that we (a) should enquire what the Russians had in mind. We should not suggest that Turkey should give up any special rights under the Montreux Convention, or that the U.S.S.R. should receive any special rights or that we ourselves should waive any of the rights secured to us by the Convention.

A copy of these instructions was sent to Sir S. Cripps. He thought it inadvisable to raise the question with the Soviet Government unless (b) we were prepared to allow some modification of the Convention in return for a Russian guarantee of Turkey, and that, unless we approached the Russians with definite proposals, they would merely raise their demands, and the result would be a deadlock favourable to the Germans. Sir H. Knatchbull-Hugessen also thought that, unless we could get some *ad hoc* Russo-Turkish agreement confined to possible emergencies arising out of the war, we should have to deal with the question of the Straits.

An answer was sent to Sir S. Cripps on July 16 that we were ready to take up Stalin's invitation to mediate between Russia and Turkey, not because we were at all hopeful of getting a new settlement with regard to the Straits but because we did not want to be obstructive and we also felt it desirable to bring Stalin 'into the open', and, if possible, to secure Russo-Turkish co-operation against the common danger of a German penetration into the Black Sea. We did not intend to make a settlement at the expense of Turkey, and if we and the Turks could not accept Stalin's proposals, we should say so. The decision whether we should even raise the matter depended on the wishes of the Turkish Government.

Sir S. Cripps, however, continued to hold the view that, unless we were prepared to make concessions about the Straits, we could not assist in securing a Russo-Turkish *rapprochement*. Meanwhile, on July 19, Sir H. Knatchbull-Hugessen telegraphed that the Turkish Government did not object to our proposed approach provided that they were not committed by it. They did not think that anything more than an *ad hoc* agreement was possible. M. Saracoglu's view was that, in face of German threats, the interests of Turkey, Great Britain, and the U.S.S.R. required that Turkey, as being neither a strong nor an aggressive Power, should retain control of the Straits. He added that as long as Great Britain retained command of the Mediterranean, it was not of vital importance whether Russia had free passage through the Straits or at least a share in their control, and that a solution ought not to be difficult if mutual confidence could be established between Russia and Turkey.

Sir H. Knatchbull-Hugessen considered that the Turkish Govern-

---

(a) N5969/30/38. (b) R6776/203/44.

ment, although they would not give up their ultimate control of the Straits, might accept an *ad hoc* compromise for protecting the Straits
(a) against German and Italian aggression. It soon became clear, however, to the Foreign Office, in trying to define the terms of such an arrangement, that the Russians would ask for more than the Turks were prepared to grant, and that the only result of a British approach might be to antagonise both parties. Hence the Foreign Office decided that it would be better to say nothing unless the Soviet Government again referred to the question. In the latter case we should ask them to define precisely what they wanted.

Towards the end of August the Turkish Ambassador in Moscow returned to Turkey. The Foreign Office recommended that he should go back to Russia as soon as possible. On September 16 Sir H.
(b) Knatchbull-Hugessen telegraphed that M. Saracoglu was considering whether he would instruct the Ambassador, on his return, to speak to the Soviet Government about the formation of a Balkan *entente*. The Ambassador would say that the last time the Soviet Government had left Turkey to do all the work, and the results were now seen. Russian co-operation was necessary in a renewed effort.

Sir H. Knatchbull-Hugessen was instructed on September 21 that we had expected the Turkish Government to tell us their views on their relations with the Soviet Government after they had seen their Ambassador, but as we had received little information from them it was difficult to give advice. We thought it of the highest importance that the Soviet Government should be left in no doubt about the intention of Turkey to act towards us as a loyal ally.

We did not see any objection to a proposal for Russian co-operation in the formation of a Balkan League as long as the Turkish Government took care that the proposal did not encourage the Soviet Government to interpret the Ambassador's instructions as a further sign of Turkish weakness. The Balkan States were too much afraid of Russian penetration to make it possible for the U.S.S.R. to participate in the formation of a Balkan *bloc*; Turkey alone could organise it.

Sir H. Knatchbull-Hugessen was also asked, if he thought it wise, to suggest that the Ambassador should tell the Soviet Government that the future of Iran, as a member of the Saadabad pact, was of interest to Turkey. We should, however, find it hard to answer a question from Turkey about our own policy in the event of a Russian threat to Iran. M. Saracoglu agreed to these suggestions, but said that the Turkish Ambassador at Moscow could not make any reference to Iran. He also realised that Turkey alone could undertake the reconstitution of the Balkan *entente*.

The Ambassador left for Moscow on October 8 and saw
(c) M. Molotov on October 17. According to the Ambassador's account

R6830, 6987, 7048/203/44. (b) R7252, 7421/703/44. (c) R7967/203/44.

of the interview to Sir S. Cripps, M. Molotov was pleased at the Turkish preparations in Thrace, and thought that these preparations would deter the Italians from attacking Greece. M. Molotov reaffirmed the friendship and loyalty of the Soviet Government to Turkey. He said that the Germans had given Russia no indication that they were sending troops into Roumania, and that, at the appropriate moment, the Soviet Government would ask for an explanation. He took particular note of the Ambassador's statements and did not mention the Straits.

On October 30 Sir S. Cripps reported that the Yugoslav Minister (a) had gained the impression from the German and Italian Ambassadors that the Axis Powers had made an offer of some kind to the Soviet Government about a share in the control of the Straits. Sir S. Cripps thought that this immediate offer might seem to be of greater value than our suggestions. He asked whether the Turkish Government could be persuaded to make a temporary concession to Russia.

In reply Sir S. Cripps was told on November 2 that, even if we could persuade the Turkish Government to make an attractive offer (b) in regard to the Straits, it was doubtful whether the Soviet Government would accept it, owing to their fear of Germany. Moreover the Russians had more interest in maintaining the *status quo* than in sharing the control of the Straits with Germany. The first object of Anglo-Turkish policy in Moscow should therefore be to convince the Soviet Government that the *status quo* could be maintained.

In any case, we had failed to discover proposals which would satisfy both Turkey and the U.S.S.R. The only really attractive offer would be a share in the physical control of the Straits, i.e. a naval base in the area, and the Turkish Government would certainly not accept this plan. We might, however, suggest that, in view of our offer of consultation on the post-war settlement, the Soviet Government would be able to raise any question about the Straits, but we could not make even this suggestion without the approval of the Turkish Government.

Sir S. Cripps replied with a different proposal. He suggested that the Turkish Government might say that, if the Soviet Government alone, or in association with the Roumanian Government, secured control of the Danube mouths and agreed to consult Turkey with regard to the passage of warships other than Russian and Roumanian into the Black Sea, Turkey would agree to consult Russia with regard to the passage of non-Turkish warships through the Straits. Sir S. Cripps thought that this plan would assist in creating difficulties between Russia and Germany over the Danube, and would give the Turkish Government advantages equivalent to those accorded to Russia.

(a) R8117/242/44. (b) R8202/242/44.

The objections to this proposal were set out in telegrams of November 7 to Sir H. Knatchbull-Hugessen and Sir S. Cripps. The proposal assumed that the Soviet Government would secure complete control of the mouths of the Danube. It seemed unlikely that they would in fact secure this control. In any case Germany would still be able to assemble submarines at Constantsa. The Foreign Office agreed with the Turkish Government that it was undesirable to raise the question of the Straits in existing circumstances.[1] Under Sir S. Cripps's proposal Turkey would be offering a substantial concession which could be justified only if she were certain of obtaining a corresponding advantage. Finally, it was doubtful whether any offer about the Straits would really affect the attitude of the Soviet Government. In view of these difficulties, Sir S. Cripps's suggestion was not adopted.

(ii)

The Italian attack on Greece: British attempts to secure Turkish and Yugoslav co-operation in support of Greece (August–December, 1940).

The Italian attack on Greece introduced a new factor, since it brought nearer to realisation the Axis control of the Balkans which the British Government were trying to prevent. In the circumstances there was no immediate likelihood of getting Russian help, but the question of Turkish co-operation was more urgent than ever.

On the entry of Italy into the war Mussolini had reaffirmed the peaceful intentions of his Government towards Greece and their other neighbours. These affirmations obviously had no value, and did not assure the Greeks. Greek fears were increased by the sinking on August 15 of the cruiser *Helle* by a submarine which was unidentified but was—rightly—believed to be Italian. At the same time the

(a) Italians opened a violent press and radio campaign demanding the cession of Epirus and the extradition from Greece of persons alleged to be responsible for the murder of a so-called Albanian 'patriot'.[2] They also accused Greece of 'unneutral' behaviour in the interest of Great Britain.

---

[1] On November 2, Sir H. Knatchbull-Hugessen had telegraphed that the Turkish Government considered it most dangerous for them to make an offer about the Straits. The

(b) Axis Powers could outbid them, and the Turkish Government would then have to make too great concessions since, once the subject had been opened, the Soviet Government could not be allowed to 'go away empty-handed'.

[2] The Greek Government in fact agreed to extradite the two persons held for this murder: but no formal request for extradition was ever put forward by the Italian Government.

(a) R7021, 7058, 7178/764/19.   (b) R8117/242/44.

Although the Greek Government did not make provocative replies to this campaign or to the sinking of their cruiser, they left no doubt that they would fight if they were attacked, and that they relied on the British guarantee. General Metaxas, the Greek Prime Minister, rejected a hint that Greece might ask for German protection. Only a (a) week after the loss of the *Helle* an Italian attack seemed imminent. General Metaxas then enquired what help Greece might expect (b) from Great Britain. He said that, in order to avoid giving the Italians a pretext for aggression, he wished Great Britain to do nothing until an attack took place. The Greek Government also avoided even the appearance of compromising their neutrality. On August 17 they asked that British warships should use special care to avoid Greek (c) territorial waters, and on August 26 they interned the crew of a British aircraft which had made a forced landing on Greek territory, although only five days earlier they had allowed an Italian aircraft in similar circumstances to continue its flight to Rhodes.

The British Government did not want to raise false hopes about the amount of help which they could provide, but General Metaxas's question required a definite reply. The Chiefs of Staff considered the (d) items of a reply on August 23. They felt that they could not go beyond a general assurance—which we had already given—that the most (e) valuable help we could provide would be to defeat Italy. This purpose would not necessarily be served by the dispersal of our forces. We (f) could not therefore undertake to send land or air forces to the Greek mainland, but we should try to prevent an Italian occupation of Crete. In any case Greece could count on our support in the general settlement after the war.

Sir M. Palairet, British Minister at Athens, was instructed to do all that he could to ensure that, in spite of this discouraging reply, the Greek Government continued to resist Italian demands even to the point of war. The Italian threats might be bluff; if, however, they were followed by a declaration of war, the diversion of Italian forces from the attack which they were apparently intending in Libya would be a gain to us while we were building up our forces.

Sir M. Palairet did not act on these instructions. He asked that we should offer more direct help in spite of the general strategic argu- (g) ment against scattering the small forces available to us. He pointed out the damaging effect on our prestige if we failed to help the only country to which we could actually supply the assistance promised in our guarantee. If we did not honour our guarantee directly, we could hardly ask Turkey to fulfil her obligations to us.

(a) R7238/764/19.   (b) R7225/764/19.   (c) R7117/764/19.   (d) R7274/764/19.
(e) R7058/764/19. (f) R7225/764/19. (g) R7284/764/19.

In view of Sir M. Palairet's appeal, the War Cabinet reconsidered
(a) the matter on August 26, but could not see their way to give more
encouraging promises. Sir M. Palairet was authorised to say that we
would do what we could to meet a request for financial help; that we
would provide naval support whenever and wherever possible, and
not merely in defence of Crete, and that we would also attack Italy
(b) heavily by air.[1] In a personal message to General Metaxas the Prime
Minister hoped that we should soon be stronger in the Mediterranean.
Throughout September and October, however, on the advice of the
(c) Chiefs of Staff, the War Cabinet refused to promise direct air
assistance on the Greek mainland, though on October 22 the Middle
East Command were authorised to hold a small force in readiness for
despatch to Crete.

(d) The Italians opened their attack on Greece at 5.30 a.m. on
October 28, half an hour before the expiry of an ultimatum presented
three and a half hours earlier, and demanding, *inter alia*, the surrender
of certain strategic points. The nature of this aggression was so little
disguised that, when the Italian Minister was asked what 'strategic
points' the Greeks were to hand over, he could give no answer.
Mussolini had in fact decided on the attack before the Italian entry
into the war against the Allies.[2]

General Metaxas at once appealed to Great Britain for immediate
help by sea to defend Corfu and in the air to defend Athens. The
Greek Minister in London also appealed to Lord Halifax, and referred to the British guarantee. Sir M. Palairet supported the Greek
requests and asked that air assistance should be given on a scale
sufficient to make Greece a base of operations against Italy. The
Greeks did not ask at this time, or throughout the winter, for the
assistance of land forces on the mainland.

Up to the date of the Italian attack the Foreign Office had inclined
to think that, owing to the lateness of the season, it might after all be
postponed until the following spring. In the afternoon of October 28,
however, the War Cabinet met to discuss what could be done
(e) to meet the Greek requests. They still felt unable to go beyond their
previous engagements or to promise fighter aircraft. During the next
few days there was a considerable change in policy. On October 31
(f) Air Chief Marshal Longmore, Commander-in-Chief of the Air Forces
in the Middle East, reported that on his own responsibility he had
arranged to send a squadron of Blenheims (of which one half were
equipped as fighters) to Greece. The Prime Minister approved this

---

[1] Lord Halifax said in the House of Lords on September 5 that Great Britain would
honour her existing guarantee. *Parl. Deb. 5th Ser. H. of L.*, vol. 117, cols. 368–9.

[2] Ciano, in his *Diaries*, (October 14) states that the ultimatum prepared for Greece
allowed her 'no way out'.

(a) WM (40)234, R7274/764/19; R7284, 7310/764/19. (b) R7229/764/19. (c) R7505,
7953/7505/19. (d) R8088, 8055, 8095. 8114, 8392/764/19. (e) WM(40)278.2, C.A.
(f) Hist.(B)1, No. 4.

action. Three days later the Greek Minister in London asked Lord (a) Halifax for the immediate despatch of aircraft, anti-aircraft and anti-tank guns, and rifles, and for British support in obtaining armaments from the United States.

The War Cabinet not only agreed to do what they could towards meeting these requests, but also, at the Prime Minister's recom- (b) mendation, to give more direct land and air help. They decided that two more squadrons of Blenheims and one of Gladiators should be sent at once, and a second squadron of Gladiators later on; if (c) necessary, a second battalion of infantry should be sent to Crete.[1]

The Prime Minister agreed that these measures would leave us dangerously weak in the Middle East. Nevertheless, although we could make specious excuses for refusing help to Greece—we could say, for example, that the guarantee had been Anglo-French, and that the plans for implementing it had been in the hands of General Weygand—we could not satisfy public opinion by subterfuges of this kind. We should also lose the Turkish alliance if our assistance to Greece were on a smaller scale than that proposed, and we had as great a strategic interest in keeping the Italians out of Athens and the Piraeus as in keeping them out of Khartoum.[2]

At this time the Prime Minister and the War Cabinet did not realise the scale of the offensive which General Wavell intended shortly to take against the Italians in the Western Desert. They therefore tended to think that the military authorities were holding back unnecessarily from sending forces to Greece. Mr. Eden, as Secretary of State for War, had arrived in Cairo on October 16 for (d) consultation with General Wavell on the strategic situation in the Mediterranean and Middle East, and on the use to be made of the reinforcements recently sent there. Mr. Eden came back on November 8, and explained General Wavell's plan. Meanwhile the Middle East (e) Command were seriously concerned at the prospective withdrawal of about a third of their fighter force on the eve of their offensive; they asked that they might keep the second squadron of Gladiators in Egypt. There were also difficulties in finding sufficient airfields in Greece and making adequate ground arrangements for the aircraft.

Thus there was another short period of hesitation, in spite of more appeals from the Greeks—including a personal message from the (f) King of the Hellenes to His Majesty the King—that they were in

---

[1] General Wavell had already sent one battalion to Crete.

[2] The Prime Minister had in mind the Italian threat to the Sudan which was later removed by the successful offensives of General Platt in Eritrea and General Cunningham in Italian Somaliland and Abyssinia. In November, 1940, the Italian land and air forces were overwhelmingly larger than those of Great Britain in the Sudan and East Africa. On the other hand the Italians could not send reinforcements owing to British control of the sea. Hence they had either to strike at once or remain on the defensive.

(a) R8212,8214/764/19.   (b) WM(40)282.2, C.A.   (c) R8269/764/19.   (d) Hist.(B)1, Nos. 6–12.   (e) WM(40)287.5, C.A.   (f) R8343/60/22.

desperate need of fighter help. The military situation in Greece, however, turned out very differently from the expectations of the friends
as well as the enemies of the Greeks. At the end of October Sir M.
Palairet had reported as the view of the British Service Attachés in
Athens that without help from outside the country would soon be
overrun, but, after a short withdrawal, the Greeks held the Italian
attacks, took the offensive in southern Albania, and succeeded in
driving back the enemy. On the night of November 11–12 British
aircraft from the *Illustrious* attacked the Italian fleet at Taranto and
put three battleships and a cruiser out of action for some months.
It now seemed desirable to send air reinforcements to Greece not
merely for defensive purposes but to take advantage of the weakness
of the Italians and also to make it more difficult for the Germans to
come south through Bulgaria to their assistance.

(a)   With these considerations in mind the War Cabinet on November 19—four days before the Greeks captured Koritza—approved the
despatch of the second squadron of Gladiators, together with twelve
more Gladiators for the use of the Greek Air Force. This second
squadron arrived in December. By this time there was another
change in the situation. The British authorities were considering the
likelihood of German action in the Balkans after the winter, if not
earlier; they wanted, if possible, to forestall the Germans by establishing a large air striking force at Salonika. The Greeks, on the other
hand, began to be nervous that a move of this kind would provoke
German attack, and therefore thought it unwise to make preparations at Salonika which the Germans would not fail to observe.[1]

In order to understand this last change of view, in which the
Greeks inclined to discourage the building up of an air striking force
for which they had previously asked, it is necessary to review the
general position in the Balkans. Here the attitude of Turkey continued to be of great importance. Turkey was bound by the terms of
the Balkan pact to assist Greece against Bulgaria, though not
necessarily against Italy. On the other hand she was pledged generally
under article 2 of the Anglo-Franco-Turkish Treaty of Mutual
Assistance to assist France and Great Britain in resisting an act of
aggression in the Mediterranean, and specifically under article 3 to aid
them in the fulfilment of their guarantees to Greece and Roumania.

The Turkish Government had already excused themselves from
fulfilling the general obligations in article 2; even if Turkish participation in the war at this time had been entirely in British interests, the
British Government were hardly in a position to insist upon the
fulfilment of the obligation in article 3. On August 18, three days
after the sinking of the *Helle*, Sir H. Knatchbull-Hugessen was

---

[1] See also below, section (iii) of this chapter.
(a) WM(40)291.2, C.A.; Hist (B)1, No. 18.

instructed to explore discreetly the chances of Turkish aid to Greece (a)
in the event of war between the latter country and Italy. The
Turkish Foreign Minister gave a non-committal answer. He said (b)
that Turkey ought to avoid anything which would offend the Soviet
Union, and that already the Turkish Government, in keeping an
army in Thrace, were doing more than Greece or Yugoslavia to
fulfil their obligations under the Balkan Entente. Sir H. Knatchbull-
Hugessen thought that, unless a spectacular British victory changed
the military situation, the Turks would do nothing to help Greece. He
also considered that on balance Turkish belligerency would not be
an advantage. The Turks, with their existing military resources, could (c)
not be expected to give direct military assistance, but, if they came
into the war, they would ask for more war material from Great
Britain, and, in particular, would require us to make up the arrears in
the delivery programme due to the defection of France. Russia might
also take advantage of Turkish preoccupation elsewhere to put forward demands in respect of the Straits. Our best policy therefore
would be to ask only that the Turkish Government should close the
Straits under article 21 of the Montreux Convention, break off
diplomatic relations with Italy and perhaps expel Italian nationals.

Sir M. Palairet did not agree with these arguments. He too wanted
to avoid an open dispute with the Turks over their obligations, but (d)
thought that the real question was whether Turkey would fight while
Greece was still able to resist the Italians, or wait until, after a Greek
defeat, she had to fight under much less favourable conditions.
Sir M. Palairet did not believe that the Russians would object to
Turkish aid to Greece; on the other hand a clear warning from
Turkey might have the effect of deterring Italy from an attack on
Greece.

The Chiefs of Staff had considered the question on August 23 in
connexion with the question of aid to Greece. They had inclined to (e)
Sir H. Knatchbull-Hugessen's view that we should not require more
than 'benevolent neutrality' from Turkey, including, if possible,
connivance at our use of Turkish territorial waters in the
Mediterranean. Our Ambassador was therefore instructed to (f)
follow this policy, though he was also to try to get a general declaration from Turkey which might hold back the Italians from an
attack. The Turkish Government avoided this issue by maintaining (g)
that the Italians were bluffing and therefore that the question of
Turkish intervention was unlikely to arise. They agreed, finally, to
make a statement at the opening of the Turkish National Assembly
on October 29.

(a) R7058/764/19. (b) R7211/764/19. (c) R7224/764/19. (d) R7254/764/19.
(e) R7274/764/19. (f) R7224, 7314/764/19. (g) R7396, 7362/764/19.

Thus, when the Italians attacked, there had been no statement. There had also been no agreement with the British Government upon a joint Anglo-Turkish declaration on the policy of Turkey if Italian aggression took place. Even at this stage the British view was that a declaration of policy might at least deter Bulgaria from joining in the attack. The Turkish Foreign Minister, however,

(a) explained to Sir H. Knatchbull-Hugessen that Bulgaria had been given a clear warning through diplomatic channels that a Bulgarian attack on Greece would bring Turkey into the war. M. Saracoglu considered that the most useful assistance which Turkey could give to Greece would be to contain the Bulgarian army in Thrace and thereby enable the Greeks to move troops to Albania from the Thracian frontier. The speech of M. Inönü, the Turkish President, to the National Assembly on November 1 was less definite than the

(b) Foreign Office had hoped. The President declared that Turkey could not allow her territory or her territorial waters or skies to be violated by either belligerent, but that the attitude of non-belligerency would not be an obstacle to 'normal relationships with all the countries which show the same measure of good-will towards us'. Nevertheless, although he announced no definite measures against Italy, the President reaffirmed Turkey's vital interest in Greece, and her loyalty to the alliance with Great Britain with whom the Turkish Government were 'carefully studying the situation'.

Meanwhile the Foreign Office had also been studying the situation in the wider context of the reports received about the meeting between Hitler and Mussolini at the Brenner Pass on October 4. From the information received by the Foreign Office about this meeting it seemed probable that the Germans intended during the winter to carry out a joint campaign with the Italians in the Mediterranean area, and that a part of the German action in this campaign would be a drive southwards through the Balkans. The announcement on October 7 of the entry of German troops into Roumania, under the pretext of assisting the reorganisation of the Roumanian army, could be taken as the first move in the plan of campaign.[1]

(c) On October 9 Lord Halifax suggested to the War Cabinet that the Chiefs of Staff should be asked for their views on this new *Drang nach Osten*, and that the Foreign Office should also try to find out the attitude of Turkey and of Russia. Owing to further rumours about German plans the Foreign Office considered it

(d) desirable to approach the Turkish Government without waiting for the report of the Chiefs of Staff and to point out that the first stages

---

[1] For the detailed views of the Foreign Office about the German plans, see above, p. 488.
(a) R8069, 8092/764/19.   (b) R8186, 8340/316/44.   (c) R7849/5/67; WM(40)268.4, C.A. (d) R8849/1213/44.

of the German plan—the occupation of Roumania and the Black Sea ports—were already being carried out.[1] Sir H. Knatchbull-Hugessen therefore spoke to M. Saracoglu on October 16. M. Saracoglu thought that a German move in the Balkans was likely, and that it would aim at securing the Roumanian oil supplies and at facilitating attacks on Russia either directly or by seizing the Straits, and on Turkey. M. Saracoglu said that Turkey would not give way to German threats. If, as a result, she were attacked, she would try at once to secure overland communication with the British forces in the Middle East. He spoke of the value of any help which the Royal Air Force might be able to provide and of the importance of co-ordinating naval action. Sir H. Knatchbull-Hugessen was impressed by M. Saracoglu's attitude, but during the next few months Turkish policy was, from the British point of view, disappointing.

This policy indeed depended to some extent on the attitude of Yugoslavia and Bulgaria. German troops could enter Greece by land only if they crossed Bulgarian or Yugoslav territory. Bulgaria was unlikely to resist a German demand for passage and might be bribed into active co-operation by an offer of an outlet on the Aegean. Yugoslavia hoped to avoid German demands, but there was no certainty that she would resist them. On the day of the Italian attack on Greece the Foreign Minister of Yugoslavia, M. Cincar Markovic, told Mr. Campbell, British Minister at Belgrade, that (a) Yugoslavia could serve Greek interests best by remaining neutral, since otherwise she might draw a German attack upon herself and upon Greece. Mr. Campbell was instructed on October 29 to say to the Yugoslav Government that we hoped that they would do what they could to help the Greeks, and in particular, that they would refuse demands for the passage of Axis troops. The Yugoslav reply was that the Greeks had already been assured that Italian troops (b) would not be allowed to pass through Yugoslav territory; Yugoslavia would also refuse in principle a similar request from Germany, though Mr. Campbell gathered that the tone of the refusal would depend upon the degree of force with which the request was backed. Mr. Rendel, British Minister at Sofia, was instructed on October 28 to say that His Majesty's Government hoped that, for reasons of self-interest and of honour, Bulgaria would remain neutral. The Bulgarian Government answered that they hoped to do so, but that the situation was 'delicate and difficult'. They were less ready to say that they would refuse a German demand for the right of passage through Bulgarian territory.

---

[1] See above, p. 489, for the simultaneous enquiries sent to Sir S. Cripps about the probable attitude of Russia.

(a) R7065/415/92. (b) R7065/415/92.

(a) The Greek successes encouraged Yugoslavia to go as far as a promise to resist by force a German attempt to cross Yugoslav territory. Nevertheless in the third week of November the situation was still uncertain. M. Molotov had seen Hitler on November 12–14. Three days later King Boris of Bulgaria went on a visit to Hitler at Berchtesgaden. Although there was no evidence that the King had agreed to join the Tripartite Pact, the Germans were evidently putting strong pressure on him.

It was thus desirable to try to persuade the Turkish Government to make public the warning which they had given privately to Bulgaria. Meanwhile Dr. Aras, the Turkish Ambassador in London, told the Foreign Office that his Government had approached Yugoslavia with a view to a joint request to Bulgaria to combine with them in resisting German penetration into Bulgaria. The Yugoslav Government had not replied. Dr. Aras therefore concluded that, even if the Bulgarian Government allowed German troops to enter the country, Turkey ought to remain passive until her armaments were completed and she could choose her own time for intervention.

(b) The War Cabinet discussed the situation on November 22. The Chiefs of Staff, partly as a result of Greek resistance, and partly under the influence of the Prime Minister's opinion that we should put pressure on Turkey, had now come round to the view that it would be desirable, on balance, to try to bring the Turks into the war at once, especially if there were any doubt whether they would in fact enter it later if Germany made a move in the Balkans. The Foreign Office thought with more consistency (since, if Turkey were unlikely to enter the war in the event of an actual German threat to Greece, she was even less likely to do so beforehand) that, if we put pressure on the Turks, we should merely get more demands for armaments which we could not supply. In any case, as Sir H. Knatchbull-Hugessen had long maintained, we should not succeed in persuading Turkey to enter the war unless her own interests were vitally threatened. Lord Halifax therefore suggested to the War Cabinet that we should not ask Turkey to declare war, but that we should confine ourselves to encouraging her to go on with the plan which she had herself initiated; that is to say, we should try to get a joint Turkish-Yugoslav declaration to Bulgaria that they would make war on her if she admitted German troops. This declaration would be followed by an invitation to Bulgaria to join in a tripartite undertaking to resist German attack or penetration.

The War Cabinet accepted this plan, and instructions were sent accordingly to Sir H. Knatchbull-Hugessen and Mr. Campbell. At the Prime Minister's request the instructions to the former were

---

(a) R8329/415/92. (b) R8586/316/44; WM(40)294.

supplemented by a plainer statement of the policy of the British Government to the effect that, on the principle of 'a bird in the hand', we wanted Turkey to come into the war as soon as possible. We were not pressing her to take any special steps to help the Greeks except by making it clear that a move by Germany to attack Greece, or a hostile movement by Bulgaria against Greece, would be followed by a declaration of war. We wanted Turkey and Yugoslavia to consult together in order, if possible, to have a joint warning ready to present to Bulgaria at the first sign of a German movement towards the latter country. If German troops crossed Bulgarian territory, with or without Bulgarian consent, it was vital that Turkey should fight at once. Otherwise the Balkan States would be destroyed one by one, and Turkey would be left alone without the possibility of British help.

Sir H. Knatchbull-Hugessen replied by repeating his view that Turkish participation at this time would be more of a liability to us (a) than an asset. He thought that the Turkish Government were beginning to realise that a German or Bulgarian occupation of Salonika would be a vital threat to Turkish security, and that they were becoming more inclined to take action to resist it, but he still doubted whether they would do anything if the Germans advanced through Yugoslavia, and did not reckon as more than 70 per cent the chances of Turkish action in the event of a German move through Bulgaria. In fact the Turkish declaration to Bulgaria was very mild, and the warning in it was conveyed only indirectly in a statement that if either country went to war, the other would be involved in it. The Yugoslav Government were equally nervous about committing themselves and at the end of December the sole definite ground for optimism in regard to Turkish action was a remark by the Turkish Deputy Chief of Staff that the country could not remain indifferent to any move which might threaten Salonika. The one chance of stiffening Balkan resistance therefore lay in trying to persuade the Turkish Government to accept and act upon this view.

(iii)

Greek and Yugoslav objections to the despatch of a British force to Salonika: death of General Metaxas: further attempts to secure Turkish collaboration in Balkan defence (December 29, 1940–February 8, 1941).

The Germans also realised the importance of Salonika, and as the Italian defeats in Albania and Libya made it less unlikely that

(a) R8697/316/44.

British aid could be sent to Greece on a considerable scale, German
(a) propaganda began to use the argument with the Balkan States that
the establishment of a British base at Salonika would be an offensive
act which Germany could not tolerate. In fact one of the strongest
reasons from the British point of view for assistance to Greece was
that Greek air bases might be used for attacking Italy, checking a
German advance southwards through the Balkan States and bombing
(b) the Roumanian oilfields. The King of the Hellenes had himself
complained in November of our failure to send air units to the
Salonika area, and had pointed out the strategic advantage of a
strong air force which might deter the Germans from moving against
Greece during the winter.

Sir M. Palairet was instructed on December 29 to put before the
(c) Greek Government the importance of preparing preliminary bases
from which a larger British air striking force could operate in
northern Greece. Unless these bases were available we might find it
impossible to operate the air forces which the Greeks might request
at a later stage of the war. Salonika in particular was the best base
for bombing operations against the Albanian ports. Without Greek
permission we should not attack from the Greek aerodromes territory
in German occupation but we must have full information in view of
a possible German attack in the spring. If General Metaxas should
ask whether we were willing to face the risk of an immediate German
attack on Greece, the answer was that we did not think such an
attack likely but that we wanted to take precautions against it by
preparing the aerodromes.

General Metaxas agreed reluctantly, and only 'in principle', to
(d) the establishment of a bomber squadron at Salonika; he asked that
we should not send it until we had fully considered the consequences
of provoking a German attack. Greece was not afraid of war against
Germany when the time came for it; after the defeat of Italy she
would be with us against Germany as we had been with Greece
against Italy, but the moment was not favourable. We must first
defeat Italy: we might then strike at the Roumanian oilfields, and
thus provoke Germany into an attack through Yugoslavia which
the Yugoslavs would certainly resist. Meanwhile, although he had
approved the making of preliminary surveys at Salonika, General
Metaxas continued to think it would be unwise actually to establish
an air base there. On the other hand he had asked for a detailed
reconnaissance of Lemnos, and agreed that it should include
Mitylene.

(a) R8764/4/7; R8878/316/44. (b) R8933/764/19. (c) R8940/764/19. (d) R11/11/19; R22/22/19.

The pace of the Greek advance in Albania had now slowed down, and the Greek Government were appealing for more material help. On January 7 the Greek Minister complained at the Foreign Office (a) that practically nothing had been done to meet a list of the most urgent requirements which his Government had submitted two months earlier. The Greeks were in particular need of lorries: we had provided very few of those promised from Great Britain or from captured Italian stocks in North Africa.

It was necessary to consider these requests, and the possibility of establishing a base at Salonika, in the light of the general situation. The Germans seemed to have given up the idea of a drive through Spain, but they were likely to send forces, and especially air reinforcements, through Italy to Africa in order to assist the Italians. Reports of German troop concentrations in Roumania suggested also an invasion of Greece, probably by way of Bulgaria. The Prime Minister thought that we should regard the provision of aid to Greece as more important than the prosecution of the campaign in Libya. We might not be able to bring help in time to save the Greeks, but we ought to try. Opinion in the United States, Russia and Turkey was watching to see whether once again we should fail to help our friends. The Defence Committee accepted the Prime Minister's view and decided that our assistance should take the form of specialist mechanised units and air forces to support the Greek divisions. They authorised the Middle East commanders to send to Salonika up to (b) three squadrons of Hurricanes, two more squadrons of Blenheims and a mechanised force including tanks, field artillery and anti-aircraft artillery. General Wavell was instructed to discuss plans with General Metaxas and to report the latter's comments.

The Foreign Office considered that in order to encourage the co-operation and stiffen the resistance of Yugoslavia and Turkey we (c) should tell the two Governments about our plans. The effect of giving the information was unexpected. The Prince Regent of Yugoslavia said that we should merely bring the Germans into the Balkans: they could get there more quickly than our forces, and would overrun the peninsula in a few weeks. Prince Paul argued that the purpose of German troop movements in the Balkans was not to retrieve the reverses of the Italians but to be ready for a British initiative at Salonika and to forestall a possible move by the U.S.S.R. The Germans would not allow an offensive front to be formed against them in Greece. Our proposal was therefore 'rash and mistaken'— a 'clumsy move' which would spoil our own and the Greek chances of success. Prince Paul again said that Yugoslavia would resist the

(a) R223/34/19. (b) Hist.(B)1, No. 40. (c) R278/236/44; R336/236/44.

passage of German troops, but later sent a message that this intention might be changed if the British Government did anything which constituted the formation of a Salonika front.

The War Cabinet did not accept these arguments.[1] They thought
(a) that the Greeks ought to decide for themselves upon the probable German reactions to increased British assistance. The Greeks, however, agreed with the Yugoslav view that the forces we proposed to
(b) send to Salonika would be large enough to provoke a German invasion and yet not sufficient to enable the invasion to be held. They welcomed all plans to improve and accelerate the supply of war materials—especially lorries and clothing; they were also glad to have the additional air squadrons—the largest number which they could absorb—but on the Salonika question they remained firm. General Metaxas explained to General Wavell that he was not refusing our assistance at Salonika. He wanted us to make secretly all preparations for landing an expeditionary force there. Nevertheless we ought not to land any troops until we could bring them in sufficient force for attack as well as for defence. General Wavell himself at this time
(c) regarded the Salonika proposal as a 'dangerous half-measure'—our troops would be insufficient to hold up a determined German advance, and we should have to send reinforcements or become involved in retreat or defeat. Meanwhile, owing to the diversion of the forces from Libya, our advance there would be halted and the Italians would have time to recover.

The Greek Government repeated their case in a formal note which
(d) was handed to Sir M. Palairet on January 18. They did not believe that the reinforcements offered to them would be strong enough to resist a German attack, expecially if, as was likely, the Bulgarians acted with the Germans. The Yugoslav Government told them that, in the event of a German attack provoked by the despatch of British troops to Macedonia, they would have to withdraw their pledge to resist a German demand for passage across Yugoslavia. The Greek note asked that a British force should be sent only if German troops crossed the Danube or entered Bulgaria. If plans were made for the transport by sea of a 'strategical reserve', there need be no risk of a rapid German advance before British help arrived. Even so the Greek Government felt obliged to 'draw the attention of His Majesty's Government most particularly to the fact that the problem of South-East Europe cannot be faced with the forces now at their disposal in

---

[1] Mr. Churchill sent a memorandum to Lord Halifax on January 14 that Prince Paul's views left him (Mr. Churchill) unchanged. 'The evidence in our possession of the German
(e) movements seems overwhelming. In the face of it Prince Paul's attitude looks like that of an unfortunate man in the cage with a tiger, hoping not to provoke him while steadily dinner time approaches.'

(a) WM(41)6.2, C.A. (b) Hist.(B)1, No. 50. (c) Hist.(B)1, No. 59. (d) R435/49/19; R309/173/92. (e) PMM.55/1.

the Near East. As for us, we shall accomplish our duty to the end. We leave it to the British Government to take into consideration our suggestions which are those of devoted and faithful friends.'

The attitude of Greece and Yugoslavia put the British Government in a difficult position. The Chiefs of Staff took the view that a German advance on Salonika through Yugoslavia could not be held, (a) and that an advance through Bulgaria could be met only if the Turks declared war as soon as the Germans invaded Bulgaria, and if British forces were established at Salonika before the Germans began their invasion of Bulgaria. In view of the Greek (and Yugoslav) objections to a prior occupation of Salonika, we had to accept the fact that we should be able only to impose a small delay on a German attempt to occupy the whole of Greece. The Defence Committee therefore decided to change our plans and to instruct the Middle East commanders to take as their immediate objectives an extension of the (b) Libyan offensive as far as Benghazi, and the capture of the Dodecanese. Meanwhile we should try to build up in the Nile Delta a strategic reserve of the equivalent of four divisions, i.e., the minimum strength required, in General Metaxas's view, to assist the Greeks to hold a German invasion.

Three weeks later there was another change in plans. The German move into Bulgaria which the British Government had inclined to expect in January did not take place, but the Greeks became increasingly nervous about German intentions and also of their own ability to defeat the Italians if the drain on Greek resources con- (c) tinued.[1] General Metaxas's death on January 29, 1941, deprived Greece of a leader who had won respect and confidence in spite of the previous widespread opposition to his internal policy. The new Commander-in-Chief, General Papagos, now talked of appealing for (d) British help not when the Germans crossed the Bulgarian frontier but when they entered Greece.

On February 8 Sir M. Palairet asked M. Koryzis, the new President of the Council, whether General Metaxas's statements of January 18 still held good. The President made the surprising answer that he had never seen these statements, but Sir M. Palairet was given a formal communication that Greek policy—including the determination to fight to the end—was unchanged. The Greek Government in their turn asked whether the British offer remained open. They put this question 'in order that the British Government may be in a position to judge whether, in spite of the sacrifice which Greece is prepared to

---

[1] After General Metaxas' death, General Papagos told the British Military Mission that in two months the Greeks would have no artillery ammunition.

(a) Hist.(B)1, No. 54.   (b) Hist(B)1, No. 62.   (c) Hist.(B)1, Nos. 87, 93, 101.
(d) R900/24/19; R923/9/9.

undergo in resisting the aggressor with the weak forces at her disposal on the Macedonian front, the British forces to be sent would be sufficient, with the forces at Greece's disposal, to check the German attack and to encourage at the same time Yugoslavia and Turkey to participate in the struggle'. They added that Germany would certainly consider the premature despatch of insufficient forces as a provocation; the launching of the German attack would be precipitated, and thus destroy 'even the faint hope that this attack might be avoided'.

Three days before the delivery of the Greek note the British army in Libya had captured Benghazi, and thus released earlier than had been expected considerable forces for use elsewhere. It therefore seemed possible to meet the requirements of the Greeks—four British divisions—to assist them in holding a German invasion. The Prime Minister and Mr. Eden considered that we could not abandon the Greeks in order to conserve our resources for helping Turkey.

(a) The Turks had evaded their responsibilities, and were doing nothing to prevent the Germans from establishing themselves in Bulgaria.

The Defence Committee therefore decided to make preparations at once to send the largest possible land and air forces from Africa to Europe in order to assist the Greeks against a probable German attack through Bulgaria. In order to concert plans with the military authorities and the Governments concerned, Mr. Eden and General Sir J. Dill, Chief of the Imperial General Staff, were asked to pay visits to Cairo, Athens and Ankara.

The decision to concentrate our resources in assistance to Greece was taken after the failure of another attempt to bring Turkey more openly to our side, but the Greek reluctance to allow a British force to establish itself at Salonika was in itself a reason for trying to persuade Turkey and Yugoslavia to act together in resisting a German attack on Greece. These efforts at persuasion continued intermittently, without much success, during January, 1941. The Foreign Office was already concerned over the attitude of Turkey. Although the Turkish General

(b) Staff clearly thought that Turkey should not allow a German threat to Salonika, there was little evidence that the Turkish Government entirely shared this view; they were indeed suggesting that the Germans had now given up the idea of an eastern campaign.

(c) Nevertheless on January 19 the Turkish Foreign Minister assured Sir H. Knatchbull-Hugessen that Turkey would go to war (i) if she were directly attacked by any Power; (ii) if Bulgaria, or Germany by an advance through Bulgaria, attacked Greece; (iii) if Salonika were threatened.

The Turkish Government, however, did not make a public declaration of their intentions, and although they and the Yugoslav

(a) Hist.(B)2), Nos. 1–2. (b) R278/236/44. (c) R481/236/44.

Government had agreed in principle to discuss common action, no dis- (a)
cussions were taking place. In any case it seemed clear that the
Germans were already establishing themselves in Bulgaria not by any
open acts of aggression but by methods of 'infiltration'. King Boris
had tried to avoid committing himself to Germany, yet he was even
less willing to accept the only practicable alternative at this time, that
is to say, he would not turn to Russia for protection against German
pressure. If, therefore, the Bulgarians quietly allowed German entry
into their country, Turkey might have another excuse for doing (b)
nothing.

In these circumstances the Chiefs of Staff pointed out that once the
Germans had firmly established their air force in Bulgaria, there
would be no hope of any satisfactory Turkish resistance. We might
therefore act in Turkey as the Germans were acting in Bulgaria, and
even follow the German technique of infiltration by sending air
formations and anti-aircraft artillery with personnel in civilian
clothes. The Prime Minister thought that we should try to persuade
the Turkish Government to accept assistance from us; he had not
regarded the capture of Benghazi or of the Dodecanese as sufficient
employment for the large forces which we now had available in the
Middle East. With the approval of the War Cabinet, the Prime
Minister therefore sent on January 31 a personal message to the
President of the Turkish Republic. He pointed out that the Germans (c)
were consolidating their position in Bulgaria and would soon be able
to dictate to Turkey under threat of bombing her. They could thus
reach Salonika unopposed, and secure air bases in Greece and in the
Greek islands which would threaten communications between
Turkey and the British forces in the Middle East, deny the use of
Smyrna to the British fleet, and close the exits from the Dardanelles.

The Prime Minister's view was that we should repeat in Turkey the
kind of measures which the Germans were taking on the Bulgarian
airfields. We could then not only defend Turkey but attack Roumanian oil supplies. The threat of British air forces within range of
Baku would restrain Russia (of whose intention we could not be wholly
sure) even from indirect aid to Germany. Turkey herself, under
the protection of British air power, would perhaps be able to deter
Germany from over-running Bulgaria and Greece, and also to
counterbalance the Russian fear of the German armies. If the
decisive position were to be saved, we must act at once.

Sir H. Knatchbull-Hugessen was instructed, in the event of a
favourable answer to the Prime Minister's message, to propose full
consultation with the Turkish Government on all aspects of policy
and on the prosecution of the war and to say that for this purpose
Mr. Eden would be willing to pay a visit to Ankara. The Turkish

(a) R557/557/92; R512/236/44. (b) R545/91/7. (c) R720/274/44.

(a) reply, however, was unfavourable. Our offer of assistance—10 air squadrons and 100 A.A. guns—seemed to the Turkish Government far too small. The President said that 'to allow the presence in Turkey, in anticipation of a German advance threatening Turkish security, of British air and artillery units would mean the entry of Turkey into the war'. This step would be against Turkish and British interests, and could not be contemplated 'within the framework of present commitments'. Turkey was also short of essential war material. The Turkish attitude would remain loyal, and of service to the common cause of the two Allied countries, and Turkey would accept everything (including personnel as 'instructors') short of military formations.[1]

Thus in the second week of February 1941, before Mr. Eden and General Dill left England, the immediate position in the Balkans and in the eastern Mediterranean was in some respects more favourable than at the time of the opening of the Italian offensive against Greece, while the prospects for the future were becoming increasingly grave. The Italians had been heavily defeated in Libya and in the Sudan. There was no threat to Cairo, or to Khartoum, and the internal situation in Egypt was satisfactory. At sea the Italians had not yet repaired the damage done to their capital ships by air attacks at Taranto in the previous November. Henceforward there was still serious danger from cruiser raids and submarine and torpedo attacks by small craft and from the attacks of shore-based aircraft, but the larger ships of the Italian navy were unlikely to venture themselves in a battle to gain control of the eastern Mediterranean. The brave resistance of the Greeks had also lowered Italian prestige and was causing serious losses in men and material.

On the other hand the fact that Italy was floundering in defeat made German intervention more probable. There were already some doubtful rumours of a coming German attack on Russia; even if these rumours were to be believed, and if the Russians did not give way to German demands, the Germans were likely to secure themselves in the Balkans before turning against Russia. The prospects of a successful invasion of Great Britain were much less, but the

---

[1] On February 17, 1941, the Turkish and Bulgarian Governments issued a declaration reaffirming their pact of friendship and stating that they proposed to have an exchange of views in the light of recent events, and that they had agreed (without prejudice to their contracted agreements with other countries) on the following points: (i) the unchanging basis of the foreign policy of both countries was to abstain from aggression; (ii) the two Governments would maintain and develop good neighbourly relations. The declaration also referred to the development of mutual trade, and expressed the hope that the press of each country would be inspired by mutual trust and confidence.

(a) R871/274/44; R898/236/44.

Germans would have more forces available for a move in south-east Europe if they decided not to attempt invasion. Their air force, though considerably damaged, was still very powerful and their armies had the immense prestige of victory in France. The Balkan States, like the smaller States of northern and western Europe a year earlier, were terrified of Germany. Roumania had already collapsed; German divisions were concentrating in the country and preparing for a southward advance. Bulgaria was falling rapidly under German control. Yugoslavia and Turkey were unwilling to do anything which might provoke a German attack. Greece was fighting the Italians, but not very hopeful that Great Britain could save her when the Germans came to the rescue of their Italian Ally.

The British Government had decided, at least in principle, to fulfil their obligations to Greece both as a matter of honour and in their own interest; a German occupation of the Greek ports and islands—including Crete—would have been a most serious embarrassment to the British connexion with Turkey and to sea communications generally in the eastern Mediterranean. If Greece and, ultimately, Turkey, were to be saved, the only hope of success lay in bold and rapid action. This action would strain British resources and weaken British military strength elsewhere in the Middle East; the risks of failure were considerable, but for moral and political reasons as well as on grounds of general strategy these risks had to be taken.

(iv)

The Eden-Dill Mission, I: the Tatoi conversations and the decision of His Majesty's Government to send an expeditionary force to Greece: Colonel Donovan's report (February 19–28, 1941).

Mr. Eden and General Dill arrived in Cairo on February 19[1] and after discussion with the Commanders-in-Chief in the Middle East flew to Athens on February 22. They reached Ankara on February 26 and came back on March 2 to Athens. They left Athens on March 6 for Cairo. Mr. Eden saw M. Saracoglu again in Cyprus on March 18 and 19, and left Cairo for London on March 25, but returned with General Dill on March 27 from Malta to Athens, and from Athens again to Cairo. The two envoys left Cairo finally on April 7.

---

[1] On this day Hitler gave orders (confirmed six days later) for the building of bridges across the Danube between Bulgaria and Roumania for the crossing of German troops on March 2. On February 18 Hitler had set up a German Afrika Korps under General Rommel.

(a)   Mr. Eden's instructions from the Prime Minister were that his first task was to help Greece; for this purpose he was to initiate any action necessary with the Middle East military authorities and with the Greek, Egyptian, Yugoslav and Turkish Governments. He was authorised to make the 'best arrangement possible in the circumstances' with the Greek Government. Two days before Mr. Eden

(b)   flew to Athens the Prime Minister recapitulated to the War Cabinet the main factors in the situation. If the Greeks were determined to resist German attack, we could not do otherwise than help them to the full extent of our power, although in fact we might not be able to keep the Germans out of Salonika. If the Greeks made terms—and we should not blame them for doing so—we would try to hold the islands. Mr. Churchill hoped that we should not have to put a large part of our army into Greece; he also thought it unlikely that large British reinforcements could arrive there before the Germans.

(c)   On February 21 Mr. Churchill sent a telegram to the two envoys reminding them that they need not feel bound to a Greek enterprise if they considered it hopeless.

    Mr. Eden's telegrams were, however, not at all pessimistic. The

(d)   Middle East commanders agreed with the Cabinet that Greece must have first call on our direct assistance, although in such case we could do little or nothing to help the Turks. They also thought that, if the Greeks would accept our help at once, there was a fair chance of halting a German advance into the country, although we probably had insufficient air resources to hold a line which would allow us to defend Salonika. General Wavell was ready to send three divisions, the larger part of one armoured division, a Polish brigade, and some specialised troops, such as anti-tank and anti-aircraft units. The total strength would include 100,000 men, 240 field guns and 142 tanks. Air Chief Marshal Longmore undertook to reinforce before the end of March the squadrons already supporting Greece by 3 squadrons of Blenheims and also to make available when required 3 night bomber squadrons based on Egypt.[1]

(e)   Mr. Eden and General Dill held conversations at the Palace of Tatoi near Athens with the King of the Hellenes, the President of the Council and General Papagos. The Greeks reaffirmed their determination to go on fighting until victory; they would fight the Germans as well as the Italians and, if necessary, they would fight alone. They had only three divisions on their Macedonian frontier, and were still afraid that, while the attitude of Yugoslavia and Turkey

---

[1] At the Tatoi meeting the British representatives said that two more squadrons of fighters might be available by the end of March.

(a) R1945/9/19.   (b) WM(41)19.1, C.A.   (c) Hist. (B)2, No. 36, Tel. 467 to Cairo; WP(41)38.   (d) Hist. (B)2, No. 35, No. 39, Cairo tels. 355, 358; R3870/1109/67 (1942), Annex 1.   (e) Hist. (B)2, No. 40, Athens tel. 262; R3870/1109/67 (1942), Annexes 2 & 3, R1522/1383/67; WP(41)38.

remained doubtful, British help on an insufficient scale would merely provoke a German attack which the combined Anglo-Greek forces could not withstand.

Mr. Eden then gave details of the forces we could provide and the time it would take to send them. He said that if we waited through fear of provoking Germany or because we were not sure of the Turks or Yugoslavs, we should be too late. After discussion between the Greek and British military representatives, M. Koryzis stated formally that the Greek Government accepted the British offer and approved the detailed arrangements reached in the military conversations.

The most important of these arrangements was that the Greeks should withdraw most of their advanced forces from Thrace and Macedonia in order to join with the British forces in defending the so-called Aliakhmon line. This position extended from the Yugoslav frontier near Lake Ostrovo along the high ground running from north of Mount Olympus to the west of the Vardar, and protecting the routes westwards and southwards from the Vardar plain. The British representatives agreed that if we could rely on Yugoslav help we might subsequently go beyond this line and defend Salonika, but that there should be an immediate withdrawal to the shorter and more defensible position to the south-west. According to the British record (though General Papagos stated later that this was not his view of the decision) the Greek representatives agreed. A second point was that the British forces should be under the command of General Papagos, but that the British commander should have the right to appeal to General Wavell who could in turn appeal to the British Government if he failed to reach agreement with General Papagos.

From their later conversations with the Greeks it seems clear that at Tatoi the British representatives were satisfied that there was a good chance of holding the Aliakhmon line even if Yugoslavia and Turkey did not enter the war. In the afternoon of February 24 the War Cabinet approved the offer made to the Greeks and the decision (a) implied in it to open a new front in Greece. The decision was not an easy one, although the strategic arguments had already been discussed and the chances and consequences of failure considered. There were, however, two new factors in the discussion. In the first place the Chiefs of Staff disagreed with the military authorities in the Middle East on the question of the vital importance of the attitude of Turkey and Yugoslavia. The Chiefs of Staff considered that if these two countries entered the war, we might hope to build up a Balkan front; without the support of one or the other of them we were unlikely to be able to save Greece. The Foreign Office

(a) WM(41)20.4, C.A.; WP(41)39 (Revise).

thought that our action might have some influence on Turkey, but that there was little hope that Yugoslavia would hold out against German demands.

The second new factor was that only a small proportion of the troops which General Wavell proposed to send to Greece were from the United Kingdom. Two divisions would be Australian, and one from New Zealand. The Australian Prime Minister, Mr. Menzies, was present at the War Cabinet meeting on February 24. He asked for assurances that the venture had a reasonable chance of success; that, if it failed, we should not lose more than the material of the armoured division, and that no Australian troops should be sent without adequate equipment. The War Cabinet finally accepted the plan subject to the willingness of the Governments of Australia and New Zealand to authorise the use of their respective troops. The two Governments gave their consent with certain reservations: (i) that the troops should be fully equipped and adequately supported, (ii) that the force proposed was believed to be adequate to the hazardous task proposed for it, (iii) that reinforcements should be provided as soon as possible. The Australian Government also laid down as a condition that plans should be prepared for the evacuation of the troops if it were found necessary.[1]

(a)   The War Cabinet considered the matter again on February 27. The Prime Minister was influenced by the optimistic views of the Middle East Command. He spoke of the political consequences for which we might hope from the proposed expedition. We hoped for the co-operation of Turkish forces which, with our own and those of the Greeks, would outnumber any force which the Germans could put into the field against us for several months. It was still possible that the Yugoslavs might join us, and we should expect to send considerable reinforcements approximately within two months.

The main arguments therefore in favour of the expedition were not only that we should be honouring our pledges to Greece but that we had also good prospects of transforming the military and political situation in our favour. The view taken of these chances seems to have been affected not only by the hopeful telegrams from Mr. Eden and (b) General Dill, but also by an American report on the prospects of the war in the Mediterranean area. Colonel Donovan, the writer of this report, had been making a tour of the Balkan capitals and the Middle East as the personal emissary of Colonel Knox, United States Secretary of the Navy. His mission had no official status—and he was not a member of the Democratic Party—but these facts showed the

---

[1] The risks of the enterprise were also explained to General Sikorski. It should be recorded that he agreed nonetheless to the employment of the Polish brigade although it was at this time the only Polish force in being.

(a) WM(41)21.2, C.A.   (b) R1483, 2157/113/67.

new 'nation-wide' character of American policy towards the war. There was no doubt that Colonel Donovan's views would carry great weight with the President and the State Department. Colonel Donovan thought it of vital importance to build up a Balkan front. He believed that the first aim of Germany was still the invasion of Great Britain, and that the Germans would have tried to maintain peace in the Balkans, if the Italian defeat had not compelled them to reckon with the possibility that British forces might establish themselves within striking distance of the Roumanian oilfields. Hence the Germans might now decide to overrun the whole peninsula before effective British aid could arrive. Colonel Donovan considered that the Balkans offered perhaps the one field of operations in which Great Britain could meet and defeat the German armies, but only on condition that Yugoslavia and Turkey, and, if possible, Bulgaria, joined in common action with the British and Greek forces. Great Britain could provide the technical and expert services needed for such concerted action, and American diplomatic influence might do much to decide the Balkan States in favour of taking it. Hence Colonel Donovan urged that Mr. Roosevelt should use his good offices to this end, and that the United States should increase their supplies of war material to Greece.

Colonel Donovan's report thus strengthened the view that the risks of an expedition to Greece were worth taking, and, conversely, that a refusal to help Greece would have a serious moral effect on the American attitude towards Great Britain. Moreover, even before the report was drafted, there had been signs of an increased American interest in the Balkans. At the end of November 1940, the State Department had refused a suggestion from the British Government that they might warn the Bulgarians against giving way to Axis pressure. Before the end of the year, however, they had spoken on these lines to the Bulgarian Minister at Washington. In the middle of January they had also agreed to instruct the United States Chargé d'Affaires at Sofia to call the attention of the Bulgarian Government to the references in Mr. Roosevelt's speeches to the aid which the United States would give to all countries resisting aggression. Mr. Roosevelt himself sent personal messages to the Turkish Prime (a) Minister and the Prince Regent of Yugoslavia on February 14.[1]

---

[1] *F.R.U.S.*, 1941, III, 815-6, and II, 944.
(a) R1278/1003/67.

(v)

*The Eden-Dill Mission, II: Bulgarian adherence to the Tripartite Pact:
final decision of the War Cabinet to send an expeditionary force to Greece,
(March 1–7, 1941).*

The relative optimism felt on the British and American sides at
the time of the Tatoi conversations was not borne out by events.
(a) Mr. Eden and General Dill found on their arrival at Ankara that
the Turks had made no progress in their conversations with the
Yugoslavs, and were unlikely to come into the war even if the
Germans invaded Greece. President Inönü impressed the British
representatives with his goodwill and his confidence in a British
victory. He repeated that Turkey would fight if attacked, but said
that, owing to their lack of war material, Turkish forces could not
carry out an offensive; hence Turkey would serve the common cause
better if she remained out of the war until she had made good these
deficiences and could employ her army with the maximum effect.
Mr. Eden and General Dill agreed that Turkey should not attempt
offensive action; they suggested that she should declare war at the
latest when Germany invaded Bulgaria. Otherwise the Germans
would be free to carry out their usual plan of dealing only with one
enemy at a time, and public opinion in Greece, Yugoslavia, the
United States and Great Britain would be discouraged by the
Turkish attitude. The Turkish answers, however, remained non-
committal. They did not say that they would not declare war; they
maintained only that they could not give an undertaking to do so.

The Yugoslav attitude was not more satisfactory. Mr. Eden had
(b) telegraphed to Prince Paul from Athens asking for his views on the
dangers inherent in German activities in the Balkans. The telegram
was an indirect appeal to Yugoslavia to join in the assistance which
Great Britain was giving to Greece.[1] The Yugoslav Ambassador at
(c) Ankara brought the reply to Mr. Eden; Yugoslavia would defend
herself against aggression or against the transit of foreign troops, but
could not yet decide what she would do if Germany moved across
Bulgaria. The Ambassador said that Great Britain could give
Yugoslavia no assistance, and that the formation of a united front
by Yugoslavia, Turkey and Greece might well provoke counter-
action by Germany.

The question whether Yugoslavia would take action if German
troops moved into Bulgaria was answered almost at once. From the

---

[1] At the Tatoi meeting it had been agreed to inform Prince Paul in general terms of the
assistance which Great Britain proposed to send, and to invite Yugoslavia to join in the
defence of Greece. After the meeting it was decided on security grounds to use less direct
language.

(a) Hist. (B)2, No. 60, Ankara tel. 414; R3870/1109/67 (1942), Annexes 5–7.
(b) R1487/73/92. (c) R3870/1109/67 (1942), Annex 8.

morning of March 1 German troops had begun to enter the country **(a)**
without pretence of concealment. On this day M. Filoff, President
of the Council of Ministers, left for Vienna to sign the Tripartite
Pact. The British Minister, at a meeting with King Boris on March 2,
pointed out the grave consequences to Bulgaria of the course she was
taking in associating herself actively with the enemies of Great
Britain. The King answered that Bulgaria had again suffered from
her geographical position: he said nothing to show that he regretted
the policy which he had adopted.

Mr. Rendel had already been given discretion to break off
diplomatic relations with Bulgaria. He decided to do so on March 5.
In his final interview with M. Filoff, he said that he regretted that
the British Government had not been able to help Bulgaria to
maintain her independence. M. Filoff replied that the Bulgarian
Government were themselves able to look after the independence of
the country. Mr. Rendel took formal note of this statement and
pointed out that it might prove important to have on record for a
future peace conference the fact that the Bulgarian Prime Minister
had assumed formal responsibility for the consequences to Bulgaria
of the policy of his Government.

Mr. Eden and General Dill returned to Athens on March 2. Here **(b)**
they learned that General Papagos had not withdrawn Greek troops
from Macedonia to the Aliakhmon line since he had assumed that
the decision to do so depended on the receipt of definite news of the
attitude of Yugoslavia. General Papagos said that, in view of the
German entry into Bulgaria, a withdrawal was not now possible
because the Germans were now much nearer and their advance
might catch the Greek troops on the move; in any case their retreat
would cause alarm amongst the Greeks in the Macedonian districts
to be evacuated. He was also unable to move troops from the
Albanian frontier without serious effect on their morale.

The envoys found that the Greeks were in general despondent,
with the exception of the King, who was calm, determined, and
helpful. Mr. Eden and General Dill pointed out that the decision to
hold the Aliakhmon line had been taken irrespective of the attitude
of Turkey and Yugoslavia, but they could get no more than an
undertaking that three Greek divisions from Macedonia and (if the
Turks agreed) seven battalions from Thrace should be sent to the
line. Even so the British military authorities continued to regard it
as possible to halt the German advance on this line. Mr. Eden
therefore used the discretionary power which he had been given to
act in an emergency, and accepted the revised Greek proposals. He
had called General Wavell to Athens to take part in the discussions

---

(a) R4411/1041/7.   (b) Hist. (B)2, Nos. 73, 76-7, Athens tels. 313, 314, 326; R3870/
1109/67 (1942), Annex 9.

(a) and the Middle East Commanders-in-Chief agreed with the decision. Mr. Eden reported these facts in a telegram of March 5.

Mr. Eden also decided, on his return to Athens, to make another
(a) attempt to persuade Yugoslavia to resist the Germans. Mr. Campbell, who had come from Belgrade to see Mr. Eden, thought there was still
(b) a chance that the Yugoslavs might be ready to help if they knew the extent of our plans for aiding Greece. Mr. Eden therefore considered that he must take the risk of letting Prince Paul know more about the plans. He gave Mr. Campbell a letter for Prince Paul. On presenting the letter Mr. Campbell was to explain that we had decided to support the Greeks with land and air forces as strongly and as rapidly as possible. While we were concentrating our forces, we should hold a covering position west of Salonika, but the Greek army in Macedonia would be defending the city, and as soon as we could do so, we should move forward to operate with them. The chances of a successful defence of Salonika must depend largely on the attitude of Yugoslavia. If Prince Paul would agree to send a staff officer to hold discussions with the Greeks, the British military authorities would join in them. Mr. Eden also gave Mr. Campbell discretion to say that the British Government were 'studying with sympathy' the case for the revision of the Yugoslav frontier with Italy in Istria, and 'were disposed to think that this case could be established and advocated by them at the Peace Conference'.[1]

(c) Mr. Eden had suggested to Prince Paul before leaving England that he might go to Yugoslavia, but the response had been that a meeting
(d) was impracticable. Later attempts to arrange a meeting also failed although the Yugoslav Prime Minister, M. Cvetković, and the Foreign Minister had seen Hitler and Ribbentrop on February 14, and Prince Paul himself went to Germany on March 4. The Yugoslav Government now agreed to send a staff officer to meet Greek and British military representatives on condition that the visit was kept
(e) secret. This officer arrived in a defeatist mood but seemed satisfied with the answers to his questions.[2]

---

[1] This step had been suggested by Sir S. Cripps. The Cabinet confirmed their approval
(f) of it on March 3. The precise terms of revision were left vague, but the Foreign Office considered that we might recognise on ethnographical grounds the Yugoslav claim to the Istrian Isthmus northwards as far as Gorizia and to the Italian Islands off the Yugoslav
(g) coast. The Foreign Office pointed out that hitherto we had adopted the rule that we could not discuss territorial changes during the war. We might, however, disregard this rule in the case of Yugoslavia if by so doing we could induce her to intervene forcibly on behalf of Greece. Obviously we had no obligation to Italy.

[2] These answers were in guarded terms, but Admiral Cunningham thought that we had
(h) given too high an estimate of the naval assistance which it would be possible for us to provide.

(a) Hist. (B)2, No. 72, Athens tel. 312.   (b) R3870/1109/67 (1942) and Annex 10.
(c) R1198/274/44.   (d) R1196, 1243/274/44; R1410, 1490, 1650, 1655, 1805, 1833, 1840, 1841/1383/67;   (e) R 3870/1109/67 (1942), Annex 11; Hist (B)2, No. 98.   (f) R589/73/92; WM(41)22, R1949/960/92.   (g) WP(41)45.   (h) Hist. (B)2, No. 125.

The War Cabinet thus had to consider the position towards the end of the first week of March in the light of Mr. Eden's information and of the unwillingness of Turkey and Yugoslavia to risk the provocation of Germany even after the Germans were massing in Bulgaria. The War Cabinet met in the afternoon of March 5, and the Defence Committee at 10 p.m. on this day. The Prime Minister (a) told the War Cabinet of the latest developments, and of the view of Mr. Eden and his military advisers that we should accept the Greek proposals. The Prime Minister said that if the Greeks had taken action, or entered into commitments, on the strength of undertakings received from us, we should have had no alternative but to go through with our plans for assisting them. The Greeks, however, did not appear to have taken any such action; they had not indeed done what we had expected them to do, i.e. withdraw divisions from the Albanian and Macedonian fronts. It was thus still open to us, if we thought it best to do so, to tell the Greeks that we would release them from any undertaking which they had given to us: they would then be free to make terms with Germany. Mr. Churchill referred to Mr. Eden's comment that our forces would be engaged in a much more hazardous operation than we had thought a week earlier. The Government would therefore have to consult the Australian and New Zealand Governments again before committing them to a Balkan campaign, but we ought not to leave them with the main burden of decision. The War Cabinet agreed that the situation had changed for the worse since they had decided to send forces to Greece, and that they might have to reconsider their decision. Since there was no need to come to a final conclusion at once, Mr. Eden should be told of their doubts, and should be asked whether the prospects generally, and the help we could provide in the time available, justified us in persuading the Greeks to resist a German attack if it were clear that our attempts to raise a Balkan combination had failed.

The Defence Committee at their meeting considered the draft of a telegram which the Prime Minister proposed to send to Mr. Eden. (b) They thought that there must have been some factors unknown to them which had influenced Mr. Eden and General Dill to take the view that there was still a good chance to hold up a German advance. The Prime Minister's opinion was that the Greeks would be unable to resist the Germans, and that there was little or nothing we could do in the time available.

In his telegram to Mr. Eden (which was despatched on the night of March 5–6) the Prime Minister asked for more precise information on (c) the reasons why he and General Dill still thought that the plan to send an expeditionary force to Greece should go forward. The Prime

---

(a) WM(41)24, C.A. (b) DO (41) 9th meeting. (c) Hist. (B)2, Nos. 78–9, Tels 607–8 to Cairo.

Minister said that it was difficult to believe that we had the power to avert the fate of Greece unless Turkey and Yugoslavia, or at least one of the two, joined us, and their collaboration now seemed most improbable. We had done our best to secure a Balkan combination against Germany, and must now be careful not to urge the Greeks, against their better judgment, into a hopeless resistance when we had only handfuls of troops which could reach Greece in time. Grave imperial issues were involved in committing Australian and New Zealand troops to an enterprise which had now become even more hazardous. The War Cabinet were therefore bound to consult the two Dominion Governments and could not be sure of their assent. They themselves saw no reason for expecting success, though they attached great weight to the opinions of General Wavell and General Dill. We must liberate the Greeks from any feeling that they ought to reject a German ultimatum, though if they were still resolved to fight, we were bound to some extent to share their ordeal.

The loss of Greece and of the Balkans would not be a major catastrophe for us, as long as Turkey remained an honest neutral. On the other hand our ignominious ejection from Greece might do us more harm in Spain and with the Vichy Government than the fact of the submission of the Balkan States which we could not have been expected to prevent with our scanty forces.[1]

(a)   The War Cabinet met again at 6 p.m. on March 6. No answer had yet been received from Mr. Eden. After Mr. Menzies had explained the difficulties from the Australian point of view, i.e. all the new factors added to the hazards of the operation, and no reason had been given why our military advisers thought it should succeed, the Prime Minister said that no decision need be taken, or indeed could be taken, until they heard from Mr. Eden. He thought it advisable to send another telegram to Mr. Eden to make it clear that the War Cabinet had to delay their decision until they had heard from him. Meanwhile the delay would not affect the operation: our troops were on the move and would not begin to arrive in Greece until March 8. The Prime Minister's own view was that we could not now go back on the agreement signed by General Dill and General Papagos unless the Greeks themselves released us.

In his second telegram to Mr. Eden (despatched during the night
(b) of March 6–7) the Prime Minister said that two points were dominant. We must not take on ourselves the responsibility of persuading the Greeks against their better judgment to fight a hopeless battle and probably involve their country in speedy ruin, although, as the

---

[1] The Prime Minister concluded with the words: 'I send you this to prepare your mind for what, in the absence of facts very different from those now before us, will probably be expressed in Cabinet tomorrow' (i.e. March 6).
(a) WM(41)25.1, C.A.   (b) Hist. (B)2, No. 90, Tel. 623 to Cairo.

Prime Minister repeated, if the Greeks were resolved to fight to the death, we must fight with them. We must, however, be able to tell the Australian and New Zealand Governments faithfully that we were undertaking this hazard not owing to 'any commitment entered into by a British Cabinet Minister at Athens, and signed by the Chief of the Imperial General Staff', but because General Dill and Wavell and the other Commanders-in-Chief were convinced that we had a reasonable fighting chance.

Mr. Eden sent a short telegram in the afternoon of March 6 that he and General Dill had re-examined the situation with the three (a) Commanders-in-Chief, and that they still thought that the decision taken in Athens was right, although it involved us in heavy commitments and grave risks. On the morning of March 7, in answer to the Prime Minister's requests, Mr. Eden sent a longer appreciation. He (b) confirmed his earlier statement that General Wavell believed that, if his forces could be transported to Greece and concentrated on the Aliakhmon line, there was a good chance of holding the enemy, who had difficulties of his own—long and bad communications through countries of doubtful friendship. On the other hand we had heavy handicaps at sea and in the air, and the risks were now greater than they had seemed even at the Tatoi meeting.[1] Moreover the issues could not be weighed solely in chances of military success. The Greeks had said that they would fight to the end even without our assistance. There had been no question of urging them to resist against their own judgment. If we left them to their fate at a time when, as everyone knew, our Libyan victories had made forces available to us, we should damage our own reputation far more gravely than we could damage it by an unsuccessful attempt to hold the Germans.

The Australian and New Zealand commanders in the Middle East also agreed[2] that we should send our expedition, in spite of the increased risks. Field-Marshal Smuts[3] took the same view, although (c) he thought that it would be very difficult to get our troops into Greece before the German assault began. He considered that we should send as large a force as possible, and that the Germans would not attempt more than a 'feint' in North Africa in the hope of keeping our troops there.

---

[1] Apart from other set-backs the laying of mines by the enemy in the Suez Canal had greatly increased the military difficulties. We had also failed in an attempt to capture the island of Casteloritzo, and the general operations planned against the Dodecanese had therefore been postponed.

[2] I have not dealt with the question (raised subsequently by the Dominion Governments) whether the consultation with their commanders was adequate.

[3] Mr. Eden, with the Prime Minister's approval, had invited Field-Marshal Smuts to Cairo to take part in the discussions.

(a) Hist. (B)2, No. 85, Cairo tel. 455.   (b) Hist. (B)2, No. 91, Cairo tel. 463; R3870/1109/67 (1942), Annexes 12–13. (c) Hist. (B)2, No. 89.

(a)   The War Cabinet met at noon on March 7. Mr. Eden's longer telegram had not arrived, and the War Cabinet had to come to a decision on the basis of his earlier telegrams, including the short message of the afternoon of March 6. They felt it extremely difficult to judge a situation which was rapidly changing for the worse, and upon which a military decision required local knowledge. They had been told the general views of the Middle East commanders, but had not heard the detailed arguments which led the commanders to believe that the enterprise had a fair chance of success.[1] Indeed the military considerations hitherto brought forward seemed to weigh against the plan, and the Chiefs of Staff could do no more than say that, although the risks were now greater, they were prepared to accept the opinion of the local commanders that the campaign would not be a hopeless venture. The Prime Minister thought that we should go on with our plan. Mr. Menzies agreed with him, though he still thought it strange that the arguments given by Mr. Eden and his military advisers told against, rather than for the case which they recommended the War Cabinet to adopt. The War Cabinet accepted the Prime Minister's conclusion that we should continue with the plan. They at once informed the Australian and New Zealand Governments. These Governments gave their consent, also with great misgivings.

(vi)

Further attempts to prevent a Yugoslav surrender to German demands and to bring about an agreement between Turkey and Yugoslavia: adherence of Yugoslavia to the Tripartite Pact, March 25, 1941.

The War Cabinet had accepted the risks of sending an expedition to Greece. They had acted on the advice of the military chiefs, but, whatever the hazards, it would not have been easy for them to have taken any other decision. If the expedition succeeded, the Germans would be committed to a front at the end of long communications; although success on this front would not settle the issue of the war, it might well turn out from the German point of view to be something like the 'running sore' of Spain in the Napoleonic war. If the expedition failed, at least we should share in the sufferings of the Greeks, and avoid the disgrace of leaving brave friends to their fate. Nevertheless the decision had been doubly difficult because the land forces

---

[1] It is remarkable that neither General Wavell nor General Dill had gone to see the ground before coming to the conclusion that there was a good chance of holding the Aliakhmon line.

(a) WM(41)26.1, C.A.

which we could send to Greece consisted mainly of Australian and New Zealand troops. They would be conveyed in British ships under protection of the British Navy and the Royal Air Force, but, in asking for authorisation to send them, the Prime Minister and members of the War Cabinet were putting a heavy responsibility, not only on themselves, but on the Governments of Australia and New Zealand. The facts that they could suggest doing so, that Mr. Menzies, the Australian Prime Minister, was present at the decisive meetings of the War Cabinet in London, and that Field-Marshal Smuts was also consulted, show the nature of the co-operation between members of the British Commonwealth.[1] The consent of the Australian and New Zealand Governments was the more striking because at this time it seemed that the Japanese might decide to enter the war, and that Australia and New Zealand might need all their available manpower for defence in their own area.[2] It was therefore out of regard for the Dominions as well as for the Greeks and themselves that the British Government tried their utmost, even at this late stage, to secure the co-operation of Yugoslavia and Turkey.

The German military attack in the Balkans did not open until a month after the War Cabinet had finally decided to persist in the plan to send an expeditionary force to Greece. During this month the main diplomatic struggle was over Yugoslavia. In spite of the pressure by the Germans, there seemed a chance that Yugoslavia might not give way to the demands which the Germans were known to be making. Popular opinion among the Serbs was anti-German, though there were ominous divisions between the Serbs and the Croats, and the Yugoslav Government knew well enough that, even if they surrendered to Germany, the Germans might well enforce territorial sacrifices upon them to the advantage of Italy.

Prince Paul's attitude, in various conversations with Mr. Campbell during the first half of March, showed the extreme difficulty in which he was placed. His own wish for a British victory appeared to be sincere. He felt, however, that he was not free to decide according to (a) his personal inclinations. He had to judge the chances of military success; his advisers told him that the country could not hold out for more than a week, and that, even with British help, the Greeks could not resist much longer. He had also to consider public opinion,

---

[1] It should be mentioned, however, that the Australian Government, while accepting the decision, protested against Mr. Eden's action in signing, without their prior consent, an agreement committing Australian troops. Mr. Churchill himself had already had this point in mind in his telegram to Mr. Eden on March 7. Mr. Menzies had also called the attention of the War Cabinet to the fact that the Australian Government had not been asked to approve the grant of discretionary power to Mr. Eden.

[2] See Volume II, Chapter XXIII.

(a) R2289/113/67.

especially in Croatia. It was therefore impossible for him to come to a decision until he was sure that there was no way out between surrender to the Germans and fighting them.

Prince Paul's choice was not long delayed. On March 14 the (a) Yugoslav Prime Minister and Foreign Minister went again to Germany. They had told Mr. Campbell that they would never agree to participate in the war on the German side, or to the passage of German troops through Yugoslav territory, but it seemed clear that they were on the point of accepting some kind of adherence to (b) the Tripartite Pact. Mr. Eden therefore decided to send Mr. Shone, the British Minister at Cairo and a personal friend of Prince Paul, to Belgrade with another letter of encouragement. On March 20 Mr. Campbell learned, however, that the Yugoslav Cabinet had in fact agreed to sign the Tripartite Pact on certain conditions. Prince Paul and the Yugoslav Prime Minister said that they hoped that the Germans might refuse these conditions, and thus put themselves in the position of aggressors. Mr. Campbell suggested that one condition should be a German declaration safeguarding Salonika, but Prince Paul had already said to him on March 18 (when he was delivering (c) Mr. Eden's letter) that the Croats would regard Salonika merely as a 'regional interest' of the Serbs. Similarly the Croats would consider as an act of unjustified aggression the attack upon the Italian armies in Albania which the British representatives were asking Yugoslavia to make.

Mr. Eden also tried to obtain Russian encouragement for the (d) Yugoslavs. On March 8 the Yugoslav Prime Minister had mentioned to Mr. Campbell that he noticed signs of a change in Soviet foreign policy and that there was evidence of German troop movements towards the Russian frontier. Three days later Mr. Campbell reported that the Yugoslav Ministers favoured the idea of a military alliance between Yugoslavia and Russia and that a special envoy whom they had sent secretly to Moscow a few weeks earlier seemed hopeful about the prospects of such an alliance. Sir S. Cripps also reported that military authorities in Moscow were advising the (e) Yugoslav Minister there to raise the question with the Soviet Government. On March 21 Mr. Eden telegraphed to Sir S. Cripps (f) suggesting that he should ask the Soviet Government whether they could do anything to encourage Yugoslavia not to give way to Germany.

Sir S. Cripps made the suggestion to M. Vyshinsky on March 22. (g) M. Vyshinsky received it 'very seriously' and said that he would

(a) R2342, 2430, 2490, 2540, 2536, 2538, 2539, 2574, 2571/113/67.   (b) R2594/113/67; R2776/2706/92; R3870/1109/67 (1942), Annex 17; R2778, 2828, 2830/2706/92. (c) R2776/2706/92.   (d) R2341/113/67.   (e) R2360, 2446/113/67.   (f) R2853/2706/92. (g) R2878/394/92.

communicate it at once to the Soviet Government. The Yugoslav Minister, on Sir S. Cripps's suggestion, made a similar approach. Late on the night of March 22–3 M. Vyshinsky summoned the Minister and told him that the Soviet Government considered that (a) the situation was already 'settled adversely', and that they could do nothing. If, however, in the course of the next days, the settlement of which he had spoken appeared not to have taken place, the Soviet Government would reconsider the matter.[1]

On March 23 Prince Paul told Mr. Campbell that the German (b) Government had given Yugoslavia until midnight of that day to sign the Tripartite Pact in a modified form.[2] On March 24 Mr. Campbell delivered letters from His Majesty the King to Prince (c) Paul and from Mr. Churchill to the Yugoslav Prime Minister, but the Prince and his Minister had decided to give way, and the latter signed the Tripartite Pact in Vienna on March 25.

Meanwhile, after his return to Cairo on March 6, Mr. Eden had tried to get some gesture from Turkey which might at least delay the (d) German attack. He suggested, on the recommendation of Sir M. Palairet, that the Turkish Government might agree to take over the Thracian positions which the Greeks were evacuating, and, in particular, the bridgeheads at Demotika and Dedeagatch.

The Turkish Government refused to move from their negative attitude. M. Saracoglu said that he realised the importance of raising Greek and Yugoslav morale, but there was little that the Turks could (e) do while they had to remain on the defensive. They could not occupy the Thracian bridgeheads, though they would not announce the fact. They had also had no response to their approaches to Yugoslavia. On March 13 Sir H. Knatchbull-Hugessen was told that, in consequence of the unopposed occupation of Roumania and (f) Bulgaria by Germany, the Turkish scheme of defence had been changed. The main stand would be made, not on the Chakmak line close to the frontier but further east, on the Enos-Midia line. This was the reason why it was impracticable to hold the Thracian bridgeheads. Although the decision left the Germans free to enter Thrace in the area between the Maritza and the Struma, it was prudent from a Turkish military point of view. British military

---

[1] See also below, p. 602.
[2] The German and Italian Governments agreed not to ask during the war for Yugoslav military co-operation under the terms of the Tripartite Pact or for the passage or transport of troops through Yugoslav territory. For the German (and Italian) negotiations with Prince Paul and the Yugoslav Government ending in their adherence to the Tripartite Pact, see *D.G.F.P.*, XII, *passim*. In return for adherence to the Pact Yugoslavia was promised Salonika after the war.

(a) R2879/394/92. (b) R2926/73/92. (c) R2855, 2897/2706/92; R3870/1109/67 (1942). (d) R1596/1596/67. (e) R2355/113/67. (f) R2447/113/67.

opinion indeed thought that the best policy would have been to concentrate on holding the Straits.

There was indeed a certain difference of view between Mr. Eden
(a) and the British Middle Eastern Command on the question of putting more pressure on Turkey. Sir H. Knatchbull-Hugessen thought that we could not force Turkey into the war against her will, and that in any case it was undesirable for her to come in until she could do so without risk of defeat. She was loyal to the alliance and had shown her loyalty by refusing to give way to the German appeals—conveyed in the usual mixture of threats and assurances— that she should come over to the Axis side; her cautious attitude towards our appeals was due to our inability to provide her with the necessary war material.

Mr. Eden, however, considered it worth while to pay another visit to Turkey in the hope of persuading the Turkish Government to take a stronger line. General Wavell and Air Chief Marshal Longmore
(b) opposed the plan. They argued that, if Mr. Eden went once more to Turkey, with nothing new to offer, the Turkish Government would be puzzled, and would assume that we were in a desperate position. Mr. Eden pointed out that a Turkish declaration of war might well be the only chance of getting Yugoslavia to fight, and that it would not necessarily draw attack upon Turkey herself. The Commanders-in-Chief then agreed that another meeting could do no harm if it were held to discuss political, not strategical, questions. They also assented to Mr. Eden's suggestion that he should try to get the Turkish Government to do something to reassure Yugoslavia and Greece by a declaration that the policy of Turkey was to preserve peace in the Balkans, and that she therefore could not be indifferent to any further act of aggression by a foreign Power in the Balkan area. Finally, on March 17 when the Yugoslavs appeared to be giving way, the Commanders-in-Chief came round to Mr. Eden's view that we should try once more to persuade the Turkish Government to send a message to the Yugoslav Government to the effect that, in the event of a German attack on Greece, they would declare war if Yugoslavia would do so.

M. Saracoglu agreed to meet Mr. Eden at Nicosia in Cyprus.
(c) Here, on March 18 and 19, he began by promising to make the communication to Yugoslavia suggested by Mr. Eden: later he retracted his promise on the ground that, if Yugoslavia rejected the approach, Turkey would be compromised to no advantage. Finally he agreed to an elaborate form of words suggesting an exchange of views. Even in this form the communication was not made. From his

(a) R2450/236/44.   (b) R3870/1109/67 (1942), Annexes 14–15.   (c) R2555/113/67; R2790, 2877/2706/92; R2720/1934/44; R2893, 2894/557/92; R3870/1109/67 (1942), Annex 16.

later statements on the subject it is clear that M. Saracoglu's colleagues thought that he had gone too far, but in any case the Yugoslav Government had committed itself by March 20 to the signature of some form of agreement with the Axis Powers.

(vii)

The coup d'état *in Yugoslavia: relations with the new Yugoslav Government: the German attack on Yugoslavia and Greece (March 27–April 6, 1941).*

In the afternoon of March 26—the day after the Yugoslav adherence to the Tripartite Pact—Mr. Churchill sent a message to Mr. Campbell telling him to continue to keep in close touch with the Prince Regent and the Ministers and to insist that by their signature of the Tripartite Pact they were handing over their country to the Germans. At the suggestion of the Foreign Office, however, Mr. Campbell was instructed at the same time not to neglect 'any alternatives to which we might have to revert' if we found that the present Government had 'gone beyond recall'. In other words, we had in mind the possibility of supporting a *coup d'état.* This possibility seems first to have been put before Mr. Eden on March 21, when it was clear that the policy of surrender to Germany did not have the support of all the members of the Yugoslav Government, and still less of the whole population. The Croat Ministers, including Dr. Maček, the leader of the Croat Peasant Party, had voted in favour of the Pact, and Croat lukewarmness had been used as the chief argument for the surrender to German demands. On the other hand three Ministers had refused to accept the Pact and had resigned: three others, of whom the Prime Minister was one, had not voted.

Mr. Campbell and Mr. Shone thought that, in view of the strength of popular feeling in Serbia, there was some chance of a *coup d'état.* (a) They telegraphed to ask Mr. Eden whether the British Government would countenance a *coup d'état* by undertaking to break off relations with the existing Government and to support a new one. Mr. Eden replied on March 22 by asking whether there was adequate leader- (b) ship for a *coup;* whether the army—whose chiefs were alleged to be defeatist—would support it, and what would happen to the Prince Regent. On March 23, however, Mr. Eden gave Mr. Campbell (c) provisional authority, and on March 24 full authority, to do what he thought fit to further a change of government or régime even by a

---

(a) R2854/2706/92.   (b) R2871/2706/92.   (c) R2896, 2916, 2872/2706/92.

coup d'état, and to get into touch with any prospective leaders in whom he had confidence. Mr. Campbell had also been told on March 22 to give to such leaders the message about a possible future revision of the Istrian frontier which he had been authorised to give to
(a) Prince Paul. Meanwhile Mr. Eden suggested through Sir M. Palairet that General Papagos should send a message to the Yugoslav army leaders—and especially to those in southern Serbia—urging them to stand firm.

On March 24 Mr. Campbell telegraphed that the best chance of
(b) a successful *coup* lay in a military movement. The existing military chiefs—with one exception—would do nothing, but one or two senior generals on the retired list might be found to lead the movement. On the other hand, if the army were to be won over, we must offer them military equipment and, if possible, make a naval demonstration in the Adriatic as evidence that we could maintain communications by sea with a Serbian army. Mr. Campbell also said that, if we were
(c) working for a *coup d'état*, we should have to be ready to break off relations with the existing Government.

Mr. Eden felt unable to authorise more than a guarded reply to
(d) any question about material assistance. We could not promise to supply more than petrol and lubricants, and later, 3-ton lorries; we had already pointed out that the Yugoslavs could get a rich haul of equipment if they attacked the Italians in Albania. Mr. Eden also
(e) thought it inadvisable for the moment to break off diplomatic relations with the Government. If there were a chance of a popular movement, the British Mission ought to be in Belgrade and able to keep in touch with it. We ought now to try openly to increase popular opposition to the signing of the pact with Germany, and we might begin indirect propaganda in favour of a revolutionary movement in Serbia.

Mr. Eden and General Dill left Cairo for London on March 25.
(f) They were delayed by bad weather at Malta, and on March 27 had news there that a Yugoslav *coup d'état* had taken place in the early hours of the morning. The Prime Minister and Minister for War had been arrested. King Peter had accepted the resignation of the three Regents, and had invited General Simović, formerly Chief of the Air Staff, to form a new Government.

On hearing this news Mr. Eden and General Dill went back to
(g) Athens. They found the Greek leaders eager to take advantage of the Yugoslav *coup* and to adopt a more ambitious strategic policy. General Papagos not only urged the formation of a line to defend

---

(a) R2873/2706/92. (b) R2987/2706/92. (c) R2962/2706/92. (d) R3131/73/92.
(e) R3044/2706/92. (f) R3870/1109/67 (1942). (g) R3870/1109/67 (1942), Annex 18.

Salonika, but spoke also of a single defensive front from the Adriatic to the Black Sea, with the Yugoslavs helping to clear the Italians from Albania and the Turks taking responsibility for western Thrace. The British representatives advised against an advance from the Aliakhmon line until more was known of the new Yugoslav policy and, in particular, until the new Government had made a declaration that they regarded the defence of Salonika as a vital Yugoslav interest. It seems, however, that General Papagos, with the consent of the British commander, General Wilson, had already moved one Greek division forward from the Aliakhmon line to the Macedonian front.

Meanwhile, as soon as he heard of the Yugoslav *coup*, Mr. Churchill had authorised Mr. Campbell to say to the new Yugoslav Govern- (a) ment that, if they were resolved to denounce the Tripartite Pact and to help Greece, His Majesty's Government would recognise them as the Government of Yugoslavia. Mr. Eden had also suggested a (b) meeting, either in Belgrade or with Yugoslav representatives in southern Serbia or at Athens, in order to concert plans of resistance, but the character and purpose of the Yugoslav revolution were not as simple as the British observers outside Yugoslavia inclined to think. Before the *coup d'état* had taken place Mr. Campbell and Mr. Shone (c) had considered that the only alternative to the existing régime would be a government supported by the army and representing predominantly Serbian interests. In fact the new Government repre- (d) sented all the nationalities in the Yugoslav State; it included, in addition to the Serbs, four Croats, two Slovenes, three Bosnians, and one Montenegrin. Thus the *coup* was a protest, not merely against the signature of the Tripartite Pact, but also against the dictatorial methods of the fallen Government and its predecessors. It was not even certain that there would be a complete reversal of foreign policy. In any case the change of government did not alter the fact that the most practicable line of defence which the British and Greek forces could establish in concert with Yugoslavia would have left Croatia and Slovenia open to the Germans. The view in London was that the Yugoslav forces might withdraw to the south of a line from Sarajevo to Nish.

The British representatives at Belgrade realised more quickly that there might not be a sudden *volte-face* in foreign policy. (e) Mr. Campbell did not see the new Prime Minister until March 29. General Simović then said that his policy towards Germany was to (f) gain time. He would neither denounce nor ratify the Tripartite Pact, and did not wish us to force him to do anything likely to provoke Germany. If, however, Germany attacked Salonika, the Yugoslav

---

(a) R3090/73/92. (b) R3133/73/92. (c) R3032/2706/92. (d) R3137,3138/73/92.
(e) R3186/73/92. (f) R4319/2706/92.

army would attack the Germans in Bulgaria and the Italians in Albania. Nevertheless he did not want to make a public declaration about Salonika. He had already told the Italians through military channels that they were in a precarious position in Albania and that it would be inadvisable for them to urge the Germans to attack Salonika.

General Simović agreed with the proposal that Mr. Eden and
(a) General Dill should come to Belgrade, but later withdrew his acceptance, and only after further representations agreed on March 30 to a very secret visit by General Dill. General Dill arrived
(b) in Belgrade on March 31. His conversations with General Simović on this day and on the following morning were constantly interrupted by other business, but the main agenda was carried through. General Dill said that we were concentrating important forces on the Aliakhmon line, and would eventually have 150,000 there; we were already somewhere near to the half-way mark. This force would have all possible help in the air, and although we could not make much use of the port of Salonika, we might be able to land a certain amount of material by night.

General Simović and General Ilić, the new Minister for War, thought that the main German attack would come from the south-west corner of Bulgaria against the south-east corner of Yugoslavia. Hence it was essential to occupy in force a position at Lake Doiran: could British forces advance to this position, and, if necessary, over the Yugoslav frontier to meet the Germans? General Dill answered that this question would have to be discussed at detailed staff talks. We had considered holding with the Greeks a fortified line along the Bulgarian frontier and the Nestos river if we could be sure of Yugoslav co-operation. Otherwise we could not go beyond the Aliakhmon line. The Yugoslavs repeated that, if we failed to hold Doiran, the Germans would come down the Vardar valley to Salonika, take the Greeks on the Bulgarian frontier in the rear, and divide the Yugoslav forces from the British.

General Simović said that the Germans regarded the Yugoslav adherence to the Tripartite Pact as effective; the Yugoslav Government proposed to leave the matter in suspense, but, as far as they were concerned, their accession to the pact had lapsed.[1]

It thus seemed that the Yugoslav Ministers regarded war with Germany as certain, but that they wanted to gain time and would not risk any move likely to provoke attack. Apart from the need to complete their military preparations, the Ministers were anxious to avoid an internal political split. The Croats and Slovenes—owing to

---

[1] The Yugoslav Government had used somewhat vague language on this point to the German and Italian Governments.

(a) R3235, 3286/73/92. (b) R3870/1109/67 (1942), Annex 20; R3354, 3355/73/92.

their exposed position—were causing difficulties, and, although there were Croat Ministers in the Government, Dr. Maček's support was not yet assured. A disunited Yugoslavia would be useless to her allies, and the need to avoid provocation (which also ruled out a visit by Mr. Eden) made it impossible to take the initiative in an attack on Albania. Finally the Yugoslavs hoped that, in the event of a German attack on Yugoslavia, Turkey would at least declare war.

General Simović agreed to the holding of secret staff discussions on April 2 at Florina on the Greek-Yugoslav frontier and to the signature of an agreement to the effect that Great Britain would give Yugoslavia all possible help if she were attacked by Germany, and that Yugoslavia would join Great Britain in assisting the Greeks if the Germans attacked them without also attacking Yugoslavia. On the next day, however, General Simović withdrew his agreement to the signature of any document and said that, without consulting his Government, he could not go beyond an exchange of views. He then discussed again the strategical dispositions, and advised against an advance beyond the Struma-Doiran line to the Nestos. He remained willing to send a representative to the proposed staff talks with full power to make plans which would be contingent on a German attack on Yugoslavia or on Salonika, but there must be no commitments on either side.

The staff meeting which took place at Florina on the night of (a) April 3-4, was not very useful. The Yugoslav representative said that, without further authorisation, he could not continue the conversations at Athens, or agree that British officers in plain clothes should reconnoitre Yugoslav territory; he made no suggestions of his own about maintaining contact, and no effective contact was established after this time with the Yugoslav Government. The last reports from Belgrade, however, before the opening of the German attack on the morning of April 6, confirmed that the Government were still hesitating. Mr. Campbell heard on April 3 that they had accepted an (b) Italian offer to mediate between Yugoslavia and Germany. The Italian Government had later made an excuse to postpone the arrival of a Yugoslav envoy, but, if the offer were renewed, the Yugoslav Government would accept it, since it was in their interest, as they believed it to be in the British interest, that, if possible, the Germans should not take further action in the Balkans. Germany could thus choose between giving up her plans for an advance in the Balkans, and thus securing Yugoslav neutrality, or continuing with these plans and bringing Yugoslavia into the war against her.

Later on April 3 General Simović said that the new Yugoslav Foreign Minister might go to Germany; the Croats (i.e. Dr. Maček's (c)

(a) R3870/1109/67 (1942), Annex 22. (b) R3408,3444/73/92. (c) R3465/73/92.

party) had now agreed to join the Government but they had done so on the understanding that Yugoslav policy should be one of peace and national security. Mr. Eden sent a message from Athens that a visit to

(a) Germany would only compromise the freedom of action of the new Government and that the best means of gaining time was to continue to tell the Italians that if the Germans attacked Yugoslavia the Yugoslavs would at once invade Albania.

The Prime Minister sent an even more strongly worded message on

(b) April 4. He said that he could not understand why the Yugoslav Ministers thought that they were gaining time. Their one hope of safety lay in winning a decisive victory in Albania by attacking the Italians in the rear and collecting the mass of equipment which would fall into their hands. Four German mountain divisions were reported to be moving from the Tyrol to Albania; these divisions would offer a very different resistance from that of the demoralised Italians.

In the event the Yugoslav Government had no chance of 'gaining time'.[1] The Germans marched against Yugoslavia and Greece without warning during the early hours of April 6. Belgrade was heavily bombed; the Government and the Diplomatic Corps left the capital, and for two or three days Mr. Campbell was out of touch with General Simović and the Foreign Minister.

(viii)

British appeals to Turkey with regard to a common front, March 27–April 6: the Russo-Yugoslav pact of non-aggression: collapse of organised resistance in Yugoslavia and Greece: withdrawal of the British forces from Greece and Crete (April 6–June 1, 1941).

In the new situation created by the Yugoslav *coup d'état*, the British Government made yet another attempt to secure at least some positive move from Turkey. Mr. Eden had telegraphed to Sir H.

(c) Knatchbull-Hugessen before leaving Malta on March 27 that if the 'Cyprus message'[2] had not been delivered, the time was now favourable for sending it. Mr. Churchill also telegraphed a personal

---

[1] At a military conference on March 27, a few hours after the Yugoslav *coup d'état*, Hitler announced to the commanders present that, without waiting for 'possible loyalty declarations' by the new Yugoslav Government, he intended '. . . to smash Yugoslavia militarily and as a state. No enquiries regarding foreign policy will be made or ultimatums presented.' The attack, which would begin as soon as possible, would be carried out with 'inexorable severity' and would also have the effect of deterring Turkey (*D.G.F.P.*, XII, No. 217).

[2] See above, p. 540.

(a) R3506/73/92. (b) R3520/73/92. (c) R3132/113/67.

message in the same sense for President Inönü that there was now a (a) chance to organise a common front so strong that Germany would hardly dare to invade the Balkans.

Sir H. Knatchbull-Hugessen was less hopeful of a change in Turkish policy. He advised against putting pressure on the Turks, and (b) thought that the delivery of Mr. Churchill's message would do more harm than good. General Marshall-Cornwall was bringing a military mission to Ankara on April 3; if this mission could promise British assistance, the Turks might see for themselves the advisability of following our advice, but we should not give the impression that we were pushing them into war.

In reply the Prime Minister sent Mr. Eden his own appreciation of the general situation in the Balkans and authorised him in the light of it to deal as he thought fit with the Turkish Government. Mr. Churchill pointed out that the united forces of Great Britain, Yugo-slavia, Greece and Turkey to withstand a German attack in the Balkans amounted to some 70 divisions; the Germans had not more than 30 divisions. Here was the best practical argument for a common front, but alternatively we could say that the Germans might well direct their attack, or part of it, against Turkey: if the Turkish Government were not prepared to make their own contribution to the security of the Balkan States, they must expect little help from others in their own need. The best plan would obviously be a declaration of unity by Turkey, Greece and Yugoslavia, and a demand to be left alone, and at the same time, a withdrawal by the Turkish army in Thrace to the Chatalja lines.

Mr. Eden sent instructions in this general sense to Sir H. Knatch-bull-Hugessen on March 29. He did not agree that by pressing the (c) Turks we were making them suspicious. We were not pushing them into war; our view was that a more resolute Turkish attitude might prevent or at least delay a German attack. We accepted the Turkish view that strategically their armies must remain on the defensive, but we had never said that, in consequence, Turkey should take no political action. We must still try to form a Balkan front, and to obtain a joint statement supported by ourselves that an attack on any one of the three Powers would be an attack on all. Turkey stood to gain most by such a statement because she was now more isolated and exposed than Yugoslavia or Greece.

For a time there was some hope that the Turkish Government would agree to a four-Power meeting to discuss a declaration and the means of giving effect to it, but the tentative approaches made both by the Yugoslavs and the Greeks came to nothing. The Yugoslavs (d) wanted to be assured that Turkey would regard an attack on Salonika

---

(a) R3341/113/67. (b) R3159/113/67; R3160/1934/44. (c) R3243/236/44. (d) R3307/113/67; R3310/1934/44; R3359, 3393, 3357, 3464/557/92; R3399/73/92; R3456/79/37.

as a *casus belli;* the Turks would not give this positive assurance. The staff conversations with General Marshall-Cornwall's mission only brought out again the difference between the political and military aspects of a Turkish declaration. Politically we wanted Turkey to join in a common front which might deter or delay the Germans and certainly encourage the Yugoslavs. On the military side the Middle
(a) East Command wished to avoid the commitments which an immedia e Turkish entry into the war would entail. The Turkish General Staff realised this latter fact; M. Saracoglu indeed told Sir H. Knatchbull-Hugessen on April 5 that the staff conversations showed how well we understood the Turkish position.

After the opening of the German attack on Yugoslavia and Greece the military aspect of the situation dominated the political considerations. There was no longer any possibility of trying to promote a common front in the Balkans as a means of keeping Germany from attack. All that now mattered was the practical question whether Turkey could help in the operations of war. Since neither we nor the Turkish Government thought that they could actually do much, the only reason for continuing our political pressure was that another Turkish default might have a bad moral effect on Greece and Yugoslavia. For this reason Mr. Eden, before leaving the Mediterranean,
(b) made a final attempt to rally the Turkish Government. He asked Sir H. Knatchbull-Hugessen to tell them of our disappointment at their attitude towards the German attack on Yugoslavia and Greece. We agreed that it might not be to our common interest that Turkey should take the offensive, but she might at least break off diplomatic relations with Germany and Italy. Before Sir H. Knatchbull-
(c) Hugessen had received this message M. Saracoglu had told him that for the time the Turkish Government had decided to remain nonbelligerent. On hearing of Mr. Eden's message, M. Saracoglu said that, although he did not think the suggestions in it were wise, he would put them before his colleagues. His own attitude was not at all forthcoming; he asked why we, for example, did not now carry out a landing in Belgium.

Henceforward the British Government made no serious effort to induce Turkish intervention in the Balkan campaign. The Yugoslavs
(d) continued to ask for British good offices in this respect, and, on reports that Bulgarian forces were taking part in the attack, Yugoslavia appealed to Turkey to fulfil her obligations under the Balkan Pact. These early reports proved to be unfounded; Bulgarian forces took no part in the attack on Yugoslavia and did not invade Greece until April 24, the day after the King and Government had left for Crete. In any case, as the campaign developed, it became

(a) R3533/1934/44; R3548/236/44. (b) R3619/1934/44. (c) R3678/1934/44. (d) R3679, 3983, 3984/1934/44.

clear that Turkish intervention could do nothing to save the situation, and events during May in Syria and Iraq[1] made it certain that Turkey would not enter the war on the Allied side.

In his final message to the Turkish Government Mr. Eden recommended an attempt at closer Russo-Turkish collaboration. (a) Here also the circumstances had changed with the sudden con- clusion of a pact of non-aggression between Yugoslavia and the U.S.S.R. The first news that the new Yugoslav Government were negotiating with the Russians came from the British Air Attaché at Belgrade and was transmitted through Mr. Campbell on April 2. (b) The Foreign Office was inclined to doubt whether the report was accurate, but Mr. Campbell confirmed it on April 3. Sir S. Cripps was instructed on April 5 to enquire about the negotiations, and, if possible, to assist in them, but before he could act on his instructions the Russo-Yugoslav pact was signed. The pact had a political importance as a stage in the definition of the Russian attitude towards Germany,[2] but it was of no military use to the Yugoslavs. They had no help from Russia, and there was no possibility that, even if the Russians had tried to do so, they could have sent help in time.

It is difficult in retrospect to understand why the Middle East Commanders-in-Chief should have considered that, even in the most favourable circumstances, the chances of holding a German advance into Greece were in themselves high enough to justify the enterprise from a military point of view. Apart from the political and military difficulties which made the Yugoslavs hesitate to abandon part of their country and the Turks to go to war while their army was insufficiently equipped, the view that German communications would be more strained than those of the Allies contradicted the experience of the Salonika expedition in the First World War. Moreover, in this earlier war, the Germans had been able to reinforce the Balkans more quickly than the Allies at a time when Germany was fighting a land war on two fronts, Italy was on the Anglo-French side and enemy air power was almost a negligible factor at Salonika. There are very strong reasons for regarding the expedition to Greece as the fulfilment of an obligation which it would have been dis- honourable to evade. From the sole point of view of strategy, however, the historian cannot but feel surprised at the degree of

---

[1] See Chapter XVII.
[2] The German Ambassador protested on April 4 against the decision to conclude the pact, but M. Molotov refused to reconsider the decision (*D.G.F.P.*, XII, No. 265).
(a) R3619/1934/44. (b) R3397, 3408/73/92.

confidence shown by the military authorities in the face of known facts.

In any case the Yugoslavs, in spite of their courage in refusing to give way to German demands, were as mistaken as the Poles a year and a half earlier in their organisation of their defence. They were indeed taken by surprise, at a critical change of régime, but the German methods were by this time so well known that, paradoxically, a surprise ought to have been expected. Even if they had had longer warning of the German attack, the Yugoslav arrangement and placing of their forces put them in a hopeless position. There were, of course, political reasons which determined the decision to meet the German attack in frontier territory, where the German armoured and highly mobile forces were at the greatest advantage. Nevertheless the result was that the scattered Yugoslav army, which might have held the mountain areas for a good many months, was broken within eleven days, and capitulated on April 17. The British Government had given a pledge of alliance to Yugoslavia immediately the German attack opened; they could not provide any material help. In the last stage of the short campaign they brought the King and his Ministers away by air to reconstitute a Yugoslav Government in Egypt. Even this step was taken against Mr. Churchill's advice. He had telegraphed (a) on April 13 that he could not understand why the King and his Government should leave the country rather than go into the mountains and carry on a guerrilla resistance in areas where the German tanks could not penetrate.

The end came hardly less quickly in Greece. Here the German attack on April 6 caught the Greek and British and Yugoslav forces before they were prepared to meet it. Most of the Greek army was still on the Albanian front; one of the three divisions earlier withdrawn to help in the consolidation of the Aliakhmon line had been moved forward to the Macedonian front. The British forces had not completed their disembarkation and long journey to the front;[1] owing to the combined German and Italian attack in Cyrenaica, which opened on March 31, and drove back General Wavell's depleted forces from their gains of the winter, the later units were not even sent to Greece. There was no strong force to hold the Monastir gap or the area south of the Rupel Pass; the Germans entered Salonika on April 8, turned the Aliakhmon line, and twelve days later reached Thermopylae—the last line of defence upon which the Allies could stand.

(b)　　On April 16 General Papagos had suggested that, in the critical

[1] Owing to the danger of air attack the port of Salonika was not used; most of the troops and supplies were disembarked at the Piraeus.

(a) R3954/3379/92.　(b) Hist. (B)3, No. 118; R4041/11/19.

situation, it would be better for the British forces to withdraw, and to save Greece from devastation. On hearing of this suggestion Mr. Churchill telegraphed to General Wavell that we could not (a) stay in Greece against the wishes of the Greek Government, and that General Wilson or Sir M. Palairet should obtain from them the endorsement of General Papagos's request.

General Wavell went to Athens on April 19. He found a difficult political situation. M. Koryzis, the Greek Prime Minister, had (b) committed suicide on April 18.[1] General Wavell was doubtful about the desirability of immediate evacuation, and said that we were (c) prepared to hold on to the Thermopylae line and to cover Athens as long as Greek resistance continued and the Greek Government wished us to do so. A decision was postponed until the King could form a new Government. On April 21 the new Prime Minister, M. Tsouderos, made a formal communication to Sir M. Palairet, (d) in which he explained that the Greek army had not the means to continue their resistance, and that without Greek co-operation, the British forces could not hold their positions for more than a few days. Hence the Greek Government was obliged to say that further sacrifice of the British Expeditionary Force would be in vain, and that its withdrawal in time to escape destruction was necessary in the common interest of the Allies.

The King was anxious, if possible, to remain on Greek territory and, in accordance with his wish, went with his Government by air to Crete on April 23. A month later they were again forced to escape from capture and, with considerable difficulty, made their way to Cairo. The loss of Crete completed the failure of the British forces in Greece, but there was, in this record of disaster, one outstanding factor in addition to the courage and determination of the Greek and British forces. In spite of the collapse of the political and military plans for the Balkans, and in spite of the German air force, nearly 50,000 of the 62,000 British and Commonwealth troops in Greece were safely withdrawn. The proportion was less in Crete, but even so the British Navy demonstrated the importance of sea-power—a weapon which the enemy had failed to challenge effectively, and which was ultimately to be their undoing.

---

[1] On the previous day M. Koryzis had told Sir M. Palairet that the Greek Government wished to do as much for us as they could do for their own troops. In fact they were ready (e) to prejudice their own troops to benefit us, since they regarded themselves as our hosts.

(a) Hist. (B)3, No. 118; R4041/11/19, (b) R4119/11/19. (c) Hist. (B)3, No. 150; R4117/11/19; R4172/96/19. (d) R4233, 4238/11/19. (e) 4064/11/19.

CHAPTER XVII

Palestine, Syria and Iraq, from the outbreak of war to
the German attack on Russia: the German-Turkish
agreement of June 16, 1941

(i)

Palestine and the policy of the White Paper.

THROUGHOUT their negotiations with Turkey from the summer
of 1939 to the German attack on Yugoslavia and Greece, the
British Government had always to remember the extent to
which Turkish policy could affect the general strategic position in the
Middle East as well as in the Balkan peninsula. If Turkey yielded to
the pressure of the Axis Powers, or were defeated by them, the way
was open for a German-Italian invasion of Syria and an attack on the
Suez Canal; the oil supplies of Iraq and Iran and the whole of the
Arabian peninsula and the Persian Gulf would fall into enemy
control.

Turkish independence and, at least, favourable neutrality were
therefore the essential background of British policy in the Middle
East. Against this background, however, the Arab States and
Palestine offered separate and difficult problems. At the beginning of
the war the position of the Allies was in many respects more favourable than in 1914. Turkey was friendly; the Arab States which
had once been part of the Ottoman Empire were under British or
French influence, and, on balance, sympathetic to the Allies. There
were 100,000 French troops in Syria, as well as large forces in North
Africa, and within a short time the British forces in Egypt were
reinforced. On the other hand, Italy, with at least 500,000 troops in
Libya and East Africa, was a potential danger to the south and
south-east as well as to the west of Egypt, and the Italian possession of
the Dodecanese threatened communications with Turkey and Allied
naval traffic in the eastern Mediterranean. Moreover in the first
World War Arab dislike of Turkish rule had given the Allies a
chance of propaganda and 'fifth column' activities throughout the
Arab populations of the Middle East. In 1939 the Germans could
make a similar use of latent or open discontent at British and French
predominance in order to stir up trouble, particularly in regard to
Syria and Palestine. They had indeed more opportunity to do so
since there was greater freedom for political agitation in the independent Arab States than in the old Turkish Empire; the Germans

had also taken measures before 1939 to extend their influence by 'planting out' agents and by offering facilities on a considerable scale for the technical training of Arabs in German institutions and in the study of German methods.

The Arab grievances over Syria were primarily against the French. At the end of the first World War the Arabs had regarded Syria (with Damascus) as an important unit in the newly liberated Arab World and possibly in the federation of Arab States to which the more politically minded enthusiasts looked forward. The award to France of a mandate for Syria had thus been a sharp disappointment. The strictness of the French régime had maintained and increased local resentment and, although the Arabs could observe the more liberal British policy in Egypt, Iraq and Transjordan, they blamed Great Britain for acquiescing in the policy of France. In 1939 the close co-operation of the two countries in war made it harder to distinguish between them.

In any case the unsolved problem of Palestine was an even more serious cause of Arab discontent. Here Great Britain was directly concerned. At the outbreak of war the British Government were still trying to find a way of meeting irreconcilable obligations to Jews and Arabs. The Germans, by their persecution of the Jews, had very greatly intensified the difficulties in Palestine. For obvious reasons, more Jews wanted to enter the country; Jewish opinion looked with greater eagerness to the possibility of a Jewish State, and the horrors of persecution deepened the consciousness of Jewish nationalism and even created a kind of Jewish chauvinism. In these circumstances the original offer made to the Jews during the first World War took on, from the Jewish standpoint, a meaning which the British Government had never intended it to possess. For this same reason the Arabs, who had also developed a national consciousness and a chauvinism of their own, were even more hostile than in the earlier years of the Mandate.

In May 1939, after failing to obtain an agreement between Jews and Arabs, the British Government published in a White Paper a statement of the policy which they intended to carry out in Palestine. The main points of this policy were as follows: (i) Within ten years there should be established an independent Palestinian State in which Arabs and Jews would share control under safeguards for the interests of each community. During the transitional period Jews and Arabs alike would be given an increasing share in the government of Palestine; (ii) Jewish immigration for the next five years would be limited to 75,000,[1] and would thereafter be continued only with the

---

[1] This quota was to be made up of an annual quota of 10,000 immigrants, together with a further 25,000 Jewish refugees to be admitted as and when His Majesty's Government thought fit.

consent of the Arab inhabitants of Palestine; (iii) the British High
Commissioner for Palestine would have power to prohibit or regulate
the sale to non-Arabs of Arab land to an extent necessary to preserve
the 'rights and position' of the Arab population. (The two main factors
here were the rapid growth of this Arab population and the rate at
which Arab land was passing into Jewish hands.)

Arab opinion did not accept the White Paper, although the policy
laid down in it went a good way towards meeting Arab grievances; in
particular, the British Government had now rejected the Jewish
interpretation of the Balfour Declaration as guaranteeing the
establishment of a 'Jewish National State'. The Zionists were much
more hostile, and the British declaration of policy was also a subject of
controversy in the House of Commons. The Liberal and Labour
parties voted against it; so did a number of Conservatives, including
Mr. Churchill. Moreover Zionist opinion was especially sensitive
since the German persecution of the Jews had been intensified in the
winter of 1938–9 after the murder of a German diplomat in Paris by a
young Jewish fanatic. In June 1939, the Permanent Mandates
Commission of the League of Nations found, by a majority of four to
three, that the policy laid down in the White Paper was not in
accordance with the terms of the Mandate. The Mandates Commission
submitted their finding to the Council of the League and, early in
August 1939, the British Government put forward their own comments with a request that these comments should be circulated to the
Council. The Council had not considered the question at the
outbreak of war, and was then prevented from doing so by
events.

The Germans at once exploited the situation. They continued to
persecute the Jews in all areas under German control; at the same
time they assisted the movement of Jewish refugees to the Black Sea
ports. Thus they encouraged the flood of illegal immigrants whereby
the Zionists hoped to nullify the British prescribed quota; they then
tried to stir up Arab hostility by pointing to the increased number of
illegal immigrants as evidence that Great Britain did not intend to
carry out the policy of the White Paper.[1]

On the British side there was deep sympathy for the Jewish
community which had suffered to such a terrible extent from
German cruelty and intolerance. There were also political arguments
for trying to satisfy Jewish opinion in the United States. On the other
hand the Arabs had as great a claim as the Jews to justice and fair
dealing, and here also there were political factors of the highest
importance which required consideration. Palestine was a small,

---

[1] Most of these illegal immigrants were not old people or children, but young men and
women in good health of the type likely to be useful in building up the Jewish position in
Palestine.

though strategically important area in the Middle East; British interests, and Allied success in the war required a large measure of Arab acquiescence and co-operation. Furthermore, although they were deliberately embarrassing the Allies in the conduct of the war, the Zionists knew that only an Allied victory could save the Jews from destruction in Palestine and elsewhere, whereas the Arabs were far from sure that, on other issues as well as that of Palestine, a German victory might not be to their advantage.

At the beginning of the war there had indeed been for a time a certain relaxation of tension in Palestine itself. The Executive of the Jewish Agency issued early in September a statement declaring the determination of the Jewish community, notwithstanding its rejection of the White Paper, to stand by Great Britain and the cause of democracy, and calling for a truce from acts of violence. Apart from certain Palestinian groups the Arabs did not put forward any statement, but in fact unrest in Palestine subsided. Zionists and Arabs, however, made indirect representations to the British Government; the Zionists asked for a revision of the White Paper policy, and the Arabs for an assurance that nothing less than this policy should be carried out.

On November 24 a delegation of the American Zionist Organis- (a) ation called on Lord Lothian to say that there was increasing disquiet among American Jews about rumours of further restrictions on Jewish immigration and of the enforcement of the rules about land sales. The Delegation apparently believed that there had been an informal promise that the 25,000 immigrants in addition to the annual quota of 10,000 were to be admitted in the first year of the quinquennium.

The Foreign Office replied that the total figure of 75,000 would (b) not be reduced but that there had been no promise to admit the additional 25,000 above the annual quota in the first year, and that the reports about land sales were probably due to the knowledge that the High Commissioner was considering legislation on the subject under the powers conferred on him. Lord Lothian was instructed to say that the British Government believed the policy laid down in the White Paper to be the most just solution of the Palestine problem and that they would continue to resist pressure from either side to modify this policy. In spite of the value of Arab support in the war, the British Government had refused to reduce the promises made to the Jews; they could not reduce the promises made to the Arabs in order to get Jewish support. They would not like to feel that Jewish support was being given to them for any other reason than that the Jews shared the ideals for which the Allies were fighting and realised that an Allied victory was in Jewish interests. 'There must be no

(a) E7874/6/31. (b) E8032/6/31.

misunderstanding as to the possibility of rewards, whether in the form of further immigration into Palestine or otherwise.'

(a)   The Foreign Office had already replied in similar terms to a letter from Dr. Weizmann,[1] and had added that the White Paper did not require—as the Zionists argued—the approval of the Council of the League, since it did not involve an amendment of the terms of the Mandate. Lord Lothian's instructions were, however, suspended

(b)   before he had acted on them and for some time no reply was given to the Zionists. Mr. Churchill had seen Dr. Weizmann before he left on a visit to the United States, and thought that Dr. Weizmann's whole desire was to bring American opinion over to the British side. Mr. Churchill held that we ought not to risk any chance of losing American support and that it was more necessary even than in 1917 to conciliate the American Jews and to secure their aid in opposing isolationist and anti-British opinion. Mr. Churchill also doubted whether we were entitled to speak with confidence about the White Paper as a just and unalterable settlement in view of the attitude of the Mandates Commission and of the Liberal and Labour opposition.

Mr. Churchill's arguments did not convince the Foreign Office. The Foreign Office view, which was set out in early January 1940, in

(c)   a memorandum for the War Cabinet, was that a declaration re-affirming the policy of the White Paper would not necessarily turn American Jewish opinion against us. If we were frank about our intentions, we might well get a favourable response. In any case the American Zionist leaders, like the British Government, had to take expediency into account; however much they might feel about Palestine, the cause of their co-religionists in Europe required them to help the Allies to victory. The loss of Jewish support might not affect American opinion as a whole; it was indeed possible that a too conspicuously pro-Allied attitude on the part of the American Jews might defeat its object by suggesting that the Jews were trying to drag the United States into the war. Furthermore if it were inexpedient to tell the American Zionists that we stood by the White Paper, it would be equally inexpedient to tell the Arabs that we did not pro-pose to stand by it. The present quiet in the Middle East was largely the result of the White Paper, and, if we allowed doubts to develop about our policy, we should undermine the basis of this tranquillity. On balance, the Arab danger was as great as the Zionist danger, and, from the geographical point of view, more serious.

As for the parliamentary opposition, the Palestine problem would remain whatever line we might take. Even on a short view it was better to keep to our policy, and to explain and defend it rather than

---

[1] Dr. Chaim Weizmann was President of the World Zionist Organisation and the Jewish Agency for Palestine.

(a) E8075/6/31.   (b) E8118/6/31.   (c) WP(G)(40)4;   WM(40)15.

to create doubt and confusion by abandoning it. It might be that this policy would never be carried out. A future Government might change it, or it might be submerged in a world disaster, but, if we won the war, a future Government could hardly offer more to the Jews than we had offered in the White Paper. They might try to do more, but Arab opposition would force them into a compromise much like that of the White Paper. We should be as conciliatory as possible to both parties, but we could not avoid some kind of answer to Jewish and Arab enquiries and we ought not to hold out to the Jews hopes which could not be fulfilled. Mr. Malcolm MacDonald, Secretary of State for the Colonies, agreed with the Foreign Office, (a) and felt even more strongly that we should reassure the Arabs. We had been blamed in the past for our failure, under Jewish pressure, to keep our promises to the Arabs. We ought therefore to show our good faith now by putting into effect the legislation about land sales.

During January and February 1940, the War Cabinet considered (b) the arguments on both sides of the question. They decided to give no hint to the Zionists that we had withdrawn from the White Paper policy and at the same time to make no new public statement about our position. They would, however, authorise the High Commissioner for Palestine to issue regulations for the control of land sales. (c) Instructions in this sense were sent to Lord Lothian, together with a warning to withhold official intimation of the regulations from the Jewish leaders until the day before their publication. On February 28, 1940, the Land Sale Regulations were published. A motion in the House of Commons against the policy of the Government on this issue was defeated by 292 votes to 129.

The War Cabinet had also considered what use they could make of the manpower and productive capacity of Palestine. In October 1939, Mr. Churchill had proposed that we should employ local man- (d) power to free for service elsewhere the ten regular battalions tied down in Palestine, and that we should build up a munitions industry (e) in the country for the Middle East. The question of recruiting Palestinian manpower was clearly a political one, and the Foreign Office, War Office and Colonial Office agreed that, in spite of the improvement in the local situation, it was unsafe to use Palestinian Jews for suppressing Arab disorder or disarming Arabs; neither a Jewish nor an Arab force could be relied upon to maintain internal security in the country. The War Cabinet accepted these conclusions on February 12, 1940, and limited the enlistment of Palestinians for war service to certain specified units of the British army. They also authorised the High Commissioner to take special measures against illegal Jewish military organisations.

(a) WP(G)(40)3. (b) WM(40)15, E460/31/31; WM(40)39, E648/31/31. (c) E658/31/31. (d) WM(39)53. (e) WP(G)(40)16; WM(40)39.

The collapse of France and the entry of Italy into the war had far-reaching effects on British policy generally in the Middle East. The area of fighting was now nearer to the Arab countries: the British military and political authorities therefore became even more anxious not to do anything which would affect our relations with the Arabs. The collapse of French resistance in Syria brought new difficulties, and the Germans continued to declare their sympathy for Arab grievances.

On the other hand, various Jewish organisations, including the Jewish Agency, made repeated offers of Jewish services to the Allied cause, directly or indirectly linked with the proposal for a Jewish national force to defend Palestine. The Colonial Office, with the
(a) approval of the Foreign Office and War Office, advised strongly against accepting the offers of the extremist 'New Zionist Organisation', which would co-operate only if the 'MacDonald' policy in Palestine were stopped, and 'all those features of previous policy which had nearly killed the magnetism of the Allied cause abroad' were reversed. The Prime Minister was anxious, however, not to reject all offers of Jewish military assistance out of hand. It might prove necessary to bring home the bulk of the British regular forces in Palestine; Mr. Churchill indeed would have been willing to go further, and to sanction the arming of the Palestine Jews for self-defence. On representations from the Colonial Office, this plan was dropped, but, at Mr. Churchill's suggestion, Lord Lloyd saw Dr. Weizmann on May 29, and agreed with him that the British Government should accept in principle the Jewish Agency's offer of assistance, on condition, first, that any Jews recruited by their efforts should be incorporated in British Army units and enlisted for general service in all theatres of war, and secondly, that Jews should be recruited in all countries and not only in Palestine. Some three weeks later His Majesty's Government accepted in principle another proposal from Dr. Weizmann, for the raising of a Palestinian force on the understanding that numerical equality should be maintained as between Arabs and Jews, and that nothing in the nature of a Jewish army should be created in Palestine.

During the summer, General Wavell on his own account sought
(b) and obtained permission to raise six companies of Palestinians for local garrison duties, with Jews and Arabs allocated to separate companies and attached to different regiments. By the end of the year, however, the main project—for the recruitment of Jews from all countries—had made little progress. It was not until mid-October
(c) that the Secretary of State for War submitted to the Cabinet a scheme

---

(a) E2044/187/31. (b) WM(40)192, E2232/187/31. (c) WP(40)404; E2766/2062/31; WM(40)269.

agreed with Dr. Weizmann for the recruitment of Jewish forces.[1] The American presidential election was then imminent and the situation in the Arab countries disquieting; hence the Cabinet, while giving general approval to the plan, agreed that it should be deferred for the time being.

During the summer, while the question of Jewish recruitment in Palestine was under discussion, there were many who felt that our first duty was rather to reassure the Arabs. It seemed impossible to evade a plain suggestion from General Nuri Pasha es-Said, the (a) Foreign Minister of Iraq, on May 25, 1940. The Foreign Minister said that, as a complement to the measures which the Iraqi Government were taking to defeat enemy propaganda, the British Government and, if possible, the French Government, should issue a clear and unambiguous statement guaranteeing immediately, or at the end of the war, the execution of the promises already given for the organisation of self-government in Palestine and Syria.

The Foreign Office pointed out in a memorandum of June 12, (b) 1940, that we could no longer continue our policy of reticence. We ought not to make new promises, but we were being asked whether we did or did not intend to carry out the policy of the White Paper, and we must answer 'yes' or 'no'. The Foreign Office proposed the following reply:

'The policy of His Majesty's Government for Palestine continues to be that laid down in the White Paper of May 1939. So far as the provisions . . . relating to immigration and land sales are concerned, these matters are already being regulated in accordance with those provisions. So far as constitutional development is concerned, His Majesty's Government have not so far been able to regard peace and order as sufficiently restored for the first step to be taken, that is to say, for Palestinians to be appointed to take charge of some of the departments of the Administration. Nor do they think it likely that this step can be taken while the present war continues. But they hope and expect that when the war is ended conditions in Palestine will quickly permit the various stages of constitutional development to follow one another on the lines which the White Paper lays down.'

Most of the members of the Cabinet who discussed this draft would (c) have accepted it—in some cases with great reluctance—but the Prime Minister thought it better to defer the question for a few days longer. On June 26 the Foreign Office again pointed out the need for (d) urgency, and after another discussion on July 3 the War Cabinet agreed to send a much shorter reply without a direct reference to the White Paper: 'His Majesty's Government do not see any reason to

---

[1] The stipulation that there should be numerical equality between Jews and Arabs does not appear in this scheme, which provided for the recruitment of up to 10,000 Jews in all, of whom not more than 3,000 should be drawn from Palestine.

(a) E2077/50/31. (b) WP(G)(40)149, E2220/20/31. (c) WM(40)167. (d) WP(G)(40) 165; WM (40)192.

make any change in their policy for Palestine as laid down in
May 1939, and it remains unchanged.' If British representatives in
the Middle East were asked what this reply meant, they were to say
that 'His Majesty's Government hope and expect that, when the war
is ended, conditions in Palestine will permit the various stages of
constitutional development to follow one another in orderly succession
on the lines laid down'. In a private telegram to Sir B. Newton,
British Ambassador in Baghdad, the Foreign Office explained that there
could be no question of promises going beyond those in the White
Paper or even of defining the policy in the White Paper more clearly.

Later in the year, the Foreign Office and Colonial Office prepared
(a) for submission to the Cabinet a proposal to proceed at once with the
first step in the White Paper policy—the appointment of a number
of Palestinian heads of departments: but this proposal seems to have
been cut short by an unforeseen development—the sinking of the
S.S. *Patria* off the Palestine coast.

The *Patria*, lying in Haifa harbour with some 1,800 illegal Jewish
immigrants on board awaiting deportation to Mauritius, sank as the
result of an explosion on November 25. The incident brought
forward once more the problem of illegal immigration, to which
recent German penetration in the Balkans had given a fresh impulse.
(b) The Colonial Secretary told the War Cabinet that during the past
eighteen months nearly half the 75,000 quota of immigrants laid
down in the White Paper had in fact reached Palestine. The Cabinet,
after considerable discussion, decided that while, as a special act of
clemency, the survivors of the *Patria* should be allowed to remain in
Palestine, there should be no further deviations from the principle
(already announced in a proclamation by the High Commissioner)
that all intercepted illegal immigrants should be sent to Mauritius
or to some other British colony for the duration of the war.[1]

(ii)

*Syria after the Franco-German armistice: abandonment of plans for a Free
French coup in the autumn of 1940: occupation of Syria by British and
Free French forces, June–July 1941: negotiations with the Free French after
the occupation of Syria: proclamation of the independence of Syria and the
Lebanon.*

Meanwhile the French armistice had brought about a critical

---

[1] The Cabinet decided that they could not explicitly either revoke or endorse a further
point made in the High Commissioner's proclamation, namely that those deported would
not be allowed into Palestine at the end of the war. They felt that it would prove impossible
to prevent these people from eventually entering Palestine. On the other hand, to suggest
that they would be allowed to enter after the war would undoubtedly encourage the
traffic in illegal immigrants.

(a) E2894, 2972/31/31. (b) WM(40)297, 299.

situation in Syria. Since it had seemed possible at first that the
French authorities there might continue resistance, the Foreign
Office had instructed the British representatives in the Middle East (a)
to discourage Arab action likely to embarrass the French. The main
requirement was that no other non-Arab Power should establish
itself in Syria and that all Arab countries should help to this end.
Even after the French High Commissioner and General Mittelhauser (b)
had decided on June 27, 1940, not to continue resistance, the Foreign
Office wanted to avoid increasing the difficulties of the French, and
therefore refused to commit themselves to an outspoken endorsement
of Arab claims. The British Government issued a declaration on
July 1 that they could not allow Syria or the Lebanon to be occupied (c)
by a hostile Power or used as a base for attacks on those countries in
the Middle East which the British Government were pledged to
defend, or to become the scene of disorders constituting a danger
to those countries. Any action which might be necessary in regard to
these requirements would be taken entirely without prejudice to the
future status of the territories under French mandate. The Turkish
Government assented to the terms of the declaration and to the
British view that Turkey should leave Great Britain to carry out any
measures which might be found necessary in Syria and the Lebanon.

In the second half of July the Foreign Office instructed Mr. Havard,
British Consul-General at Beirut, on the terms which we should (d)
require if we were to arrive at a temporary *modus vivendi* with the
French authorities. As a condition of economic concessions—such as
a clearing arrangement with Palestine—we insisted on the maintenance of order, with due regard to the susceptibilities of Arabs
throughout the Levant, and on freedom to present our case through
the Syrian press, though we would undertake not to direct propaganda against France or against the French authorities in Syria. We
also required that, whatever the orders of the Vichy Government, the
French in Syria should resist German or Italian attack; that they
should keep open for through traffic railway communications between
Syria and neighbouring countries, and that they should not allow
anti-British propaganda or activities in the territory under their
control. M. Puaux, the French High Commissioner, seemed at first (e)
to be willing to co-operate on this basis, but under instructions from (f)
Vichy his attitude quickly changed. We therefore decided to apply
economic pressure. At the end of August M. Puaux made a speech (g)
blaming British policy for the economic difficulties of Syria. At the
same time there appeared to be signs that the French in Syria might
organise a *coup d'état* against the Vichy supporters and invite one of (h)

(a) E2170/2170/89. (b) E2200/2170/89. (c) WM(40)187; E2200/2170/89. (d) E2240/
2170/89. (e) E2318/2170/89. (f) E2333, 2786/2170/89. (g) E2541/2170/89. (h) E2570/
2170/89; E2606, 2700, 2567/2157/89; E2674/2170/89; E2745/2029/65.

the Free French leaders to take control of the country. General Catroux therefore went out on September 29 to the Middle East to test opinion, and, if the moment seemed favourable, to organise a Free French movement.

This plan came to nothing. Even before General Catroux reached Cairo, the French authorities in Syria had arrested a number of sympathisers with General de Gaulle. The failure of the Free French at Dakar on September 23 had a depressing effect, and by the
(a) middle of December General Catroux admitted that nothing could be done before the spring. In the same month General Dentz was appointed High Commissioner for Syria and Commander-in-Chief in the Levant, and General Verdilhac became Deputy Commander-in-Chief. The new High Commissioner was more likely to obey strictly the instructions from Vichy.

During this time British resources in the Middle East were so much strained that there was no question of using British forces to assist a movement in Syria. For this reason and also because they did not want to aggravate still further their relations with the Vichy Government the British Government considered that any *coup* in Syria should be carried out wholly by the Free French. The Foreign Office were also anxious, in view of the dangerous possibilities of Arab excitement, that nothing should be done which would lead to the weakening of French control—either Vichy or Free French— to a point where internal security could no longer be maintained.
(b) The Free French agreed with these views; on October 8 General Catroux said that it would be 'inopportune and rash' to provoke a local rising.

Later, when the hopes of winning over the French had begun to fade, General Catroux began to consider bidding for the support of the Arab population. In December he came to the view that a *coup*
(c) would succeed only if it were carried out by joint Franco-British action, with the active support of the Arabs. Although he could easily obtain the assistance of the latter, the Vichy French troops would fight, and the combined Free French and British resources were not sufficient to justify an attempt. In order to secure Arab support in the future, he suggested that the best plan would be to issue a declaration in the name of Free France promising Syria and the Lebanon independence, with safeguards for essential French rights, under an arrangement similar to those safeguarding British rights in the Anglo-Egyptian treaty. The Foreign Office fully approved of this proposal for a declaration. They thought that it would be unwise to start an Arab revolt, but they wanted to establish contact with the Syrian nationalist leaders in order to

---

(a) E3084/2170/89. (b) E2745/2029/65. (c) E3084/2170/89; E2980/2157/89.

prevent them from drifting, like the Mufti of Jerusalem,[1] to the Axis side.

During the early months of 1941 there were differences of view between General de Gaulle and the British authorities, and to some extent among the British and French authorities themselves, about the Syrian question. On the British side there was indeed agreement that the best solution would be the adherence of Syria to the Free French, since we could not occupy the country, even for the duration of the war, without appearing to break our pledge that we had no designs on French colonial territory. A spontaneous declaration in favour of the Free French was, however, unlikely, and until we had sufficient forces available we could not encourage a movement in Syria which might require British help. Sir M. Lampson and (a) General Wavell, with General Catroux's support, considered that we should play for time by offering General Dentz a barter agreement and by trying to keep the Arab leaders quiet with money and advice, and that we should let the French authorities know that we wanted to help them to keep internal order.

There were indeed other considerations in favour of an attempt to reach some agreement or *modus vivendi* with General Dentz. Owing (b) to the long semi-desert frontier, and to the 'open door' of a neutral Turkey, the economic blockade of Syria was not easy to enforce; in any case our efforts to enforce it were harming ourselves as much as or more than they harmed the French in Syria. We also wanted to secure a land route for sending supplies into Turkey, and therefore needed a passage through Syrian territory. Early in the year General Catroux, with British agreement, had written to General (c) Dentz suggesting that if he would give a secret undertaking that in the event of a German attack on Turkey Syria would rejoin the Allied cause, the counterpart would include guarantees of the position and rights of France in Syria, both now and at the Peace Conference, and the abstention by the Free French from any enterprise in Syria. General de Gaulle, on the other hand, proposed a (d) more active anti-Vichy policy, and was supported by the British Mission to the Free French of which General Spears was in charge. General de Gaulle did not hope much from the economic negotiations,

---

[1] Haj Amin al Husseini was appointed Mufti (i.e. interpreter of the canonical Muslim law) of Jerusalem in 1921 by Sir Herbert Samuel (then High Commissioner in Palestine). He later became also Chairman of the Arab Higher Committee, which was set up by him in 1922 and consisted of his own nominees. Partly owing to the long-standing feud beween the Husseinis and the rival Jerusalem family of Nashashibi, which came to represent the more moderate elements among the Palestinian Arabs, and partly owing to his own aptitude for intrigue, the Mufti became deeply involved in opposition to the British authorities. In 1937 the Arab Higher Committee was declared illegal; the Mufti then left Palestine and, on the outbreak of war, associated himself openly with the Axis Powers.

(a) E955/11/89. (b) E2965/2170/89(1940); E407/407/89; E964, 1346/76/89; E1132/298/89. (c) E754/62/89. (d) E1554, 1571, 1966/76/89; E1795/34/89; E1797, 1800/298/89.

but he was confident that, if he had full facilities for his propaganda, he could bring Syria over to the Free French.

The conflict of views continued until the outbreak of the Iraqi revolt at the end of April. At this time the Germans had secured control of the Balkans, and there was an increased danger that they might get a foothold in Syria.[1] In this new situation the British authorities in the Middle East and at home had to decide what to do.

(a) At a meeting in Cairo on May 5 Air Chief Marshal Tedder urged the importance of keeping the enemy out of the Syrian airfields and, on the political side, Sir M. Lampson considered that a German occupation of Syria would have serious consequences throughout the Middle East. General Catroux, who had hitherto been in favour of a delaying policy, now said that if Syria were attacked, he proposed to present himself at the frontier with the six battalions of Free French forces available to him, and to appeal to the Vichy troops to join him in resisting the Germans or at least to give passage to the Free French.

General Wavell, however, said that he could send only a small force to support a Syrian campaign in view of the German reinforcement of the Italians in Libya and the loss of men and material in Greece. Even the small force would not be available for Syria if it were required in Iraq. General Wavell thought that, in any case, it should not go to Syria unless the Vichy troops there resisted German attack. He also considered that an attempt on the part of the Free French to take the lead in operations would cause the greatest resentment among the French population.

Until May 8 the Prime Minister and the Chiefs of Staff had upheld General Wavell's view that the Free French must be kept in check.

(b) On the evening of May 8, however, the Defence Committee in London came to the conclusion that there was no practicable alternative to General Catroux's plan even if we could give no more than minor air support to the Free French. At the same time they felt that the Free French should not act until General Dentz had shown himself unwilling to resist a German air landing.

(c)   On May 12 and 13 the British authorities learned that German aircraft on their way to assist Rashid Ali and the Iraqi rebels had been seen on Syrian airfields and that French arms and ammunition were being sent by rail from Syria to Iraq.[2] In these circumstances the Defence Committee immediately authorised the Royal Air Force

---

[1] See also Volume II, Chapter XXI, section (ii). For an interesting report on German activities in Syria and Franco-German collaboration by Herr Rahn, a diplomat in charge of a special mission to Syria, see *D.G.F.P.*, XIII, No. 165. Rahn arrived in Aleppo on May 9, and left Syria on the night of July 11–12.

[2] See also below, p. 580, and Volume II, chapter XXI, section (ii).

(a) E2018, 2025/76/89. (b) DO (41) 26th meeting. (c) Hist. (B)4, Nos. 83–4, 95–7; E2148/298/89; E2151/2116/89; E2192, 2227, 2281, 2410/2118/89; Hist. (B)4, No. 103; DO(41) 29th meeting.

to attack the Syrian airfields. They also asked the United States Government to transmit to the Vichy Government the text of a statement made by Mr. Eden in the House of Commons on May 15 that the full responsibility for these attacks on Syrian airfields rested with the French Government, since their action in allowing the German flights was a clear breach of the armistice terms and inconsistent with the undertakings which they (the French Government) had given. A communication in similar terms was made to General Dentz.

For the next ten days the political and military situation remained confused. The French authorities in Syria were reported to be moving their troops from the Palestinian frontier into the Lebanon. These reports suggested that, although there seemed little chance that the French would oppose a German landing by air, they would not offer strong opposition to the entry of Allied forces into the country. The road to Damascus therefore seemed open. Sir M. Lampson telegraphed on May 19 further reports that our bombing attacks on the (a) German aeroplanes in Syrian airfields had impressed the Arab population. Sir M. Lampson therefore thought that, if the French really were withdrawing their forces into the Lebanon, the moment was favourable for intervention by the Free French with or without British support.

General Wavell still hesitated, but Mr. Churchill insisted that, in (b) spite of the risks of failure, the attempt should be made. Mr. Churchill had in mind an armed political inroad of the kind which the Germans had nearly succeeded in carrying out in Iraq. The inroad was, however, postponed for more than a fortnight, since there had been another change in the situation. Field-Marshal Smuts telegraphed on May 21 that in his view the German threat (c) to Egypt from Syria was more dangerous than the threat from Libya. Field-Marshal Smuts hoped that British support of the Free French would be strong enough to ensure that there was not another failure like that at Dakar. On the other hand there appeared to be no truth in the previous reports of a French withdrawal of troops from (d) the frontier; thus the chances of a *coup* based on a rally of the Vichy troops to resist an invader grew less, and at the same time Allied prestige was affected by the German successes in Crete, though the German losses in Crete made an immediate air-borne attack on Syria less likely. The Germans had in fact decided to move out of Syria.

Meanwhile Mr. Eden[1] instructed Sir H. Knatchbull-Hugessen to

---

[1] Mr. Eden had sent a minute to the Prime Minister on May 19 that, if the Free French were to be used in Syria, they should be used at once, since every day's delay would weaken their determination and the chances of a favourable reception from any part of General Dentz's forces (Churchill Papers 422/6, P.M. 41/13).

(a) E2353/76/89. (b) E2378/76/89; DO(41) 32nd meeting; Hist. (B)4, No. 151; E2400/76/89. (c) E2617/76/89. (d) Hist. (B)4, Nos. 163–5.

(a) suggest that Turkey should support an Allied move into Syria by a temporary occupation of Aleppo and the surrounding districts—including the airfields in northern Syria—in order to protect Turkish rail communications with the Persian Gulf. Sir H.

(b) Knatchbull-Hugessen doubted whether an approach of this kind was expedient, since it might renew the suspicions of the Turks that we were trying to bring about a direct breach between Turkey and Germany. The Foreign Office replied that, in spite of this risk, the suggestion could safely be made if we took care to avoid giving the impression that we were too weak to deal with Syria by ourselves, and if we emphasised our wish to consult Turkey at the outset of operations, and also mentioned that we and the Turks had already discussed Aleppo during the military conversations of the previous winter.

(c)   Sir H. Knatchbull-Hugessen spoke to M. Saracoglu on June 2. He asked for the Turkish views on our proposal, and for their wishes with regard to the northern districts of Syria bordering on Turkey and, in particular, in regard to Aleppo and the railway through it. M. Saracoglu said that there were certain past injustices which Turkey would like to see removed. Sir H. Knatchbull-Hugessen said that M. Saracoglu was looking at the matter from the point of view of permanency, but the British Government had in mind only a temporary measure. M. Saracoglu said he understood this. M. Saracoglu did not reject the proposals, and did not seem unduly perturbed at the possibility of clashing with German interests. Four days later, M. Saracoglu stated that the Turkish Government could not accept the proposal since it might involve them in war with

(d) France, and possibly with Germany. They were, however, increasing their forces on the Syrian border and would ensure that news about these reinforcements leaked out.

The British Government and the Free French authorities in the Middle East had agreed for some time that an Allied entry into Syria must be accompanied, if not preceded, by a proclamation of independence for Syria and the Lebanon. There was however some doubt whether the Allies should aim primarily at an appeal to the French in Syria or to the local inhabitants. On May 19, when he

(e) thought that British help would be on a very small scale, Mr. Churchill had pointed out that it would be impracticable to appeal concurrently to both parties in Syria. If the French army in Syria would come over to us, and work with the Free French forces until the end of the war, we could hold over Syrian claims for consideration at the Peace Conference. If the French army would not join us, we should have to get the Syrian Arabs on our side by

---

(a) E2598/76/89.   (b) E2667/76/89.   (c) E2766/76/89.   (d) E2877/62/89.   (e) Un-numbered P.M. Minute, in Cabinet Office printed series of P.M. Minutes.

proclaiming an independent, sovereign, Arab State in Syria in permanent alliance with Great Britain and Turkey. We should also have to put the facts plainly to General de Gaulle. The Prime Minister's view that, if the French army in Syria came over to us (but not otherwise), we might respect for the time the French mandate implied that we could not make a declaration of Syrian independence until we knew whether the French had refused to join us. The Foreign Office, however, pointed out that we had already agreed with the Free French authorities that they should issue a declaration simultaneously with, or even before, the entry of the Free French forces into Syria.

The discussions in Cairo over the terms of the proclamation showed the same uncertainty. General Catroux's first draft contained phrases unlikely to appeal to the Arabs. Finally, when it became clear that the Vichy troops were intending to oppose an Allied entry, the proclamation was addressed primarily to the Arabs. General de Gaulle (a) agreed with its terms, and General Catroux issued it on June 8— the day on which the Anglo-French forces entered Syria.[1] General Catroux announced that he had come to put an end to the mandatory régime; henceforward the population of Syria and the Lebanon would be 'sovereign and independent peoples', free either to constitute separate States or to join together in a single State. In either case their status would be guaranteed by a treaty defining also their relations with the Free French. The proclamation promised an immediate share in the advantages enjoyed by the free countries associated with Great Britain, including the opportunity to engage in trade with them. On the same day Sir M. Lampson published a declaration in Cairo associating His Majesty's Government with General Catroux's declaration and giving it their support.

It was also necessary to regulate with Generals de Gaulle and Catroux the relations between the French and British authorities in Syria during the period of occupation. The terms of an agreement reached in Cairo were that General Catroux would be responsible for (b) all negotiations to implement the proclamation, except in respect of its economic clauses, and that the General's advice would be taken in all dealings with the administration and Government of Syria and the Lebanon, and on all questions affecting French and Syrian officials. Until the treaty or treaties referred to in the proclamation had been concluded, and as long as British troops were in occupation of the country, the final decision would rest with the Commander-in-Chief, Middle East.

---

[1] For the text of the proclamation, see Annex I to this Chapter.
(a) E2379, 2740, 2851/76/89.   (b) E2801/76/89.

The military operations in Syria lasted nearly five weeks, and cost heavy casualties to the Free French, Australian, British and Indian forces. Nevertheless, Damascus was captured on June 21 and Damour on July 9 against strong opposition from the Vichy troops. Two days later the Vichy authorities asked for an armistice, and on July 14 Syria and the Lebanon came under Allied control. There followed a period of serious disagreement over the policy to be adopted during the joint Anglo-French occupation. In spite of the assurance of Syrian and Lebanese independence by the Free French leaders and its endorsement by the British Government, trouble soon arose on the

(a) matter with the Free French. Even before the opening of the campaign General de Gaulle made it plain that he regarded the British endorsement of the French proclamation as superfluous in a political issue which was the exclusive concern of France and the populations of her mandated territories. General de Gaulle had also proposed to designate General Catroux as High Commissioner. The British Government wanted to avoid a term which might have associations with the French mandatory régime. Mr. Churchill therefore persuaded General de Gaulle to use the term 'Delegate-General and Plenipotentiary'.

General de Gaulle complained that he was not sufficiently consulted about the terms of the armistice offered to the Vichy forces

(b) under General Dentz, and that these terms included conditions which the Free French could not accept. He objected in particular to the clauses promising repatriation to those members of the Vichy forces who wished to go back to France, and limiting the facilities allowed to the Allies to persuade the troops in question to join the Free French. On the British side, the military commanders complained that General de Gaulle did not keep to the agreement allocating responsibilities between the Free French and the British authorities or to the undertakings given to the Arabs in General Catroux's proclamation. The British Government thus had the difficult task of upholding these promises and at the same time avoiding anything which would give the impression that General de Gaulle had compromised the rights of France.

(c) On June 29 General de Gaulle sent a personal telegram to Mr. Churchill expressing anxiety about a possible 'diminution of the position of France' in Syria and the Lebanon, and about the introduction into these areas of 'tendencies and action' which were 'purely British'. General de Gaulle wished that all British officials concerned in the matter should be brought under a mission with a single head who would treat with General Catroux, 'and certainly not independently of him', on all questions in which Franco-British co-operation was necessary.

(a) E2821, 2849, 2878/76/89; Hist (B)5, Nos. 67, 85, 89. (b) E3410/62/89. (c) E3436/62/89.

General Wavell was dissatisfied with General de Gaulle's attitude. (a)
He pointed out that General de Gaulle had issued his decrees
appointing General Catroux a 'Delegate-General and Plenipotentiary on all Middle Eastern Affairs and Commander-in-Chief of the
Free French Forces in the Middle East' without consultation with
himself (General Wavell) and that the letters of instruction accom-
panying the decrees did not mention the powers of the British
military commanders. It was in fact clear that General de Gaulle
regarded the Free French as full inheritors of the rights exercised by
the Vichy authorities and that, in view of the unpopularity of the
French régime, his unwillingness to recognise the existence of an
Arab problem might have serious consequences.

At the beginning of July the War Cabinet sent Mr. Oliver Lyttelton
to the Middle East as Minister of State with Cabinet rank. One of
Mr. Lyttelton's main functions was to co-ordinate political affairs in
the Middle Eastern theatre of war. He was instructed to make it clear (b)
that the chief element in British policy with regard to Syria was the
grant of independence. We intended that this policy should be
carried out; hence we could not be satisfied that the treaties promised
to Syria and the Lebanon should provide merely for a modification in
the status and functions of the French civil authorities. Our sole
interest—apart from ordinary trade—was to keep the Germans out of
Syria and to win the war, but from this point of view the Arabs were
of greater importance than the Free French. Thus we could not
allow long delays in negotiating treaties which would satisfy the
Arabs and convince them that they had not merely exchanged one
set of Frenchmen for another set. The Chiefs of Staff had also
instructed General Sir C. J. Auchinleck, on his appointment to
succeed General Wavell, that for the time at least the British Officer
Commanding in Palestine, and not General Catroux, must be the
final authority on Syrian administration.

Relations with General de Gaulle were now much strained, and on (c)
July 21 the General threatened to withdraw all Free French troops
from co-operation with the Allied forces. At last, between July 24 and
August 8, Mr. Lyttelton succeeded in reaching an agreed inter- (d)
pretation of the armistice convention of July 14 which laid down the
basis of Anglo-French military co-operation. The clauses relating to
policy within Syria affirmed the right of the Free French to keep in
being such of the *troupes spéciales de Levant*[1] as they thought fit, and to
be responsible for all the forces concerned in the internal administration of Syria. General de Gaulle acknowledged the right of the

---

[1] The *troupes spéciales* were locally recruited volunteer forces. They were only bound to
serve in the Levant States.

(a) E3540, 3570/62/89; E3484/1964/89.   (b) E3685/62/89.   (c) E4044/62/89.   (d) E4146,
5265/62/89.

British High Command in the Levant to take all measures of common defence necessary against the common enemy, and Mr. Lyttelton renewed the assurances that Great Britain had no interest in Syria or the Lebanon except to win the war. Free France and Great Britain were pledged to the grant of independence of these countries, and when this step had been taken we should admit that France had there a position predominant over that of any other European Power.[1]

(a) This agreement did not put an end to friction between the British and the Free French over Syria. On August 28 General de Gaulle left Cairo for London; his last act was to prohibit General Catroux in his absence from dealing directly with the British authorities, but his own departure, and his discussions in London did much to calm the atmosphere. Even so, at his interview with Mr. Churchill on Sep-

(b) tember 12, General de Gaulle spoke of the humiliations endured by his representatives from British military authorities who appeared to be trying to diminish the role of the Free French in Syria. General de Gaulle, before leaving for England, had told Mr. Lyttelton that the Syrians and Lebanese did not wish to negotiate treaties immediately, and that the matters likely to cause trouble were not political but those—notably the supply of wheat and sugar—which concerned the British more directly than the French. On September 27, however, General Catroux proclaimed Syrian independence in a declaration that the country should henceforth enjoy all the rights and exercise all the prerogatives of a sovereign State, including the appointment of Syrian diplomatic representatives and the creation of Syrian armed forces, subject only to the restrictions caused by the existence of a state of war. On November 26 General Catroux issued a similar declaration with regard to the Lebanon. The British Government on October 28 and December 27 respectively, recognised the independence of the two Republics as defined in General Catroux's declarations.[2] Nevertheless British reports on local opinion in Syria and in the Arab countries generally continued to draw attention to the widespread belief that, although they might concede the forms of independence, the Free French were still far from granting the substance.

---

[1] For text of the Lyttelton-de Gaulle agreements, see Annexes II and III to this Chapter.

[2] These declarations did not, in fact, terminate the French mandate, since it could be surrendered legally only to the League of Nations. The British Government, in recognising the independence of Syria, agreed that General de Gaulle should notify the Secretary-General of the League of Nations, *inter alia*, that 'the proclamation of Syrian independence leaves the Mandate in being; and that General de Gaulle will exercise, taking into account the present situation, the powers of French High Commissioner in Syria'. The Foreign Office, however, unlike the Free French authorities, were anxious that this point should receive no prominence. See also Volume IV, Chapter LII, section (iii).

(a) E5083/1964/89. (b) Z7883/3725/17.

(iii)

Anglo-Iraqi relations to the coup d'état *of Rashid Ali.*

At the outbreak of war Iraq was hardly less important than Egypt to the security of the British position in the Middle East. The geographical position of the country gave it a strategical value in relation to the oil supplies and pipelines from Iran as well as from its own oilfields. The country lay across an enemy advance through Iran. The routes between the Mediterranean and Basra, by land, air, and river, were necessary for the movement of troops and supplies, and the Government of India was directly concerned with the freedom of the Persian Gulf from enemy control.

Iraq was bound to Great Britain by a treaty signed on June 30, 1930, when Great Britain gave up her mandate over the country. According to article 4 of this treaty each of the two parties promised to come to the aid of the other as an ally in the event of war; the aid from Iraq was laid down as the provision on Iraqi territory of all facilities and assistance, including the use of railways, rivers, ports, aerodromes, and means of communication.

For some years before the war the Germans had taken great trouble to win over Iraqi opinion. They had entertained prominent Iraqis lavishly in Baghdad, and invited them to Berlin where they were shown displays of German might. The German successes in Europe before 1939, and their intensive propaganda, had made a deep impression, especially on the intelligentsia and army officers. On the other hand there existed a feeling of friendship for Great Britain amongst the most stable elements in the towns, and, with few exceptions, among the Sheikhs who, collectively, with their well-armed tribes, exercised real power in the country. The Regent, Amir Abdulillah, was friendly, though somewhat weak. General Nuri, who was friendly to Great Britain, and had been carrying the main burden of securing the fulfilment of the treaty, gradually lost power to the pro-Axis party under Rashid Ali, an ambitious politician of anti-British views. The army fell under the influence of four pro-Axis sympathisers who were known as the 'Golden Square', and who ultimately became more powerful than Rashid Ali himself. Their activities were supported by the exiled Mufti of Jerusalem and his retinue. Iraq was in the forefront of the politics of the Arab world, and, with some of her most delicate problems still unsolved, proved more susceptible than Egypt to enemy propaganda directed towards the Arab states, and less affected by fears of Italian designs.

The Iraqi Government had broken off relations with Germany in 1939. In March, 1940, General Nuri was replaced by Rashid Ali. In spite of British representations Rashid Ali refused in June, 1940, to break off relations with Italy. As the German military successes increased, public opinion in Iraq became more amenable to enemy propaganda. At the end of October the Government were believed at least to be considering proposals from Germany which included the resumption of diplomatic negotiations and the introduction of anti-Jewish legislation. These proposals—whatever they may have been—came to nothing, but at the opening of the Iraqi parliament on November 5, 1940, the speech from the throne contained only a perfunctory reference to the alliance with Great Britain. Sir B.

(a) Newton, the British Ambassador, had been assured in June that the Iraqi Government would not oppose the landing of British troops in the country; at the beginning of October, he thought that a landing might be resisted.

(b) Sir B. Newton had urged, even before the Italian entry into the war, that we should send troops to Iraq in order to counter a tendency on the part of the Iraqi Government to repudiate their engagements.

(c) The War Cabinet agreed on July 1 that a division should be sent from India, but General Wavell in the Middle East and General Cassels in India doubted whether one division would be enough, especially if its despatch should provoke a move on the part of Russia.

(d) The Foreign Office, however, continued to ask that a force might be sent if only to accustom the Iraqis to their presence, and thus make it easier to send more troops later on. In the end, however, the need to reinforce the army in Egypt was so great that the division from India was diverted for this purpose; but the military authorities, although they could not spare any troops, were also concerned over the drift of

(e) the Iraqi Government away from the alliance, and urged the Foreign Office to do what they could to secure the removal of Rashid Ali and also to counter the activities of the Mufti. The War Cabinet approved in November, 1940, the recommendations of the Chiefs of Staff that we should try to influence the Iraqi Government by offers of economic and financial aid, that we should send out to Baghdad a special diplomatic mission headed by a strong personality known to and respected by the Arabs, and that we should consider, as a gesture, opening up lines of communication although we could not yet send a large force to Iraq.

The Foreign Office did their best to try to get rid of Rashid Ali, but their efforts were affected by the absence of military backing. They decided to send out Sir Kinahan Cornwallis as Ambassador.[1] Even so they had to delay his appointment because the Iraqi Government complained of the representations made by Sir B. Newton in Baghdad;

---

[1] Sir K. Cornwallis had served in Egypt and the Sudan and had been Adviser to the Iraqi Ministry of the Interior from 1921 to 1935.

(a) E2105/448/93. (b) E1970/367/31. (c) WM(40)189, E2228/448/93. (a) E2315/448/93. (e) E2802, 2957, 3012/448/93; E2900, 3099/367/31; E2940/2029/65; E2961/1123/93; WM(40)284.

an immediate change of ambassadors, therefore, might have seemed a concession to Iraqi pressure. The military authorities also found it impossible to spare the troops for opening up a line of communication. The British victories in the western desert, however, had their effect on Iraqi opinion. On January 31, 1941, Rashid Ali was forced to (a) resign and his place was taken by General Taha Pasha al Hashimi. The new Prime Minister was unable or unwilling to show more zeal in the fulfilment of the Anglo-Iraqi treaty. Relations with Italy were not broken off; the Golden Square continued to dominate the army and to hold the most important military commands in the capital.

In the first week of March 1941, Mr. Eden met at Cairo Tewfikal Suwaidi, Foreign Minister in General Taha Pasha's Government. Mr. Eden said that Great Britain required a more co-operative attitude, and in particular, the immediate breaking off of relations with Italy. The Foreign Minister seemed willing to agree, but explained the difficulty of getting the co-operation of the army. He said that since the beginning of the war Great Britain had kept the Iraqi army short of war material, and that it had become more difficult to break with Italy at our request. If he were given time he would try to win over the army leaders; otherwise he would attempt to remove them. If he failed to do so he would resign.

Meanwhile Rashid Ali was reported to be planning a *coup d'état* in the interest of the Axis, with the support of the Mufti and the four officers of the Golden Square. On March 26 the Government brought matters to a crisis by ordering the removal of the four officers from combatant commands in Baghdad. Five days later, and on the day after the prorogation of the Iraqi Parliament, Rashid Ali and the military clique carried out their *coup*, and established themselves in (b) power.

On April 2 the new British Ambassador, Sir K. Cornwallis, arrived in Baghdad. He found that the Regent had taken refuge in the American Legation, and had then gone from the Legation to Habbaniyah whence he intended to fly to Basra. The Regent's (c) escape made it impossible for Rashid Ali to give an appearance of legality to his *coup*, since without a royal decree neither his own appointment nor the resignation of General Taha Pasha was constitutionally valid. Nonetheless on April 3 the General's resignation (d) was announced in the Iraqi press and Rashid Ali took control of the Government offices in Baghdad in the name of the revolutionary party. The British Government refused to recognise the new régime, (e) and suggested to the American, Egyptian, Turkish and Saudi Arabian Governments that they also should refuse recognition. On April 5 the B.B.C. broadcast that 'His Majesty's Government regard (f)

(a) E320/1/93. (b) E1244/1/93. (c) E1251/1/93. (d) E1249, 1253/1/93. (e) E1254/1/93. (f) E1276/1/93.

the present situation [in Iraq] as completely unconstitutional, and must await the formation of a properly constituted Government'.

(iv)

The revolt of Rashid Ali: the restoration of the Regent.

(a) Sir K. Cornwallis had assumed at the time of his arrival that any Government which we should sponsor would be based on the support of the Regent, but when three days later the Regent had reached

(b) Basra, and was staying on board a British warship, there was clearly no chance that he could resist the rebels without British armed assistance. His supporters had fled the country or gone into hiding. The key posts in the capital and the provinces had been filled by Rashid Ali's nominees.

Sir K. Cornwallis thought that we had three possible courses of action: (i) We might intervene by force to get rid of the new régime; the head of the British Military Mission considered that strong air measures and the use of a mechanised force against the army in Baghdad would be enough. Sir K. Cornwallis recommended that, if we chose this policy, we should tell Rashid Ali that we would have no official relations with his régime; that we were considering what measures were necessary to protect our interests and treaty rights, and that, as a mark of our lack of confidence, we were taking steps to remove the British community from Baghdad.

(ii) We might merely refuse to have official relations with the régime and try to squeeze Rashid Ali as much as possible. We should suffer in prestige by our failure to support the Regent and the constitution, and the country was likely to fall rapidly under Nazi influence. On the other hand the Germans would find it hard to increase their resources in Iraq, and we could always consider the possibility of restoring the position when we were able to do so.

(iii) We might recognise the régime. Sir K. Cornwallis regarded this third course as unthinkable, and advocated the first course if we could spare the necessary forces.

General Wavell, however, explained that, owing to the critical

(c) situation in Cyrenaica and the opening of the Balkan campaign, he could spare practically nothing from the Middle Eastern theatre of war, although, in a case of extreme urgency, he would move one British battalion by road from Palestine to defend the camp at Habbaniyah. General Wavell believed on April 7 that the Regent might still recover his position if he had the moral support of a firm

---

(a) E1263/1/93. (b) E1292, 1337/1/93. (c) E1359, 1385/1/93.

British declaration in his favour, and if this declaration were backed by the largest air demonstration which could be carried out by the aircraft already in Iraq. General Wavell thought that we must accept the risk of failure, since our resources did not allow us to restore the Regent by force.

After General Wavell's views had been received in London, an (a) urgent request was sent to India for any troops which could be spared. The Government of India at once agreed to send forces which would amount eventually to a division, and of which the first detachment could arrive about April 20. The detachment was almost ready to leave for another destination and could therefore be diverted forthwith. On April 10 the Foreign Office told Sir K. Cornwallis of the coming of these reinforcements. He was instructed to keep the news strictly secret until the troops had arrived and then to make the most of their arrival. The Foreign Office also asked what argument Sir K. Cornwallis proposed to use in justification of our right to introduce the troops, since the matter was not fully covered by our treaty rights. We had the right to use lines of communication through Iraq, and to send reinforcements to Basra aerodrome in an emergency, but only after consultation with the Iraqi Government. There was no doubt about the emergency, yet we could not obtain the prior consent of the Iraqi Government; in any case we did not recognise Rashid Ali. The Foreign Office thought that we should say that recent developments in Iraq had shown the grave danger that, owing to direct or indirect Axis influence, our line of communications through Iraq and our treaty position generally might be imperilled, and that we must act at once to meet this unexpected emergency.

The Foreign Office had already begun to doubt whether it would be wise to use our forces in open support of the Regent. Sir K. Cornwallis had reported that the Regent's situation was (b) getting worse; he telegraphed on April 11 that the moment for swift and summary action against Rashid Ali had passed. The Regent, although well-liked, did not arouse any widespread popular enthusiasm. On April 10, after the Parliament had agreed to replace the Regent by one of his nominees, Rashid Ali had declared (c) in the name of his Government that Iraq intended to honour her treaty with Great Britain in the letter and the spirit. Rashid Ali had thus deprived us of the excuse that the landing of troops was in defence of our treaty rights. It was therefore important that, when we took action, we should do so in accordance with the terms of the treaty or in consequence of an Iraqi refusal to implement the treaty on some clear-cut issue.

Sir K. Cornwallis suggested that he should give Rashid Ali formal (d) advance notice of the coming of our troops, and should say that the

---

(a) E1347/1/93. (b) E1386, 1408, 1410/1/93. (c) E1382, 1411/1/93. (d) E1414/1/93.

military situation outside Iraq required the rapid passage of troops through to Palestine and that in accordance with our treaty rights we were opening up lines of communication at once. If Rashid Ali failed in this test of his good faith, we should be free to do whatever we thought fit, but we ought not to associate the opening of the lines of communication with the support of the Regent's cause or to accompany it with threats. It was likely that Rashid Ali would ask us to recognise his Government in return for accepting the landing

(a) of our troops. Sir K. Cornwallis now considered that it would be expedient, in spite of the loss of prestige, to agree to some form of recognition contingent upon the fulfilment of Iraqi treaty obligations if we could thereby get our troops into the country without incident.

(b)   The Government of India thought that if we gave advance notice of the coming of our forces, Rashid Ali would have time to organise resistance to their landing; it would therefore be necessary to recast

(c) our whole plan of landing. The Foreign Office and the Chiefs of Staff, on the other hand, agreed with Sir K. Cornwallis. At first, after a

(d) meeting of the Defence Committee on April 13 at Chequers, at which the Foreign Secretary and the Secretary of State for India were present, Sir K. Cornwallis was told not to say anything about the landing to Rashid Ali until the ships were expected to be sighted.

(e)   Sir K. Cornwallis pointed out that Rashid Ali must at least be allowed an opportunity to countermand the standing orders of the Iraqi forces at Basra to oppose an attempted landing. He was there-

(f) fore instructed to choose his own time for giving the notice, and, when he gave it, to say that, if we had unconditional Iraqi co-operation in opening up our lines of communication, as a sign of Rashid Ali's intention to abide loyally by the treaty, we would enter at once into informal relations with his Government and accord full recognition to it as soon as its position had been regularised.

(g)   On the evening of April 16, after finding that there were already rumours that British troops were on their way, Sir K. Cornwallis used his discretionary power to speak to Rashid Ali on the subject. To his surprise Rashid Ali took the news well; he seemed pleased at the offer of recognition and agreed to give all facilities for the movement of the troops.

(h)   The first detachments landed without incident, but it soon became clear that Rashid Ali and the 'Golden Square' were going to cause

(i) trouble. On April 18 the Iraqi Government told Sir K. Cornwallis that they agreed to the disembarkation of troops on condition (i) that measures should be taken to hasten their passage through the country; (ii) that reasonable notice should be given of the arrival of

---

(a) E1439/1/93. (b) E1456/1/93. (c) COS(41) 132nd meeting; E1457/1/93. (d) DO(41) 13th meeting; E1414/1/93. (e) E1467/1/93. (f) WM(41)40, E1439/1/93. (g) E1524/1/93. (h) E1568, 1593/1/93. (i) E1565, 1616/1/93.

further detachments, and that the total strength of the British forces in Iraq at any one time should not be more than one mixed brigade; (iii) that no more troops should disembark until those who had already landed had passed through the country. Three days later these conditions (which had been expressed at first as 'wishes') were laid down in a note.

On April 22 the Foreign Office sent to Sir K. Cornwallis a telegram (a) embodying Mr. Churchill's view of the situation in Iraq. Mr. Churchill pointed out that our chief interest in sending troops to Iraq was to establish and cover a great assembly base at Basra. We had invoked our treaty rights to ensure a peaceful landing, but, if necessary, we should have used force. Our position at Basra did not rest solely on the treaty with Iraq, but also on a new event arising out of the war. We could not undertake to send the troops northwards or to move them through to Palestine, and we could not recognise a right to require such undertakings 'in respect of a Government which has itself usurped power by a *coup d'état*, or in a country where our treaty rights have so long been frustrated in the spirit'.

On the following day the British military commander at Basra (b) came to Baghdad in order to discuss the position with the Iraqi Chief of Staff. He explained the need for time to organise a base, and said that a battalion of British troops was being flown from Basra to Habbaniyah. He also gave notice that more troops belonging to the formations which had already arrived would be disembarking within the next few days. The Chief of Staff seemed anxious to avoid trouble, but asked that something should be done quickly to show that we did not intend to keep troops permanently at Basra.

On April 24 Sir K. Cornwallis, with the approval of the Foreign (c) Office, informed the Iraqi Foreign Minister verbally that he had authority to enter into informal relations with the new Government. He said that the British Government were favourably impressed by the attitude of the Ministers and hoped that by giving further evidence of their loyalty to the treaty they would make possible the establishment of formal relations. The Foreign Minister promised to do all that he could to improve Anglo-Iraqi relations, but again asked for full and early recognition and for the rapid passage through the country of the troops landed at Basra.

On April 28 the Iraqi Government were notified of the impending arrival of 2,000 more troops (mostly of non-combatant units). They (d) replied by telephone to Sir K. Cornwallis that they could not agree to the arrival of these troops. During an interview on the same afternoon Rashid Ali and the Foreign Minister said to Sir K. Cornwallis that the Iraqi Cabinet had considered the question, and would not allow any more troops to land until the detachments

(a) E1623/1/93. (b) E1686/1/93. (c) E1723/1/93. (d) E1782, 1790/1/93.

already disembarked had moved on or were out of the country. They also refused to enter into further discussions concerning the treaty until the Ambassador had presented his credentials (i.e. until the British Government had formally recognised the new Government). In any case they insisted that the treaty did not give the British Government the right to maintain forces in Iraq, even in war time, other than the guards required for the treaty air bases; the retention of a force at Basra was a violation of the treaty which the Iraqi people could not tolerate.

Sir K. Cornwallis warned Rashid Ali that, in spite of his objections, the troops would certainly be landed and that the consequences of opposition or obstruction would be serious. He found Rashid Ali's attitude so threatening that he decided at the interview to send British women and children away from Baghdad. The two Iraqi Ministers gave an assurance that facilities would be given for them to leave the country in safety. A scheme for evacuation had already been prepared, and by the evening of April 29 the party of some 240 women and children reached Habbaniyah whence they were to be flown to Basra during the next few days.

(a)   During the night of April 29–30, however, in spite of these promises, Iraqi forces surrounded the air base at Habbaniyah and early on the morning of April 30 their commander sent a declaration that Great Britain had violated the treaty with Iraq, and a warning that his forces would shell aircraft attempting to leave the airfield (b)   or armoured cars leaving the camp. Sir K. Cornwallis at once replied with a written protest to the Iraqi Government, and added that, if they did not immediately withdraw their forces from the neighbourhood of Habbaniyah, they must be held responsible for the consequences.

From this point the situation rapidly became one of open hostilities; by May 3 the Ambassador, his staff and the greater part of the British community of Baghdad were unable to leave the Embassy.[1] Communications by wireless or cypher telegram were cut off, and the Iraqi authorities requested that the British flag should not be flown from the Embassy. It was hoisted accordingly in the Embassy garden.

The news of the outbreak of hostilities at Habbaniyah was followed (c)   by offers of mediation from the Turkish and Egyptian Governments. The Turkish Government was especially anxious for a quick and friendly settlement. The Iraqi Minister at Ankara, who was a brother of Rashid Ali, had tried with some success to convince M. Saracoglu that the new Iraqi Government meant to carry out loyally the terms

---

[1] The United States Minister, Mr. Paul Knabenshue, at considerable personal risk, gave refuge to more than 150 members of the British community who were unable to reach the British Embassy.

(a) E1802, 1817/1/93. (b) E1815/1/93. (c) E1907, 1912, 1919, 1920/1/93.

of the treaty and that the crisis was due entirely to the attempts of the British to exceed their treaty rights.

General Wavell thought at first that we should accept the offers of mediation because we had not enough troops to spare for upper Iraq (a) and a defeat there would have most serious effects elsewhere. The Foreign Office and the Chiefs of Staff agreed, however, that we could not agree to mediation or avoid dealing with the situation ourselves. We knew that Rashid Ali had been negotiating with the Axis Powers and had been waiting for their support. The arrival of our troops at Basra had forced him into action before enemy support had reached him. We therefore had a good chance of getting rid of him if we acted quickly. Sir H. Knatchbull-Hugessen was therefore instructed (b) to tell the Turkish Government that we could not agree to proposals for the abandonment of our treaty rights, and that Turkish inter-vention could be of value only in inducing Rashid Ali to arrange the unconditional withdrawal of the Iraqi troops at Habbaniyah. The best plan would be for the Turkish Government to try to secure the replacement of Rashid Ali and the military clique by a more friendly and more trustworthy administration. The Turkish Govern-ment, however, were unwilling to act on any of these suggestions.

Although the Foreign Office and the Chiefs of Staff decided to take a firmer line than General Wavell had suggested, they also shared the views of General Wavell and Sir K. Cornwallis that we should avoid antagonising the Iraqi people. We should not declare war on Iraqi or bomb Iraq cities, or interfere more than was necessary in the civil administration of the country. As long as the Iraqi administration met our requirements, we should leave it alone. We had not the resources for a military occupation of the country or even of all its key points; in any case an attempt of this kind would give an opportunity to Axis propaganda. The Government of India, who were specially concerned over the safety of the oilfield areas and the communications leading from them to the Persian Gulf, and who had provided most of the forces in Iraq, would have preferred a full occupation of the country, but such a plan was impracticable. It was also essential to reassure the friendly Arab tribes that we did not intend to destroy Iraqi independence. We should make it clear that we were merely refusing to accept a compromise with Rashid Ali and his clique and that we could not agree to a return to the unsatis-factory position in which Iraq was governed by a few politicians in Baghdad without reference to the general interests of the country.

The military situation improved more quickly than might have been expected. The population in general showed no wish for a war of 'liberation', and the rebels never had any important or dramatic

---

(a) Hist. (B)4, Nos. 20, 21, 32, 40; DO(41) 24th and 25th meetings; E2051, 2104, 2109, 2110/1/93. (b) E1907, 1909/1/93.

success which might have brought waverers over to their side. In particular, the tribes, with hardly an exception, refused to listen to their appeals. Owing to their preoccupation with the attack on Crete, which opened on May 20, the Germans could not divert much of their available air force to Syria and Iraq; their heavy losses in air-borne troops and material during the Cretan operation prevented them from turning at once to Iraq at the beginning of June. In any event they would probably have been too late.[1] The critical days in the revolt were from April 30 to May 7. On May 7 the small garrison at the Habbaniyah aerodrome was reinforced by air from Basra, and drove the Iraqi rebel forces away from the high ground commanding the station. On May 10 the fort at Rutbah was recaptured from the rebels, and on May 13 a hastily organised relief column crossed the Iraqi frontier, and six days later took the town of Fallujah on the Euphrates between Habbaniyah and Baghdad. The rebels made a determined counter-attack on May 21, but were driven back, and the relief column reached the approaches to Baghdad on May 30. The Regent, who had gone to Palestine, went back to Iraq on May 22; on the following day the Foreign Office learned that he had sent a representative to Basra, and that a number of well-known Sheikhs had declared their loyalty to him. When the relief column reached Baghdad, Rashid Ali, the Mufti, and the other leaders of the revolt left the country; the German[2] and Italian Ministers went with them, and the Regent was free to come back to Baghdad.

(a) Meanwhile the Mayor of Baghdad and other Iraqi notables not compromised with Rashid Ali had set up an *ad hoc* committee to negotiate the end of hostilities. They signed an agreement on May 31 with the British military authorities providing that the

---

[1] The Germans had maintained contact with Rashid Ali, but before the spring of 1941 had not gone beyond propaganda and general exploitation of anti-English feeling. On March 7, 1941, a German Foreign Office memorandum on policy towards Arab countries considered that they were for the present beyond operational reach and that a political declaration in favour of a great Arab State was difficult owing to the need to avoid trouble with the French over Syria or controversy with the Italians. The memorandum suggested that arms might be sent through Turkey to Iraq on the pretext that they were in transit for Iran and Afghanistan (*D.G.F.P.*, XII, No. 133).

On April 18 the Germans heard that the Iraqi Government had made an immediate appeal to the Italian Minister in Baghdad for arms. Ribbentrop drew up a memorandum for Hitler, but Hitler doubted whether the Germans could send air assistance. Steps were taken later to provide this assistance which involved the use of Syrian aerodromes (see above, p. 564–5). One measure was to instruct German ships at Bandar Sharpur (Iran) to sink themselves in the Shatt-el-Arab in order to impede the movement of British supplies to Basra. The German Minister at Baghdad was told on May 31 that German aeroplanes would probably reach Mosul on June 1. He replied that they could not safely land at Mosul or Kirkuk, and must operate through Syria. Later on May 31 all German forces were withdrawn to Aleppo. The French authorities in Syria then strongly urged that German aircraft and personnel should leave Syria at once in order to avoid any pretext for British and Gaullist attacks. See *D.G.F.P.*, XII, Nos. 528, 543, 566–7, 581.

(b) [2] The German Minister had returned to Baghdad at the beginning of the revolt.

(a) E2724, 2749/1/93. (b) E2331/1/93.

Iraqi army should retain its arms and equipment, but that all units should go at once to their normal peace-time stations. British prisoners were to be released; German and Italian service personnel were to be interned, and the British military authorities given immediate facilities for unimpeded through communication by rail, road and river.

On June 1 the Regent came back to Baghdad, and a revolt which, (a) if wrongly handled, might have shaken at a critical time the whole British position in the Middle East, ended in a way which enhanced British prestige.

(v)

The German-Turkish agreement of June 16, 1941.

During the long negotiations with Turkey before the opening of the German attack in the Balkans, there had been on the British side a certain under-current of anxiety about the pressure which the Germans were known to be putting on the Turkish Government to join the Axis side. The reasons for this pressure were obvious. Turkey was as important to German plans of attack as to British plans of defence, and, for that matter, a complete Turkish surrender to the Axis would have been even more dangerous to the U.S.S.R.

At the beginning of March 1941, the Germans made a particular effort to win over the Turkish Government. Hitler sent a personal message on March 4 through Herr von Papen, the German (b) Ambassador at Ankara, to President Inönü. He tried to explain in this message that Germany had no territorial interest in the Balkans, and that she was concerned there only with measures to resist British attempts to secure a foothold in the European continent. As soon as these measures had succeeded, German troops would be withdrawn from Bulgaria and Roumania. German and Turkish interests required close economic collaboration, and there need be no opposition between the two countries in regard to the post-war territorial settlement. Germany would thus do nothing to harm Turkey as long as the Turks themselves took no steps which would necessitate a change in the German attitude.

The Turkish reactions to this message seemed, from a British point of view, entirely satisfactory. M. Saracoglu showed Hitler's letter at once to Sir H. Knatchbull-Hugessen, and said that he would reply to it only 'pour des raisons protocolaires'. The Turkish Government (c) did not send an answer to Hitler until March 12. They then expressed

---

(a) E2747/1/93.   (b) R2117/113/67; R2029/1934/44.   (c) R2178, 2464/113/67.

their regret that the Germans had not carried out their previous undertakings not to enter the Balkans.[1] In reply to the German promise not to attack Turkey unless Turkish action changed the situation, they gave similar assurances to Germany.

The Germans renewed their pressure after the collapse of resistance in Yugoslavia and the British defeats in Greece. The situation was

(a) indeed especially serious when Papen came back to Ankara on May 13 after a visit to Berlin. The Iraqi revolt had broken out, and the Foreign Office had information that the Germans were intending to come through Turkey, with or without Turkish consent, to the aid of the rebels. The collapse of the revolt eased matters from the Turkish point of view, but the Germans were now close at hand and Great Britain could give very little help against them. The Germans

(b) were also able to threaten Turkey with a Russo-German agreement at Turkish expense. The Turkish Government kept Sir H. Knatchbull-Hugessen informed of the German demands, but said that they felt bound to enter into discussions with Germany and perhaps to exchange assurances with her as the best means of preventing a Russo-German deal.

The Foreign Office thought that the Germans were probably trying to weaken both Turkish and Russian resistance by playing on Turkish fears. The obvious way to counter this German trick was for the Turks themselves to approach the Soviet Government. The Turkish Government, however, were unwilling to do this. Mr. Eden

(c) sent a personal message to M. Saracoglu on June 2 suggesting that we might sound the Soviet Government on their view of the German efforts to bring pressure on Turkey. On the same day Mr. Eden

(d) said to M. Maisky that he would be willing to obtain information from the Turkish Government about the German demands if the Soviet Government doubted the expediency of a direct enquiry on their part.

(e)   Neither the Soviet nor the Turkish Government responded to these British suggestions, but the Foreign Office considered that Turkey might be trying to gain time until the British military position

(f) in the Middle East improved. On June 12, however, Papen once more offered Turkey an agreement to the effect that the two countries would respect the integrity and inviolability of each other's territories and maintain amicable contact on all questions touching their common interests in order to bring about an understanding on the solution of such questions.

---

[1] This account of the Turkish reply to Hitler was not altogether accurate. The reply noted the change which had come about in German policy in the Balkans, and pointed out that Turkey was in no way responsible for such change, but there was no statement of regret that Germany had not carried out her undertakings not to enter the Balkans (*D.G.F.P.*, XII, No. 161).

(a) R5266/1934/44; R5332/5332/44; R5356/113/67. (b) R5366, 5367, 5368, 5456/1934/44. (c) R5571, 5692, 5718/1934/44; R5558/112/44. (d) N2570/3/38. (e) R5848/112/44; R5925, 6082/1934/44. (f) R6141/1934/44; R6148/5182/44.

Sir H. Knatchbull-Hugessen, on hearing of this draft from M. Saracoglu, pointed out that the terms went beyond a mere pledge of neutrality in a Russo-German war (for which the Germans had already asked). On the other hand Papen was disappointed that the Turks refused to accept the draft without a preamble safeguarding the existing agreements of the two parties. The Germans accepted this condition, and asked for the immediate signature of the agreement. Sir H. Knatchbull-Hugessen then argued that Turkey would be doing just what the Germans wanted if she allowed the Russians to see that they could expect no help from her in the event of a German attack.[1] M. Saracoglu answered that, in spite of our efforts, and of the menacing German concentrations on the Russian frontier, the Soviet Government had given no signs of approaching Turkey; in other words, there was still room for doubt whether the Russians might not agree to a 'deal' with Germany.

The Foreign Office realised that they could not prevent the Turkish Government from coming to an agreement with Germany. They tried once again to point out the dangers in the Turkish course. The Germans were rushing Turkey at a time when the movement of their troops showed that they were not intending an attack on Turkish territory, and when our own position in the Middle East was improving. The agreement—whatever its terms—would make a very bad impression, not only throughout the Middle East but in Great Britain and the United States.

The Foreign Office did not expect these arguments to deter the Turks from their policy. Hence the only course open to us was to try to ensure that the actual terms of the agreement did not affect Turkish obligations under the treaty with Great Britain. M. Saracoglu had already given verbal assurances that this treaty would be respected, and that the agreement with Germany would not contain concessions (such as the right to send troops or war material through Turkey) prejudicial to our interests. The Foreign Office attempted to (a) get a public statement on the subject, and, if possible, the inclusion in the agreement of a clause specifically referring to our treaty rights. The treaty was signed on June 18. The Turkish Government would not make a public declaration in the sense desired by His Majesty's (b) Government, but on June 19 M. Saracoglu told Reuter's correspondent at Ankara that the Anglo-Turkish treaty was one of the agreements covered generally by the reservation clause in the preamble to the agreement with Germany. Nevertheless the official announcement of the agreement two days later was accompanied by

---

[1] On May 28 M. Saracoglu had told Sir H. Knatchbull-Hugessen that Herr von Papen had not mentioned Russia by name, but that he had spoken of any 'new war' in which (c) Germany might be engaged.

(a) R6141, 6170, 6233/1934/44. (b) R6347, 6350, 6468/1934/44. (c) R5692/1934/44.

Turkish and German statements recalling in extravagant terms the long-standing friendship between the two countries.[1]

(a)   The War Cabinet decided that, since they could not prevent the conclusion of the agreement, they would not 'nag' about it. The main fact was that Turkey remained neutral, and had not actually joined the German side. The Foreign Office was anxious that the

(b)   British press should not abuse Turkey, and that we should continue to send the supplies promised under our agreement. If we cut off these supplies, in spite of the Turkish assurance that they had not compromised their treaty with us, the Turks would think either that we did not trust them or that our own military position was such that we could not spare the supplies. The War Cabinet agreed to continue the despatch of supplies, though the situation was altered to some extent by the opening of the German attack on Russia.

ANNEX I

(1)

Proclamation by General Catroux in the name of General de Gaulle

Cairo, le 8 juin, 1941.

Syriens et Libanais. A l'heure où les forces de la France Libre unies aux forces de l'Empire Britannique, son Alliée, pénètrent sur votre territoire, je déclare assumer les pouvoirs, les résponsabilités et les devoirs du représentant de la France au Levant. Ceci au nom de la France Libre, qui s'identifie avec la France traditionelle et authentique, et au nom de son chef, le Général de Gaulle. En cette qualité je viens mettre un terme au

---

[1] The Germans did not demand immediate passage for men or material through Turkey, but the German Ambassador at Ankara was instructed on May 17 to ask for a secret treaty (in addition to an open treaty) which would allow unlimited right of passage (*D.G.F.P.*, XII, No. 529). With the collapse of the Iraqi rebellion the transit question was less urgent, but on June 1 von Papen was sent the draft of a treaty with a secret protocol (*ib.*, No. 583). The Turkish Government held out successfully for a statement in the preamble to the effect that the treaty was 'without prejudice to existing obligations of the two countries' (*ib.*, No. 648). There was no secret protocol, and in reporting the Turkish insistence on the statement about existing obligations, Papen let the Turks know that Germany would be disappointed 'in every respect' at the 'meagre result of the negotiations' (*ib.*, No. 620).

(a) WM(41)60.   (b) WP(41)141;   WM(41)63;   DO(41) 44th meeting.

régime du mandat et vous proclamer libres et indépendants. Vous serez donc désormais des peuples souverains et indépendants et vous pourrez soit vous constituer en Etats distincts soit vous rassembler en un seul Etat. Dans les deux hypothèses votre statut d'indépendance et de souveraineté sera garanti par un traité où seront en outre définis nos rapports réciproques. Ce traité sera négocié dès que possible entre vos réprésentants et moi. En attendant sa conclusion notre situation mutuelle sera celle d'alliées étroitement unies dans la poursuite d'un idéal et des buts communs. Syriens et Libanais. Vous jugerez par cette déclaration que si les forces Françaises Libres et les forces Britanniques franchissent vos frontières ce n'est pas pour opprimer votre liberté, c'est pour l'assurer. C'est pour chasser de la Syrie les forces d'Hitler. C'est pour empêcher que le Levant devienne contre les Britanniques et contre nous une base offensive de l'ennemi. Nous ne pouvons permettre, nous qui combattons pour la liberté des peuples, que, submergeant peu à peu votre pays, les ennemis puissent s'emparer de vos personnes et de vos biens et faire de vous des esclaves. Nous ne permettrons pas que des populations que la France a promis de défendre soient jetées entre les mains du maître le plus impitoyable que l'histoire ait connu. Nous ne permettrons pas que les intérêts séculaires de la France au Levant soient livrés à l'ennemi. Syriens et Libanais. Si, répondant à mon appel, vous vous ralliez à nous, vous devez savoir que le Gouvernement Britannique d'accord avec la France Libre s'est engagé à vous consentir tous les avantages dont jouissent les pays libres qui leur sont associés. C'est ainsi que le blocus sera levé et que vous entrerez sur-le-champ en relations avec le bloc de la livre sterling, ce qui ouvrira les plus larges possibilités à votre commerce d'importation et d'exportation. Vos achats et vos ventes avec tous les pays libres se feront librement. Syriens et Libanais. La France vous déclare indépendants par la voix de ceux de ses fils qui combattent pour sa vie et pour la liberté du monde.

(2)

Declaration by His Majesty's Government supporting General Catroux's proclamation

General Catroux, on behalf of General de Gaulle, Chief of the Free French, has issued a declaration to the inhabitants of Syria and the Lebanon before advancing with the object of expelling the Germans. In this he declares the liberty and independence of Syria and the Lebanon. He undertakes to negotiate a treaty to ensure these objects.

I am authorised by His Majesty's Government in the United Kingdom to declare that they support and associate themselves with the assurance of independence given by General Catroux on behalf of General de Gaulle to Syria and the Lebanon.

I am also authorised to give you the assurance that, should you support and join the Allies, His Majesty's Government in the United Kingdom offer you all the advantages enjoyed by free countries who are associated with them. Thus the blockade will be lifted and you will enter into immediate relations with the sterling *bloc*, which will give you enormous and immediate advantages from the point of view of your exports and imports. You will be able to sell your products and to buy freely in all free countries.

MILES LAMPSON
His Britannic Majesty's Ambassador, Cairo,
on behalf of His Majesty's Government
in the United Kingdom

Cairo, June 8, 1941

ANNEX II

Exchange of letters between the Minister of State, Cairo, and General de Gaulle concerning the interpretation to be placed by the British and Free French Authorities upon the Syrian Armistice Convention

(1)

Minister of State to General de Gaulle

Cairo, July 24, 1941

MY DEAR GENERAL,

I send you herewith the text of the agreement drawn up yesterday by our representatives which defines the interpretation to be placed by the British and Free French authorities upon the Syrian Armistice Convention. This agreement is authoritative and supersedes or overrides any other interpretation of the convention as between the British and Free French authorities.

It is agreed that in the event of it being found by the Disarmament Commission that there has been substantial violation of the Armistice Convention by the Vichy forces, we shall declare that, as a sanction, the British and Free French authorities consider themselves free to take any steps they see fit to rally Vichy troops to Free France. In that event article 2 of the enclosed agreement would become null and void.

This exchange of letters should not be published except by our mutual consent.

May I learn whether you agree? As soon as I receive your letter to this effect the agreement will become binding upon the military and civil authorities concerned.

Yours sincerely,

OLIVER LYTTELTON

Enclosure in (1)

Arrangement fixing the Interpretation to be given by the British and Free French Authorities to the Armistice Convention of July 14 putting an end to Hostilities in the Levant

Article 1

It is recognised that the Free French Command has a pre-eminent interest in all questions affecting the Vichy troops. This interest shall be taken into special consideration in all matters concerning the stationing and cadres of the troops, and in particular the transfer of troops or individuals which may be necessary will be settled by understanding between the two commands concerned.

Article 2

Article 8 of the Armistice Convention provides that the alternative of rallying to the Allied cause or of being repatriated will be left to the free choice of each individual. This liberty of choice can only mean that the Free French authorities will be allowed to explain their point of view to the personnel concerned with the same fullness and freedom granted to the Vichy authorities by the fact of the presence of Vichy officers and non-commissioned officers with their men.

Any arrangement which may have been made and which may conflict with the Armistice Convention on this point can in no way derogate from the principle established by the armistice. All measures of stationing and encadrement necessary to give full effect to article 8 will be applied.

Article 3

As regards repatriation of the Vichy forces, the British Command will take into consideration the desires of the Free French Command so that full effect may be given to the terms of article 8 concerning free choice.[1]

Article 4

It is recognised that the war material is French property, The handing over will be effected by agreement between the two commands.

The Free French Command will give priority to employment of this material in the Middle East.

The Free French Command, by agreement with the British Command, will place at the disposal of the latter the material which it cannot utilise in the near future, account being taken of the constitution of the necessary reserves. The Free French Command, in agreement with the British Command, will be able to reassume possession of this material if it finds itself able to utilise it itself.

Free French technicians will be added to the British armourers and technicians for the purpose of receiving and examining the material.

---

[1] *Note* in original: The period considered necessary by the Free French command for the purpose of the repatriation of the bulk of those who do not rally is about six weeks.

Any sabotage will engage the responsibility of the person concerned and of the superior officers, who will be excluded from any guarantee afforded by the Armistice Convention.

Article 5
The military services of the Vichy troops will continue to carry out their duties in accordance with the orders of the occupation authorities.

Article 6
All the military establishments (supply service, signals, artillery, medical, equipment, repair workshops, dumps and establishments of the Air Force, yards and establishments of the Navy) will continue according to the orders of the occupation authorities to be run by their administration and personnel, who will be responsible for the preservation and maintenance of the establishments and of the material as is provided in the case of the material referred to in Article 4.

This responsibility will only terminate upon regular discharge.

Article 7
The special troops of the Levant which the Free French Command consider it useful to keep in being will form part of the Free French Forces.

Article 8
In view of the great importance for military operations which attaches to the maintenance of order in the Jebel Druse, it is agreed that the French Delegate-General will concert with the British Commander-in-Chief on all important measures concerning the maintenance of order in that area.

Article 9
Under reserve of the agreement to be established as regards the collaboration of the French and British services concerning security, it is recognised that the question of the civilians referred to in article 8 will fall within the competence of the French authority.

(2)

General de Gaulle to Minister of State

Beyrouth, le 27 juillet, 1941

CHER CAPTAIN LYTTELTON,

Je reçois votre lettre du 24 juillet 1941 et le texte de l'accord que nos représentants respectifs ont établi comme interprétation de la Convention d'Armistice en Syrie. Je me fais un plaisir de vous dire que j'approuve ce texte qui, dès à présent, engage les autorités militaires et civiles françaises qu'il concerne.

D'autre part, je prends acte de votre accord sur la sanction à prendre à l'égard des éléments français dissidents dits 'de Vichy', s'il est établi que ces éléments ont, comme je le pense, effectivement violé la convention.

Il est entendu que ni votre lettre du 24 juillet, ni ma réponse, ne seront publiées sans que nous y consentions tous les deux.

Bien sincèrement à vous,

C. DE GAULLE

ANNEX III

Exchange of letters between the Minister of State, Cairo, and General de Gaulle concerning the collaboration between the British and the Free French Authorities in the Middle East

(1)

Minister of State to General de Gaulle

Cairo, July 25, 1941

MY DEAR GENERAL,

I am sending you herewith the text of an agreement and of a supplementary agreement concerning the collaboration between the British and the Free French authorities in the Middle East, which we drew up together this morning.

I should like to take this opportunity of assuring you that on the British side we recognise the historic interests of France in the Levant. Great Britain has no interest in Syria or the Lebanon except to win the war. We have no desire to encroach in any way upon the position of France. Both Free France and Great Britain are pledged to the independence of Syria and the Lebanon. When this essential step has been taken and without prejudice to it, we freely admit that France should have the dominant privileged position in the Levant among all European nations. It was in this spirit that we approached the problems under discussion. You will have seen the recent utterances of the Prime Minister in this sense, and I am glad to reaffirm them now.

I shall be happy to learn that the enclosed texts have your full agreement and approval.

Yours sincerely,

OLIVER LYTTELTON

Enclosure (a) in (1)

Agreement concerning the Collaboration between the British and Free French Authorities in the Middle East

Article 1

The Middle East constitutes a single theatre of operations. The defensive and offensive operations of the Allies in this theatre shall be co-ordinated.

Further, by reason of the special obligations of France in the territory of the Levant States, it is primarily to the defence of this territory that Free France has decided to devote, in the present general situation, the French forces in the Middle East and the Syrian and Lebanese forces.

Article 2

Any plan of operations which entails the employment of French forces jointly with the British forces, or which directly affects the territory of the Levant States, shall be drawn up in common by the British command and the French command.

In view of the large preponderance at the present time of the British forces in comparison with the French forces in the Middle East, it is for the British command in the Middle East theatre of operations to draw up plans and to fix the role to be played by the French forces in joint operations. The British command in the theatre of operations in the Middle East will determine this role by delegation from General de Gaulle. The same delegation will apply to any force ('echelon') forming part of the British command subordinated to the Commander-in-Chief in the Middle East, when the Commander-in-Chief has charged such a force to direct operations which interest the territory of the Levant States or entail the employment of French forces. At the same time, if the French command considers that the plan drawn up or the role assigned to the French forces is incompatible with its special responsibilities concerning the Levant States, it will refer to General de Gaulle. The question shall then be decided by agreement between His Majesty's Government in the United Kingdom and General de Gaulle.

Article 3

The command of the British and French forces operating in the same zone of action is normally exercised by a British officer or by a French officer, according as the British forces or the French forces preponderate there. In any case, the organic links of units, large or small, will be maintained as far as possible. The French officer or the command of French forces subordinated to a British officer exercises the right of and receives facilities for reporting directly on its situation, assignment and requirements to the superior unit of its own army, and to remain in direct liaison with that unit. Such communications may be in secret form.

Article 4

Whatever may be the proportion and assignment of the British forces and the French forces, the territorial command (direction or military control of public services, general security, gendarmerie, police, exploitation of local resources, etc.) belongs to the French authority in Syria and the Lebanon.

The British forces which may operate in the territory of Syria and the Lebanon and the French forces which may operate in other territories of the Middle East may themselves assure there their tactical security and utilise all resources which are necessary for their needs. They do so, so far as possible, with the assistance of the territorial command.

In enemy territory the territorial command is shared between the British authorities and the French authorities in accordance with the proportionate relationship between the British and French forces in the various parts of the territory concerned.

Article 5

In any case, the British forces and the French forces depend respectively and exclusively from the British command and the French command in all matters concerning discipline, organisation of troops and services, assignment of personnel and material, turn-out, postal censorship, etc.

Enclosure (b) in (1)
Supplementary Agreement concerning the Collaboration between British and Free French Authorities in the Middle East

Article 1

General de Gaulle recognises that the British High Command in the Levant is empowered to take all measures of defence which it judges necessary to take against the common enemy.

If it should happen that any of these measures should appear to be contrary to the interests of France in the Levant, the question would be submitted to the British Government and to General de Gaulle.

Article 2

General de Gaulle accepts the principle of raising additional Desert Troops for the requirements of operations.

He does not rule out, if it appears indispensable, the attachment of certain specialised British officers in the Desert Units.

He sees no objection to the employment in the Syrian Desert of Desert Troops recruited in the Nejd, Transjordania, Iraq or other territories by the British authorities.

Article 3

A section of the British Military Security Service will be attached to the Sûreté générale of the Levant States with the object of ensuring liaison with the British command and with the security services of the adjoining States and of concerting with the French service the general measures which the British command may consider necessary.

(2)

General de Gaulle to Minister of State

Beyrouth, le 27 juillet, 1941

CHER CAPTAIN LYTTELTON,

Je reçois qotre lettre du 25 juillet. Je suis heureux de prendre note des assurances vue vous voulez bien m'y donner concernant le désintéressement de la Grande-Bretagne en Syrie et au Liban et le fait que la Grande-Bretagne reconnaît par avance la position dominante et privilégiée de la France au Levant lorsque ces Etats se trouveront indépendants.

Le texte de l'accord et du supplément à cet accord que je trouve annexé à votre lettre et que nous avons arrêté ensemble au Caire le 25 juillet sera mis immédiatement en application par les autorités militaires françaises qu'il concerne.

Bien sincèrement à vous,

C. DE GAULLE

ANNEX IV

Exchange of letters between the Minister of State, Cairo, and General de Gaulle concerning British policy in Syria and the Lebanon

(1)

Minister of State to General de Gaulle

Cairo, August 7, 1941

MY DEAR GENERAL,

At the conclusion of our talk today I am happy to repeat to you the assurance that Great Britain has no interest in Syria or the Lebanon except to win the war. We have no desire to encroach in any way upon the position of France. Both Free France and Great Britain are pledged to the independence of Syria and the Lebanon. When this essential step has been taken, and without prejudice to it, we freely admit that France should have the predominant position in Syria and the Lebanon over any other European Power. It is in this spirit that we have always acted. You will have seen the recent utterances of the Prime Minister in this sense. I am glad to reaffirm them now to our friends and allies, who have our full sympathy and support.

On our side, I am happy again to receive your assurances of the determination of Free France, as the friend and ally of Great Britain and in accordance with the agreements and declarations which you have already made, to pursue relentlessly to the finish the war against the common enemy. I am happy that we should thus reaffirm our complete understanding and agreement.

Yours sincerely,

OLIVER LYTTELTON

(2)

General de Gaulle to Minister of State

Beyrouth, le 7 août, 1941

MON CHER CAPTAIN LYTTELTON,

Je reçois la lettre que vous voulez bien m'écrire comme conclusion de notre entretien d'aujourd'hui. Je suis heureux de prendre acte des assurances que vous m'y donnez de nouveau concernant le désintéressement de la Grand-Bretagne en Syrie et au Liban et le fait que la Grande-Bretagne y reconnaît par avance la position prééminente privilégiée de la France lorsque ces Etats se trouveront indépendants conformément à l'engagement que la France Libre a pris à leur égard.

Je m'empresse de vous répéter à cette occasion que la France Libre, c'est-à-dire la France, est résolue à poursuivre la guerre, aux côtes de la Grande-Bretagne, son amie et son alliée, jusqu'à la victoire complète contre nos ennemis communs.

Bien sincèrement à vous,

C. DE GAULLE

CHAPTER XVIII

Anglo-Russian relations in 1941 to the opening of the German attack on the U.S.S.R.

(i)

Mr. Eden's proposal to send a letter to Stalin: Sir S. Cripps's conversation of February 1 with M. Molotov: the question of the Baltic ships.

IN spite of the British efforts to improve Anglo-Russian relations during the period after the Russo-Finnish war and, particularly, during the latter half of the year 1940, there had been no obvious sign of change for the better. The German advance into Roumania and the Italian attack on Greece had not made the Soviet Government less distant in their attitude towards Great Britain or more forthcoming in their treatment of minor questions such as the Baltic ships. On the other hand the relations between the U.S.S.R. and Germany appeared to be as close as at any time since the signature of the Russo-German agreement of 1939. On January 10, 1941, this agreement was renewed in a Pact of Friendship; the pact provided for the settlement of questions connected with the annexation of the Baltic countries and problems connected with the Russo-German frontier in occupied Poland. At the same time a new Russo-German trade agreement was signed in Moscow. On January 21 an extension of the Fisheries Agreement with Japan was announced in Moscow and described by the Tass agency as 'undoubtedly a step forward in the improvement of Russo-Japanese relations'.

On February 1, 1941, M. Molotov saw Sir S. Cripps, but the interview merely confirmed the unwillingness of the Soviet Government to take any step towards an Anglo-Russian *rapprochement*. An interview between Sir S. Cripps and M. Vyshinsky on March 22 was equally unhelpful. In April Sir S. Cripps made two further attempts at an approach, but without success.

(a)   Meanwhile, as early as January, and increasingly from the middle of March onwards, the Foreign Office began to receive reports pointing to the possibility of a German attack on Russia. There was no doubt about the military concentrations to which the reports referred, but the purpose of these concentrations was less certain. They might be part of a German 'war of nerves' to weaken the Soviet Government into accepting complete co-operation with Germany.

(a) N107/78/38.

It was impossible for the British Government to decide whether the Soviet Government would give way to German threats or whether the Germans would attack Russia if their demands were not accepted. On April 5 the Soviet Government signed a pact of non-aggression and friendship with the new Yugoslav Government established after the deposition of Prince Paul for his approval of Yugoslav adherence (March 25) to the Tripartite Pact.[1] On April 13 a Russo-Japanese pact of neutrality was signed.[2] Neither pact gave any clear indication whether Russia would resist German demands. The Russians provided no help to Yugoslavia against the German attack of April 6 and an article in *Pravda* denied that the Russo-Japanese agreement was either directed against Germany or signed under German pressure. The public speeches of the Russian leaders early in May warned their countrymen to be prepared for defence, but the Soviet Government did nothing to improve relations with Great Britain. On May 9 indeed they announced the withdrawal of recognition from the Belgian, Norwegian and Yugoslav Legations in Moscow 'owing to their countries' loss of sovereignty'. A few days later the Tass agency announced the renewal of diplomatic relations with Iraq.[3]

From this time until the opening of the German offensive, there was an increasing volume of evidence that Hitler had decided to attack Russia, and that nothing short of a complete Russian surrender would avert the attack. On June 13 Mr. Eden asked M. Maisky to tell the Soviet Government that, in the event of a German attack on the U.S.S.R., we should be prepared to send a mission of the three services to Russia and to do what we could to meet Russian economic needs. M. Maisky's answer was to suggest that, while our message presupposed intimate Anglo-Russian co-operation, the conditions of such collaboration did not exist.

In view of the failure to secure an economic agreement with the U.S.S.R., the British Government, at Sir S. Cripps's suggestion, had tightened to a certain extent the contraband control of goods to Russia, but Mr. Eden had continued the policy of avoiding all provocation in communications to the Soviet Government. He had asked Sir S. Cripps not to send his proposed letter[4] to M. Mikoyan because he was afraid that the Soviet Government might assume that the letter represented a change in policy on his assumption of office. On December 29 Mr. Eden suggested to Sir S. Cripps that he (Mr.

---

[1] See above, p. 549.

[2] See Volume II, Chapter XXIII, section (ii).

[3] Ten days after the opening of hostilities between British forces and the supporters of Rashid Ali.

[4] See above, pp. 497–8.

(a) Eden) might send a short personal message to Stalin recalling their meeting in 1935 and saying that he was determined to work for better relations between Great Britain and the U.S.S.R. and that he hoped for a similar disposition on Stalin's part. A message of this kind would disprove the thesis that the Foreign Office were not doing their best to improve Anglo-Russian relations.

Mr. Eden did not expect that the message would bring any sensational results but it might help to dispel doubts in the mind of Stalin about the sincerity of our wish for co-operation. The message might also help Sir S. Cripps to get through the barrier set up by M. Molotov. Although Stalin had not sent a written answer to the Prime Minister's message of the previous July, he had given Sir S. Cripps a valuable interview in which he had made an authoritative statement on Russian foreign policy.

(b)   Sir S. Cripps replied on December 31 that he considered a message unwise. In view of the leakage[1] of information about Stalin's interview in July he (Sir S. Cripps) would not have any chance of delivering the message personally. The message would therefore be sent only by letter or through M. Molotov. The former course was not sufficiently dignified, and would not produce an answer. The latter course would establish contact only with M. Molotov who would take the chance of being critical and of reaffirming Russian demands with regard to the Baltic questions. In any case, unless we made a definite proposal, the Soviet Government would interpret the message as a sign of weakness on our part and would use it as an opportunity to strengthen their Baltic demands. The Soviet Government knew that we wanted to improve relations with them: friendly messages did not affect their realist policy. Sir S. Cripps was sure that we must await the turn of events before attempting anything more than a settlement of Baltic questions. Our present policy of reserve and 'non-helpfulness' was more likely to make the Soviet Government take some step in our direction; they were suspicious of us and fundamentally no more friendly to us than to the Germans.[2]

---

[1] There appear to be no papers in the Foreign Office archives referring to any such 'leakage'.

[2] On January 21, 1941, M. Maisky asked Mr. Eden to suggest a date for luncheon with him. Mr. Eden consulted the Foreign Office about this invitation. The Northern Department pointed out that M. Molotov had not seen Sir S. Cripps for three and a half months, although he often saw the German, Italian and Japanese Ambassadors. A refusal of M. Maisky's invitation might be a hint at our views about the boycott of Sir S. Cripps in Moscow. Mr. Collier (the head of the Northern Department) also called attention to M. Maisky's 'calculated indiscretions'. A foreign diplomat had said to Mr. Collier that 'if any
(c) other ambassador conducted himself like Maisky, he would be *persona non grata*'. Mr. Eden decided to accept the invitation, but to speak to M. Maisky on the treatment of Sir S. Cripps in Moscow.
(d)   Although M. Maisky's indiscreet and propagandist conversations with journalists continued to cause difficulty, the Foreign Office considered that it was better to take no action about them. M. Maisky's 'calculated indiscretions' were part of his usual technique. We could not have a 'stand-up row' over the matter, and any mild complaints would merely make M. Maisky think that his indiscretions had succeeded in embarrassing us.

(a) N7558/40/38. (b) N29/3/38 (1941). (c) N7484/40/38 (1940). (d) N502/3/38.

In view of Sir S. Cripps's opinion Mr. Eden decided not to send a message, and until the end of January 1941, there was no discussion on general political questions between the two countries.

In a conversation with M. Maisky on January 29 Mr. Eden said (a) that Sir S. Cripps was not being treated with the consideration which His Majesty's Ambassador had the right to expect in Moscow. M. Molotov had not asked to see Sir S. Cripps since October 1940. M. Maisky answered that M. Molotov was not only Foreign Secretary but also Prime Minister and that he himself had only seen the Prime Minister once. Mr. Eden refused to accept this explanation. He said that M. Molotov 'on countless occasions recently' had seen the German and other foreign Ambassadors, and that he must ask M. Maisky to report his complaint to the Soviet Government.

As a result of these representations, M. Molotov sent for Sir S. (b) Cripps on the evening of February 1. He began the conversation by speaking at length of the physical impossibility of meeting personally all the foreign representatives and of the competence of his assistants, especially M. Vyshinsky, to handle most questions. Sir S. Cripps said that M. Mikoyan had failed to answer our trade proposals and that M. Vyshinsky had disclaimed authority to discuss major political proposals.

M. Molotov then complained that, since Sir S. Cripps's appointment, we had shown no desire to improve relations in practice and indeed had taken some definitely unfriendly steps, e.g. with regard to the Baltic States, where the British attitude was in unfavourable contrast with that of Sweden. The political proposals communicated to M. Vyshinsky had not been evidence of a wish for improved relations and M. Vyshinsky had said that they did not provide a basis for a general settlement. Sir S. Cripps pointed our that M. Vyshinsky had expressed this view merely as his own personal opinion. An argument then took place about the extent to which M. Vyshinsky's statement of opinion could be taken as indicating the views of the Soviet Government. M. Molotov tried to maintain that Sir S. Cripps should have taken M. Vysinsky's hint in this sense, while Sir S. Cripps said that he had been given no opportunity of discussing with M. Molotov possible modifications in the proposals before the Soviet Government came to a decision about them.

M. Molotov contested Sir S. Cripps's suggestion that, if a general understanding were reached, it would be easier to dispose of secondary questions. He also repeated his complaint that the attitude of the British Government had disappointed his expectations and had led to a 'quite sad' situation. He went on to complain about the leakages at the time of the negotiations of 1939 and the proposals of the autumn

---

(a) N382/3/38. (b) N402/3/38.

of 1940.[1] He denied that M. Maisky could have been to blame for these leakages (i.e. in 1940) because he had not known the proposals in detail. The leakages were obviously attributable to someone who wished to embroil Anglo-Soviet relations.

Sir S. Cripps reported that the interview was polite, though 'quite unproductive'. M. Molotov's only purpose seemed to be to dispose of the contention that he was inaccessible and to give some semblance of a reply to our political proposals while pretending that the reply had already been given. He made no specific references to the Baltic ships or to any other particular question.

(a)   In later telegrams Sir S. Cripps expressed the view that M. Molotov merely wanted to counter a possible argument that his refusal to see Sir S. Cripps had prevented the settlement of outstanding questions and to give the appearance that he was confirming a reply already given by M. Vyshinsky to our political proposals. He gave no reason for the rejection of the political proposals and did not mention any item in them. He refused to say anything about the economic proposals and repeated twice that the Soviet Government had had considerable hopes of Sir S. Cripps's appointment, but that all their expectations had come to nothing and that matters were even worse than before Sir S. Cripps's arrival. He did not suggest a method by which existing difficulties might be solved. Towards the end of the conversation Sir S. Cripps tried to discuss the merits of our political proposals; M. Molotov 'showed himself frankly bored and impatient, finally announcing that he had no more to say'.

Sir S. Cripps concluded that, for the time, the Soviet Government did not desire a general political or economic agreement with us, and that M. Molotov had wanted to create a sense of Sir S. Cripps's personal failure in order to stimulate him to settle the Baltic questions. The Soviet Government wanted to 'finalise' their position in the Baltic States in order to avoid discussion of the matter at the peace settlement.

(b)   The questions arising out of the Russian annexations of the Baltic States had remained a source of controversy and disturbance.[2] On October 8 Sir S. Cripps had suggested to the Foreign Office a settlement on the lines that the British Government would admit the interest of the Soviet Government in the Baltic ships, and would eventually release £100,000 of the Baltic gold as provisional payment for the use of the ships; the Russian claims to the remainder of the

---

[1] The Foreign Office believed that these leakages in the autumn of 1940 were due to an American journalist.

[2] See above Chapter XV, sections (iv) to (vi).

(a) N411, 829/3/38.   (b) N6811, 6819/2039/59.

frozen assets and the British claim to compensation would be the subject of negotiations which would begin not later than March, 1941. Sir S. Cripps suggested that we should requisition all the ships. M. Maisky, however, protested strongly against this action, and, in (a) view of his protests, and of Sir S. Cripps's approach to the Soviet Government on the subject of a general agreement, the ships were, for the time, not put into service.

After Sir S. Cripps had held more inconclusive discussions with (b) M. Vyshinsky, the War Cabinet decided on November 12 to say that the ships had been formally requisitioned and were in use, and that we would pay the usual charter rates into a blocked account from which the owners could be recompensed when the question of ownership had been settled. The War Cabinet agreed that Soviet policy would not be influenced by any action taken by us in a minor matter of this kind.

Sir S. Cripps was instructed accordingly on November 16. He was also asked to find out without further delay the arrangements proposed by the Soviet Government for the repatriation of those members of the crews who wished to go home and to take Russian citizenship.

Sir S. Cripps carried out his instructions on November 19. (c) M. Vyshinsky's only reply was to recall the protest of the Soviet Government against the requisitioning of the ships and to say that it was useless to raise the question of laying aside funds, etc. since the requisitioning decided the whole matter. M. Maisky also protested on December 6 against the requisitioning order and said that the (d) Soviet Government were particularly concerned about the crews. He suggested that they might be sent back in one of the five Baltic ships in Eire ports. Sir S. Cripps was asked on December 18 to put this question to M. Vyshinsky, but no progress towards a settlement was (e) made during the rest of the month.[1]

During this time the Soviet Government had allowed the question of the Baltic gold to fall into the background; the requisitioning of the Baltic ships and, particularly, the repatriation of their crews remained a matter of lengthy discussion during the first six months of 1941. On January 6 Mr. Eden gave M. Maisky a note to the effect (f) that we could not ensure that the ships in Eire ports would become available, but if the Soviet Government could obtain any of them, we would undertake not to interfere with their use for the repatriation of those crews who wished to go back to the U.S.S.R. In present circumstances we were not prepared to reopen any other question

---

[1] I have not dealt at length with the voluminous correspondence and legal arguments over these Baltic questions. The correspondence in the latter half of December included some telegrams of a controversial kind from Sir S. Cripps disapproving of the policy of His Majesty's Government in the matter.

(a) N6883, 6985/2039/59.   (b) N6893, 7088/2039/59; WM(40)287; N6979/2039/59.
(c) N7234/2039/59.   (d) N7382/2039/59.   (e) N7503/2039/59.   (f) N104/50/59.

arising out of the requisitioning of Baltic shipping in British ports.

The Baltic ships in Eire ports were, however, held up owing to claims of ownership brought to the Irish courts. M. Maisky therefore
(a) asked on February 15 whether we could use two of the ships in British ports. Mr. Butler explained that this course was impossible and that we had better try to find a neutral ship. On February 20
(b) Mr. Butler suggested that repatriation might be arranged in a Swedish ship.[1]

(c) On March 5 Mr. Butler told M. Maisky that a Swedish ship would probably be available in April; but later in the month this arrangement also broke down because the Swedish Government were unwilling to send a ship to repatriate Swedish sailors owing to the
(d) German sinking of ships with 'safe-conducts'. On April 3 the War Cabinet agreed that we should offer one of the requisitioned ships for the repatriation of the seamen if the Soviet Government would grant facilities to British subjects[2] in Sweden and Finland to travel through the U.S.S.R. on their way to the Middle East.

The end of this long controversy can be summarised in a few words. M. Maisky protested at the condition of the ship offered for the repatriation of the seamen, and at the cost of the repairs necessary to make her seaworthy. The Soviet Government, however, finally
(e) agreed on June 2 to an arrangement whereby they would pay for fitting out the ship and the British Government would pay for the repairs. The Soviet Government would also agree to the repatriation of British subjects from Sweden and Finland other than volunteers to Finland. The ship was not ready to sail at the time of the German attack on Russia. After this attack His Majesty's Government suggested that the plan might be dropped.
(f) M. Maisky agreed with this suggestion and with proposals that the crews should be told to serve in British and Allied ships and that the ship allocated for repatriation should be handed over to the Soviet Government and used for the transport of goods to the U.S.S.R.

---

[1] M. Maisky also asked whether thirty members of the Russian trade delegation in Great Britain could return in the same ship. He said that these officials would need cabins, but that the sailors could 'sleep anywhere'. One diplomatic member of the trade delegation would need a specially good cabin. Mr. Butler answered that he had thought everyone in the Soviet Union was treated alike. M. Maisky said this was so 'within limits'. The Ministry of Shipping had informed the Foreign Office that they were unable to arrange to transport the crews to Turkey or to the Persian Gulf. The Soviet Government were unwilling to send a ship of their own to bring back the men.

[2] These 300–400 British subjects included volunteers to Finland and naval ratings from H.M.S. *Hunter* who had escaped from Narvik.

(a) N639/3/38. (b) N663/50/59. (c) N823/50/59. (d) WM(41)35. (e) N2574/50/59. (f) N3478/50/59.

(ii)

Views of the Foreign Office on the question of concessions to Russia: the Prime Minister's message of April 3 to Stalin: Sir S. Cripps's memorandum of April 18, 1941.

On hearing of Mr. Eden's visit to the Middle East[1] in February 1941, Sir S. Cripps asked him whether he would fly to Moscow for a (a) few days on condition that Stalin would see him, and that facilities were provided for a direct flight. The Prime Minister telegraphed his comments on this suggestion to Mr. Eden. He thought that a 'mere visit' would be of no use unless we had some success in the Balkans. On the other hand, if the Russians thought that 'we would win, all would be well, but then [Mr. Eden's] visit would be unnecessary, and they would come to us'. An invitation from Stalin to meet him at Odessa would be 'a serious proposition, but why should he do that when the odds seem so terribly against us in Greece?' Mr. Eden replied to Sir S. Cripps that, apart from the difficulty of finding time for a visit to Moscow, he had always agreed with Sir C. Cripps that it would be bad policy to 'run after' the Soviet Government. Their policy towards us would be decided finally by the measure of our success against Germany; they could not now pursue an independent policy even if they wished to do so. On the other hand, if the Soviet Government cared to suggest that he (Mr. Eden) should meet M. Molotov at Odessa or in the Crimea, he would accept the invitation.

No such invitation was given. Mr. Eden therefore did not go to (b) Russia, but Sir S. Cripps flew to see him in Turkey. Sir S. Cripps arrived at Ankara on February 28. It would appear that he reported to Mr. Eden his view that we should attempt a settlement of the Baltic questions. Mr. Eden agreed on general grounds that the time had come for an approach to the Soviet Government, and promised to consider the Baltic questions on his return to London. Sir S. Cripps also suggested that the Turkish Government should try to improve their relations with Russia.

After his return to Moscow Sir S. Cripps asked M. Vyshinsky whether His Majesty's Government could do anything to remove (c) the lack of mutual confidence which prevented the Soviet and Turkish Governments from discussing together the situation brought about by the German advance in the Balkans. On March 10 M. Vyshinsky told Sir S. Cripps that the Soviet Government had communicated to Turkey a declaration that there was no reason for (d) Turkish suspicions of Russia, and that, in the case of attack by a

---

[1] See above, Chapter XVI.

(a) N675/3/38. (b) N733/3/38. (c) R2129/112/44. (d) R2248/112/44.

foreign Power, Turkey could reckon on the full understanding and neutrality of the U.S.S.R.

(a)   Sir S. Cripps regarded this declaration as of great importance; he thought that the Turkish Government should send a cordial answer, and ask more definitely for Russian assistance. The Foreign Office, however, pointed out that the Russian declaration did not mean much. The wording excluded the case of Turkish entry into the war, even in self-defence, before she were definitely attacked, and the promise of understanding and neutrality did not suggest a guarantee of assistance. Previous discussions had shown that the price of any such guarantee might be too high. The Turkish Government secured—with some difficulty—the publication of the terms of the declaration, and gave reciprocal assurances to the U.S.S.R., but there was no reason to assume that it implied a change in Russian policy.

On the night of March 21 Mr. Eden telegraphed to Sir S. Cripps suggesting that he might approach the Soviet Government on the question of Yugoslavia. Mr. Eden thought that with Soviet encouragement the Yugoslav Government and people might refuse to give way to German pressure. Sir S. Cripps raised the matter on March 22

(b) and M. Vyshinsky said that he would communicate the request to his colleagues. Later in the evening M. Vyshinsky told him that the Soviet Government could do nothing.[1] He also said that there was no possibility of an Anglo-Russian discussion of general political questions such as the position of Yugoslavia. Our action with regard to stopping exports to Russia from the United States of America[2]

---

[1] See also above, p. 539.

(c)   [2] Early in January, 1941, the British Embassy in Washington had been instructed to ask the United States Government to restrict to normal figures the export to Russia of wheat, cotton, copper, petroleum and oil-field equipment. The question was given greater urgency owing to the Soviet-German trade agreement of January 10, 1941, which provided for greatly increased Russian deliveries to Germany, especially of oil and grain. Soon after his arrival in Washington Lord Halifax spoke to Mr. Hull on the subject, and asked that the United States Government should set up machinery to limit to normal pre-war figures exports to Russia of oil, oil-drilling machinery, cotton, copper, wheat, lard, and edible oils. It was pointed out that Russia had only just begun to buy significant quantities of diesel oil and lubricating oil (both important German deficiencies) and that her large purchases of oil-field equipment (some $12,000,000 worth was on order) were designed to expand her production in order to meet her commitments to the Germans (who could not supply the equipment) and were thus having the direct result of supplying Germany with oil, though it was the policy of the United States Government no less than of ourselves to prevent such supply. As regards cotton, the Russians had imported 34,000 tons from the United States in the last quarter of 1940: they had not imported any in the years 1937–9. Continued imports at this rate would mean that the United States would be supplying the entire German war-time cotton requirements. American copper exports to Russia had risen from a negligible quantity in 1937–8 to 24,000 tons in 1939 and 56,000 tons in 1940: continuance at this rate would enable Russia (who could be self-supporting in 1941 and had large stocks) to meet a considerable proportion of the estimated German deficiency. Wheat purchases, which had been negligible in 1937–8, had been at an annual rate of 108,000 tons in 1939 and 1940. In the new trade agreement Russia had undertaken to treble her exports of grain to Germany. In view of Germany's deficiency in fats and Russia's undertaking to deliver increased quantities it was significant that the Russians had recently

(a) R2326, 2368/112/44.   (b) N1229, 1598/3/38.   (c) N318, 494, 515, 546, 937, 1887/37/38.

showed our attitude towards the Soviet Government and until this policy of hostility were changed no discussions could take place.

Sir S. Cripps then explained the attitude which we were compelled to adopt on economic questions. In spite of our offers, the Soviet Government had not shown themselves willing to improve their economic or political relations with us on a reciprocal basis. We therefore had to consider the situation from the point of view of our buying interests. Russia was one of the main channels of supply to Germany. We did not know what goods were supplied. Hence we had to assume that all goods sent to the U.S.S.R. might go to Germany. Our action at Washington was thus directed not against Russia but against Germany. We were open to suggestions, but in view of the reception given to our proposals, the initiative must now come from the Russian side.

Sir S. Cripps thought that the interview showed that the pressure of our blockade was being felt; that M. Vyshinsky's attack was milder than he had expected, and that he had moved considerably in our direction.

The Foreign Office did not agree with Sir S. Cripps's qualified optimism or with his often repeated view that it would be expedient to offer concessions, e.g. on the Baltic questions, or that such concessions would have any general effect upon Russian policy towards ourselves or Germany. The Foreign Office considered that the Soviet (a) Government would be guided by events and would regard an approach by us as weakness. If an approach were to come from the Soviet Government we ought not to hurry to meet it with offers, but to ask what they were prepared to do to check the German aggression which threatened them as much as anyone else. If the Russians

---

been buying lard and edible oils, of which they had not previously bought any in the United States. Some 12,000 tons of coconut oil was now awaiting shipment to Vladivostok.

Mr. Hull promised to consider some kind of rationing. Meanwhile, on January 21, the United States Government had withdrawn the so-called 'moral embargo' (imposed at the beginning of the Russo-Finnish war) on the export to Russia of aircraft, aeronautical equipment, and material essential to aircraft manufacture, including aluminium and molybdenum and equipment for the production of high-grade aviation fuel. All these items were, however, still subject to export licences, and Lord Halifax reported that he had been told that no export licences were being issued for commodities previously covered by the 'moral embargo'.

During February, March, and April, 1941, a number of export licences for other goods, including a shipment of oil-drilling machinery, were in fact withdrawn. On April 26 Lord Halifax reported that the United States Government had now decided on the following policy as regards their exports to Russia. As far as manufactured goods were concerned, the Russians already had on order 52 million dollars' worth: 35 million dollars' worth of this was subject to export licences, which would not be given: a further 15 million dollars' worth was subject to supply priorities, which would not be given. Of a further 49 million dollars' worth of orders which the Russians wished to place, only $3,700,000 worth would be given export licences. As regards raw materials, they would still be able to get cotton, which did not need export licences: some other raw materials were now under embargo because of American defence needs, and of the rest exports would be restricted to amounts in accordance with normal pre-war trade.

(a) N1323/1323/59; N1386/3/38.

made a suggestion for effective action, we could then decide (in consultation with the United States) what price we could afford to pay. Until the Soviet Government gave up their policy of appeasing Hitler, we could not hope to reach a real understanding with them.

(a) The considerations for and against making another approach to the Soviet Government were affected at the end of March by a new factor in the situation. On the night of March 31–April 1 a report was received from Belgrade that Hitler had told Prince Paul of Yugoslavia that he intended to attack Russia on June 30. The Foreign Office thought that we should transmit this report to the Soviet Government only if we were sure that they would understand it to mean that the German attack would take place irrespective of any concessions which they might make. Even so they might not change their attitude of subservience to Germany. They might argue that the attack would not come until Hitler had finished with us, and that they were safe because Hitler never would have finished with us.

(b) On the night of April 2–3 Lord Halifax telegraphed that Mr. Welles had given him a report of the statement by Hitler to Prince Paul[1] of his intention to attack Russia. Mr. Welles also said that Göring had told Mr. Matsuoka in Berlin that Germany intended to attack Russia immediately after the attack on Great Britain, even if this latter attack failed.

(c) In view of these reports and of other information about German troop movements the Prime Minister decided to send a warning to Stalin in the following terms:

'I have sure information from a trusted agent that when the Germans thought they had got Yugoslavia in the net, that is to say after March 20, they began to move three out of the five Panzer divisions from Roumania to southern Poland. The moment they heard of the Serbian revolution this movement was countermanded. Your Excellency will readily appreciate the significance of these facts.'

The Prime Minister wished Sir S. Cripps to deliver this message personally to Stalin. He agreed also with a suggestion from the Foreign Office that Sir S. Cripps might point out that the Soviet Government should make use of this postponement of Hitler's threat to them. The delay which had been caused by the Yugoslav *coup d'état* showed the advantages which would follow from anything like a

---

(d) [1] On April 6 Mr. Eden telegraphed from Athens that the King of Greece had said that Prince Paul was quite clear that Hitler had spoken strongly against Russia and had explained that he would have to take military action in order to secure the raw materials which he needed. Hitler said that he would choose his own time for the attack.

(a) N1316/78/38. (b) N1354/78/38. (c) N1366/78/38. (d) N1430/78/38.

united front as well as the fact that the forces of the enemy were not unlimited. The obvious way for the Soviet Government to strengthen themselves would be to give material help to Turkey and Greece and through Greece to Yugoslavia. German difficulties in the Balkans might thereby be increased to an extent sufficient to delay the German attack on the U.S.S.R. of which there were so many signs.

Sir S. Cripps was warned not to imply that we wanted help. Our purpose was to make the Soviet Government realise that sooner or later Hitler intended to attack them, and that the war against Great Britain would not stop him unless he were also in some special embarrassment in the Balkans. Hence the Soviet Government had every interest in preventing Hitler from settling the Balkan problem as he wished.

Sir S. Cripps replied on April 5 that it was out of the question (a) for him to try to deliver a message personally to Stalin. Sir A. Cadogan therefore asked the Prime Minister whether he would like the message to be given to M. Molotov. The Prime Minister gave instructions to this effect on April 6, and Sir S. Cripps was informed accordingly on the following day.

Meanwhile Sir S. Cripps had telegraphed on the night of April 6–7 (b) that he felt sure that the Soviet Government were aware of the considerations set forth in his instructions and that they were acting on them. It would therefore be unwise to interfere at a moment when everything was going as well as possible in our direction. Sir S. Cripps had in mind the Russo-Yugoslav pact of non-aggression and friendship announced on April 6, and articles in the Soviet press on the pact. He sent another telegram on April 8 that, in view of these (c) developments and of the fact that at his (Sir S. Cripps's) suggestion the Yugoslav Minister had told Stalin and Molotov of Hitler's statement to Prince Paul, he thought it a grave mistake to give Mr. Churchill's message. M. Molotov would interpret the message as an attempt by us to make trouble between Russia and Germany.

Sir A. Cadogan referred Sir S. Cripps's telegrams to the Prime Minister. Mr. Churchill replied on April 10 that it was his 'duty to have these facts conveyed to the Head of the Russian State. It makes no difference to the importance of the facts that they or their channel is unwelcome. Make sure that M. Stalin has my message.'

Sir S. Cripps was instructed on April 11 that the Prime Minister still considered that his message should be delivered. Although Stalin already knew the German threat to Russia, it was important for him to realise that the engagement of German armoured divisions in the Balkans had deferred the threat and given Russia a breathing-space. The more support which the Balkan States could obtain, the longer would they be able to tie up Hitler's forces.

(a) N1397/78/38.   (b) N1429/78/38.   (c) N1510/78/38.

(a)   Sir S. Cripps replied on the night of April 12–13 that just before receiving these instructions he had sent a personal letter to
(b)   M. Vyshinsky reviewing the succession of failures on the part of the Soviet Government to counteract German encroachment in the Balkans and urging in the strongest terms that the U.S.S.R. must decide upon an immediate and vigorous policy of co-operation with the countries still opposing the Axis there (i.e. in the Balkans). Unless they took this decision, they would miss the last chance of defending their own frontiers in alliance with others.[1]

Sir S. Cripps had sent this letter owing to the difficulty of a more direct approach to Stalin after M. Vyshinsky's statement that the attitude of the British Government precluded the discussion of the political situation. He had made it clear that his letter expressed his personal views but he had added that he was sure that there was nothing in the letter with which the British Government would disagree. Sir S. Cripps felt certain that the letter would be shown to Stalin at once. If therefore he gave the Prime Minister's message to M. Molotov, the effect would be to weaken the impression created by his letter to M. Vyshinsky. The Soviet Government would not understand why so short and fragmentary a commentary on facts already known to them should be conveyed in so formal a manner and without any suggestion for action on their part.

The Foreign Office could not understand Sir S. Cripps's attitude. After refusing to communicate the Prime Minister's message for ten days he had written, on his own authority, a 'full-dress' letter to M. Vyshinsky formally raising the whole political issue. M. Vyshinsky's refusal to discuss the political situation obviously was a difficulty, but this refusal should have kept Sir S. Cripps from writing his letter. The Prime Minister's message invited no discussion and would not have been open to the same objections, but it was now unnecessary to deliver the message. On the other hand, if M. Vyshinsky's response were favourable, Sir S. Cripps should give him the substance of the message.

Mr. Eden sent Sir S. Cripps's telegram to the Prime Minister on April 15 with the comment that there was something to be said for not giving the message. Mr. Churchill, however, replied on the same day that he had set special importance on the delivery of the message, and could not understand Sir S. Cripps's opposition. 'The Ambassador is not alive to the military significance of the facts.'

Mr. Churchill's instructions reached the Foreign Office on April 16. On April 18 he again asked whether his message had been delivered. Mr. Eden answered that owing to his absence at

---

[1] The Germans appear to have obtained (from an undisclosed source) a copy of this and earlier letters about the end of March from Sir S. Cripps to Vyshinsky (*D.G.F.P.*, XII, No. 383).

(a) N1573/78/38. (b) N1848/78/38.

Sandringham a telegram of instructions to Sir S. Cripps had been delayed. The telegram was sent to Sir S. Cripps on April 18. He replied on April 19 that he had sent the text of the message to (a) M. Vyshinsky without any comments. On April 23 Sir S. Cripps telegraphed that M. Vyshinsky had written to him to the effect that the message had been given to Stalin.

Meanwhile Sir S. Cripps had followed his letter of April 11 to M. Vyshinsky with further action on his own initiative. He reported (b) on April 17 that he expected the German Ambassador to come back to Moscow with a new offer to the Soviet Government on a large scale in return for whole-hearted Russian co-operation and with a veiled threat in case of a refusal of the offer. The apparent unwillingness of Turkey to do anything and the indecision of His Majesty's Government about making a bid for closer relations left the Soviet Government subject only to Axis pressure. In view of the Yugoslav collapse and our own great difficulties in Greece and North Africa, the Soviet Government had every inducement to side definitely with Germany if the Germans did not ask too much (e.g. demobilisation or the surrender of territory). Sir S. Cripps repeated that he had asked constantly that we should remove the Baltic difficulties in order that, at the critical moment, we might play some part in influencing the action of the Soviet Government. The critical moment had come, or was very near, but unfortunately he (Sir S. Cripps) could do nothing. He proposed, however, to see M. Molotov, and to put as direct a question as possible to him on future Russian action. This question could not cause harm, and the answer might enable Sir S. Cripps to make some estimate of Russian intentions.

Sir S. Cripps thought it likely that M. Molotov would refuse to see him. This forecast was correct. Sir S. Cripps therefore drew up a memorandum for M. Molotov and gave it to M. Vyshinsky on April 18. The memorandum summarised the course of events since (c) Sir S. Cripps's interview with M. Molotov on February 1. Sir S. Cripps then referred to his discussions in October and November 1940 with M. Vyshinsky. In these talks he had said that

'. . . it was not outside the bounds of possibility, if the war were protracted for a long period, that there might be a temptation for Great Britain (and especially for certain circles in Great Britain) to come to some arrangement to end the war on the sort of basis which has again recently been suggested in certain German quarters, that is, that Western Europe should be returned to its former status, while Germany should be unhampered in the expansion of her "living space" to the east.[1] Such a suggestion might also receive a response in the United States of America. In this connexion it must be

---

[1] It should be noted that Sir S. Cripps had no authority to make this statement.

(a) N1725/3/38. (b) N1667/3/38. (c) N1692, 1828/3/38.

remembered that the maintenance of the integrity of the Soviet Union is not a direct interest of the British Government as is the maintenance of the integrity of France and some other Western European countries.

At the moment there is no question whatever of the possibility of such a negotiated peace so far as His Majesty's Government are concerned. Nevertheless the security of Eastern Europe—so far as it has any security—depends ultimately upon the continued resistance of Great Britain in the west and on the maintenance of Britain's command of the seas. So long as these persist, the opening of a major front by Germany in the east is at least a hazardous operation, far more dangerous than would be the case after a cessation of hostilities in the west.

The more recent developments of the war, and the apparent decision of Hitler to postpone the attempt to invade England, have in the view of His Majesty's Government increased the likelihood of German pressure to the east; and, according to their information, this view is confirmed from a great many independent sources in other countries, notably in Germany itself.

For assuming—as I believe to be the case and as all our information, including the statements of the German leaders themselves, leads us to believe—that Hitler now contemplates a war lasting several years, he must—as he himself has said—assure an adequate supply of food and raw materials from some source other than those which he at present controls. Unless—which is most unlikely—he can himself gain command of the seas, he can in fact only obtain these supplies in a volume in any way comparable with his requirements from or through the Soviet Union.

There would therefore seem to be two major possibilities as regards the development of the Eastern European situation. That is to say, Hitler could obtain his supplies in one of two ways: either by agreement with the Soviet Union, or, if he cannot ensure the obtaining and carrying out of such an agreement, then by using force to try and take what he requires.

With regard to the first eventuality I need only say that it will obviously make it necessary for His Majesty's Government to tighten up their blockade wherever they can do so.

In the second eventuality we should have a mutual interest, since Great Britain is already opposing its force to Hitler's. In that event His Majesty's Government would in their own interests want to do their utmost to assist in preventing Hitler from achieving his aim and thus delaying the final Allied victory. We should therefore be anxious to do our best to assist the resistance of the Soviet Union economically and in any other way practicable, for instance, the co-ordination of aerial activity.

It may be that the Soviet Government regards the position as still too hypothetical to justify its coming to any decision. Judging, however, by the many indications which we have received from usually reliable sources, such a seizure by force of the sources of supply in the east is not a hypothesis at all, but is part of the planned German development of the war for the spring of this year.

His Majesty's Government at least regard this contingency as sufficiently probable to require their most careful consideration and the immediate exploration of the various courses of action which might be necessitated, and which must consequently influence their future plans and dispositions.

If it were the case that the Soviet Union contemplated acceding to the first alternative and so constituting herself a source of supply to Germany to the limit of her capacity for the rest of the war, then clearly His Majesty's Government would have to adapt their future policies to that basis.

If, on the other hand, the Soviet Union has the intention of resisting such a demand, or the equivalent demand for the cession of such territory as would yield the needed supplies, then His Majesty's Government might well wish to embark upon quite different lines of policy, and to suggest the adoption by the United States of a policy following a direction similar to their own.

I do not propose to ask your Excellency what the Soviet Government intend to do, because I fully realise how difficult such a question might be to answer. But I do wish to ask, in the light of the above considerations, whether the Soviet Government is now interested in bringing about an immediate improvement of its political and economic relations with His Majesty's Government, or whether, on the contrary, the Soviet Government is content that those relations should remain on the present wholly negative basis for the remainder of the war.

If the answer to the first part of the question is in the affirmative, then in my view there is no time to be lost if such an improvement is to be of use to either party. If, on the other hand, the answer to the second part of the question is in the affirmative, then I should with very deep regret feel compelled to reconcile myself to the fact that the future policies of His Majesty's Government must be formulated upon that basis, so far as both the war and the post-war period are concerned.'

Meanwhile Mr. Eden had seen M. Maisky on April 16 and (a) explained to him the efforts made by us to induce the Yugoslav Government to reach an agreement with us before the development of the German attack. Mr. Eden told M. Maisky of Hitler's statement to Prince Paul and said that, in our opinion, Russia also was threatened by Germany's boundless military ambitions. It seemed therefore desirable to consider whether there was any possibility of an Anglo-Russian *rapprochement*. M. Maisky complained that the Soviet Government had shown a desire for better relations in a number of minor questions, but had not been encouraged by our

(a) N1658/3/38.

negative attitude over such matters as the repatriation of the Baltic seamen.

Mr. Eden said that he had in mind something on a larger scale. M. Maisky said that the Baltic question was the main stumbling block in our relations with the U.S.S.R. and that, if this stumbling block were removed, progress would be possible. Mr. Eden replied that he could not discuss the Baltic question on the basis that after agreement had been reached on the subject the Soviet Government might then review their relations with us. A Baltic settlement must be part of a larger arrangement to which Russia would make a comparable contribution. We were not necessarily asking for things for ourselves; we did at least suggest that the U.S.S.R. should help our friends, e.g. by the supply of war material to Turkey.

M. Maisky thought an agreement possible if we would formulate our requirements and say what we were prepared to do. Mr. Eden said that we were not prepared for a unilateral gesture, but that he would consider M. Maisky's suggestion.

(a) Sir S. Cripps's report of M. Vyshinsky's reception of his memorandum did not encourage hope of an agreement. Sir S. Cripps gave M. Vyshinsky a copy of his memorandum as a record of his verbal statement. M. Vyshinsky did not like it. He said that the necessary prerequisites of a wide political discussion did not exist, and that the situation remained as it had been on March 22. On the Russian side there was no question of improving relations because the Soviet Government had done nothing to worsen them. M. Vyshinsky asked why Sir S. Cripps thought that the Soviet Government did not want good relations with the British Government. Sir S. Cripps gave as his reason the attitude of the Soviet Government towards Germany and the help given by them to Germany. M. Vyshinsky said that the Soviet Government had been annoyed and indignant at our attitude over the Baltic questions and, for this reason, M. Molotov had refused to see him. M. Vyshinsky thought that there was nothing new or material in Sir S. Cripps's memorandum but he promised to submit it to his Government.

Sir S. Cripps said that M. Vyshinsky could be practically certain that the British Government would not consider a settlement of the Baltic questions apart from 'some more general enlargement of friendly relations'. M. Vyshinsky said that he accepted this view. Sir S. Cripps replied that the British Government were studying the Baltic questions again and that his report of M. Vyshinsky's conversation might influence them. This remark embarrassed M. Vyshinsky. He tried to elude the point by saying that he was sure that the conversation would influence the British Government favourably.

(a) N1692/3/38.

Sir S. Cripps thought it better to await M. Vyshinsky's answer before giving a definite opinion. He considered, however, that the Soviet Government had not turned at all in our direction as a result of the latest events, although they had also not turned towards Germany.

In spite of this conclusion Sir S. Cripps repeated at length to the Foreign Office on April 19 his views on the desirability of opening negotiations as soon as we could reckon that our action would cause (a) a deterioration in Russo-German relations and the Soviet Government had given us an opportunity by referring again to the obstacles in the way of an agreement.

On April 21 Mr. Eden told the War Cabinet that he wished to try (b) to open up discussions with the Soviet Government, though he was not confident about good results. The Soviet Government still regarded the Baltic questions as the 'main stumbling block'. Mr. Eden thought that we should make no concessions in the matter unless we obtained something definite in return.

On the following day the Prime Minister wrote to Mr. Eden, after reading Sir S. Cripps's latest statement of his proposals: (c)

> 'None of this seems to me to be worth the trouble it has taken to send. They [i.e. the Soviet Government] know perfectly well their dangers and also that we need their aid. You will get much more out of them by letting these forces work than by frantic efforts to assure them of your love. This only looks like weakness and encourages them to believe they are stronger than they are. Now is the moment for a sombre restraint on our part, and let them do the worrying. Above all, we ought not to fret the Americans about it.'

Mr. Eden agreed with this view. On April 26, therefore, Sir S. Cripps was instructed that the Soviet Government already knew our willingness to discuss the Baltic questions as part of a general agreement. The fact that they had made no move in the matter showed that they had not yet decided to revise their fundamental policy towards Germany.

(iii)

Information about German intentions with regard to Russia, April 20–May 24: views of the Foreign Office on possible action to strengthen Russian resistance to German pressure.

The Prime Minister's message to Stalin had mentioned only one of many reports received by the British Government with regard to German preparations for an attack on the U.S.S.R. These reports had

---

(a) N1725/3/38. (b) WM(41)42; N1781/3/38. (c) N1725/3/38.

been among the main reasons why Mr. Eden had approached M. Maisky about the possibility of an Anglo-Russian *rapprochement*. The Soviet Government had not responded favourably to this approach. None the less, the evidence of German preparations remained extremely strong.

(a)   On April 20 Sir S. Cripps was sent[1] a summary of the evidence and of the conclusions which the Foreign Office had drawn from it. The measures taken by Germany included a further call-up of men for military service (this call-up involved serious long-term economic risks); the development of aerodromes in Poland; the mapping of the Russo-German frontier (from a point east of Warsaw to Slovakia) by air photography; the printing of Russian currency notes; the training of Russian refugees from Roumania for administrative work, and the reorganisation of Ukrainian and White Russian émigrés; the extension eastwards of air raid precautions and the construction of shelters, an increase in the German forces in Poland and East Prussia (since March 26) from 55 to 65 divisions, i.e. from $1\frac{3}{4}$ to 2 million men; 'fifth column' activity in the Ukraine and the Caucasus.

Sir S. Cripps was told that these reports might be part of the German war of nerves. A German invasion would result in such chaos throughout Russia that the Germans would have to reorganise everything in the territories which they might occupy. Meanwhile they would lose their supplies from Russia. The loss of material transferred across the Trans-Siberian railway would be even more important. Although the resources of Germany were immense, they would not allow her to continue her campaign in the Balkans, maintain the existing scale of air attacks against us, take the offensive against Egypt and at the same time invade and reorganise a large part of the U.S.S.R. The main German handicap would be a lack of fighter aircraft for all these theatres of war. On the other hand a rapid success in the Balkans would enable Germany to throw most of her fifteen heavy armoured divisions against Russia. Even so there would be almost a month's delay after the end of a Balkan campaign. There was as yet no information about the movement of German aircraft towards the Russian frontiers; if the necessary preparations had been made in Poland, aircraft could be moved there at the shortest notice. The German General Staff appeared to be opposed to a war on two fronts and in favour of disposing of Great Britain before attacking Russia, but the decision rested with Hitler.

---

[1] Throughout this section I have dealt only with the more important reports of German intentions. It is now known from German sources that Hitler had ordered definite preparations for an invasion of Russia, with the probable date of June 1. On hearing of the Yugoslav *coup d'état*, Hitler postponed the invasion date to approximately June 22. This date was confirmed on April 30.

(a) N1364/78/38.

Sir S. Cripps replied to this telegram on the night of April 23–4. (a)
He thought that the basic hostility of the U.S.S.R. to Germany had
not been lessened by the approach of danger. If anything, this
hostility had increased. The military leaders, who were beginning to
be a force outside the Communist party, were convinced that there
would be war, but were anxious to postpone it at least until nearer
the winter. The Soviet Government would give way to Germany to
any extent not vitally affecting their preparations for war. If Hitler
were willing to be satisfied with assurances and promises, he need not
attack Russia; but he must attack her, if he wanted to secure a real
control of Russian supplies and transport. The whole question therefore depended on the extent of Hitler's demands. The present actions
of both Governments were just as consistent with 'pressure-politics' as
with preparations for war. The only possible counterweights to
German pressure were Russian fears (a) that Turkey might join the
Axis, (b) that the United States might turn towards Japan and
completely cut off all supplies.[1]

On April 26 Sir S. Cripps reported that, according to a statement (b)
by the Italian Ambassador in Moscow, the return of the German
Ambassador on April 27 with a delegation—presumably of economic
experts—would mean a Russo-German 'show-down' within a fortnight. The point was not that Russia had failed to fulfil her promised
deliveries to Germany but that the German needs were increasing
with every country which they invaded. These needs could be met
only by Russia. The German demands would therefore be acute, and,
in the event of a Russian refusal, Germany would have to take the
necessary guarantees, i.e. she would have to secure the key positions
in the Russian economy. Sir S. Cripps thought that this view coin-
cided, except on the question of guarantees, with the opinion of all
neutral and friendly diplomats in Moscow.

On May 2 Sir S. Cripps reported that the German Counsellor of (c)
Embassy in Moscow, in conversation with a reliable neutral on
April 30, had said that a German attack on Russia was in present
circumstances entirely out of the question. The Germans wanted
more economic help from Russia, but the Russians had carried out
all their undertakings and the German Government could rely on
them to carry out a new agreement. The Germans would not move
in a new direction until they had completed their campaign against
Egypt and the Middle East. They were entirely confident about this

---

[1] The Foreign Office found Sir S. Cripps's meaning obscure. Mr. Collier thought that
(a) meant that the Russians must fear that if they did not help Turkey to stand up to
German pressure she might give way and allow the use of her territory as a base for a
German attack on the U.S.S.R. In (b) the word 'towards' was probably an error for
'against'. Sir S. Cripps himself added that Turkey herself appeared unwilling to help in
making Russia commit herself definitely in that direction (i.e. assisting Turkey), and the
United States were not talking to the Japanese or putting any pressure on them.

(a) N1761, 1762/78/38. (b) N1819/78/38. (c) N1978/78/38.

campaign and did not expect Turkey to fight. All they wanted from the Turkish Government was the denunciation of the Anglo-Turkish treaty. Sir S. Cripps thought the Counsellor's statement represented a new propaganda line. The Germans might be afraid that they had overplayed their hand, and might be trying to 'smooth down' the temper which they had created in Russia.[1] On May 6 Sir S. Cripps reported that, according to Yugoslav information, German (a) preparations in Roumania indicated the possibility of operations against Russia in the very near future; German officers spoke of mid-June as the date.

Although information of this kind continued to be received during May, the Foreign Office were still unable to judge whether Germany would go beyond threats and pressure. There was no doubt that this pressure was being exercised; unconfirmed reports mentioned negotiations in Berlin. On May 13 Sir S. Cripps suggested that any (b) disclosures from Hess[2] might be used to stiffen Russian resistance (a) by increasing the fears of the Soviet Government that they might be left alone to 'face the music' or (b) by encouraging them to think that their position was less dangerous if they resisted now and in company with others. Sir S. Cripps meant under (a) revelations from Hess about a tendency in influential German circles towards a compromise peace with Great Britain, and under (b) revelations about positive German preparations for a direct attack on Russia or for undermining the Russian régime.

The Foreign Office considered, however, that action on the lines suggested by Sir S. Cripps might drive Stalin completely to the German side. In particular hints of a compromise peace would be far too dangerous. Furthermore Sir S. Cripps appeared to be 'jumping to conclusions' about Hess. Sir S. Cripps was told on May 17 that the Foreign Office would let him know if and when Hess produced any

---

[1] On May 5 Sir S. Cripps reported that, according to a 'fairly reliable colleague', the (c) German Ambassador in Moscow was 'depressed'. Hitler had told him in Berlin that in view of Russia's 'behaviour towards the Japanese Government' he had reinforced his armies on the Russian front 'as a precaution'. The Ambassador had not seen M. Molotov since his return from Berlin, since he had nothing to say to him. If M. Molotov wanted to know anything from him, he could send for him. Sir S. Cripps added that, according to reports received through a domestic channel at the German Embassy, the Ambassador was 'packing', and that he might therefore be giving place to a stronger Nazi with better qualifications to carry out a policy of threats and pressure. On May 13 Sir S. Cripps (d) reported, again from information given by a neutral colleague, that, in his one short interview with the German Ambassador, Hitler had violently denounced the Russo-Yugoslav pact. The Ambassador thought, however, that Hitler had not yet made up his mind to attack Russia. It is, in fact, more probable that the Ambassador, who was unfavourable to the policy of war with Russia, realised at this time that Hitler was determined on attack. See *D.G.F.P.*, XII, No. 443.

[2] The National Socialist leader Hess flew to Scotland on the night of May 10–11. He disclosed nothing of value about German intentions towards Russia.

(a) N2030/78/38. (b) N2171/78/38. (c) N2020/78/38. (d) N2172/78/38.

material suitable for the purpose which he (Sir S. Cripps) had in mind.[1]

On May 23 Lord Halifax telegraphed that, according to reports of May 21 from Berlin, German troops were assembled in force on the (a) Russian frontier, but in recent trade negotiations the Soviet Government had assented readily to German demands for a large increase in the supply of material from Russia. The rumours of an imminent German attack on Russia might have been circulated deliberately by the Germans. These rumours were now largely replaced by reports that Russia was about to sign a far-reaching economic agreement with military implications. The extreme view of these implications was that Russia would allow the passage of German troops and material to areas east of Suez and might take action against India. One explanation of the Russian attitude was that the Soviet Government, feeling their weakness, were gradually giving way and proposing to allow Germany economic privileges in the Ukraine and the region of Baku. Ribbentrop was said to be in favour of an arrangement of this kind; the German General Staff were thought to oppose it because it would give Russia time to improve her military position. The military authorities therefore wanted to attack at once, but Hitler had not yet come to a decision.

At the end of May it was clear at least that Hitler intended to make the most far-reaching demands on Russia, and possibly to attack her even if he could have obtained without war all the concessions for which he was likely to ask. The British Government did not rate highly the chances of a successful Russian defence against German attack;[2] the prospects of a complete Russian surrender were even more serious. It was therefore more desirable than ever to attempt a *rapprochement* which might strengthen Russian resistance to German demands, but the Russians themselves had resisted every approach made by us.

Hence there seemed little hope of improvement. M. Molotov had refused to see Sir S. Cripps; M. Vyshinsky had shown no interest in Sir S. Cripps's proposals. Sir S. Cripps himself telegraphed on May (b) 27 that his hopes had been a little shaken by signs of Russian weakening. The Russian attitude seemed to the Foreign Office to be (c)

---

[1] On June 10 Sir S. Cripps was informed that we were putting about a report that Hess's flight was evidence of a growing split in Germany over the policy of collaboration with (d) Russia. If Hitler continued this policy, he would insist on short-term benefits, since he knew that sooner or later he would have to abandon the policy and break any promises he had made to the Russians. Russia would then have made vital concessions, and, having lost potential friends, would have to face Germany alone and in a weakened state.

[2] The Foreign Office view that the Germans would defeat Russia was taken generally by the Service departments. The Ministry of Economic Warfare thought at this time that the Germans would not incur heavy casualties or any high degree of military exhaustion in (e) defeating the Red Army. The Prime Minister did not share the prevailing pessimism about Russian powers of resistance.

(a) N2388/78/38. (b) N2466/78/38. (c) N2566/3/38. (d) N2787/78/38. (e) N2234/78/38.

due to fear of Germany, and at a time when events were going against us it was hard to think of an approach likely to convince the Soviet Government. The Germans had landed airborne troops in Crete on May 20 and secured a dominating position; on May 27 General Wavell reported that he had ordered the withdrawal of the troops defending the island; a German-Italian attack in Libya had recaptured the Halfaya Pass on May 27–8.

(a)   Mr. Eden invited M. Maisky to see him on June 2 in order to discuss the international situation. Mr. Eden began by asking M. Maisky why the Soviet Government should have chosen the moment of Rashid Ali's revolt to appoint a Minister to Iraq. M. Maisky thought that the Minister had not taken up his post, and that he would now go to the newly-appointed Iraqi Government. Mr. Eden said that we were determined to maintain our position throughout the Middle East, including Iran and Afghanistan. We knew that Germany was trying to bring British and Russian interests into conflict in these regions, but, with a mutual Anglo-Russian understanding, there was no reason why she should succeed.

In answer to questions from M. Maisky, Mr. Eden said that we had the situation in Iraq under control and were prepared to meet any danger in Syria. Our armies were being reinforced and the arrival of American aircraft in the Middle East gave us adequate means of dealing with a German attack. If the Germans diverted to the U.S.S.R. a part of their air force at present concentrated against us in the Middle East we would take action to relieve the pressure against Russia. The Turks were holding out against German demands. M. Maisky asked whether these demands were political as well as economic. Mr. Eden thought that Germany would follow her usual practice of beginning modestly and then asking for more. He offered to enquire from the Turkish Government on M. Maisky's behalf about the German demands if the Soviet Government felt uncertain whether Turkey would welcome a direct Russian enquiry.[1]

M. Maisky spoke of the information which Mr. Eden had given him about German concentrations against Russia. He thought that this information might be correct, but found it hard to believe that the concentration was more than a part of the 'war of nerves'.[2] He then said that he took Mr. Eden's communication as evidence that we wanted to improve Anglo-Russian relations. Could we not pursue matters a little further and try to reach agreement on the Baltic question?

Mr. Eden said that we could not make unilateral concessions and that he did not believe in 'a policy of appeasement towards Soviet

[1] See above, p. 582.
[2] Mr. Eden thought that M. Maisky was 'trying to convince himself' when he maintained that Germany did not intend to go to war with Russia.
   (a) N2570/3/38.

Russia or anyone else'. M. Maisky asked whether we could not draw up a statement of the concessions we were prepared to make on the Baltic question and those for which we hoped in return from the U.S.S.R. Mr. Eden said that he would consider this suggestion. Meanwhile he wished M. Maisky to find out whether the Soviet Government would be able to assure us that their Middle Eastern policy was similar to our own and that they did not intend to join with Germany against us in Iran or Iraq.

(iv)

Further estimates of German intentions with regard to Russia: Mr. Eden's interviews of June 10 and 13 with M. Maisky: warning from His Majesty's Government to the Finnish Government: German attack on Russia, June 22: Mr. Churchill's broadcast of June 22, 1941.

Until the end of May a Russian surrender seemed more probable than resistance to German demands.[1] A memorandum written in the Ministry of Economic Warfare on May 28, however, pointed out that, if the German aim were to obtain full economic control of (a) Russia, war was almost certain. The arguments suggesting surrender were that Russian deliveries to Germany could not be increased without an improvement in Russian production and means of transport. In order to secure this improvement Germany would ask for her own experts to be put into Russian industrial and transport organisations. If this measure were insufficient, the Germans would require these experts to be allowed to share in the supreme control of Russian industry and transport. Stalin would give way to this demand rather than face invasion and defeat.

The memorandum pointed out that the Germans knew too much about Russian economic conditions to spend time in asking for concessions which would be useless. Russian exports to Germany did not represent a true economic surplus; they were secured only by cuts in the domestic demand. These cuts could be greater, but a real increase in agricultural production could take place only very slowly. Russian technique in metallurgical mining and in oil production was on the whole in advance of German technique and there was not much room for increased production. Similarly the railways were already carrying about as much traffic per mile of track as the

---

[1] The Chiefs of Staff, who, up to the end of May, did not think that the German preparations gave 'reliable indications of imminent hostilities', agreed in the first fortnight of June that war was practically certain, and that the German attack would probably begin in the second half of June.

(a) N7500/78/38.

German railways, and the Germans could not do much to remedy the defects of minor personnel which limited the efficiency of the services.

Hence the only way of improvement, from the German point of view, would be to put German experts into the Russian central planning organisation. The Germans would have to recast Soviet planning, reallocate labour, capital and transport. This would mean reversing the tendencies of three 5-year plans, winding up the vast armaments and engineering industries in Russia, and stopping the construction of strategic railways and fortifications. This procedure would amount to the forcible disarmament of Russia, and to this Stalin could never agree. It was assumed that he was afraid of invasion because, if he were defeated, he and his party would lose power, but he was not fool enough to think that he could maintain power after the Germans had made it impossible for him to produce arms. Therefore, either the Germans would not ask for complete economic control and would be satisfied with a higher rate of deliveries or, if they insisted on control, a Russo-German war was inevitable, and the Germans would know that it was inevitable.

The Foreign Office considered, in a memorandum submitted to
(a) Mr. Eden, the various reports and memoranda on the question. The memorandum examined the motives which Hitler might have for making war. These motives might be economic, political or military. On the economic side it appeared that Hitler could obtain by negotiation practically everything which Russia could supply. War would reduce if not dry up Russian supplies for a considerable time.

On the other hand, if Hitler were preparing for a long war, he might argue that he would have to start organising Europe on a different and more permanent basis as an economic and autarchic unit. He would therefore want complete control of the economic resources of European and Asiatic Russia. He might think that the demand for these concessions would mean war, and, consequently, a temporary loss of supplies. In this case his motives for war would be political.

Hitler might also wish to capitalise his victories by a *Gleichschaltung* of the whole of Europe, and thus to transform the Soviet system into something like a Russian equivalent of National Socialism. He would consider that the elimination of Russian Communism would rally the National Socialist party in Germany and be welcome to large sections of the populations throughout Europe and assist in reconciling them to German domination. He would hope that a crusade against Communism might turn American

(a) N2893/78/38.

and even our own public opinion in his favour. Finally, the replacement of the existing Soviet Government by a new Government closely linked with the Axis would greatly facilitate co-operation with the Japanese. Hitler probably thought that this move would discourage the United States and might even keep them out of the war.

All these political motives would call for early action. On the military side Hitler might say that owing to the climate he could not attack Egypt from Libya in high summer, and that he might as well attack Russia (otherwise he could not attack her till next spring). Hitler would be taking risks, but if the Russians surrendered quickly to diplomatic or military pressure, he might get all the political advantages at which he was aiming and also the military advantages resulting from access to the Caucasus. If Russia put up an effective resistance, Hitler doubtless expected to be able to arrange a compromise settlement without adverse effect upon his general strategic position in the Atlantic or eastern Mediterranean.

It was inconceivable that Hitler should think the Russian army, which was constituted purely for defence, was a threat to his flank in eastern Europe, but this army immobilised 50 German divisions and the Germans might consider it worth while to free these divisions. Hitler could then demobilise part of his army, relieve the labour shortage within Germany and show these facts as propaganda evidence that Germany regarded the war as over and was preparing to organise Europe on a peace footing.

On June 9 the Joint Intelligence Committee produced a paper dealing with the military, political, and economic effects of a Russo- (a) German war. They examined the strength, value and equipment of the Russian armed forces, and concluded that, although their numbers were large, much of their equipment was out of date. They considered that the Russian forces had certain inherent failings which would serve them ill against the Germans, and that their value for war was low, though they were at their best in defence and had vast territories on which to fall back. The Germans could find 100 divisions against Russia without much difficulty, but the diversion of armoured forces and aircraft would prevent them from undertaking simultaneously large-scale operations elsewhere. The German soldier would prefer to invade the U.S.S.R. rather than to invade England. The probable course of the war would be a combination of advances (a) to Leningrad through the Baltic States, (b) north of the Pripet marshes to Moscow, (c) south of the Pripet marshes to the Ukraine. The Germans might hope to occupy the Ukraine and possibly to reach Moscow in 4–6 weeks.[1] The military effects of the outbreak of war would be the postponement of an attempt to invade Great Britain, a large dispersal of German forces, a reduction in the numbers of German aircraft available for attacks on Atlantic shipping or the bombing of Great Britain, a dangerous reduction in German fighter strength in the west, and a temporary removal of the German threat against us in the Middle East.

During the fortnight before the German attack the evidence seemed to point towards war rather than towards a Russian surrender. In other words, it became increasing clear—although until the actual attack it was never certain—that Hitler had decided in favour of dealing with Russia once and for all, without giving her a chance
(a) to surrender to the most stringent German demands. The Swedish view on June 7 was that Germany would force a 'show-down' with Russia about June 15. M. Boheman thought that there was an even chance of war.

Information from the United States tended to confirm this view.
(b) Mr. Welles told Lord Halifax that the State Department had received substantially identical reports from Finland, Stockholm and Bucharest and, less definitely, from Rome and Berlin. The Stockholm report was based on a statement from M. Dahlerus that Göring had told him of Germany's intention to attack Russia almost at once. Germany had delivered an ultimatum asking for Russian demobilisation and the establishment of a separate government in the Ukraine, the control of the Baku oilfields, and, apparently, an outlet on the Pacific. The explanation of this move was that Germany had to safeguard herself with regard to food supplies, etc., before American production could be fully developed and while the internal situation in Russia was insecure. Hence, if the Germans were ever to strike, they must do so at once. Mr. Welles thought that these stories might be part of the German 'pressure technique' and that Russia would agree to almost anything except demobilisation. If the Germans attacked Russia, Mr. Welles expected the Japanese also to attack her and to forgo 'southern adventures'.

(c) On June 10 M. Maisky told Mr. Eden that the Soviet Government had instructed him to say they were not negotiating with the Germans and would not make a military alliance with them. Mr. Eden said that he had thought some economic negotiations were in progress. M. Maisky said that ordinary informal talks might be going on, but that there were no large-scale negotiations.

---

[1] In a revised version of this paper on June 14 the time-table for the advance to Moscow
(d) was given as 3–4 weeks, or as long as six weeks, and the necessary postponement of the attempt to invade Great Britain as 4–6 weeks after a 3–4 weeks *Blitzkrieg* or 6–8 weeks after a longer war against Russia.

(a) N2680/78/38. (b) N2707/78/38. (c) N2712/122/38. (d) N3047/78/38; JIC (41) 234 (Revise).

M. Maisky had not received an answer to Mr. Eden's questions of June 2 about the Russian attitude towards the Middle East and towards German concentrations. Mr. Eden said that we did not know the purpose of these concentrations, but that, in the event of a Russo-German war, we should do everything in our power to attack by air German-occupied territories in the west. M. Maisky 'nodded, but made no comment'. Mr. Eden understood from M. Maisky's statement that the German concentrations were due to the Russian refusal to negotiate.[1]

On the evening of June 13 Mr. Eden invited M. Maisky to see him. (a) Mr. Eden said that during the previous forty-eight hours reports reaching us about German concentrations against Russia had increased in significance. After consultation with the Prime Minister, Mr. Eden had decided to make a communication to M. Maisky to the effect that, although we did not know whether these concentrations were merely for the purpose of a war of nerves, we wished to tell the Soviet Government that, in the event of a German attack on the U.S.S.R., we should be prepared to send a mission to Russia representing the three fighting services. We did not pretend to any superiority in the art of war over Russian commanders, but our mission might be a help as it would be composed of officers who had had the most recent experience of fighting the Germans. We should also be prepared to give urgent consideration to Russian economic needs. We could not tell whether Japan would join in an attack on Russia, but we were ready to discuss both the general and economic requirements of Russia and technical details such as the best routes of supply.

After asking for details of our reports on German concentrations, M. Maisky said that Mr. Eden had previously mentioned the possibility of air action by us if German forces were engaged in Russia. Mr. Eden answered that we would consider whether we could take air action from Great Britain against enemy-occupied country.

M. Maisky thought that we had exaggerated the German concentrations and that Germany was not intending to attack Russia. Our message to the Soviet Government presupposed intimate Anglo-Russian collaboration; did the conditions for such collaboration exist? The Soviet Government would react more favourably if the message were accompanied by action on our part showing that we desired more friendly relations.

Mr. Eden replied that we thought the situation extremely urgent. We could either say nothing until hostilities opened or we could

---

[1] Mr. Eden reported that the interview was 'somewhat stiff throughout, which may in part have been due to the presence of the Counsellor of the Soviet Embassy, and to his knowledge, as well as M. Maisky's, that I should have preferred to see the Ambassador alone'.

(a) N2793/78/38.

explain frankly now what our attitude would be in the event of war. We thought the latter course more fair, although we knew that the Soviet Government might not agree with our diagnosis of the danger now facing them.

(a)
(b) In view of the increasing number of reports about the imminence of a German attack, the British Government considered it desirable to consult the United States Government on the possibility of American help to the Soviet Government in the event of war. Lord Halifax spoke to Mr. Welles on the subject on June 15. Mr. Welles said that there would be no objection of principle, but that there were practical difficulties. Russia would want machine tools, war material, copper, rubber, etc., i.e. the commodities needed by the United States and ourselves. Mr. Welles thought that Japan would attack Russia, and declare a blockade. This question would also raise problems for the United States.

(c) The British Government also thought it necessary to warn the Finnish Government that we should wish Finland to remain as passive as possible in a Russo-German war. It was probably too much to hope that the Finnish Government would try to prevent the use of their territory as a base of German operations, but they ought not to give active co-operation. Mr. Vereker was therefore instructed on the night of June 14–15 to give the following message to the Finnish President and Marshal Mannerheim:

> 'Since Germany is our enemy we shall oppose her and those fighting with her wherever we can. If therefore Finland joins a Russo-German war on the side of Germany, she will forfeit British support and sympathy, and we shall have to subject her to every form of economic pressure in our power. Owing to the uncertainty of the present political situation we are detaining ships now on their way to Petsamo. As soon as the attitude of the Finnish Government becomes clear to His Majesty's Government, they will be prepared to examine the question of the continued detention of the ships in the light of the political and military situation then prevailing.'

(d) On the night of June 18–19 further information[1] of German plans were received through M. Dahlerus. M. Dahlerus told Mr. Mallet

---

(e) [1] On June 20 the Japanese Ambassador in Moscow told the United States Ambassador that M. Molotov had said to him on June 19 that he was expecting demands which the Soviet Government could not accept. The Japanese Ambassador thought that Japan would not come into the war at once, but would come in later. The Germans had told the Japanese Ambassador that they expected to finish the war with Russia in two months. The Japanese Ambassador expected the Soviet Government to leave Moscow without making provision for the Diplomatic Corps or for the maintenance of order. He also thought that the Red Army was anxious to fight, and would begin well, but that, when things began to go against them, there would be mass surrenders.

(a) N2793/78/38.   (b) N2831/78/38.   (c) N2832/78/38.   (d) N2950/78/38.
(e) N3066/78/38.

that in the course of a conversation lasting five hours Göring had said to him that Germany would have to fight a long war and must therefore ensure her supplies from Russia, and could not risk a stab in the back or the undermining of the New Order. A Russo-German war was inevitable and could best be undertaken at a time when the Soviet Army was relatively unprepared. M. Dahlerus thought that, up to June 14, the Germans had made no demands on Russia; these demands would be made in the near future, possibly within the week, since Göring was going to Berchtesgaden. The Germans would probably ask for the rectification of the pre-war frontiers of Finland, the Baltic States and Roumania, the demobilisation of the Russian army in certain areas such as the Caucasus and the Ukraine, and the control of the administration and reorganisation of these areas. As an excuse for their ultimatum, the Germans were likely to say that the Soviet Government had not fulfilled their treaty obligations to deliver certain goods to Germany and had not co-operated in the spirit of the Russo-German pact (e.g. their encouragement of the Turks, Yugoslavs and Bulgarians). Stalin might be tempted to accept the demands but would not dare to do so because, if he accepted them, the army would start a revolt against him.[1]

Thus to the moment of the German attack, there was no definite and conclusive evidence that Germany intended to attack Russia and not merely to use diplomatic and military threats to intimidate the Soviet Government. None the less, this evidence was such that His Majesty's Government were not taken by surprise on June 22 at the news of the German invasion of Russia. They had warned the Russian Government of the likelihood of an attack. They had already made it clear that, if the attack took place, they would offer all the assistance in their power to the Soviet Government and armies. The offer was made known to the world in a broadcast by the Prime Minister on the very day of the German attack. The broadcast ended with the words that the invasion of Russia was a prelude to the invasion of Great Britain. 'The Russian danger is therefore our danger, and the danger of the United States.'

---

[1] The German negotiations with Turkey (see above, pp. 581–4) also pointed to the imminence of a German move against Russia.

Dd.142654 K32 10/69   SBN 11 630052 3*

2000/t